lonely planet

Taiwan

Robert Storey

D0448271

Taiwan

4th edition

Published by
Lonely Planet Publications
Head Office: PO Box 617, Hawthorn, Vic 3122, Australia
Branches: 150 Linden Street, Oakland CA 94607, USA
10a Spring Place, London NW5 3BH, UK
1 rue du Dahomey, 75011 Paris, France

Printed by
Colorcraft Ltd, Hong Kong

Photographs by

Martin Moos
Robert Storey
Chris Taylor

Front cover: Book on Clan History (China Tourism Press, The Image Bank)

First Published
November 1987

This Edition
September 1998

Although the authors and publisher have tried to make the information as
accurate as possible, they accept no responsibility for any loss, injury or
inconvenience sustained by any person using this book.

National Library of Australia Cataloguing in Publication Data

Storey, Robert.
Taiwan.

4th ed.
Includes index.
ISBN 0 86442 634 8.

1. Taiwan – Guidebooks. 2. Taiwan – Description and travel. I. Title.

915.1249045

text © Robert Storey 1998
maps © Lonely Planet 1998
photos © photographers as indicated 1998

Robert Storey

Robert has had a colourful and chequered career, starting with his first job as a monkey-keeper at a zoo. He later worked his way through school by repairing slot machines at a Las Vegas casino. After graduating from the University of Nevada with a worthless liberal arts degree, he became a professional, unemployed traveller. In Taiwan, he ran out of funds so embarked on a new career writing text books for teaching English (*Creative Conversation* and *The Traveler's Guide to English*). He also published *Understanding Chinese Characters*, an aid to teaching Chinese to foreigners, before going on to author and co-author 13 books for Lonely Planet. Robert now lives in a small farming community (population 50) in Taiwan, and is looking forward to the publication of his first novel, *Life in the Fast Lane*. His hobbies are computer hacking, raising fish and spraying politically incorrect herbicides on his weeds.

From the Author

I'd like to express my gratitude to the following travellers, expats and Taiwanese locals: Guy Taylor, Bill Rubens, Andy Clarke, Pamela Hung, Chris Taylor, Chris Curren, Phelim Kyne, Chiu Miaoling, Li Chihkuo, Chen Hsiuchen, Lee Schondorf, George Lu, Douglas Habecker and Huang Chingcheng.

From the Publisher

This edition of Taiwan was coordinated by Joyce Connolly with help from Michelle Glynn, Miriam Cannell, Sally Dillon, Lara Morcombe and Justin Flynn. The maps were drawn by Maree Styles with help from Sarah Sloane, Mark Germanchis and Gadi Farfour. Trudi Canavan did the design and layout as well as many of the illustrations. Paul Piaia supplied the climate charts, David Kemp designed the cover and Kerrie Williams helped with the indexing. Thanks also to Dan Levin for setting up the soft fonts, to Quentin Frayne for editing the language section and to Charles Qin for checking the final script.

Warning & Request

Things change – prices go up, schedules change, good places go bad and bad places go bankrupt – nothing stays the same. So, if you find things better or worse, recently opened or long since closed, please tell us and help us make the next edition even more accurate and useful.

We value all the feedback we receive from travellers. Julie Young coordinates a small team who read and acknowledge every letter, postcard and email, and ensure that every morsel of information finds its way to the appropriate authors, editors and publishers.

Everyone who writes to us will find their name in the next edition of the appropriate guide and will also receive a free subscription to our quarterly newsletter, *Planet Talk*. The very best contributions will be rewarded with a free Lonely Planet guide. Excerpts from your correspondence may appear in new editions of the guide; in our newsletter; or in updates on our Web site – so please let us know if you don't want your letter published or your name acknowledged.

Thanks

Many thanks to all the travellers who took time to write to us about their experiences in Taiwan. Your names appear on page 420.

Contents

Map Legend

BOUNDARIES

.... International Boundary
.... Provincial Boundary
.... Disputed Boundary

ROUTES

A25 ..... Freeway, with Route Number
.... Major Road, with tunnel
.... Minor Road
.... Minor Road - Unsealed
.... City Road
.... City Street
.... City Lane
.... Train Route, with Station
.... Metro Route, with Station
.... Cable Car
.... Ferry Route
.... Walking Track

AREA FEATURES

.... Building
.... Cemetery
.... Desert
.... Market
.... Park, Gardens
.... Pedestrian Mall
.... Reef
.... Urban Area

HYDROGRAPHIC FEATURES

.... Canal
.... Coastline
.... Creek, River
.... Lake, Intermittent Lake
.... Rapids, Waterfalls
.... Salt Lake
.... Swamp

SYMBOLS

⊙	**CAPITAL** .... National Capital	✈	.... Airport
◎	**CAPITAL** ...... Provincial Capital	✢	.... Airfield
●	**CITY** .... City	⠄⠂	.... Archaeological Site
●	**Town** .... Town	⑤	.... Bank
●	Village .... Village	✕	.... Battle Site
		🏝	.... Beach
■	.... Place to Stay	🏰	.... Castle or Fort
⚊	...... Camping Ground	⌒	.... Cave
🚐	.... Caravan Park	🕌 ✝	.... Church
⌂	.... Hut or Chalet	⌒⌒⌒	.... Cliff or Escarpment
		⌐	.... Golf Course
▼	.... Place to Eat	✛	.... Hospital
🍺	.... Pub or Bar	🗼	.... Lighthouse
		✕	.... Mine
		▲	.... Mountain or Hill
		🏛	.... Museum
		🌲	.... National Park
		←	.... One Way Street

⚘	.... Pagoda
🅿	.... Parking
)(	.... Pass
⛽	.... Petrol Station
★	.... Police Station
✉	.... Post Office
❖	.... Shopping Centre
◎	.... Spring
🏛	.... Stately Home
🏊	...........Swimming Pool
☎	.... Telephone
🗼	.... Temple
⊙	.... Toilet
▣	.... Tomb
ⓘ	.... Tourist Information
⊖	.... Transport
⬛	.... Trekking Shelter
🐾	.... Zoo

Introduction

A province of China or an independent nation – Taiwan is an island in search of its identity. Born out of the Chinese civil war which never quite ended, Taiwan has existed as a de facto nation since 1949.

Facing constant threats from China and 'derecognition' by almost every other nation, Taiwan has not only survived, but prospered. China bellows and occasionally fires missiles, but the Taiwanese shrug and continue to do what they do best – make money.

The island has one of the world's most dynamic export-oriented economies and as such is a familiar destination for many business travellers. Just a few decades ago, Taiwan was known for the production of low-technology goods, like clothes and cheap toys. Today, Taiwan lives on the export of electronics and computers. No longer considered to be in the Third World, economists refer to Taiwan as one of Asia's 'Little Dragons' or 'Little Tigers'.

Having become a de facto country almost by default, Taiwan has carved out a political and economic niche for itself that far surpasses its physical size. The island is home to a colourful, complex and fast changing society. While visitors to China often remark on how much the country has changed over the past decade, people familiar with both places wonder if China isn't simply following in Taiwan's footsteps. If that is so, the possibilities are intriguing because in the space of one generation, Taiwan has changed from dictatorship to democracy and has created prosperity from poverty.

The images that impact on visitors first are congested cities, rushing traffic, teeming markets and neon signs. Look a little deeper and you'll find Buddhist and Taoist temples, Confucian ceremonies, calligraphy exhibitions and the world's best Chinese art. One of the biggest surprises to visitors is that traditional Chinese culture is more genuinely preserved in Taiwan than in mainland China.

Early Portuguese sailors gave Taiwan the

name 'Ihla Formosa', which means 'Beautiful Island' – you'll appreciate why if you can escape the cities. The island has spectacular natural scenery with incredible mountains and thick forests. Hiking trails, hot springs, waterfalls and towering cliffs overlooking the sea are abundant. Off the coast, the remote islands of the Taiwan Straits offer an even more relaxed pace.

When the Taiwanese travel abroad, it's often with a tour group. This makes a solo traveller far from home an oddity, and people will be curious about you. The Taiwanese fear loneliness above all else and so they will go out of their way to make you feel welcome. The people of Taiwan are among the most friendly on the planet and it's their hospitality that is perhaps the greatest asset of this remarkable island.

Facts about Taiwan

HISTORY

The Aborigines

Little is known of Taiwan's earliest history, but with the results of radiocarbon dating of primitive utensils it has been estimated that people have inhabited Taiwan for at least 10,000 years. The first inhabitants of the island were not Chinese, even though Taiwan has always been on the periphery of the Chinese Empire. Although Chinese history dates back more than 3000 years, there was no significant Chinese migration to Taiwan until the 15th century. Taiwan's earliest inhabitants – simply known as 'aborigines' – appear to have migrated from the Pacific islands, as their features closely resemble those of the peoples of the nearby Philippines.

When the Chinese arrived in Taiwan, there were two distinct groups of aborigines. One lived on the rich plains of central and south-western Taiwan and the other lived in the mountains.

Arrival of the Chinese

From the Sui dynasty (589-618) until the Ming dynasty (1368-1644), the Chinese name for Taiwan was Hsiao Liuchiu, even though Taiwan was not as yet claimed by China. From the 15th century on Chinese people from Fujian province migrated to Taiwan in ever increasing numbers. Fujian is just across the straits from Taiwan, and the Fujian dialect is almost identical to modern-day Taiwanese. As their numbers grew, the Fujianese occupied the land most suitable for agriculture (Taiwan's west coastal plain), driving the aborigines towards the mountains and the rocky east coast. The Fujianese have always been the keenest of Chinese travellers, and today they can be found all over South-East Asia.

Along with the Fujianese came a small but steady stream of ethnic Chinese known as the Hakka. Coming from Henan province in northern China, the Hakka first moved to Guangdon and Fujian provinces in the south to escape severe persecution in their homelands. The name Hakka means 'guests' and, as guests in search of a home, they gradually trickled into Taiwan. Today, the Hakka are a minority in Taiwan – only their nearly forgotten dialect distinguishes them from the Taiwanese majority.

European Imperialism

In 1517 the first Europeans – Portuguese sailors – landed on Taiwan's shores and were so impressed by the beautiful scenery that they named it Ilha Formosa, which means 'Beautiful Island'. The name Formosa is still used, though nowadays the island is better known by its Chinese name, Taiwan, which means 'Terraced Bay'.

Following the tradition of imperialism that was popular at the time, the Dutch invaded Taiwan in 1624. The Dutch established the first capital on Taiwan, at what is now the city of Tainan in the south-western part of the island. Two years later the Spanish grabbed control of north Taiwan, but they were expelled by the Dutch in 1641.

Taiwan had no real army to resist the Dutch occupation, but events on the Chinese mainland soon changed all that. Blood was flowing in China as the up-and-coming Qing (Manchu) dynasty armies set about destroying the Ming dynasty supporters. Cheng Chengkung, also known as Koxinga, was one Ming supporter who fled to Taiwan. He left in 1661 with 35,000 troops in 400 war junks and successfully expelled the Dutch from their stronghold in Tainan.

The Manchu Period

Koxinga's forces had hoped to launch an invasion to recapture the mainland from the Manchus, but instead the Manchu armies captured Taiwan in 1682. For the next 200 years there was substantial migration from Fujian province across the Taiwan Straits. These immigrants brought their culture and language with them, and these still dominate Taiwan today. Taiwan remained a county of Fujian province from 1684 until 1887 when, with a population of more than 2.5 million, it became a province of China.

Japanese Imperialism

In 1894 a dispute over Korea led to the Sino-Japanese War. Taiwan, being somewhat remote, managed to avoid most of the dislocations of the battle on the mainland. But when China was defeated in 1895, Taiwan became one of the spoils of war and was ceded to Japan. Although the Japanese brought law and order, they also brought harsh rule. Many of Taiwan's residents objected and rebelled against this rule, proclaiming Taiwan an independent republic later that year. The Formosan Republic, the first republic in Asia, was short-lived as the Japanese quickly and brutally crushed it. For the next 50 years Taiwan remained part of Japan. The Japanese influence was extensive and even today many of the older people speak Japanese.

Although the Japanese ruled with an iron fist, they were also efficient and contributed substantially to Taiwan's economic and educational development. During Japan's rule Taiwan became more developed than mainland China. The Japanese built roads, railroads, schools and hospitals, and improved agricultural techniques. However, WWII created a great demand for men and raw materials to feed Japan's war machine. The Japanese drafted tens of thousands of Taiwanese into the Japanese army, many of whom were killed or wounded. The western Allies also bombed Japanese military installations in Taiwan, though the island was lucky enough to escape the carpet bombing that Japan endured. By the time the war ended, Taiwan's economy, along with those of mainland China and Japan, was in ruins.

The Republic of China

Birth of the Republic Events in mainland China were destined to impact on Taiwan's future. China's last dynasty – the Qing dynasty – collapsed in 1911 following a

Dr Sun Yatsen, founding Father of the Republic of China (ROC)

nationwide rebellion led by Dr Sun Yatsen, who became the first president of the Republic of China (ROC). Sun Yatsen did not lust for power, but instead stepped down in favour of Yuan Shikai. Unfortunately, Yuan Shikai did not share Sun Yatsen's vision of a democratic China and he attempted to promote himself as a new emperor. He was unsuccessful and died of cancer in 1916.

A period of civil war ensued while various rival warlords and factions struggled for power. Unity was eventually restored when the Kuomintang (the KMT, or Nationalist Party) forcibly took power. The Nationalist army was led by Chiang Kaishek, who preferred the title 'Generalissimo'. However, the KMT soon found itself beleaguered by Japan's growing militancy and the Communist rebellion, and in 1931, Japanese forces occupied Manchuria. In 1937, they invaded the Chinese heartland.

Under the Yalta Agreement, China regained sovereignty over Taiwan after Japan's defeat in WWII. At first the Taiwanese were happy

Chiang Kaishek, leader of the KMT, led the move to Taiwan from China.

to be rid of the Japanese military and welcomed the KMT, but their joy soon faded when Chiang Kaishek sent the corrupt and incompetent General Chen Yi to be Taiwan's governor. Chen Yi's misrule came to a head on 28 February 1947, when anti-KMT riots broke out and were brutally repressed – somewhere between 10,000 and 30,000 civilians were killed. The incident, now known as '2-28' (for the date when it occurred), remained a forbidden topic of discussion in Taiwan until the lifting of martial law in 1987.

The 'Two Chinas' In 1949, the Communists wrested control of the Chinese mainland from the KMT and established the rival People's Republic of China (PRC). The KMT, now firmly under the control of Chiang Kaishek, fled to Taiwan, taking with them their flag and ROC constitution. Thus began the still unsettled saga of 'two Chinas' – the ROC and the PRC.

About 1.5 million Chinese, including 600,000 soldiers, moved to Taiwan after the Communists captured the mainland. As a result, the island's population grew from around six million in 1946 to 7.5 million in 1950. In 1950, disgraced former governor Chen Yi was executed on Chiang's orders.

As they fled, KMT troops were able to hold onto three small islands just off the Chinese mainland – Kinmen (Quemoy), Matsu and Wuchiu – which still remain under the control of Taiwan. An invasion of Taiwan was fully expected, but the Communist army became bogged down in the Korean War. The USA (fearing Communist world domination) sent its 7th Fleet into the Taiwan Straits to thwart any invasion plans the Communists may have had.

The KMT maintained from the beginning that their stay in Taiwan was temporary – that they would retake mainland China from the Communists 'very soon', and that, in the meantime, no political opposition could be permitted. Such policies did not necessarily endear the KMT to the native Taiwanese. Nevertheless, the KMT proved itself capable of repairing Taiwan's war-torn economy. An excellent land-reform program was introduced in the 1950s which resulted in a far more equitable income distribution than is found in most Asian countries. Rapid industrialisation in the 1960s made Taiwan one of the wealthiest economies in Asia.

In October 1971, the ROC lost the China United Nations seat. A further blow came in January 1979, when the USA withdrew recognition of the ROC in favour of the PRC regime on the mainland. Most countries have now withdrawn diplomatic recognition of the ROC. In spite of this, most of the capitalist world maintains very strong unofficial economic ties with Taiwan.

Chiang Kaishek died from a heart attack in 1975, at the age of 87. His son, Chiang Chingkuo, became president of the ROC in 1978 after an uncontested election. He was re-elected in 1984 and served a second term till his death in January 1988.

From the 1980s to the present day, mainland China has kept relentless pressure on other countries not to sell military hardware to Taiwan. This has caused some serious rows, most often with the USA. China says arms sales to Taiwan are 'interference in the internal affairs of China'. China has also tried to get other countries to break economic links with Taiwan, but few have done so. Taiwan has consistently denounced these policies, which are referred to as 'Chinese-Communist united-front tactics'.

Political Reform In 1986, a political upheaval occurred with the formation of the Democratic Progressive Party (DPP), despite a government ban on new political parties. After much debate, the KMT – under the specific orders of President Chiang Chingkuo – decided not to interfere with the DPP. A large number of DPP candidates were elected in 1986 and were permitted to take their seats in the legislature, thus creating Taiwan's first true opposition party.

In 1987, 38 years of martial law ended. It was one of the last acts of Chiang Chingkuo before his death. He was succeeded by Lee Tenghui, the first Taiwanese-born person to hold the post of president.

President Lee's first important act was to solve the problem of the 'ageing deputies' – KMT legislators who were elected in the mainland before the Communist takeover. Unable to stand for re-election, they were frozen in office for over 40 years, absurdly claiming to represent their constituents in the mainland. In December 1991, those still living (there were more than 460) were finally forced to retire, and the first free election to the National Assembly was held. This made Lee very popular and earned him the unofficial title of 'Mr Democracy'.

With the ageing deputies gone, reforms quickly followed. Almost all restrictions on the press were lifted. Raucous parliamentary debates and free elections soon allowed the Taiwanese to claim that their society was one of the most liberal in Asia.

With free debate now permitted, the Taiwanese leadership soon accepted reality and gave up its position that Taiwan would 'retake the mainland'. However, China has not given up its position that it will 'retake

Taiwan'. The leaders of the PRC have stated unequivocally that there is only 'one China', and that the People's Liberation Army (PLA) will invade Taiwan if the island ever makes a formal declaration of independence.

With this in mind, the Taiwanese have been careful to continue referring to their country as the ROC. Officially, the Taiwanese agree that there is only one China, which is currently divided between the PRC and ROC, but 'someday' the Chinese nation will be reunited. Unofficially, many young Taiwanese people favour establishing a fully independent Republic of Taiwan, but so far the majority has been willing to live with the status quo.

Unfortunately, the status quo may not be good enough. While officially claiming to be part of China, the Taiwanese upped the ante in 1994 by lobbying the United Nations to grant a seat to the ROC. As far as China was concerned, this was tantamount to a declaration of independence. Lee Tenghui angered China further by making a high profile visit to the USA in late 1995 as a precursor to his re-election campaign. China went ballistic – literally – and conducted a series of missile tests in the hope of intimidating Taiwanese voters to vote for 'pro-China' candidates in the December 1995 parliamentary elections. A second round of war games, conducted during the March 1996 presidential elections, were held to scare off voters from supporting President Lee Tenghui. Chinese missiles plunged into the sea just 25km off the coast of Taiwan.

China's 'missile diplomacy' pretty much achieved the opposite of what the Chinese leadership intended. The USA parked two aircraft carriers just off the coast to thwart any actual invasion plans. Independence sentiment in Taiwan greatly increased as a direct result of China's threats and 'war games'. Voters rallied to President Lee and returned him to power with 54% of the vote in a four way race. The DPP candidate, Peng Mingmin, ran on an unabashed independence platform and came in second with 21% of the vote. The most pro-China candidate, Lin Yanggang, received 15%. The remaining 10% went to pro-Buddhist Chen Li-an.

Recent Developments President Lee's glory did not last long. One of his first official acts following re-election was to fire Ma Yingjeou, the popular Justice Minister who had received widespread praise for his crackdown on corruption. Lee's greatest political problem, however proved to be something totally unexpected – crime. In 1996, a high profile crackdown on underworld godfathers won some kudos, but the political benefits were soon dissipated when many of the gangsters were quickly released from prison for 'medical reasons'.

The first big shockwave came in November 1996, when Liu Pang-you (magistrate of Taoyuan County) was killed along with seven others in a gangland execution in the garage of Liu's mansion. That December, the nation was further horrified by the savage rape and murder of 47-year-old Peng Wanru, a well-known women's rights activist and member of the DPP. In 1997, the brutal kidnapping and murder of Pai Hsiaoyen – daughter of famed Taiwanese TV star Pai Pingping – brought up to 70,000 demonstrators onto the streets of Taipei to protest the breakdown in law and order. China's takeover of Hong Kong on 1 July 1997 sent more jitters through Taiwan. The second half of the year was gloomy with the growing Asian currency crisis. Taiwan's currency value dropped by about 15%, but overall Taiwan came out of the crisis in better shape than almost every other country in the region.

The other major event of 1997 was a six-day visit to Taiwan by the Dalai Lama. China sternly objected to the visit and demanded it be stopped, but the Taiwanese authorities issued the visa despite Beijing's protests (see the Asian Flu boxed text in the Facts for the Visitor chapter).

China began 1998 by extending an olive branch to Taipei, offering to resume talks which had been suspended (by China) during the 1995 missile crisis. Part of the motive behind the new peace offer might have been that China was facing a severe banking crisis

of its own, and could ill-afford any further confrontations that would have scared off Taiwanese investors.

GEOGRAPHY
Shaped roughly like a leaf, the island of Taiwan is only 160km across the Taiwan Straits from mainland China.

The maximum length of the island is 395km, and the maximum width is 144km. Taiwan's total land area of 32,260 sq km is surrounded by a 1448km coastline. Though the island is small, its mountains are extremely high, reaching 3952m at Yushan (Jade Mountain), which is higher than Mt Fuji in Japan. Indeed, apart from the Himalayan region, Yushan is the highest peak in North-East Asia.

The mountains rise straight out of the sea on Taiwan's east coast, while the west side of the island is a flat and fertile plain, much more hospitable to human habitation. Over 90% of Taiwan's population resides there. However, the mountainous eastern side of the island is far more scenic.

In addition to the island of Taiwan itself, there are a number of smaller offshore islands which have become popular with tourists. These include Orchid Island, Green Island, the Penghu Islands (which numbers 64, including islets), Hsiao Liuchiu, Kinmen, and Matsu (18 including islets).

Taiwan, like mainland China, lays claim to 53 rocks, shoals and reefs above Brunei in the South China Sea, known as the Spratly Islands. The Spratlys are also claimed by Malaysia, Vietnam, the Philippines and Brunei. The claims wouldn't be taken too seriously except that there is *possibly* oil under these islands, which has led to heavy fortification of the area. Taiwan maintains a military base on the largest islet in the Spratly group to enforce its claim.

On the northern front, Taiwan has had a long running dispute with Japan and mainland China over the Tiaoyutai Islands (Japan calls them the Senkaku Islands) which lie to the north-east of Taiwan. The islands were indeed part of China once, but were annexed by Japan in 1895 (the year Taiwan was also annexed). When the Japanese were forced out of Taiwan at the end of WWII, they held onto the Tiaoyutai chain and the Americans acquiesced.

Taipei, at the very northern end of Taiwan, is the largest city and the seat of the national government. Other large cities include Kaohsiung, Taichung and Tainan – all on the west side of the island.

GEOLOGY

Taiwan is on the western edge of the Pacific 'rim of fire', where the Philippine tectonic plate collides with the Eurasian landmass. Where two plates collide like this, you expect to find steep mountains, earthquakes and sometimes volcanoes. This is indeed the case in Taiwan – steep limestone mountains rise dramatically out of the sea on the east (Pacific) coast. The mountains were mostly created by fault action, though a few have volcanic origins. All of Taiwan's volcanoes are now extinct, though numerous hot springs remain as a reminder of the recent geological turbulence. Orchid Island and Green Island off the east coast are totally volcanic in origin.

A major fault line runs down the east coast, the source of frequent tremors which reverberate throughout the island. Noticeable minor earthquakes occur several times a year, but there have been no devastating geological disasters in Taiwan's recent history. In 1995, an earthquake demolished a school in Taitung County, but fortunately this occurred at night when no students were inside. However, the potential for a deadly earthquake remains a threat, especially on the east coast.

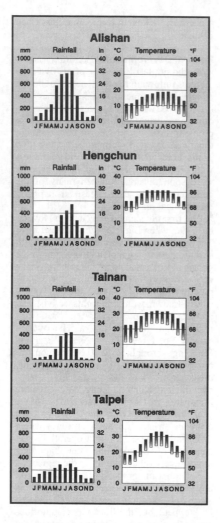

CLIMATE

Taiwan is a subtropical island with two – rather than four – seasons. For such a small place, the climate varies considerably. There are basically three climatic regions: the north and east coastal region, the south-west coastal region, and the mountains.

In the north and east coastal region, which includes Taipei, there isn't really a dry season. Winter is cool, occasionally chilly, and is characterised by heavy cloud cover and frequent drizzle. Statistically, more rain falls during summer but, ironically, the skies tend to be sunny most of the time. Summer rain comes in short, torrential thunder showers mostly during the afternoon. Summers are sticky and very hot.

The south-west has two distinct seasons. Summer is hot and humid, with frequent afternoon thunder showers. Winter is very dry and sunny, with pleasantly cool days.

The mountains get the most rain of all, especially during summer. The summer rain tends to fall in short-lived thunder showers, starting about 2 pm and often ending by 4 pm. Places at higher altitudes often experience an afternoon fog. During winter the weather tends to be drier on the west side of the mountains than on the east side. Temperatures can get very low above 2000m, and winter snow is common above 3000m.

A striking feature of Taiwan's winter is the monsoonal wind *(hánliú)* from Central Asia, which can send the temperature plummeting 10°C or more in just a few hours. You might be comfortably wearing a T-shirt and shorts in the morning, but by noon you'll have to put on long trousers and a coat. At such times it can snow in the mountains.

The Penghu Islands in the Taiwan Straits are lashed with severe winds during winter. Kinmen and Matsu are surprisingly cold in winter, thanks to their proximity to the icy mainland.

Spring is warm and mild but there is frequent rain throughout the country. This is known as the 'plum rain' and can continue through to August.

Summer is typhoon season. The brief autumn (October and November) is the most delightful time to visit the whole region, including mainland China, though typhoons are possible in October. Autumn temperatures are ideal, and this is the driest time of year, especially in the south-west.

ECOLOGY & ENVIRONMENT

Painful as it is to admit, Taiwan is infamous for its poor record on environmental protection. The industrial revolution, rapid population growth, rubbish dumping, dense motor vehicle traffic and unplanned urban development have all had a major impact.

The good news is that there is growing awareness of the issue and environmental protesters have grown ever more shrill in their demands to clean things up. The dirtiest industries have been forced to shut down operations, though most have simply moved across the Taiwan Straits to mainland China where protesters don't dare raise their voices. Taiwan's rather lame Environmental Protection Agency (EPA) is making slow progress in cracking down on polluting industries and vehicles. Some efforts at recycling have begun. Taiwan may someday get its act together on protecting the environment, but that day is probably still several years away.

FLORA & FAUNA
Flora

Thanks to its subtropical climate, Taiwan is covered with some very lush vegetation, at least in those parts of the island which have managed to escape urban development. The mountain areas and the east coast are especially rewarding for nature enthusiasts. However, many native species have been pushed aside by exotic imports. Approximately 55% of Taiwan is forested or cultivated woodland. The high mountain forests are predominantly cypress, though juniper, fir, pine, spruce, bamboo, azalea and many hardwoods are common. Camphor trees, which at one time provided the base material for Taiwan's thriving camphor industry, have all but disappeared. In the past, camphor was Taiwan's leading export; unfortunately, this is no longer the case.

Fauna

Taiwan's wildlife has not fared well. Development along the west coast has ruined the wetlands which once provided a habitat for Taiwan's numerous birds. During WWII the Japanese heavily logged Taiwan's forests for the war effort, with devastating consequences for wildlife.

The good news is that Taiwan's sparsely inhabited east coast and mountainous interior have largely been reforested, providing a much improved habitat for animals. Mammals like the Formosan brown bear, sambar (a species of deer), Reeve's muntjac (a very small deer) and Formosan serow (a type of wild goat) are protected, but your chances of seeing any of them are rare. Birds have been the chief beneficiary of the reafforestation program – they can now be seen in abundance.

Offshore islands such as Penghu and Green Island have largely escaped the ravages of civilisation, which has helped preserve their local bird life too.

National Parks
(guójiā gōngyuán)
It was only as recently as the 1980s that Taiwan began to think about preserving its natural treasures. As awareness of the issue grew, six national parks were established. The first was Kenting *(kěndīng)* National Park, on 1 January 1984. This was rapidly followed by Yushan *(yùshān)*, Yangmingshan *(yángmíngshān)*, Taroko Gorge *(tàilǔgé)*, Shei-Pa *(xuěbà)* and Kinmen *(jīnmén)* national parks.

Taiwan's national parks are not true wilderness areas. You will find houses, hotels, telephones, roads and other intrusions of modern civilisation in them. However, new developments are strictly controlled – houses cannot be built, for example, without permits which are extremely difficult to obtain. Hopefully, this will stop the recent trend for Taiwan's nouveaux riches to build villas in scenic spots purely for real estate speculation. Although one very controversial road was built in Yushan National Park after it was established, the emphasis now is on constructing walking trails.

The mountainous east coast of Taiwan is now at least semiprotected as the East Coast National Scenic Area; there are even plans to construct a bicycle path there. Off the west coast are the Penghu Islands, now designated the Penghu National Scenic Area. The area east of Keelung is the North-East Corner National Scenic Area.

GOVERNMENT & POLITICS
Power is distributed among five major branches of government called *yuan*: the Legislative (National Assembly), Executive, Judicial, Examination and Control.

The first three are self-explanatory. The Examination Yuan oversees Taiwan's formidable system of exams, which determines access to education, jobs, business licences, the civil service and so on. The Control Yuan is a watchdog agency which tries to keep things honest.

The president is chosen by the legislature, though there is much debate on changing the constitution to allow the direct election of the president. The president appoints the premier, who wields considerable power because they appoint the heads of Taiwan's many ministries which oversee the ubiquitous bureaucracy. Important ministries include Economic Affairs, Education, Finance, Foreign Affairs, Interior, Justice, National Defence, and Transportation and Communications. The ministries themselves are multi-tiered bureaucracies, with numerous agencies, bureaus, commissions and directorates, some of which seem to perform no useful function whatsoever (what exactly does the Mongolian & Tibetan Affairs Commission do?).

Taiwan is still officially a province of China. Thus, there is a largely forgotten provincial government with its capital at Chunghsing Village in Taichung County. In 1997, Taiwan's constitution was amended to reduce the provincial government's role to a few ceremonial posts. This act angered mainland China, as it seemed like an indirect way of saying that Taiwan was no longer a province of China but an independent nation.

Many claim that Taiwan is the first Chinese democracy. This point can be debated, but there are few countries in Asia which have a more open political system than Taiwan. This is a very recent change – Taiwan was essentially a dictatorship until martial law was lifted in 1987. Today there is universal suffrage and the voting age is 20.

Taiwan has an ever increasing number of political parties emerging. There are also a few independent legislators, the so-called 'non-partisans' *(dǎngwài)*.

The Kuomintang
(guómín dǎng)
The KMT has controlled the ROC since the

CHRIS TAYLOR

MARTIN MOOS

MARTIN MOOS

MARTIN MOOS

CHRIS TAYLOR

CHRIS TAYLOR

The Taiwanese are a friendly and diverse group of people who place great importance on family values and religion. Traditions such as the *xiuxi* (siesta; top left) and communication with spirits through mediums (bottom right) flourish alongside the country's technological advancements. The nine aboriginal tribes also retain a strong identity which they promote through their native dress and crafts (middle left).

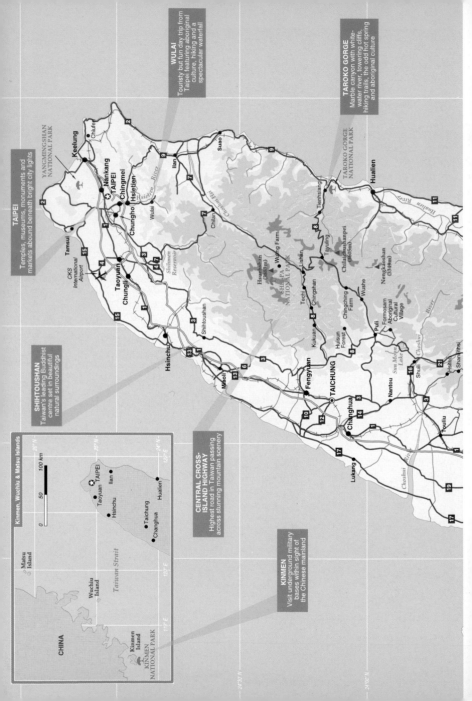

TAIPEI
Temples, museums, monuments and markets abound beneath bright city lights

WULAI
Touristy but fun day trip from Taipei featuring aboriginal culture, hiking and a spectacular waterfall

TAROKO GORGE
Marble canyon with white-water river, towering cliffs, hiking trails, the odd hot spring and aboriginal culture

SHIH-TOUSHAN
Taiwan's leading Buddhist centre set in beautiful natural surroundings

CENTRAL CROSS-ISLAND HIGHWAY
Highest road in Taiwan passing across stunning mountain scenery

KINMEN
Visit underground military bases within sight of the Chinese mainland

Kinmen, Wuchiu & Matsu Islands

0   50   100 km

CHINA

Matsu Island

Wuchiu Island

Taiwan Strait

Kinmen Island

KINMEN NATIONAL PARK

TAIPEI

Taoyuan Ilan
Hsinchu
Taichung
Changhua

Hualien

119°E   120°E   121°E   122°E

26°N
25°N
24°N

YANGMINGSHAN NATIONAL PARK

Keelung
Chiufen
Nankang
TAIPEI
Chingmei
Chungho Hsiehtien
Tamsui
CKS International Airport
Taoyuan
Chungli
Hsinchu
Maoli
Shihtoushan
Fengyuan
TAICHUNG
Changhua
Nantou
Lukang
Touliu

Ilan
Suao
Wulai
Chilan
Shihmen Reservoir

Wuling Farm
Hsuehshan (3886m)
SHEIPA NATIONAL PARK
Lishan
Tayuling
Chilaichupei (3605m)
Teehi
Chingstan
Nengkaoshan (3349m)

Teehsiang
Hualien
TAROKO GORGE NATIONAL PARK

Kukuan
Hulsun Forest
Chingching Farm
Wushe
Puli
Formosam Aboriginal Cultural Village
Sun Moon Lake
Shuili
Hsitou
Shanlinhs

Choshui River
Hualien River
Choshui River
Hsintien River
Choshui River

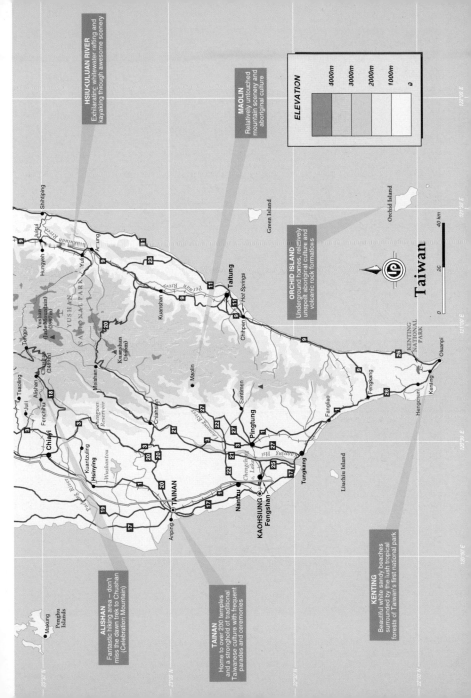

HSIU-KU'LUAN RIVER
Exhilarating whitewater rafting and kayaking through awesome scenery

MAOLIN
Relatively untouched mountain scenery and aboriginal culture

ELEVATION

	4000m
	3000m
	2000m
	1000m
	0

ORCHID ISLAND
Underground homes, relatively unspoilt aboriginal culture and volcanic rock formations

Taiwan

0   50
0   40 km

ALISHAN
Fantastic hiking area – don't miss the dawn trek to Chushan (Celebration Mountain)

TAINAN
Home to over 200 temples and a stronghold of traditional Taiwanese culture with frequent parades and ceremonies

KENTING
Beautiful white sandy beaches surrounded by the lush tropical forests of Taiwan's first national park

Penghu Islands

Makung

Shihtiping

Hungyeh

Lungpu

Tsaoling

Jui

Alishan

Fenchihu

Chushan
(2489m)

Yushan
(Jade Mountain)
(3997m)

YUSHAN
NATIONAL PARK

Juisui

Hsiukuluan River

Arung

Yuli

Chiayi

Kuantzuling

Hsinying

Wushantou

Tsengwen
Reservoir

Meishan

Kuanshan
(3668m)

Kuanshan

Maolin

Tseng-wen River

Kuanshan

Peinan River

Taitung

Chihpen
Hot Springs

TAINAN

Anping

Nantzu

KAOHSIUNG

Fengshan

Chianan

Chingtsao
Lake

Kaoping River

Pingtung

Santimen

Tungkang

Liuchiu Island

Fangliao

Fengkang

Hergun

Kenting

Oluanpi

KENTING
NATIONAL PARK

Green Island

Orchid Island

Lanyang River

Penkang River

CHRIS TAYLOR

MARTIN MOOS

CHRIS TAYLOR

CHRIS TAYLOR

CHRIS TAYLOR

Taiwan boasts a smorgasbord of culinary delights for all tastes and budgets. Explore the myriad food stalls (bottom left) that line the streets and offer everything from traditional Chinese breads (top right) and noodles (bottom right) to more exotic delicacies like pickled wasps (top centre). To complement your food, try a refreshing sugar cane juice (top left).

time of its official founding in 1911. They're still in control, but at the time of writing they only had a slim, one-seat majority in the National Assembly. The KMT's grip on power is definitely slipping, and the party could well be headed into opposition following the next parliamentary and presidential elections.

The party's biggest weaknesses have been dealing with corruption and alleged links to organised crime, both of which have greatly undermined public confidence in them. The party has implemented a number of anti-corruption reforms and 'strike hard' anticrime campaigns. However, it's often been a case of too little, too late. Another headache for party leaders are factions, such as the elderly conservatives still intent on 'retaking the mainland'. However, the KMT's old warriors have been greatly reduced by natural attrition and defections to the New Party.

On the positive side, the KMT's economic policies have proven to be very sound. The party also has considerable financial resources of its own – it's believed to be the world's richest political party. Delivering the bacon has always been the KMT's trump card, and most observers still think it would be wrong to count the party down and out.

The Democratic Progressive Party
(mínjìn dǎng)
The DPP has emerged as the chief opposition party. With little interest in retaking the mainland, they have instead promised to 'retake Taipei'. Indeed, they did so in 1994 when the DPP's candidate Chen Shuibian managed to capture the post of mayor in a three way election.

Although the DPP contains many sincere and talented people, the party is riven by factions, some of which commit incredible acts of political buffoonery. For many years, DPP politicians were best known for throwing things and getting into fistfights with KMT legislators while the TV cameras rolled. More recently, the party has tried to clean up its image, but unsubstantiated allegations, name calling, and bringing in truckloads of betel nut-chewing yahoos for

protest rallies have become DPP hallmarks. Many DPP politicians are unabashed socialists who have shown little understanding of the free marketry that underpins Taiwan's prosperity. The DPP's policies have already succeeded in scaring off a number of major foreign investors.

Nevertheless, the DPP has its strengths and it could well wind up as Taiwan's ruling party. To its credit, the DPP has swiftly expelled any party members suspected of corruption, and their politicians, once elected, have tended to act more responsibly than their heated rhetoric has suggested.

The most divisive issue in politics is Taiwanese independence. Officially, the DPP is committed to holding a referendum on independence if the party gains power. China's nuclear weapons and the fast growing two-way trade between Taiwan and the mainland dampens enthusiasm (even among DPP legislators) for rocking the boat. For now, most Taiwanese prefer to waffle on the issue, saying that independence is a good idea but the time 'isn't right yet'.

The New Party
(xīndǎng)
Voters fed up with both KMT inefficiency and DPP antics were given a ray of hope with the formation of the New Party (NP). Originally a reformist faction of the KMT, known as the KMT New Alliance, the NP broke away to become a separate party in August 1993. The NP did quite well in the 1995 National Assembly elections, campaigning on a pro-business anticorruption platform. Unfortunately, the young reformers in the NP soon found themselves engaged in a desperate ideological struggle with the party's elderly flag wavers, which the latter seem to have won. Today, the NP are regarded as ultraconservative and as staunchly favouring reunification with the mainland. The majority of Taiwanese voters are dismayed by the NP's pro-China platform. Support for the party is shrivelling and some of the party's most popular politicians have quit. At the time of writing, the NP were locked into a

fierce internal debate, with many questioning whether the party could survive.

Taiwan Independence Party
(jiànguó dǎng)

After garnering 21% of the vote in the 1995 presidential election, DPP candidate Peng Mingmin and his supporters left the DPP and formed the Taiwan Independence Party (TIP). This was because they felt that the DPP's support for Taiwan's independence was wavering. At the time of writing the TIP held no seats in the National Assembly.

The Green Party
(lǜ dǎng)

In 1997, yet another party emerged on the political scene, the Green Party. Like the DPP, they promise to shut down all of Taiwan's nuclear power plants if they gain the majority. The Green Party has yet to capture even a single legislative seat, but it would be wrong to say that they will have no impact on Taiwan's political map. Ironically, like the TIP, their main effect could be to siphon off votes from the DPP.

Labour Party
(gōng dǎng)

Taiwan also has a tiny Labour Party, though they currently hold no seats and many wonder if the party should be taken seriously. To date the Labour Party's most memorable

Not Your Everyday Politician
The Labour Party's most memorable candidate was Hsu Hsiaotan, a young dancer with a propensity for stripping in public. She spent three months in prison for making a porno movie, and many believe that her prosecution on this charge was politically motivated. Ms Hsu's flamboyant campaign was unsuccessful, but she came within 107 votes of being elected to the National Assembly. She retired from politics and married in 1997 – at the wedding reception, her 'wedding dress' consisted of a couple of pasties and a fig leaf. ∎

candidate was Hsu Hsiaotan – see the 'Not Your Everyday Politician' boxed text.

ECONOMY

The business of Taiwan is business. Rising from an economy shattered by WWII, the island has experienced rapid economic growth. Taiwan has been classified as a 'newly industrialised economy' (NIE). It was formerly known as a 'newly industrialised country' (NIC) until mainland China threw a tantrum, pointing out that Taiwan is not a country, but is actually part of China.

Annual per capita income has risen to over US$12,000 and the annual economic growth rate is still a respectable 6%. The engine behind this economic success story is largely foreign trade. Not long ago, the label 'Made in Taiwan' was associated with cheap plastic toys that broke easily; these days Taiwanese manufacturers have moved upmarket into high quality electronics and computers. Taiwan's exports in 1997 were valued at over US$125 billion, just US$23 billion less than mainland China. Despite testy relations with China, the mainland is now Taiwan's largest export market.

Although many foreigners assume that Taiwan has a capitalist, free market economy like Hong Kong, it is in fact regulated by a number of cumbersome bureaucratic controls and more social programs than most people realise. The state heavily subsidises education, transportation and health care. A lot of government money has gone into public health, family planning, agriculture and reafforestation, and Government workers, of which there are far too many, enjoy generous benefits and pensions. It's true that there are no welfare schemes of the type found in western Europe although, if the DPP has its way, Taiwan may indeed (for better or worse) take on all sorts of new social welfare spending. Social welfare or not, nobody seems to be starving. Indeed, except for some rural backwaters like Orchid Island, Taiwan seems to have almost no poverty at all.

Another role the government plays in the economy is seen in the many large government owned monopolies controlling such industries as tobacco, liquor, sugar, salt and rail transportation. In this sense, Taiwan's economy is more socialist than most imagine. However, the economy is undergoing a slow but steady process of deregulation.

One of the government's most frequently stated aims is to make Taiwan into an Asia-Pacific Regional Operations Centre (APROC). To accomplish this, Taiwan has been slashing away at its bureaucracy and opening up its service industries (such as banking and telecommunications) which were former government monopolies. Probably the biggest hurdle to the APROC's success is the lack of direct shipping and transportation between Taiwan and mainland China. Eventually, such links will be established – assuming that Taiwan doesn't declare independence and ignite a war with China.

In addition to the legitimate economy, there is an enormous black economy present in Taiwan. The chief culprit is the licensing and tax bureaucracy which makes compliance with the law so arduous – and, for some small businesses, impossible – that many businesses prefer to operate illegally. For example, it's next to impossible to obtain a licence to operate a youth hostel (even though the government operates youth hostels), so almost every private hostel is illegal. The high price of real estate and construction means that many buildings have illegal rooftop add-ons built with flimsy materials and inadequate electrical wiring – frequent fires are the result. Many factories are illegally built on land zoned for agriculture. In any case, most penalties for noncompliance are lenient or nonexistent.

Another major reason why businesses remain illegal is to avoid taxes. This is, in fact, an ancient Chinese tradition. Also, Taiwan's tax system bears little relation to western models – taxes may be assessed arbitrarily according to the amount of office space used and the number of employees hired, rather than based on profits. Murky accounting schemes are common – using homes as office space, double bookkeeping, employing workers off the books and so on. Small business has always been Taiwan's biggest employer and the foundation of the economy, but the government is constantly crying out about the need to develop big business. The newspapers seem to support this theme, often pointing to South Korea as a good example of how big business should be the backbone of the economy. Ironically, the newspaper editorials in South Korea point to Taiwan as an example of why small business should be the backbone of the economy.

POPULATION & PEOPLE

A combination of the postwar baby-boom and an increase in the average life expectancy (76 years) – due to better health conditions – has pushed the population of Taiwan to about 21.5 million. Thanks to government-instituted family planning and increased financial security, the annual population growth rate has slowed to about 0.9% and is still falling, but Taiwan's population density is 666 people per sq km, making it one of the most crowded places in the world.

In 1949, about 70% of the population was considered to be Taiwanese; today that figure is 85%. For definition purposes, Taiwanese means someone of more or less Chinese descent whose family was in Taiwan before the KMT arrived en masse following WWII. Those who arrived after WWII are simply called 'mainlanders', but their numbers are diminishing due to natural attrition and intermarriage with the native Taiwanese. The Hakka, who originally comprised perhaps 5 to 10% of the population, have also intermarried to such an extent that they are no longer a visible minority.

Today, Taiwan's aborigines represent nearly 2% of the population. Many aborigines have converted to Christianity even though intermarriage between aborigines and members of the ethnic-Chinese majority does occur, it is far less common than marriages between Taiwanese and westerners. There are 10 tribes – the Ami, Atayal, Bunun, Paiwan, Puyuma, Rukai, Shao, Saisiat, Tsou and Yami – each of which has its own language. Like indigenous people elsewhere, Taiwan's aborigines have suffered from ridicule and scorn. However, the situation has improved in the 1990s, and aboriginal culture has become very popular. Aboriginal art is in demand and aboriginal music has hit the top of the charts (see The Times They are A-Changin' boxed text). Things aboriginal are so 'in' that ethnic-Chinese newlyweds frequently dress up in aboriginal costume for wedding photos.

EDUCATION

Literacy in Taiwan is over 93%, and most of the illiterate are elderly people who missed their chance at education due to WWII.

The Taiwanese are obsessed with higher education, and admission to a university is determined by life-or-death exams. To pass these exams, a whole industry of private cram schools has emerged, a boon to those wanting to teach English. Pity the poor students who have to spend all their evenings, weekends and holidays attending these schools. Higher education in Taiwan has a definite emphasis on science and technology – about 35% of Taiwan's 500,000 university students are studying engineering.

Foreigners who have a reasonably good level of proficiency in Chinese can be admitted to a university in Taiwan and receive a degree after completing a course of study. However, with such keen competition for university places, only a small percentage is allotted to foreigners, mostly overseas Chinese who are exempted from the formidable examinations. On the other hand, it's

The Times They are A-Changin'

Taiwanese musicians have long been at the forefront of the music scene in Asia, and many stars have flourished. As is often the case, changing attitudes have directly impacted on the success of the stars and their music. Today the Taiwanese are gradually shifting away from their Chinese roots and focusing more attention onto their own home grown culture. Nowhere has this change been more apparent than in the music scene.

Theresa Teng *(dèng lìjūn)*, one of Taiwan's most popular singers, began her profession in 1963 at age 13, performing for bored soldiers at military outposts in isolated places such as Kinmen and Matsu. She was often photographed in military uniforms, and was prone to making fiercely anti-communist public statements. Although there's no doubt her music career got a kick-start from her father, a high-ranking military officer, Theresa's talent soon became apparent, and her fame spread far beyond the Taiwanese armed forces. In her prime, Theresa Teng had millions of loyal fans in Chinese communities in the west, Hong Kong, Japan and – ironically – mainland China.

With the lifting of martial law in 1987, it suddenly became possible for the Taiwanese to legally visit the mainland. Most musicians took advantage of the thaw in relations to perform for mainland Chinese audiences. Theresa, however, resolutely refused. This may have been a matter of principle, or it may have had something to do with the fact that after the age of 30, she rarely performed publicly for profit. Her concerts in the 1980s were mostly performances at orphanages, retirement homes and – as always – military bases. Furthermore, in the late 1980s she wasn't in Asia very often, having moved to France.

Theresa never married, but she had a French boyfriend, who was considerably younger than herself. He was with her in 1995 when she died from a sudden asthma attack at Chiang Mai in Thailand. She was 42 years old.

Her body was returned to Taiwan. Theresa's tomb and a nearby statue of her have been built in the hills above Highway 2 on the north coast of the island. Like Elvis Presley's Graceland Mansion in Memphis, Tennessee, Theresa's statue is a place of pilgrimage. A steady stream of cars, taxis and tour buses bring Theresa's loyal fans, many of whom come from abroad. Her mellow tunes – played on a hidden outdoor stereo system – continually drift through the air.

More recently, the Taiwanese music market has been dominated by successful aboriginal musicians. It used to be an unpleasant fact that to be economically successful, Taiwan's aborigines had to look and behave as Chinese as possible. True, some aborigines were able to earn a living by selling aboriginal arts and crafts, while others survived by performing aboriginal song and dance shows for tourists. But overall, the best way for Taiwan's aborigines to move up the economic ladder was to hide their ethnic origins.

Taiwan's political and economic opening in the 1990s ushered in a sea of changing attitudes. Although the unemployment rate among the aboriginal population is still high, being an aborigine is now considered chic.

very easy for foreigners to enrol in private academy Chinese-language classes (see Courses in the Facts for the Visitor chapter).

ARTS
Traditional Chinese arts and culture have been well preserved in Taiwan – indeed, far more so than in mainland China.

Music
Traditional These days, the majority of people in Taiwan are more into MTV than traditional music. Nevertheless, the playing of traditional musical instruments is still studied in Taiwan (see Courses in the Facts for the Visitor chapter). Most of the instruments are stringed or flute-like and have a melodious sound. However, the instruments you are most likely to encounter while travelling are the gongs and trumpets used at temple worship ceremonies and funerals.

Common traditional instruments include:

two-stringed fiddle	*èrhú*
three-stringed fiddle	*sānxuán*
four-stringed banjo	*yuèqín*
two-stringed viola	*húqín*
flute (vertical)	*dòngxiāo*
flute (horizontal)	*dízi*
piccolo	*bāngdí*
four-stringed lute	*pípá*
zither	*gǔzhēng*
trumpet (for ceremonies)	*suǒnà*
gongs (for ceremonies)	*dàluó*

One of the first and most successful of the aboriginal pop stars is Sherry Chang *(zhāng huìmèi)*, better known by her aboriginal nickname A-Mei (see Modern Music on the next page). Sherry's younger sister, Saya *(zhāng huìchūn)* teamed up with her cousin Raya *(chén qiūlín)*, to form a hot new music duet called Amei-mei (officially misspelled Amy-my), meaning 'Amei's little sister'. Their style is reminiscent of Britain's Spice Girls, and without a doubt their youth and stunning good looks have helped make them the darlings of Taiwanese MTV. Given the fickleness of the MTV market, it's hard to say how long they will remain in the limelight, but at the time of writing they were doing very well indeed.

One interesting new aboriginal band is Power Station *(dònglì huǒchē)* which consists of two men, Yen Chihlin *(yán zhìlín)* and You Chiuhsing *(yóu qiūxīng)*. Both are members of the Paiwan tribe in Santimen, Pingtung County. Their style is reminiscent of 60s American hippies – shoulder-length hair, blue jeans, T-shirts, earrings and beaded jewellery. Both play guitar, and their songs often deal with the sadder side of life. This is far from the usual formula in the Taiwan music scene, where stars look like well-dressed college students and their lyrics follow the well-trodden 'happy-happy' romantic theme. Their music may reflect their difficult life. Yen Chihlin built his own house by hand, worked his way through school and was a low paid optician's assistant before he made his break as a musician. You Chiuhsing was a construction worker, but found his calling when his mother bought him his first guitar. Like Sherry Chang, they were discovered by a recording company while performing in a pub. ∎

COURTESY OF FORWARD MUSIC

Modern The Taiwanese seem to prefer soft ballads. Hard rock is seen as being too harsh and grating, but there are a few Taiwanese stars who alternate between hard and soft styles (usually on the same album).

Until the lifting of martial law in 1987, Taiwanese lyrics were essentially banned from the airwaves. This has all changed, and Taiwanese ballads have become popular.

You can get a reasonably good idea of the latest music trends in Taiwan by tuning into the Asian cable station, Channel V.

Not all of Taiwan's pop stars are from Taiwan. A number were born overseas (or moved overseas after becoming successful). Others are from Hong Kong, but have settled (at least part-time) in Taiwan. Some of the big names in the Taiwanese pop scene during the 1990s have been:

Coco Lee *(lǐ wén)* was born in Hong Kong but moved to the USA at age 10 and is now a US citizen. She speaks Cantonese, Mandarin, French and English. Most of her songs are recorded in Mandarin, but she has released one album in English *(Brave Enough to Love)*. Interestingly, she never intended to become a singer – but her biochemistry studies at the University of California have been derailed due to her overnight success. In 1993, after winning a 'new talent singing contest' on a visit to Hong Kong, she was offered a recording contract with Capital Artists. In 1996, she signed up with Sony Taiwan and was catapulted to the top of the charts, where she remains at the time of writing. She sings rhythm and blues.

Emil Chou *(zhōu huájiàn)*, or Chau Wah Kin in Cantonese, made his career in Taiwan. He was so successful there that practically nobody knew he was from Hong Kong until he released his debut Cantonese album *(The Real Emil Chou)* in 1993.

Harlem Yu *(yú chéngqìng)* is a native Taiwanese who sings in Mandarin and composes his own music. Harlem has hosted music TV shows in Taiwan, and in June 1996, he became the first Asian artist to be invited to London to perform in the MTV Unplugged concert. Harlem has been presented with the Top Asian Artist Award, sponsored by Billboard Magazine and Channel V.

Inou Shizuka *(yī néngjìng)*, also known as Annie, grew up in Japan, then moved to Taiwan. She's well known for being the girlfriend of Taiwanese pop star Harlem Yu, but she has also had some hits of her own. She often sings in movies.

Kao Shengmei *(gāo shèngměi)* is, like Sherry Chang, an aborigine from Taiwan. She sings in both Mandarin and Taiwanese, and is known for her soft, romantic melodies. She was at the top of the charts in the mid-1990s, but her stardom was beginning to fade by the late 1990s.

Lim Giong *(lín qiáng)* made a name for himself by being one of the first rock stars to sing in Taiwanese. He did a few punk rock songs for the soundtrack of the movie *Goodbye, South, Goodbye* (produced by Hou Hsiaohsien; see Cinema later in this section) and has also acted in several other Hou films. His music varies from mellow pop to punk (sometimes within the same song!).

Sherry Chang *(zhāng huìmèi)* is also known as A-Mei. A Taiwanese aboriginal woman who was the island's hottest star at the time of writing. Some of her better known songs include Bad Boy, Sister and Make Me Free.

Tarcy Su *(sū huìlún)* is a Taiwanese singer who has made it in Hong Kong despite the fact her Cantonese is accented. Her singing style varies from soft to almost rock'n'roll. Tarcy's most popular albums seem to be *Lemon Tree* and *The Duck*.

The Boss Band is a heavy-metal group. Local Records, a new label which specialises in Taiwanese underground music, has produced a 10-band compilation CD including The Boss Band and others.

Wu Bai *(wǔ bǎi)* and his band, China Blue, have left a big impression on Taiwan's music scene. Many say that his best album is *Wu Bai's Live (wǔ bǎi de live)* – it rocks! The style varies from blues, to mellow, to hard rock. Wu Bai is extremely versatile, and sings in both Taiwanese and Mandarin.

Literature

If you're interested in the Chinese side of Taiwan's history, then you'll find plenty of ancient Chinese literature in Taiwan to satisfy you. If you're looking for literature produced in Taiwan itself, the pickings are slim and it's all fairly recent.

The three most famous early Chinese literary works are: *The Water Margin (shuǐhú zhuàn)*, translated as *Rebels of the Marsh*; *The Dream of the Red Chamber (hónglóu mèng)*, translated as *The Dream of Red Mansions* and *The Story of the Stone*; and *Journey to the West (xīyóu jì)*. The English translations are readily available in Taiwan.

Another classic is *Jin Ping Mei*, a racy story about a wealthy Chinese man and his six wives – it's banned in China but available in Taiwan. The *I Ching (yì jīng)*, or *Book of*

Changes, is used to predict the future, but is regarded by the Chinese (and New Agers) as an ancient source of wisdom.

The Art of War (bīngfǎ), written by Sun Tzu *(sūnzi)*, is an ancient Chinese classic. It was studied by Chiang Kaishek's nemesis, Mao Zedong (too bad Chiang didn't read it), and is still required reading for modern military strategists in the west.

It's only in the second half of the 20th century that Taiwanese authors have left their mark (not too surprising, since Taiwan was annexed by Japan during the first half of the 20th century). One book which has captured much attention in the west is *The Ugly Chinaman*, by Bo Yang. The author, a journalist during Taiwan's martial law era, was imprisoned for publishing a cartoon that displeased Chiang Kaishek. He hits hard on what he considers to be the negative aspects of Chinese culture – conformity, oppression and fear of authority. It's a riveting tale. Bo Yang still lives in Taiwan and his books are freely available there (they are banned in mainland China).

No other Taiwanese author has managed to achieve Bo Yang's fame in the west, mainly because most Taiwanese books aren't translated into English. One which has made it into English is *A Family in Taiwan*, by Ling Yu (photographs by Chen Ming-Jeng). It presents life in Taiwan as exemplified by the daily life of a 12-year-old girl and her family.

Chinese Stories from Taiwan: 1960-1970, edited by Joseph Lau & Timothy Ross, was published in 1976. It's still in print, but it carries a rather steep price tag of US$58.

Bamboo Shoots After the Rain: Contemporary Stories by Women Writers of Taiwan, was made into an English language hardback by Ann C Carver & Sung-Sheng Yvonne Chang. It was published in 1991 by the Feminist Press and can usually be obtained by special order through bookshops.

Taijiquan
(tàijíquán)

Taijiquan, or slow motion shadow-boxing, has been popular in China for centuries and in recent years has become quite trendy in western countries, where it's known as 'taichi'. It is basically a form of exercise, but is also an art and a form of Chinese martial arts. Taijiquan movements are similar to kungfu *(gōngfū)*, but the latter is performed at much higher speeds, with the intention of doing bodily harm, often with the aid of weapons. There are several different styles of taijiquan, such as *chen* and *yang*.

Taijiquan is very popular among the older generation and with young women trying to keep their bodies beautiful. The movements are supposed to develop the breathing muscles, promote digestion and improve muscle tone.

Taijiquan, dancing in the park, and all manner of exercises are customarily done just as the sun rises, which means that if you want to see or participate in them, you have to get up early. Parks and most university campuses are good places to see taijiquan

You can join in with taijiquan 'workouts' at virtually any town park shortly after dawn.

being performed. In Taipei the best places to see taijiquan are the Chiang Kaishek Memorial Hall, the Sun Yatsen Memorial Hall, Taipei 2-28 Park, the hills around the Grand Hotel, Yangmingshan Park and the Sungshan Nature Reserve. Some people, for lack of a better place, perform their taijiquan on the footpath or the roof of their homes. There are organised taiji classes and foreigners are usually welcome to participate. To find a class, simply turn up at a large park early in the morning and ask a taiji practitioner where you can join in.

Martial Arts
(wǔshù)

While kungfu is the only martial art that is truly Chinese, you can find several imported varieties, from Japan and Korea, in Taiwan. The different forms of martial arts include aikido *(héqìdào)*, taekwondo *(táiquándào)*, judo *(róudào)* and karate *(kōngshǒudào)*. There are a number of martial arts schools in Taiwan – if you're interested in joining a class ask the tourism bureau to help you find one.

Qigong
(qìgōng)

As much an art form as a traditional Chinese medical treatment, *qigong* is not easily described in western terms, but it's rather like faith healing. *Qi* represents life's vital energy, and *gong* comes from kungfu. Qigong can be thought of as energy management and healing. Practitioners try to project their qi to heal others.

It's interesting to see qigong practitioners at work. Typically, they place their hands above or next to their patient's body without actually making physical contact. However, there are many who claim that they have been cured of serious illness without any treatment other than qigong, even after more conventional doctors have told them their condition is hopeless.

In Taiwan, you are most likely to see qigong practised in the ever-popular kungfu movies, where mortally wounded heroes are miraculously revived with a few waves of the hands.

Does qigong work? It isn't easy to say, but there is a theory in medicine that all doctors can cure a third of their patients regardless of the method used. So perhaps qigong also gets its 33% cure rate.

Cinema

Taiwan exports lots of things, but award-winning films are definitely not the island's speciality. Occasionally Taiwanese directors walk away with some awards at film festivals, but it's going to be a while before Taipei is declared the 'Hollywood of Asia'.

That said, film fanatics may want to dig through the video stores in search of Taiwanese hits. Most serious films are subtitled in English even if they aren't targeted at the export market.

Without a doubt, Taiwan's most renowned film director is Ang Lee *(lǐ ān)*. His first feature film was *Pushing Hands* (1992), closely followed by *The Wedding Banquet* and *Eat Drink Man Woman* (1994), which became arthouse classics. A theme running through all three films was culture clashes (children versus parents, Taiwanese suffering culture shock abroad etc). Ang Lee's career got a major boost when he directed *Sense and Sensibility* (1997), the award-winning film based on the Jane Austen novel and produced with an all-star cast. Ang Lee's latest work is *The Ice Storm* (1997), and no doubt more masterpieces will follow in the future.

Actress Sylvia Chang *(zhāng àijiā)* has starred in Ang Lee's films and in numerous Hong Kong-produced movies. She has started directing some films of her own. *Siao Yu* (1995) somewhat mimics Ang Lee's themes in that it depicts a Chinese person trying to adapt to life in America. The formula changed, however, with a funny, lightweight comedy *Tonight Nobody Goes Home* (1996).

Hou Hsiaohsien *(hóu xiàoxián)* is another Taiwanese director worthy of serious attention. Born in mainland China in 1947, Hou and his family fled the Communists in 1949 and came to Taiwan. Although Hou was at first dismissed as an another unwelcome 'mainlander', his earlier films look much like an exploration of Taiwan's history. The film that really put him in the limelight (and upset the government) was *A City of Sadness (bēiqíng chéngshì)*, which portrayed the horrific events surrounding the famed '2-28 Massacre'. Other films by Hou include *The Puppetmaster*, *Good Men Good Woman*, *Dust in the Wind*, *The Sandwich Man*, *A Summer at Grandpa's*, *The Green Green Grass of Home* and *The Time to Live and the Time to Die*. His latest film, *Goodbye South Goodbye* (1996), moves away from the Taiwanese history theme.

One director who gets abuse from film critics is Chu Yen-ping *(zhū yánpíng)*, also known as Kevin Chu. Chu is sometimes referred to as the 'King of Taiwanese pop culture'. A large number of his films, such as *Super Mischievous*, *Shaolin Popeye*, *The Clown*, *China Dragon* and *Ninja Kids*, appeal mainly to school children and parents who haven't grown up. Yet Chu gets the last laugh – his films are consistently the most popular box office draws in Taiwan. Plots can revolve around kungfu fighters, slapstick comedy, soldier stories, teenage melodrama, or lusty adult themes. If there is one thing you can say about Chu, it's that he's versatile.

Theatre

Chinese theatre draws on very different traditions from western theatre. The crucial difference is the importance of music to Chinese theatre, and thus it is usually referred to as opera. Traditional Chinese opera *(píngjù)* and the closely related Taiwanese opera are an integral part of Chinese culture that every visitor to Taiwan should experience at least once. The dialogue is all in Mandarin Chinese or, for Taiwanese opera, Taiwanese. The acting, colourful costumes, music and atmosphere are thrilling, even if you can't understand what is being said. In a few operas staged for foreigners, an English translation of the dialogue is flashed on a screen near the stage. But in most cases, no translation is available.

Contemporary Chinese opera has a 900 year continuous history, having evolved from a convergence of comic and balladic traditions in the Northern Song period. From this beginning, Chinese opera has been the meeting ground for a disparate range of forms: acrobatics, martial arts, poetic arias and stylised dance.

Operas were usually performed by travelling troupes whose social status was very low in traditional Chinese society. Their status was on a par with prostitutes and slaves and their children were barred from social advancement by a government decree that made them ineligible to participate in public service examinations. Chinese law also forbade mixed-sex performances, forcing actors to perform the roles of the opposite sex. Opera troupes were frequently associated with homosexuality in the public imagination, contributing further to their 'untouchable' social status.

Despite this, opera remained a popular form of entertainment, although it was considered unworthy of the attention of the scholar class. Performances were considered an obligatory adjunct to New Year celebrations and marriages, and sometimes to funerals and ancestral ceremonies.

Opera performances usually take place on a bare stage, with the actors taking on stylised roles that are instantly recognisable to the audience. The four major roles are the female role, the male role, the 'painted-face' role (for gods and warriors) and the clown.

Chinese opera is used to preach virtue and will usually be played near a temple to entertain the gods. Televised operas are gradually displacing live performances, but they are a poor substitute for the real thing.

SOCIETY & CONDUCT
Traditional Culture

Hidden behind a facade of gridlocked traffic, cable TV and McDonald's golden arches, there is still a strong undercurrent of traditional Chinese culture in Taiwan. Simply scratch below the surface and you'll find it.

Geomancy The Chinese word for geomancy is *fengshui*, which means 'wind-water', but the concept has little to do with climate. To be in correct geomancy is to be in proper physical harmony with the universe. This not only includes the living, but the spiritual world as well. If a Chinese person finds that their business is failing, a geomancer might be consulted. Sometimes the solution will be to move the door of the establishment; at other times it may be to relocate an ancestor's grave.

Many Chinese worship their departed ancestors and build elaborate tombs for them. A geomancer should be consulted when this is done. If this isn't done and misfortune strikes, then a geomancer may be called in and the tomb may have to be moved. Taiwan even celebrates a holiday known as Tomb Sweep Day, when people must clean the grave site of their ancestors.

Chinese Zodiac (*huángdàodài*) As in the western system of astrology, there are 12 signs in the Chinese zodiac. Unlike the western system, signs are based on the year

Culture Shock

When travelling abroad, the physical differences from your home country can be a source of endless delight. The exotic language, the interesting food, the strange but charming social customs – all make foreign travel fascinating and exciting. But not everything you encounter overseas will be so charming. Many travellers come prepared to deal with minor hazards, such as jet lag, diarrhoea and athlete's foot, but few recognise the symptoms of culture shock.

Tourists who only go abroad for a few days or weeks have little to fear, but those who are abroad for months or years are certain to suffer from some form of culture shock. This condition has been extensively studied by many psychologists, sociologists, anthropologists and government organisations. The symptoms and stages of culture shock are well documented and predictable.

Some people are more susceptible to culture shock than others, and much depends on which countries you are visiting. As a general rule, the more alike two cultures are, the less problem there will be in adapting from one to the other.

If you're not from Asia and stay there for a long time, you can expect to encounter the first two (and possibly the third) stages of culture shock. Ironically, you may experience reverse culture shock when returning to your home country after a long stay overseas. The three stages of culture shock are:

Enrapture On arrival, most people are totally dazzled with the exotic surroundings. 'Wow, I'm in Taiwan!' is a common reaction. Everything is different, interesting and exciting. A new paradise has been discovered, and many newcomers will even say things like: 'This country is more civilised than mine. There's a lot we can learn from this country'. This may or may not be true, but it's doubtful that you will really understand Taiwan and its culture after only a few days or weeks. If you stay for a long time though, you will probably reach stage two, which is:

Disillusionment Paradise lost. The happiness bubble bursts. Things begin to irritate you – maybe the food, language, climate or people's ideas and attitudes. Travellers at this stage start complaining, often bitterly, about every petty thing.

These will pile up until the visitor ends up wishing for nothing but a plane ticket home, back to a 'sensible country'. Many do indeed leave, reducing the length of their intended stay. Others, both tourists and foreign residents, withdraw from the local culture entirely and seek out the refuge of their fellow expatriates. It's worth noting that Chinese people living abroad also do this, which is why many western cities have a Chinatown. The tendency to look for something familiar in a foreign land is common. Expats in Asia often choose to live in 'foreigners' ghettos', eating familiar western foods and failing to learn the local language and culture.

Some develop an outward superiority complex – 'We are superior to these natives'. They constantly write letters 'home' and always seem to be checking their mailbox for responses. They search relentlessly for news from their home country, showing no interest in local news. Some hide indoors with books or music tapes, or simply sleep all day, afraid to go out of the door. Instead of getting out and enjoying the experience of living in a foreign country, expats working in Taiwan often rather than the month of birth, though the exact day and time of birth are also carefully considered in charting astrological paths.

Fortune tellers are common in Taiwan. Making use of astrology and palm and face reading, fortune tellers claim they can accurately predict the future. If you want to try out this service, you will almost certainly need an interpreter, since few fortune tellers in Taiwan speak English.

If you want to know your sign in the Chinese zodiac, look up your year of birth in 'The Chinese Zodiac' boxed text over the page; future years are also given so you know what signs are coming up. However, it's a little more complicated than this, because Chinese astrology goes by the lunar calendar. New Year falls in late January or early February. So, if your birthday is in January you will be included in the zodiac year before the calendar year of your birth.

It's said that the animal year chart originated when Buddha commanded all the beasts of the earth to assemble before him. Only 12 animals came and they were each rewarded by having their names given to a

fall into a rut, a boring daily routine of working, eating, sleeping and complaining. Chronic fatigue, a bad temper and frequent whingeing are all signs of emotional depression. And that is the ultimate result of culture shock: depression.

The traveller can simply go home or at least move on to another country. An expat working overseas on a contract may not have this option. Married couples 'stuck overseas' are likely to take out their frustration on each other, and divorce is sometimes the result. The best solution, of course, is to try to reach the third stage:

Adaptation Taiwanese people often ask a foreigner, 'So, how do you like my country?' And the reply they often get is 'First of all it's too hot. Secondly, I can't understand what people are saying. Thirdly, it's chaotic and no one obeys the traffic rules and...'

Face it. You cannot change Taiwan; you must adapt to it. If you fail to adapt, you'll suffer the consequences of isolating yourself from the society you've chosen to live in.

One suggestion I like to give to foreigners living in Taiwan – don't bottle yourself up; get out and explore. Even within the city limits of Taipei, there are opportunities for hiking (Yangmingshan, Sungshan Nature Reserve etc). There are special-interest clubs (bungy jumping, computers, rock climbing, swimming, bowling, martial arts, Toastmasters, Hash House Harriers etc; see Activities in the Taipei chapter for more details). Taiwan also has a very active nightlife – take advantage of it. Glueing yourself to a TV set or sitting around a hostel feeling sorry for yourself will only make you feel worse.

An important factor in adapting to a new culture is learning the local language. Communication is the key. Indeed, learning a foreign language should be considered one of the great benefits of living overseas. Study everything you can find about Taiwan.

This advice sounds easy to follow, but actually it's not. Only a small number of westerners ever gain a true understanding of, and adapt well to living in, Asia. For most, a trip to Asia is a love-hate experience.

There is also the opposite danger. Some foreigners are so heavily influenced by the local culture that in a sense they 'go native'. This is not necessarily a good adaptation. If it reaches the point whereby you thoroughly reject your native culture and disparage your home country to the point where you don't want anything more to do with it or its people, then you are suffering from another form of culture shock. For lack of a better term, I'll call it the 'rejection syndrome'. It's not a healthy sign at all.

The rejection syndrome is a common ailment among wandering westerners who are drifting through Asia 'in search of themselves' and who think they've discovered 'true enlightenment' by adopting eastern cult religions and rejecting all things western. Indeed, some come to believe that they now possess some exclusive wisdom that makes them superior to other westerners. To put it more simply, they suffer from an inflated ego. What these 'enlightened' individuals fail to see is that western culture, for all its faults, has many strong points, which is why it's so pervasive in the world today. Seeking knowledge in the east is a fine idea; many Asians go to the west seeking the same thing. The best advice would be to borrow the strong points of all the cultures you encounter and adapt them to your own needs. ∎

The Chinese Zodiac

Rat	1924	1936	1948	1960	1972	1984	1996
Ox/Cow	1925	1937	1949	1961	1973	1985	1997
Tiger	1926	1938	1950	1962	1974	1986	1998
Rabbit	1927	1939	1951	1963	1975	1987	1999
Dragon	1928	1940	1952	1964	1976	1988	2000
Snake	1929	1941	1953	1965	1977	1989	2001
Horse	1930	1942	1954	1966	1978	1990	2002
Goat	1931	1943	1955	1967	1979	1991	2003
Monkey	1932	1944	1956	1968	1980	1992	2004
Rooster	1933	1945	1957	1969	1981	1993	2005
Dog	1934	1946	1958	1970	1982	1994	2006
Pig	1935	1947	1959	1971	1983	1995	2007

specific year. Buddha decided to name each year according to the order in which the animals arrived – the first was the rat, then the ox, tiger, rabbit and so on.

Lunar Calendar (*nónglì*) There are two calendars in use in Taiwan. One is the Gregorian or solar calendar (*yīnlì*), which westerners are familiar with; the other is the Chinese lunar calendar. The two calendars do not correspond with each other because a lunar month is slightly shorter than a solar month. To keep the two calendars in harmony, the Chinese add an extra month to the lunar calendar every 30 months, essentially creating a lunar leap year. Thus, the Chinese lunar New Year – the most important holiday – can fall anywhere between 21 January and 28 February on the Gregorian calendar.

Calendars showing all the holidays for the current year are readily available in Taiwan. These calendars look just like the ones westerners are familiar with, but the lunar dates are shown in smaller numbers.

Renao (*rènào*) It's hard to translate *renao* into English. It means something like 'lively', 'festive', 'happy' and 'noisy' – especially 'noisy'. Many Taiwanese people seem immune to noise. You'll notice that department stores and restaurants have background music blaring at around 100 decibels. This is used to attract customers, whereas in western

countries it would surely drive them away. Lighting firecrackers is also very renao.

Many people in Taiwan have asked me why Americans like to live in the suburbs and commute to the city for work. 'The city is so much more exciting (renao),' they say, 'so why would anyone want to live out in the lonely countryside?' I have met a number of people in Taiwan who must work in the country, but they live in the city where housing is much more expensive, and commute every day to the country. 'Why?' I ask. 'Because,' they say, 'the city is a good place to raise children.'

Guanxi The closest English word to *guanxi* (*guānxì*) would be 'relationship'. However, guanxi has a stronger meaning, similar to the English expression 'You scratch my back and I'll scratch yours'. To build up good guanxi, you have to do things for people: give them gifts, take them to dinner, grant favours and so on.

Once this is done, an unspoken obligation exists. It is perhaps because of this unspoken debt that people automatically try to refuse gifts. They may not wish to establish guanxi with someone, because, sooner or later, they may have to repay the favour. Even after it is 'repaid', guanxi is rarely terminated. It is a continuing process of mutual gift-giving, back-scratching and favouritism that can last a lifetime.

Guanxi also helps if you know the right people, as it can help you avoid a lot of red tape and may be mutually beneficial to all parties involved. This is very important in traditional Chinese society, where stifling bureaucracy can make it difficult to accomplish anything.

Of course, guanxi exists everywhere, and it's stronger on the Chinese mainland than in Taiwan, so you are likely to encounter it eventually. Those doing business with local people should be particularly aware of guanxi.

Age Do you know how old you are? Many Chinese say you are already one year old on the day you're born. So if you're a 30-year-old in the west, you're 31 in Taiwan.

Dos & Don'ts
Face In Asia, having 'big face' is synonymous with prestige, and prestige is important throughout the continent. All families, even poor ones, are expected to have big wedding parties and throw money around like water in order to gain face. The fact that this can cause bankruptcy for the young couple is considered far less serious a problem than losing face.

Much of the Taiwanese obsession with materialism is really to do with gaining face, not material wealth. There are many ways to gain points in the face game: owning nice clothes, a big car (even if you can't drive), a piano (even if you can't play), imported cigarettes and liquor (even if you don't smoke or drink) or a golf club membership (even if you don't know where the golf course is). Therefore, when choosing a gift for a Taiwanese friend, try to give something with snob appeal such as a bottle of imported liquor, perfume, cigarettes or chocolate. Things imported from the USA, Europe or Japan are good options that will please your host and help win you points in the face game.

Flattery Flatter your host and guest to give them big face. Words of praise like, 'You're so intelligent and humorous (or beautiful etc)'

will go down well. If you speak three words of Chinese someone will surely say, 'You speak Chinese very well'. The proper response should be self-deprecating: 'Oh no, my Chinese is very bad' (probably true). Boasting is a real faux pas. Remaining humble is very much a part of the Confucian tradition. The Chinese are famous for their humility and you will often hear Taiwanese saying things like 'Oh, I'm so ugly and stupid!'. Be sure not to agree with such comments, even in jest.

Being modest is a ticket to being accepted, especially because many Chinese seem to have stereotypes of westerners being very proud.
Christopher Fuhrman

Looking Good If you saunter around the cities in a dirty T-shirt, shorts and floppy sandals you'll probably attract some rude stares. The rule to follow is to look neat and clean, even if dressed in shorts and sandals. This is especially important when visiting people, eating in restaurants or going to discos and nightclubs – you may be refused entrance if your outfit isn't up to standard.

Though you might occasionally see a Taiwanese person with a beard, it's a rarity. The clean-shaven look is in. As one western visitor noted:

I can testify that having a beard plus being a foreigner can cause one to be stared at, especially by young children who will cry out in fear or shock. Once I was reassured by my Chinese translator, 'Don't worry. He just thinks you are a large dog'.
Philip Lake

A sandal with a strap across the back of the ankle is considered more acceptable than thongs. Thongs are for indoor wear. True, you will see people wearing thongs outdoors, but some restaurants, theatres and other establishments may refuse you admission unless your feet are properly 'strapped in'.

Sunbathing is a peculiarly western custom that the Taiwanese don't understand at all. The Taiwanese, along with most Asians, think that white skin is much more beautiful than suntanned skin; 'proper' Chinese women always carry a parasol. A suntan is associated with manual labour and farm work, which are considered to be low-class occupations by the Taiwanese. On a hot, sunny day in Taiwan, when the western expatriates head to the beach or swimming pool to bask in the sun, the Taiwanese stay indoors. They are more likely to go to the swimming pool at night, when there is no risk of getting a tan.

The Taiwanese may consume their fair share of porno videos, and nude dancing shows are more common than anyone likes to admit, but attitudes are still pretty conservative when it comes to public bathing. Bikinis are becoming more popular on the beaches, but be aware that they're still rare.

Name Cards Name cards are very popular in Taiwan – it's all part of the face game. Get some printed before or immediately after you arrive in Taiwan – you'll have plenty of opportunities to hand them out. Every professional will need a name card, even a professional dishwasher can have a name card saying they're a sanitary engineer.

In Taiwan, name cards should be printed with English on one side and Chinese characters on the other. If you get name cards or anything else printed in Taiwan, check the English carefully after it's typeset because misspellings are common.

Don't be caught short without name cards if you are doing business in Taiwan. You will almost certainly lose face if you mumble something about having run out of cards. Keep them in your wallet at all times.

Left-Handedness The left hand is not considered to be unclean as in other parts of Asia, so it is OK to touch people with it. However, conformity is valued over individualism in much of Taiwan and being left-handed is considered as 'odd'. Children who are naturally left-handed are discouraged from using their left hand. If you are left-handed, you may draw comments when you sign your name or write a letter.

Family & Children Family is the basic foundation of Chinese society and children are highly prized. If you travel with children in Taiwan, everywhere you go someone will want to play with your kids.

Asian parents are very indulgent with their children and tend to baby them right into adulthood. It is not unusual to meet people in their late 20s still living at home. Taiwanese parents are appalled that western parents leave teenage children at home while they go away for the weekend, or that they let their children move out of the family home at the age of 18. The Taiwanese are also amazed that western teenagers in high school and college often work part-time to help pay for their education, apartment or car.

Basically, children are expected to be sheltered from most adult responsibilities until after they finish school. Perhaps as a result, most Taiwanese are overly dependent on their parents by western standards.

The parent-child relationship is very strong in Taiwan throughout a person's lifetime, and trouble within the family is never discussed publicly. Avoid punishing your kids in public. If you need to discipline a child, do it in private. Public spankings will quickly draw a crowd of indignant onlookers. When the parents get old and can no longer care for themselves, they usually live with their children rather than being packed off to retirement homes as in many western countries. These strong family ties are in some respects one of the best characteristics of Asian society.

Taiwan is a patriarchal society, in line with Chinese Confucian tradition. When a woman marries, her ties with her family are partially severed and she joins her husband's family – though, interestingly, she doesn't usually give up her maiden name. If the couple still live at home after marriage, it will be with the husband's family, never the wife's family.

A divorce is considered the ultimate catastrophe. If a couple does get divorced, the father automatically gets custody of the children if he wants them. In the not-too-distant past (in the 1980s), a divorced person was basically considered 'damaged goods', but Taiwanese society is changing and these days divorce no longer holds the same stigma.

Weddings Marriage ceremonies are big business in Taiwan, as the large number of wedding shops attests. If you spend any length of time in Taiwan, you're likely to be invited to a wedding. The wedding invitation is invariably red – a happy colour – and it usually brings with it the obligation to present money to the newlyweds. Therefore, it is often referred to as a 'red bomb'.

Should you receive a red bomb from a Taiwanese friend, you'll be happy to know that the money you are expected to give is used to pay for the fabulous 10-course meal that will be served at the wedding party. You needn't bring any other gifts, just the money. The money should be cash – not a cheque – and it *must* be placed in a red envelope. It must be red because a white envelope is a sign of death. Red envelopes should be used any time you give money to somebody, such as for a birthday, a gift or even if you just owe it to them. Never give NT$4000 as the number four is taboo. The typical amount expected these days is about NT$1000 per person. It's OK to give more, but make sure that the second digit of the total amount is *not* an odd number (for example NT$1100 is bad) because a married couple is an even pair – an odd number indicates that the couple will separate. It's OK to bring an uninvited friend with you, but be sure to put an extra NT$600 in the envelope for each guest and let the host know in advance so enough food can be ordered. Be sure to write your name on the envelope so the newlyweds know who it's from.

Wedding parties do not last very long; usually just a little over an hour. Everyone tends to eat and run, allowing very little time for talking and socialising. Guests are permitted to take extra food home in plastic bags that the restaurant provides.

Bad Omens Certain things are considered to be bad omens in Taiwan. The Taiwanese are very sensitive to death signs, so don't talk about accidents and death as if they might really occur. For example, never say 'Be careful on that ladder or you'll break your neck': that implies it will happen. Chinese people almost never leave a will, because to write a will indicates the person will die soon. If you wrote a will in Taiwan, it would be virtually impossible to find a local to witness your signature for you. They will not want anything to do with it.

In Chinese, the number 'four' sounds just like the word for death. As a result, hospitals never put patients on the 4th floor. If you give someone flowers, always give red flowers, not white. In Chinese symbolism, white – not black – is the colour associated with death. Many Chinese are afraid to receive a clock as a gift, a sure sign that someone will die soon. The Taiwanese are really into longevity and death is a taboo topic.

The belief in omens probably explains why Chinese geographical names always mean something wonderful, like 'Paradise Valley', 'Heaven's Gateway' or 'Happiness Rd'. There is one national park in the USA the Taiwanese never visit – Death Valley.

The Chinese (lunar) New Year has its special taboos and omens which affect your fortune in the coming year. During New Year's Day don't wash clothes or you will have to work hard in the coming year, and don't sweep dirt out of the house or you will sweep your wealth away. Be sure not to argue during New Year, or you will face a year of bickering.

Young people and urban dwellers are far less likely to pay heed to taboos and omens than the older generation and rural residents.

Red Ink Don't write in red ink. If you want to give someone your address or telephone number, write in any other colour. Red ink conveys a message of unfriendliness. If you're teaching in Taiwan it's OK to use red pen to correct students' work, but if you need to write extensive comments or suggestions on the back of the paper, use some other colour.

continued on page 34

Temples of Taiwan

There are over 5000 temples in Taiwan, ranging in size from a back-alley hut to a monumental, multistoreyed structure that would dwarf some of the cathedrals of Europe. These temples can be broken down into three basic categories – Taoist, Buddhist and Confucian. The simpler Confucian temples are easily distinguishable, while Taoist and Buddhist temples have partially merged, often with the deities of both religions prominently displayed side by side. Sometimes a statue of Confucius will also be on display.

The Matsu Temple in Makung, Pengu Islands, was founded in 1623 and is the oldest temple in Taiwan. There are a few others which are more than 300 years old, but overall, Taiwan's temples are not as old as those in Mainland China. On the other hand Taiwan did not experience the Cultural Revolution (1966-70), which saw the destruction of many temples and the persecution of worshippers in mainland China. Therefore, Taiwan's temples today are still active places of worship.

Taoist

Taoist temples are the most colourful in Taiwan and Taoists tend to put on a good party, with frequent ceremonies, parades, firecrackers, incense burning, crashing of cymbals, exorcisms and offerings to the ghosts.

Monks and nuns are notably absent, though there is often a caretaker in residence. Inside the temple there will be a small courtyard or chamber with a large incense burner. Typically, bowls of fruit and other edible offerings to the spirits will be displayed, behind which an altar will be framed by red brocade embroidered with gold characters.

The eaves of Taoist temples curve upwards at each end and are usually decorated with divine figures and lucky symbols such as dragons and carp. The temples almost always have an 'oven' where ghost money is incinerated, this ensures that the spirits are well financed. Depending on the size and wealth of the temple, there could also be gongs, drums, side altars and adjoining rooms with shrines to different gods, chapels for prayers to the dead and funerary plaques. The basic premise behind this elaborate mysticism and ritual is to ensure good fortune and blow away bad demons.

Among the better known Taoist deities are Matsu (mǎzǔ), goddess of the sea, and the red-faced Kuankung (guāngōng), also known as Kuanti and Kuanyu. Fishermen often pray to Matsu for a safe journey, while Kuankung is believed to offer protection against war. Kuankung is based on an historical figure, a soldier of the 3rd century. You can read more about him in the Chinese classic *The Romance of the Three Kingdoms*.

Incense burners, like this one at the Lungshan Temple, Taipei, are constantly surrounded by a haze of smoke. Devotees will place two to three sticks of incense in each burner around the temple to appease the gods.

The ash within the burner itself will often represent many years of worship and if a temple should change location some of this ash will be taken to the new site.

Buddhist

By contrast, Buddhist temples are relatively sedate. The most common deities you will see in a Buddhist temple are Kuanyin (guānyīn), the goddess of mercy, and Shihchia (shíjiā), from the Indian Sakyamuni, who represents the Buddha, Siddhartha Gautama (Siddhartha was his given name; Gautama was his surname; Sakya is the name of the clan to which his family belonged). The Buddha is frequently displayed in a basic triad, with a Bodhisattva (a Buddhist saint who has arrived at the gateway to nirvana but has chosen to return to earth to guide lesser mortals along righteous paths) on either side. There are often large, fierce-looking statues of warriors brandishing swords placed near the temple doors. These are temple guards, not deities. Larger Buddhist temples are essentially monasteries with nuns and monks in residence; they are strict

MARTIN MOOS

Temple roofs, like this one in Luerhmen, are intricately detailed with colourful figures. Dragons represent strength, wisdom and good fortune while the phoenix symbolises peace and prosperity.

CHRIS TAYLOR

CHRIS TAYLOR

Left: Incense drying in the sun completes many a Taiwanese street scene. This is particularly true during Ghost Month when devotees ward off the wandering spirits from hell by burning extra incense.

Right: Hui-bi painted on a temple wall, literally meaning 'make way' (for the gods).

CHRIS TAYLOR

Matsu, seen here in Tainan's Matsu Temple, is one of the most popular deities in Taiwan. The goddess of the seas and heavenly protector is often represented in a sitting position wearing a crown and holding a sceptre or tablet.

CHRIS TAYLOR   CHRIS TAYLOR

Religious devotees place two to three sticks of incense in each of the pots strategically placed throughout temples, creating a misty and atmospheric shroud of smoke.

CHRIS TAYLOR   CHRIS TAYLOR

Offerings to the gods and ancestors include the burning of wads of ghost money (left) and donations of food and possessions (right) that equip the spirits for the afterworld; in return devotees receive protection and advice.

CHRIS TAYLOR   CHRIS TAYLOR

Traditional ceremonies are performed by priests (right) during religious festivals such as the birthday of Confucius. Performances, including traditional music recitals (left) and Chinese operas, are also staged in and around temples.

vegetarians who pass their time working in well-tended gardens. Most Buddhist monasteries offer modest dormitory accommodation to pilgrims (see Shihtoushan in the North Taiwan chapter). However it's important to realise that these are not provided as backpacker accommodation and you should only consider staying at such places if you are prepared to respect the simple Buddhist lifestyle. Some monasteries now routinely turn down requests to stay from foreigners because they have had problems with backpackers playing music, smoking dope and sleeping with the opposite sex. Monks and nuns lead a quiet and austere lifestyle, their guests are expected to do the same.

Some Buddhist monasteries have attached hospitals (much as the Catholics and Adventists operate hospitals). The most striking and unique feature of Buddhist temples is the pagoda. These pagodas have been used to store religious artefacts and documents, but their most important function is to house the ashes of the deceased. In ancient China, pagodas were constructed of wood, making them susceptible to destruction by fire and decay. Later, more durable materials such as stone, brick and concrete were introduced – this is the style you will see in Taiwan today.

Confucian

Confucian temples are simple and quiet. There are no monks or nuns in residence, just a temple caretaker. There is only one ceremony held each year, in celebration of the birthday of Confucius, on 28 September. This ceremony begins at about 4 am and lasts for two hours. It's a solemn affair with dignitaries and many worshippers in attendance many of whom hope to acquire some of a sacrificial pig's, goat's or ox's fur, since this is believed to impart wisdom.

Incense is never burnt in the modest Confucian temples nor are firecrackers used.

Other Places of Worship

There are other temples and shrines in Taiwan which do not represent any particular denomination, but were built simply to honour great heroes or martyrs (such as The Eternal Spring Shrine in Taroko Gorge). The Taiwanese also worship their ancestors, so you're bound to see many elaborate altars and tombs dedicated to departed relatives all over Taiwan.

Temple Etiquette

Temples have no set time for prayers and there are no communal services except for funerals. Worshippers come to the temple whenever they want to make offerings, pray for help or give thanks.

One great thing about visiting temples in Taiwan is that they are nearly always open and you don't have to pay to get in. It's not necessary to take your shoes off unless the floor is carpeted – look to see what others do. You are allowed to photograph temple interiors, but be respectful of people praying. I have seen some quite outrageous behaviour by foreigners in temples, such as ridiculing the deities, taking 'souvenirs', or climbing up onto a Buddha's lap to have a photograph taken, and I even know of one place where initials were carved into a wooden temple image. When visiting temples dress neatly, be quiet and behave respectfully so that travellers who come after you will continue to be welcomed.

Confucius was a teacher, not a god, who spent his life travelling around war-torn China, spreading philosophies that reflected his pacifist views. He believed that human nature was truly good and that governments should be for the benefit of the people, not just individuals.

The wisdom of Confucius was not fully appreciated until after his death in 479 BC.

continued from page 31

Funerals Hopefully, you won't be attending many of these. However, if someone you know dies, there are certain formalities that must be observed. If you receive a card informing you of the death of a friend or business associate, you are expected to send money, just as if you had received a wedding invitation. The money is used to cover the funeral costs. About NT$600 to NT$1000 is a typical amount. Of course you don't have to send money, but if you value the relationship with the deceased's family you'd better pay up. In return, you will probably receive a cheap gift. I once received a towel (worth about NT$50) for my NT$1000 donation. Alternatively, if you're planning to attend the funeral you can take your donation with you to the ceremony – you are not expected to pay twice.

You aren't expected to attend funerals unless specifically invited, and if you send money, you can be excused. If you do go, you'll find it very different from those in the west (especially if the deceased was a Taoist). The dearly departed can only be buried on an auspicious day, which may not occur until a couple of months after death. During this time, the family sets up some sort of altar, usually in the street next to the house, where stacks of flowers and gifts (tinned food, beer and boxes of MSG are the usual items) donated by friends are collected. During this period, family members of the deceased usually wear a black ribbon pinned to their clothes at all times to indicate that they're in mourning.

If you're attending a funeral, try to find out in advance what is expected. I say that because there are different types of funerals.

A conservative, traditional Chinese funeral is a solemn affair, as a funeral is in the west. However, the ceremony is very different. Children draped in white robes, with white hoods over their heads, surround the casket and hold a white rope to keep out any bad spirits.

That's the conservative funeral – other families prefer a more festive occasion. You may be asked to bring a white (it *must* be white) envelope stuffed with cash. This is to pay for the party, which can be even more festive than those held for weddings. Your hosts may employ the services of an 'electric organ flower car' *(diànzǐqín huāchē)*, which is a brightly decorated truck with an organ in the back. Beautiful young women clad in the scantiest bikinis will sing songs, and sometimes even strip off their bikinis. This is supposed to entertain the spirits. To remind everyone that this is indeed a funeral, people may be employed to cry. After the chanting, singing and stripping ceremonies, there's normally a little parade through the streets followed by a big feast.

It is perfectly acceptable to bring flowers to a funeral. Again, bring white flowers, not red.

Showing Anger Venting your rage in public is bad form. Screaming and yelling will draw an instant crowd and some of the onlookers will regard you as uncivilised. Rather than solving your problem, you may create more trouble for yourself. Smile. A lot of westerners really blow it on this point. Maybe you want to say 'This food isn't what I ordered!', but if you need to complain about something, then do so in a polite, almost apologetic tone.

The Taiwanese are very successful at controlling their emotions in public. Even when greatly distressed, they try to look cheerful. Harmonious social relations are greatly stressed in Taiwan. Even when people disagree with what you are saying, they often pretend to agree or just smile rather than confront you.

Westerners, on the other hand, tend to be argumentative and quick to complain when things don't go right. In the eyes of many Asians, this behaviour is rough mannered or rude.

Speaking Too Frankly In Asia, people don't always say what they mean. They often say what they think the other person wants to hear – this is necessary to preserve face. Getting straight to the point and being blunt is not appreciated in Taiwan. If a local asks you 'Do you like my new car?', be sure to say you love it, even if it's a piece of junk.

The Taiwanese stress polite manners and smooth social relations, so you should avoid direct criticism of others. It's better to make up a story or avoid the topic rather than confront someone with unpleasant facts that will cause embarrassment.

Personal Questions Taiwanese people will often strike up a conversation with a total stranger by asking questions such as: 'Are you married?', 'How many children do you have?', 'How much money do you make?', 'May I know your name, address and telephone number?' or 'What is your blood type?'. To be asked such questions in western society would be most unsettling, but in Taiwan it is quite normal and is considered to be friendly.

The blood type question seems to have come from the Japanese influence (most Japanese consider blood type so important that they would never marry someone whose blood type was 'wrong'). The money question, however, is very Chinese.

How do you respond if you don't wish to reveal your blood type, how much money you make or your personal family history to a complete stranger? Simply make up whatever answer you feel comfortable with. No need to say how much money you make, just make up a figure. But don't blow up and yell, 'None of your business!'. That would be a major faux pas on your part. The person asking the question was only trying to be friendly, not nosy.

Gift Giving This is a very complex and important part of Chinese culture. When visiting people it is important to bring a gift, perhaps a tin of biscuits, flowers, a cake or chocolate. As a visiting foreigner, you will find that people want to give you gifts. While sitting in a restaurant or just walking on the street, I've had total strangers come up to me and hand me candy, cigarettes and chewing gum. The first time it happened to me, I thought the guy was just a pushy door-to-door salesman so I handed the goods back to him with

an abrupt 'I don't want to buy it'. I'm afraid I insulted the poor guy – a good example of cultural misunderstanding.

Gift giving is a fascinating ordeal. Your host will invariably refuse the gift. You are expected to insist. The verbal volleyball can continue for quite some time. If the host accepts too readily, then they are considered to be too greedy. They must first refuse and then you must insist.

You: Here's a little gift I bought for you.
Host: No, no, it's not necessary.
You: Oh please, I want you to have it.
Host: No, you shouldn't waste your money on me.
You: Never mind, I've already bought it. It's my honour to give it to you.
Host: No, you should keep it for yourself.
You: Oh, but I insist that you take it.
Host: But I am not worthy of such a gift.

And so on ad infinitum. When receiving a gift, never open it in front of the person who gave it to you. That makes you look greedy. Express your deep thanks, then put it aside and open it later.

Removing Shoes One thing that the Taiwanese detest is a dirty floor. Never mind that the outside of a home might look like a toxic waste dump: the inside must be spotlessly clean, especially the floor. This tradition seems to have been inherited from the Japanese during their occupation of Taiwan, and it's slowly fading. Nevertheless, at least half the homes in Taiwan are 'shoes off'. There are usually slippers by the entrance door: if this is the case, remove your shoes and wear the slippers. Your hosts may say, 'Never mind, just wear your shoes inside', but they aren't speaking frankly, they're being polite. If everyone else takes their shoes off, you should too. When using the bathroom, there is usually another set of slippers especially for bathroom use because the floor is often wet.

Most foreigners don't seem to mind this custom because it feels good to take your shoes off on a hot day. Unfortunately, the slippers provided are often too small for western feet.

Dust Besides a dirty floor, another thing the Taiwanese detest is dust (surprising, considering how polluted Taiwan's cities are). You will often see motorcyclists and cyclists wearing surgical masks to protect themselves from dust, although they're largely oblivious to the chemical pollutants spewing from motor vehicles. Students too will often avoid sitting at the front of the classroom because they fear the dust from the blackboard – as well as being afraid of the teacher, of course.

Handing Paper to Somebody Always hand a piece of paper to somebody with both hands, as this shows respect. This is especially true if that person is somebody important, like a public official, your landlord or a business associate. If you only use one hand, you will be considered rude.

Smiling A smile in Taiwan doesn't always mean the person is happy. Smiling is a proper response to an embarrassing situation. The waitress who smiles at you after spilling tea in your lap isn't laughing at you. The smile is offered as an apology. If you get angry, she may smile more. This does not mean she is amused. If you lose your temper, then you have committed a major social error. Smile.

RELIGION

Many religions are practised in China, and all the major ones have been carried over to Taiwan. One outstanding fact from Chinese history is that the Chinese have never engaged in religious wars. The main religions of China are Buddhism, Taoism and Confucianism. Most Taiwanese consider themselves at least nominally Buddhist-Taoist-Confucianist, which makes for some pretty interesting temples (see the Temples of Taiwan section earlier in this chapter).

Buddhism

(fó jiào)
One of the world's great religions, Buddhism originally developed in India, from where it spread all over east and South-East Asia. With this spread of influence, the form and concepts of Buddhism have changed significantly. Buddhism today has developed into numerous sects, or schools of thought, but these sects are not mutually exclusive or antagonistic towards one another.

Buddhism was founded in India in the 6th century BC by Siddhartha Gautama, partly as a reaction against Brahmanism. Born as a prince, Siddhartha lived from 563 BC to 483 BC. During his early years, he lived a life of luxury, but later became disillusioned with the world when he was confronted with the sights of old age, sickness and death. He despaired of finding fulfilment on the physical level, since the body was inescapably subject to these weaknesses. Dissatisfied with the cruel realities of life, he left his home at the age of 29 and became an ascetic in search of a solution. At the age of 35, Siddhartha sat under a banyan tree, and in a deep state of meditation, attained enlightenment. He thus became a 'Buddha', meaning 'Enlightened One'. It was claimed that Gautama Buddha was not the first Buddha, but the fourth, and he is not expected to be the last.

The central theme of Buddhist philosophy is the belief that all life is suffering. All people are subject to the traumas of birth, sickness, feebleness and death; the fear of what they most dread (incurable illness or personal weakness); and separation from what they love. The cause of suffering is desire – specifically the desires of the body and the desire for personal fulfilment. Happiness can only be achieved if these desires are overcome, and this requires following the 'eight-fold path'. By following this path the Buddhist aims to attain nirvana. Volumes have been written in attempts to define nirvana; the *sutras* (the Buddha's discourses) simply say that it's a state of complete freedom from greed, anger, ignorance and the various other chains of human existence.

The first branch of the eight-fold path is 'right understanding': the recognition that life is suffering, that suffering is caused by desire for personal gratification, and that suffering can be overcome. The second branch is 'right mindedness' – cultivating a mind free from sensuous desire, ill will and cruelty. The remaining branches require that one refrain from abuse and deceit; show kindness and avoid self-seeking in all actions; develop virtues and curb passions; and practise meditation.

Many westerners misunderstand certain key aspects of Buddhism. First of all, it should be understood that the Buddha is not a god but a human being who claims no divine powers. In Buddhist philosophy, human beings are considered their own masters and gods are irrelevant.

Reincarnation is also widely misunderstood. It is not considered desirable in Buddhism to be reborn into the world. Since all life (existence) is suffering, one does not wish to return to this world. One hopes to escape the endless cycle of rebirths by reaching nirvana.

Buddhism reached its height in India by the 3rd century BC, when it was declared the state religion of India by the emperor Ashoka. It declined sharply after that as a result of factionalism and persecution by the Brahmans.

Numerous Buddhist sects have evolved in different parts of the world. Classical Buddhists will not kill any creature and are therefore strict vegetarians. They believe that attempting to escape life's sufferings by committing suicide will only bring more bad karma and result in rebirth at a lower level. Yet there are other Buddhist sects that hold opposite views. During the 1960s, for example, Vietnamese Buddhists made world headlines by publicly burning themselves to death to protest the war. Somehow, the various sects of Buddhism manage not to clash with each other.

Buddhism reached China around the 1st century AD and became its prominent religion by the 3rd century. Ironically, while Buddhism expanded rapidly throughout East Asia, it declined in India.

Buddhism in China is mixed with other Chinese philosophies such as Confucianism and Taoism. The Chinese, in particular, had a hard time accepting the fact that they should not wish to return to this life, as they believe in longevity. As many as 13 schools of Buddhist thought evolved in China, the most famous, perhaps, being Chan, which is usually known in the west by its Japanese name, Zen.

Taoism
(dào jiào)

Unlike Buddhism, which was imported from India, Taoism is indigenous to China. It is second only to Confucianism in its influence on Chinese culture. The philosophy of Taoism is believed to have originated with Laozi, whose name is variously spelled Laotze, Laotzu or Laotse. Laozi literally means 'The Old One', a fitting description since he lived in the 6th century BC. Relatively little is known about Laozi, and many question whether or not he really existed. He is believed to have been the custodian of the imperial archives for the Chinese government, and Confucius is supposed to have consulted him.

Understanding Taoism is not simple. The word *tao* (pronounced 'dào') means 'the Way'. It's considered indescribable, but signifies something like the essence of which all things are made.

A major principle of Taoism is the concept of *wuwei* or 'doing nothing'. A quote attributed to Laozi, 'Do nothing, and nothing will not be done', emphasises this principle. The idea is to remain humble, passive, nonassertive and nonaggressive.

Chien Szuma, a Chinese historian who lived from 145 BC to 90 BC, warned, 'Do not take the lead in planning affairs, or you may be held responsible'. Nonintervention, or live and let live, is the keystone of the Tao. Harmony and patience are needed, action is obtained through inaction. Taoists like to note that water, the softest substance, will wear away stone, the hardest substance. Thus, eternal patience and tolerance will eventually produce the desired result.

Westerners have a hard time accepting this. The western notion of getting things done quickly conflicts with this aspect of the Tao. Westerners note that the Chinese are like spectators, afraid to get involved. The

Chinese say that westerners like to complain and are impatient. Taoists are baffled at the willingness of westerners to fight and die for abstract causes, such as a religious ideal.

It's doubtful that Laozi ever intended his philosophy to become a religion. Chang Ling is said to have formally established the religion in 143 BC. Zhuangzi (also spelled Chuangtzu or Chuangtse) is regarded as the greatest of all Taoist writers. You can find a collection of Zhuangzi's work in *The Book of Zhuangzi*, *The Book of Chuangtzu* and *The Book of Chuangtse* which are available in English.

Taoism later split into two divisions, the 'Cult of the Immortals' and the 'Way of the Heavenly Teacher'. The former offered immortality through meditation, exercise, alchemy and various other techniques. The Way of the Heavenly Teacher had many gods, ceremonies, saints, special diets to prolong life and offerings to the ghosts. As time passed, Taoism became increasingly wrapped up in the supernatural, witchcraft, self-mutilation, exorcism, fortune telling, magic and ritualism.

Confucianism
(rújiā sīxiǎng)
Confucius is regarded as China's greatest philosopher and teacher. The philosophy of Confucius has been borrowed by Japan, Korea, Vietnam and other neighbouring countries. Confucius never claimed to be a religious leader, prophet or god, but his influence is so great in China that Confucianism has come to be regarded as religion by many.

Confucius (551-479 BC) lived through a time of great chaos and feudal rivalry known as the Warring States Period. He emphasised devotion to parents and family, loyalty to friends, justice, peace, education, reform and humanitarianism, and preached against practices such as corruption, excessive taxation, war and torture. He also emphasised respect and deference to those in positions of authority, a philosophy later heavily exploited by emperors and warlords. However, not everything said by Confucius has been universally praised – it seems that he was also a male chauvinist who firmly believed that men are superior to women.

Confucius preached the virtues of good government, but his philosophy helped create China's horrifying bureaucracy which exists to this day. On a more positive note, his ideas led to the system of civil service and university entrance examinations, where positions were awarded on ability and merit, rather than from noble birth and connections. He was the first teacher to open his school to students on the basis of their desire to learn rather than their ability to pay for tuition.

The philosophy of Confucius is most easily found in the *Lunyu* or the *Analects of Confucius*. Many quotes have been taken from these works, the most famous perhaps being the Golden Rule. Westerners have translated this rule as 'Do unto others as you would have them do unto you'. Actually, it was written in the negative: 'Do not do unto others what you would not have them do unto you'.

No matter what his virtues, Confucius received little recognition during his lifetime. It was only after his death that he was canonised. Emperors, warlords and mandarins found it convenient to preach the Confucian ethic, particularly the part about deference to those in authority. Thus, with official support, Confucianism gained influence as a philosophy and has attained almost religious status. Mengzi (formerly spelled Mencius; 372-289 BC) is regarded as the first great Confucian philosopher. He developed many of the ideas of Confucianism as they were later understood.

Although Confucius died some 2500 years ago, his influence lives on. The Chinese remain solidly loyal to friends, family and teachers. The bureaucracy and examination systems still thrive, and it is also true that a son is almost universally favoured over a daughter. It can be said that much of Confucian thought has blended into Chinese culture as we see it today.

Religious Ceremonies
Numerous forms of worship exist in Taiwan. Many people have altars in their houses and

you can frequently see people performing a worship ceremony *(bàibài)* in front of their homes. A worship ceremony can take many forms as they're performed for varying reasons. Often, you will see somebody burning pieces of paper, which represent money. If the money has a silver square in the middle it's 'ghost money'; if it has a gold square it's 'god money'. The money is usually burned to satisfy a 'hungry ghost' from the underworld (hell) so that it will not bother you or members of your family. The money could also be for a departed relative who needs some cash in heaven. Truck drivers often throw ghost money out of the window of their vehicles to appease the 'road ghosts', to ensure that they don't have an accident. Some people place the ashes of ghost money in water and drink the resulting mixture as a cure for disease.

Another custom practised is the burning of paper models of cars and motorcycles so the dear departed may have a means of transport in heaven. Incense is frequently burned, often placed on a table with some delicious-looking food which is meant for the ghosts. However, after the ghost has had a few nibbles, the living will sit down to a feast of the leftovers. It's also possible to rent or borrow carved images of the deities to take home from the temple for home worship ceremonies.

If you visit a temple in Taiwan, you will probably encounter some strange objects that you may not have seen before. One such object is a box full of wooden rods *(qiān)*. Before praying for something you desire, such as health, wealth or a good spouse, you must select a rod from the qian. Then pick up two kidney-shaped objects called *shimbui*

(shimbui is a Taiwanese word, not a Mandarin one). Drop them on the ground three times. If two out of three times they land with one round surface up and one flat surface up, then your wish may be granted. If both flat sides are down, then your wish may not be granted. If both flat sides are up, god is laughing at you.

Many festivals are held throughout the year in accordance with the lunar calendar. Some festivals only occur once every 12 years, at the end of the cycle of the 12 lunar animals. Some festivals occur only once every 60 years. This is because each of the 12 lunar animals is associated with five elements: metal, wood, earth, water and fire. The full cycle takes 60 years (5 x 12) and at the end of this time there is a 'super worship' festival, which may involve tens of thousands of participants.

You can frequently see a Taoist street parade in Taiwan, complete with crashing cymbals and firecrackers. The purpose is usually to celebrate a god's birthday.

Look closely at the temples in Taiwan and you will see some Chinese characters inscribed on every stone, engraving, painting and statue. These characters are not those of the artist, but rather the names of the people who have donated money to purchase that particular temple ornament. Should you donate some money to a temple, you may also have your name engraved in stone.

Other than monks and nuns, practically nobody in Taiwan receives any formal religious education. Therefore, the majority of the population understands little of the history and philosophy behind Buddhism and Taoism.

Facts for the Visitor

PLANNING
When To Go
Travelling in Taiwan is good at any time of the year, but summer is high season, which means higher airfares, not to mention hot and humid weather. A time to avoid is Chinese (lunar) New Year when all transport is packed to overflowing, stores and restaurants are closed and hotels double their prices. Other major holidays can cause transport bottlenecks. Of all months of the year, October has the most pleasant weather, but three public holidays fall during this time bringing dramatic but short-lived chaos. November is the best time to visit, when the weather is still mild and tourists are relatively scarce. Some foreigners like to visit during Ghost Month (late August or early September) when the temples are active and the Chinese are too superstitious to travel.

Maps
Buying a good map of Taiwan before you actually arrive can be difficult. Most maps published outside Taiwan are not up to date. If you really want a map before arriving in Taiwan, Nelles is probably the only worthwhile option. Alternatively, if you're going to be exploring the great outdoors in Taiwan, consider buying operational navigation charts which show the topography and are extremely useful for remote areas.

Every bookshop in Taiwan sells maps and atlases, but most are exclusively in Chinese characters. The tourism bureau has a collection of bilingual maps which have the advantage of being free.

What to Bring
Bring as little as possible. Keep in mind that you can and will buy things as you travel, so don't burden yourself down with a lot of unnecessary junk. Drill holes in the handle of your toothbrush if you have to – anything to keep the weight down.

That advice having been given, there are some things you will want to bring from home. But the first thing to consider is what kind of bag you will use to carry everything. If looks aren't important, then nothing is more convenient to carry than the trusty old backpack. A frameless backpack has the advantage of being very easy to load on and off luggage racks. A framed model is easier on your back if you are walking long distances. Travel packs with shoulder straps that zip away into a hidden compartment and internal frames are a modern innovation; they're halfway between the regular backpack and a shoulder bag.

Most travellers prefer an inexpensive, medium-sized, internal-frame backpack. After all, why spend a fortune on an expedition backpack when it might get lost, stolen or damaged? If this does happen to you, a reasonably cheap replacement can be bought in Taiwan.

If you're a business traveller and want to look the part, a shoulder bag still makes more sense than a cumbersome suitcase.

From May to October the lightest summer clothes will do, except if you plan to visit the mountains, where it can get quite cold at night during any time of the year. Good quality wet-weather gear will also come in handy all year for hikers, cyclists and motorcyclists.

Business travellers need to be spruced up – ties, jackets and white shirts for men, smart dresses for women.

A medical checklist of things to bring is supplied in the Health section later in this chapter. The following is a checklist of everyday travel items. Most are readily available in Taiwan, but the list is here for you to consider while you are packing your bag:

shorts, T-shirt, trousers/skirts and shirts, pullover, rain gear, underwear, socks, sunhat, toilet paper, shaving gear (men), tampons (women), nail clipper, comb, towel, water bottle, small knife, sewing kit, day-pack, wristwatch, swimsuit, name cards, small torch (flashlight).

SUGGESTED ITINERARIES
Three Days

Three days in Taipei will allow for a full day visit to the National Palace Museum and its environs, leaving two days to explore the many temples and shrines dotted around the city. There is also the option of a day trip to Wulai or Yangmingshan which will give you a peek at the countryside. A trip to one of Taipei's colourful night markets is a great way to while away the evening until the many bars and clubs come to life.

One Week

The one week visitor entering through Taipei has enough time to enjoy the city highlights and explore some of Taiwan's spectacular scenery. Start in Taipei (as described above) and allow a fourth day for a trip to Wulai, a mountain resort offering an introduction to the aboriginal culture of Taiwan. A train journey down the east coast to Hualien and Taroko Gorge offers dramatic, mountainous scenery. From Taroko Gorge you can catch a bus westwards along the Central Cross-Island Highway to Lishan, a peaceful mountain retreat. Continuing west from here you will reach the coastal city of Taichung from where you can return to Taipei for your flight out.

Two Weeks

Since many western nationals can enter Taiwan for two weeks without a visa, the two week visit is a popular option. Follow the one week option above as far as Taroko Gorge, perhaps (if visiting during the warmer months) adding on a day's rafting on the Hsiukuluan River. From the gorge continue down the east coast to Taitung, where you can fly to remote Orchid Island and get a real insight into Taiwan's aboriginal history. On your return to Taitung you may want to visit Chihpen Hot Springs (if the weather is cold), otherwise take a bus straight down to Kenting where national parkland surrounds the beaches on Taiwan's southern tip. From there head northward along the west coast to Kaohsiung – a great city for nightlife and the jumping-off point for the aboriginal village

of Santimen. The next stop from here is Tainan, home to some of the largest and most interesting temples in the country. Your time may be running short, but if possible allow two more days to get up to the mountain resort of Alishan before pushing on to Taipei to catch your flight out.

One Month

A one month visit will allow you to catch most of Taiwan's major sights. Follow the above recommended two week itinerary until you get as far as Kaohsiung. Then, if you're visiting during the warmer months, begin an exploration of the islands of the Taiwan Straits. This could take a week of your time if you want to thoroughly explore Penghu and Kinmen.

After returning to the mainland, visit the many temples of Tainan, followed by Chiayi and Alishan. Returning from Alishan, you could pay a visit to Fenchihu and Juili, both relaxing places surrounded by bamboo forests. Another expedition into the mountains can be launched from the small city of Touliu to the hiking area of Tsaoling. Mountain and hot-spring enthusiasts may want to take a bus trip to Shuili, before heading on to Tungpu in Yushan National Park. Return to Shuili and visit Sun Moon Lake and the nearby Formosan Aboriginal Cultural Village. If you're tired of the mountains, head directly to Taichung for some nightlife, otherwise go to Puli and catch a bus up to Chingching Farm, a rural area that has become a tourist attraction. Another option is to hike up to Hohuanshan (Harmonious Happiness Mountain) and then head down to Taichung by bus the next day.

Using Taichung as a base, take a day trip to the historic port of Lukang. If you're still enjoying the mountains, Lishan on the Central Cross-Island Highway is easily accessible from Taichung. Otherwise, head north to Hsinchu (the jumping-off point for Shihtoushan) before continuing north to Taipei. If you've still got time remaining before you have to catch your flight out, consider flying from Taipei to Matsu or explore Tamsui, a suburb in Taipei, or Yang-mingshan National Park.

Two Months

If you've got two months, you'll have sufficient time to explore virtually every sight mentioned in this book. No real itinerary is necessary – just go and enjoy!

HIGHLIGHTS

The National Palace Museum in northern Taipei boasts the greatest collection of Chinese art in the world. All visitors to Taiwan should allow at least one full day to explore some of the 720,000 piece collection. Real enthusiasts should allow even longer. With 15,000 exhibits on display at any given time – the pieces are regularly rotated to allow the whole collection to be displayed – it's impossible to tire of this place.

For the athletically inclined, Taiwan offers many climbing and trekking opportunities. Some of Taiwan's highest peaks such as Yushan, Hsuehshan, Tapachienshan, Nengkaoshan and Kuanshan certainly offer a challenge. Less strenuous hikes can be found in the Alishan and Tungpu areas.

For those who prefer to stick to the road, there's plenty of spectacular scenery to see, past rivers and waterfalls and through mountains (sometimes literally), from the comfort of a car or bus. The Central Cross-Island Highway over Hohuanshan is Taiwan's highest road and offers some incredible views (when the weather cooperates). Taroko Gorge on the east coast is an area of outstanding beauty with many walking trails, canyons and waterfalls. Hot springs abound in Taiwan, which lies on the edge of the Pacific 'Rim of Fire'. Good areas to enjoy a soak in these springs include Yangmingshan, Chihpen, Kuantzuling and Antung.

Taiwan still has a strong, if not somewhat depleted, aboriginal population and there are many centres where you can gain a good understanding of, and insight into, their culture. Choose between the more popular and touristy places like Wulai or traditional villages such as Maolin.

Buddhism, Taoism and Confucianism are the three main religions of Taiwan and there are thousands of temples all over the place. Temple fans shouldn't miss out on Tainan which, with over 200 temples and a long and colourful history, is the best place to truly appreciate Taiwanese culture and religious ceremonies.

Taiwan's islands are great places to get away from the hustle and bustle of the cities. In particular, the newly opened islands of the Taiwan Straits, some of which are only 3km from the Chinese mainland, have fascinating, historical military sites.

TOURIST OFFICES
Local Tourist Offices

Taiwan's Republic of China (ROC) Tourism Bureau (guānguāng jú) publishes all sorts of helpful maps, booklets and brochures which are available free of charge to tourists. Most of the tourist information provided is in English and Chinese, but French, Japanese and German information is available. The most convenient place to pick up these free goodies is at the information desk on arrival at the airport.

The Taiwan Visitor's Association or TVA (☎ 2349-1635; fax 2771-7036) shares an office with the main ROC Tourism Bureau in Taipei and, apart from their telephone numbers, there's not much difference between the two organisations. The TVA does, however, seem to run Taiwan's overseas tourist offices.

There is a tourist information hot line based in Taipei (☎ 2717-3737) with English-speaking operators who can help with Taiwan-wide transport schedules, cultural and special events and other tourist enquiries. This service also acts as an emergency translation service if you need assistance summoning the police or an ambulance. Additionally, the operators will pass on any tourism-related complaints that you may have to the relevant authorities. This popular and frequently busy service is available from 8 am to 8 pm every day of the year.

You can visit the ROC Tourism Bureau at its main office (☎ 2349-1500), 9th floor, 280

Chunghsiao E Rd, Section 4. It's not hard to find, but there is no sign outside the building.

For the addresses of tourism bureaus outside Taipei, see the regional chapters of this book.

Tourist Offices Abroad

Taiwan's overseas tourist bureaus are incorporated into the various 'trade offices' that Taiwan maintains around the world. See the Embassies section later in this chapter.

VISAS & DOCUMENTS
Passport

As the Chinese say, 'A journey of 1000 miles begins with a single step'. If you're planning to visit Taiwan, the first step will be getting a passport. If you already have one but it is within a few months of expiration, get a new one before you begin the journey – Taiwan and many other countries will not issue a visa if your passport has less than six months validity remaining. Also, be sure your passport has plenty of blank space for visas and stamps – you can have extra pages added at your country's embassy or consulate.

Losing your passport is disasterous – getting a new one means a trip to your embassy or consulate and usually a long wait while they send faxes or telexes (at your expense) to confirm that you exist. Since there are so few consulates in Taiwan, you'll have to try to work through some of the 'trade offices' (see the Embassies section later in this chapter) which will most likely send the paperwork to the nearest consulate – probably Hong Kong. This process can take several weeks. If you're going to be in Taiwan for a long period of time, it might be wise to register your passport at your national consulate (or 'business office' as it might be called in Taiwan) which will expedite matters should you need a replacement.

Visas

Taiwan allows visa-free stays of up to 14 days for citizens of the following countries: Australia, Austria, Belgium, Canada, France, Germany, Japan, Luxembourg, Netherlands, New Zealand, Portugal, Spain, Sweden, UK and USA. You must have an onward or return ticket and your passport must have at least six months validity remaining. Visa-free entry is available at any one of Taiwan's international entry points: the airports at Taoyuan and Kaohsiung and the seaports of Keelung and Kaohsiung.

If you wish to stay in Taiwan longer than 14 days or if you don't qualify for a visa-free stay, then get a visa. In general, most westerners will receive a single-entry visa valid for one to two months, which cannot be extended. Unfortunately, just what you can expect to receive when you apply for a visa is becoming increasingly unpredictable. Taiwanese visa offices have wide latitude to decide who gets what. The Taiwan visa issuing office in Bangkok has become notorious for either rejecting people or issuing two-week visas only. On the other hand the Hong Kong office recently eased its rules. This could change tomorrow – it all seems to depend on whoever is in charge, and visa staff are rotated every few years.

To apply for a visa, you will need to present your passport and three photos. Sometimes you'll also need to show your plane ticket to prove that you have booked an onward flight from Taiwan. A visa can normally be issued in one day.

There are two kinds of visas, 'visitor' and 'entry' (resident). Most travellers will be issued visitor visas, of which there are two types, single-entry and multiple-entry. These usually permit a stay of 60 days, though Bangkok-issued visas will generally only be valid for 14 to 30 days.

Single-entry visitor visas are easy to obtain, but a multiple-entry visitor visa is usually only issued in your native country and is almost impossible to get while travelling in nearby Asian countries such Thailand, Singapore or South Korea. Your chance of getting a multiple-entry visa partly depends on your nationality, but luck has a lot to do with it too.

Visa Extensions A 60 day visitor visa can be extended twice, each time for 60 days, gaining you a maximum stay of 180 days in

Taiwan. The two-week visitor visas or visa-free stays cannot be extended. However, all extension applications require a very good reason. Studying Chinese at a government-approved language centre is a valid reason. If you're in the hospital having triple-bypass surgery, that's also a valid reason. In all cases, supporting documentation is required – the authorities will not simply take your word for it.

Sightseeing is not a valid reason – even the Tourism Bureau recognises that you can see most of what Taiwan has to offer within 60 days. Teaching English illegally or busking on a street corner to raise funds are likewise not valid reasons for a visa extension. In general, visa extensions are granted grudgingly, and only if you have supporting documentation.

When applying for an extension, you must go to the Foreign Affairs Police. There are Foreign Affairs Police offices in each county seat and one in each of the five special municipalities – Taipei, Keelung, Taichung, Tainan and Kaohsiung. You need to bring your passport of course, but no photos. Don't go during or near the lunch hour (hours!) – from about 11.30 am to 2 pm. See the regional chapters of this book for details of Foreign Affairs Police offices.

If you overstay your visa by even one day you won't be able to leave the country until you clear up the matter. If you overstay by only a few days, you won't get into any serious trouble as long as you can provide a valid reason, such as illness or missing your flight. If this happens to you, report it as soon as possible to the Foreign Affairs Police at the main police station in whatever city you are in. You will have to pay a fine of around NT$600, and your name gets written down in a nasty looking big black book at CKS international airport. If you're a first-time offender, you can expect a one year suspension of visa-free stays (meaning you can't get back into Taiwan without a visa for one year). Overstaying can jeopardise your chance of getting a new visa too, so it's not recommended if you intend to see Ihla Formosa again.

Resident Visas Also known as entry visas, resident visas are difficult to come by. In the past, you could gain permanent residence and a US$1 million reward (payable in gold) by stealing a military jet from mainland China and flying it to Taiwan – however, this method no longer works.

Resident visas are usually issued only to people coming to Taiwan to work for an approved company, to full-time students at a university, to spouses of ROC citizens, and to certain missionaries, researchers and big-time investors. If you come to Taiwan to study Chinese at a university, it's possible to gain a resident visa eventually, but not during the first semester of study (however, the school can help you get two visa extensions on your visitor visa). In all cases, applying for a resident visa will require supporting documentation.

Marrying an ROC national generally gets you a resident visa, but does not necessarily gain you the right to work. If you're female, it's usually no problem because the authorities recognise the job of 'homemaker' as legitimate. For men who marry Taiwanese women, gaining residence is possible only if the husband shows that he has sufficient foreign funds to pay all the living expenses for the family.

Within Taiwan, the place to apply for a resident (entry) visa is the Department of Consular Affairs (☎ 2343-2888), Ministry of Foreign Affairs (*wàijiāo bù*), 3rd floor, 2-2 Chinan Rd, Taipei. The approval (or refusal) process normally takes about three months. Once you (hopefully) receive approval, take your forms back to the Ministry of Foreign Affairs. You'll be issued more forms and then you'll have to make a brief trip abroad to pick up your entry visa (most people go to Hong Kong). When you return, you can apply for an Alien Resident Certificate (ARC; see next section).

Alien Resident Certificate (*jū liú zhèng*) Those lucky few with entry (resident) visas are required to apply for an ARC within 30 days of their arrival in Taiwan. This permits you to live in Taiwan for a specified period.

The certificate must be renewed each year at a cost of NT$1000.

Alien residents who depart the island must apply for a re-entry visa. Failure to do this will result in the loss of resident status and you'll have to do the entry visa shenanigans all over again. There are two types of re-entry visas; a single re-entry visa costs NT$1500 while a multiple re-entry visa valid for one year will cost NT$2000 – obviously you should get the latter if you expect to make more than one trip abroad per year. At the time of writing the fee is being waived for citizens of the USA and countries that have diplomatic relations with Taiwan. You can apply for a re-entry visa at the Foreign Affairs Police station just as soon as you receive your ARC.

Photocopies

It's a good idea to always keep photocopies of your passport data pages, birth certificate, credit cards, airline tickets, other important documentation and the serial numbers of your travellers cheques. Keep these copies in an envelope in a separate part of your luggage and, to be extra cautious, leave another copy at home.

If you're travelling with your spouse, a photocopy of your marriage licence just might come in handy should you become involved with the law, hospitals or other bureaucratic authorities.

If you're planning on working or studying in Taiwan, it could be helpful to have copies of transcripts, diplomas, letters of reference and other professional qualifications with you.

If you want to work at a university, you will have to show the Ministry of Education your *original* diploma. Private schools and companies are usually less fussy, but that's not guaranteed.

Mountain Permits

If you hike or travel in certain remote mountain areas of Taiwan, a permit might be required. This tradition started back during the martial law era, when permits were needed to travel to almost all remote spots in Taiwan (including outlying islands such as Green Island and Kinmen). Nowadays, different reasons for requiring these bits of paper are given. Excuse No 1 is that it will protect the environment – supposedly carrying this paper in your pocket will prevent ecological damage as you trample through meadows, toss litter and ignite forest fires. Excuse No 2 is that it's for your own protection – presumably somebody will look for you if you applied for a permit and then disappeared.

In reality, the purpose of the permit is to give the bureaucracy something to do. It also gives them an opportunity to practise their English when the rare foreigner shows up to apply for these cherished documents.

There are two types of mountain permits, one of which is very easy to obtain and another that involves more hassle. The difficult one is called a class A pass or permit *(jiǎzhǒng rùshānzhèng),* the easier option is to obtain a class B pass or permit *(yǐzhǒng rùshānzhèng).*

Class B permits can usually be obtained in a few minutes, right at the roadside entrance or trailhead, after you've filled out a simple form. It's no hassle to get a class B pass, and if you can't read Chinese the police will probably fill out the form for you. These days there are very few places that still require these permits, and hopefully they will soon become extinct.

To apply for a class B mountain permit, you need some sort of ID. Your passport will do, but Taiwanese ID cards are preferred. Acceptable Taiwanese ID includes a driving licence or ARC. The processing fee is NT$10. The pass will be issued on the spot.

Class A mountain permits are required for climbing all mountains over 3000m in elevation. There must be three of you – lone individuals cannot get one. When you apply you should bring along originals and photocopies of your passport and ARC (if you have one). You also need a letter from an 'alpine association' (see further in this entry). Once you've gathered all the necessary documentation together, present it to the Foreign Affairs Police or any local township police station (*jǐngchá jú*) but *not* to a branch police station (*pàichū suǒ*). With the right papers, you can be issued the permit on the spot for NT$10.

If you go with a mountain club, they will apply for the permit and make all the arrangements for you. The best club for arranging this is the Chinese Taipei Alpine Association (☎ 2591-1498/2594-2108; *zhōnghuá shānyuè xiéhuì*), 10th floor, 185 Chungshan N Rd, Section 2, Taipei; another is the Mountaineering and Hiking Association (☎ 2751-0938), 50-A Lungchiang Rd, Taipei. If you want to hire a licensed mountain guide, the Alpine Association can also arrange this. You must submit the following documents to the association: itinerary (one copy); member list (five copies); photocopies of members' passports (one copy of each). The climbing party is expected to pay the guide's expenses including food, accommodation and transport. You must obtain suitable climbing gear, which you can buy, rent or borrow. In other words, don't expect to climb Yushan in thongs and a T-shirt.

Onward Tickets

Sometimes you'll need to show your plane ticket to prove that you have booked an onward flight from Taiwan. Any destination will do – it needn't be a return ticket to your home country. Often, no one will bother asking to see it at the visa office, but it might be required when you reach the check-in counter.

Travel Insurance

Although you may have medical insurance in your own country, it is probably not valid in Taiwan. But ask your insurance company anyway – they might cover you for Taiwan. You also might be automatically covered if you hold a valid International Student Identity Card (ISIC), GO 25 International Youth Travel Card (GO 25 Card) or International Teacher Identity Card (ISTC) – ask at the place where you purchased the card.

A travel insurance policy is a very good idea – the best ones protect you against the cancellation penalties on advance-purchase flights, against medical costs through illness or injury, theft or loss of possessions and the cost of additional air tickets if you get really sick and have to fly home. Obviously, the more extensive the coverage, the higher the premiums, but at a minimum you should at least be covered for medical costs due to injuries. Read the small print carefully since it's easy to be caught out by exclusions – eg injuries caused by 'dangerous activities' like skiing or cycling might be excluded.

If you undergo medical treatment, be sure to collect all receipts and copies of your medical report, in English if possible, for your insurance company.

Student travel offices are one place to enquire about relatively inexpensive insurance policies. Better travel agencies also sell travel insurance policies – do a little checking around before you buy. Again, read the fine print – the coverage may be cheap but very limited.

Driving Licence & Permits

If you stay in Taiwan for more than two months, you are expected to obtain a Taiwanese driving licence. It is *not* required for you to have a residence visa for Taiwan to be issued with a licence.

A Taiwanese driving licence is valid for six years. Separate licences are issued for cars and motorcycles. To ride motorcycles over 50cc you must have a valid motorcycle licence. Motorcycles under 50cc can be ridden without a licence but the rider must be at least 18 years of age.

You'll save yourself a lot of trouble if you bring along your licence from home – you can use it to get the Taiwanese licence without having to take a written exam or driving test. You'll also need half a dozen black and white photos of yourself, approximately 3cm x 2cm in size. If you do not have an ARC, then first visit the Foreign Affairs Police and obtain a 'Report for Alien Lodging' (*wàiqiáo zhùsù bàogào dān*). The address you put on this report will also be put on your driving licence, so don't use a hotel address. The next step in the process is to take an eye exam – this can be done at any authorised public hospital. Now equipped with your passport, home country driving licence, photos, residence/lodging documents and eye exam report, visit the Department of Motor Vehicles (*jiānlǐ suǒ*) and you should receive your licence in about an hour. The whole process should cost around NT$500 per licence.

If you plan to be driving in Taiwan but will not be taking up residence, then obtain an International Driving Permit (IDP) before you leave home. In some countries these are issued by your motor vehicles department, but in many cases you must obtain it from your local automobile association. In some countries these are valid for one year only, but other places may give you three years or more. Make sure that your permit states that it is valid for motorcycles if you plan to be driving a motorcycle over 50cc in Taiwan.

The Taiwanese Motor Vehicle Department can also issue IDPs, but they will only do this if you've first obtained a Taiwanese driving licence.

You must carry your vehicle registration document with you at all times when driving in Taiwan. A liability insurance card is also required for cars, but not motorcycles. You can get this card from an insurance agent, the cost will depend on the coverage you require. At the time of writing, one year's basic insurance (NT$1.2 million liability) for a van was about NT$2400.

Hostel Card

At the time of writing, International Youth Hostel Federation (IYHF) cards were of little use in Taiwan. However, the government has been toying with the idea of establishing a network of IYHF hostels in the hopes that this might enhance Taiwan's international prestige. Just if or when this might occur is hard to say. If you already have a valid card, you can bring it along on the odd chance you might actually get to use it, but it certainly is *not* worthwhile to buy one just for Taiwan.

Student & Youth Cards

International Student Identity Cards (ISIC) and International Teacher Identity Cards (ITIC) are issued through representative offices of the International Student Travel Confederation (ISTC). To qualify for an ISIC, you need to be a full time student but there is no age limit. Full time teachers and faculty can apply for an ITIC. You can apply for these cards through various student travel organisations in your home country. To get the ISIC, you need an official letter from your school confirming that you are indeed a student (or teacher, as the case may be).

If you are *not* a student or teacher but are aged 25 or under, then you can qualify for a GO 25 International Youth Travel Card (GO 25 Card). These are issued by representative offices of the Federation of International Youth Travel Organisations (FIYTO). These cards essentially offer the same benefits as the ISIC and ISTC.

Student travel offices in various cities and university campuses can provide you with application forms to apply for these cards.

ISIC cards can be issued at Youth Travel International (☎ 2721-1978; fax 2721-2784; *guójì xuéshēng qīngnián lüyóu*), Suite 502, 142 Chunghsiao E Rd, Section 4, Taipei – a student ID card or a university letter of acceptance is required.

ISIC cards are of very limited use in Taiwan. The airlines in Taiwan are not keen to give student discounts. Within Taiwan, you will need some sort of Chinese student ID to get discounts. You may be able to get such an ID card if you study Chinese at a Taiwan university, but don't count on it. They aren't happy about giving these cards to part time students.

International Health Card

Useful (though not essential) is an International Health Certificate to record any vaccinations you've had. These can also be issued in Taiwan at any health department.

EMBASSIES
Taiwan's Embassies Abroad

Visas are usually obtained from the embassy of the country you wish to visit, but in the case of Taiwan there are only a few countries which maintain diplomatic relations with it. As there are so few ROC embassies in the world, Taiwan's government gets around this by maintaining a number of 'nongovernmental offices' in many countries. Apart from their visa-issuing role, these offices are important links in Taiwan's vital international trade. You can get a visa for Taiwan at any of the following offices:

Australia
Taipei Economic & Cultural Office, Canberra branch (☎ (02) 6273-3344) Unit 8, Tourism House, 40 Blackall St, Barton, ACT 2600
Canada
Taipei Economic & Cultural Office, Ottawa branch (☎ (613) 231-5080) 45 O'Connor St, Ottawa, Ontario KIP 1A4
France
Association pour la Promotion des Echanges Commerciaux et Touristiques avec Taiwan (ASPECT; ☎ 01 44 39 88 20) 78 Rue de l'Université, 75007 Paris
Germany
Taipei Wirtschafts und Kulturburo, Berlin branch (☎ (30) 861-2754/861-2576) Berlinerstr. 55, D-10173, Berlin
Ireland
Taipei Economic & Cultural Office (☎ (01) 678-5413) 1st floor, 10-11 South Leinster St, Dublin 2
Japan
Taipei Economic & Cultural Office, Tokyo branch (☎ (03) 3328-7811) 20-2, Shiroganedai 5-Chome, Minato-Ku, Tokyo 108
Netherlands
Taipei Economic & Cultural Office (☎ (070) 346-9438) Javastraat 46-48, 2585 AR, The Hague
New Zealand
Taipei Economic & Cultural Office, Wellington branch (☎ (04) 473-6474), PO Box 10250, The Terrace, Wellington
UK
Taipei Representative Office (☎ (0171) 396-9152), 50 Grosvenor Gardens, London, SWI 0EB
USA
Taipei Economic & Cultural Representative Office (TECRO), Washington branch (☎ (202) 895-1800), 4201 Wisconsin Ave, NW, Washington, DC 20016-2137

Foreign Embassies in Taiwan

Because Taiwan has diplomatic relations with only a handful of countries, the following offices in Taipei are not true embassies. These 'unofficial organisations' can issue visas and replace lost passports. However, because they are not real embassies, they may have to send paperwork abroad which can cause big delays (the Japanese pseudo-embassy needs 2½ weeks to process a visa!). This is not always the case – some pseudo-embassies do the paperwork in house even if it does 'upset' China. Remember that rules can change, so always check on how long the procedure will take before handing over your passport and visa application – some travellers have been caught short waiting weeks for an onward visa while their Taiwanese visa expired.

Pseudo-embassies in Taiwan are:

American Institute in Taiwan (AIT)
(☎ 2709-2000; fax 2702-7675; *měiguó zài tái xiéhuì*) 7 Lane 134, Hsinyi Rd, Section 3, Taipei
Australian Commerce & Industry Office
(☎ 2720-2833; fax 2757-6040; *àozhōu shānggōng bànshìchù*) room 2605, 26th floor, International Trade building, 333 Keelung Rd, Section 1, Taipei
British Trade & Cultural Office
(☎ 2322-4242; visas 2322-3235; *yīngguó màoyì wénhuà bànshìchù*) 9th floor, 99 Jenai Rd, Section 2, Taipei
Canadian Trade Office
(☎ 2547-9500; visas 2514-0056; *jiānádà màoyì bànshì chù*) 13th floor, 365 Fuhsing N Rd , Taipei
France Asia Trade Association
(☎ 2545-6061; *fàguó zài tái xiéhuì*) 10th floor, 205 Tunhua N Rd , Taipei
German Cultural Centre
(☎ 2365-7294; *déguó wénhuà zhōngxīn*) 11th floor, 24 Hsinhai Rd, Section 1, Taipei
German Trade Office (☎ 2506-9028; *déguó jīngjì bànshì chù*) 4th floor, 4 Minseng E Rd, Section 3, Taipei
Ireland Institute of Trade & Investment
(☎ 2725-1691; *aìěrlán màoyì cùjìn huì*) 7B-09, Taiwan World Trade Centre building, 5 Hsinyi Rd, Section 5, Taipei
Japan Interchange Association
(☎ 2741-2116; *rìběn jiāoliú xiéhuì*) 10th floor, 245 Tunhua S Rd, Section 1, Taipei
Korea Trade Centre
(☎ 2725-2343; visas 2758-8320; *hánguó màoyì zhōngxīn*) room 2214, 333 Keelung Rd, Section 1, Taipei
Netherlands Trade & Investment Office
(☎ 2713-5760; *hélán màoyì tóuzī bànshìchù*) room B, 5th floor, 133 Minseng E Rd, Section 3, Taipei

New Zealand Commerce & Industry Office
   (☎ 2757-7060; *niŭxīlán shānggōng bànshì chù*)
   25th floor, 333 Keelung Rd, Section 1, Taipei
Philippines – Manila Economic & Cultural Office
   (☎ 2778-6511; *mănílā jīngjì wénhuà bànshìchù*)
   4th floor, 107 Chunghsiao E Rd, Section 4, Taipei

CUSTOMS

Customs inspections in Taiwan have gone from being severely traumatic to very easy. Reasonable quantities of items for personal use can be brought in duty free with no trouble.

The rules say that you should declare all computers, TVs, stereos and video recorders. At least on those items that you are likely to take out again (eg portable computers) there should be no duty to pay.

Officially, arriving passengers are permitted a duty free allowance of NT$6000 worth of personal merchandise – in practice, this is usually stretched considerably. This limit does not include foreign currency, gold, alcohol and tobacco, all of which are treated separately.

Customs rules regarding gold, silver and foreign currency are straightforward. Any amount of foreign currency can be brought in but it must be declared on arrival. Otherwise, only US$5000 in cash or the equivalent amount in another foreign currency can be taken out on departure. Travellers cheques and personal cheques are not considered to be cash and so do not have to be declared.

Declare any gold and silver that you bring into Taiwan. You cannot bring in more than US$5000 of these metals without an import permit. However, if you arrive in Taiwan carrying gold or silver in excess of the permitted quantity, you may place it in storage under the custody of customs and a receipt will be issued – don't lose it! On departure the gold or silver will be returned on presentation of the receipt. However, you will have to depart from the same place you arrived.

If you are carrying taxable items but only intend to stay 45 days or less, you can place your goods in bonded baggage until your departure. If you do this you won't be required to pay duty. If you want or need the dutiable item for use during your stay in Taiwan, it is possible to pay the duty and have the money returned to you on departure. This is a hassle, but some people do it.

Anyone aged 20 or over can bring in a litre of alcohol and either 200 cigarettes, 25 cigars or 500g of tobacco duty free.

Any literature deemed pro-communist or subversive may be confiscated. You aren't supposed to bring in anything made in mainland China – it's almost impossible not to break this rule, but remove obvious labels to avoid trouble. Pornography is prohibited (competes with the locally produced stuff). You can't bring toy guns into Taiwan even though they are a major export and available from any toy store in Taiwan.

Needless to say, real guns, ammunition and narcotic drugs are prohibited items. Most backpackers don't carry guns and ammunition, but hashish and heroin have landed more than a few travellers in prison. Foreigners caught with large quantities of drugs have received life prison sentences, and in extreme circumstances the death penalty is still enforced. Even a small quantity of narcotics for personal use is likely to land you behind bars for several years.

MONEY
Costs

As Taiwan's standard of living has increased, so have prices. The cost of most goods and services has reached the level of many European countries, but Taiwan is still much cheaper than Japan … for now.

How much does it cost to visit Taiwan? Excluding the airfare, you can probably manage to survive on less than NT$1000 per day if you stay in hostels (see Accommodation later in this chapter), buy food from noodle vendors or cheap cafeterias, take buses rather than taxis and resist the urge to go shopping. If you require a higher standard of living, it could easily cost several times as much. Taipei is marginally more expensive than elsewhere in Taiwan, but then Taipei has budget travellers' hostels which are scarce elsewhere.

Carrying Money

Pickpockets and snatch thieves are not a serious problem in Taiwan, but this doesn't mean that you should be careless with your cash. Valuables (including passports and tickets) should be kept out of reach from sticky fingers, and if possible in a secure place. Devices that can help thwart grasping hands include pockets sewn on the inside of your trousers, velcro tabs to seal pocket openings, a moneybelt under your clothes or a money pouch under your shirt.

Cash

While US dollars is the preferred currency, it's possible to exchange some other foreign currencies in Taiwan. However, it's difficult or impossible to get rid of foreign coins – most banks will not accept them.

Travellers Cheques

US dollar travellers cheques are the easiest to exchange. Some banks in Taipei can handle other major currencies such as pounds sterling, Japanese yen or Australian dollars, but don't count on it. You get a slightly better rate on travellers cheques than you do with cash.

Visa customers who need assistance can dial a free emergency assistance number in Taiwan (☎ 080-651019). American Express customers can also call for assistance on ☎ 2719-0606.

ATMs

ATM cards from a number of foreign banks will work in *some* Taiwanese ATMs. Look for machines advertising international bank settlement systems such as GlobalAccess,

Asian Flu

Hong Kong – formerly a British colony – reverted to Chinese rule on 1 July 1997, amid great fanfare. Fireworks were launched and politicians made speeches declaring the beginning of the 'Chinese century'. Many commentators talked about the 'rise of Asia' (and, by default, the decline of the west). For China it was a great party; for the Taiwanese it was further confirmation of their vulnerable status.

A small dose of reality came the very next day, when Thailand sharply devalued its currency. In the weeks that followed other Asian currencies and stockmarkets fell like dominoes – South Korea, Indonesia, the Philippines and Malaysia were all ravaged by the economic crisis. The currencies and stocks of Japan, Singapore and Taiwan also took a bashing, though they didn't fare as badly as the others. The high performing economies of east Asia – collectively known as the economic 'tigers' – suddenly took ill. Thus began the Asian financial crisis, more commonly referred to as the 'Asian flu'.

In the weeks and months that followed, economists were sent scrambling for their computers, trying to figure out what went wrong. Gradually, a picture of sorts emerged.

Throughout much of east Asia, expectations about future growth became extravagant and capital was cheap. Too many companies with murky accounting systems took advantage of the euphoria, and overborrowed. Unprofitable corporations colluded with corrupt governments and mismanaged, state-run banks. Money was poured into highly speculative investments, especially real estate. Foreign speculators were willing to dole out cash, believing nothing could go wrong. However, when bad signs started appearing, the speculators collectively panicked and headed for the exits. Overly enthusiastic when times were good, they were overly pessimistic when things looked bad. It was the herd mentality – everyone withdrew their cash so fast that real estate values and stocks plummeted overnight.

The New Taiwan dollar lost about 15% in the panic, but Taiwan emerged from the crisis in better condition than almost every other nation in east Asia. As it turned out, Taiwanese companies had not overborrowed and most of their debt was in local currency (as opposed to US dollars). Therefore, the devaluation didn't hurt much – in fact it even helped boost Taiwan's export-based industries.

Within a few months, a new political angle developed – the Taiwanese found themselves being courted by their east Asian neighbours, who were in desperate need of foreign investment. Taiwanese officials – previously unable to get visas for neighbouring countries because of China's objections – suddenly started receiving invitations to visit. This 'financial diplomacy' was harshly denounced by China. 'Some Taiwan political figures have travelled to many countries in the region in an attempt to profit from these countries' difficult situations, and to serve their own political purpose,' raged Qian Qichen, China's foreign minister. Thus, it appears that Taiwan has managed to ride out the crisis to emerge as an even stronger economic force in the region. ∎

Cirrus, Interlink, Plus, Star, Accel, The Exchange and Explore (Taipei's train station is one place to find these machines). International banking facilities are definitely easier to find in major cities so if you're heading into tiny backwaters take enough cash to last till you reach the next major centre.

Credit Cards

Major international credit cards such as American Express, Diners Club, Master-Card, Visa, JCB and others can be used at big hotels, a few fancy restaurants, major department stores, airline booking offices and at some car-rental agencies. Don't expect to get much use from your credit card at the local noodle shop or betel nut stand. You can get cash advances from most of the Taiwanese credit card issuers.

International Transfers

Having money wired to you seems to work OK. Normally, an international transfer takes one or two days to complete. Fees vary between banks, but it costs approximately NT$300 per transaction.

Sending money out of Taiwan seems to work just as well, though you have to pledge not to send out more than US$5 million!

Domestic Transfers

Wiring money between domestic banks in Taiwan is straightforward enough, though virtually all banks require you to fill out forms which are entirely in Chinese. The transfer fee is only NT$30.

One system of money transfer that is almost unique to Taiwan is the use of 'postal remittance account numbers' (yóuzhèng huàbō zhànghào). That is, if you know somebody's postal account number, you can deposit money to that account and the recipient will be sent a receipt stating the amount deposited plus the name, address and phone number of the depositor. The depositor is also issued with a receipt. This is the system of choice if you subscribe to Taiwanese magazines and newspapers, pre-pay hotel rooms in advance, purchase goods by mail etc. Indeed, many Taiwanese companies will only accept this method of payment. Virtually all post offices – even the smallest ones – offer this service.

Currency

The official unit of currency is the New Taiwan dollar (NT$), which totals 100 cents. Coins in circulation come in denominations of 50 cents (rare), NT$1, NT$5, NT$10 and NT$50; notes come in denominations of NT$50, NT$100, NT$500 and NT$1000.

US dollars and other major foreign currencies are *not* widely accepted in shops and hotels. Though some people may exchange them for you, they are only doing so to be helpful – it's certainly not a common practice. You'll perplex most shop owners if you try to pay for goods and services with anything but local currency.

It's best to use up your NT dollars or exchange them at the airport before leaving Taiwan. Although Taiwanese currency can be exchanged in other countries, the rates given are usually poor.

Currency Exchange

Some exchange rates at the time of publication included:

Australia	A$1	= NT$21.08
Canada	C$1	= NT$23.26
China	Y1	= NT$4.08
France	FF1	= NT$5.67
Germany	DM1	= NT$19.01
Hong Kong	HK$1	= NT$4.37
Japan	¥100	= NT$24.50
New Zealand	NZ$1	= NT$18.09
Philippines	P1	= NT$0.87
Singapore	S$1	= NT$20.31
Switzerland	SFr1	= NT$22.96
UK	UK£1	= NT$55.19
USA	US$1	= NT$33.86

Changing Money

Foreign currency and travellers cheques can be changed at the two international airports and at large banks. It can be difficult or even impossible to cash travellers cheques in rural areas, so take care of this in the cities.

Most banks in Taiwan will *not* handle

foreign exchange. Only the major banks are involved in this business, including the International Bank of China (ICBC) and Bank of Taiwan.

Many banks charge a fee for each travellers cheque cashed, but it varies. ICBC charges NT$60 per transaction, no matter how many cheques are involved. On the other hand, the Bank of Taiwan charges NT$10 per cheque, so those with small denomination cheques lose out. The best practice is to change money in large cities, not in small backwaters. All banks, including the one at the airport, give the same exchange rate.

Taiwan does not have the ubiquitous private moneychangers like you find in Hong Kong. Some hotels will provide foreign exchange, but only for their guests.

Normal banking hours are from 9 am to 3.30 pm Monday to Friday and from 9 am to noon on Saturday. The bank at CKS airport is supposed to remain open whenever there are international flights departing or arriving. The bank at Kaohsiung international airport theoretically follows the same policy but seems to be unreliable. On departure from either airport, you must change money before heading through immigration – there is no moneychanger beyond the immigration checkpoint.

Black Market

Changing money used to be a real cloak-and-dagger adventure in Taiwan, but that has become a thing of the past. Now that Taiwan has liberalised the banking business, there is no longer any reason to change money with shady characters in back alleys.

It's still possible to change money at some jewellery stores – you have to enquire to find out which stores will do it. They only handle cash, not travellers cheques, and they only deal in major currencies like US dollars or Japanese yen. There are abundant rumours of counterfeit bills, but it's not a major problem. You won't make money this way – indeed, you'll be charged a small commission of around 1% which is included in the quoted exchange rate. The only reason to

change money on this 'black market' is that these places are open when the banks are closed.

Tipping & Bargaining

Good news for the budget minded: tipping is not customary in restaurants, taxis or most other places in Taiwan. The only time you must definitely tip is when you are helped by a hotel bellhop or a porter at the airport. The usual tip is NT$50 per bag. Most of the bigger hotels or restaurants will automatically add a 10% service charge to your bill, plus a 5% Value-Added Tax (VAT) – smaller places almost never do that.

Some good-natured bargaining is permissible in street markets, and occasionally in small shops (but don't count on it). Ironically, you can sometimes negotiate a slight discount in a large department store simply by asking for it. In Taiwan, most department stores lease space to smaller vendors rather than trying to run the whole. If you speak to the manager of the particular department you are shopping in you may get a discount, but this usually only happens if you are making an expensive purchase like a suit, TV set or some furniture. The highest discount you can expect anywhere is around 10%.

Taxes & Refunds

If you're working legally, you are required to file an income tax return in February or March each year. The deadline is 31 March, but this can be extended (after application) to 30 April. If you stay 183 days or more in one calendar year, you are considered a resident for tax purposes. Note that if you arrive in Taiwan after 2 July, you cannot qualify as a resident before the year finishes since there will be less than 183 days till the end of the year. Being a resident is an advantage – you are taxed at a much lower rate (6%) than nonresidents (20%).

If you were taxed at the nonresident rate but become a resident within the tax year, you will almost certainly qualify for a refund. To receive this, you must of course file an income tax return. The refund cheque will eventually (quite some months later) be mailed to your record of address in Taiwan. Persuading the tax bureau to send your refund cheque to an overseas address is currently impossible.

POST & COMMUNICATIONS
Postal Rates

Domestic express letters should be delivered within 24 hours. Rates are NT$5 for letters (up to 20g), and NT$12 for 'prompt delivery' *(xiànshí zhuān sòng)* which is twice as fast as regular mail. There is also a domestic super-express mail *(kuài dì)* which is very expensive, but your letter is guaranteed to be delivered anywhere nationwide (except remote mountain areas) in just a few hours. International Express Mail Service (EMS; *guójì kuài jié*) is available in Taiwan – count on a minimum charge of NT$280. Another service you might use is registered mail *(guàhào)*, available for both international and domestic letters. You can send a domestic registered letter with return receipt *(guàhào fūhuìzhí)* for NT$28. Or if you want to cover all options, you can send it express and registered with return receipt *(xiànshí guàhào fūhuìzhí)*.

The rates on aerograms and international letters vary according to destination; see the Postal Rates from Taiwan table above.

Printed matter *(yìnshuà pǐn)*, including photographs, can be sent at a much cheaper rate than letters. If you want to send some photos home it will be much cheaper to send them in a separate envelope stamped 'printed matter'. Be sure to write 'airmail' on the envelope as well. You cannot seal the envelope with glue but it can be stapled closed. This is so the postal inspectors can open it and check that you didn't slip a letter inside. If you do hide a letter inside and it's discovered, it will be returned or sent by surface mail, and will probably take two months to arrive.

Small objects can be sent as a 'small parcel' *(xiǎo bāo)* at a much cheaper rate than normal letters. The parcel can be stapled or closed with string, but it cannot be taped shut.

The cheapest postcards cost around NT$2

Postal Rates from Taiwan			
Destination	*Airmail*	*Aerogram*	*Postcard*
Asia & Australia Hong Kong,	NT$13	NT$11	NT$10
Macau & China	NT$9	NT$8	NT$6
South America	NT$17	NT$14	NT$12
Europe & Africa	NT$17	NT$14	NT$12
USA & Canada	NT$15	NT$12	NT$11

and are available at the counter of the main post office in Taipei and other major cities.

Sending Mail

Post offices are open Monday to Friday from 8 am to 5 pm. They are also open on the first and third Saturday of each month, but they always remain closed on Sunday and public holidays.

Taiwan's postal service is fast and efficient. For domestic letters, you can count on delivery to almost any place on the island within two days. International mail is also fast – about seven days to the USA or Europe, fewer to Hong Kong or Japan.

When mailing a letter overseas from Taiwan, use the red mailboxes. The left slot on the box is for international airmail and the right slot is for domestic express. Green mailboxes are for domestic surface mail; the left slot is for 'out of town', and the right slot is for local letters. Should you mistakenly put the letter in the wrong box or slot, don't panic, it will be delivered, but could be delayed for a couple of days.

Most large post offices offer a very convenient packing service if you want to send a parcel. They'll box and seal it up for a nominal charge, saving you the time and trouble of hunting for a cardboard box and string. Unfortunately, they don't keep any padding at the post office, so bring some old newspaper with you if your goods are fragile. If you pack your own parcel, you must seal it with string – the post office will not accept parcels that are not tied. Stationery, grocery and hardware stores sell a very strong plastic string for just this purpose.

Private Couriers A rapid international service is offered by United Parcel Service (☎ 2883-3868; fax 2883-3890) and Federal Express (☎ 080-075075/2536-9038). Both companies have offices in the same building at 361 Ta'nan Rd, Shihlin district, Taipei 111. Both companies also provide pick-up services from the major cities. Contact the Taipei branches for details.

Freight Forwarders If you're shipping something too large or heavy to be handled by the post office or courier service, or if you are moving your home furnishings abroad, you need the services of a freight forwarder. Most of these companies should offer a door-to-door service. Most advertise in the *China News* and *China Post*. Some reputable ones include:

Crown Van Lines (☎ 2762-2500; fax 2761-2378) 4th floor, 165 Minsheng E Rd, Section 5, Taipei

Four Winds (☎ 2571-0564; fax 2521-3005) room 2, 7th floor, 100 Linsen N Rd, Taipei

Green Van International (☎ 2827-3052) 6th floor, 280 Wenlin N Rd, Peitou, Taipei

Jacky Maeder (☎ 2782-3360; fax 2651-7933) 2nd floor, 778 Pateh Rd, Section 4, Taipei

Orient Pacific (☎ 2834-3108) 2nd floor, 31 Chungcheng Rd, Section 1, Shihlin district, Taipei

Transworld ˋ(☎ 2836-1000/2836-5000; fax 2831-9942) 4th floor, 64 Chengchen Rd, Section 2, Shihlin district, Taipei

Receiving Mail

You can receive letters addressed *poste restante* (general delivery) at any post office. Addresses not in Chinese characters must use the Wade-Giles Romanisation system rather than Pinyin or Yale – the post office knows where Kaohsiung is but they've never heard of 'Gaoxiong'.

Telephone

Taiwan's government-owned monopoly was officially 'privatised' in 1997. Originally known as the Directorate General of Telecommunications (DGT), it was spun off and repackaged as Chunghwa Telecom. Whatever it's called, the service is just about what you'd expect from a government-owned monopoly – expensive and mediocre. The government has been promising to introduce some real competition by the turn of the century – just which century they are referring to is not yet clear.

First the good news – lines are generally good and you can almost always get connected immediately. Compared to some countries where calling across the street can take half a day, Taiwan's phone system seems to be highly functional.

Public Phones Calls made from public pay phones usually work OK, though there are a few which can be used for local calls only. These are usually pulse (rotary) dial (as opposed to touch-tone), and if you get this type of phone you'll be cut off after three minutes – feeding more coins in will not buy you more time. Fortunately, these old phones are becoming rare.

The newer pay phones have a digital display meter that tells you how much money you have put into the phone. You can clearly see how much money remains. When the meter reads zero, you get disconnected but to avoid this you can always feed in more coins.

Best of all are the phones that use a phone card *(diànhuà kǎ)* which you insert into a slot when you want to make a call. Phone cards cost NT$100 and can be bought in convenience stores, railway stations, bus stations or other places where you see the phones that accept these cards. You can also buy them from any telephone company branch office. Most (but not all) of the card phones permit you to make international calls – this is clearly indicated on the phone in English and Chinese. Of course, NT$100 doesn't give you much time to make an international call, but you can change cards without breaking the conversation by pushing the button to the left of the keypad and inserting a new card. At least, you can in theory – sometimes it doesn't work and you get cut off when the card expires.

One of the phone company's more dim-witted ideas has been the so called 'IC Card' phones. The idea behind an IC card is that it doesn't limit you to NT$100 as a phone card

Getting Your Own Phone

Frustration with Chunghwa Telecom really kicks in if you decide to live in Taiwan for a while and want to get a phone installed. In some cities it takes 10 days to get a phone line – in other places, three months. You have to buy the line rather than simply rent it – the cost varies from region to region, but at the time of writing it was about NT$3000. The rate has fallen considerably; in the 1980s it was NT$15,000.

The phone company has an annoying habit of changing your phone number every few years without advance warning, and the recorded message advising people of the change is only valid for one month. Getting your new phone number into the directory assistance computer seems to take at least six months!

You can apply to have an itemised phone bill but you will have to pay extra for this. Hang on to your bill payment receipts if you don't want to be charged twice. You can ask the phone company to deduct the payments directly from your Taiwanese bank account and they will send you a receipt every month showing how much was deducted.

Cellular phones are available but they are expensive and the exchanges are so overworked that it's often impossible to get your calls through. There is also a huge waiting list for cellular phone numbers – the phone company has promised to resolve this problem 'in the near future'.

More bad news – telephone rates are high in Taiwan, a fact which has brought considerable criticism from politicians, the newspapers and irate customers. However the rates have been dropping and the situation should continue to improve with privatisation and deregulation, though full free market competition between phone companies is probably still several years off.

Callback Services If you will be staying in Taiwan for more than a few months and make frequent overseas calls, it's worth considering a callback service. Virtually all such services are based in the USA (even if not American-owned), to take advantage of their cheaper phone rates, but they are accessible from other countries. Some of the choices available from the USA include Justice Technology, Kallback, Kallmart and New World.

Pagers It's estimated that 22% of the people in Taiwan have pagers (*hūjiàoqì* or *BB code*). Until recently, this market was the exclusive domain of Chunghwa Telecom. However, the government has authorised two new private firms to enter the market. All sorts of new services are expected to be introduced – voicemail, Chinese character messages, stock quotes, international roaming service etc. At the time of writing, the only service available was simply the ability to send someone your phone number (and not even your name).

Unlike some other countries, the current paging system is fully automated – you can page someone from any touch-tone phone without speaking to an operator. Most people in Taiwan know the system, so get a local to show you how to do it.

One warning – the phone systems in some hotels make it impossible to page from your room. In this case, you'll have to dial from a public pay phone or ask the hotel operator to page for you.

If you want to get your own pager, apply at any telephone company office. The cost is about NT$300 per month plus a refundable deposit.

Private Phone Call Rates Domestic long-distance rates are:

	Weekdays	Saturday	Sunday & Public Holidays
Full Rate	8 am to 7 pm	8 am to 1 pm	not applicable
40% Discount	7 to 11 pm	1 to 11 pm	8 am to 11 pm
65% Discount	11 pm to 8 am	11 pm to 8 am	11 pm to 8 am

A call from Taipei to Kaohsiung costs NT$5 per minute at the full rate, or NT$1.70 per minute at the cheapest night-time rate.

International call rates are:

	Weekdays	Saturday	Sunday & Public Holidays
Full Rate	8 am to 11 pm	8 am to noon	not applicable
Discount Hours	11 pm to 8 am	noon to midnight	all day

You are charged for every six seconds you are connected. A call from Taiwan to the USA costs NT$2.40 for every six seconds at the full rate, or NT$2 during the discount hours. ∎

does. Unfortunately, rather than being a debit card (like a phone card), it's a credit card. To obtain an IC card, you have to be a legal resident of Taiwan with a good credit rating, and then apply at the phone company. Very few people bother to apply, which means that the phone company is unwilling to spend the required fortune to install the special phones all around Taiwan that are needed to make this system work. The few IC card phones that exist are expensive white elephants (or rather, grey elephants) which sit unused, gathering dust at railway and bus stations. Would it not have made more sense to sell phone cards in denominations of NT$1000? For people who do not have permanent residence in Taiwan, an IC card is not even an option.

Privately owned red or green pay phones found in some hotels (especially youth hostels) are tricky to use. You must pick up the receiver *before* inserting the coin or else you will lose it – furthermore, when you are connected, you must push a button on the phone so the money goes down. If you fail to push the button, you will be able to hear the other party but they will not be able to hear you. These phones cannot be used to make international calls.

Local calls from public and private telephones all cost NT$1 for two minutes. For long distance calls, the rates from public phones are double the cost of those from private phones (see the Getting Your Own Phone boxed text on the previous page for details on call rates).

Overseas Calls To make an overseas operator-assisted call from a private phone, first dial 100 to reach the overseas operator. Anytime you use the overseas operator it's going to cost you big bucks, but person to person calls cost even more. Direct dialling is *much* cheaper. Direct dialling overseas is possible from private phones and from International Subscriber Dialling (ISD) phones. You can find ISD phones at the telephone company, some railway stations, bus stations and sometimes even the local shop.

To dial direct, the international prefix is

002, followed by the country code, area code and the number you want to dial.

Numbers starting with the prefix 080 are toll free numbers. Much rarer are 008 prefixes, which are for international toll-free numbers.

Many hotels will charge a large fee to make a reverse charge call on top of the fee that the phone company charges, so you're better off calling from a public pay phone.

An easy way to make reverse-charge calls or to bill a call to a credit card is to use a service called International Operator Direct Connection (IODC). This service is only offered to a few countries. One easy way to make an IODC call is to use a special telephone on which you simply push a button to be immediately connected to an operator in that country – these special phones can be found in airports and a few major hotels. You can also make an IODC call on an ordinary telephone by dialling the IODC operator. See the following list:

Calls to Operator	Phone No
Australia	(008-061-0061)
Austria	(008-043-0043)
Belgium	(008-032-0099)
Canada	(008-012-0012)
Denmark	(008-045-0045)
Germany	(008-049-0049)
Hong Kong	(008-085-2111)
Indonesia	(008-062-0062)
Israel	(008-097-0097)
Italy	(008-039-0039)
Japan	(008-081-0051)
Macau	(008-087-0853)
Malaysia	(008-060-0060)
Netherlands	(008-031-0031)
New Zealand	(008-064-0064)
Philippines	(008-063-0063)
Portugal	(008-035-0351)
Singapore	(008-065-6565)
South Africa	(008-027-0027)
South Korea	(008-082-0082)
Thailand	(008-066-0066)
UK	(008-044-0044)
USA (AT&T)	(008-010-2880)
USA (MCI)	(008-013-4567)
USA (Sprint)	(008-014-0877)

Calling reverse charge or with a credit card offers no savings at all, and in fact is likely to be more expensive than direct dialling. Furthermore, reverse-charge calls are billed at the same consistent rates 24 hours a day, seven days a week, so you are unable to take advantage of night and weekend discounts.

Area Codes Taiwan's area codes all start with a '0' and are assigned by county (see the Telephone Area Codes map). To call Taiwan from abroad, the country code is 886. However, when calling from abroad you must remember to omit the zero from the area code.

Finding Phone Numbers There is an English-language telephone book covering Taipei and most other cities available from Chunghwa Telecom on request. The book is not very complete – only major companies are listed – but it's better than nothing; it's free for telephone account holders.

There is also a privately produced phone book for the whole of Taiwan, which costs a hefty US$45 with listings also restricted to companies. Look for it in the major English-language bookshops.

Some useful phone numbers are:

English Directory Assistance	☎ 106
Chinese Local Directory Assistance	☎ 104
Chinese Long Distance Directory Assistance	☎ 105
Complaint Hot Line	☎ 09021-3737
Overseas Operator	☎ 100
Fire & Ambulance	☎ 119
Police Emergency	☎ 110
Reverse-Charge Calls	☎ 108
Telephone Repair	☎ 112
Time	☎ 117
Weather	☎ 166

Internet Telephone Calls The cheapest (if not the most convenient) way to make overseas calls is through the Internet. Getting this to work requires making prior arrangements with the person you wish to call, having the proper software, a computer, fast modem connection and a bit of luck. A program

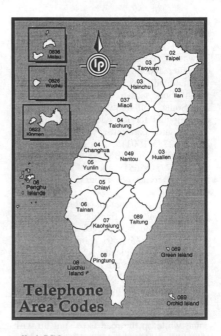

Telephone Area Codes

called ICQ (www.mirabilis.com) makes it easier to set up. For the noncomputing public, things are improving fast – direct telephone to telephone calls via the Internet are now possible. A caller has to dial a local Internet Service Provider (ISP) and then dial the international number. The call is then sent via the Internet to the destination country where it is converted back into a regular local phone call. There are various publications which explain how to make Internet telephone calls, but it's beyond the scope of this travel guide.

Fax, Telegraph & Email
There is a fax service available from the Chunghwa Telecom main office in major cities. The cost is NT$50 per page within Taiwan, and NT$200 per page for international faxes. Unfortunately, the phone company does not provide an incoming fax service. Major hotels also offer this service but will charge outrageous prices. You can

also send telexes and cables (telegraph) from the telecom office.

Email has gained wide popularity in Taiwan. If you're travelling with a portable computer and modem, all you need is an International Direct Dial (IDD) line with an RJ-11 phone jack to call to your favourite ISP. Some well known international ISPs offering this service with a local node in Taiwan are: CompuServe (☎ 2651-6899; data ☎ 2785-1001), America Online (data ☎ 2356-0786) and IBM Net (☎ 2776-7700; data ☎ 2778-6565). Other ISPs may offer a 'roaming service' – ask your ISP at home for details.

Taiwan has numerous cybercafes. The biggest problem is finding them, because they have a tendency to regularly move or go out of business. Costs for using computers at a cybercafe are typically NT$200 per hour, but it varies. There are a few places where you can use online computers for free – Taipei train station and some branches of the NOVA computer arcade.

Probably the easiest and cheapest way to email while on the road is to sign up with Rocketmail (www.rocketmail.com/), NetAddress (netaddress.usa.net) or Yahoo (mail.yahoo.com) for a free account. These services are free because you have to put up with advertising. Once you have an account, you can then access your email from a cybercafe.

If you're willing to spend US$15 per year, you can get all your email routed to any address of your choice by signing up with Pobox (www.pobox.com) – this service can also be used to block advertising and mail bombs.

If you're residing in Taiwan on a more-or-less permanent basis, you may want to set up an account with a local ISP.

Taiwan's largest ISP is HiNet, owned by Chunghwa Telecom. Unfortunately, being part of the huge, bureaucratic company means that HiNet's customer service tends to be shoddy. HiNet insists that you have an ARC to set up an account in your name. One nice feature of HiNet is that there is a local access node in every county, so you can access your email anywhere in Taiwan without making a long distance call. HiNet also has roaming agreements with several ISPs abroad, so you can gain access in places such as the USA, Canada and Hong Kong.

Other ISPs in Taiwan are less fussy – as long as you pay your bill, they don't care if you're a legal resident or not. SeedNet is the second largest ISP and also offers a local access node in every county. SeedNet has offices in three cities: Taipei (☎ 2733-6454), 3rd floor, 293-3 Fuhsing S Rd, Section 2; Taichung (☎ 254-7805), Room 11, 6th floor, 262 Henan Rd, Section 2; and Kaohsiung (☎ 336-4884), section A, 18th floor, 8 Minchuan 2nd Rd.

Transend (☎ 2706-9089; www.transend.com.tw), 5th floor, 236, Fuhsing S Rd, Section 2, Taipei, is the only ISP that seriously attempts to accommodate English speakers. Transend has nodes in Taipei and Taoyuan.

If you're a teacher or student at a university in Taiwan, you may qualify for a free Internet account with TANet which is run by the Ministry of Education. Apply at the computer centre in your university.

BOOKS

Books dealing exclusively with Taiwan are scarce. Most people with an interest in this part of the world want to read about China. Taiwan, being only one small province of China (officially), hardly merits a footnote as far as most authors are concerned.

Most of the following books can be found in Taiwan or ordered through western bookshops. Another possibility is to order through Amazon (www.amazon.com).

Lonely Planet

For those who wish to incorporate a trip to Taiwan with its neighbouring countries, Lonely Planet also publishes *North-East Asia on a shoestring* with individual chapters on all the countries in North-East Asia (including Taiwan). Lonely Planet's *Mandarin phrasebook* will help you chat with the locals and make the most of the sights, festivals and culture of Taiwan.

Guidebooks

Taipei, a Times edition, has good photos with interesting text and historical information.

Insight Guides' *Taiwan* has some practical but very out-of-date tour information. The cultural stuff is interesting and the photographs are excellent.

China by Bike: Taiwan, Hong Kong, China's East Coast, by Roger Grigsby, is a good read covering exactly what the title implies.

Culture Shock!: Taiwan by Chris & Ling-Li Bates is a good, entertaining read that will help prepare you for visiting Taiwan.

History & Politics

The Soong Dynasty by Sterling Seagrave will give you a good understanding of why the KMT are in Taiwan and not in mainland China. The book is absolutely fascinating and a must for anyone trying to make sense of the political situation that exists today.

Lords of the Rim also by Sterling Seagrave is a fascinating insight into the world of the so called 'Overseas Chinese' (which includes Taiwan).

Face Off: China, the United States, and Taiwan's Democratisation by John W Garver focuses on mainland China's 'missile diplomacy' during Taiwan's 1995 and 1996 elections.

Taipei (Belhaven World Cities) by Roger Mark Selya is a 294 page scholarly work tracing Taipei's development from 1949 to 1995. It's thorough, but the US$70 price tag is a bit discouraging.

Taiwan: Nation-State or Province? by John Franklin Copper has a self-explanatory title and is now in its second edition.

Language Study

A good dictionary is an essential learning tool for anyone who is even considering tackling the Chinese language.

The *Concise English-Chinese Chinese-English Dictionary* by AP Cowie & A Evison is one of the best available for beginners right through to advanced students. This is one of the classics, available in several versions, with Pinyin pronunciation throughout.

The recently published *Chinese Character Genealogy – A Chinese-English Dictionary* by Rick Harbaugh is particularly good if you want to understand the etymology of Chinese characters.

The *ABC Chinese-English Dictionary: Alphabetically Based Computerized* by John Defrancis is unique in that it is arranged by word pronunciation rather than by character pronunciation. It's most useful for those students who purely want to learn how to speak Chinese.

The *Far East Chinese-English Dictionary* is published in Taiwan and uses the traditional characters only. It's arranged by radicals (stroke order) but includes a Pinyin index as well as Taiwan's own *bopomofo* phonetic system. Make sure you buy the newest edition as the older ones use the cumbersome Wade-Giles Romanisation system. It's a particularly good dictionary for intermediate to advanced students of Chinese. A companion, *Far East English-Chinese Dictionary*, is available but this one is harder to use because it doesn't show the pronunciation of Chinese characters.

General

The *Guide for Doing Business in Taiwan* is published by the American Chamber of Commerce and has good stuff on business etiquette. Contact the chamber in Taipei (fax 2542-3376).

The *Directory of Taiwan* is published annually by the *China News*, one of Taiwan's two English-language daily papers. The book is basically a laundry list of the names, addresses and telephone numbers of organisations and businesses in Taiwan. There's a good deal of useful information in there (like dial-a-taxi phone numbers, addresses of hospitals and government agencies etc).

If it's business information you're after, the China External Trade & Development Council (CETRA) in Taipei publishes a number of titles including *Taiwan Trade Opportunities*, *Taiwan Products*, *Doing Business with Taiwan* and *Importers and Exporters in Taiwan*. It's dry reading, but if it's what you need contact CETRA (☎ 2341-9211).

Business Taiwan: A Practical Guide to Understanding Taiwan's Business Culture by Peggy Kenna & Sondra Lacy is a scant 64 pages, but it's cheap and gets to the point. The same authors have published similar abbreviated business guides to China, South Korea and Germany.

CD-ROMS

There are plenty of CD-ROMs published in Taiwan, but few are in English. With some effort, you should be able to find something. Hong Kong is perhaps a better place to find CD-ROMs published in English but dealing with Chinese topics.

The ROC Tourism Bureau in Taipei has a freebie CD-ROM that introduces Taiwan. Stock is limited, so there's no certainty that you will be able to get one. The overseas branches of the bureau may have library copies for viewing.

The National Palace Museum, US$60, is available in Taiwan at the museum's gift shop or from Lambert Publishing Co (lambert@lambert.com.tw), 6th floor, 201-24 Tunhwa N Rd, Taipei.

There are several good interactive CD-ROMs on the market which are useful for learning to speak and read Chinese. For more information contact the Far East Book Company Ltd (☎ 2311-8740), 66-1 Chungching S Rd, Section 1, Taipei; the China Guide Company (www.china-guide.com); or CD-ROM dealers.

CETRA publishes some directories on CD-ROM. The best thing to do is contact the Council's book sales department (email: books@cetra.org.tw). The CD-ROMs are also available through some of Taiwan's representative offices abroad.

ONLINE SERVICES

The Internet changes so fast that almost anything one can say today may be out of date tomorrow. You could try going online and searching using the words 'Taiwan', 'China' or 'Chinese', but this will likely bring up many thousands of hits, most of them worthless. Some of the more useful sites follow:

www.lonelyplanet.com This is Lonely Planet's award-winning site, containing destination updates, recent travellers' letters and a useful traveller's bulletin board.

www.tbroc.gov.tw The ROC Tourism Bureau's Web site in English is worth a peek.

www.sinica.edu.tw/tit/index.html The site for *Travel in Taiwan* magazine has all sorts of useful information for tourists.

www.icrt.com.tw This English-language site maintained by International Community Radio Taipei (ICRT) is the place to catch up on activities, concerts and other happenings in Taiwan.

www.webcom.com/bamboo/chinese The venerable Carlos McEvilly has one of the best Chinese linguistic sites around.

www.zhongwen.com Rick Harbaugh has put together a superb online etymological dictionary of the Chinese language on this site.

www.community.com.tw If you're thinking of taking up residence in Taiwan check out this Community Services Centre site.

www.hotel.cybertaiwan.com This site has information on Taiwan's hotels.

FILMS

Taipei's annual Golden Horse Film Festival is a major Asian entertainment event which film fanatics will want to attend. The festival begins around the last week of November and runs until just before Christmas. There are plenty of foreign presentations so you could end up watching Czech or Finnish films with Chinese subtitles, check before you purchase your ticket if you would prefer a particular language. The situation can change, but at present all festival films are screened at the China Theatre (☎ 2331-2305), 127 Hsining S Rd, Section 1, Taipei. Advance tickets are available from several sources in Taipei – try Era International, 46 Pateh Rd, Section 1.

The Taiwanese have produced plenty of films (see Cinema under Arts in the Facts about Taiwan chapter). Films about Taiwan produced by foreigners are thin on the ground indeed.

NEWSPAPERS & MAGAZINES

Taiwan produces two English-language

newspapers: the *China Post* and the *China News*. Neither is very complete, and you can read through them quite quickly as there are typically only 16 pages per edition (half of which is devoted to advertising). The *China News* is marginally better thanks to its fine weekend entertainment guide published every Friday. Both papers can be purchased at convenience stores and some bookshops and hotels.

Sinorama Magazine (guānghuá) is a bilingual monthly magazine, available in either Chinese-English or Chinese-Spanish editions. It's certainly one of the more intelligent magazines published in Taiwan, and just about the only one for foreigners which discusses sensitive topics like social and political issues. The Chinese-English edition is available from better bookshops in Taiwan and even some places in Hong Kong, but the Chinese-Spanish edition is only available by subscription. You can subscribe to either edition by contacting *Sinorama Magazine* (☎ 2392-2256; fax 2397-0655), 8th floor, 15-1 Hangchou S Rd, Section 1, Taipei 100, Taiwan.

The *International Herald Tribune* can be purchased in Taiwan at major hotels, bookshops or by subscription. The *Asian Wall Street Journal* is printed in Taiwan and is readily available.

Travel in Taiwan is a magazine that gives a good rundown on sights around the island. It costs NT$100 per issue, but free copies are available from the Tourism Bureau.

The two biggest Chinese-language dailies are the *China Times (zhōngguó shìbào)* and *United Daily News (liànhè rìbào)*.

RADIO & TV

Taiwan has one English-language radio station, International Community Radio Taipei (ICRT) which broadcasts 24 hours a day on AM at 576MHz, and FM at 100MHz.

There are three broadcast TV stations in Taiwan – CTS, CTV and TTV. Most shows are in Chinese; even foreign shows are dubbed. English-language programs are sometimes shown late at night, usually starting from 10 pm. Unfortunately, all three stations tend to broadcast their English programs at the same time. Check the local English-language newspapers for the schedule.

Much of Taiwanese TV is directed towards children, especially advertising, with adult shows focused on kungfu and soap operas. Expatriates living in Taiwan will tell you there's nothing more mindless than Taiwanese TV (apparently they haven't seen North Korean TV), but the situation has vastly improved with the introduction of cable TV which the Taiwanese call 'channel 4' *(dì sì tái)*. Cable has been a real boon to expat couch potatoes, though many foreign programs are still dubbed into Chinese. Just how many stations you get to see with a cable hookup varies but count on at least five in English and several in Japanese. At least in the larger cities, cable carries HBO movies, Disney channel, Discovery channel, Sports channel and CNN reports of terrorism and air crashes.

If you have access to a video player there are plenty of English-language movies available for rent from numerous shops in any city in Taiwan.

If you wonder why Chinese characters are displayed on the TV screen during a Chinese dialogue, it is because many older Chinese people from the mainland can read and write the characters but cannot speak Mandarin.

VIDEO SYSTEMS

In a nutshell, the problem with video systems is that the various countries of the world cannot agree on a single TV broadcasting standard. Taiwan subscribes to the NTSC broadcasting standard, the same as Canada, Japan, Korea, Latin America and the USA. Competing systems not used in Taiwan include SECAM (France, Germany, Luxembourg) and PAL (Australia, New Zealand, the UK and most of Europe). Some of the more expensive TV sets are capable of switching between all three major video systems, but this is not a standard feature.

NTSC expats take note – bringing a TV set or video player from home can still lead to problems because Taiwan's broadcast frequencies are different. The video player and

TV must run at the same frequency to work together – even if both are NTSC. The frequency can be adjusted by a technician.

PHOTOGRAPHY & VIDEO
Film & Equipment
All major brands of colour print film such as Kodak, Fuji and Konica are available at reasonable prices in Taiwan. One hour colour photo processing stores are abundant and the quality is about the same standard as in western countries.

Slide film, mostly Ektachrome and Fujichrome, is available and most places selling film will also be able to provide slide processing services. Agfachrome is rare, while Kodachrome is not available at all and cannot be processed in Taiwan. Prints made from slides often do not turn out very well – it's better to have this done elsewhere than Taiwan.

Black and white film is available in Taiwan at reasonable prices. The quality of monochrome photo processing varies considerably, but it's done by hand and is generally poor. There are some types of black and white film (eg Ilford) which can be processed by colour print film machines. If you need good-quality black and white film processing done in Taiwan, you'll have to look for a specialist – expect to pay a premium.

Taipei is a good place for purchasing photographic equipment. Prices are OK and warranties are usually honoured. However, if you plan on taking the equipment out of Taiwan, be sure you have some sort of international warranty.

Photography
Taiwan is in many ways a photographer's paradise. Even the urban landscapes are great for shots of people, temples, bright lights, bustling markets, monuments etc. The biggest problem is likely to be the weather – Taipei, for example, can have grey rainy skies for weeks on end. To avoid disappointment, be well prepared with fast film, a flash and whatever else you need for indoor or poor light photography.

Video
For the average amateur video photographer, Taiwan offers no special problems. Recharging your batteries will probably be the biggest concern (see Electricity later in this chapter).

Restrictions
Military bases are the only areas where you'd be advised to keep the camera tucked away. Otherwise, Taiwan is mostly free of restrictions on photography and videotaping – even shots from aircraft are OK.

Photographing People
There are three basic approaches to photographing people. One is the polite 'ask for permission and pose it' shot, which is sometimes rejected. The second is the 'no holds barred and upset everyone' approach. The third is the surreptitious, 'standing 1km away with a metre-long telephoto lens' approach.

If you have befriended a Taiwanese, they will generally be more than happy to model for you. Candid shots of people, however, are not welcomed by everybody.

The Taiwanese (like most Asians) are very people oriented – they have a near obsession with collecting photos of themselves posing in front of something. Thus, virtually everyone in Taiwan has hundreds or thousands of photos of themselves, usually posed in the same rigid position, hands at the sides etc, and they can't understand why people take pictures of scenery which are considered 'boring'.

Airport Security
All X-ray machines in Taiwan are marked 'film safe'. However, extremely light sensitive film (ASA1000 or higher) could be fogged by repeated exposures to X-rays – you may wish to carry such film in your hand luggage rather than have it zapped.

TIME
Taiwan is eight hours ahead of GMT/UTC. Daylight-saving time is not observed.

When it's noon in Taiwan, it's 8 pm the

previous day in Los Angeles, 11 pm the previous day in New York; and 4 am in London. It's also noon in Singapore, Hong Kong and Perth; and 2 pm in Sydney. During daylight-saving time, these times are one hour off.

Calendar

Year zero for the Kuomintang is 1911 – the year when the Republic of China was founded. All official documents in Taiwan use 1911 as a reference point in establishing the date. Thus the year 1998 is 87 (1998 minus 1911) – in other words, the 87th year since the founding of the Republic. This can really scare you when you look at the expiration dates printed on food and medicines!

In Taiwan the date is written in the order: year, month, day. So 20 October 1998 would be written 87/10/20.

ELECTRICITY
Voltage & Cycle

Taiwan uses the same standards for electric power as the USA and Canada – 110V, 60Hz AC. If you bring appliances from Europe, Australia or South-East Asia, you'll need an adaptor or transformer.

However, 220V is available in many buildings in Taiwan solely for the use of air-conditioners. Most new houses and apartments have at least one 220V outlet, usually next to a window or hole in the wall where you'd expect to mount an air-conditioner. A few unwary foreigners have managed to blow up their TVs and radios by plugging into these.

Plugs & Sockets

Most 110V plug sockets have two vertical slots, closely resembling the system used in the USA, except that there is no third prong for ground (earth). The few 220V sockets you'll encounter are designed for three prongs, one of which should be horizontal.

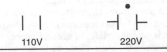

110V   220V

The previous diagram shows the two types of sockets you'll find in Taiwan.

WEIGHTS & MEASURES

Officially Taiwan subscribes to the international metric system (an imperial conversion table appears on the inside back cover of this book). However, ancient Chinese weights and measures still persist. The most likely ones that visitors will encounter are the *tael* (*liǎng*) and the *catty* (*jīn*).

One catty is 0.6 kg (1.32lbs). There are 16 taels to the catty, so one tael equals 37.5g (1.32oz). Most fruits and vegetables in Taiwan are sold by the catty, while teas and herbal medicines are sold by the tael.

The other unit of measure that you might encounter is the *ping*. Pings are used to measure area, and one ping is approximately 1.82 sq metres (5.97 sq ft). When buying cloth or carpet, the price will be determined by the number of pings. Ditto for renting an apartment or buying land, except for farmland which is sold by the *fen* (293.4 pings).

LAUNDRY

Doing laundry is often a big headache for travellers in Taiwan. Some of the youth hostels offer laundry services and others have a machine (often broken) for your use. There are plenty of laundry services in Taiwan, but most are slow, expensive and geared towards ironing and dry cleaning. The best places for fast and cheap laundry services are those around universities catering to the student population. They charge by the weight of the clothes and some have a 4kg minimum. Student laundry services don't include ironing or dry cleaning.

HEALTH

Travel health depends on your predeparture preparations, your daily health care while travelling and how you handle any medical problem that does develop. While the potential dangers can seem quite frightening, in reality few travellers experience anything more than an upset stomach. Except for traffic accidents, a visit to Taiwan poses few serious hazards to your health. Nevertheless, there are some special health conditions and precautions worth noting, and the further off the beaten track you go the more necessary it is to take precautions. Be aware that there is often a greater risk of disease with children and during pregnancy.

Predeparture Planning

Immunisations The only vaccination you really need for Taiwan is yellow fever and that's only if you're coming from a yellow fever infected area (most of sub-Saharan Africa and parts of South America). The World Health Organization considers Taiwan to be free of risk from infection with yellow fever or malaria.

Discuss your individual requirements with your doctor, but vaccinations you could consider for a trip to Taiwan include:

- **Typhoid** This is an important vaccination to have where hygiene is a problem, so is not really necessary for a visit to Taiwan, unless you plan to spend a lot of time in remote areas. It's available either as an injection or oral capsules.
- **Diphtheria & Tetanus** Diphtheria is a throat infection and tetanus is a wound infection; both diseases can be fatal. Everyone should have these vaccinations. After an initial course of three injections, boosters are necessary every 10 years.
- **Hepatitis B** This disease is spread by blood or by sexual activity. The risk of infection is greatest among travellers who will be working in health-related areas or hope to make frequent sexual contact with the locals. A hepatitis B vaccination involves three injections, the quickest course being over three weeks with a booster at 12 months.
- **Japanese B Encephalitis** This mosquito-borne disease is not common in travellers, but occasionally occurs in Taiwan, so you may want to consider the vaccination. It involves three injections over 30 days. The vaccine is expensive and has been associated with serious allergic reactions so the decision to have it should be balanced against the low risk of contracting the illness.

Health Insurance Make sure that you have adequate health insurance. See Travel Insurance under Visas & Documents earlier in this chapter for details.

Travel Health Guides

If you are planning to be away or travelling in remote areas for a long period of time, you may like to consider taking a more detailed health guide.

Staying Healthy in Asia, Africa & Latin America, Dirk Schroeder, Moon Publications, 1994. Probably the best all-round guide to carry; it's compact, detailed and well organised.
Travellers' Health, Dr Richard Dawood, Oxford University Press, 1995. Comprehensive, easy to read, authoritative and highly recommended, although it's rather large to lug around.
Travel with Children, Maureen Wheeler, Lonely Planet Publications, 1995. Includes advice on travel health for younger children.

There are also a number of travel health advice sites on the Internet. The Lonely Planet Web site (www.lonelyplanet.com) has links to the World Health Organization and the US Center for Diseases Control & Prevention.

Other Preparations Make sure you're healthy before you start travelling. If you are going on a long trip make sure your teeth are OK. If you wear glasses take a spare pair and your prescription.

If you require a particular medication take an adequate supply, as it may not be available locally. Take part of the packaging showing the generic name, rather than the brand, which will make getting replacements easier. Have a legible prescription or letter from your doctor to show that you legally use the medication.

Basic Rules

Food There is an old colonial adage which says: 'If you can cook it, boil it or peel it you can eat it ... otherwise forget it'. Vegetables and fruit should be washed with purified water or peeled where possible. Seafood is one of Taiwan's specialities and is generally good. However, shellfish such as mussels, oysters and clams should be treated with caution as should undercooked meat, particularly mince. Steaming does not necessarily make shellfish safe for eating.

If a place looks clean and well run and the vendor also looks clean and healthy, then the food is probably safe. In general, places that are packed with travellers or locals will be

Taiwan's architecture has been subjected to many colonial influences: compare a traditional Taiwanese window (top right) with a Japanese-style window in Kinmen (bottom left). However China has been the predominant cultural icon and colourful village doors (bottom right), covered in Chinese script advertising trades such as calligraphy (top left), reflect this.

MARTIN MOOS

ROBERT STOREY

ROBERT STOREY

Top: Surrounded by beautiful parkland, Taipei's Chiang Kaishek Memorial is the centrepiece for a cultural complex that serves as a peaceful retreat as well as an entertainment venue.
Bottom Left: Furnaces for burning 'ghost money', like this one in Taipei, are all over Taiwan.
Bottom Right: The straightfaced guards at the Martyrs' Shrine, Taipei, are difficult to distract.

Chinese Herbal Medicine

In virtually every town and on nearly every street of the main cities of Taiwan, you can find shops peddling traditional herbal medicine *(zhōngyào)*. Although Taiwan has plenty of doctors and an abundance of modern hospitals, many Taiwanese like to back up western medicine with a few herbs 'just in case'. Some herbs are taken to cure disease while others are taken as preventive measures to ward off colds and flu. Some herbs serve as aphrodisiacs while others are longevity treatments. No matter what your ailment, a Chinese herbalist is certain to have some remedy for your condition.

Many people are surprised to learn that the ingredients of some herbal medicines include spices like ginger, cinnamon, anise, nutmeg and the dried skins of particular fruits. Some, such as ginseng and rosehip, are well known in the west. Adherents of herbal medicine claim that you don't use a single herb but rather a combination of herbs to produce the desired result. The herbs, when properly mixed, are believed to have a synergistic effect. That is, the whole is greater than the sum of its parts.

Another important property of herbal medicine is that the effects are supposed to be gradual, not sudden or dramatic. That is, you start taking herbs at the first sign of illness, such as a scratchy throat, or even before you get sick as a preventive measure. So in the cold and flu season you might build up resistance by taking herbs before you even have your first cough or sniffle.

When reading about the theory behind Chinese medicine, the word 'holistic' appears often. Essentially, this means that Chinese medicine seeks to treat the whole body rather than focusing on a particular organ or disease. Using appendicitis as an example, a Chinese doctor may try to fight the infection using the body's whole defences, whereas a western doctor would simply cut out the appendix. While the holistic method sounds great in theory, in practice the western technique of attacking the problem directly often works better. In the case of appendicitis, surgery is very effective. On the other hand, in the case of migraine headaches, asthma or chronic stomachache, herbs may well be more effective in the long run.

Central to Chinese medicine is the Yin and Yang theory. Stated briefly, all things in the universe have two aspects, a Yin aspect and a Yang aspect. Examples would include female and male, cold and hot, night and day, down and up, passive and active, and so on. In terms of illness, the Chinese often speak of 'too much fire' which is very Yang, or of being cold which is Yin. Weakness is Yin, hypertension is Yang. The trick is to keep these two forces in balance.

Many Taiwanese practise *jìnbǔ*, the consumption of tonic food as well as herbs, in order to build strength, and in some cases to increase their sexual potency. It is a widely held belief in Taiwan that sex wears down the body and that frequent sex will result in a short life. To counter the wear and tear of sexual activity you should eat snake, since snakes are long and strong. Poisonous snakes are considered the most effective. An elixir made from deer antlers (also long and strong) is a good medicine for men whose virility is on the wane. Another treatment requires drowning bees in a strong alcoholic drink. Drinking the resulting potion will bring out the machismo in any man. The flesh of a tiger will also really give your hormones a recharge, but the sale of tiger, along with other endangered species, is illegal in Taiwan.

Herbs are not candy, and the reckless consumption of these and any other medicines can be harmful. Many Taiwanese people take herbs for years hoping to build up a resistance to illness; instead they wind up destroying their liver because many of the herbs are partially toxic. Liver disease is a major cause of death in Taiwan.

On the other hand, there are some herbal treatments that have been undeniably successful. One example of a dramatic herbal cure is the bark of the cinchona tree, which is used to make the antimalarial drug quinine. The Chinese also discovered qing haosu (Artemesinine), another malaria treatment which has generated much interest in medical circles. The dried seed of papaya has proved effective in battling dysentery. Scurvy, caused by vitamin C deficiency, can be cured with rosehip, while other vitamin-rich herbs can cure beriberi, night blindness, pellagra and rickets. Ginger root, placed in soup, seems to be helpful as a mild decongestant for colds. Other herbs such as mint and menthol soothe a sore throat, while liniment relieves sore muscles. Some herbs work well for an upset stomach, while all over the world people regularly use the oil of cloves to numb an aching tooth. ■

Medical Kit Check List

Consider taking a basic medical kit including:

☐ **Aspirin** or paracetamol (acetaminophen in the USA) – for pain or fever.

☐ **Antihistamine** (such as Benadryl) – useful as a decongestant for colds and allergies, to ease the itch from insect bites or stings, and to help prevent motion sickness. Antihistamines may cause sedation and interact with alcohol so care should be taken when using them; try to take one you know and have used before.

☐ **Antibiotics** – useful if you're travelling well off the beaten track, but they must be prescribed; carry the prescription with you.

☐ **Loperamide** (eg Imodium) or Lomotil – for diarrhoea; prochlorperazine (eg Stemetil) or metaclopramide (eg Maxalon) – for nausea and vomiting.

☐ **Rehydration** mixture – for treatment of severe diarrhoea and dehydration; particularly important for travelling with children.

☐ **Antiseptic** such as povidone-iodine (eg Betadine) – for cuts and grazes.

☐ **Multivitamins** – especially for long trips when your dietary vitamin intake may be inadequate.

☐ **Calamine lotion** or **aluminium sulphate spray** (eg Stingose) – to ease irritation from bites or stings.

☐ **Bandages** and Band-aids.

☐ **Scissors, tweezers** and a **thermometer** (note that the carriage of mercury thermometers is prohibited by airlines).

☐ **Cold and flu tablets** and throat lozenges. Sudafed (Pseudoephedrine hydrochloride) may be useful if flying with a cold to avoid ear damage.

☐ **Insect repellent, sunscreen, chap stick** and **water purification tablets**.

fine, while empty restaurants are questionable. The food in busy restaurants is cooked and eaten quite quickly with little standing around, and is probably not reheated.

Water Tap water is not too bad in Taiwan, but the government does recommend that it be boiled before drinking. Most Chinese do boil their water anyway out of habit, even when it is not necessary. Tea or coffee should also be OK, as the water should have boiled.

Water Purification The simplest way of purifying water is to boil it thoroughly. Vigorously boiling should be satisfactory; however, at high altitude water boils at a lower temperature, so germs are less likely to be killed. Make sure you boil it for longer in these environments.

Consider purchasing a water filter for a long trip. There are two main kinds of filter. Total filters take out all parasites, bacteria and viruses, and make water safe to drink. They are often expensive, but they can be more cost effective than buying bottled water. Simple filters (which can even be a nylon mesh bag) take out dirt and larger foreign bodies from the water so that chemical solutions work much more effectively; if water is dirty, chemical solutions may not work at all. It's very important when buying a filter to read the specifications, so that you know exactly what it removes from the water and what it doesn't. Simple filtering will not remove all dangerous organisms, so if you cannot boil water treat it chemically.

Chlorine tablets (Puritabs, Steritabs or other brands) will kill many pathogens, but not some parasites like giardia and amoebic cysts. Iodine is more effective in purifying water and is available in tablet form (such as Potable Aqua). Follow the directions carefully and remember that too much iodine can be harmful.

Medical Problems & Treatment

Self-diagnosis and treatment can be risky, so you should always seek medical help. Although we do give drug dosages in this section, they are for emergency use only. Correct diagnosis is vital. You can buy almost any medication across the counter in Taiwan. Pharmacies *(yàojù)* are everywhere in the cities, but can be hard to find in some rural areas.

Antibiotics should ideally be administered only under medical supervision. Take only the recommended dose at the prescribed

Nutrition

If your food is poor or limited in availability, if you're travelling hard and fast and therefore missing meals, or if you simply lose your appetite, you can soon start to lose weight and place your health at risk.

Make sure you keep your diet well balanced. Cooked eggs, tofu, beans, lentils (dhal in India) and nuts are all safe ways to get protein. Fruit you can peel (eg bananas, oranges or mandarins) is usually safe (melons can harbour bacteria in their flesh and are best avoided) and a good source of vitamins. Try to eat plenty of grains (including rice) and bread. Remember that although food is generally safer if it is cooked well, overcooked food loses much of its nutritional value. If your diet isn't well balanced or if your food intake is insufficient, it's a good idea to take vitamin and iron pills.

In hot climates make sure you drink enough – don't rely on feeling thirsty to indicate when you should drink. Not needing to urinate or small amounts of very dark yellow urine is a danger sign. Always carry a water bottle with you on long trips. Excessive sweating can lead to loss of salt and therefore muscle cramping. Salt tablets are not a good idea as a preventative, but in places where salt is not used much adding salt to food can help. ■

intervals and use the whole course, even if the illness seems to be cured earlier. Stop immediately if there are any serious reactions and don't use the antibiotic at all if you are unsure that you have the correct one. Some people are allergic to commonly prescribed antibiotics such as penicillin or sulpha drugs; you should carry this information (eg on a bracelet) when travelling.

Environmental Hazards

Altitude Sickness Lack of oxygen at high altitudes (over 2500m) affects most people to some extent. The effect may be mild or severe and occurs because less oxygen reaches the muscles and the brain at high altitude, requiring the heart and lungs to compensate by working harder. Symptoms of Acute Mountain Sickness (AMS) usually develop during the first 24 hours at altitude but may be delayed up to three weeks. Mild symptoms include headache, lethargy, loss of appetite, dizziness and difficulty sleeping. AMS may become more severe without warning and can be fatal. Severe symptoms include breathlessness, a dry, irritative cough (which may progress to the production of pink, frothy sputum), severe headache, lack of coordination and balance, confusion, irrational behaviour, vomiting, drowsiness and unconsciousness. There is no hard-and-fast rule as to what is too high: AMS has been fatal at 3000m, although 3500m to 4500m is the usual range.

Treat mild symptoms by resting at the same altitude until recovery, usually a day or two. Paracetamol or aspirin can be taken for headaches. If symptoms persist or become worse, however, *immediate descent is necessary*; even 500m can help. Drug treatments should never be used to avoid descent or to enable further ascent.

The drugs acetazolamide (Diamox) and dexamethasone are recommended by some doctors for the prevention of AMS, however their use is controversial. They can reduce the symptoms, but may also mask warning signs; severe and fatal AMS has occurred in people taking these drugs. In general we do not recommend them for travellers.

To prevent acute mountain sickness:

- Ascend slowly – have frequent rest days, spending two to three nights at each rise of 1000m. If you reach a high altitude by trekking, acclimatisation takes place gradually and you are less likely to be affected than if you fly directly to high altitude.
- It is always wise to sleep at a lower altitude than the greatest height reached during the day if possible. Also, once above 3000m, care should be taken not to increase the sleeping altitude by more than 300m per day.
- Drink extra fluids. The mountain air is dry and cold and moisture is lost as you breathe. Evaporation of sweat may occur unnoticed and could result in dehydration.
- Eat light, high-carbohydrate meals for more energy.
- Avoid alcohol consumption as it may increase the risk of dehydration.
- Avoid sedatives.

Fungal Infections Fungal infections occur more commonly in hot weather and are usually found on the scalp, between the toes (athlete's foot; known to the Chinese as 'Hong Kong feet') or fingers, in the groin area and on the body (ringworm). You get ringworm (which is a fungal infection, not a worm) from infected animals or people. Moisture encourages these infections.

To prevent fungal infections wear loose, comfortable clothes, avoid artificial fibres, wash frequently and dry carefully. If you do get an infection, wash the infected area at least daily with a disinfectant or medicated soap and water, and rinse and dry well. Apply an antifungal cream or powder like tolnaftate (Tinaderm). Some inexpensive brands available in Taiwan include Fundex and Nysco UU ointment. Try to expose the infected area to air or sunlight as much as possible and wash all towels and underwear in hot water, change them often and let them dry in the sun.

Heat Exhaustion Dehydration and salt deficiency can cause heat exhaustion. Take time to acclimatise to high temperatures, drink sufficient liquids and do not do anything too physically demanding.

Salt deficiency is characterised by fatigue, lethargy, headaches, muscle cramps and giddiness; salt tablets may help, but adding extra salt to your food is better. Liberal use of soy sauce will do the trick.

Anhydrotic heat exhaustion, caused by an inability to sweat, is quite rare. It is likely to strike people who have been in a hot climate for some time, rather than newcomers.

Heatstroke This serious, occasionally fatal, condition can occur if the body temperature rises to dangerous levels and the body's heat-regulating mechanism breaks down. Long, continuous periods of exposure to high temperatures and insufficient fluids can leave you vulnerable to heatstroke.

The symptoms are feeling unwell, not sweating very much (or at all) and a high body temperature ($39°C$ to $41°C$ or $102°F$ to $106°F$). Where sweating has ceased the skin becomes flushed and red. Severe, throbbing headaches and lack of coordination will also occur, and the sufferer may be confused or aggressive. Eventually the victim will become delirious or convulse. Hospitalisation is essential, but in the interim get them out of the sun, remove their clothing, cover them with a wet sheet or towel and then fan them. Administer fluids if they are conscious.

Hypothermia Too much cold can be just as dangerous as too much heat. If you are trekking at high altitudes or simply taking a long bus trip over mountains, particularly at night, be prepared. You should always be prepared for cold, wet or windy conditions even if you are just out walking or hitching.

Hypothermia occurs when the body loses heat faster than it can produce it and the core temperature of the body falls. It is surprisingly easy to progress from very cold to dangerously cold due to a combination of wind, wet clothing, fatigue and hunger, even if the air temperature is above freezing. It is best to dress in layers; silk, wool and some of the new artificial fibres are all good insulating materials. A hat is important, as a lot of heat is lost through the head. A strong, waterproof outer layer (and a 'space' blanket for emergencies) are essential. Carry basic supplies, including food containing simple sugars to generate heat quickly and fluid to drink.

Symptoms of hypothermia are shivering, exhaustion, numb skin (particularly toes and fingers), slurred speech, irrational or violent behaviour, lethargy, stumbling, dizzy spells, muscle cramps and violent bursts of energy. Irrationality may take the form of sufferers claiming they are warm and trying to take off their clothes.

To treat mild hypothermia, first get the person out of the wind and/or rain, remove their clothing if it's wet and replace it with dry, warm clothing. Give them hot liquids – not alcohol – and some high-kilojoule, easily digestible food. Do not rub victims, instead allow them to slowly warm themselves. This should be enough to treat the early stages of hypothermia. The early recognition and treatment of mild hypothermia is the only way to prevent severe hypothermia, which is a critical condition.

Jet Lag Jet lag is experienced when a person travels by air across more than three time zones (each time zone usually represents a one-hour time difference). It occurs because many of the functions of the human body (such as temperature, pulse rate and emptying of the bladder and bowels) are regulated by internal 24 hour cycles. When we travel long distances rapidly, our bodies take time to adjust to the 'new time' of our destination, and we may experience fatigue, insomnia, disorientation, anxiety, impaired concentration and loss of appetite. These effects will usually be gone within three days of arrival, but to minimise the impact of jet lag:

- Rest for a couple of days prior to departure.
- Try to select flight schedules that minimise sleep deprivation; arriving late in the day means you can go to sleep soon after you arrive. For very long flights, try to organise a stopover.
- Avoid excessive eating (which bloats the stomach) and alcohol (which causes dehydration) during the flight. Instead, drink plenty of non-carbonated and non-alcoholic drinks such as fruit juice or water.
- Avoid smoking.
- Make yourself comfortable by wearing loose-fitting clothes and perhaps bringing an eye mask and ear plugs to help you sleep.
- Try to sleep at the appropriate time for the time zone you are travelling to.

Motion Sickness Eating lightly before and during a trip will reduce the chances of motion sickness. If you are prone to motion sickness try to find a place that minimises movement – near the wing on aircraft, close to midships on boats, near the centre on buses. Fresh air usually helps; reading and cigarette smoke don't. Commercial motion-sickness preparations, which can cause drowsiness, have to be taken before the trip commences. Ginger (available in capsule form) and peppermint (including mint-flavoured sweets) are natural preventatives.

Prickly Heat If your skin develops painful red pin pricks, you probably have prickly heat. This is an itchy rash caused by excessive perspiration trapped under the skin. It usually strikes people who have just arrived in a hot climate. Keeping cool, bathing often,

Everyday Health
Normal body temperature is up to 37°C or 98.6°F; more than 2°C (4°F) higher indicates a high fever. The normal adult pulse rate is 60 to 100 per minute (in children it's 80 to 100, in babies it's 100 to 140). As a general rule the pulse increases about 20 beats per minute for each 1°C (2°F) rise in fever.

Your respiration (breathing) rate can also indicate illness. Count the number of breaths per minute: between 12 and 20 is normal for adults and older children (up to 30 for younger children, 40 for babies). People with a high fever or serious respiratory illness breathe more quickly than normal. More than 40 shallow breaths a minute may indicate you have pneumonia. ∎

drying the skin and using a mild talcum or prickly heat powder or air-conditioning may help. If all else fails, a trip to Taiwan's high, cool mountains will do wonders for your itching skin.

Sunburn In the tropics, the desert or at high altitude you can get sunburnt surprisingly quickly, even through cloud. Use a sunscreen (fàng shài yòu), hat and blockout for your nose and lips. Calamine lotion or Stingose are good for mild sunburn. Protect your eyes with good quality sunglasses, particularly if you will be near water, sand or snow.

Infectious Diseases
Diarrhoea (lā dùzi) Simple things like a change of water, food or climate can all cause a mild bout of diarrhoea, but a few rushed toilet trips with no other symptoms is not indicative of a major problem.

Dehydration is the main danger with any diarrhoea, particularly in children or the elderly as it can occur quite quickly. Under all circumstances fluid replacement (at least equal to the volume being lost) is the most important thing to remember. With severe diarrhoea a rehydrating solution is preferable to replace minerals and salts lost. Commercially available oral rehydration salts (ORS) are very useful; add them to boiled or bottled water. In an emergency you can make up a solution of six teaspoons of sugar and a half teaspoon of salt to a litre of boiled or bottled water. You need to drink at least the same volume of fluid that you are losing in bowel movements and vomiting. Urine is the best guide to the adequacy of replacement – if you have small amounts of concentrated urine, you need to drink more. Keep drinking small amounts often. Stick to a bland diet as you recover.

Lomotil or Imodium can be used to bring relief from the symptoms, although they do not actually cure the problem. Only use these drugs if you do not have access to toilets and if you *must* travel. For children under 12 years Lomotil and Imodium are not recommended. Do not use these drugs if you have a high fever or are severely dehydrated.

If you continue to suffer and show signs of fever or have blood and pus in your stool, then you may have a more serious form of diarrhoea (dysentery), and you may require antibiotics. In these situations avoid the gut-paralysing drugs like Imodium or Lomotil. Such illnesses require urgent medical attention, which means getting a stool test at a hospital laboratory.

Amoebic dysentery is gradual in onset, and fever may not be present. It will persist until treated and can recur and cause other health problems. **Giardiasis** is another type of diarrhoea. The parasite causing this intestinal disorder is present in contaminated water. The symptoms to look out for are stomach cramps, nausea, a bloated stomach, watery, foul-smelling diarrhoea and frequent gas. Giardiasis can appear several weeks after you have been exposed to the parasite. The symptoms may disappear for a few days and then return; this can go on for several weeks. Tinidazole, known as Fasigyn, or metronidazole (Flagyl) are the recommended drugs. Treatment is a 2g single dose of Fasigyn or 250mg of Flagyl three times daily for five to 10 days.

HIV & AIDS *(àisì bìng)* Infection with the Human Immunodeficiency Virus (HIV) will probably develop into the Acquired Immune Deficiency Syndrome (AIDS), which is a fatal disease. HIV is a major problem in many countries. Any exposure to blood, blood products or body fluids may put the individual at risk. The disease is often transmitted through sexual contact or the sharing of dirty needles – vaccinations, acupuncture, tattooing and body piercing can be potentially as dangerous as intravenous drug use. HIV/AIDS can also be spread through infected blood transfusions, though in Taiwan this is not a problem as the country has an effective blood-screening program.

Fear of HIV infection should never preclude any treatment for serious medical conditions.

Note that before you can receive a resident visa for Taiwan you must undertake an HIV test; foreigners who test positive for HIV are deported.

Intestinal Worms These parasites are most common in rural, tropical areas. The different worms have different ways of infecting people. Some may be ingested in foods including undercooked meat and some enter through your skin. Infestations may not show up for some time, and although they are generally not serious, if left untreated some can cause severe health problems later. Consider having a stool test when you return home to check for these and determine the appropriate treatment.

Sexually Transmitted Diseases (STDs; *xìng bìng*) The sexual revolution has reached Taiwan, along with the diseases that go with it. Gonorrhoea, herpes *(pàozhèn)* and syphilis are among these diseases; sores, blisters or rashes around the genitals, discharges or pain when urinating are the more common symptoms. In some STDs, such as wart virus or chlamydia, symptoms may be less marked or not observed at all especially in women. Syphilis symptoms eventually disappear completely but the disease continues and can cause severe problems in later years. While abstinence from sexual contact is the only 100% effective prevention, using condoms is also effective. The treatment of gonorrhoea and syphilis is with antibiotics. The different sexually transmitted diseases each require specific antibiotics. There is no known cure for herpes or AIDS.

Typhoid Typhoid fever is a dangerous gut infection caused by contaminated water and food. It has not been a problem in Taiwan for several decades but if you do contract it medical help must be sought.

In its early stages sufferers may feel they have a bad cold or flu on the way, as early symptoms are a headache, body aches and a fever which rises a little each day until it is around 40°C (104°F) or more. The victim's pulse is often slow relative to the degree of fever present – unlike a normal fever where the pulse increases. The sufferer may also experience vomiting, abdominal pain, diarrhoea or constipation.

In the second week the high fever and slow pulse continue and a few pink spots may start to appear on the body; trembling, delirium, weakness, weight loss and dehydration may occur. Complications such as pneumonia, perforated bowel or meningitis may develop.

The fever should be treated by keeping the victim cool and giving them fluids as dehydration should be watched for. Ciprofloxacin 750mg twice a day for 10 days is good for adults.

Chloramphenicol is the recommended drug in many countries. The adult dosage is two 250mg capsules, four times a day. Children aged between eight and 12 years should have half the adult dose; and younger children one-third the adult dose.

Insect-Borne Diseases
Dengue Fever *(tōnggǔrè)* This disease was once eradicated in Taiwan, but there have been outbreaks during the summer months in recent years. There is no preventative drug available for this mosquito-spread disease, which can be fatal in children. The best prevention is to avoid mosquito bites. A sudden onset of fever, headaches and severe joint and muscle pains are the first signs

before a rash develops. Recovery may be prolonged.

Japanese B Encephalitis This viral infection of the brain is spread by mosquitoes. Most cases occur in rural areas as the virus exists in pigs and wading birds. Symptoms include fever, headache and alteration in consciousness. Hospitalisation is needed for correct diagnosis and treatment. There is a high mortality rate among those who have symptoms; of those that do survive many are intellectually disabled.

Cuts, Bites & Stings
Bedbugs & Lice Bedbugs live in various places, particularly in dirty mattresses and bedding, as evidenced by spots of blood on bedclothes or on the wall. Bedbugs leave itchy bites in neat rows. Calamine lotion or Stingose spray may help.

All lice cause itching and discomfort. They make themselves at home in your hair (head lice), your clothing (body lice) or in your pubic hair (crabs). You catch lice through direct contact with infected people or by sharing combs, clothing and the like. Powder or shampoo treatment will kill the lice and infected clothing should then be washed in very hot, soapy water and left in the sun to dry.

Bees & Wasps Wasps *(hǔtóufēng)* and bees *(mìfēng)* are common in the tropics. Wasps are especially nasty, and if you see a wasp nest, the best advice is to move away quietly. They won't attack unless they feel threatened, so don't do anything foolish like poking their nest with a stick. Every year, several people in Taiwan are killed or injured by swarms of angry wasps; the victims are most often children who throw rocks at the nests. Should you be so unfortunate as to be attacked by wasps, the only sensible thing to do is run like hell.

Bee and wasp stings are usually painful rather than dangerous. Calamine lotion or Stingose spray will give relief and ice packs will reduce the pain and swelling. However, people who are allergic to bee and wasp stings may experience severe breathing difficulties and require urgent medical care. People with this allergy are also susceptible to bites by red ants. If you happen to have this sort of allergy, you'd be wise to throw an antihistamine and epinephrine into your first-aid kit.

Cuts & Scratches Wash well and treat any cut with an antiseptic such as povidone-iodine. Where possible avoid bandages and Band-aids, which can keep wounds wet. Coral cuts are notoriously slow to heal and if they are not adequately cleaned, small pieces of coral can become embedded in the wound and cause infection.

Mosquitoes Mosquitoes *(wénzi)* are a year-round annoyance almost anywhere in Taiwan, especially at night when you're trying to sleep. Electric insect zappers are not too useful (mosquitoes are not attracted to light). A more effective and portable innovation is the 'electric mosquito incense' *(diàn wénxiāng)*, known in English as 'vapour mats' or 'mosquito mats'. Vapour mats and the electric heater *(diàn wénxiāng zuò)* are sold in grocery stores and supermarkets all over Taiwan – every 7-Eleven store stocks them. The vapour mats do emit a poison – breathing it over the long term may have unknown health effects, though naturally the manufacturers insist that it's safe.

Mosquito incense coils *(wénxiāng)* do the same thing as the vapour mats and require no electricity, but the smoke is nasty. Mosquito repellent is somewhat less effective than incense, but is probably less toxic and gives protection outdoors where incense is impractical. Look for brands that contain DEET (diethyl toluamide). Some effective brands include Off! and Autan. Sleeping under an electric fan all night (not recommended during winter) will also keep the mosquitoes away. A mosquito net will work fine provided you have some means to drape it over your bed (not easy).

Poisonous Plants A minor but painful hazard is caused by a type of stinging nettle,

a plant called 'bite people cat' *(yǎorénmāo)*. In fact, touching this plant is much more painful than a cat's bite. The pain and swelling typically takes three days to go away. Taiwanese nettles are a rather ugly plant with splotches on the leaves and are common at around 1500m elevation. Should you accidentally touch one, you'll never forget what it looks like.

When hiking, cover your ankles and legs to protect them from the sting of the 'bite people cat' nettle.

Snakes *(shé)* Taiwan's subtropical weather is perfect for snakes – which explains the island's thorough assortment of deadly, poisonous snakes. Probably the most common is the small but venomous bamboo snake. They are green and camouflage themselves in the bushes and trees, and are not necessarily restricted to bamboo trees. Another interesting snake is the '100 pacer', so called because if it bites, you can expect to walk about 100 paces before dropping dead. There are also cobras, though the most likely place to see one is on a dinner plate in Taipei's exotic night markets. Other common poisonous serpents include the banded krait, Taiwan habu and Russell's viper. Less common, but no less poisonous, are coral snakes, the Oshima's habu and Chinese mountain pit viper. *All* sea snakes are poisonous and are readily identified by their flat tails.

Now that you're thoroughly paranoid, try to remember the following: almost all species of snakes are timid and will flee from humans. Even those which are not timid are unlikely to attack a big creature like a human unless you inadvertently step on one of them. Snakes eat insects, birds, rodents and frogs, not people. They only bite humans when they feel threatened. Don't be a fool and attack a snake with a stick – that's the most likely way to get bitten. Whenever you see a snake on a walking trail, it's best to make some noise to scare it off so it can't be attacked by a vicious hiker. Some Taiwanese hikers attach a small bell to their pack to scare off snakes – not a bad idea if you can tolerate all that damn noise.

To minimise your chances of being bitten always wear boots, socks and long trousers when walking through undergrowth where snakes may be present. Don't put your hands into holes and crevices, and be careful when collecting firewood.

Snake bites do not cause instantaneous death and antivenenes are usually available. Immediately wrap the bitten limb tightly, as you would for a sprained ankle, and then attach a splint to immobilise it. Keep the victim still and seek medical help, if possible take the dead snake with you for identification. Don't attempt to catch the snake if there is a possibility of being bitten again. Tourniquets and sucking out the poison are now comprehensively discredited.

Spiders & Scorpions You really don't need to worry about spiders (*zhīzhū*), but you may encounter a large spider which looks much like a tarantula. They live in trees and it's easy to bump right into them. Fortunately, they are neither poisonous nor aggressive and will usually flee from humans.

Taiwan is also the habitat of the vinegarroon, or whip scorpion. The stinger points straight up like a radio antenna rather than being curved and segmented as in the common scorpion. As nasty as they look, they are not venomous. Still, it's not a good

idea to pick one up and play with it – when confronted by a human, they assume an aggressive posture with claws and stinger bristling. Although it's debatable how capable they are of inflicting a wound on a human, they do spray a smelly solution of acetic acid which can irritate the skin (hence the name vinegarroon).

Less Common Diseases

The following diseases pose a small risk to travellers, and so are only mentioned in passing. Seek medical advice if you think you may have any of these diseases.

Cholera This is the worst of the watery diarrhoeas and medical help should be sought. Outbreaks of cholera are generally widely reported, so you can avoid such problem areas. *Fluid replacement is the most vital treatment* – the risk of dehydration is severe as you may lose up to 20L a day. If there is a delay in getting to hospital then begin taking tetracycline. The adult dose is 250mg four times daily. It is not recommended for children under nine years nor for pregnant women. Tetracycline may help shorten the illness, but adequate fluids are required to save lives.

Hepatitis (*gān yán*) Hepatitis is a general term for inflammation of the liver. It is a common disease worldwide. The symptoms are fever, chills, headache, fatigue, feelings of weakness and aches and pains, followed by abdominal pain, vomiting, loss of appetite, nausea, dark urine, jaundiced (yellow) skin, light-coloured faeces and the whites of the eyes may turn yellow. **Hepatitis A** is transmitted by contaminated food and drinking water. If you contract it, you should seek medical advice, but there is not much you can do apart from resting, drinking lots of fluids, eating lightly and avoiding fatty foods. People who have had hepatitis should avoid alcohol for some time after the illness, as the liver needs time to recover.

Hepatitis E is transmitted in the same way as hepatitis A, and it can be very serious in pregnant women.

There are almost 300 million carriers of **hepatitis B** in the world. It is spread through contact with infected blood, blood products or body fluids, for example through sexual contact, unsterilised needles and blood transfusions, or contact with blood via small breaks in the skin. Other risk situations include having a shave, a tattoo, or having your body pierced with contaminated equipment. The symptoms of type B may be more severe and may lead to long term problems. **Hepatitis D** is spread in the same way, but the risk is mainly through shared needles.

Hepatitis C can lead to chronic liver disease. The virus is spread by contact with blood – usually via contaminated blood

Acupuncture & Other Chinese Healing Techniques

Can you cure people by sticking needles into them? The Chinese think so and they've been doing it for thousands of years. Now the technique of acupuncture *(zhēnjiū)* is rapidly gaining adherents in the west. In recent years, many westerners have made the pilgrimage to China either to seek treatment or to study acupuncture. While acupuncture is also employed in Taiwan, it is by no means as common as on the Chinese mainland.

Getting pierced with needles might not sound pleasant, but if done properly it doesn't hurt. Knowing just where to insert the needle is crucial. Acupuncturists have identified more than 2000 insertion points, but only about 150 are commonly used.

The exact mechanism by which acupuncture works is not fully understood. The Chinese talk of energy channels or meridians which connect the needle insertion point to the particular organ, gland or joint being treated. The acupuncture point is sometimes quite far from the area of the body being treated. (Acupuncture is even used to treat impotence, but I've never wanted to ask just where the needle is inserted.)

Like herbal medicine, acupuncture tends to be more useful for the treatment of long term conditions (like an ear infection) rather than sudden emergencies (like a broken bone). However, acupuncture can be used in an emergency condition. For example, some major surgical operations have been performed using acupuncture as the only anaesthetic. (In such cases, a small electric current (from batteries) is passed through the needles.) This is a good example of how western medicine and Chinese medicine can complement each other.

While some satisfied patients give glowing testimonials about the prowess of acupuncture, others are less impressed. The only way to really find out is to try it.

Other Chinese healing techniques also focus on tapping into the body's energy channels, but using methods other than needles, for example

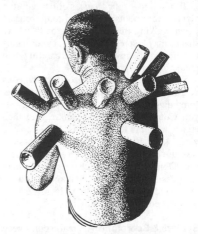

An alternative for those squeamish about needles is the bamboo suction treatment.

massage *(ànmó)*. One traditional Chinese massage method employs bamboo suction cups placed on the patient's skin. A burning piece of alcohol-soaked cotton is briefly put inside the cup to drive out the air before it is applied. As the cup cools, a partial vacuum is produced, leaving a nasty-looking but harmless red circular mark on the skin. The mark goes away in a few days. Other methods include blood-letting and scraping the skin with coins or porcelain soup spoons.

A related technique is called moxibustion. Various types of herbs, rolled into what looks like a ball of fluffy cotton, are held just near the skin and ignited. A slight variation of this method is to place the herb on a slice of ginger and then ignite it. The idea is to apply the maximum amount of heat possible without burning the patient. This heat treatment is supposed to be good for diseases such as arthritis. ■

transfusions or shared needles. Avoiding these is the only means of prevention.

Tetanus *(pò shāng fēng)* Tetanus can occur when a wound becomes infected by a germ which lives in soil and in the faeces o horses and other animals. It enters the body via breaks in the skin. All wounds should be cleaned promptly and adequately and an antiseptic cream or solution applied. Use antibiotics if the wound becomes hot, throbs or pus is seen. The first symptom may be discomfort in swallowing, or stiffening of the jaw and neck; this is followed by painful convulsions of the jaw and whole body. The disease can be fatal.

Tuberculosis (TB) TB is a bacterial infection usually transmitted from person to person by coughing but may be transmitted through consumption of unpasteurised milk. Milk that has been boiled is safe to drink, and the souring of milk to make yoghurt or cheese also kills the bacilli. Travellers are usually not at great risk as close household contact with the infected person is usually required before the disease is passed on.

Women's Health
Gynaecological Problems STDs are a major cause of gynaecological problems. Symptoms include a smelly discharge, painful intercourse and sometimes a burning sensation when urinating. The male sexual partner must also be treated. Medical attention should be sought and remember, in addition to these diseases, HIV or hepatitis B may also be acquired during exposure. Besides abstinence, the best thing is to practise safe sex using condoms.

Antibiotic use, wearing synthetic underwear, sweating and taking contraceptive pills can lead to fungal vaginal infections when travelling in hot climates. Maintaining good personal hygiene, and wearing loose-fitting clothes and cotton underwear will help to prevent these infections. Fungal infections, characterised by a rash, itch and discharge, can be treated with a vinegar, yoghurt or lemon-juice douche. Nystatin, miconazole

or clotrimazole pessaries or vaginal cream are the usual treatment.

Pregnancy It is not advisable to travel to some places while pregnant as some vaccinations normally used to prevent serious diseases are not advisable in pregnancy eg yellow fever. In addition, some diseases are much more serious for the mother (and may increase the risk of a stillborn child) in pregnancy eg malaria.

Most miscarriages occur during the first three months of pregnancy. Miscarriage is not uncommon, and can occasionally lead to severe bleeding. The last three months should also be spent within reasonable distance of good medical care. A baby born as early as 24 weeks stands a chance of survival, but only in a good modern hospital. Pregnant women should avoid all unnecessary medication, however vaccinations and malarial prophylactics should still be taken where needed. Additional care should be taken to prevent illness and particular attention should be paid to diet and nutrition. Alcohol and nicotine, for example, should be avoided.

TOILETS
Toilet paper is seldom provided in public toilets so keep a stash of your own with you at all times. If you do forget to take some there are vending machines that dispense paper – keep some change handy. In most places you will not be charged to use the toilet, but payment (around NT$5) can be asked for occasionally.

Try to remember the Chinese characters for male and female toilets.

男	女
Men	Women

The issue of what to do with used toilet paper can be confusing. In general, if there's a plastic-lined waste-basket next to the toilet, this is where you should throw the paper. Don't throw paper in the basket if it's not lined. The problem is that many hotels have antiquated plumbing systems that were designed in the pre-toilet paper era. Also there are no sewerage treatment plants in rural areas – the waste empties into an underground septic tank where toilet paper will really create a mess. Some hotel staff will get really angry if you do flush paper down the toilet (and plug up the works). For the sake of international relations, be considerate and use the waste-basket.

And while we're on the subject of toilets, in most Asian countries, including modern Taiwan, you will encounter squat toilets. For the uninitiated, a squat toilet has no seat for you to sit on while you read the morning paper … in other words it's a hole in the floor with a flush. While it takes some practice to become proficient at balancing yourself over a squat toilet, at least you don't need to worry if the toilet seat is clean. Furthermore, the experts who are employed to study such things (scatologists?) claim that the squatting position is better for the bowels.

While most people in Taiwan now have western-style toilets in their homes, many public toilets still have the squat variety. While you are balancing yourself over one of these devices, take care that your wallet, keys and other valuables don't fall out of your pockets into the abyss.

WOMEN TRAVELLERS

Women travelling in Taiwan should not attract any special attention beyond that which is normally displayed to a foreign traveller. However, it is not usual for women from Taiwan to smoke or drink, so those foreign women that do will probably attract a few stares.

In the past there have been periodic reports of young, unescorted females who have been raped and/or robbed by a taxi driver, usually at night. Most taxi drivers are OK, but there are just enough bad ones to warrant a warning.

Probably the safest thing you can do to avoid this situation is call a radio-dispatch taxi (telephone numbers are listed under the main cities in this book). Alternatively, have a friend write down the taxi's licence plate number, the time and your location, in full view of the driver, before you enter the vehicle.

When entering a taxi have a quick check to make sure the inside door and window handles are attached, so you can escape or call for help if necessary. In a hatchback, it may be worth checking that the back seat cushion doesn't pull out – attackers have been known to hide accomplices in their car boot (trunk).

Finally, don't be overly paranoid. These attacks do happen, but they are not that common as the police have cracked down hard on wayward taxi drivers in recent years. Nevertheless, a little bit of caution is a good idea.

GAY & LESBIAN TRAVELLERS

Taiwan does have a gay and lesbian community, and in June 1997, Taipei's first Gay Pride Festival was held in the city's 2-28 Memorial Park. Taipei and the larger cities have a range of gay and lesbian venues which include bars, saunas and nightclubs, and often straight venues will host a gay and lesbian night once a week – check the local press for details.

The main gay and lesbian publication is the bi-monthly *G & L Magazine* which is available from most bookshops. Unfortunately this magazine is published in Chinese only, for more English-language information on Taiwan check out the Utopia Web site (www2.best.com).

DISABLED TRAVELLERS

The biggest problem facing disabled travellers is Taiwan's formidable traffic. Those with walking disabilities will be especially displeased with Taipei's system of pedestrian overpasses and underpasses – there are lots of stairs to climb.

If it's any compensation, parking spots for vehicles with disabled drivers or passengers are becoming increasingly common. There are also cutouts in footpaths to assist wheelchairs – it's just too bad that there are so few footpaths.

Disabled access is sometimes provided in newer buildings, but older buildings may not have lifts or even wheelchair ramps.

Some museums and theme parks offer special discounts for disabled persons.

SENIOR TRAVELLERS

Getting across a street in a Taiwanese city can challenge the athletic abilities of a youthful Olympic star. For senior travellers, it's that much worse.

As mentioned in the previous section, there are a lot of pedestrian crossings in Taipei that require you to climb stairs. Senior mountain climbers may enjoy the exercise, but those with frail knees probably won't.

However, the Confucian tradition of respecting ones elders is very much alive in Taiwan. So while seniors might get creamed by a motorcycle gorilla on Taiwan's crowded streets, in most cases the errant driver will make a big deal about profusely apologising.

Some museums, zoos, theme parks and other touristy attractions offer special discounts for seniors. Bring along a driving licence or passport etc as ID, although in most cases your word will be accepted.

TRAVEL WITH CHILDREN

The Taiwanese are very children oriented. That is to say, virtually everyone wants children, so kids tend to be fussed over and are a bit spoiled and pampered. If you do bring kids to Taiwan it's likely that they will be a constant source of attention, opening up plenty of opportunities to interact with the Taiwanese. Some more positives – there are discounts for children at most public places, and there are no special health considerations for children visiting Taiwan.

On the downside, Taiwanese cities are not particularly child-friendly. First there is the traffic mess, then there are few parks or public playgrounds and finally, if your kids don't speak Chinese, finding long term playmates will be difficult. Also, most Taiwanese children spend a lot of their spare time attending cram schools, so don't have time to play.

Then there is the issue of kidnapping, a major threat if parents are perceived as being wealthy. While kidnapping victims tend to be mainly wealthy Taiwanese families, a few foreigners (mostly Japanese corporate executives) have had their children held for ransom. None of this need concern the average backpacker, but if you're bringing the kids to Taiwan, the best advice is to try and look poor.

Lonely Planet's *Travel with Children* by Maureen Wheeler provides good, additional advice including a rundown on health precautions to be taken with kids and advice on travel during pregnancy.

Despite the foregoing, don't be overly paranoid. Essentially, bringing the kids along to Taiwan is probably not any riskier than taking them to Europe, Australia or the USA. The biggest problem is likely to be boredom.

USEFUL ORGANISATIONS

CETRA assists people coming to Taiwan on business and maintains good international business libraries in Taipei and Kaohsiung (see Information listed under the regional chapters of this book).

The Government Information Office (☎ 2341-9211), 3 Chunghsiao E Rd, Section 1, Taipei, issues press releases and organises information for journalists.

The American Institute in Taiwan (AIT) has information for expats as does the American Chamber of Commerce in Taiwan. These organisations can also offer information relevant to other nationalities.

All Foreign Affairs Police speak English and can provide assistance to travellers in emergencies. They also process visa extensions. Contact details for the Foreign Affairs Police offices can be found in the Information sections of the regional chapters of this book.

DANGERS & ANNOYANCES
Crime

If you believe the newspapers, Taiwan is a hotbed of criminal activity. Although it is no doubt less safe than it used to be, Taiwan is one of the safer places in Asia in terms of street crime. However, travellers should be aware that kidnappings (see Travel with Children earlier in this chapter) and attacks on women (see Women Travellers earlier in this chapter) do occur in Taiwan. Travellers cheques are safer than cash, but be sure to have a receipt and/or written record of the serial numbers. Many of the better hotels have a safe where you can deposit your valuables rather than carrying them around with you. If you're staying for a long time, you can rent a safe deposit box from a bank.

Although street muggings are exceedingly rare, there is a serious problem with residential burglaries in the cities. Youth hostels are not immune, especially since they tend to leave their doors unlocked. Also, it's sad but true that some of your fellow travellers can be an even greater threat to your possessions than the locals – never leave valuables lying around the hostel dormitory.

Foreigners rarely seem to be the target of crime, especially since they usually have less money than the locals. Wearing expensive jewellery is not advised, nor is dressing to announce your wealth.

LEGAL MATTERS

If you run into legal trouble, you should first try to contact your country's 'trade office' in Taipei (see the list of 'pseudo-embassies' under Embassies earlier in this chapter). There's no guarantee that your government can get you out of trouble, but you can at least get some legal advice and have your family informed of your predicament.

Taiwan takes a very dim view of drugs, including marijuana. Foreigners have been busted for both possession and smuggling – the latter can carry the death penalty. There are notices on Taiwan's customs forms and in international airports warning of these severe penalties – you'd be wise to pay heed.

The other legal problem that often affects foreigners is working illegally. Although it's unfair, the severity of the penalty seems to depend on your nationality. People from poor third world countries (the Philippines and Thailand in particular) are regularly busted for doing illegal manual labour, and can face long jail terms. Westerners caught teaching English illegally will usually just receive a fine or, at worst, have their visas suspended and have to leave Taiwan within a few days.

One final problem which occasionally affects foreigners has to do with invalid or forged passports. Again, it's people from the third world who suffer most. Some people who are stateless or otherwise don't have legal documents simply buy their papers on the black market. The newspapers have reported cases of undocumented workers from Thailand spending over five years in prison because they arrived in Taiwan with forged passports and could not arrange the legal documents to return home. The Thai government has shown no interest in resolving these cases.

BUSINESS HOURS

At the time of writing, Taiwan's business hours were undergoing a major change. Previously, the typical Taiwanese wage earner worked 44 hours a week – weekdays from 8 or 8.30 am to 5 or 5.30 pm, and Saturday from 8 am until noon. Taiwan is now gradually moving to a 40 hour work week, but only once every two weeks. This means that the 2nd and 4th Saturday of every month will be a full day off, and the 1st and 3rd Saturday will remain as a half day. This change has already been implemented in government offices, and large companies are expected to follow (though most have not done so yet).

In smaller companies, the situation is considerably less clear. Many small shops keep long hours, typically from 8 am to 10 pm. Small family-owned restaurants may even be open from 6 am to 11 pm, sometimes closing between 2 and 5 pm for a siesta. In large cities, convenience stores stay open 24 hours. Department stores are open every day from around 10 or 11 am till about 10 pm. Banks are open from 9 am to 3.30 pm Monday to Friday and from 9 am to noon on Saturday, but again the Saturday hours may change soon.

The Taiwanese take lunch very seriously. Most businesses and all government offices close for the siesta from about noon to 1.30 pm. Don't expect to get anything done during this time. If you walk into an office during the lunch break, don't be surprised to find the whole staff asleep. Not being aware of this, on my second day in Taiwan I walked into a travel agency at 1 pm, only to find all the office workers slumped over their desks. My first thought was that there must be a gas leak! I was in a near state of panic until somebody woke up and asked me why I was there during the siesta.

PUBLIC HOLIDAYS & SPECIAL EVENTS

Taiwan's decision to move to a 40 hour work week will cause a reduction in the number of public holidays, but exactly which holidays will be cancelled remains unclear. In theory, there will be just as many calendar holidays as before. In practice, most public holidays will be moved to the nearest 2nd or 4th Saturday of the month which, for most workers, will have the same effect as cancelling the day off. This is to help reduce the impact on businesses, many of whom fear that increasing holidays will lower productivity and so reduce Taiwan's international competitiveness.

For this reason, all bets are off when it comes to predicting which days will be public holidays in Taiwan. With that caveat in mind, the following is the official dispensation as it stood at the time of writing.

Solar Calendar Holidays

Founding Day *(yuándàn)* The founding day of the Republic of China falls on 1 January. Many businesses and schools remain closed on 2 January as well.

2-28 *(èr èr bā)* This, Taiwan's newest public holiday (established 1997), commemorates the events of 28 February 1947, when thousands of Taiwanese were massacred in a military crackdown against political dissent. Establishing this as a public holiday was the brainchild of the DPP, and it's still very controversial. It's entirely possible that this holiday could be cancelled.

Youth Day *(qīngnián jié)* Youth Day falls on 29 March. Of course, all schools are closed on this day.

Tomb Sweep Day *(qīng míng jié)* A day for worshipping ancestors; people visit and clean the graves of their departed relatives. They often place flowers on the tomb and burn ghost money for the deceased. It falls on 5 April in most years, 4 April in leap years.

Teacher's Day *(jiàoshī jié)* The birthday of Confucius is celebrated as Teacher's Day on 28 September. There is a very interesting ceremony held at every Confucius Temple in Taiwan on this day, beginning at about 4 am. However, tickets are needed to attend this ceremony and they are not sold at the temple gate. The tickets can sometimes be purchased from universities, hotels or tour agencies, but generally they are not easy to obtain.

National Day *(shuāngshí jié)* As it falls on 10 October – the 10th day of the 10th month – National Day is usually called 'Double 10th Day'. Big military parades are held in Taipei near the Presidential Building. At night there is a huge fireworks display by the Tamsui River. It's one of the more interesting times to visit Taipei. The rest of the country tends to use this day to head to the beach, karaoke bar, pub etc.

Retrocession Day *(guāngfù jié)* Taiwan's Retrocession Day, 25th October, celebrates Taiwan's return to the ROC after 50 years of Japanese occupation.

Chiang Kaishek's Birthday *(jiǎnggōng dànchén jìniàn rì)* Chiang Kaishek's birthday falls on 31 October. Because it coincides with Halloween, it's a good time for expat parties in Taipei.

Sun Yatsen's Birthday *(guófù dànchén jìniàn rì)* Sun Yatsen is regarded as the father of his country. His birthday is celebrated on 12 November.

Constitution Day *(xíngxiàn jìniàn rì)* Most westerners and many Chinese consider this to be a Christmas *(shèngdàn jié)* holiday since it falls on 25 December, but this isn't a Christian nation and the official designation is Constitution Day.

Lunar Calendar Holidays
There are only three lunar public holidays: the Chinese New Year, the Dragon Boat Festival and the Mid-Autumn Festival, but many festivals are also held according to the lunar calendar (see Cultural Events following this section).

Chinese (Lunar) New Year *(chūn jié)* The Chinese celebrate New Year on the first day of the first moon. Actually, the holiday lasts three days but many people take a full week off work. It is a very difficult time to book tickets, as all transport and hotels are booked to capacity. Workers demand double wages during the New Year and hotel rooms triple in price.

The Lunar New Year will fall on the following dates: 16 February 1999, 5 February 2000, 24 January 2001, 12 February 2002 and 1 February 2003.

Dragon Boat Festival *(duānwǔ jié)* On the fifth day of the fifth moon, colourful dragon boat races are held in Taipei and in a few other cities – they're shown on TV. It's the traditional day to eat steamed rice dumplings *(zòngzi)*.

The Dragon Boat Festival will fall on the following dates: 18 June 1999, 6 June 2000, 25 June 2001, 15 June 2002 and 4 June 2003.

Mid-Autumn Festival *(zhōngqiū jié)* Also known as the Moon Festival, this takes place on the 15th day of the eighth moon. Gazing at the moon and lighting fireworks become very popular at this time. This is the time to eat tasty moon cakes *(yué bìng)*, which are available from every bakery.

This festival will fall on the following dates: 5 October 1998, 24 September 1999, 12 September 2000, 1 October 2001, 21 September 2002 and 11 September 2003.

Cultural Events
All major cities have municipal cultural centres where cultural events are stage, and all have schedules of their current programs. Major bookshops also have this information.

Taiwan's festivals are held according to the lunar calendar.

Lantern Festival *(yuánxiāo jié)* Also known as Tourism Day, this is not a public holiday, but is still a very colourful celebration. Hundreds of thousands of people use this time to descend on the towns of Yenshui, Luerhmen and Peikang to ignite fireworks – making them good places to visit or avoid, depending on how you feel about fireworks and crowds.

The Lantern Festival falls on the 15th day of the first moon: 2 March 1999, 19 February 2000, 7 February 2001, 26 February 2002 and 15 February 2003.

Kuanyin's Birthday *(guānshìyīn shēngrì)* The birthday of Kuanyin, goddess of mercy, is on the 19th day of the second moon and is a good time for temple worship festivals.

This event is due on the following dates: 5 April 1999, 24 March 2000, 13 March 2001, 1 April 2002 and 21 March 2003.

Matsu's Birthday *(māzǔ shēngrì)* Matsu, goddess of the sea, is the friend of all fishermen. Her birthday is widely celebrated at temples throughout Taiwan. Matsu's birthday is on the 23rd day of the third moon, and will fall on the following dates: 8 May 1999, 27 April 2000, 16 April 2001, 5 May 2002 and 24 April 2003.

Ghost Month *(guǐ yuè)* Ghost Month is the seventh lunar month. The devout believe that during this time the ghosts from hell walk the earth making it a dangerous time to travel, go swimming, get married or move to a new house. If someone dies during this month, the body will be preserved and the funeral and burial will not be performed until the following month. As Chinese people tend not to travel during this time, it's a good time for visitors to travel around the island and avoid crowds. It is also a good time to see temple worship. On the first and 15th day of the Ghost Month, people will be burning ghost money and incense and placing offerings of food on tables outside their homes; the 15th day is usually the most exciting. Ghost Month is the best time to visit a Taoist temple – an experience not to be missed.

The first day of Ghost Month will fall on the following dates: 11 August 1999, 31 July 2000, 19 August 2001, 9 August 2002 and 29 July 2003. To save you counting, the 15th day of Ghost Month will fall on the following dates: 25 August 1999, 14 August 2000, 2 September 2001, 23 August 2002 and 12 August 2003.

Lovers' Day *(qíngrén jié)* Ironically, the Chinese equivalent of St Valentine's Day falls during Ghost Month. The tradition is to go out for the evening, though Valentine cards, chocolates and the like are just starting to catch on. Classy restaurants, pubs, discos and theatres do very good business on this night. Later in the evening, the parks are totally packed with young lovers trying to 'get away from it all'.

Lovers' Day is the seventh day of the seventh moon, and will fall on: 17 August 1999, 6 August 2000, 25 August 2001, 15 August 2002 and 4 August 2003.

ACTIVITIES
Hiking
(páshān)
With dozens of peaks over 3000m elevation, Taiwan offers some outstanding opportunities for walking and mountaineering.

Hiking Clubs There are many clubs in Taipei and other big cities. Some are nonprofit clubs associated with universities, but most are commercial outfits. The clubs typically take a whole busload of hikers out for about NT$500 a head for day hikes. They charge considerably more for overnight trips. Most things are included: transport, lodging, meals and mountain permits. The only bad thing about these clubs is that at times their trips can be rather crowded. The Taiwanese like to do things in groups, so you may get 50 or 100 or more people hiking together. Fortunately, overnight trip groups are usually smaller, involving about 20 people or less.

To find these clubs, enquire at any shop which sells backpacking equipment. Additionally, all universities in Taiwan have hiking clubs, but these are usually for students and faculty only. Also bear in mind that most of these clubs are thoroughly Taiwanese and few people will speak English.

Safety Issues The most immediate threat to hikers in Taiwan comes from the unpredictable weather. It rains frequently, especially in the spring and summer months. The weather can be beautiful one minute, then the clouds and fog come out of nowhere and it starts pouring. Therefore, adequate waterproof clothing is a must. Cheap plastic rain boots with lugged soles, widely available in Taiwan, are great for keeping the feet dry too.

Hypothermia can occur in Taiwan's mountains even during summer if you're unprepared. It is surprisingly easy to progress from very cold to dangerously cold with a combination of wind, wet clothing, fatigue and hunger, even if the air temperature is above freezing. It helps to dress in layers; silk, wool and some artificial fibres are all good insulating materials. A hat is important, as a lot of heat is lost through the head. A strong, waterproof outer layer to keep you dry is essential. Carry basic supplies, including food with simple sugars to generate heat quickly, and lots of fluid.

The rain and steep mountains produce another hazard – landslides. In most cases, you won't have to worry about them if you stick to the trails, but be warned that trails and even roads are subject to landslides, especially during the rainy season.

Typhoons are another weather hazard to be aware of in Taiwan (see the Typhoons boxed text in the East Coast chapter).

Surfing
(chōnglàng)
Being a subtropical island, you'd expect

Taiwan to be a surfers' paradise. Actually, there are only a few spots on the island considered to be suitable for surfing. The west coast is a dead loss – the water in the Taiwan Straits is just too calm to generate sufficient waves (unless you want to try it during a typhoon!).

The east coast has far better waves, but it's also rocky and plagued by dangerous riptides. Still, there are a few sandy beaches sheltered by coves that have started to attract surfers. In particular, Taipei, Ilan and Taitung counties and Kenting National Park, at the very southern tip of Taiwan, are good surfing areas (see the regional chapters for details).

Windsurfing
(fēngfán)
Windsurfing is also starting to catch on. Unlike surfing, big waves are not necessary, though wind is essential. Windsurfing equipment is available for rent at Kenting National Park and Chipei Island in the Penghu Islands.

Grass-Skiing
(huá cǎo)
Taiwan is mountainous but as it doesn't get much snow local skiers have had to improvise, and so grass-skiing was born. Grass-skis look like a cross between normal downhill-skis and the treads on army tanks. The sport is said to be somewhat dangerous – grass is less forgiving than snow so skiers fall even harder than normal. It seems that no one has attempted grass-ski jumping yet – now *that* would be a challenge! Other variations on the theme include grass-toboggans and grass-sleds.

The degree of danger depends largely on the gradient and length of the slope, as well as the skill of the participants. There are a number of venues – the hills above Tamsui are popular. All are commercial resorts, but the fees charged are not outrageous. If helmets, shoulder pads and other safety equipment are supplied, you're advised to wear them. If not, consider investing in them as they are cheaper than medical bills.

Parasailing
(huá xiáng yì)
You can pursue this sport anywhere if you have the right equipment, but there are a few established spots with equipment rentals and instructors. One place to look is Sai Chia Paradise in Pingtung County (see the South-West Taiwan chapter).

Whitewater Rafting
(fànzhōu)
Taiwan's small size means there are very few big rivers, but the presence of mountains and heavy rainfall makes for some interesting runs, especially after a major typhoon.

The main venue for whitewater rafting trips is the Hsiukuluan River in Hualien County. The Laonung River in Kaohsiung has hosted a few commercial river runners, but not many. A few hardy souls have taken off on their own and rafted the river through Huisun Forest.

Kayaking has also gained popularity in recent years with a few clubs emerging (see Activities in the Taipei chapter).

Bungy Jumping
(gāokōng tán tiào)
First promoted by Oxford's Dangerous Sports Club in 1979, this craze has now come to Asia. Bungee International in Taipei introduced the sport to Taiwan (see Activities in the Taipei chapter).

Tenpin Bowling
(bǎolíng qiú)
Tenpin bowling has taken off in a big way in Taiwan, and in larger cities you can even find bowling alleys open 24 hours. Westerners with big feet might consider investing in a pair of bowling shoes – the ones available for rent tend to be a little tight.

Golf
(gāo'ěrfū qiú)
The art of poking a white ball around a lawn receives considerable prestige in the face-conscious Asia. Due to its snob appeal (and the high cost of real estate) green fees in Taiwan are anything but cheap.

Ideally, golf courses *(gāo'ěrfū qiú liànxí chǎng)* should be built on land that is at least semi-flat – steep mountainsides make the game a bit trickier. Since much of Taiwan's unused land is in the mountains, this has posed a problem for country club developers. Most of Taiwan's existing golf courses have been built illegally on land zoned for agriculture. The course owners have been allowed to obtain the necessary permits after presenting the government with a *fait accompli*. This practice has raised more than a few eyebrows.

All that having been said, the news for golfers (if not environmental activists) is good. Most of the large west coast cities in Taiwan have several excellent golf courses within an hour's drive of their downtown areas. At last count there were 37 golf courses in Taiwan. Since 1990, there has been a ban on creating new courses, but there is pressure to lift this ban.

More abundant than golf courses are golf practice driving ranges *(gāo'ěrfū qiú liànxí chǎng)*. These can be found on the outskirts of any large or medium-sized city. Needless to say, practice ranges are much cheaper than an 18 hole golf course.

For further information contact the ROC Golf Association (☎ 2711-7482/2711-3046; fax 2711-4178), 75 Lane 187, Tunhua S Rd, Section 1, Taipei.

COURSES
Language
Taiwan is an excellent place for the study of Chinese, and some schools also teach Taiwanese. The vast majority (around 90%) are in Taipei, but Taichung, Kaohsiung and Tainan offer alternatives. There are both government and privately run centres. The government places are good but tend to be advanced, inflexible and will really push you. The private ones will allow you to progress at a more leisurely pace and offer a good deal of flexibility in choice of teachers, curriculum, textbooks and scheduling.

See Language Courses under the regional chapters for information on schools which offer foreigners the opportunity to study Chinese.

Music
The playing of traditional musical instruments is still studied in Taiwan. Courses are normally taught in the Chinese departments of various universities around the island, and a number of the students are foreigners. Probably the best place to study traditional Chinese music is at the Chinese Cultural University at Yangmingshan in Taipei (see Universities in Taiwan in the Facts about Taiwan chapter).

WORK
English Teaching
Word has spread far and wide through the travellers' grapevine that big bucks can be made teaching English in Taiwan. Some years ago when I first came to Taiwan, foreigners were such a rare commodity that I was practically kidnapped by some eager students shortly after my arrival at the airport. Recruiters from the various language schools came knocking on my door so often I almost had to beat them off with a stick.

That was then and this is now. There are thousands of foreigners teaching English in Taiwan, so students aren't going to come and break down your door. However, it is still possible to find work if you go out and look for it. The pay is still pretty good (typically starting at NT$400 per hour), but if you've got to keep making frequent trips to Hong Kong or if you have to sign up for unwanted Chinese lessons to keep immigration off your back, it cuts into your profits. Plus if you're caught working illegally, you can be fined and deported.

In view of the foregoing, consider the virtues of getting a legal teaching job. It takes about three months of bureaucratic wrangling to complete all the paperwork (see Visas and Documents earlier in this chapter for more details), but is worthwhile provided you want to commit yourself to spending at least a year in Taiwan. Legal teaching jobs are most easily arranged through private 'cram schools' *(bǔxíbān)*. However, not all cram schools are legal, and not all are licensed to hire foreigners. Those which are properly licensed are mostly big chains with branches all over the island.

One of the first things you'll have to decide is whether or not you'd rather teach adults or children. As a general rule, teaching adults is more interesting but teaching children pays better and these jobs are more readily available.

Some of the best known chain schools for teaching adults are ELSI, Global Village and Jordan's. For children's classes, the biggies are Hess and Joy. However, there are numerous others, if you dig deeply for them.

Teaching at a university is normally very relaxed and pays well. However, universities are more fussy about credentials than cram schools. Normally, a master's degree or PhD is required to land these plumb jobs. Although not absolutely mandatory, universities prefer that your advanced degree is in a relevant subject – to teach English conversation, relevant subjects would include linguistics, TESL (TEFL) or education.

Even if you can clear all the hurdles and land a legal job, it's also worth noting that teaching English is not always as easy as it sounds. Getting the job is only half the battle; keeping it is the other. If you're a capable teacher and your students are good, it can be a pleasure. Unfortunately, it's quite likely that you'll get many students whose English is poor. Some people love teaching English, but many travellers say they find it boring at best.

Buskers & Musicians

Buskers were tolerated in Taipei for a while, but the police have cracked down and this means of fundraising is now likely to get you deported. The authorities have even cracked down on foreigners playing in nightclubs – only performances advertised as a 'charity benefit' are permitted to have foreign musicians. Of course, very famous western stars (eg Michael Jackson) have been permitted to perform but only through a Taiwanese sponsor who agrees to hand over several million dollars in taxes.

Other Work

There are other jobs besides teaching, but you usually need some sort of high-tech skill or qualification to get these. A large number of engineers, electronic technicians and computer programmers have found work in Taiwan. The Foreign Affairs Ministry has a list of what they term to be 'acceptable' professions, not all of which are technical – 'corporate executive' or 'ambassador to Taiwan' are possibilities, though getting these plum jobs is not particularly easy.

ACCOMMODATION

Prices have risen to the point where the only true budget accommodation left is the dormitory. The best way to save money on accommodation is to travel with a companion. Most hotels in Taiwan charge nothing extra for two people as long as you're willing to share a double bed. Hotels usually charge by the number of beds in the room, not by the number of people sleeping in them. Most 'single rooms' in Taiwan are what westerners usually call doubles – there is one large bed which can accommodate two people. Twin rooms have two separate beds and typically cost 50% more.

The question you'll most likely be asked first at any reception desk is *'Nǐ yào zěnme yàngde fángjiān?'*, meaning 'What kind of room do you want?'. If you're after 'the cheapest', then learn to say *'zuì piányìde'*. If the room you're shown is too dismal, you could ask for something 'a little better' *(hǎo yìdiǎnde)*. If you think the price quoted is too high, tell them it is 'too expensive' *(tài guì)*. You can also ask them to give it to you 'a little cheaper' *(kěyǐ suàn piányì yìdiǎn ma)*.

Discounts are an option, especially during low season, weekends or bad weather (like typhoons). Resort areas generally earn their bread and butter during weekends and holidays, so you can usually get a hefty discount (typically 30%) during off-peak times. The discount will usually be offered to you as a matter of course – you won't even have to ask for it. Bargaining a larger discount *may* be possible, but you shouldn't count on it. There is certainly no room for vociferous bargaining – Taiwan is not a third world country. Hotel proprietors may knock off 10% or they may simply give you a cheaper room, but in general prices are not subject to haggling. If you bargain for more than 30 seconds then you're really just arguing, which is a waste of time and is likely to result in you being asked to leave.

Reservations

At the bottom end of the scale, reservations are usually not accepted and those planning to stay in hostels can usually find a bed. To save yourself some running around you can telephone ahead from the airport. The people at the information desk in the airport will do this free of charge. It's certainly better to call ahead rather than scramble from place to place in search of a room.

Good discounts can be found through the Internet; try (www.hotel.cybertaiwan.com), which is Cybertaiwan's web site.

Camping

Camping, though not the most comfortable, is the cheapest way to live. All national parks have camping grounds. A few of the established grounds are in fact adjacent to youth hostels, providing a means of accommodating any overflow. In some cases, tents are already set up so you needn't bring your own, but you'll have to pay a fee for their use. A recent trend has required campers to bring their own tents and sleeping bags, though there still may be a local place to rent equipment.

Camp sites come in two varieties, one with a wooden platform (*píngtái mùbǎn yíngwèi*) which you set the tent up on, or a grass camp site (*cǎopíng lùyíng yíngwèi*) where you set the tent up directly on the grass. Camp sites with a wooden platform usually cost more. Fees for a grass camp site are about NT$200 and wooden platform sites are NT$300. However, discounts may apply on weekdays or during low season.

Free camping grounds do exist, even in established parks. Sometimes they're free during the low season (usually winter) but fees apply during the high season.

In back country areas, there is usually no objection to setting up a tent just about anywhere free of charge. Of course, don't expect toilets or hot showers.

You need to consider how much equipment you're willing to carry. Tents and sleeping bags are bulky, heavy items that most travellers would rather leave at home. You can get away without a sleeping bag during summer as long as you stay below 1000m elevation; above that, it gets very cold at night. Above 2000m, the temperature can dip below freezing and, in addition to a good sleeping bag, you'll need a foam pad to act as a buffer between you and the icy cold ground.

Give some thought as to what type of tent to bring. Afternoon and evening showers are a common feature in Taiwan, so you need something that's waterproof. At low elevations like beach areas, you also need something that's bugproof.

You need to keep your backpack and other equipment dry too. A rain cover or plastic garbage bags will do the trick.

Rental Accommodation

First the bad news – prices have been going up, so rentals aren't cheap. This is particularly true in big cities, especially Taipei.

The good news is that it's fairly easy to find a place to rent, and it's not difficult to find roommates if you need to split the cost. If you're going to work for someone, your employer might even help you find something. Places where foreigners hang out (language schools, pubs, popular restaurants etc) may have a notice board with people looking for roommates. Students should definitely check out the notice boards around universities where foreigners study Chinese. Places for rent are usually advertised on red paper with black characters, fastened to any likely object in the neighbourhood such as a telephone pole. Finding an apartment to rent through a newspaper advertisement is possible too. In most cases, you'll need the assistance of a Chinese speaker – ads are seldom in English.

The advertisements for apartments that

one sees in the English-language newspapers are usually for luxury flats – in other words, expensive. However, some of the realtors which also advertise in the papers might have cheaper listings. The Chinese papers are generally a better source of information on budget apartments. Notice boards stuck up at universities are good for finding rooms and roommates. Advertisements usually make mention of the size of the apartment as measured in 'pings' (see the earlier Weights & Measures section for details). A typical apartment is about 30 pings.

As any realtor will tell you, the price of real estate depends on three things: location, location and location. Rents in working-class neighbourhoods in Taipei are typically around NT$20,000 for a small three bed-room apartment, but in neighbourhoods like Tienmu it can easily be double this. In a rural area, the same house could cost NT$4000, but there are few work or study opportunities in such places. Students will typically rent a studio apartment (tàofáng), which can cost from NT$5000 to NT$10,000 per month.

Most landlords want one month's rent as a deposit and some will even ask for two months', but the whole amount is almost always refundable if you leave the apartment in one piece. Taiwan does not have the ridiculous custom of demanding 'key money' (extortionate nonrefundable deposits) as in Japan and Korea, nor are there restrictions on where you can live or who you can live with (as in mainland China).

As an alternative to renting an apartment, many travellers working in Taipei and Kaohsiung stay at government-run youth hostels, most of which give discounts to long term renters (see Hostels later in this section).

Homestays

You can sometimes rent rooms in the homes of local people, called homestays (mínsù). The standard of accommodation varies – it could be an attic floor that you'll have to share with several other people. Nevertheless, homestays are significantly cheaper than hotels and possibly more fun. You're most likely to encounter this practice in resort areas on weekends and holidays when regular hotels book out. Sometimes home owners will display a sign (in Chinese), but this isn't common because they fear trouble from the tax and licensing authorities. Finding a homestay is usually accomplished by asking around.

Hostels

There are essentially two types of hostels in Taiwan – private and public. Private ones are mostly found in Taipei and Kaohsiung, with a few other fledglings occasionally popping up and closing again. The Catholic church has a few (Kenting and Taroko Gorge), but the rest tend to be run by a single owner who might live on the premises. These places offer both dormitory beds and small private rooms with a shared bath. Sometimes the dorms will only have two beds, but they could just as easily have four, six or occasionally eight. Prices for a dorm bed are typically from NT$200 to NT$300 per night, with discounts available if you rent by the week.

Taiwan's government-run youth hostels are operated by various branches of the bureaucracy. Some are not truly operated by the government, but rather by the KMT which owns the China Youth Corps (CYC; jiùguótuán). CYC operates the various youth activity centres (qīngnián huódòng zhōngxīn) around the island (see the China Youth Corps Hostels map on page 88). Other types of hostels include teachers' hostels (jiàoshī huìguǎn), government workers' hostels (gōngjiào huìguǎn), police hostels (jǐngguāng sùshè), armed forces hostels (guójūn yīngxióng guǎn), labourers' recreation centres (láogōng yùlè zhōngxīn) and dormitories run by the forest service (línwù jú). You do not actually need to be employed by the government to use these hostels, but an ID card showing that you are a teacher or civil servant will get you a discount. There are also so called 'public hostels' (guómín lǚshè) – these are nothing more than expensive government-owned hotels.

Few hostels are connected with the International Youth Hostel Federation (IYHF), therefore you do not need an IYHF card.

Dorm-style accommodation in private hostels costs between NT$200 and NT$300. Most of these places have private rooms available, but prices for these are usually no cheaper than a private hotel. Reservations are advisable, especially during holidays – the CYC hotels in particular are often booked solid.

Call rural youth hostels before heading out to them as they can be closed in winter or after landslides. If you're desperate for somewhere to stay you can seek shelter at schools, churches or temples, but this should be reserved for emergencies only. Another option if you're stuck is to ask the police – they might at least offer you a cup of tea.

When all the beds are full, some remote mountain hostels allow travellers to 'camp out' on the dining room floor for a small 'camping fee' (perhaps NT$50). This seems to be an on-again/off-again practice depending on who is running the hostel.

The Taipei International can book a bed ahead for you in other CYC hostels around the island. If booking by telephone, the hostels will ask for you to send a postal money order.

Guesthouses

Guesthouses (dà lǚshè or lǚshè) is a catch-all phrase for older hotels. These places may be a bit run-down, but they're acceptable if you're not too fussy. Although there's no frills, many are air-conditioned and have private bathrooms. Starting prices can be as low as NT$500.

Older guesthouses sometimes have very cheap Japanese-style tatami rooms, a legacy of the 50 years of Japanese occupation in Taiwan. A tatami room consists of straw mats or quilts laid out on the floor. Be sure to take your shoes off before entering these places! Even if you don't speak a word of Chinese, just say the word tatami (tātāmǐ). They may say they have 'no tatami', in which case you could find out if they have a dormitory (tuántǐfáng). If they don't, then ask for a room with shared bath (pǔtōngfáng). Rooms with private bath (tàofáng) cost more.

Hotels

Hotels (dà fàndiàn) can easily cost more than NT$3000 per night at the top end. Mid-range hotels will charge from around NT$1000 to NT$2000 for a twin room.

All resort area hotels have discounts from Monday to Friday, excluding holidays. The usual discount is 20% but sometimes it can be as much as 50%. However, the most generous discounts tend to be at the hotels which have the highest rates anyway, so the bargain may not be as good as it looks.

Many of the resort hotels in the mountains or those next to beaches have dormitories (tuántǐfáng), but these are usually reserved for large groups. In resort areas, weekdays are slow and the management may permit you to sleep in the dormitory, but on the weekends or holidays you will be joined by other people. If the hotel you are staying at is booked out by a tour group, you might be asked to move into another room which may be more expensive; in some cases there may be no other rooms available and you might have to leave. The management isn't trying to be nasty or xenophobic, but if a large tour group arrives and you happen to be occupying a needed dormitory room, somebody has got to move. Most of these resort hotels only survive on weekend business.

It is very difficult to contact your western friends in other hotels or even in the same hotel by giving their name. The best results are obtained by asking face to face rather than by telephone. Having a room number greatly increases your chance of success. Knowing when your friend checked in is also helpful. The problem is communication – most Chinese desk clerks have no idea how to deal with western names. Rather than lose face by admitting this, the usual response to an enquiry will be: 'he checked out', even if 'he' is a 'she'.

One thing to keep in mind is that the Taiwanese bathe in the evening rather than in the morning. In less expensive hotels the hot water might not be turned on until the evening. This is generally only a problem in rural areas – urban hotels almost all have 24 hour hot water.

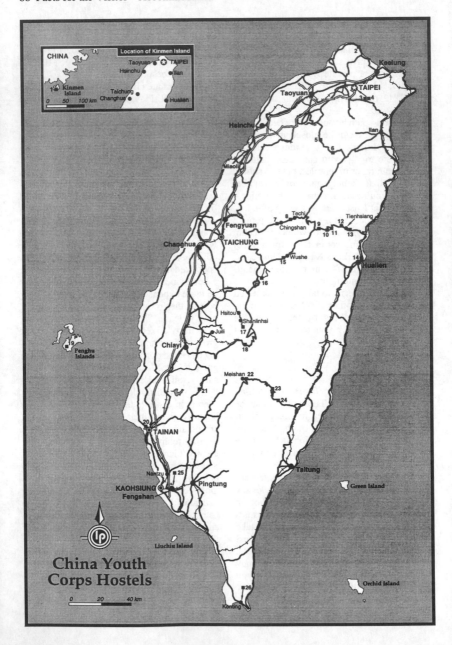

CHINA YOUTH CORPS HOSTELS 救國團

1 Kinmen Youth Activity Centre
金門青年活動中心
2 Chinshan Youth Activity Centre
金山青年活動中心
3 Chientan Youth Activity Centre
劍潭青年活動中心
4 Taipei International (TIYAC)
台北國際青年活動中心
5 Fuhsing Youth Activity Centre
復興青年活動中心
6 Paling Mountain Hostel
巴陵山莊
7 Chingshan Mountain Hostel
青山山莊
8 Techi Mountain Hostel
德基山莊
9 Tayuling Mountain Hostel
大禹嶺山莊
10 Kuanyun Mountain Hostel
觀雲山莊
11 Tzuen Mountain Hostel
慈恩山莊
12 Loshao Mountain Hostel
洛韶山莊
13 Tienhsiang Youth Activity Centre
天祥青年活動中心
14 Hualien Student Hostel
花蓮學苑
15 Wushe Mountain Hostel
霧社山莊
16 Sun Moon Lake Youth Activity Centre
日月潭青年活動中心
17 Hsitou Youth Activity Centre
溪頭青年活動中心
18 Alishan Youth Activity Centre
阿里山青年活動中心
19 Penghu Youth Activity Centre
澎湖青年活動中心
20 Tainan Student Hostel
台南學苑
21 Tsengwen Youth Activity Centre
曾文青年活動中心
22 Meishan Youth Activity Centre
梅山青年活動中心
23 Yakou Youth Activity Centre
啞口青年活動中心
24 Litao Youth Activity Centre
利稻青年活動中心
25 Chengching Lake Youth Activity Centre
澄清湖青年活動中心
26 Kenting Youth Activity Centre
墾丁青年活動中心

Expensive hotels will often have English signage, but cheaper places usually will not. Probably the most important Chinese characters that you can learn represent the words for 'guesthouse' (*lǚshè*) and 'hotel' (*dà fàndiàn*). You will save yourself a good deal of hassle by learning to recognise these. See the Language chapter later in this book.

Hot-Spring Hotels There are many hot springs in Taiwan which unfortunately tend to be commercialised. That is, the hot water is pumped into a pool or tub, rather than left in its natural environment. Some hotels pump the water into private tubs in individual rooms. However, some of the better resorts have outdoor pools in beautiful natural settings. In general, these are great places to stay.

Fortunately, you do not always have to rent a hotel room to use the hot-spring facilities. Outdoor public pools are a much cheaper option. It's also possible to rent a room for a two hour 'rest' at half the normal rate – this gives you a chance to take a private soak if you like. Places that have private pools usually have swimsuits for sale. Renting swimsuits – once popular – has gone out of fashion due to an unreasonable fear of AIDS. To find a hotel that has hot-spring facilities, look for the hot-springs symbol.

旅社

Cheap
Hotel/Guesthouse

Hot Springs Symbol

Saunas

It might sound strange, but many of Taiwan's saunas (*sān wēn nuǎn*) offer an acceptable alternative to hotels (at least for men). As a rule, men's saunas are open 24 hours a day. With women's saunas, the situation is less certain – a few stay open all night but most operate from around 8 am to 10 pm.

Typically, saunas charge around NT$300 for day use, or NT$500 if you stay all night. You can spend a full evening steaming, soaking, watching videos and sleeping in lounge chairs wearing a bathrobe (supplied free) or nothing at all. Lockers are provided so you can safely secure your valuables – you receive a locker key on a chain which can be worn around your neck.

Massage services are available for an extra fee, and in *most* cases this is legitimate massage, not simply a front for prostitution. Manicures, facial mudpacks and various other beauty treatments, along with tea and snacks, are usually available, but there may be an extra charge for these. The prices for all extra services are clearly posted on the wall (in Chinese only) – always ask the price first to avoid nasty suprises when the bill is presented to you just before leaving.

The big problem is finding these places. They go in and out of business with regularity, and some of the elegant ones deteriorate until they really do become fronts for prostitution. Additionally, many saunas don't call themselves saunas at all (not even in Chinese) because of problems with the tax and licensing bureaucracies; the neon sign might say 'market' or 'restaurant'. Saunas are listed in this book, but in many cases it may be prudent to recruit the help of a local when looking for these places.

FOOD
Restaurants
Restaurants are anywhere and everywhere, and in cities you can find something to eat 24 hours with little effort. Pay careful attention to prices, especially with seafood. The Chinese try to impress each other by ordering exotic fish which costs the earth, so don't just point to a fish that somebody else is eating and say you want that one, always check the price first. It could be NT$100 – or NT$3000, even if you buy it from what looks like a cheap food stall in the night market – even a small lobster can cost as much as NT$3000.

Breakfast is the cheapest meal if you are eating Chinese food. Western breakfasts are considerably more expensive. In resort areas all food can be pricey, so check out the grocery stores. Most hotels, bus and train stations have a machine providing hot and cold water so if you buy cheap noodles in a styrofoam bowl for NT$25 you can make a cheap, filling meal. You could also carry your own coffee or tea.

Cafeterias *(zìzhù cān)* offer cheap and generally good meals for lunch and dinner, but get there either just before noon or around 5.30 pm for the best selection. As soon as the crowd arrives, the good stuff quickly disappears – the leftovers sit around for hours stewing in the hot Taiwanese weather so you might get sick if you eat this stuff at 3 pm.

Many western-style fast-food restaurants are ubiquitous in the cities though they haven't encroached upon rural areas. Fast food tends to be much more expensive than Chinese food as it holds considerable snob appeal to the face-conscious Taiwanese.

Chinese Cuisine
If Chinese food continues to receive rave reviews, it's for a very good reason. Through the generations, the Chinese have perfected a unique style of cooking, which they regard as a fine art. As anyone who has been to Taiwan will tell you, the Taiwanese love to eat.

As always, the language barrier can be a hurdle, and the translations of menus into English is not an exact science (what exactly is 'complicated soup'?). Even packaged foods have mystifying labels: 'chocolate sand' turned out to be chocolate sandwich cookies and 'hot spicy jerk' was spicy beef jerky. A popular soft drink made by a Japanese joint venture is called 'Pocari Sweat'. Advertisements help shed some light on the issue; one restaurant in Taipei innocently advertised its hamburgers as 'the best piece of meat between two buns'.

Don't chuckle too hard at other people's English blunders; foreigners manage to give the Taiwanese quite a laugh when ordering in Chinese. Once, when trying to explain to the waitress what vegetables I wanted, I asked if she had venereal disease *(cài huā)* instead of cauliflower *(huā cài)*. Chinese translations of common food-related phrases and popular Taiwanese dishes are given in the Language chapter later in this book.

Certain foods are sold at particular times of the day or year. Bread, fruit and pungent tofu are sold mostly at night. Soybean milk, steamed buns and clay-oven rolls *(shāobǐng)* are sold only in the morning. Spring rolls *(chūnjuǎn)* are sold mostly during April; moon cakes during the Mid-Autumn (or Moon) Festival; rice dumplings *(zòngzī)* are at their best during the Dragon Boat Festival. 'Red turtle cakes' are for birthdays and temple worship. Snake meat and snake blood are mostly served in the night markets.

It's true that some Taiwanese eat dog and it's for the same reason that they once ate tiger and other exotic animals – because it is believed to have medicinal value. As a medicine, it is expensive and therefore no one is going to sneak it into your fried rice as a replacement for beef, so you can put this fear to rest. If you want to eat dog, you have to seek out a restaurant that specialises in it. Such restaurants are hard to find – eating dog is not popular with the current generation (the older folks are less squeamish). Dog meat is most readily available in winter, since the Chinese believe it can prevent colds. If you prefer Fido with his tail wagging, try the medicinal (and very tasty) angelica chicken *(dāngguī jī)* or angelica duck *(dāngguī yā)* instead, which are served from street stalls or night markets.

Chinese cooks make liberal use of monosodium glutamate (MSG). Very few people have problems with this, but some westerners complain that they are allergic to it. Heart patients in particular must avoid salt because of its sodium content, and MSG is loaded with sodium. If you are really worried about MSG, just tell the cook you don't want it by saying *(búyào wèijīng)*. Most cooks will readily comply.

Main Dishes

There are many different styles of Chinese cooking, originating from the different regions of China which are well represented in Taiwan.

There are four major styles of Chinese cuisine: Beijing-Shandong, Sichuan-Hunan, Shanghainese and Cantonese-Chaozhou. There are also various offshoots, of which Fujian Taiwanese is one. In most cases, you probably won't know or care which style you're eating, but for the benefit of culinary connoisseurs, a brief rundown follows.

Taiwanese Being a subtropical island, Taiwan has a rich supply of rice, sugar and seafood, all basic staples in Taiwanese cooking. Some local specialties include simmered cuttlefish, oyster omelettes, fried dried fish with peanuts and squid balls.

Sichuan-Hunan Sichuan food is the hottest of the four major categories – it's great stuff if you like spicy food, but keep the drinking water handy! Specialities include frogs' legs and smoked duck. Other dishes to try are shrimps with salt and garlic; dried chilli beef; bean curd with chilli; fish in spicy bean sauce; and aubergines in garlic.

Hunan food is a variation, often hot and spicy like Sichuan cuisine, usually with duck, chicken and seafood on the menu.

Beijing-Shandong Beijing and Shandong cuisine comes from the cold northland of China. Since this is China's wheat belt, steamed bread, dumplings and noodles figure prominently rather than rice.

The most famous speciality is Beijing duck, served with pancakes and plum sauce. Another northern speciality is Mongolian hotpot, composed of assorted meats and vegetables cooked in a burner right on the dining table – it's so good in Taiwan that it's hard to believe it can be so bad in Mongolia. Hotpot is usually eaten during winter. Bird's-nest soup is another speciality of Shandong cooking.

Shanghainese Shanghainese cooking is noted for its use of seafood, but is heavy and oily. Many westerners say it's disgusting,

Eating Etiquette

Rather than greeting someone by saying 'How are you?', many Taiwanese people will open a conversation by asking 'Have you eaten yet?'. This may seem like a strange question to ask someone at 10 am, but food plays a major role in Chinese society (could this have something to do with the famines in their history?).

Proper hosts *must* feed their guests. A polite guest *must* refuse (to avoid appearing greedy) and then, even if they genuinely aren't hungry, they will be force-fed. The host will do everything short of putting a funnel into their guest's mouth and shoving the food in. One of the more entertaining scenes encountered in Taiwan goes something like this:

Host: Here, have something to eat.
Guest: Oh, no thank you, I just ate.
Host: Oh, but you must, I insist. Have some cake, some fruit.
Guest: No, no, I'm on a diet.
Host: But you must. Don't be shy. Have something.
Guest: Really, it's not necessary ... *(ad infinitum)*.

The best solution to this dilemma is to wait until you are hungry to visit people. This is especially true as such formidable hospitality not only means that you must eat with the appetite of a normal person, but your host will see to it that you eat until you reach bursting point – and then they will insist that you have some more. A phrase you'll soon learn to dread is *duō chī yīdiǎn* (eat some more).

In addition, while the Taiwanese don't expect foreigners to understand all of their dining customs, there are a few rules to be aware of.

Proper etiquette demands that you hold your rice bowl close to your face rather than leaving it on the table – exactly the opposite of what would be considered proper behaviour in western countries. This only applies to bowls, not to plates. It is also acceptable to spit out fish bones and pile them on the table next to your plate.

People in Taiwan rarely use forks, spoons are usually for soup, and eating with a knife is almost unheard of except in western-style restaurants serving steak. If you haven't already mastered the skill of using chopsticks, you'd better get practising (see diagrams below). When not eating, never leave your chopsticks pointing down into the bowl. Always place them across the top of the bowl or on the table. To the Chinese, leaving chopsticks sticking vertically into the bowl looks like sticks of incense in a bowl of ashes – a clear death sign.

There is also proper etiquette involved when using a toothpick – you should use two hands, one to operate the pick and one to block the view of this process. Personally, I think using two hands makes the whole thing far more conspicuous, but local custom demands you do it this way.

If dining out, be prepared for a rather amusing scene when it's time to pay the bill. If you are with a group of people, don't be suprised if they all rush up to the cash register, each one insisting on paying for the entire group. It can turn into quite a battle as they all pull out their money and simultaneously try to stuff it into the hands of the bewildered cashier. As a foreign guest, everyone will insist that they pay for you. Keep smiling and insist that you should pay. It's unlikely that they will let you, but part of the ritual is to pretend that you really want to. ■

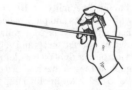

Place the first chopstick between the base of your thumb and the top of your ring finger. (Bend fingers slightly.)

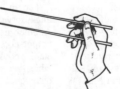

Hold the second chopstick between the top of your thumb and the tops of your middle and index fingers.

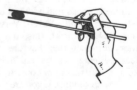

Keeping the first chopstick and your thumb still, move the other chopstick up and down using your middle and index fingers.

tasteless and greasy, but the liberal use of spices can make it almost palatable. Eels are popular, as is drunken chicken, cooked in wine. Other things to try are some of the cold meat and sauce dishes, ham and melon soup, bean curd (tofu) and brown sauce, braised meat balls, deep-fried chicken and pork ribs with salt and pepper.

Cantonese-Chaozhou This is southern Chinese cooking – lots of steaming, boiling and stir-frying. Dim sum is a snack-like variation, usually served for lunch rather than dinner, consisting of all sorts of little delicacies served from pushcarts wheeled around the restaurant floor. It's justifiably famous and highly addictive stuff.

The Cantonese are famous for making just about anything palatable; specialities are abalone, dried squid, 1000-year eggs (made by soaking eggs in horse's urine), shark's fin soup, snake soup and dog stew. Other culinary exotica include anteaters, pangolins (a sort of armadillo that is becoming endangered), cats, rats, owls, monkeys, turtles and frogs. One saying is that the Cantonese eat anything with four legs – except the table. Another Chinese joke is that the Cantonese are industrious people – capable of doing any job except zookeeper.

Despite the unusual ingredients, Cantonese food has long been a favourite in the west – Chinese restaurants around the world often include a rich selection of Cantonese dishes on the menu.

Vegetarian

Vegetarian restaurants in Taiwan come in two varieties, Buddhist and non-Buddhist. There is no easy way to recognise the non-Buddhist ones other than to be able to read the Chinese for 'vegetarian' (súshì cāntīng).

By contrast, it's extremely easy to spot the Buddhist vegetarian restaurants – look for the Buddhist symbol.

卍

When buying packaged items at a grocery store (biscuits, noodles etc), the Buddhist symbol indicates that no animal products were used.

Fast Food

All of the well-known fast-food chains (McDonald's, Wendy's, KFC, Pizza Hut etc) can be found in the big and mid-sized cities. There isn't much hope of finding these places in the countryside though, at least not yet.

You probably think that fast food in Taiwan will taste just like it did back home. In most cases that's true. However, pizzas with corn and pineapple toppings are a notorious Taiwanese innovation. Even McDonald's has localised it's menu – the pancake breakfasts and egg muffins have been replaced with Taiwanese-style corn soup. Another surprise is the lack of salt packets – if you ask for salt, you'll probably be given pepper instead. However, when it comes to hamburgers, French fries, chicken and Coca-Cola, they do indeed taste 'just like at home'.

Pizza Hut in Taiwan offers a great deal on weekdays between 2 and 5 pm. During these times, for NT$138 you can order a qīng-sōngbā which is a meal made up of a small pizza and all-you-can-eat from the salad bar (this special deal is not on the menu, so ask). Chinese fast-food chains also exist – most are easily forgettable. The fried chicken tends to be saturated in grease, and the French fries are made from sweet potatoes (and more grease). The 'hamburgers' might literally be made from ham, and the ketchup contains enough sugar to give you diabetes. The one thing you can count on is the ubiquitous 'corn soup' – one begins to wonder if there isn't some law requiring it to be on the menu.

Self-Catering

You can put together a cheap meal at any convenience store – check out the tea-eggs (eggs boiled in tea), instant rice and noodle dishes which can be heated in their microwave oven. The steamed meat buns at 7-Eleven stores are some of the best in Taiwan, especially the spicy ones (orange wrapper on bottom).

There are other pretenders to the throne – Japanese-run chains such as Family Mart, Nikko Mart etc, all try to compete in the 24 hour convenience store sweepstakes.

If you've got your own cooking facilities, Taiwan's supermarkets can supply most of your needs. However, if you've got a craving for western delicacies such as cheese and salami, you'll have to explore some of the rare speciality shops selling imported foods.

Desserts

Fruit, rather than cake, ice cream or other sweets, is usually served at the end of the meal. This is not to say that Taiwan suffers from a shortage of sweets. The Taiwanese produce some wonderful junk food. Fruit with shaved ice and syrup *(bābǎo bīng)* is a personal favourite, especially during the hot, sticky summers. Variations include tofu (bean curd) pudding with peanuts and ice *(huāshēng dòuhuā bīng)* or ice with red mung beans and milk *(hóngdòu niúnǎi bīng)*. The papaya milkshakes *(mùguā niúnǎi)* are superb. Sesame seed candy *(zhīmá táng)* is almost as ancient as China itself.

Be careful though, because looks can deceive. You may bite into what looks like a dreamy, creamy pastry, only to find it filled with salted pork and green beans. Then there are things on a stick called *yāmǐxiě* which look like popsicles – in fact, they're made from sticky rice mixed with duck's blood!

Fruit

Taiwan's subtropical climate means you can expect a year-round abundance of fruit. However, prices are generally high, reflecting a shortage of workers willing to grow and harvest the stuff (most young Taiwanese disdain farm life). It's also a reflection of the power of the Taiwanese farm lobby that they manage to keep out most cheaper imports. Imports do exist though, mostly cool-climate fruits like apples and pears which do not grow well in Taiwan. There are also some exotic tropical imports, like durians from Thailand and 'red dragon fruit' *(hóng lóng guǒ)* from Vietnam.

The Chinese almost never eat the skin on apples, pears and grapes. If you do, expect to draw a few amused stares and comments. They feel the same way about uncooked vegetables, like carrots. They figure only rabbits do that.

Many foreigners who have never eaten sugarcane before make complete fools of themselves the first time they try (much to the amusement of the Chinese). Do not eat the outer (purple coloured) skin of sugarcane – it must be removed with a peeling knife. Also, don't actually eat the sugarcane, chew it to extract the sweet juices and then spit out the pulp. If you swallow the pulp, you'll practically choke (but the Chinese audience will have a giggling fit).

DRINKS

Nonalcoholic Drinks

Tea Chinese tea is justifiably famous and Taiwan produces many top grade varieties. All over the island you'll find tea shops selling the stuff in bulk.

Black tea, called 'red tea' by the Chinese, is the type most westerners are familiar with. Black tea is fully fermented – that is, the tea is kept at around 27°C for several hours before being heated to 95°C to complete the drying process.

Green tea is not fermented at all. In order to kill the microbes the tea leaves are steamed immediately after the tea is picked, then they're rolled, crushed and dried.

Oolong (literally, black dragon) tea is a partially fermented tea and is considered to be prime quality. Some oolong teas fetch such incredibly high prices that they're almost worth their weight in gold. As oolong tea is so highly prized, there is a tendency among tea vendors to label other teas 'oolong'. Different grades of oolong include *lóngjǐng* (dragon well), relatively mild stuff; *tiě guānyīn* (iron goddess of mercy), which is stronger; and *dōngfāng měirén* (oriental beauty), which is heavy on the caffeine.

In addition to these basic teas there are blends available; for example, jasmine tea is a mixture of green tea and flowers. The possible combination of blends is endless.

Finding good tea is only half the battle. To enjoy tea, one has to know how to prepare it. Most Taiwanese are dumbfounded by the western custom of putting milk and sugar in tea. They drink it straight, and the more bitter the taste, the better.

There are several methods of preparing tea. The most popular way for a group to drink tea is 'old man style'. A tiny teapot is stuffed full of tea leaves and scalding hot water is poured inside. After a very short steep, the tea is quickly poured into a small flask to cool, it's then served in very tiny cups which allow the tea to cool faster. More boiling water is poured into the teapot and a second brew is prepared. As the tea gets weaker, the time needed for steeping is progressively longer. Eventually, the leaves are discarded and the pot can be stuffed with fresh leaves again. Beautiful tea sets to make 'old man tea' can be bought cheaply in Taiwan.

The easiest way to prepare tea is to put the leaves directly into a cup or large teapot, pour boiling water into it, and then let it steep for no less than six minutes. The longer it steeps the more bitter it will become. Tea bags are also available, mostly being the familiar imported brands like Lipton.

Taiwanese tea is high in caffeine, and some of the more expensive oolong and green teas will make your head buzz. Herbal teas have no caffeine, but you won't find these in Taiwanese tea shops – look in grocery stores and supermarkets. Some common types are hibiscus tea (not bad), wheat tea (tastes a lot like coffee), chrysanthemum tea (awful stuff), ginger tea (spicy but excellent) and ginseng tea. The more absurd the health claims written on the box, the higher the price – one expensive brand of ginseng tea claims to cure 'chronic thirst'.

Teahouses are common in Taiwan, especially in the countryside. Typically you pay around NT$130 to NT$400 for the tea and each person pays a cover charge of NT$100 (called a 'water fee'). These are great places to while away the hours chatting or reading and refilling the pot with hot water as often as you like.

Coffee Taiwan does not produce any coffee of its own. The coffee you buy in Taiwan is imported and, at least in classy coffee shops and restaurants, is grotesquely overpriced. Nevertheless, hanging out in a coffee shop with friends is a pleasant and popular pastime. The coffee itself comes in a tiny cup which costs as much as a whole dinner, maybe NT$150 (if lucky, you might get one free refill), so if you're hungry order the dinner instead. Ironically, the dinner often includes a free cup of coffee, but this is normally iced coffee already flavoured with (too much) sugar and milk. If you ask for hot coffee instead, you'll be charged an extra NT$150. Coffee shops usually have excellent ice-cream sundaes which are better value than the coffee. The atmosphere is relaxed and sometimes a band is provided, especially on Saturday night.

If all you want is a cheap cup of coffee, then go to McDonald's. Not only is it cheap to begin with at NT$30 a cup, but refills are free.

Doutor's, the Japanese coffee chain, has branches in most Taiwanese cities. At NT$35 a cup, it's not too pricey though there are no free refill bargains here. By way of compensation, Doutor's offers a wide selection of coffee blends. Doutor's also bakes some mean cakes, making it a good venue for breakfast.

If you set yourself up in Taiwan for a long stay and want to brew your own coffee, most coffee shops (including Doutor's) will sell you beans. Popular blends are readily available and electric coffee bean grinders and brewing machines can be purchased from big department stores at a reasonable cost.

Soft Drinks During Taiwan's long hot summers, one of the great pleasures is indulging in icy drinks. Even at the local convenience store you'll find a range of unusual beverages such as iced green tea. Even better are 'ice shops' which serve such exotica as carrot juice and papaya milkshakes.

All the usual western carbonated drinks can be found, but sugar free versions are harder to come by. Usually you can score

Diet Coke in major cities, but it's a rare item out in the hinterlands. Decaffeinated cola is nonexistent. Don't forget to check out the local brands either – Taiwanese sarsaparilla is especially recommended.

Cordial (concentrated fruit syrup) that you dilute with water is one of Taiwan's little known specialities. The most popular with westerners seems to be passionfruit *(bǎixiāngguǒ)*. Other flavours to look for include hibiscus *(luòshén huā)* and sour plum *(suān méi)*. You'll generally find these in the larger supermarkets.

Alcoholic Drinks

Only one beer is actually brewed in Taiwan and this is simply called 'Taiwan Beer'. While not the world's best, it's not too bad and is reasonably cheap. A recent trend (starting in 1996) has been to import western beers in bulk and repackage them in containers to look almost identical to Taiwan Beer. These new 'clones' include Superior Beer, Good Cornmeal Beer, Premium Beer, Essential Beer and the strangely named 'I Want Beer'. With the exception of Premium Beer, most of the clones are considered inferior to the native brew. The Alcohol and Tobacco Monopoly – the owners of the Taiwan Beer label – has considered legal action against the clones for trademark infringement but so far they've refrained from doing so.

You can, of course, buy imported western beers in their original containers, though these tend to be considerably more expensive than Taiwan Beer.

Apart from beer, Chinese booze doesn't attract much of a following among westerners. Most liquors are rather harsh, although some make a fairly good mixed drink. Taiwanese rum in particular mixes well with Coke or Pepsi, but the Chinese prefer it straight from the bottle. The strongest stuff, called Kaoliang, is made out of sorghum. It's 65% alcohol and makes a reasonably good substitute for paint thinner. The most popular liquor is Shaoshing, distilled from rice with a 15% alcohol content. Taiwan produces a good sweet red grape

wine and plum wine. There is also a white grape wine which some westerners like.

If you attend a feast or dinner party, be careful of getting drawn into the 'finger game' *(huá jiǔ quán)*. It's a drinking game and the loser is obliged to empty the glass – lose too many times and you'll need to be carried out the door.

As a westerner, you may find yourself being toasted. Someone will lift his glass and say *gān bēi*, which literally means 'dry glass'. If you accept the challenge, see the local herbal medicine shop for some hangover remedies. If you would rather not get wasted, just answer *suí yì*, or 'as you like'. You can then just take a sip.

Women are not expected to drink in Taiwan so expect a few rude stares if you are a female drinker. There is no minimum age for purchasing alcohol or for drinking it.

ENTERTAINMENT
MTV

Music & TV (MTV) clubs offer the chance to see movies on video in either a large group room or in the privacy of your own little cubicle. It's not quite the same as MTV in the west – the films may be full-length feature films. These clubs were extremely popular, but most have run afoul of the copyright law and have been shut down by the government. A few still exist – their legal status is questionable, but some clubs claim to have secured rights from the copyright owners.

KTV
(kǎlā OK)

Derived from the Japanese word *karaoke* (empty music) and MTV, KTV is one big amateur singing contest to the accompaniment of a videotape.

KTV has taken Asia by storm while most westerners find it as interesting as watching concrete dry. Clearly there is some vast cultural difference here that could provide the basis for a budding anthropologist's doctoral dissertation.

If you visit a KTV you will certainly be asked to perform. No matter how badly you sing, you will undoubtedly receive polite applause. The Taiwanese love to hear foreigners sing even if they can't understand a word you say. However, if your singing is truly awful, for the sake of international relations, don't subject the audience to more than one song.

You won't have much trouble locating a KTV – they seem to be everywhere. All upmarket hotels have them as do some midrange hotels. One variation on the theme is Hotel TV (HTV), where your hotel room is equipped with a karaoke machine. Some of Taiwan's few passenger ferry boats even have KTV onboard.

Most KTVs are also bars – alcohol is served, and a few can even be pick-up joints or fronts for prostitution. Each KTV has its own character and it's hard to make any judgements until you walk in the door.

Pubs & Discos
(píjiǔ wū, jiǔbā)
Pubs and discos have become increasingly popular in the large cities. Some places have taped music while others feature live bands. In a few places (mostly Taipei), there are pubs which cater to foreigners by offering English-language and western-style menus with western rock music playing in the background. Prices in pubs and discos tend to be on the high side.

Barbershops
(lǐfǎ tīng)
This is meant more as a warning than a 'how to' guide. A trip to a barbershop in Taiwan can be a delightful experience. Choose from the many services offered: haircut, shampoo, blow-dry, manicure and massage of the head, neck and shoulders. Men can have a shave and you can even have the wax cleaned out of your ears. Prices can be as low as NT$250, though you could spend up to as much as NT$2000 in a luxurious place.

Barbershops are generally for men; there are beauty parlours *(měiróng yuàn)* for women. But many places are unisex.

Alas, things aren't always what they seem. In some 'barbershops' not a hair gets cut nor a whisker gets shaved – they are nothing but brothels! More than a few travellers have wandered into barbershops innocently looking for a haircut, and wound up making complete fools of themselves.

How to distinguish a real barbershop from a house of ill repute? Usually, you can judge from the outside. Real barbershops have windows that you can look through so you know what's going on inside. Brothels have mirrored glass or no windows at all. The pimp standing outside is also a giveaway. Brothels have gaudy bright lights and sometimes a neon butterfly. To the Taiwanese, a butterfly symbolises a man who cheats on his wife, 'fluttering' from flower to flower.

SPECTATOR SPORTS
In Taiwan, where real estate is expensive and scarce (at least in urban areas), large outdoor stadiums are notable for their absence. A contributing factor is that most Taiwanese spectators hate being outdoors in the scorching summer sun (or chilly winter drizzle). For these reasons, the Taiwanese seem to be more attracted to indoor sports.

Of the indoor sports, basketball *(lán qiú)* seems to be one of the most popular. Other indoor games which attract a following (and are often broadcast on TV) include martial arts *(wǔshù)* and table tennis *(pīngpōng qiú)*. There is also some interest in western-style boxing and wrestling.

Professional baseball *(bàng qiú)* is played outdoors, usually at night to avoid the merciless summer sun. Each team is allowed five foreign players, so it's not uncommon to see a few old has-beens from the major American leagues. Although the outdoor stadiums are small and seats are limited, games are poorly attended so getting a ticket is seldom a problem. One reason for the popularity of baseball may be due to the fact that the gambling addicted Taiwanese like to place bets on the outcome of the games.

International tennis *(wǎng qiú)* and soccer *(zú qiú)* matches are often broadcast on cable TV. During the soccer World Cup, Taiwanese viewers stay glued to their TV screens.

American-style football, cricket and

rugby have all failed in their attempts to capture to the imagination of the Taiwanese.

THINGS TO BUY

Taiwan is no longer the bargain centre it used to be. In this era of the 'globalised economy', prices in the west are much the same as in Taiwan or even cheaper.

Thus, the main reason to embark on a shopping expedition in Taiwan is to find something that is unavailable or rare in your home country. If you're into arts and crafts, Taiwan produces exotic items such as jade jewellery, calligraphy scrolls, watercolour paintings, Buddhist-style incense burners, carved name seals (chops), pottery and tea sets for serving 'old man's tea'.

Traditional Chinese-style clothing can be beautiful, but in Taiwan it's a speciality and generally costly. The locals prefer western outfits because they're 'modern'.

Keep in mind that clothing sizes are different in Taiwan. Most things, such as shoes, gloves, clothing and even bicycles, are smaller than in the west. An 'extra large' in Taiwan is about equal to medium in the west. Don't believe the sales assistants when they say, 'It will stretch'. It won't. Also, take a good look at the English slogans written on the T-shirts – some of them are nonsensical.

With half the population on motorcycles, Taiwan offers some real bargains on motorcycle accessories. If you're a biker, this is worth checking out. Motorcycle wet-weather gear, for example, is cheap and totally waterproof – look for these rain suits in grocery stores and supermarkets. Quality varies by brand name and price – check carefully. Remember too that a medium-sized westerner will probably want an extra large size. The maroon coloured rain suits are meant for women while blue ones are for men – if a

Name Chops
(yìnzhāng)

Traditional Chinese name chops or seals have been used for thousands of years. It is likely that they were created as a simple form of identification, especially as many people would have been illiterate and Chinese characters are so complex.

A chop served both as a form of identification and as a valid signature. All official documents in China needed to be validated with a chop.

Today, most Taiwanese are literate, but the tradition is still kept alive. In fact, without a chop it is difficult or impossible to enter into legally binding contracts in Taiwan. A chop is used for bank accounts, safe-deposit boxes and land sales. If you extend your visa in Taiwan, the official who grants the extension must use their chop to stamp your passport. Only red ink is used for printing a name chop.

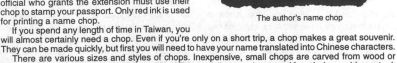

The author's name chop

If you spend any length of time in Taiwan, you will almost certainly need a chop. Even if you're only on a short trip, a chop makes a great souvenir. They can be made quickly, but first you will need to have your name translated into Chinese characters.

There are various sizes and styles of chops. Inexpensive, small chops are carved from wood or plastic. Chops costing several thousand New Taiwan dollars can be carved from jade, marble or steel.

Security is an issue with name chops so most people keep many different chops to confuse possible thieves, though they run the risk of confusing themselves as well. They may use one chop for their bank account, another for contracts and another for a safe-deposit box. Fortunately, most banks allow foreigners to use a signature for documentation and identification. The people who carve chops don't check your ID, so obtaining a fake or forged chop could be very easy. However, creating someone else's name chop for illegal purposes is treated as document forgery, a very serious crime in Taiwan. ■

man wears a maroon rain suit, he's quite likely to be laughed at. Motorcycle shops sell a wide variety of superb wheel locks, utility racks and panniers.

Straw and bamboo mats are great during the summer, especially for keeping you cool while you sleep . If you live in a hot climate and drive a car, look for the seat covers made from small wooden balls stitched together. Small shops which specialise in straw, bamboo and rattan furniture are the best places to look for this kind of stuff.

With electronic goods and cameras, ask if there is a warranty. For 'grey-market' goods (imported by someone other than the authorised agent), there might be no warranty at all.

Rip-Offs

Getting ripped off is seldom a problem in Taiwan. No matter how many bad experiences you may have had in mainland China or Hong Kong, don't assume that Taiwan is the same – it's not. Foreigners may occasionally be overcharged, mainly by elderly people who haven't heard that WWII has ended. But as a general rule if the store says it's jade, it will be jade, not coloured glass. If they say it's a genuine Rolex watch, then it will be real, not a fake. If merchandise is sold with a warranty, it will generally be honoured.

Nevertheless, not everyone is honest. If you think you've been ripped off, try some negotiation. You may be able to obtain a refund or exchange from the store itself especially if you act immediately. Finally, in cases of outright fraud, file a complaint with the Foreign Affairs Police.

Getting There & Away

AIR
Airports & Airlines

Taipei is the principal gateway to the island of Taiwan, but there is also an international airport in Kaohsiung.

A number of major airlines do not fly to Taiwan. This is not because they don't want to, but because the government of mainland China has threatened them with retaliation (loss of landing rights in China) if they provide services to Taiwan. The policy of the Chinese government is that it alone has the right to negotiate aircraft landing rights for all of China, including Taiwan. To get around this, some airlines have simply created new subsidiaries solely to serve the Taiwan market: for example, Japan Airlines created Japan Asia Airways. Many airlines have bowed to China's wishes, though a few –

Warning

The information in this chapter is particularly vulnerable to change: prices for international travel are volatile, routes are introduced and cancelled, schedules change, special deals come and go, and rules and visa requirements are amended. Taiwan's continued economic growth has also been accompanied by steadily advancing inflation. Please recognise that the prices quoted in this book are subject to sudden change. Airlines and governments seem to take a perverse pleasure in making price structures and regulations as complicated as possible. You should check directly with the airline or a travel agent to make sure you understand how a fare (and any ticket you may buy) works. In addition, the travel industry is highly competitive and there are many lurks and perks.

The upshot of this is that you should get opinions, quotes and advice from as many airlines and travel agents as possible before you part with your hard-earned cash. The details given in this chapter should be regarded as pointers only and are not intended to be a substitute for your own careful, up-to-date research. ■

backed by their governments – have refused to yield.

Taiwan is also forced to play the game. Taiwan's flag carrier, China Airlines, created a privatised subsidiary called Mandarin Airlines just for flying to those countries which had agreed to China's demands. China Airlines was also pressured into removing the ROC flag from their aircraft and replacing it with a plum flower. Taiwan's other major international carrier is the privately owned EVA Airways, which has a reputation for sumptuous service.

For checked luggage, most airlines allow a maximum weight of 20kg – any more than that and you could be hit with an overweight charge of 1% of the 1st class fare for each additional kilogram. On flights between Taiwan and North America, many airlines allow 30kg for luggage (check your ticket).

Carry-on baggage is theoretically limited to 5kg, though it is rarely weighed. However, most airlines do enforce a size restriction with a maximum of 56 x 36 x 23cm.

Buying Tickets

With the exception of the major holiday periods (especially Chinese New Year), there is no shortage of air services to Taiwan. However, apart from those from Hong Kong and Macau, there are still no direct flights between Taiwan and mainland China.

The price of the air ticket alone can gouge a great slice out of anyone's budget, but you can reduce the cost by searching for discounted fares. Discounting is a widespread practice and the only people likely to be paying full fare are travellers flying in 1st or business class.

There are plenty of discount tickets which are valid for 12 months and allow multiple stopovers with changeable dates. These tickets allow maximum flexibility. All sorts of special packages are available that allow a prolonged stopover in Taipei en route to somewhere else, often at no additional cost or perhaps for only an extra US$50. Return tickets are usually significantly cheaper than two one-way fares.

When looking for bargain air fares, you should go to a travel agent rather than directly to the airline, which can only sell fares at the full list price. But watch out – many discount tickets have restrictions (the journey must be completed in 60 days, no flights during holidays, and so on). It's important to ask the agent what restrictions, if any, apply to your ticket.

The danger with discount ticket agents is that some of them are unsound. Sometimes these travel agents fold up and disappear after you've handed over the money and before you've got the tickets. When purchasing a ticket from a small-time operator, it's wise to take a few precautions. Talk to other recent travellers – they may be able to recommend a reliable travel agent and stop you from making some of the same old mistakes.

You're safer if you pay with a credit card: if they don't accept credit cards, that's a danger sign, though it's not absolute proof of dishonesty. Agents who only accept cash should hand over the tickets straight away; they should not tell you to 'come back tomorrow'. After you've made a booking or picked up the tickets, call the airline and confirm that the booking was made. All this might sound like excessive paranoia, and perhaps it is, but remember that it's your money on the line.

You may decide to pay more than the rock-bottom fare by opting for the safety of a better known travel agent. Firms such as STA Travel, which have offices worldwide, Council Travel in the USA or Travel CUTS in Canada are not going to disappear overnight and they offer competitive prices to most destinations.

If you purchase a ticket and later want to make changes to your route or get a refund, you need to see the original travel agent. Airlines only issue refunds to the purchaser of a ticket, and if you bought your ticket from a travel agent, then that agent is the purchaser, not you. Many travellers do in fact change their route halfway through their trip,

so think carefully about buying a ticket which is not easily refundable.

APEX The Advance Purchase Excursion (APEX) fares are relatively cheap, but you are locked into a fairly rigid schedule. Such tickets must be purchased at least three weeks ahead of departure, do not permit stopovers and may have minimum and maximum periods of stay as well as fixed departure and return dates. Unless you are definite about your return date, it's best to purchase APEX tickets on a one-way basis only. There are stiff cancellation fees if you try to get a refund on an APEX ticket.

Group Tickets The so-called 'group tickets' are well worth considering. You usually do not need to travel with a group. However, once the departure date is booked it may be impossible to change: you can only depart when the 'group' departs, even if you never meet or see another group member.

The good news is that the return date can usually be left open, but there may be other restrictions: you might have to complete the trip in 60 days, or perhaps can only fly off season or during weekdays. As always, it's important to ask the travel agent what conditions and restrictions apply to any tickets you intend to buy.

Open Jaw Tickets These are a variation on the return ticket theme. For example, this ticket might allow you to fly from your home country to Taipei and fly back again from Kaohsiung. This saves you the time and expense of backtracking to Taipei to catch your return flight.

Round-the-World Tickets Buying Round-the-World (RTW) tickets is considered to be trendy – having one will gain you instant prestige. These tickets are usually offered by an airline or combination of airlines and allow you to take your time (from 90 days up to a year) moving from point to point in the same direction, for the price of one ticket. Sometimes this works out to be cheaper than a return ticket or buying all of your tickets separately as you go along, but it eliminates the possibility of doing part of the trip overland, unless you organise this when booking the ticket.

Added drawbacks are that you must book the first sector in advance and cancellation penalties then apply. As well, since you are usually booking the dates of your individual flights as you go and are already committed to certain carriers, you can get caught out by the lack of flight availability and may have to spend more or less time in a place than you originally intended.

The actual cost depends on the route you take and the number of stopovers you have.

A typical budget ticket with five stops currently costs about US$1310, while seven stops pushes it up to US$1850.

Circle Pacific Tickets Circle Pacific tickets use a combination of airlines to circle the Pacific, combining Australia, New Zealand, North America and Asia. As with RTW tickets there are advance purchase restrictions and limits to how many stopovers you can make. These fares are likely to be around 15% cheaper than RTW tickets.

Student, Teacher & Youth Fares Some of the airlines offer student discounts on their

Air Travel Glossary

Baggage Allowance This will be written on your ticket and usually includes up to two pieces of luggage with a combined weight of up to 20kg to go in the hold, plus one item of hand luggage.

Bucket Shops These are unbonded travel agencies specialising in discounted airline tickets.

Bumped Just because you have a confirmed seat doesn't mean you're going to get on the plane (see Overbooking).

Cancellation Penalties If you have to cancel or change an Apex or other discounted ticket, there are often heavy penalties involved; insurance can sometimes be taken out against these penalties. Some airlines impose penalties on regular tickets as well, particularly against 'no-show' passengers.

Check In Airlines ask you to check in a certain time ahead of the flight departure (usually one to two hours on international flights). If you fail to check in on time and the flight is overbooked, the airline can cancel your booking and give your seat to somebody else.

Confirmation Having a ticket written out with the flight and date you want doesn't mean you have a seat until the agent has checked with the airline that your status is 'OK' or confirmed. Meanwhile, you could just be 'on request'.

Discounted Tickets There are two types of discounted fares – officially discounted (such as promotional fares) and unofficially discounted. The lowest prices often impose drawbacks like flying with unpopular airlines, inconvenient schedules or unpleasant routes and connections. Discounted tickets only exist where there is fierce competition.

Economy Class Tickets Economy class tickets are usually not the cheapest option, though they do give you maximum flexibility and are valid for 12 months. If you don't use them, most are fully refundable, as are unused sectors of a multiple ticket.

Full Fares Airlines traditionally offer 1st class (coded F), business class (coded J) and economy class (coded Y) tickets. These days there are so many promotional and discounted fares available that few passengers pay the full economy fare.

Independent Inclusive Tour Excursion An Independent Inclusive Tour Excursion (ITX) is often available on tickets to popular holiday destinations. Officially it's a package deal combined with hotel accommodation, but many agents will sell you one of these for the flight only and give you phoney hotel vouchers in the unlikely event that you're challenged at the airport.

Lost Tickets If you lose your airline ticket the airline will usually treat it like a travellers cheque and, after inquiries, issue you with another one. Legally, however, an airline is entitled to treat it like cash and if you lose it then it's gone forever. Take good care of your tickets.

No-Shows No-shows are passengers who fail to show up for their flight. Full-fare passengers who fail tickets (up to 25%) to holders of student cards, youth cards and teacher cards. In addition to the card, some airlines may even ask for a letter from your school. These discounts are generally only available on ordinary economy class fares. You wouldn't get one, for instance, on an APEX or a RTW ticket since these are already discounted.

Airlines usually carry babies up to two years of age at 10% of the relevant adult fare, as long as they don't occupy a seat; a few may carry them free of charge. For children between the ages of two and 12 the fare on international flights is usually 50% of the full fare or 67% of a discounted fare, which includes a baggage allowance. These days most air fares are likely to be discounted.

Frequent Flyer Most airlines offer frequent flyer deals that can earn you a free air ticket or other goodies. To qualify, you have to accumulate sufficient mileage with the same airline.

First, you must apply to the airline for a frequent flyer account number (some airlines will issue these on the spot or by telephone if you call their head office). Every time you buy an air ticket and/or check in for your flight, you must inform the clerk of your

to turn up are sometimes entitled to travel on a later flight. The rest are penalised (see Cancellation Penalties).

On Request This is an unconfirmed booking for a flight.

Overbooking Airlines hate to fly empty seats and since every flight has some passengers who fail to show up, airlines often book more passengers than they have seats. Usually excess passengers make up for the no-shows, but occasionally somebody gets bumped. Guess who it is most likely to be? The passengers who check in late.

Point-to-Point Tickets These are discount tickets that can be bought on some routes in return for passengers waiving their rights to a stopover.

Promotional Fares These are officially discounted fares like Apex fares, available from travel agents or direct from the airline.

Reconfirmation At least 72 hours prior to departure time of an onward or return flight, you must contact the airline and 'reconfirm' that you intend to be on the flight. If you don't do this the airline can delete your name from the passenger list and you could lose your seat.

Restrictions Discounted tickets often have various restrictions on them – Apex is the most usual one. Others are restrictions on the minimum and maximum period you must be away, such as a minimum of 14 days or a maximum of one year.

Stand-By This is a discounted ticket where you only fly if there is a seat free at the last moment. Stand-by fares are usually only available on domestic routes.

Tickets Out An entry requirement for many countries is that you have a ticket out of the country. If you're unsure of your next move, the easiest solution is to buy the cheapest onward ticket to a neighbouring country or a ticket from a reliable airline which can later be refunded if you do not use it.

Transferred Tickets Airline tickets cannot be transferred from one person to another. Travellers sometimes try to sell the return half of their ticket, but officials can ask you to prove that you are the person named on the ticket. This is unlikely to happen on domestic flights, but on an international flight tickets may be compared with passports.

Travel Agencies Travel agencies vary widely and you should choose one that suits your needs. Some simply handle tours, while full-service agencies handle everything from tours and tickets to car rental and hotel bookings. If all you want is a ticket at the lowest possible price, then go to an agency specialising in discounted tickets.

Travel Periods Some officially discounted fares, Apex fares in particular, vary with the time of year. There is often a low (off-peak) season and a high (peak) season. Sometimes there's an intermediate or shoulder season as well. Usually the fare depends on your outward flight – if you depart in the high season and return in the low season, you pay the high-season fare. ■

frequent flyer account number, or else you won't be credited for it.

Save your tickets and boarding passes, as it's not uncommon for the airlines to fail to give you the proper credit. You should receive a regular statement by post informing you of the mileage you've accumulated. Once you've accumulated sufficient mileage to qualify for freebies, you should receive vouchers by mail. Many airlines have 'blackout periods', or times when you cannot fly for free (Christmas and Chinese New Year are good examples). The worst thing about frequent flyer programs is that they tend to lock you into one airline, and that airline may not always have the cheapest fares or most convenient flight schedules.

Courier Flights Courier flights are a great bargain if you're lucky enough to find one. The way it works is that an air freight company takes over your entire checked baggage allowance. You are permitted to bring along a carry-on bag, but that's all. In return, you get a steeply discounted ticket.

There are other restrictions: courier tickets are sold for a fixed date and schedule changes can be difficult or impossible to make. If you buy a return trip ticket, your schedule will be even more rigid. You need to clarify beforehand just what restrictions apply to your ticket, and don't expect a refund once you've paid for it.

Booking a courier ticket takes some effort. They are limited in availability, and arrangements have to be made a month or more in advance. You won't find courier flights on all routes either. Major routes like London-Taipei or New York-Taipei offer the best possibilities.

Courier flights are occasionally advertised in the newspapers, or you can contact air freight companies listed in the phone book. You may even have to go to the air freight company to get an answer since they aren't always keen to give information over the phone. Another possibility (at least for US residents) is to join the International Association of Air Travel Couriers (IAATC). The

membership fee of US$45 gets members a bimonthly update of air courier offerings, access to a fax-on-demand service with daily updates of last minute specials and the bimonthly newsletter, *The Shoestring Traveler*. For more information contact: IAATC (☎ (407) 582 8320), 8 South J St, PO Box 1349, Lake Worth, FL 33460, USA. However, you should be aware that joining this organisation does not guarantee you a place on a courier flight; it only guarantees you a newsletter.

Buying Tickets Online The Internet boom has created a market for air tickets which can be purchased online. However, buying tickets online can be a mixed blessing. You can spend an awful amount of time tracking down the ticket you want, only to find you could have got something cheaper by visiting your nearest travel agent.

Nevertheless, 30 minutes of Web surfing can help you find out approximately what to expect in the way of budget fares and schedules. If nothing else, it's good research for when you're ready to start negotiating with your favourite travel agency. Furthermore, it's a good way to find the addresses and telephone numbers of local discount travel agencies. If you're looking to purchase tickets on the Net, a couple of good sites are Travelocity (www.travelocity.com) and Preview Travel (www.previewtravel.com).

The airlines also have their own Web sites. This is no place to look for discounts, but airline Web sites can be interesting nonetheless for flight information. A few to try include British Airways (www.british-airways. com), Canadian Airlines (www. cdnair.ca), China Airlines (www.china-airlines.com), EVA Airways (www.evaair. com.tw), Air France (www.airfrance.fr), United Airlines (www.ual.com), Mandarin Airlines (www.mandarin-airlines.com), Air New Zealand (www.airnz. com) and Singapore Airlines (www.new-asia-singapore. com).

For other useful travel Web sites, see the listings under individual countries in this chapter.

Back-to-Front Tickets These should be avoided. Back-to-front tickets are best explained by example. If you are living as an expat in Taipei (where tickets are somewhat expensive) and you want to fly to the UK for a holiday (where tickets are cheaper), you can (theoretically) book and pay for a ticket, by cheque or credit card, through an agent in the UK. You can then ask the agent or a friend to mail the ticket to you in Taiwan.

The problem is that the airlines have computers and will know that the ticket was issued in London rather than Taipei and will refuse to honour it. Consumer groups have filed lawsuits over this practice with mixed results, but in most countries the law protects the airlines, not consumers. In short, the ticket is only valid starting from the country where it was issued. The only exception is if you pay the full Taiwanese fare, thus foregoing any possible discounts that UK travel agents can offer.

Be careful that you don't fall foul of these back-to-front rules when purchasing tickets by post or through the Internet.

Second-Hand Tickets You'll occasionally see advertisements on various youth hostel bulletin boards and sometimes even in newspapers for 'second-hand tickets'. That is, somebody purchased a return ticket, or one with multiple stopoffs, and now wants to sell the unused portion of the ticket.

The prices offered often look very attractive indeed. Unfortunately, these tickets are worthless, especially for international flights. The name written on the ticket must match the name on the passport of the person checking in. Some people reason that the seller of the ticket can check you in with their passport, and then give you the boarding pass – wrong again (at least in Taiwan)! The Taiwanese immigration will ask to see your boarding pass, and if it doesn't match the name in your passport then you won't be able to board the flight. This may not be a problem when departing from countries with less diligent immigration authorities, but it's still a risk.

What happens if you purchase a ticket and then change your name? It can indeed happen. Some people change their name when they get married (or divorced), while others change their name simply because they feel like it. If the name on the ticket doesn't match the name in your passport, you could have problems. A few people have had their honeymoon plans dashed this way. To avoid trouble, be sure you at least have documentary proof (your old passport, marriage certificate etc) to prove that the old you and the new you are the same person.

Travellers with Special Needs

Most international airlines can accommodate special situations – travellers with disabilities, people with young children, children travelling alone and special dietary preferences (vegetarian, kosher etc) – but you must let them know in advance so that they can make the relevant arrangements.

The reputable international airlines will usually provide nappies (diapers), tissues, talcum powder and all the other paraphernalia needed to keep babies clean, dry and half-happy. 'Skycots' are also provided, if requested in advance, and can hold a child weighing up to 10kg.

Guide dogs for the blind will often have to travel in a specially pressurised baggage compartment with other animals, away from their owner; smaller guide dogs may be admitted to the cabin. All guide dogs will be subject to the same quarantine laws (six months in isolation etc) as any other animal when entering or returning to countries currently free of rabies such as Taiwan and Australia.

Deaf travellers can ask for airport and in-flight announcements to be written down for them.

Australia

The high season for most flights from Australia to Asia is from 22 November to 31 January; if you fly out during this period expect to pay more for your ticket.

Generally speaking, buying a return ticket works out cheaper than paying for separate one-way tickets for each stage of your journey, although return tickets become more expensive as their validity lengthens. Most return tickets to Asia have a 28 day, 90 day or 12 month validity.

Quite a few travel offices specialise in discount air tickets. Some travel agents, smaller ones particularly, advertise cheap air fares in the travel sections of weekend newspapers, such as the *Age* and the *Sydney Morning Herald*.

Two well-known discount agents are STA Travel and the Flight Centre. STA Travel (www.sta-travel-group.com) has offices in all major cities and on many university campuses, but you don't have to be a student to use its services. The Flight Centre (www.-flightcentre.com.au) have dozens of offices throughout Australia and New Zealand and they have recently opened up a new chain of agencies, Student Flights, catering specifically for backpackers and students. Both STA Travel and the Flight Centre regularly publish brochures with their latest deals.

Philippine Airlines offers one-way/return air fares between Australia and Taipei for US$444/660 (with a transit stop in Manila). Cathay Pacific flies a similar route (via Hong Kong) for US$655/912.

New Zealand

The Flight Centre (☎ (09) 309-6171) has a large central office at 3A National Bank Tower, 205-225 Queen St, Auckland.

At the time of writing, low-season (same as Australia) one-way/return fares to Taipei were US$652/888.

The UK

Discount air ticket agents are affectionately known as 'bucket shops' in the UK. Despite the somewhat sleazy name, there is nothing under-the-counter about this business. It's a good idea to look in the Sunday papers and *Exchange & Mart* for cheap flights ads. There are also a number of magazines in the UK which have good information about flights and agents. These include: *Trailfinder*, free from the Trailfinders Travel Centre in Earl's Court; and *Time Out*, a London weekly entertainment guide widely

available in the UK. The best deals are available in London.

When purchasing a ticket from a bucket shop that looks a little unsound, make sure they are bonded and belong to the Association of British Travel Agents (ABTA) and have an Air Travel Organiser's Licence (ATOL).

Some recommended London bucket shops to try include: Trailfinders Travel Centre (☎ (0171) 938-3366), Council Travel (☎ (0171) 437-7767), Platinum Travel (☎ (0171) 937-5122) and STA Travel (☎ (0171) 938-4711). Campus Travel (☎ (0171) 730-7285; www.campustravel. co.uk) has 44 UK offices, 150 worldwide. Flight Bookers (☎ (0171) 757-2444; www. flightbookers.co.uk) is another biggie.

Internet Travel Services (www.its.net/ ta/home.htm) have a very good Web site with many travel agencies listed. The list includes courier companies in the UK.

At the time of writing, KLM-Royal Dutch Airlines had the best rates on London-Taipei flights (one-way/return for US$635/ 1100). Other discount tickets are available on flights offered by Philippine Airlines, Swissair and British Airways. Also check out Taiwan's EVA Airways.

Continental Europe

Fares similar to those from London are available from other western European cities. Amsterdam is a particularly good departure point as there are direct flights to Taipei with KLM and China Airlines.

The Netherlands, Belgium and Switzerland are good places for buying discount air fares. In Antwerp, WATS has been recommended. In Zürich, you can try SSR (☎ (01) 297-1111) or Sindbad (☎ (01) 734-0000). In the Netherlands, NBBS (☎ (20) 638 17 26) is a reputable agency.

In France, OTU is a student organisation with 42 offices around the country. You can contact their Paris office (☎ 01 43 36 80 47). Another recommended agent in Paris is Council Travel (☎ 01 42 66 20 87).

In Germany, there's STA Travel in Berlin (☎ (030) 3 11 09 50) at Goethestr. 73 with another in Frankfurt (☎ (069) 43 01 91) at Berger Str. 118.

In Sweden, STA Travel (☎ (018) 14 54 04) is at Bangardsgatan 13, 75320 Uppsala.

The USA

There are some very good open tickets which remain valid for six months or one year (opt for the latter unless you're sure of your length of stay) but don't lock you into any fixed dates beyond your initial departure. For example, there are cheap tickets between the US west coast and Hong Kong, allowing stopovers in Japan, Korea or Taiwan, with departure dates that can usually be changed for no extra cost, and giving you one year to complete the journey.

However, be careful during the high season (summer and Chinese New Year) because seats will be hard to come by unless they are reserved months in advance.

The *New York Times*, the *LA Times*, the *Chicago Tribune* and the *San Francisco Examiner* all produce weekly travel sections in which you'll find any number of travel agents' ads. The magazine *Travel Unlimited* (PO Box 1058, Allston, MA 02134) publishes details of the cheapest air fares and courier possibilities for destinations all over the world from the USA.

Discounters in the USA are known as 'consolidators' (though you won't see a sign on the door saying 'Consolidator').

It's not advisable to send money (even cheques) through the post unless the agent is very well established. Some travellers have reported being ripped off by fly-by-night mail order ticket agents.

Council Travel (☎ (800) 226-8624; www. ciee.org) is America's largest student travel organisation, but you don't have to be a student to use them. Council Travel have an extensive network in all major US cities – look in the phone book or check out their Web site.

One cheap and reliable travel agent on the US west coast is Overseas Tours (☎ (415) 692-4892; www.overseastours.com) which is based in Millbrae, California. Another good and recommended agency is Gateway

Travel (☎ (214) 960-2000; (800) 441-1183), which is based in Dallas, Texas, but has branches in many major US cities.

At the time of writing, travel agents quoted one-way/return fares from the US west coast to Taipei as US$612/1050 on Philippine Airlines and US$663/1124 on Malaysian Airlines. Most other airlines were asking nearly 30 to 50% more. From New York to Taipei, the lowest quoted fare was US$990/1600. Be aware that these budget fares are for flights with some stopovers – eg Philippine Airlines (who only fly from the west coast) stop in Manila, and sometimes Honolulu, which can add anywhere between three and 10 hours to the total flight time. All fares are likely to rise during summer and Chinese New Year.

Canada

As in the USA, Canadian discount air ticket sellers are known as 'consolidators'. Air fares from Canada tend to be at least 10% higher than those from the USA.

The Toronto *Globe & Mail* and the *Vancouver Sun* carry travel agents' ads. Travel CUTS are Canada's national student travel agency and they have offices in all major cities. You don't have to be a student to use their services. You can find them in the phone directory, call their Toronto office (☎ (416) 977-5228) or visit their Web site (www. travelcuts.com).

Other agencies that have received good reviews are Avia (☎ (514) 284-5040) in Montreal and Mar Tours (☎ (416) 536-5458) in Toronto.

At the time of writing one-way/return Vancouver-Taipei discount tickets were available for US$658/1145. From Toronto, the lowest quoted rates were US$826/1312.

Asia

Hong Kong The Hong Kong-Taipei and Hong Kong-Kaohsiung routes are two of the busiest (and most lucrative) in Asia, with over a dozen flights daily. However, the two routes are dominated by a duopoly of China Airlines and Cathay Pacific. Both airlines charge the same rates, which are typically around US$232/344 for one-way/return tickets.

Some other airlines (eg Japan Asia, British Airways, Singapore Airlines etc) offer slightly cheaper rates, but these flights only operate a few times a week and become heavily booked.

Some agents worth trying for discount tickets include: Traveller Services (☎ 2375-2222), room 1012, Silvercord Tower 1, 30 Canton Rd, Tsimshatsui; and Shoestring Travel (☎ 2723-2306; fax 2721-2085) flat A, 4th floor, Alpha House, 27-33 Nathan Rd, Tsimshatsui.

Indonesia Bali is a popular tourist destination for the Taiwanese, so flights there are frequent. However, flights from Jakarta are even cheaper. One-way/return fares from Denpasar (Bali) start at US$691/1069. Starting from Jakarta, fares are US$551/969.

In Jakarta, Jalan Jaksa is the area to look for travel agencies specialising in discount tickets.

Japan Numerous airlines offer direct flights between Taipei and Tokyo, Osaka and Naha (Okinawa). In Tokyo, try Council Travel (☎ (03) 3581-5517) or STA Travel (☎ (03) 5391-2889). The one way/return fare from Tokyo to Taipei was quoted as US$505/906. There is also an STA branch in Osaka (☎ (06) 262-7066).

Macau You can fly from Macau to either Taipei or Kaohsiung on EVA Air, TransAsia or Air Macau. Fares are almost exactly the same as for Hong Kong. If you purchase your ticket in Taiwan, the airlines sometimes throw in a free ferry ticket to Hong Kong.

A couple of places in Macau doing discount tickets can be found on the ground floor (new wing) of the Lisboa Hotel. These include Amigo Travel (☎ 337333) and Estoril Tours (☎ 710361).

Malaysia Malaysian Airlines offer frequent services on the Kuala Lumpur-Taipei route. At the time of writing one-way/return fares were US$390/600. If flying between Taiwan

and Europe on Malaysian Airlines, you must make a transit stop in Kuala Lumpur and so have the option of arranging a free Malaysian stopover.

One place where it is possible to buy tickets is STA Travel (☎ (03) 248-9800), Lot 506, 5th floor, Plaza Magnum, 128 Jalan Pudu, Kuala Lumpur.

Philippines Philippine Airlines has direct flights connecting Manila with Taipei and Kaohsiung.

The cheapest ticket between Taiwan and the Philippines is between Kaohsiung and the Filipino city of Laoag. This is the sole international route for Uni Air, the mostly domestic Taiwanese airline. If departing from Taiwan, NT$200 will buy you a return ticket and two nights in Uni Air's luxury hotel in Laoag.

Taiwan's Far Eastern Air Transport flies the Kaohsiung-Subic Bay route, which is another good way to enter the Philippines without having to deal with Manila.

All other flights between the Philippines and Taiwan are Manila-Taipei; one-way/ return fares are US$183/334.

Singapore The Taipei-Singapore route is extremely busy. China Airlines and Singapore Airlines have most of the traffic, and at the time of writing quoted one-way/return fares of US$310/620.

A good place to buy cheap air tickets in Singapore is Harharah Travel (☎ 337-2633). Also try STA Travel (☎ 737-7188), 171C Bencoolen St. Other agents advertise in the *Straits Times* classifieds.

South Korea Bad relations between Taiwan and South Korea have had a major impact on the airline business. None of the South Korean airlines are allowed to land in Taipei and the Taiwanese airlines do not fly to Seoul. The result is that the Taipei-Seoul route is currently served by only two airlines: Cathay Pacific and Thai Airways International (THAI). One-way/return rates were quoted on Cathay Pacific as US$148/218, while THAI were charging US$148/236.

Some recommended Seoul discount travel agencies include: Joy Travel Service (☎ 776 9871; fax 756 5342), 10th floor, 24-2 Mukyo-dong, Chung-gu, Seoul (behind City Hall); and Korean International Student Exchange Society (KISES; ☎ 733 9494; room 505) and Top Travel (☎ 739 5231; room 506), both on the 5th floor of the YMCA building on Chongno 2-ga (next to Chonggak subway station). In It'aewon, you can try O&J Travel (☎ 792 2303; fax 796 2403) on the 2nd floor, above the Honey Bee Club.

Thailand Khao San Rd in Bangkok is known as budget travellers' headquarters and the place to look for bargain ticket deals. You could also try STA Travel (☎ (02) 233-2582), Wall St Tower, Room 1406, 33 Surawong Rd, Bangrak, Bangkok. One-way/return fares from Bangkok to Taipei are US$234/246.

Vietnam Vietnam Airlines, Pacific Airlines, EVA Airways and China Airlines offer direct services between Ho Chi Minh City/Hanoi and Taipei/Kaohsiung. Pacific Airlines are the cheapest. Vietnam is generally an expensive country for buying air tickets, so try to get them elsewhere. If you're flying to Vietnam from the USA or Europe, China Airlines offer a particularly good deal which allows you to transit Taipei for free. Budget tickets between Vietnam and Taipei can be as low as US$370 return.

In Saigon, Fiditourist (☎ 835-3018), 195 Pham Ngu Lao St, District 1, is a reasonable place for tickets. Fares between Saigon and Taipei are US$742 return.

SEA

Taiwan does not seem to be included on the international luxury cruise circuit. The only international passenger ferry serving the island connects the ports of Keelung and Kaohsiung to Okinawa in Japan. Taiwan has three other international seaports (Taichung, Hualien and Suao), but you can only arrive or depart from those ports if you're on a cargo ship.

Living with the Dragon

Any nation that thinks it can maintain diplomatic relations with both the Republic of China (Taiwan) and the People's Republic of China (China) is swiftly reminded of reality – China will not tolerate it. Lithuania tried (and failed). China is adamant – Taiwan is a 'renegade province' of China. Only some 20-odd tiny nations are brave enough to maintain diplomatic relations with the ROC, and most of them do it to receive financial aid from Taiwan's government (call it 'dollar diplomacy').

At the insistence of China, Taiwan was expelled from the United Nations on 25 October 1971, suspended from the International Atomic Energy Agency in 1972 and expelled from the International Monetary Fund and World Bank in 1980. So far, China has also frustrated Taiwan's efforts to join the World Trade Organisation (WTO).

Taiwan's athletes are only permitted to participate in Olympic Games under the title 'Chinese Taipei', and when they win a medal, the ROC national anthem cannot be played nor the flag raised. China continues to threaten any nation that grants visas to Taiwanese officials – when President Lee Tenghui visited the USA in 1995, China called it 'an act of war', threatened to nuke Los Angeles, and went as far as firing live missiles to within 25km of Taiwan's coast. China has promised to 'wash the island in blood' if Taiwan ever declares independence.

Dealing with the dragon is Taiwan's number one concern. China's 1997 takeover of Hong Kong sent shivers down the spines of the Taiwanese. The ROC military has built up considerable firepower in the hopes of deterring an invasion, but no one really thinks that Taiwan could win a war with China.

Oddly, while the two sides snarl at each other, money flows liberally across the Taiwan Straits. Indeed, China has surpassed the USA as Taiwan's leading export market. The two-way trade is heavily slanted in Taiwan's favour, and the Taiwanese are believed to be the biggest 'foreign' investors in China. Such trade and investment probably reduces tensions – after all, nobody is keen to blow up their business partner. The Taiwanese have the dragon by the tail, and they continue to hold on for dear life. ∎

Japan

There is a weekly passenger ferry, run by the Arimura Line, that operates between Taiwan and Naha on the Japanese island of Okinawa. From Naha, there are many passenger ferries to Japan's major port cities: Tokyo, Osaka, Fukuoka and Kagoshima.

Economy class on the ferry is cheaper than flying. The ferry runs overnight, departing Okinawa one day and arriving in Taiwan the next. Sometimes it will make brief stops at the islands of Miyako and Ishigaki, but the schedule for this is irregular. If you really want to visit those islands you'll probably have to backtrack from Okinawa. From Taiwan, ferry departures alternate between the ports of Keelung and Kaohsiung, leaving once weekly from each port.

Tickets are available from some travel agents in the port cities that the ferry departs from, but it's usually just as easy to go straight to the ferry company itself. In Japan the Arimura Line has offices in Naha (☎ (098) 864-0087) and Osaka (☎ (06) 531-9269).

In Taiwan you can purchase tickets from the Nanchang Boat Company (☎ (02) 424-8151; *nánchāng chuán wù gōngsī*), Jen-5 Rd, Keelung and the Haitian Boat Company (☎ (07) 330-9811; *hǎitiān chuán wù gōngsī*), 9th floor, room 11, 232 Chengkung 1st Rd, Kaohsiung.

Departures from Keelung are on Tuesday at 10 pm (board boat at 8 pm). Departures from Okinawa to Keelung are on Monday and Friday at 8 pm (board boat at 6 pm). The one-way economy fare is NT$2540.

Departures from Kaohsiung to Okinawa are on Sunday at noon (board the boat at 9 am). Departures from Okinawa to Kaohsiung (via Keelung) are on Friday at 8 pm (board the boat at 6 pm). The one-way economy fare from Kaohsiung to Okinawa is NT$2920.

DEPARTURE TAX

When leaving Taiwan, whether by sea or air, you will be liable for a departure tax of NT$300, which must be paid at the point of departure in local currency.

ORGANISED TOURS

Many western travel agencies are obsessed with tours to mainland China, but those dealing with Taiwan are thin on the ground. In most cases, you'll simply have to book your own air tickets in your home country, and contact a local Taiwanese travel agent to arrange for them to meet you or your group on arrival.

For more information on Taiwanese tour operators see Organised Tours in the Getting Around chapter.

Getting Around

Intercity buses, trains and planes serving the major routes are frequent, fast and reliable. You should have no problem getting to wherever you wish to go except on a Sunday or public holiday, when all means of transport can be very crowded.

Travelling on the local buses and trains, rather than in a private car or taxi, allows plenty of opportunity to meet the locals. Some of them will be happy to practise their English with you, even though you may not be so keen, and you can always use the opportunity to practise your Chinese.

AIR
Due to Taiwan's small size there is little need to fly within the country, unless you are in a big hurry or plan to visit some of the smaller islands around Taiwan (Penghu, Orchid Island etc). However, many people are in a hurry and flying is popular. As a result, the domestic air service is well developed.

Weekends and holidays are busy times – if you haven't made an advance booking then you can try flying stand-by *(hòubǔ)*. This is run on a first come, first served basis, so if you're flying stand-by you should arrive at the airport early. If you already have a reservation, be sure that you check in at least 30 minutes before departure time, otherwise the airline could reallocate your seat to waiting stand-by passengers.

Warning
Passengers travelling on Taiwan's airlines should be aware that they will face possible life sentences in jail if they are caught using mobile phones or other electronic equipment during flights. This tough regulation was introduced by the Taiwan Civil Aeronautics Administration in 1998, in an attempt to prevent fatal accidents caused by electronic equipment interference with aerial communications systems. ■

It is a requirement that you present identification (either a passport or Alien Resident Certificate) when you check in for a domestic flight in Taiwan. This requirement was introduced in May 1998, after a lunatic tried to set fire to himself, and the aircraft he was on, during a domestic flight.

It's significantly cheaper to purchase domestic air tickets from travel agencies rather than directly from the airlines. Travel agents typically give discounts of 30% or more. Be aware that many discounted air tickets are not refundable, though the departure date and time can be changed. Some discount tickets are refundable, though you may be charged a 10% service fee – it's best to check this when you book. Tickets purchased from the airlines at full fare will be fully refundable. Some travel agents will only issue refunds if you have not written your name on the ticket. Most travel agents in Taiwan will leave a blank space where the ticket says 'Name', and you'd be wise not to write anything there until check-in time. A ticket with no name can even be legally resold to another person (the opposite situation from international air tickets).

The standard of service offered by domestic travel agencies varies widely. Some will just want to sell you a blank ticket (no name, no date) and then expect you to call the airline and make the booking yourself – in such cases you *do not* actually have a reserved seat until you've made the phone call and have obtained a computer number from the airline! Other agencies are much better and will do all the work for you.

Most of the airlines will not accept telephone bookings within two hours of a flight departure time. In that case, you'll have to go to the airport and make the booking at the service counter. However, they will accept a blank discounted ticket from a travel agency so you do not necessarily have to purchase a full-fare ticket from the airline.

There are 10 domestic airlines in Taiwan,

including Far Eastern Air Transport who also have one international service to the Philippines. Smoking is not permitted on any domestic flights. No meals are served, but you do get a soft drink and piece of cake.

BUS

On the major routes at least, Taiwan's bus service is frequent, dependable and comfortable. However, just how fast it gets you around depends on the traffic. The North-South Freeway has a posted speed limit of 100km per hour, but at times the traffic slows to only 1km per hour. Avoiding travel during rush hours, weekends and holidays is highly advised. A trip from Taipei to Kaohsiung takes 4½ hours by bus, which is faster than the train, unless there is a big accident on the freeway (a frequent occurrence), in which case it could take six to 10 hours. The buses make a 10 minute stop en route at a freeway rest area, where stale food can be purchased at inflated prices.

In rural areas, the bus service has deteriorated sharply in recent years thanks to Taiwan's 'car revolution'. As more people buy cars, fewer take the bus, forcing the bus companies to reduce their services. Also, when the Taiwanese go on holiday and decide to leave the car at home, they usually go by tour bus rather than using the public buses.

Ironically, in urban areas bus service use is on the increase mainly because the parking problem is now so severe that many people don't dare to bring their car into the city.

On all buses you should save your ticket stub. You must turn it in to the driver or conductor when you get off the bus or you will have to pay the full fare again!

Classes

There are two types of bus companies: public and private. Public buses are run by the Taiwan Bus Company *(tíqì kèyùn)*, and there are two classes: the kuokuang *(guóguāng hào)* and the chunghsing *(zhōngxīng hào)*. The chunghsing is the cheaper of the two. The kuokuang has a toilet on board and is a smoother ride than the chunghsing, but both

cover the route in the same amount of time. Some of the newer chunghsing buses also have toilets on board, but there's no guarantee of this.

The kuokuang and chunghsing are both air-conditioned year-round and, as there is no way to turn the air-con off, are often too cold. Rather than freezing for several hours, some travellers carry tape to stick over the vents – the bus company is not amused.

Private bus companies are numerous but the standard of service varies widely. The largest private bus company is the Tonglien Bus Company. In order to attract customers, some of the private bus companies offer video movies and occasionally other entertainment (even stand-up comedians).

Smoking is not permitted on the government-owned buses, private bus companies usually don't care if you smoke or not – this is particularly true on the video buses. On all long-distance buses, you can eat and drink to your heart's content.

Reservations

For government-owned buses, tickets can be purchased up to four days in advance. On private buses, it depends on the bus company. On normal days, advance-sale tickets should not be necessary, but it's not a bad idea to get a ticket ahead of time if you want to travel during the weekend or on major public holidays.

TRAIN

Train services are frequent and generally good, though not quite up to the standards of Japan and Europe. There are two major lines: the west coast line, which is electrified; and the east coast line, which still uses diesel trains. There are also several spur tracks to places like Alishan and Shuili. The trains are more expensive than the buses.

Food is available on trains in the form of packaged snacks and precooked lunch boxes *(biàndāng)*. The quality of the lunch boxes has gone from bad to ghastly, but it beats starving (marginally). Food bought on the train and in or around the train and bus stations tends to be more expensive than elsewhere, but not too outrageously so. However, there is free hot tea on the train and you can help yourself. If you're going to be spending a long time on a train, it's best to buy something to eat and drink before you board.

Smoking is not permitted on the trains, though you can sometimes get away with it in the space between the cars.

Make sure you save your ticket when you get off the train as you need to turn it in at the gate when you leave the train station. If you lose it, you have to pay a large fine.

Timetables (shí kè biǎo) are available but they are only written in Chinese. Timetables which cover the entire railway system cost NT$25 – there are simpler timetables for NT$15 which just cover the express trains. The timetables can be purchased at the service counter in almost any train station.

There are left luggage rooms in every major train station which charge NT$17 per item per day. An exception is Taipei's main train station which only has lockers; these are gradually being introduced elsewhere.

Classes

Currently, there are four classes of train and it is fair to say that you get what you pay for. In descending order of comfort they are:

ziqiang (zìqi ng hào)
    A very fancy express with air-con; it usually has a dining car.
zuguang (jǔguāng hào)
    Has air-con but is slightly slower than Ziqiang.
fuxing (fùxīng hào)
    Has air-con, but is slower and not as luxurious as Juguang.
putong (pǔtōng chē, píngkuài, duì kuài or diànchē)
    Cheap but slow. Not all Putong trains run the entire length of the line. For example, you'd be hard pressed to find a Putong train in Taipei that is heading all the way south to Kaohsiung. It's more likely that you'd have to purchase a Taipei-Changhua ticket and then a separate Changhua-Kaohsiung ticket. If you're going to travel in Putong class, you'd probably better save it for short runs.
    Most Putong trains do not have air-con, but since the windows can be opened and these trains are very slow, it's better for photographers. Another advantage Putong trains have over the more luxurious trains is that no one likes to catch these trains, so on a Sunday or holiday it's still easy to find a seat when the express trains are packed.

Reservations

On the fast trains (Ziqiang, Juguang and Fuxing) it is often wise to buy your ticket a day or two in advance, especially on weekends and holidays. There is no need to buy advance tickets on the Putong trains as there are no reserved seats. If no seats are available, you are permitted to board any train but will have to stand.

Costs

You can receive a 15% discount on return tickets, but the ticket must be used within 15 days of purchase. If you don't use the return portion of a round-trip ticket, you can refund it (minus the 15% discount you previously received) within 15 days of purchase.

If you are rushing for the train, you can board without a regular ticket if you have bought a platform ticket for NT$4. You must then find the conductor and upgrade your ticket. The same applies if you buy a cheap ticket and then decide to get on a more expensive train. When you find the conductor, you must say 'upgrade ticket' (bǔ piào) and tell them where you wish to get off.

TAXI

The reputation of long-distance taxi drivers is not a good one. The drivers hang around bus and train stations chewing betel nut, gambling and spitting on the footpath while hustling passengers into their cars.

If you speak Chinese, you may enjoy listening to their sales pitch as they solicit customers. They often approach people standing in line at a ticket window and say something like, 'The bus you want is out of order' or 'It has just left' or 'It drove off a cliff' or whatever. Most people ignore them and wait for the bus to arrive, on time, five minutes later.

You are most likely to use long-distance taxis in remote parts of the country where they are the only form of transport, or during holidays when buses become cattle cars. At these peak times, the taxi drivers congregate right next to the bus or train stations and try to solicit business. Meters are not used and you can also expect to pay more at peak times, but it is very likely that you'll be able to share the taxi with other passengers and split the cost. This is a common practice and fully expected by the drivers. You can even tell the driver you'll only take the taxi if he can round up some more passengers.

CAR & MOTORCYCLE

You might ask yourself whether or not you really need a car. For affluent tourists or a group splitting the cost, a car could be useful for getting to some remote areas not easily accessible by public transport. In cities like Taipei or Kaohsiung either renting or buying a car is an insane idea. Traffic barely moves, parking space is more difficult to find than the Holy Grail and the chance of getting a ticket or having an accident is far greater than in rural areas. As for the Taiwanese, the main reason why many buy cars is for face. Foreign residents with fragile egos also drive cars for the same reason. In the cities you can save yourself a mountain of cash and aggravation by taking taxis.

A motorcycle can be useful in Taiwan, but there are a few drawbacks. Chief among these is the possibility of getting killed. Also, motorcycles aren't all that comfortable in Taiwan's frequently rainy weather. On the other hand, finding a place to park a motorcycle is far easier than for a car, and a motorcycle can give you a lot of freedom, particularly in the countryside where public transport is poor or nonexistent.

Touring the island by motorcycle is most enjoyable during the summer season when the warm breeze makes riding pleasant. However, it can be a real drag during a winter thunderstorm in the mountains when the temperature comes close to freezing.

Road Rules

Anarchy! The golden rule observed by all Taiwanese drivers is to pass the car in front of you. There's a pot of gold waiting for the first one across the finish line.

All right, the above may be a slight exaggeration, but not by much. There are other rules besides winning the Grand Prix. The problem is that figuring out just what the police expect of you is no easy task. The police appear to be more interested in filling quotas than solving the traffic problem. Enforcement of the law is sporadic – fines are dished out at random for the most minor infractions, while the most serious traffic violations continue to go unpunished. It's not unusual to see police randomly stopping cars and hitting the drivers with fines for stopping too close to the kerb, while drivers who run right through red lights are ignored. Taipei experimented with giving the police a commission on every ticket written to encourage strict law enforcement – this led to an explosion of random ticket writing with no visible improvement in safety.

The vast majority of traffic tickets that are issued are for turning right on a red light. In most countries of the world (at least those where people drive on the right-hand side of the road), turning right against a traffic light is legal. In Taiwan, it's illegal. The police

Fights

The Taiwanese are among the most hospitable people in the world, especially towards foreigners, but fights resulting in bloodshed can sometimes occur. Most fights between foreigners and the Taiwanese usually have something to do with the traffic. A typical example of what can happen is that a taxi will come within an inch of hitting a foreigner on a motorcycle. The foreigner won't like that and will catch up with the taxi at the next traffic light, where they will dismount and kick the side of the taxi, putting a dent in the door. The taxi driver won't like this, and will get out of the taxi with a tyre lever and will put a dent in the foreigner's head.

In such a case, most Taiwanese people would clearly say that the foreigner was in the wrong. True, the taxi was speeding, ran through a red light and was driving on the wrong side of the road, but that's typical driving procedure in Taiwan. Attempts to enforce the law by foreigners is not appreciated. If you're going to drive in Taiwan, you need to learn that ancient Chinese virtue – tolerance. ■

take particular delight in enforcing this moronic rule since everyone breaks it, thus making their job of filling ticket-writing quotas much easier. Motorcycles are *required* to park on the pedestrian footpaths, which means pedestrians usually have to walk in the motorcycle lane. The police frequently tow away motorcycles even when they're legally parked (chaining your motorcycle to a pole helps prevent this). Cars are often parked in the motorcycle lane, thus blocking it completely.

The most obnoxious policy is the use of hidden cameras to catch traffic violators. The citation will be charged against the owner of the vehicle, no matter who was driving at the time. It takes the slumbering bureaucracy many months to finally send the citation by mail, but if not paid promptly the fine will be automatically tripled! By this time, the driver of the vehicle may have long left Taiwan, leaving the unfortunate owner of the vehicle holding the bag – a big headache for the car rental agencies.

Officially, driving is on the right-hand side of the road, though judging by many drivers this appears to be optional.

Driving at night with no lights is popular because Taiwanese drivers believe (erroneously) that the headlights consume more petrol. Driving on the footpath also seems to be acceptable. Tickets for driving faster than the speed limit are seldom issued, except on the freeways where there are radar traps waiting for unsuspecting motorists.

Taiwan has a seat-belt law, but most people ignore it and enforcement is virtually nonexistent. However, the fines – when enforced – can be stiff. Driving without a seatbelt on ordinary roads can cost you NT$1500. On freeways, the fine can be from NT$3000 to NT$6000. There is also a fine of NT$500 for carrying children under the age of six without fastening them securely in a children's safety seat. Another fine of NT$3000 is enforced for leaving a child under six unattended in a car.

There are over 10 million motorcycles in Taiwan, one for every two people. This rates as the world's highest per capita motorcycle ownership, a fact which is immediately obvious from the moment you step off the airport bus. It's quite possible that Taiwan also boasts the world's highest accident rate. Should you contemplate riding on two wheels, get medical and life insurance and have your will updated.

Safety helmets are required by law, though this rule is only sporadically enforced in major cities (and not at all in rural areas). A helmet with a face shield will not only help keep your head in one piece, but it will also protect your eyes from flying bugs, gravel and rain. Riding with your headlight on is not required by law, but it makes you more visible (unfortunately, everyone will keep reminding you to turn off your lights to 'save petrol'). Since rainy weather is almost guaranteed sooner or later, equip yourself with waterproof clothing and boots. Don't forget your hands either – a pair of waterproof gloves is a necessity in Taiwan's cold, wet conditions.

Rental

If you've got the cash and want to hire a car, you'll find plenty of rental agencies ready, willing and able to put you in the driver's seat. When you rent a car, be sure that it's fully insured against accidents and theft, and that the rental company will cover repairs and towing costs. If you're renting for a long time, discounts should be available. Car rental agencies are listed under the Getting Around sections of the regional chapters.

Rental fees vary wildly depending on what vehicle you rent and for how long. Typical half-day rentals cost from NT$800 to NT$1500. A full day will set you back between NT$1300 and NT$2500. There are discounts for long-term renters: typically 10% for three to seven days; 20% for eight to 20 days; and 30% for anything over three weeks. Some car rental agencies limit you to a 400km mileage per day, charging an extra NT$2 per kilometre in excess of this, but you'll seldom have an opportunity to drive so far on a small island like Taiwan.

The quoted car rental fees will always include third party liability insurance, which is required by law. Normally this covers your liability to others for injuries up to NT$1.2 million. For an extra fee you can buy comprehensive insurance (called CDW in Taiwan). This covers loss due to such things as fire, theft and collision, and currently costs between NT$400 and NT$900 per day depending on the vehicle you rent. In Taiwan, CDW is not very comprehensive – usually NT$10,000 is deductible from all claims, and for theft there may be another 35% deductible.

In large cities like Taipei, motorcycles are difficult to rent. It's much easier to rent them in small cities and rural areas, especially tourist resorts like Orchid Island, Hualien, Kenting, Penghu and Green Island. Rentals in these places cost from about NT$300 to NT$400 per day.

Purchase

Buying a motorcycle and reselling it a few months later is a popular option. The big hurdle is that you need a resident visa in order to legally register the motorcycle in your own name. Because the registered owner is legally liable for traffic violations, you won't find many Taiwanese willing to allow you to register the motorcycle in their name. Since most foreigners don't have legal residence, they avoid the problem by purchasing a 'foreigner's bike' – that is a motorcycle that is registered to a foreigner who left Taiwan long ago. The motorcycle simply gets passed from one foreigner to another, without any change of registration papers. The legalities of this are dubious and it's not recommended, but that's the way things usually go in Taiwan.

The best all-round touring motorcycle you can legally buy in Taiwan is the Sanyang (Honda) or Kwangyang 125cc or 150cc. Four-stroke engines are definitely superior to the two-stroke models (the latter are noisy and polluting). Except for 50cc models, two-stroke motorcycles are no longer produced in Taiwan because they cannot meet pollution limitations. Even the 50cc two-stroke models may eventually be forced off the road.

Motorcycles larger than 150cc would be more comfortable for long distances, but the government does everything to discourage these. Taxes on large engine motorcycles are prohibitive, and there are none manufactured domestically. You'll find it very difficult to even purchase one.

The 125cc four-stroke engines use very little petrol, they are reliable and repairs of any kind are very cheap. Motor scooters are a poor choice for long distances – the small wheels are dangerous on rough roads and your posterior will quickly vibrate into marshmallow.

Motorcycles are not permitted on freeways, no matter how large the engine. You can transport a motorcycle by train – indeed, this is very common. The Taiwanese spend ages wrapping their motorcycles in cardboard and tape before giving it to the railway freight office – which hardly seems worth the effort for the tiny scratch it might get.

Buying a used vehicle from a private individual (as opposed to a car or motorcycle shop) presents some extra bureaucratic hurdles. The biggest is Taiwan's household registration system. Every citizen of the Republic of China (ROC) is issued a household registration certificate *(hùkoǔ)* at the time of birth – the certificate lists their city and county of residence. If they move to another city, they must wait six months before they can transfer the hùkoǔ to the new location, and doing so involves quite a bit of bureaucratic wrangling so most people don't bother. The hùkoǔ is like a stone around the neck. Taiwanese must return to their 'home' (the place where the hùkoǔ was issued) to perform various bureaucratic requirements – to vote, buy a house, register a motor vehicle etc. So if you're in Taipei and you buy a motorcycle from someone whose hùkoǔ was issued in Kaohsiung, either you, the other party or even a third party will have to return to Kaohsiung to process the paperwork. This person will need the original and new owner's identity cards and name chops (seals) to allow them to process the paperwork at the original owner's county of legal residence.

BICYCLE

Rental

Bicycles can be rented in Kenting and a few other beach resorts, but in general the Taiwanese are not big on cycling and rentals are rare.

Purchase

Taiwan is a major producer and exporter of touring and mountain bikes, the well known brands being Giant and KHS. These are generally cheap, though the top quality models carry premium price tags. However, shops usually only stock the smaller frame sizes. If you need a larger frame they may have to order it for you; this should probably only take one or two days.

Taking the bike home with you or to another country is feasible – airlines generally accept bikes as a part of your baggage allowance if it's properly boxed.

Bicycle touring is most sensible on the east coast where the traffic is relatively light. The west coast plains are relatively boring, hot, dusty and have an abundance of traffic – not ideal for cycling. However, if you do want to ride down the west coast, follow Highway 3 – it's mountainous, but scenic and not heavily used by motor vehicles. A few hardy travellers have tackled the mountains on the scenic cross-island highways, which can be very rewarding if you're in good physical condition. Some mountain roads are still gravel, and for those places a mountain bike makes far more sense than a street-style 10 speed bike.

You can transport your bicycle around Taiwan on the trains for about half the price of a passenger ticket. Your bike must ride in the freight carriage, and it will probably not go on the same train that you do. The freight office in the train station can estimate when your bike will arrive, but take the estimate with a grain of salt – it's often several hours later.

As for city riding, you'll have to put up with insane traffic, noise and pollution. Bicycle theft is a problem – keep yours securely chained to a pole or, if possible, park it indoors.

HITCHING

Hitching is never entirely safe in any country in the world, and we don't recommend it. Travellers who decide to hitch should understand that they are taking a small but potentially serious risk. However, many people do choose to hitch, and the advice that follows should help to make their journeys as fast and safe as possible.

It is certainly possible to hitchhike in Taiwan. Indeed, you may have no other choice in remote areas now that the rural bus service has all but collapsed.

In urban areas it's a different story – the bus service is good and hitching is nearly impossible within the complicated grid of city roads. In cities, most people will assume that you want to get to the bus station, and that's where they'll take you – you'll need a good command of Chinese to explain otherwise. Most Taiwanese will be shocked if they learn that you're only hitching to save money – the main reason they would have picked you up in a city is because they assumed you were lost.

Hitching can be problematic even in rural areas. Country people are friendly and will usually pick you up, though on rare occasions you may be asked to pay for your ride. Communicating can be a problem since English-speakers are a small minority, in which case you can pass the time giving English lessons. If you can't speak Chinese, you and the driver will probably spend the whole journey grinning at each other.

Attacks on hitchhikers are almost unheard of, though this is probably because the Taiwanese never hitchhike. As elsewhere in the world, single women are more vulnerable and may prefer to travel with a companion rather than hitching solo.

The biggest danger to hitchhikers is getting picked up by drunks. It's happened to me a few times, and the last time was pretty exhilarating. A motorcyclist pulled over. The driver was friendly enough – he even pulled a bottle of Kaoliang out of his coat pocket and offered it to me. The problem was that he kept zigzagging all over the twisting, precipitous mountain road we were travelling on. Worse still, he was speeding, turning his head to talk to me, driving with one hand and holding the bottle of Kaoliang with the other. The brakes weren't working very well and music blasted us from a stereo he had built into his motorcycle. After five minutes of this, I was suffering from a severe case of sensory overload and finally had to get off.

BOAT

There are several ferry trips which can be made to the islands around Taiwan, and they are covered in the regional chapters of this book. Some destinations that can be reached by boat include the Penghu Islands, Liuchiu Island, Orchid Island and Green Island.

LOCAL TRANSPORT

Bus

The city bus service is generally excellent in Taipei, workable in Taichung, almost workable in Kaohsiung and pathetic in Tainan. Elsewhere, it's pretty decrepit if it exists at all. Fares are typically from NT$10 to NT$15. See the Getting Around sections of the individual cities for further information.

Bus drivers (and taxi drivers) in Taiwan are known for their fiery temperament. Perhaps it has something to do with the frustration of driving – insanity tends to be contagious. Regardless of the reason, it seldom pays to get into an argument with drivers over their rudeness and mad driving tactics. Stories of drivers arguing with passengers (and finally assaulting them) are not uncommon – if your driver starts waving a tyre iron in your face, it's best to terminate the conversation quickly and head for the door.

Taxi

You won't have to look for a taxi in most large cities, they will be looking for you. Just stand on a street corner, raise your hand to scratch your nose, and three or four of them will stop. However, this does not apply during rush hour and heavy rainstorms when competition for taxis is keen.

The taxi service is generally good, but there are two negative points that you must deal with; the drivers seldom speak a word of English, and many of them wish to demonstrate their Formula One racing skills. The first difficulty can be overcome easily enough if you speak Chinese, have a Taiwanese person with you or have your destination written down in Chinese characters. Be sure to also have the name and address of your hotel written in Chinese for the return trip.

The second problem is a little more difficult to solve, but you can try several tactics. The first is to look for an old driver, as they are usually wiser (how else did they survive so long?) than a young driver. Also look for simpler taxis rather than those with racing stripes, air scoops and Christmas lights. Finally, you can tell the driver to slow down by saying *kāi màn yìdiǎn, hǎo bù hǎo*. If that doesn't work, you can always ask to get out by saying *xià chē*.

The taxis in Taipei, Taichung, Tainan and Kaohsiung are required to have meters. In the big cities the metered fare is set by the government and there is no bargaining; just make sure that the meter is used. However, with country taxis you should agree on the fare before you get in. The typical price is around NT$150 for any place within the town or city, and the drivers usually won't bargain. When going out into the countryside the rates might not be as straightforward, so the golden rule is to never get into an unmetered taxi until you've settled on the price. In general, country taxis cost more than urban taxis because the drivers can seldom get a return fare.

Meters charge for both time and distance. In Taichung, Tainan and Kaohsiung, it's NT$60 at flag fall, which covers the first 1.5km. Each additional 300m then costs NT$5. If the taxi gets stuck in traffic, there is an additional NT$5 waiting charge clocked up every three minutes.

In Taipei, things are a little different. To begin with, the rates are slightly higher – flag fall is NT$50 which includes the first 1.65km, then it's NT$5 for each additional 350m. A 20% surcharge is added to the metered fare between 11 pm and 6 am.

Finally, there is a mandatory 'tip' of NT$15 to be paid over and above the metered amount.

Taxis waiting at train stations and airports have a right to add NT$50 to the metered fare. This is supposed to compensate them for having to line up and wait for a long time for a fare (though sometimes this takes less than 10 seconds). In addition, some drivers will insist on a minimum charge of NT$250 or more. This doesn't mean they will add NT$250 to the metered fare, but they do want you to spend at least that much. If you're only making a short trip, you'll come out the loser. The best advice is to walk a block or two from the station or airport and hail a passing cab.

Except for Taipei's mandatory NT$15, tipping is not necessary and never expected. Most taxi drivers do quite well for themselves.

Never ask taxi drivers for directions, and take anything that they tell you with a heap of salt. They'll often tell you that the place you want to go to is 'too far' and that you must take a taxi, whereas in reality it's just one block away.

The Ministry of Communications has complaint hot lines for taxis in Taipei (☎ (02) 2729-1181, 2767-8217, 2394-9007, 2683-7869) and Kaohsiung (☎ (07) 761-4621, 363-1040, 771-5349). Be sure you correctly write down the taxi's number displayed on the rear window or licence plate before making a complaint. Drivers can be fined for rude service or cheating on fares. If you're in a city with no complaint hot line, you can contact the Foreign Affairs Police. They are generally sensitive about complaints by foreigners and will try to assist you. However, make sure you really have cause to complain – some cases of 'rudeness' and 'cheating' are due to bad communication.

ORGANISED TOURS

Most Taiwanese tourists prefer organised tours to individual travel. The tour guide wears a smart uniform, carries a brightly coloured flag and speaks through a megaphone. Those who take the tours get to wear bright yellow caps with visors and sing songs together. It's customary to dress formally (black suits and ties for the men) – you'd think the participants were attending a funeral rather than going on holiday. The tours are usually spending sprees with frequent 'rest stops' at shopping plazas. Many people claim that the tour companies get a commission from the vendors for bringing in customers – it certainly looks suspicious when more time is spent in souvenir shops than at sightseeing spots. A huge lunch at a fancy restaurant is a major feature of Taiwanese tours and is always included in the tour price. The actual sightseeing part of the tour tends to be rushed – most of the time is spent shopping, eating and posing for group photos.

It's only fair to add that a few tour operators are used to dealing with groups of westerners and have customised their itineraries to suit western tastes. The description above applies mainly to tour packages geared towards local, overseas Chinese and Japanese tourists.

Packaged tours take the work out of travelling (some say it takes the travel out of travelling). You won't get to experience the country in depth when you safari by tour coach, but at least you won't be lonely. You'll also spend a significant chunk of money. If packaged tours interest you, these can easily be booked in Taipei and a few other cities. Some reputable tour agencies include:

Edison Travel Service
(☎ (02) 2563-5313; fax 2563-4803) 4th floor, 190 Sungchiang Rd, Taipei
Everbest
(☎ (02) 2523-7740; 2562-9985) 5th floor, 20 Nanking E Rd, Section 2, Taipei
Golden Foundation Tours Corporation
(☎ (02) 2773-3266; fax 2773-4994; email gftours@tptsl.seed.net.tw) 8th floor, 134 Chunghsiao E Rd, Section 4, Taipei
Gray Line
(☎ (02) 2541-6466; fax 2522-1960) China Express Transportation, 4th floor, 46 Chungshan N Rd, Section 2
Huei-Fong Travel Service
(☎ (02) 2551-5805; fax 2561-1434) 8th floor, 36 Nanking E Rd, Section 2, Taipei
Southeast Travel Service
(☎ (02) 2571-3001; fax 2564-2256; email segi@ms6.hinet.net) 60 Chungshan N Rd, Section 2, Taipei

Tours Available from Taipei		
Tour	*Duration*	*Price*
Taipei and National Palace Museum	half-day	NT$600
Taipei Culture Tour	half-day	NT$850
Taipei Night Tour	half-day	NT$1000
Tamsui Tour	half-day	NT$850
Wulai	half-day	NT$850
Northern Coast	half-day	NT$750
Window on China, Tzuhu and Shihmen Reservoir	one day	NT$2250
Taroko Gorge	one day	NT$3750
Sun Moon Lake and Formosan Aboriginal Culture Village	overnight	NT$4800
Sun Moon Lake, Formosan Aboriginal Culture Village, Kaohsiung and Kenting	three days and two nights	NT$8000
Sun Moon Lake, Formosan Aboriginal Culture Village, Taroko Gorge and Hualien	three days and two nights	NT$8000
Round-the-Island	four to eight days	from NT$11,000

Youth group tours can be arranged for rates as low as US$1000 per day, including accommodation, food and transport around Taiwan. Accommodation is in group-style dormitories, with four to 10 people per room. These tours are mainly aimed at overseas Chinese students and these groups tend to be large – *very* large.

An overseas Chinese student who was on one of these tours told me the tour was nicknamed 'The Love Boat' (apparently teenage romance is a big attraction). If you are active with a youth group that might be interested, contact China Youth Corps (☎ (02) 2543-5858; *jiùguótuàn*), 219 Sungchiang Rd, Taipei. These tours are heavily subscribed during the summer holidays and Chinese New Year.

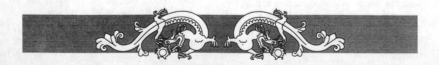

Taipei 台北

Not too long ago, the valley of the Tamsui River was home to rice and vegetable farmers but today it's the site of Taipei, the bustling centre of commerce, government and culture in Taiwan. Almost without exception, Taipei – meaning 'North Taiwan' – is the first stop for visitors arriving in Taiwan; it is also home for most western expatriates. As far as most people are concerned, this is the heart of Taiwan and the place where things happen.

The city proper has a population of 2.9 million, but the surrounding Taipei County adds another three million to the total. It's easily the most densely populated place in Taiwan and resident numbers are growing rapidly. The population increase is due primarily to an influx of people from other parts of Taiwan who are attracted to the city by the economic and educational opportunities available there. This has driven the cost of land to astronomical levels, making Taipei an expensive place to live and work. The high price of housing and office space is beginning to have an effect – many companies are relocating to other parts of the island to escape the sky-high rents. The government is also making an effort to move industry and educational institutions to other parts of the island. Nevertheless, most people in Taiwan still believe that if you want to make it big, you must live in Taipei.

Taipei has its share of problems – crime and drug addiction have increased sharply. More noticeable are the environmental problems such as overcrowding, noise and incredible traffic jams. Unless the wind is blowing, the air is almost toxic. The sky-rocketing price of real estate has made home ownership an impossible dream for the working classes. In an attempt to deal with the onslaught of people, industry and auto-mobiles, there is a tremendous amount of construction going on in the city – at any one time half the streets seem to be torn up. A gigantic new subway system has been half

built, but many think it will be obsolete by the time it finally reaches completion.

Whether or not you like Taipei depends on how you feel about big, booming cities. Taipei is not known for its architectural excellence – many of the buildings are just plain ugly. At the same time, for such a large city it's a very friendly place, with adventure and discovery around every corner. Travellers often develop a love-hate relationship with Taipei – they hate it so much that they

HIGHLIGHTS

- **National Palace Museum** – allow a day to wander through this treasure-trove of over 720,000 Chinese artefacts
- **Martyrs' Shrine** – witness the pomp and ceremony of the changing of the guard at this serene monument – you can even join in if you like!
- **Lungshan Temple** – don't miss this popular Taoist temple that is always a riot of colour and activity
- **Night Markets** – hunt out those shopping bargains and culinary delights at some of the city's many colourful markets

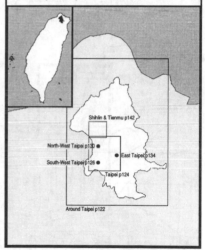

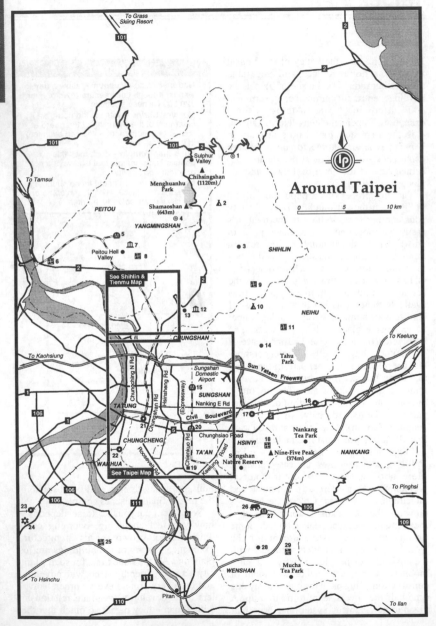

To Grass
Skiing Resort

101

2

2

To Tamsui

101

101

2
Sulphur
Valley
Chihsingshan
(1120m)
○ 1

Menghuanhu
Park

PEITOU

Shamaoshan
(643m)
○ 4

YANGMINGSHAN

Å 2

M 5

fi 7

Peitou Hell
Valley

8

2 6

2

See Shihlin &
Tienmu Map

○ 3

SHIHLIN

9

13

fi 12

Å 10

NEIHU

11

CHUNGSHAN

14

Tahu
Park

To Keelung

To Kaohsiung

Chungching N Rd

Chungshan Rd

Hsinsheng Rd

(Expressway)

Sungshan
Domestic
Airport

15

SUNGSHAN

Nanking E Rd

Sun Yatsen Freeway

16

1

106

1

TATUNG

21

(Civil) Boulevard

5

20

17

5

Nankang
Tea Park

CHUNGCHENG

Chienkuo Rd

Chunghsiao Road

TA'AN

18

Nine-Five Peak
(374m)

HSINYI

NANKANG

Keelung Road

22

WANHUA

Roosevelt Rd

19

Sungshan
Nature Reserve

See Taipei Map

23

106

24

106

111

9

26

M
27

106

To Pinghsi

109

25

28

29

Mucha
Tea Park

To Hsinchu

111

WENSHAN

110

Pitan

To Ilan

LP

Around Taipei

0   5   10 km

2

AROUND TAIPEI 台北市

1 Matsao Hot Springs
   馬槽溫泉
2 Chingshan Camping
   Ground
   菁山營地
3 Pingdengli Orchard
   平等里觀光果園
4 Hushanli Hot Springs
   湖山里溫泉
5 New Peitou MRT Station
   新北投站
6 Kuantu Temple
   關渡宮
7 Folk Arts Museum; Shann
   Garden; Mongolian
   Barbeque Restaurant
   北投文物館
8 Chaoming Temple
   昭明宮
9 Pishan Temple
   碧山寺
10 Pishan Camping Ground
   碧山露營場

11 Golden Dragon Temple
   金龍寺
12 National Palace Museum;
   Shunyi Taiwan Aboriginal
   Museum
   故宮博物館、
   順益台灣原住民
   博物館
13 Movie Studio; Soochow
   University
   電影文化城、
   東吳大學
14 Fuhsing Dramatic Arts
   Academy
   復興劇校、內湖路
   2段177號
15 Chungshan Middle School
   MRT Station
   中山國中站
16 Nankang Train Station
   南港火車站
17 Sungshan Train
   Station
   松山火車站
18 Sheng'on Temple
   松山自然保育區、
   聖恩宮

19 Taipei International Youth
   Activity Centre (TIYAC)
   國際青年活動中心
20 Chunghsiao-Fuhsing MRT
   Station
   忠孝復興站
21 Taipei Train Station
   台北火車站
22 Wanhua Train
   Station
   萬華火車站
23 Panchiao Train Station
   板橋火車站
24 Lin Gardens
   林家花園
25 Yuantung Temple
   圓通寺
26 Mucha Zoo
   木柵動物園
27 Taipei Zoo MRT
   Station
   動物園站
28 Chengchih University
   政治大學
29 Chihnan Temple
   指南宮

stay for months and never get out of the city at all. Even if you like Taipei, one thing is for sure – it's an expensive place to hang out unless you're working there.

Taipei's winter is grey, drizzly and chilly. From June to September the myriad buildings and thermal pollution, from cars and air-conditioners, turns the city into one big heat sink. October is the best month, but the only thing you can count on about Taipei's weather is that you can't count on it.

Taipei is the economic, cultural and trendsetting heart of Taiwan, if you haven't seen Taipei then you haven't seen Taiwan.

Orientation

Taiwan's cities – and Taipei in particular – might at first seem like confusing sprawls to the uninitiated. A good map helps, and it's also useful to carry a small pocket compass to keep yourself oriented.

Sprawling as Taipei might be, addresses are based on a logical system. In fact, it's more logical than the system normally used in western countries. Naturally, it's easier if you can speak, read and write Chinese, but it isn't absolutely necessary. It's certainly helpful to have your destination written down in Chinese characters and, of course, always carry the name card of your hotel with you so you can find your way back.

Taipei city (as opposed to Taipei County) is divided into 12 urban districts, and these districts appear on most postal addresses so they are worth knowing. The districts *(qū)* are Chungcheng, Chungshan, Hsinyi, Nankang, Neihu, Peitou, Shihlin, Sungshan, Ta'an, Tatung, Wanhua and Wenshan. Within these districts are neighbourhoods, the better known ones being Tienmu, Dinghao and Waishuanghsi.

The city is also divided into compass

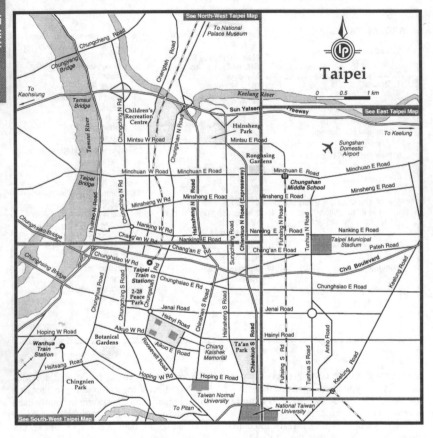

points. Chunghsiao and Pateh Rds bisect the city into its north and south grids. All major roads that cross Chunghsiao and Pateh Rds are labelled accordingly. Thus, we have Linsen N Rd and Linsen S Rd, Yenping N Rd and Yenping S Rd etc.

Chungshan Rd bisects the city into east and west grids. Most roads to the east of Chungshan Rd are labelled east and those to the west are labelled west. Thus, we have Nanking E Rd and Nanking W Rd.

Finding Addresses Major roads, such as Chungshan N Rd, are divided into sections.

In Taipei there is Chungshan N Rd, Section 1, Section 2, Section 3 and so on right up to Section 7. In some places, instead of writing 'Wufu Rd, Section 3', they might write 'Wufu-3 Rd', but the meaning is the same. A section is normally about three blocks long. When trying to find an address you really have to pay attention to which section you are in.

Then there are lanes. A lane, as the name implies, is a small side street – and they never have names, just numbers. A typical address might read: No 16, Lane 20, Chungshan N Rd, Section 2, Chungshan district. The No

---

Perverted Romanisation

One traveller wrote to LP to complain about our use of the 'perverted' Wade-Giles Romanisation system in the *Taiwan* guide. Perverted? A Romanisation system may not be entirely adequate, but can it be described as 'perverted'?

Perhaps. The Wade-Giles system has everyone confused. Even the government officials who enforce its use don't have the foggiest notion of how to Romanise their own names. Street signs in Taipei are inconsistent – one side of the street has one Romanised name while the opposite side has another. Maps and brochures produced by the Tourism Bureau consistently give different spellings for the same place – 'Hsuehpa' National Park or 'Shei-Pa' National Park?

Let's forget for the moment that Taiwan's largest city is really spelled T'aipei, not Taipei (that at least is easy to guess). Is it Changrong Rd or Changjung Rd? Keelung or Chilung? Tamsui, Tanshui or Danshuei? Nanking Rd or Nanching Rd? Chiuju Rd, Jeoru Rd or Jiuru Rd? These fun questions and more await unwary travellers trying to make sense of Taiwanese maps and street signs. Pity the poor postal clerks who have to sort out this mess and make sure that the mail gets delivered to the right place.

Things really start to get interesting when the Taiwanese newspapers take a stab at Romanising the names of people and places in mainland China. Is the capital of China spelled Beijing, Peking, Peiching or Peiping? Tourists can visit the ancient city of Xi'an, Hsian or Sian, depending on what mood the editor is in. Did Deng Xiaoping die or was it Teng Hsiaoping? Mao Zedong or Mao Tsetung?

Every now and then someone has the brilliant idea of trying to persuade the government to drop Wade-Giles in favour of the more accurate Pinyin system. So they seek out whichever government officials are available, imploring them to make the change. Unfortunately, they soon discover that: (a) no government officials have heard of Wade-Giles; (b) they don't know what Pinyin is either, but if mainland China uses it then they definitely don't want it; (c) no one is willing to take responsibility for making such a change; and (d) no one cares anyway. ■

---

16 is the house number, and Lane 20 is the name of the lane which intersects with Section 2 of Chungshan N Rd. That's not too difficult, but is there an easy way to locate Lane 20?

Fortunately, there is. As you walk along Chungshan N Rd, Section 2, keep your eye on the house numbers. Lane 20 should intersect with Chungshan N Rd just near a building bearing the street address number 20. Once you understand this system, it becomes very easy to find the lane you are looking for. Even-numbered lanes are on the same side of the street as even house numbers.

Occasionally, you'll have to find an alley. An alley is a lane which runs off a lane. Again, the same system is used. Alley 25 will intersect with a lane, and the house at the corner of this intersection should be number 25. A typical address could be 132 Alley 25, Lane 20, Chungshan N Rd, Section 2, Chungshan district, Taipei. It may look complicated, but it's very systematic.

Budget travellers, in particular, should learn this method of finding places, as many of the inexpensive hostels in Taipei are in these small lanes.

To confuse matters further, a building may have more than one entrance. If you have an address that is written as 34-2 Shuang Cheng St; this means that you will want the second entrance at building No 34.

It's worthwhile spending your first day in Taipei exploring the city on foot – it's an exciting place with plenty to see. Chungshan N Rd is a good place to start, as it is full of shops, restaurants and tempting bakeries. If you are looking for a cheap meal, get off the main street and into the narrow lanes and alleys where you will find all sorts of tiny restaurants selling a variety of inexpensive Chinese delicacies. The Dinghao neighbourhood in east Taipei and Kungguan near National Taiwan University are other good walking areas.

Information

Tourist Offices The ROC Tourism Bureau (☎ (02) 2349-1500) *guānguāng jú*), 9th floor, 280 Chunghsiao E Rd, Section 4, is not

TAIPEI

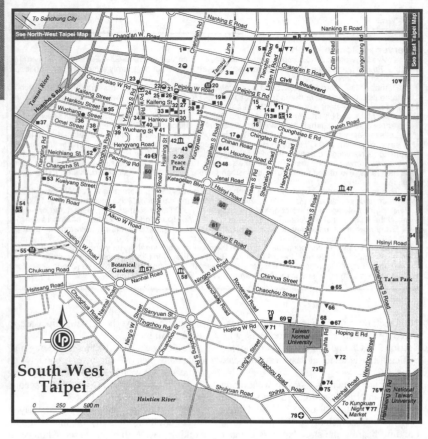

32 Paradise, Royal,
Keyman's Hotels; Hotel
Flowers
南國大飯店、
皇家大飯店、
懷寧旅店 、
華華大飯店
33 Chuan Chia Huam Hotel
全家歡賓館、懷寧街
6號4樓
34 Pan American Hotel
泛美大飯店
35 East Dragon Hotel
東龍大飯店
37 Riverview Hotel
豪景大酒店
53 Best Western Kilin Hotel
麒麟大飯店

PLACES TO EAT
 4 Seoul Korean Barbecue
中山北路1段33巷4號
 7 Chuansheng Vegetarian
Restaurant
林森北路111號
 9 Zum Fass Restaurant
林森北路119巷55號B1
10 Coriya Restaurant
可利亞
11 Meilin Vegetarian
Restaurant
北平東路14號
38 TGI Friday's
星期五美式餐廳
40 Doutor's Coffee
Shop
羅多倫咖啡店
41 TGI Friday's
星期五美式餐廳
66 Santa Fe Cafe
潮州街150號
71 Coriya Restaurant
可利亞
72 Shihta Night Market;
Grandma Nitti's
師大夜市、
師大路93巷8號
73 In Between Cafe
師大路92巷1號
76 Tequilla Sunrise
Restaurant
新生南路3段42號
77 TU Cafe
溫州街91號

OTHER
 2 North Bus Station (Taiwan
Bus Company)
台汽北站
12 Shantao Temple
善導寺
15 Provincial Police
Administration (Mountain
Permits)
警政署
17 Ministry of Foreign Affairs
外交部
20 Taipei Train Station
台北車站
21 East Bus Station (Taiwan
Bus Company)
台汽東站
22 West Bus Station (Taiwan
Bus Company)
台汽西站
23 North Gate
北門
24 GPO
郵政總局
26 NOVA Computer Arcade
NOVA資訊廣場
27 Mitsukoshi Department
Store
新光三越百貨
30 Far Eastern Air Transport
Booking Office
遠東航空售票處
36 Cinema St
武昌街二段、
電影戲院街
39 Foreign Affairs Police
警察局外事課
42 Taiwan Provincial Museum
台灣省博物館
43 Buses to Wulai
往烏來公車站
44 Chinese Handicraft Mart
中華工藝館
45 Chienkuo Holiday Jade
Market
建國假日玉市
46 Opium Den
仁愛路3段32號
47 Chang Foundation
Museum
鴻禧美術館
48 National Taiwan University
Hospital
台大醫院
49 Bank of Taiwan
台灣銀行

50 Presidential Building
總統府
51 Armed Forces Cultural
Activity Centre
國軍文藝活動中心
52 Tower Records
淘兒唱片行
54 Lungshan Temple
龍山寺
55 Wanhua Train Station
萬華火車站
56 Little South Gate
小南門
57 National Museum of
History; National Science
Hall; National Arts Hall
歷史博物館
58 Postal Museum
郵政博物館
59 National Central Library
中央圖書館
60 National Theatre
國家戲劇院
61 National Concert
Hall
國家音樂廳
62 Chiang Kaishek Memorial
Hall
中正紀念堂站
63 Chunghwa Telecom Head
Office
電信總局
64 Chienkuo Holiday Flower
Market
建國假日花市
65 DV8
金華街223號
67 Lucky Bookstore
師大書苑
68 Mandarin Training Centre
(Taiwan Normal
University)
師大國語中心
69 Spin Disco Pub
和平東路1段91號B1
70 45 Pub
和平東路1段45號
74 Wellcome
Supermarket
頂好超市
75 Mami Store
媽咪商店
78 Tri-Service General
Hospital
三軍總醫院

far from the Sun Yatsen Memorial Hall. This is a good place to pick up some of the free and limited English-language maps available.

There is another small branch of the Tourism Bureau in the Taipei train station, but this is largely Chinese speaking and is geared towards domestic tourists. However, they will try to help you if you're lost.

There is a tourist information hot line (☎ 2717-3737) which accepts calls from 8 am to 8 pm every day of the year. The operators speak English and can provide useful information such as the schedule of cultural events and exhibitions, and they even have current bus and train timetables. They also provide an emergency translation service if you need to summon the police or an ambulance and will also forward your complaints to the relevant authorities. The biggest problem with this number is that it is frequently busy.

Visa Extensions Visas can be extended in Taipei at the Foreign Affairs Police (☎ 2381-7494; *wàishì jǐngchá*), 96 Yenping S Rd, close to Chunghua Rd in south-western Taipei.

Mountain Permits The usual place to apply for mountain permits is the Foreign Affairs Office at the Taiwan Provincial Police Administration, 7 Chunghsiao E Rd, Section 1, directly across the street from the Lai Lai Sheraton Hotel.

Foreign Consulates Taiwan has limited diplomatic relations with foreign countries. For a list of pseudo-embassies that can deal with issues such as lost passports see Embassies in the Facts for the Visitor chapter.

Money The International Commercial Bank of China (ICBC) is the best place to change money, as it has numerous branches strategically placed throughout the city and can handle almost any brand of travellers cheques.

Central Taipei
(☎ 2311-8298) 6 Chunghsiao W Rd, Section 1
Chungshan
(☎ 2511-9231) 15 Chungshan N Rd, Section 2
Dinghao
(☎ 2771-1877) 233 Chunghsiao E Rd, Section 4
Nanking
(☎ 2751-6041) 198 Nanking E Rd, Section 3
Shihlin
(☎ 2834-5225) 126 Chungshan N Rd, Section 6
Tienmu
(☎ 2871-4125) 193 Chungshan N Rd, Section 7

Another place to change money is the Bank of Taiwan. Expect more forms to fill out here than at the other banks. Major branches in Taipei include:

Central Taipei
(☎ 2314-7377) 120 Chungching S Rd, Section 1
Chungshan
(☎ 2542-3434) 150 Chungshan N Rd, Section 1
Dinghao
(☎ 2707-3111) 560 Chunghsiao E Rd, Section 4
Shihlin
(☎ 2836-7080) 248 Chungshan N Rd, Section 6

It's said that many gold shops on Yenping Rd (north and south) are black market money exchange facilities. Rumours of counterfeit bills abound. Apart from the ATMs dotted around the city, there is nowhere to change money outside of banking hours.

Post & Communications The Taipei GPO, called the North Gate Post Office, is on Chunghsiao W Rd close to the train station. There is a separate window for poste restante services.

It is possible to make international direct-dial phone calls from the Taipei train station with a phonecard.

Chunghwa Telecom has many branches around the city where you can apply for their service connections (including Internet accounts), make international calls and send fax messages, telegrams and telexes. The largest branch is at 28 Hangchou S Rd, Section 1. Some other branches are: 162 Tunhua S Rd, Section 2; World Trade Centre, 5 Hsinyi Rd, Section 5; and 168 Poai Rd.

Online Services The municipal government of Taipei has staked out a presence on the Internet (www.tpg.gov.tw).

You can get free (yes, free!) use of Internet

computers inside the Taipei train station. However, these machines are not operational all day, and may not be available for use during holidays. You'll just have to take pot luck. Furthermore, there are no seats – you have to surf while standing. Still, it's a free way to check your email.

Other places charge for the service but costs are reasonable, plus you can sit in comfort and enjoy drinks and snacks.

The Garfield Internet Cafe (☎ 2874-2098), 2nd floor, 103 Tienmu W Rd, Tienmu, Shihlin district, has one Mac and three PCs. The staff speak English.

T-Zone Computer Store (☎ 2392-2122), 54 Chunghsiao E Rd, Section 1, next to the Lai Lai Sheraton Hotel, not far from Taipei train station, has a small cybercafe on the 2nd floor.

Travel Agencies Following are some of the discount agencies in Taipei dealing with international travel. Many other travel agencies post adverts in the English-language newspaper, the *China Post*. I've personally been using Jenny Su Travel for years, and have found it reliable, but no doubt many others offer the same competitive rates. Many, however, will quote very low group ticket prices over the phone which will not be available when you actually go to finalise the booking. Some of the more reputable agencies are:

Astor Tours
    (☎ 2545-8199) 2nd floor, 303 Fuhsing N Rd
Come First Travel
    (☎ 2506-6606) 9th floor, 176 Nanking E Rd, Section 2
Glory Travel
    (☎ 2571-8696) 12th floor, 98 Nanking E Rd, Section 2
Interlink Travel
    (☎ 2578-0611) 11th floor, 68 Kuangfu N Rd
Jenny Su Travel
    (☎ 2594-7733/2596-2263; fax 2592-0068) 10th floor, 27 Chungshan N Rd, Section 3
Linda's Special
    (☎ 2522-3268) Room 901, 9th floor, 98 Nanking E Rd, Section 2
TC Travel
    (☎ 2521-4255) 5th floor, 66 Sungchiang Rd

Not surprisingly, it's easier to find agencies selling discount air tickets for domestic travel in Taiwan near the entrance to Sung-shan domestic airport. Just across from the entrance of the airport is Chuntian Travel (☎ 2545-8887; *chūntiān lǚyóu*), 262 Tunhua N Rd. This place deserves kudos for its friendly service. The office is open daily from 6 am until 10 pm.

In the same vicinity is Tianshun Travel Agency (☎ 2547-1117; *tiānshùn lǚxíngshè*), 201 Minchuan E Rd, Section 3.

Bookshops Caves Books (☎ 2537-1666; *dūnhuáng shūjú*), 103 Chungshan N Rd, Section 2, has long been a favourite of the expat community in Taiwan. One strong feature of this store is the excellent collection of books on the study of Chinese. There is another Caves nearby at 81 Chungshan N Rd, Section 2, but this is for Chinese books only, although there is a good stationery section upstairs. Perhaps more useful is the Caves (☎ 2874-2199) in Tienmu at 5 Lane 38, Tienyu St. There is also another branch in Neihu (☎ 2790-1932) on the 7th floor, 180 Chengkeng Rd, Section 4.

Taiwan's largest bookstore belongs to Eslite (☎ 2775-5977; *chéngpǐn shūdiàn*), 245 Tunhua S Rd, Section 1, on the north-east corner of Jenai Rd. There are numerous smaller branches scattered around town, but the selection of English books at these branches is definitely more limited. Still, if you'd like to browse, the dispensation is as follows:

Central
    (☎ 2237-0310) Asiaworld Department Store, 2nd, 4th and 5th floor, 50 Chunghsiao W Rd, Section 1
Hsimenting
    (☎ 2388-6588) 3rd floor, 54 Emei St
Kuangfu
    (☎ 2773-0095) basement, 286 Kuangfu S Rd
Nanking
    (☎ 2717-2688) 3rd floor, 2-1 Lane 269, Nanking E Rd, Section 3
Taiwan University
    (☎ 2362-6132) 98 Hsinsheng S Rd, Section 3

TAIPEI

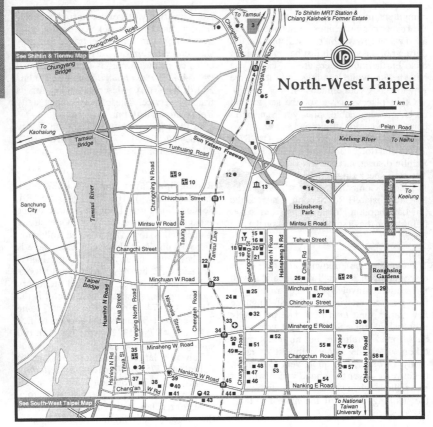

To Shihlin MRT Station &
Chiang Kaishek's Former Estate

To Tamsui

North-West Taipei

0   0.5   1 km

See Shihlin & Tienmu Map

Chungyang Bridge

To Kaohsiung

Tamsui Bridge

Chungcheng Road

Chengteh Road

Chungshan N Road

Sun Yatsen Freeway

Tunhuang Road

Keelung River   To Neihu

Peian Road

Chungching N Road

Chiuchuan Street

Mintsu W Road

Changchi Street

Minchuan W Road

Tamsui River

Sanchung City

Talung Street

Tamsui Line

Taipei Bridge

Huanho N Road

Tihua Street

Yenping North Street

Ninghsia Street

Chengteh Road

Minsheng W Road

Hsinyi N Rd

Tihua St

Chang'an W Rd

Nanking W Road

See South-West Taipei Map

Shuangcheng St

Linsen N Rd

Hsinsheng N Rd

Chilin Rd

Tehui Street

Hsinsheng Park

Mintsu E Road

Minchuan E Road

Chinchou Street

Minsheng E Road

Changchun Road

Nanking E Road

Sunghang Road

Chienkuo N Road

Ronghsing Gardens

Keelung

To Keelung

See East Taipei Map

To National Taiwan University

Tienmu 1
   (☎ 2874-6977) 3rd floor, 34 Chungshan N Rd, Section 7
Tienmu 2
   (☎ 2873-0966) 3rd floor, 188 Chungchen Rd, Section 2
World Trade Centre
   (☎ 2345-5577) 2 Hsinyi Rd, Section 5

New Schoolmate Books (☎ 2700-7000; *xīn xué yǒu shūjú*), also known as NSB or Sensaio Books, is at 259 Tunhua S Rd, Section 1, on the south-east corner of the roundabout at the intersection with Jenai Rd. Some have called this the McDonald's of

bookshops – it's a chain store with a large choice of English-language glossy covered best sellers, magazines and Chinese books. The Tienmu branch (☎ 2873-5566) at 36 Tienmu E Rd is near Taipei American School. Note that there are numerous other branches in Taipei which do *not* carry English titles.

The Lucky Bookstore (☎ 2392-7111; *shīdà shūyuàn*), 129-1 Hoping E Rd, Section 1, is very popular with foreigners studying Chinese in Taipei as it's in the same building as the Mandarin Training Centre of Taiwan Normal University. Prices here are slightly

NORTH-WEST TAIPEI
台北巿西北部

PLACES TO STAY
7 Grand Hotel
   圓山大飯店
8 Chientan Youth Activity
   Centre
   劍潭青年活動中心
15 Riviera Hotel
   歐華大飯店
16 President Hotel
   統一大飯店
19 Empress Hotel
   帝后大飯店
21 Imperial Inter-Continental
   Hotel
   華國洲際大飯店
22 Santos Hotel
   三德大飯店
24 Fortuna Hotel
   富都大飯店
25 Hotel New Asia
   新亞大飯店
26 Ritz Landis Hotel;
   Kuanshihyin Restaurant
   亞都麗緻大飯店、
   觀世音素菜餐廳
27 Amigo Hostel
   吉林路235號4樓
29 Miramar Hotel
   美麗華大飯店
31 Golden China Hotel;
   Taj Palace Restaurant
   康華大飯店、
   塔吉印度餐廳
37 Hotel 6F
   銀寶賓館、
   延平北路1段121號
38 Fortune Hotel
   福君大飯店、
   重慶北路1段62號
41 Queen Hotel
   皇后賓館、長安西路
   226號
43 Senator Hotel
   信州大飯店、
   長安西路83號

44 Golden Palace Hotel
   金府大飯店
46 Delight Hotel
   大欣大飯店、
   中國國際商業銀行
47 Hotel Royal
   老爺大酒店
48 Grand Formosa Regent
   Hotel
   麗晶酒店
49 Formosa Hostel I
   中山北路2段20巷16號
   3樓
50 Formosa Hostel II
   中山北路2段62巷5號
   2樓
51 Ambassador Hotel
   國賓大飯店
52 Gloria Hotel
   華泰大飯店
53 Beauty Hotel
   美的大飯店
54 First Hotel
   第一大飯店
55 Gala Hotel
   慶太大飯店
57 Leofoo Hotel
   六福客棧
58 Capital Hotel
   首都大飯店

PLACES TO EAT
17 YY's Kitchen & Steak
   House
   中山北路3段49號
39 Food Circle
   圓環
56 Peppers Restaurant
   松江路187-1號

OTHER
1 Central Auto (Car Rentals)
   承德路4段164號
2 Fin's Sealife Taipei
   台北海洋生活館
3 Shihlin Night Market
   士林夜市
4 Chientan MRT Station
   淡水捷運線、劍潭站

5 Yuanshan Sports Centre
   圓山育樂中心
6 Martyrs' Shrine
   忠烈祠
9 Paoan Temple
   保安寺
10 Confucius Temple
   孔子廟
11 Yuanshan MRT Station
   淡水捷運線、圓山站
12 Children's Recreation
   Centre
   兒童育樂中心
13 Fine Arts Museum
   美術館
14 Lin Antai Old Homestead
   林安泰古厝簡介
18 My Place Pub;
   The Farmhouse
   雙城街32港
20 Malibu West Bar
   雙城街25巷9號
23 Minchuan W Rd MRT
   Station
   淡水捷運線、
   民權西路站
28 Hsingtien Temple
   行天宮
30 Eliza Sauna (women)
   伊莉莎仕女
   休閒廣場、
   建國北路2段120號
32 Caves Books
   敦煌書局
33 Mackay Memorial Hospital
   馬偕醫院
34 Shuanglien MRT Station
   淡水捷運線、雙連站
35 Chenghuang Temple
   城隍廟
36 Tihua St Market
   迪化街
40 Tianlong Sauna (men);
   Wellcome Supermarket
   天龍三溫暖、
   頂好超市
42 Tonglien Bus Station
   統聯客運站
45 Chungshan MRT Station
   淡水捷運線、中山站

discounted and the selection is heavily
geared towards students' tastes.

Nearby is Crane Publishing Company
(☎ 2393-4497/2394-1791), 6th floor, 109

Hoping E Rd, Section 1. You can't see the shop from the street – take the lift to the 6th floor and you're there. This branch is open daily from 9 am to 6 pm. The company operates another branch (☎ 2322-5437) at 59 Chungching S Rd, Section 2 (just south of Nanhai Rd) and is open daily from 10 am to 7 pm. Crane is heavily into publishing educational books – English teachers can get a 20% discount. Even for nonteachers, there's quite a good collection of classical English literature.

Sung Kang Computer Book Company (☎ 2708-2125; *sōnggāng diànnǎo shūdiàn*) specialises in – you guessed it – computer books. Unlike most computer bookshops in Taipei, this place has computer manuals in English. The store is on the 3rd floor, 337 Tunhua S Rd, Section 1, near the intersection with Hsinyi Rd.

Most of the foregoing bookstores are also good places to pick up tickets for concerts and other cultural events.

Libraries The China External Trade Development Council (CETRA) maintains an international Trade Data Library on the 4th floor, 333 Keelung Rd, Section 1, Hsinyi district, in the high rise building adjoining the World Trade Centre.

The American Institute in Taiwan (AIT) has a Trade Unit Library in the same building as the CETRA Trade Data Library. This small library offers business, telephone and other directories covering the USA. It also has some useful material on American import regulations.

The National Central Library (☎ 2361-9132), adjacent to the Chiang Kaishek Memorial Hall at 20 Chungshan S Rd, is Taiwan's largest. The facilities are stunning – even if you don't like libraries, just wander around and admire the architecture. Both Chinese and English periodicals are available. The 6th floor of the library has a complete set of highly detailed topographic quadrangle maps of Taiwan, produced by the government. These maps are not for sale to the public, but you can photocopy them within the library.

The Taipei Municipal Library's (☎ 2755-3029) very impressive building is at 125 Chienkuo S Rd, Section 2, between Hoping and Hsinyi Rds.

Academia Sinica (☎ 2789-9326), 128 Yen Chiu Yuan Rd, Section 2, Nankang district, has the most modern facilities for serious researchers. The library is in the far eastern part of Taipei. You can reach it from the centre on bus No 270.

The Information and Computing Library (☎ 2737-7737), Science & Technology building *(kējì dàlóu)*, 13th floor, 106 Hoping E Rd, Section 2 has a collection of up-to-date computer books and magazines. Perhaps more useful is the shareware collection, which you are permitted to copy freely onto floppy disks sold at the library. On the 10th floor of the same building is the somewhat less useful Institute for Information Industry Library (☎ 2737-7133).

Universities The National Taiwan University *(táidà)* is the largest and, reputedly, best institute of higher learning in Taipei. The campus serves as an official park, so you can stroll through it, visit the bookshop and use the library. If you want to meet Chinese students, then you will find that most of those here are friendly and anxious to practise their English.

The National Taiwan University is in the Kungkuan neighbourhood. Buses that stop near the campus include bus Nos 0-South, 10, 30, 52, 60, 236, 251, 252, 253, 311 and 501.

Laundry There are heaps of laundries in Taipei, though they tend to be in back alleys and have no English signs. If you can't spot one yourself, get a Chinese-speaking person to help you.

Logical places to look for inexpensive laundry services are in the alleys around National Taiwan University and Taiwan Normal University *(shīdà)*. One of many is *shīdà zìzhù xǐyī* (☎ 2362-1047), 72 Lungchuan St. Lungchuan St is one block east of Shihta Rd and runs parallel to it.

Medical Services The Adventist Hospital has English-speaking doctors and caters for foreigners, but it's very expensive – if you have health insurance you might be covered. Central Clinic and Mackay Memorial Hospital are private, very good and somewhat cheaper. The other hospitals listed are government-run and relatively cheap for the high standard of service provided. However, they can get very crowded – bring plenty of reading material and expect long waits.

Adventist Hospital
(☎ 2771-8151; *tái ān yīyuàn*) 424 Pateh Rd, Section 2
Cathay General Hospital
(☎ 2708-2121; *guótài zōnghé yīyuàn*) 280 Jenai Rd, Section 4
Central Clinic (☎ 2751-0221; *zhōngxīn zhěnsuǒ*) 77 Chungsiao E Rd, Section 4
Chang Gung Memorial Hospital
(☎ 2713-5211; *cháng gēng yīyuàn*) 199 Tunhua N Rd
Mackay Memorial Hospital
(☎ 2543-3535; *mǎjiē yīyuàn*) Chungshan N Rd, Section 2
National Taiwan University Hospital
(☎ 2397-0800; *táidà yīyuàn*) 7 Chungshan S Rd
Tri-Service General Hospital
(☎ 2365-9055; *sānjūn zhōng yīyuàn*) 40 Tingchow Rd, Section 3
Veterans General Hospital
(☎ 2871-2121, English-language ext 3530; *róngmín zǒng yīyuàn*) 201 Shihpai Rd, Section 2
Yangming Hospital (☎ 2835-3456; *yángmíng yīyuàn*) 105 Yusheng St

Emergency English-speaking police can be contacted at several branch offices: Central area (☎ 2311-9940/2311-9916, ext 264); Chungshan area (☎ 2511-0956); and Tienmu area (☎ 2871-4110/2871-4440). As elsewhere in Taiwan, the Chinese-speaking numbers for an emergency are ☎ 110 for the police and ☎ 119 for fire and ambulance.

If the above doesn't work, call the tourist information hot line (☎ 2717-3737).

Useful Organisations The Community Services Centre (☎ 2836-8134/2835-6907; fax 2835-2530), 25 Lane 290, Chungshan N Rd, Section 6, Shihlin, is run by expats and provides support covering everything from new resident orientation to adult education classes.

Maybe you dread going there, but sometimes you've got to face the music. The tax office (☎ 2311-3711, ext 116-118) is at 2 Chunghua Rd, Section 1. Operating hours are from 8.40 am to noon and from 1.40 to 5 pm. It's closed on Sunday, alternate Saturdays and public holidays.

The American Chamber of Commerce (☎ 2581-7089; fax 2542-3376), Room 1012, Chia Hsin building Annex, 86 Chungshan N Rd, Section 2, Taipei 104, should interest anyone with long term business interests in Taiwan. Non-US citizens can join up with the chamber as associate members and receive their newsletter.

The China External Trade Development Council (CETRA), 6th floor, 333 Keelung Rd, Section 1, Taipei 110, is a government organisation responsible for developing Taiwan's foreign trade. The council also organises trade shows at the adjacent World Trade Centre and is a fountain of business information. CETRA also provide a traders' hot line (☎ 2725-5960).

Left Luggage The Taipei train station does *not* have a left luggage office. However, it does have lockers in the basement. The cost is NT$30 per day for small lockers and NT$60 for large ones. The new day begins at 10 pm (as far as the lockers are concerned) and you will have to feed the locker another day's fee to retrieve your bag after that time. You can store bags here for a maximum of three days.

The Sungshan train station in east Taipei has a left luggage office charging NT$17 per bag per day. The office is open daily from 7 am to 10 pm. It's advisable to take a passport or some other identification with you even though the staff won't always insist on seeing it.

You should also find left luggage offices at train stations in most of the other large cities in Taiwan, but the hours will be shorter, from around 8 am to 8 pm, and they will probably close over lunch time.

TAIPEI

East Taipei

Sungshan Domestic Airport

0   0.5   1 km

EAST TAIPEI 台北東部

PLACES TO STAY
11 Sherwood Hotel
西華大飯店
23 Magnolia Hotel; Kiss La
Boca
中泰賓館
25 City Hotel
北城大飯店
29 Brother Hotel
兄弟大飯店
30 Asiaworld Plaza Hotel
環亞大飯店
31 Rebar Holiday Inn Crowne
Plaza
力霸皇冠假日大飯店
37 Baguio Hotel
碧瑤大飯店
49 Asia Pacific Hotel
亞太大飯店
52 United Hotel
國聯大飯店
56 Grand Hyatt Hotel
凱悅大飯店
61 Charming City Hotel
香城大飯店
68 Howard Plaza Hotel
福華大飯店
71 Hotel Dynasty
朝代大飯店
74 Far Eastern Plaza Hotel
遠東大飯店

PLACES TO EAT
5 Fahua Vegetarian
Restaurant
法華素菜餐廳
8 Tandoor Indian Restaurant
合江街73巷10號
9 Subway Sandwiches
復興北路346號
12 Lulu Bar & Restaurant
民生東路3段113巷9號
13 Hard Rock Cafe
民生東路3段115號
14 Tony Roma's Restaurant
民生東路3段156號
17 Swensen's Restaurant
雙聖西餐
18 L'Amico Restaurant
民生東路4段55巷10號
19 Hollywood Baby Diner;
Citibank
花旗銀行、民生東路
4段56巷1弄2號

24 G'day Cafe
興安街180號
32 Coriya Restaurant
可利亞
36 Dan Ryan's Chicago Grill
敦化北路8號
42 SOGO Department Store;
TGI Friday's
太平洋崇光百貨、
星期五美式餐廳
45 Ploughman's Inn
敦化南路1段232巷8號
46 Malibu Cafe
仁愛路4段91巷5號
48 Pasta West East
安和路1段7號
53 Capone's Dinnerhouse
忠孝東路4段312號
59 TGI Friday's; Wally Gym
星期五美式餐廳
60 Pizza Hut
必勝客
63 Swensen's Restaurant
雙聖西餐
73 Ciao Pasta House
和平東路3段75號

OTHER
1 Buses to CKS airport
台汽客運松山機場站
2 Tianshun Travel
天順旅行社
3 Chuntian Travel
春天旅遊
4 VIP Car Rental
民權東路3段148號
6 Chungshan Middle School
MRT Station
捷運木柵線
中山國中站
7 Eliza Sauna (women)
伊莉莎仕女
休閒廣場、
復興北路400號
10 My Other Place Pub
復興北路303號
15 American Express
美國運通銀行
16 Bank of America
美國商業銀行
20 Wellcome Supermarket
頂好超市
21 Air Force General
Hospital
空軍總醫院

22 Chang Gung Memorial
Hospital
長庚醫院
26 China Airlines
中華航空
27 911 Disco Pub
遼寧街119號
28 Nanking E Rd MRT Station
南京東路站
33 Jaoho St Night Market
饒河街夜市
34 Department of Motor
Vehicles
台北監理所
35 Municipal Stadium
市立體育場
38 Adventist Hospital
台安醫院
39 Chunglun Bus Station
台汽中奮站
40 Indian Beer House
印地安啤酒屋
41 Chunghsiao-Fuhsing MRT
Station
忠孝復興站
43 Tower Records;
Wellcome Supermarket
淘兒唱片行、
頂好超市
44 Central Clinic
中心診所
47 Eslite Books
誠品書店
50 Q Bar
忠孝東路4段
216巷19弄16號
51 ROC Tourism Bureau
觀光局
54 Sun Yatsen Memorial
國父紀念館
55 City Hall
台北市政府
57 World Trade Centre
世貿中心
58 Convention Centre
國際會議中心
62 Cathay General Hospital
國泰醫院
64 Eliza Sauna (women)
伊莉莎仕女
休閒廣場、
仁愛路4段112港5號B1
65 New Schoolmate Books
新學友書店

continued over

TAIPEI

66	Far Eastern Department	69	American Institute in	72	Tunghua Night Market
	Store		Taiwan (AIT)		通化街夜市
	遠東百貨		美國在台協會	75	Technology Building MRT
67	TU Pub	70	Ta-an MRT Station		Station
	復興南路1段249號B1		大安站		科技大樓站

Lungshan Temple
(lóngshān sì) 龍山寺

This is a superb example of a temple dedicated to Kuanyin, the goddess of mercy.

Lungshan (Dragon Mountain) Temple was originally built in 1738, in the district that was then known as Mengchia (now renamed Wanhua). In 1815 an earthquake levelled Mengchia, along with the temple, but the Kuanyin statue survived and a new temple was reconstructed around it. The temple was wrecked again by a typhoon in 1867 but was once again restored. In 1945, US bombers hit the temple during a raid against Japanese troops.

The temple was rebuilt yet again, and remains today as one of the most popular in Taipei. It's extremely colourful and is packed with worshippers most of the time; the air is heavy with smoke from burning incense and 'ghost money'. Adjacent to the temple is an active market, and two blocks away is the touristy Snake Alley.

Lungshan Temple is at 211 Kuangchou St, off Kueilin Rd, and is open daily from 5 am to 10 pm. You can get there on bus Nos 0-West, 25, 38, 49, 234, 265 and 310.

Confucius Temple
(kǒngzǐ miào) 孔子廟

Compared to Taiwan's ornate Buddhist and Taoist temples, the Confucius Temple is a modest place. There are no statues or deities and the only time it comes to life is on 28 September, the birthday of Confucius (Teacher's Day), when there is an interesting festival held at dawn. If you're around at this time, check the tourist offices or your hotel to see if you can get a ticket to this festival. Probably the easiest way to get to the temple (at 275 Talung St) is via the Tamsui subway line to Yuanshan station. From there it's a

short walk. Alternatively bus Nos 41, 250, 288, 302 and 601 pass by the temple.

Paoan Temple
(do'ān gōng) 保安宮

Just a short walk from the Confucius Temple is the Paoan Temple at 61 Hami St. The temple was originally built around 1765, making it Taipei's oldest temple. Like any good Taoist temple, the interior is a riot of colours and deities, and it's particularly active during the 15th day of the lunar month. To get here use the same transport as described for the Confucius Temple in the previous section.

Hsingtien Temple
(xíngtiān gōng) 行天宮

This temple is dedicated to Kuankung *(guāngōng)*; the god of war and martial arts and the patron saint of businesspeople. Kuangkung was actually a general who lived from 162 to 219 AD. While Confucius, regarded as the saint of literature, is revered for his wisdom, Kuankung is known for his physical strength.

Hsingtien Temple is at 109 Minchuan E Rd, Section 2, at the intersection with Sungchiang Rd (north-east corner).

Chenghuang Temple
(chénghuáng miào) 城隍廟

The Chenghuang (City God) Temple is a small but very ornate and lively Taoist place of worship. Most cities in Taiwan have a temple dedicated to the city god, who protects local residents and brings good fortune. If possible, try to visit this temple on the city god's birthday, in this case the 13th day of the fifth moon, when there are loud and lively celebrations.

Chenghuang Temple is at 61 Tihua St,

Section 1, which is west of Taipei train station. You can walk from the station, but buses which pass nearby include Nos 9, 14, 206, 255, 274, 302, 304 and 601.

Shantao Temple
(shàndǎo sì) 善導寺

This unusual looking temple is instantly recognisable by its nine storey, squarish pagoda. The pagoda, which vaguely resembles a layer cake, houses some Buddhist art works.

The temple is at 23 Chunghsiao E Rd, Section 1, which is a 10 minute walk east of Taipei train station.

Shunyi Taiwan Aboriginal Museum
(shùnyì táiwān yuánzhùmín bówùguǎn)
順益台灣原住民博物館

The museum (☎ 2841-2611) is privately owned (built by Mitsubishi!). The exhibits cover four storeys, plus the basement. On display in the entrance is an interesting topographical map showing the main cities and sights of Taiwan along with the territories and villages of the nine aboriginal tribes. The museum has exhibits representing aborigine

Paiwan pots, like this one used for divination, are displayed in the Shunyi Taiwan Aboriginal Museum.

customs as well as objects of sacrifice, divination and exorcism. Aborigine crafts, dwellings, the weapons and utensils of daily life, and costumes and ornaments worn by the various tribes give an extra insight into this fascinating culture. There is also a small cinema in the basement showing movies on aboriginal themes.

The museum is at 221 Chihshan Rd, Section 2, Shihlin district, adjacent to the National Palace Museum (see the National Palace Museum section later in this chapter). Operating hours are from 10 am to 6pm, but it's closed on Monday. It's also closed for a full month from 20 January to 20 February. Admission costs NT$150; a 20% discount is available to holders of a paid ticket from the National Palace Museum. All the handout materials are in Chinese and Japanese only, but English-language tours of the museum are available if booked in advance.

Fine Arts Museum
(měi shù guǎn) 美術館

Exhibits at the Fine Arts Museum are rotated every few months, and they include many works by foreign artists. Exhibits have covered everything from Australian aboriginal art to rare Mayan artefacts from Mexico. The museum's gift shop sells works by local artists, often reasonably priced – typically between NT$1500 and NT$3000. The gift shop also sells calligraphy brushes, ink stones, ceramic tea cups and various unidentifiable objects made from metal scraps welded together.

The big problem with this museum is that virtually everything – including explanations on exhibits and most of the books in the gift shop – is in Chinese only.

Photography is prohibited inside the museum.

The Fine Arts Museum (☎ 2595-7656) is at 181 Chungshan N Rd, Section 3, just south of the Grand Hotel. It's open from 10 am to 6 pm Tuesday to Sunday. Bus Nos 216, 217, 218, 220, 224, 247, 277, 301 and 310 pass by the museum. Catching the subway to Yuanshan station (Tamsui line) will also get you very close. Admission costs NT$30.

National Palace Museum
故宮博物館

Taipei's National Palace Museum holds the world's largest collection of Chinese artefacts, around 720,000 items in all. Since the museum only has space to display around 15,000 pieces at any given time, the majority of the treasures are kept well protected in air-conditioned vaults, buried in secure caves deep within the mountainside. The museum's exhibits are rotated once every three months, enabling 60,000 pieces to be displayed each year, which effectively means that it would take nearly 12 years to see the entire collection. Real enthusiasts could find this a bit frustrating.

The wealth of the collection explains why it is widely regarded as the world's leading centre for the study of Chinese art. The museum is also the recognised home of Chinese culture and tradition.

History

During the Song dynasty (960-1279) Emperor Dai Cong decided he wanted to monopolise China's art treasures. Therefore, he sent teams of servants into the countryside to search for, and ultimately confiscate, paintings, sculptures, pottery, wood carvings, calligraphy scrolls, books and everything else an emperor could want. The tradition thrived right up to the Qing dynasty (1644-1911). During these times the 'donations' were regularly shuttled back and forth between palaces in Beijing and Nanjing, finally coming to rest in the 1400s, when Emperor Yong Le established Beijing's Forbidden City. The collection was to remain there for the next 500 years.

The Forbidden City was just that – entry without an invitation was forbidden. As far as the imperial art treasures were concerned, they remained for the exclusive viewing of emperors and empresses along with a select group of their consorts.

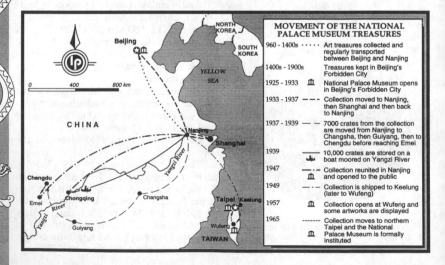

MOVEMENT OF THE NATIONAL PALACE MUSEUM TREASURES

960 - 1400s	·····	Art treasures collected and regularly transported between Beijing and Nanjing
1400s - 1900s		Treasures kept in Beijing's Forbidden City
1925 - 1933	🏛	National Palace Museum opens in Beijing's Forbidden City
1933 - 1937	– – –	Collection moved to Nanjing, then Shanghai and then back to Nanjing
1937 - 1939	——	7000 crates from the collection are moved from Nanjing to Changsha, then Guiyang, then to Chengdu before reaching Emei
1939	⚓	10,000 crates are stored on a boat moored on Yangzi River
1947	–·–· 🏛	Collection reunited in Nanjing and opened to the public
1949	– ·· – ·	Collection is shipped to Keelung (later to Wufeng)
1957	🏛	Collection opens at Wufeng and some artworks are displayed
1965	········· 🏛	Collection moves to northern Taipei and the National Palace Museum is formally instituted

China's revolution of 1911 theoretically put emperors out of business and the Kuomintang (KMT) in power, but it wasn't until 1924 that Emperor Puyi was served his eviction notice and left the Forbidden City for good. In 1925, for the first time, the Forbidden City's gates were thrown open to ordinary Chinese citizens. The emperors' palace was thus transformed into the central showcase of China's new National Palace Museum.

Unfortunately, the Beijing-based museum only had a life span of about eight years. In September 1931, the Japanese occupied Manchuria, setting up a puppet state with Puyi as the symbolic head. Relations between China and Japan continued to go downhill, and in 1933 the KMT realised that war was increasingly likely. The possibility of having the entire collection of the National Palace Museum fall into Japanese hands was something the Chinese couldn't swallow, so the goods were packed up and hauled by train to Nanjing for safe keeping. A month later they were transferred to a warehouse in Shanghai. In 1937, the collection was transferred back to Nanjing, just in time to avoid the Japanese invasion of Beijing and Shanghai – the opening shots of China's entry into WWII.

Some of the collection was shipped by rail southwards to Changsha, then on to Guiyang, finally coming to a halt in Chengdu. Even then, the collection was not safe – Japanese bombers pounded Chengdu frequently – so in 1939 the crates moved once again to the remote village of Emei. Meanwhile another 10,000 crates were loaded onto a boat and spirited out of Nanjing, just as the Japanese began their attack. The boat remained moored in the Yangzi River near Chongqing until the war ended.

Despite all the bombings and land battles, virtually the entire collection survived intact. In 1947, the collection was moved back to the KMT capital of Nanjing and was once again displayed to the public in December of that year. By January 1949, the Communists had all but defeated the KMT's army in the north and were advancing southwards. Once again the KMT were concerned about the art collection falling into the 'wrong' hands, so the collection was shipped out to the Taiwanese port of Keelung. Unfortunately the KMT's withdrawal was so hasty that about 700 crates had to be left behind in Nanjing.

Silver Wine Cup
This unique piece was created by Chu Pi-shan, an artist who lived between the late Yuan and early Ming dynasties. It is considered to be a fine representation of the high standard of silverwork created during the Yuan dynasty.

The finely worked cup characterises Chang Ch'en, who, according to Chinese folklore, rode a wooden raft up the Yangzi River, intending to find its source and a way to control the flow that brought devastating floods to China each year.

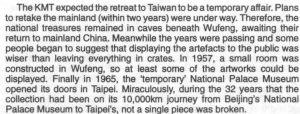

The KMT expected the retreat to Taiwan to be a temporary affair. Plans to retake the mainland (within two years) were under way. Therefore, the national treasures remained in caves beneath Wufeng, awaiting their return to mainland China. Meanwhile the years were passing and some people began to suggest that displaying the artefacts to the public was wiser than leaving everything in crates. In 1957, a small room was constructed in Wufeng, so at least some of the artworks could be displayed. Finally in 1965, the 'temporary' National Palace Museum opened its doors in Taipei. Miraculously, during the 32 years that the collection had been on its 10,000km journey from Beijing's National Palace Museum to Taipei's, not a single piece was broken.

Although physical fighting between the mainland and Taiwan had ceased, the war of words continued. The Communists harshly criticised the KMT for 'stealing' this priceless collection of Chinese treasures and demanded that it be returned. The KMT had an easy answer to that – it's doubtful that much would have survived China's Cultural Revolution of the 1960s. The Communists had virtually extinguished China's cultural heritage, and the KMT felt justified in claiming the moral high ground. Thus, the artefacts remain in Taipei.

The Collection
The collection changes so regularly that it is impossible to predict what will be on display at any given time. There are also special exhibitions

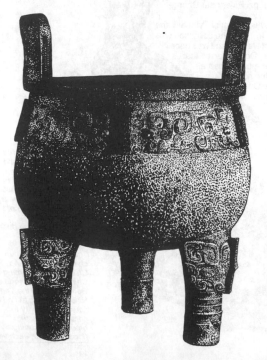

Bronze Ting
A 'ting' is a three legged, round-bodied, two handled cooking vessel. Initially made from pottery over 7000 years ago, the ting had long legs so it could be placed over a fire. A pole was passed through the handles of the ting so that it could be carried.

The ting soon became a symbol of power and sovereignty. The emperor of the Hsia dynasty, Yu the Great, had nine bronze tings – each representing one of the nine states under his rule – that later became crown treasures.

Tings were decorated with varying patterns, including masks of animals – real or imaginary – that symbolised the characteristics and traditions of different tribes.

held, with artworks from other world reknowned museums on display. An overview, with examples of what you could expect to see, is given in the following paragraphs.

Some of the oldest artefacts in the collection date from the Neolithic period and include pottery pieces which clearly demonstrate the different regional styles that emerged from China. The museum is widely known as the home of the world's most comprehensive collection of jade and it has many tools, carvings and decorative pieces on display. Some of the finest pieces used a carving process called *ch'iao-tzou*, whereby the artist incorporated the natural colouring of the jade into the design.

China didn't experience its Bronze Age until about 4000 years ago. However once discovered, the Chinese made good use of bronze to create a variety of vessels. One of the more interesting pieces on display is the San-P'an. This vessel was designed as a peace treaty between two states arguing over borders. Inscribed with over 300 characters, it is the oldest peace treaty in the world today. During the Warring States period (453-221 BC), lacquerware pieces started to replace those traditionally made from bronze. Commonly red in colour, there are thought to have been over 200 different types of lacquerware.

The Chinese invented the use of porcelain and there are many exquisite artworks to be seen here. Although it was created in the west, enamel was adapted by the Chinese to create *ching-t'ailan*; a mix with cobalt blue which produces a stunning and vibrant effect.

One of seven copies of the largest collection of books ever created in the world, the *Ssu-k'u ch'uan-shu* (Complete Library of Four Classifications) resides under the National Palace Museum roof. Over 5000 people were employed, for a period of more then 15 years, to create the books which were finished about 200 years ago. In all, 3451 individual works were used to compile this collection which is divided into four classifications: Chinese classics, history, philosophy and literature.

Other artworks that you will undoubtedly see on display are ivory pieces, calligraphy, paintings (including portraits of Chinese Emperors and Empresses), silk weavings, silverware and gilt statues.

Information

The National Palace Museum (☎ 2881-2021) is at 221 Chihshan Rd, Section 2, in the Waishuanghsi neighbourhood of Taipei. The museum is open from 9 am to 5 pm every day of the year; admission is NT$80. There are good tours of the museum in English, twice daily at 10 am and 3 pm, starting from the information desk in the main lobby.

Photography is prohibited inside the museum, which has a gift shop, restaurant, coffee shop and teahouse. A visit to the traditional-style teahouse is highly recommended (see Teahouses in the Places to Eat section of this chapter).

Just to the east of the museum steps is Chihshan Garden, which has fine Song dynasty landscaping and is a nice place to relax. Admission costs NT$10.

The museum is too far to walk from the centre of the city – take bus Nos 213, 255 and 304. If you take No 304, get off at the terminus; you will have to ask to be dropped off at the museum on the other buses. The museum is a long way into another bus zone from the city, so you will have to pay a double fare (NT$30).

Recently, selected pieces have been sent on the road around Taiwan. If you can't make it to the museum itself, you can always check with cultural centres in the larger cities for forthcoming National Palace Museum exhibitions.

TAIPEI

Shihlin &
Tienmu

0   250   500 m

See North-West Taipei Map

Chang Foundation Museum
(hóngxī měishùguǎn) 鴻禧美術館
This museum (☎ 2356-9575) is unusual in
that it's privately owned by the Chang family. The emphasis of the exhibits is on ancient
Chinese art with a rich assortment of ceramics dating back over 2000 years. While some
people object to private art collections, the
Chang's deserve some credit for putting
theirs on display to the public. The collection
gets very good reviews from travellers, and
some even say it's better organised than the
much larger National Palace Museum.

The museum is in the basement at 63 Jenai

Rd, Section 2, between Hsingsheng S Rd and
Chinshan S Rd. You can catch bus No 36 or
37 to the museum from the east entrance of
the Taipei train station. Admission costs
NT$100, students receive a 50% discount.
Opening hours are from 10.30 am to 4.30 pm
Tuesday to Sunday. The museum closes
during the first two weeks of July.

Taiwan Folk Arts Museum
(běitóu wénwù guǎn) 北投文物館
The museum (☎ 2891-2318/2893-1787), 32
Yuya Rd, is in a quaint set of buildings that
looks much like a traditional Japanese

SHIHLIN & TIENMU
士林、天母

PLACES TO EAT
2 Antonio's Pizzeria
   天母西路56號
5 TGI Friday's; Eslite Books;
   Kona Connection
   星期五美式餐廳、
   誠品書店
6 Burger King
   漢堡大王
7 Round Table Steak &
   Pizza
   圓桌武士西餐
12 Swensen's Restaurant;
   Support & Solutions
   (Appleshop)
   雙聖西餐、天母東路
   48號
14 Ticino Swiss
   Restaurant
   天母東路82巷2號
15 Subway Sandwiches
   中山北路6段467號
16 Jake's Country Kitchen
   中山北路6段705號
20 Uli's Euro Deli
   克強街17號
25 Lanka Restaurant
   士林區忠義街48號

26 Post Home Restaurant
   中山北路6段35巷31號
30 Swensen's; Round Table
   Pizza
   雙聖西餐、
   圓桌武士西餐
31 McDonald's
   麥當勞
32 Skylark Restaurant
   中山北路4段544號

OTHER
1 Veterans General Hospital
   榮民總醫院
3 Caves Books
   敦煌書局
4 Tienmou Yuehou Grocery
   Store
   天母益和商店
8 Wellcome Supermarket
   頂好超市
9 Taipei Japanese School
   台北日僑學校
10 Taipei American School
   台北美國學校
11 New Schoolmates Books
   新學友書局
13 Pig & Whistle Pub; Green
   Bar
   天母東路78號、
   天母東路84號

17 Shihpai MRT Station
   淡水捷運線、石牌站
18 Mingteh MRT Station
   淡水捷運線、明德站
19 Tienmu Swimming
   Pool
   天母游泳池
21 Bank of Taiwan
   台灣銀行
22 Community Services
   Centre
   中山北路6段
   290巷25號
23 Wellcome Supermarket
   頂好超市
24 Yangming Hospital
   陽明醫院
27 Chihshan
   淡水捷運線、芝山站
28 Astronomical Museum
   天文科學館
29 Shin Kong
   Hospital
   新光醫院
33 Shihlin MRT
   Station
   淡水捷運線、士林站
34 Chiang Kaishek's Former
   Estate
   士林官邸

teahouse (there is in fact a teahouse here). Over 5000 items are on display here. You'll have to remove your shoes before entering.

To get to the museum, in the Peitou district of north-west Taipei, take bus No 216, 217, 218, 266 or 269 to Hsin Peitou, from there change to bus No 230 which will take you to the museum. You can also get to Hsin Peiton on the Tamsui subway, from where you will still need to catch bus No 230.

Admission costs NT$100. The museum is open weekdays from 9 am to 5 pm, weekends from 9 am to 7.30 pm.

Astronomical Museum
(tiānwén kēxué guǎn) 天文科學館
This museum introduces astronomy to the masses. There are four floors of exhibits plus an adjacent Space Theatre and 3D Theatre.

The telescopes on the roof are available to the public for stargazing on Saturday and Sunday nights.

The museum (☎ 2831-4551) is at 363 Chiho Rd, Shihlin district, an area of town known for its astronomical rents. The museum is open Tuesday to Friday from 9 am to 4 pm, and Saturday to Sunday from 9 am to 8 pm. The museum is closed on Monday. Admission costs NT$40, plus NT$100 each for the Space and 3D theatres.

You can get to the Astronomical Museum by taking the Tamsui subway line to the Chientan station.

Postal Museum
(yóuzhèng bówùguǎn) 郵政博物館
For stamp enthusiasts, the Postal Museum (☎ 2394-5185) is at 45 Chungching S Rd,

Section 2. It's open from Tuesday to Sunday, except for the day after national holidays.

For collectors, the real action takes place not inside in the museum, but right in front of it. On weekends, private collectors and vendors stake out the front of the museum, forming their own impromptu stamp market. If this isn't enough, there are seven stamp shops within two blocks of the Postal Museum.

Presidential Building
(zhŏngtŏng fŭ) 總統府
Close to the 2-28 Peace Park is the Presidential Building. Normally, there is not much to see here, but on Double 10th Day (10 October or National Day) there are enormous rallies and impressive military parades held at this site. If you're in Taipei at this time it may be worth checking out. The area is lit up for several weeks after Double 10th, presenting an excellent opportunity for night photography.

On the evening of Double 10th, one of the world's most dazzling displays of fireworks is held over an island in the middle of the Tamsui River. You can watch the fireworks from Huanho S Rd near the Chunghsing Bridge; they start around 7.30 pm, but get there earlier to secure a good viewing place. The fireworks run for one hour.

Buses that go here include Nos 0-East, 0-West, 0-South, 3, 5, 18, 38, 204, 209, 227, 235, 236, 241, 244, 251, 270 and 604.

Sun Yatsen Memorial Hall
(guófù jì niàn guăn) 國父紀念館
The Sun Yatsen Memorial Hall is an interesting place for history buffs, as it is stocked with many photographs taken during the early part of the 20th century in mainland China. Dr Sun Yatsen is an important figure in China's history. He is highly regarded as a national hero and the father of his country due to the key role he played in the 1911 revolution and the creation of the Republic of China. He is revered by both the KMT and the Communist Party for his role in overthrowing China's last dynasty.

The Sun Yatsen Memorial Hall contains an auditorium used for staging cultural events. The memorial is on Jenai Rd, Section 4, near the ROC Tourism Bureau.

Buses which stop close to the Sun Yatsen Memorial Hall are Nos 31, 212, 232, 235, 240, 254, 259, 263, 266, 270, 281, 282, 504 and the Chunghsiao Rd bus line. Bus No 212, from Taipei train station, is probably the most frequent.

Martyrs' Shrine
(zhōng liè cí) 忠烈祠
The Martyrs' Shrine is a fairly peaceful place with colourful buildings set against a backdrop of hills. It was built to honour those who died in various wars fighting for the ROC. There are two rifle-toting members of the military police who stand guard at the gate in formal dress – absolutely rigid, not moving a muscle or blinking an eye – while tourists harass them. It's a testament to these guys that they don't run amok and bayonet a few of their camera-clicking tormenters.

The changing of the guards is quite a spectacle – too bad you can't ask the guards just what time this occurs. It seems to be about once every two hours and the whole elaborate ceremony takes about 10 minutes. You can march with the guards if you wish – there's always some tourists who do this, and none (so far) have been reprimanded.

The Martyrs' Shrine is just under a 10 minute walk east along Peian Rd from the Grand Hotel. You can get there on bus No 213, 247, 267 or 287.

Chiang Kaishek Memorial
(zhōngzhèng jì niàn táng) 中正紀念堂站
The Chiang Kaishek Memorial is a large walled compound fronted by a traditional Chinese arched gate. Within the walls is a large park dominated by the towering **Chiang Kaishek Memorial Hall**, a huge and ornate piece of architecture which some of the generalissimo's critics sarcastically refer to as the 'Chiang Kaishek Temple'. Inside the hall is a white statue of Chiang Kaishek, and downstairs you'll find a museum devoted to his acheivements.

Also inside the compound is the **National**

Concert Hall (*guójiā yīnyuè tīng*) and the **National Theatre** (*guójiā xìjù yuàn*).

In the morning, the park is a very popular venue for joggers and practitioners of *taijiquan* (Chinese shadow boxing). During the Lantern Festival (two weeks after Chinese New Year), the Chiang Kaishek Memorial is illuminated at night with thousands of coloured lights and fireworks.

The Chiang Kaishek Memorial is on Hsinyi Rd, Section 1. The main hall is open daily from 9 am until 5 pm. Buses which pass nearby are Nos 18, 20, 22, 48, 60, 70, 204, 209, 236, 237 and the Hsinyi Rd line.

Lin Antai Old Homestead
(*lín āntài gǔcuò jiǎnjiè*) 林安泰古厝簡介
This fully restored traditional Taiwanese homestead is remarkable for simply having survived amidst Taipei's urban building boom. Most of the building materials were imported from mainland China's Fujian province.

The traditional Taiwanese house follows the design seen in mainland China. A three sided courtyard (*sānhéyuán*) is the most common style, though in crowded urban areas you might find a fully enclosed courtyard (*sìhéyuán*). Traditional houses were built with the principles of Chinese geomancy in mind – the entrance, for example, had to face south-west. Until recently, there were many such houses in Taiwan, but these days the Taiwanese prefer modern concrete boxes. If you explore the remote mountain areas of Taiwan you can still find traditional houses, but they are not easily accessible and most are in poor condition. Without preservation efforts, this style of architecture seems destined to disappear.

There are some temples which predate it, but the Lin Antai Homestead is the oldest residential building in Taipei. The original dwelling was built in 1783, and this was gradually expanded over the generations as the family's size grew. It reached its present size in 1823.

The structure was not always at its present site. Originally, it was built in Taipei's Ta'an district several kilometres to the south. It would have been demolished in 1978 during the widening of Tunhua S Rd, but officials were persuaded to preserve it. The preservation proved to be more difficult than anyone had imagined – the whole building had to be dismantled brick by brick, in reverse order of construction. The roof came down first, followed by the walls, floors and foundations. Every piece had to be numbered, blueprints had to be made, everything had to be carefully packed away and then it was stored.

In 1984, the decision to reconstruct the building in Pinchiang Park (*bīnjiāng gōngyuán*) in the Chungshan district, just east of Hsinsheng N Rd, and north of Mintsu E Rd was made. The only unfortunate thing about this is that it's right under the landing path for Sungshan airport – aircraft come in so low it's a wonder they don't knock the chimney off.

Buses that can take you to the homestead include Nos 33, 222, 279, 283 and 286. Bus No 222 is probably most convenient – you can catch it from Chungshan S Rd. If you're feeling energetic, you could walk from the Fine Arts Museum. Admission is free.

City Gates
Looking at Taipei's skycrapers and bustling streets today, it's almost hard to imagine that it was once a small village. It was – like most sizable villages in ancient China – surrounded by a wall with gates that were closed at night. The wall has long disappeared, but two gates have survived the urban onslaught. The largest is the North Gate (*běi mén*) at the intersection of Chunghsiao W and Yenping Rds. The other is the Little South Gate (*xiǎo nán mén*) at Aikuo W and Yenping S Rds. Neither gate is terribly impressive – the North Gate looks especially forlorn buried beneath an on-ramp to the Chunghsiao Bridge. Still, if you're in the neighbourhood, it is worth pausing for a few moments to see the gates and reflect on just how much Taipei has changed over the last century.

Chiang Kaishek's Former Estate
(*shìlín guāndǐ*) 士林官邸
Chiang Kaishek fled the Chinese mainland

in 1949 and made this palatial estate his home until his death in 1975.

The estate remained closed to the public until 1996, when Taipei's Mayor Chen Shuibian decided to turn it into a park. This set off a legal dispute with Chiang's wife, Soong Mayling, who, at nearly 100 years of age, was still alive even at the time of the research of this book. Soong claims title to the property. However, Mayor Chen made the case that the land was 'stolen' from the citizens of Taiwan.

At present, the solution has been a compromise. The estate's grounds are open to the public, but Madame Soong retains title to the family home which is gated, guarded and definitely off limits to the public. No one actually lives in the house – Madame Soong lives in New York.

The estate has been a big hit with tourists, and Mayor Chen certainly got a lot of popular political support by gaining control of it for the citizens of Taipei. It's definitely worth visiting, if for no other reason than to see how well Chiang and family lived.

The estate is in the Shihlin district, a short walk east of Chungshan N Rd, Section 5. Buses running up Chungshan Rd pass by, including bus Nos 61, 203, 220, 260, 267, 279, 280, 285, 310 and 606. The grounds are open on weekdays from 8.30 am until 5 pm, and from 8 am to 6 pm on weekends and holidays. For more information on the estate, call the management office (☎ 2881-2512/ 2881-2912).

2-28 Peace Park
(èrèrbā hépíng gōngyuán) 二二八和平公園
Once known as 'New Park' the name was changed in 1997 by Taipei's Mayor, Chen Shuibian. The park's new theme is to honour anti-Kuomintang (KMT) protestors and innocent bystanders who were murdered in the military crackdown that began on 28 February 1947.

The pleasant tree-shaded grounds contain a lake, a pagoda, pavilions and an increasing number of 2-28 memorabilia. On the north side of the park is the **Taiwan Provincial Museum** (☎ 2397-9396; shěnglì bówùguǎn)

at 2 Hsiangyang Rd. This has interesting displays of artefacts made by Taiwan's aborigines. Of special interest is an excellent, well organised display of herbs on the main floor. The museum is open from 9 am to 5 pm Tuesday to Sunday.

This park was also the venue for Taiwan's first Gay Pride Festival in 1997. The park is within walking distance of the Taipei train station.

Botanical Gardens
(zhíwù yuán) 植物園
The Botanical Gardens, on Nanhai Rd, south of the central area, are a pleasant retreat from the noisy city. There is a beautiful lotus pond in the gardens; it's one of those adjacent to the **National Museum of History** (☎ 2361-0270; lìshǐ bówù guǎn), **National Science Hall** (kēxué guǎn) and **National Arts Hall** (yìshù guǎn) – all of which are worth looking into.

Travellers give the National Museum of History high marks. It's sort of a scaled-down version of the National Palace Museum. It has a good pottery collection and is open daily from 9 am to 5 pm; admission is NT$20 for adults (half price for students). You can get there on bus Nos 0-West, 1 and 204.

Children's Recreation Centre
(értóng yùlè zhōngxīn) 兒童育樂中心
As the name implies, the Children's Recreation Centre (☎ 2593-2211) is for kids. It's basically a park divided into two sections, the World of Yesterday and World of Tomorrow. The World of Yesterday has an ancient Chinese village, statues depicting the life of Taiwan's aborigines and a kiddie's entertainment area. The World of Tomorrow reminds me of an old TV show called 'Mr Wizard', in which general science was introduced. This place is built on the site of the former Taipei Zoo (an opposition legislator once suggested that the National Assembly should be moved here!).

The Children's Recreation Centre is opposite the Fine Arts Museum, so you can use the same transport to get here. It's open daily from 9 am to 5 pm. Admission costs NT$30 for adults and NT$15 for children. Also here is the **Space Theatre** (*tàikōng jùchǎng*) which seats 500 people and charges an additional NT$100 for adults and NT$50 for children. If you purchase a Space Theatre ticket you get into the rest of the facilities for free. There are additional costs for various kiddie rides within the recreation centre.

Topview Taipei Observatory
(*xīnguāng mótiān zhǎnwàngtái*)
新光摩天展望台
On the top (46th) floor of the Shin Kong Life Insurance building there is an observatory (☎ 2388-6132) which offers a great vantage point to look out on the city's smog and overcast skies. However, the weather does occasionally cooperate, and when it does you'll get a nice view of the traffic-clogged streets 244m below.

The Shin Kong Life Insurance building towers above the Mitsukoshi Department Store at 66 Chunghsiao W Rd, Section 1. This is directly opposite (south of) the Taipei train station. The observatory is open from 11 am to 10 pm on weekdays, 10 am to 10 pm on weekends and holidays. Admission costs NT$120.

Movie Studio
(*zhōngyǐng wénhuà chéng*) 中影文化城
Also known by its official name of the China Motion Picture Cultural Village (☎ 2881-7886/2882-1022), the Movie Studio is within walking distance of the National Palace Museum, in the Waishuanghsi neighbourhood of the Shihlin district, and therefore is easy to visit. Basically, it's a movie set where the buildings are all designed in the traditional style of ancient China. If you watch TV in Taiwan, you are sure to see some Chinese kungfu dramas – this is where they are filmed. The buildings are a good introduction to Cinese architecture and you may also have the chance to see some filming. There is also a wax museum (*làxiàng guǎn*).

The movie set is open to public daily from 8.30 am to 10 pm. Admission for adults costs NT$200, but student discounts are available.

There is an attached cinema that charges an additional NT$100 if you purchase the ticket separately, or you can buy a combined ticket to the Movie Studio and the cinema for NT$270.

The studio is a 10 minute walk heading west from the National Palace Museum, on your left-hand side. The official address is 34 Chihshan Rd, Section 2, Shihlin, and a big sign in Chinese (no English) marks the spot. Right next to the Movie Studio is Soochow University (*dōngwú dàxué*), but there isn't much to see there.

Fin's Sealife Taipei
(*táiběi hǎiyáng shēnghuó guǎn*)
台北海洋生活馆
Although it's crammed into a small space, this aquarium has 15 large tanks (so far) housing over 200 species of marine creatures. There is an underwater passage that you walk through to see fish swimming above. The aquarium (☎ 2880-3636), 128 Chiho Rd, Shihlin district, gets good ratings from most visitors. The easiest way to get there is via subway to the Chientan station. Admission to the aquarium costs NT$300 for adults, NT$250 for students. Opening hours are from 9 am to 10 pm daily.

Markets
Section 1 of Tihua St (*díhuà jiē*) is known for its many shops specialising in dried foods and Chinese herbs. It's an old part of Taipei, and though it looks somewhat worse for wear, it's a very interesting neighbourhood to visit. It's particularly interesting from about noon to 10 pm during the two weeks preceding Chinese New Year, when it's thronged with shoppers. The market area is along the same part of Tihua St as Chenghuang Temple.

Also very interesting is Huayin St (*huáyīn jiē*), just to the north of the North bus station. This street and some of the adjacent alleys are a treasure trove of everything from shoes, clothes and handbags to tools, clocks and motorcycle accessories. Take a good look into Lane 220, Chang'an W Rd, which intersects with Huayin St.

In Neihu, a suburban district to the north-east of Taipei, is the hypermarket Makro (*wànkèlóng*). If you wish to shop here you must be an authorised reseller with a membership card.

Chienkuo Holiday Flower Market This colourful outdoor market (*jià rì huā shì*) is held on Saturday, when there are relatively few customers, but expands enormously on Sunday and holidays. The market is held under an overpass on Chienkuo S Rd, between Jenai and Hsinyi Rds. Buses which stop nearby include Nos 36, 37, 48, 65, 263, 270, 275 and 298 and those on the Hsinyi and Jenai Rds lines. The operating hours are roughly from 10 am until 8 pm.

Chienkuo Holiday Jade Market This market (*jià rì yù shì*) is underneath the overpass at the section of Pateh and Hsinsheng S Rds. Even if you don't want to buy jade, it's interesting to come here and look.

Snake Alley Although it's a bit like a carnival, many people still like to visit Huahsi Night Market, better known as Snake Alley (*huáxī jiē*). The presence of busloads of tourists has driven up prices in this very lively night market, but the atmosphere more than makes up for this.

What you get for your inflated tourist dollars is the opportunity to see skilled snake handlers playing with real live cobras as if they were wind-up toys. You can sample snake soup or drink a cup of snake bile – definitely not for the squeamish, nor are they cheap. This is also the place to stock up on snake-penis pills and powdered gall bladder. Because Chinese herbalists claim that snake meat acts as an aphrodisiac (see the Herbal Medicine boxed text in the Facts for the Visitor chapter), Snake Alley has long been associated with brothels. However, the brothels have been shut down, which has no doubt hit the market for aphrodisiacs.

Even if you're not in the market for a reptile's gall bladder, Snake Alley is a busy night market. Particularly good buys here are the cheap music cassettes (see Music in the

Facts for the Visitor chapter), though they mostly offer Chinese music. The market gets going around 7 pm and closes sometime after midnight. The market is in the Wanhua area and you can get there on bus No 0-West, 25, 38, 49, 65, 231, 242, 264, 265, 310 or 601.

Night Markets One of the oldest and largest evening markets is the **Shihlin Night Market** (*shìlín yèshì*). It's to the north-west of the Grand Hotel, just to the west of Wenlin Rd and starting from the south side of Chungcheng Rd. This market is open during the day, but it really comes alive around 7 pm and normally shuts down from around 10 to 11 pm – even later on weekends.

The **Tunghua Night Market** (*tōnghuà jiē yèshì*) is in east Taipei, one block south of Hsinyi Rd, Section 4, between Tunhua and Keelung Rds. This long alley is one big eating orgy in the evenings.

The **Jaoho St Night Market** (*ráohé jiē yèshì*) is in the Sungshan district at the northern end of Keelung Rd. This is one of the newest and largest markets in the city.

The **Kungguan Night Market** (*gōngguǎn yèshì*), Roosevelt Rd, Section 4, by Hsinsheng S Rd and National Taiwan University, is popular with students. The 'market' is a collection of stores and sidewalk vendors spread through small alleys. The same applies to **Shihta Rd Night Market** (*shīdà lù yèshì*) by Taiwan Normal University.

Exercise Clubs
If late-night carousing is running you down, you can get back in shape at various health and fitness centres around town.

The Arts Health Club (*yàlìshāndà jiànkāng xiūxián jùlèbù*) is open to both men and women, offering heated swimming pools, saunas, exercise machines and dance classes – this is a place to pamper yourself. It's also one of the most expensive clubs in Taipei and the facilities are posh. Membership costs from NT$5000 per month to NT$32,000 per year – obviously the annual fee is a much better deal for long termers. There are four branches around town: Nankang (☎ 2660-0033); Chunghsiao (☎ 2762-3866); Tachih

(☎ 2532-5588) and Hsinyi (☎ 2345-5155); The company's main office is in the basement at 163 Keelung Rd, Section 1.

Wally Gym (☎ 729-3809), 2nd floor, 13 Keelung Rd, Section 2, has become a popular place with expats. The first three month membership costs NT$5500, and it's NT$4000 per quarter thereafter. The gym is open daily from 10 am to 11 pm and is close to the World Trade Centre.

The Clark Hatch Fitness Centre (☎ 2741-6670), 86 Tunhua S Rd, Section 1, is one of many branches in various corners of the world.

Saunas

A couple of blocks north of Taipei train station is the Tianlong Sauna (☎ 2522-2277; *tiānlóng sān wēn nuǎn*), 8th floor, 73 Chungching N Rd, Section 1. It's for men only and it costs NT$500 to spend the whole night there.

Eliza Plaza (*yīlìshā shìnǚ xiūxián guǎngchǎng*) is a 24 hour women's sauna which has three branches in Taipei: the Chienkuo branch (☎ 2506-9045), basement, 120 Chienkuo N Rd, Section 2; Fuhsing branch (☎ 2516-0191), 400 Fuhsing N Rd (at Minchuan E Rd); and Jenai branch (☎ 2705-2002), basement, 5 Lane 112, Jenai Rd, Section 4.

Swimming

There is an outdoor swimming pool in Youth Park (*qīngnián gōngyuán*) in south-west Taipei, but expats really like the swimming pool in Tiemu. All outdoor pools are open during the summer months only. Some of the big hotels have an arrangement whereby you can pay a monthly fee which gains you access to their swimming pools, tennis courts, exercise rooms and other recreational facilities.

Tenpin Bowling

The most popular tenpin bowling venue with Taipei's expat community is Yuanshan Sports Centre (☎ 2881-2277; *yuánshān bǎolíng qiúguǎn*), 3rd floor, 6 Chungshan N Rd, Section 5, Shihlin, near the Grand Hotel. This place also boasts a snack bar, pool,

rollerblades, roller disco, air hockey, video games and (brace yourself) karaoke.

Bungy Jumping

Bungee International (☎ 2332-5523; fax 2366-1674) has an office on the 7th floor, 98 Hsinsheng S Rd, Section 3 (near National Taiwan University). The club travels to wherever they can find a convenient bridge or crane to jump from (most often in Taoyuan County). The cost is NT$2000 for the first jump and NT$1000 for each jump thereafter. Bungee International is also expanding into water-skiing and 'skurfing' (surfing on a board pulled by a jetski). Contact the club for full details.

Hash House Harriers

This club is mainly for foreign residents of Taipei – if you're just passing through you might not be enthusiastically welcomed. Hash House Harriers is a loosely strung international club with branches all over the world. It appeals mainly to young people, or the young at heart. Activities typically include a weekend afternoon easy jog followed by a dinner and beer party which can carry on until the wee hours of the morning.

Taipei's Hash is very informal – there is no club headquarters and no stable contact telephone or address. The best place to find the Hash is to look in the monthly magazine *This Month in Taiwan*.

That disclaimer given, there is usually a run held every Saturday at 2 pm, and every Sunday at noon. The usual meeting place is the Post Home Restaurant (☎ 2835-6991), 32 Lane 35, Chungshan N Rd, Section 6. This is just behind Ricardo Lynn Furniture (*qiáodà jiājù*) at the corner of Fukuo and Chungshan N Rds. Again, you should always call ahead to check this – otherwise, you might be the only one to show up.

Computer Clubs

The Taipei User's Group (TUG) is the largest English-speaking club for computer users in Taiwan. Theoretically there are meetings every month, though sometimes this doesn't happen. You can receive information on the club by calling ☎ 2695-2318.

ClubMac is, of course, for Macintosh users. Contact Wolfgang Schubert (☎ 2895-3452; fax 2894-9894) for further details.

Toastmasters

This is an informal club with meetings at varying times all over Taipei. It's mainly a chance for the locals to practise their English by giving speeches on some topic of interest. It's a good way to socialise with the locals and the odd foreigner who shows up.

Look in *This Month in Taiwan* or the *Taipei Pocket Guide* for details.

Language Courses

If you wish to study in Taipei it's possible to get a foreign university degree credit through the Stanford Centre, but applications must be made six months prior to the start of the term in September – it is much easier to gain admission to other schools in Taipei. The Mandarin Training Centre at Taiwan Normal University has a rigorous and competitive program which many students swear by.

Following is a list of language centres licensed to teach Chinese to foreigners:

Chinese Cultural University
(☎ 2356-7356) Mandarin Learning Centre, 6th floor, 9 Roosevelt Rd, Section 2
Chinese Language Development Association
(☎ 2312-1313/2312-0632; email aperfect@ms15.hinet.net) 4th floor, 1-2 Wuchang St, Section 1
Flag Language Institute
(☎ 2331-3000/2311-1100) Room 1, 3rd floor, 61 Yenping S Rd
Mandarin Daily News
(☎ 2391-5134) 100 Fuchou St
My School
(☎ 2394-5400; email mayya@tpts5.seed.net.tw) 2nd floor, 126-8 Hsinsheng S Rd, Section 1
Pioneer Language Institute
(☎ 2363-3535/2363-3849) 6th floor, 200 Hoping E Rd, Section 1
Stanford Centre
(☎ 2363-9123) Inter-University Program, c/o National Taiwan University, 1 Roosevelt Rd (PO Box 13-204, Taipei)
Taipei Language Institute (TLI)
(email: tli@transend.com.tw)

Roosevelt Rd (☎ 2367-8228)
Hsinyi Rd (☎ 2341-0022)
Kaohsiung branch (☎ (07) 215-2965)
Shihlin district (☎ 2832-8256)
Taichung branch (☎ (04) 225-4681)
Taiwan Normal University
(☎ 2391-4248) Mandarin Training Centre, 129 Hoping E Rd, Section 1
Tamkang University Language Centre
(☎ 2356-7356) 18 Lishui St (by Taiwan Normal University), Ta'an district
Wendy's Office
(☎ 2371-8277, 2705-9768) Room 6, 4th floor, 41 Chunghsiao W Rd, Section 1

Places to Stay – budget

In expensive Taipei, budget defines any place with rooms costing NT$1000 or less per night.

Hostels There are a number of privately operated hostels in Taipei, and they all charge similar prices. Most of the beds are in dormitory-style rooms although there are a few private rooms (the latter fill up quickly). The hotel reception area at CKS international airport has name cards for the hostels (which is helpful as they often have a map on the back).

The *Happy Family Hostel I* (☎ 2375-3443) is on the 4th floor, 16-1 Peiping W Rd, about a stone's throw from Taipei train station. The friendly management make an effort to keep it clean in spite of the constant flow of travellers. Dorm beds here cost NT$220 and there are a couple of single rooms costing NT$320. There are discounts available for weekly and monthly rentals.

Under the same management is the *Happy Family Hostel II* (☎ 2562-1735/2563-3341), 2-1 Lane 56, Chungshan N Rd, Section 1; it's a short walk away from the train station, look for the small sign that says 'HF'. This is in fact the main hostel, larger than Happy I, and the facilities are better here. The place has a very homey feel and has a washing machine and kitchen. Dorm beds cost NT$240, and there are several private single rooms that cost from NT$350 to NT$450. Doubles cost NT$550. Again, ask about long term rates.

Another clean and well-managed hostel is the *Formosa Hostel I* (☎ 2562-2035), 3rd floor, 16 Lane 20, Chungshan N Rd, Section 2. Bookings should be arranged through the *Formosa Hostel II* (☎ 2511-6744), 2nd floor, 5 Lane 62, Chungshan N Rd, Section 2, which is where the manager lives. Facilities at both hostels include a kitchen and washing machine. Dorm beds cost NT$200 per day. Single rooms are available for NT$350 per day, and twins (actually two-bed dorms) cost NT$230 per person per day. Ask about discounts for weekly rentals.

The *Amigo Hostel* (☎ 2542-0292/2571-0612), 4th floor, 235 Chilin Rd is also a good deal. It's clean, has air-con and a TV and video. From the train station take bus No 502 and get off at the corner of Minchuan E Rd and Chilin Rd, opposite the Ritz Landis Hotel (*yàdū dà fàndiàn*). Bus No 49 from the train station also stops nearby. Dorm beds cost NT$220.

The *Taipei Hostel* (☎ 2395-2950), 6th floor, 11 Lane 5, Linsen N Rd, is the oldest hostel in Taipei and it shows. This is the bottom end of budget hostels in Taiwan, but at least it's cheap. Dorm beds cost NT$200 and singles/doubles cost NT$400/450 daily. Like all the other hostels, there are discounts for long termers.

CYC Hostels China Youth Corps (CYC) operates two hostels (dubbed youth activity centres) which are intended for students and rarely have room for travellers. Foreigners are welcome, but most of those who stay here are tour groups of overseas Chinese. The prices for doubles and twins are really not much cheaper than a lower end hotel. The group rooms (basically dormitories) are cheap but are designed for group use – if you can round up five friends then it's a great deal. There are telephones and TVs in each room, plus air-con and plenty of hot water. The facilities are very clean.

Nearby is the granddaddy of all KMT hostels, the *Chientan Youth Activity Centre* (☎ 2596-2151; fax 2595-1861; *jiàntán qīngnián huódòng zhōngxīn*), 16 Chungshan N Rd, Section 4. Doubles cost NT$1300 per room, quads cost NT$1900, six-bed dorms are NT$2200 (NT$366 per person) and

eight-bed dorms are NT$2400 (NT$300 per person).

Taipei International Youth Activity Centre (TIYAC; ☎ 2362-1770; fax 2363-4104; *táiběi guójì qīngnián huódòng zhōngxīn*), 30 Hsinhai Rd, Section 3, serves as the headquarters for all KMT hostels. Many foreign students studying at the nearby National Taiwan University base themselves here. Twins cost from NT$800 to NT$1300, five-bed dorms cost NT$1250 (NT$250 per person).

Hotels Huaining St (*huáiníng jiē*) is south of the train station and is the happy hunting ground for relatively cheap hotels. One of the best bargains is the *Paradise Hotel* (☎ 2331-3311; *nánguó dà fàndiàn*), 7 Huaining St, where doubles cost between NT$700 and NT$800. Just across the street is the very plush-looking *Chuan Chia Huam Hotel* (☎ 2381-4755; *quánjiā huān bīnguǎn*), 4th floor, 6 Huaining St, where doubles cost from NT$1000 to NT$1200.

One block to the west is Chungking S Rd, which has a few places worth checking out. The *New Mayflower Hotel* (☎ 2311-0212; *huáměi dà fàndiàn*), 1 Chungching S Rd, Section 1, has doubles for NT$1000.

Further west is the *East Dragon Hotel* (☎ 2311-6969; *dōnglóng dà fàndiàn*), 23 Hankou St, Section 2, which is slightly plusher. Doubles cost from NT$1080 to NT$1320, twins cost from NT$1320 to NT$1600 and suites cost NT$2400. Facilities here include foreign currency exchange and a coffee shop.

Chang'an W Rd, one block north of Taipei train station, is another place to look for cheap hotels. One of the cheapest in the neighbourhood is the *Queen Hotel* (☎ 2559-0489; *huánghòu bīnguǎn*) on the 2nd floor at No 226. Doubles cost from NT$600 to NT$700. There's no English sign, so look out for the street number.

Very close to the Queen is the *Dragon Garden Hotel* (☎ 2556-7576; *lóngyuán dà fàndiàn*), 55-57 Taiyuan Rd. At NT$650 for a double, it's an excellent bargain.

The *Fortune Hotel* (☎ 2555-1121; *fújūn*

dà fàndiàn), 62 Chungching N Rd, Section 1 (at Chang'an W Rd), is a large place that frequently accommodates budget tour groups though they usually have room for individual travellers. Doubles are NT$1050.

Also in this vicinity is the *Senator Hotel* (☎ 2558-6511; *xìnzhōu dà fàndiàn*), 83 Chang'an W Rd, where doubles cost from NT$1000 to NT$2000. The same people run the *Hotel 6F* (☎ 2555-1130; *yínbǎo bīnguǎn*), on the 6th floor at 251 Chang'an W Rd; doubles cost from NT$850 to NT$1000. Both hotels are clean and pleasant enough, but the Senator has a better location.

One alley to the north of the Taipei Hostel, at 12 Lane 9, Linsen N Rd, is the *Life Hotel* (☎ 2391-5271; *láifú bīnguǎn*) which has doubles for NT$800.

Places to Stay – middle

By Taipei standards, a 'mid-range' hotel should have at least some double rooms in the NT$1100 to NT$3000 range. Most of the hotels listed have minimum facilities which include: swimming pools; conference and business facilities, travel and laundry services, foreign currency exchange, bars, restaurants, coffee shops and some even have karaoke.

Check with the hotels directly if you have specific requirements and be sure to ask about discounts – many hotels have special deals, especially if you're staying three or more days (look over the room carefully first to be sure you want to stay that long).

The *Delight Hotel* (☎ 2565-2155; *dàxīn dà fàndiàn*), 2-2 Lane 27, Chungshan N Rd, Section 2, is in a quiet alley. Its low price puts it almost, but not quite, into the budget range. Double rooms cost between NT$1190 and NT$1680.

The *Keyman's Hotel* (☎ 2311-4811; fax 2311-5212; *huáiníng lǚdiàn*), 1 Huaining St, is an excellent little business hotel just south of Taipei train station. The price here ranges from NT$1730 to NT$2660.

Just next door to Keyman's is the *Royal Hotel* (☎ 2311-1668; *huángjiā dà fàndiàn*), 5-1 Huaining St with doubles for NT$1250.

Cosmos Hotel (☎ 2361-7856; *tiānchéng*

dà fàndiàn), 43 Chunghsiao W Rd, Section 3, has good facilities and is the closest mid-range hotel to Taipei train station. Doubles cost from NT$1800 to NT$2400, twins from NT$2200 to NT$2800 and suites between NT$4000 and NT$4500.

The *Baguio Hotel* (☎ 2781-3121; *bìyáo dà fàndiàn*), 367 Pateh Rd, Section 2, is superb for this price range and gets good reviews from most travellers. Doubles/twins/suites cost NT$2300/2600/3000.

The *Beauty Hotel* (☎ 2541-6148; *měide dà fàndiàn*) is at 56 Changchun Rd. Doubles cost from NT$1600 to NT$2000 and twins cost from NT$2200 to NT$3500. Facilities here are on the lean side with not much more than a restaurant.

The *Capital Hotel* (☎ 2507-0168; *shǒudū dà fàndiàn*), 187 Changchun Rd, is a relatively large mid-range place. Doubles cost between NT$2700 and NT$3700 and twins/suites cost NT$3500/4000.

Very close to the Capital is the *City Hotel* (☎ 2501-7601; *bevichéng dà fàndiàn*), 279 Changchun Rd, with good business facilities. Doubles/twins are NT$2800/3200.

The *Charming City Hotel* (☎ 2704-9546; *xiāngchéng dà fàndiàn*), 295 Hsinyi Rd, Section 4, has doubles from NT$2060 to NT$2460, and twins/suites for NT$2560/2660.

The *Hotel Dynasty* (☎ 2708-1221; *cháodài dà fàndiàn*), 41 Fuhsing S Rd, Section 2, has complete facilities and gets very good reviews. Doubles/twins/suites are NT$3200/3600/4800.

The *Golden Palace Hotel* (☎ 2531-6171; *jīnfú dà fàndiàn*), 8th to 11th floors, 1 Nanking W Rd, is a large place. Doubles cost between NT$1800 and NT$2200 and twins cost from NT$2000 to NT$2800.

The *Pan American Hotel* (☎ 2314-7305; *fànměi dà fàndiàn*), 88 Hankou St, Section 1, has doubles from NT$1340 to NT$1755 and twins from NT$1940 to NT$3550. The facilities here are slim considering the prices charged; there's only a restaurant and travel and laundry services.

The *Hotel China Taipei* (☎ 2331-9521; fax 2381-2349; *zhōngguó dà fàndiàn*), 14 Kuanchien Rd, is large, plush and very close to Taipei train station. Doubles/twins/suites cost NT$2500/2700/4000.

The *Empress Hotel* (☎ 2591-3261; fax 2592-2922; *dìhòu dà fàndiàn*), 14 Tehuei St, has doubles/twins for NT$2600/NT$3200 and suites for NT$5000.

The *First Hotel* (☎ 2541-8234; fax 2551-2277; *dìyī dà fàndiàn*), 63 Nanking E Rd, Section 2, has doubles from NT$2300 to NT$2700, twins from NT$2900 to NT$3200 and suites cost from NT$4600 to NT$6500.

Hotel Flowers (☎ 2312-3811; fax 2312-3800; *huáhuá dà fàndiàn*), 19 Hankou St, Section 1, is central and close to the Taipei train station. Doubles and twins cost from NT$2400 to NT$3000 and suites cost from NT$3500 to NT$5000.

The *Gala Hotel* (☎ 2541-5511; fax 2531-3831; *qìngtài dà fàndiàn*), 186 Sungchiang Rd, is a very serviceable business hotel, with Doubles/twins/suites for NT$3000/3200/4800.

The *Best Western Kilin Hotel* (☎ 2314-9222; fax 2331-8133; *qílín dà fàndiàn*), 103 Kangting Rd, has doubles for NT$1800, twins from NT$2200 to NT$3200 and suites from NT$3200 to NT$4000.

The *Astar Hotel* (☎ 2551-3131; *yàshìdū fàndiàn*), 98 Linsen N Rd, has doubles/twins/singles for NT$2000/2200/2800.

The *Merlin Court Hotel* (☎ 2521-0222; fax 2551-0521; *huámào dà fàndiàn*), 15 Lane 83, Chungshan N Rd, Section 1, is on a relatively quiet lane. Doubles/twins cost NT$2500/2800.

The *Hotel New Asia* (☎ 2511-7181; fax 2522-4204; *xīnyà dà fàndiàn*), 139 Chungshan N Rd, Section 2, has a good range of facilities. Doubles/twins cost NT$2300/2500 and suites cost from NT$3600 to NT$4600.

The *YMCA* (☎ 2311-3201; *jīdūjiào qīngnián huì bīnguǎn*), 19 Hsuchang St, is big with visiting youth groups and boasts a very central location near the Taipei train station. Doubles cost from NT$1500 to NT$1700 and twins cost from NT$1700 to NT$1900.

The *Emperor Hotel* (☎ 2581-1111; fax 2531-2586; *guówáng dà fàndiàn*), 118 Nanking E Rd, Section 1 has doubles/twins for NT$3000/3200 and suites for NT$6800.

This place has good facilties and credit cards are accepted.

The *Hotel China Yangmingshan* (☎ 2861-6661; fax 2861-3885; *yángmíngshān zhōng guó dà fàndiàn*), 237 Ketzu Rd, is up in the hill near Yangmingshan National Park. It has complete facilities, which are especially worthwhile if you like sports (there are tennis courts, a swimming pool and hot springs) and clean air. This place can compete with some of the top-end hotels, the only drawback being the distance from town. Doubles cost NT$3000, twins cost between NT$3200 and NT$3600 and suites cost from NT$7000 to NT$10,000.

Places to Stay – top end

Many upmarket hotels impose an additional 10% service charge and 5% Value-Added Tax (VAT) onto their quoted prices. On the other hand, you may be able to negotiate lower prices than those quoted here. All places accept credit cards. All of the hotels listed have standard services which include: car parking, airport transfers, foreign currency exchange service, business and conference facilities, coffee shops, bars, resataurants, hair salons, gymnasiums, swimming pools, travel and laundry services and shopping arcades. Some even have women's and non-smoking floors. Check with the hotel if you require a specific facility.

The *Ambassador Hotel* (☎ 2555-1111; fax 2561-7883; *guóbīn dà fàndiàn*), 63 Chungshan N Rd, Section 2 has doubles/twins/suites for NT$5200/5800/12,000.

The *Asia Pacific Hotel* (☎ 2772-2121; fax 2721-0302; *yàtài dà fàndiàn*), 172 Chunghsiao E Rd, Section 4, has doubles/twins for NT$3570/4620.

The *Asiaworld Plaza Hotel* (☎ 2715-0077; fax 2713-4148; *huányǎ dà fàndiàn*), 100 Tunhua N Rd, is the second largest hotel in Taipei. Twins cost from NT$5800 to NT$7700 and suites cost from NT$11,500 to NT$140,000.

The *Brother Hotel* (☎ 2712-3456; fax 2717-3334; *xiōngdì dà fàndiàn*), 255 Nanking E Rd, Section 3, charges from NT$3800 to NT$4600 for doubles and NT$4600/8500 for twins/suites.

The *Far Eastern Plaza Hotel* (☎ 2378-8888; fax 2377-7777; *yuǎndōng guójì dà fàndiàn*), 201 Tunhua S Rd, Section 2, is phenomenal – 43 storeys of luxury complete with swimming pool on the roof. Doubles and twins cost from NT$6900 to NT$9000 and suites from NT$10,000 to NT$59,000. This place has a 130 shop arcade.

The *Fortuna Hotel* (☎ 2563-1111; fax 2561-9777; *fùdū dà fàndiàn*), 122 Chungshan N Rd, Section 2, is a very serviceable business hotel. Doubles cost from NT$3400 to NT$3800, twins are from NT$3800 to NT$4200 and suites cost from NT$6500 to NT$23,100.

The *Gloria Hotel* (☎ 2581-8111; fax 2581-5811; *huátài dà fàndiàn*), 369 Linsen N Rd has doubles for NT$3600, twins from NT$4150 to NT$4600 and suites from NT$5700 to NT$9000.

The *Golden China Hotel* (☎ 2521-5151; fax 2531-2914; *kānghuá dà fàndiàn*), 306 Sungchiang Rd, has twin rooms costing from NT$3200 to NT$3600 and suites from NT$7000 to NT$10,000.

The *Grand Hotel* (☎ 2596-5565; fax 2594-8243; *yuánshān dà fàndiàn*), 1 Chungshan N Rd, Section 4, has spacious grounds and looks like a Chinese palace. It's so attractive that tourists come here just to take photos of the ornate exterior. The lowest priced rooms fall into the mid-range price category because they are in the centre of the hotel so don't have windows, but all the other rooms have magnificent views which is one of the reasons to stay here. Doubles cost NT$3000, twins cost from NT$4000 to NT$7000 and suites cost from NT$8000 to NT$10,000.

The *Grand Hyatt Hotel* (☎ 2720-1234; fax 2720-1111; *kǎiyuè dà fàndiàn*), 2 Sungshou Rd (near City Hall) is the largest hotel in Taipei. Doubles and twins cost from NT$6900 to NT$8500 and suites cost from NT$9500 to NT$50,000.

The *Hilton Hotel* (☎ 2311-5151; fax 2331-9944; *xī ěrdùn dà fàndiàn*), 38 Chunghsiao W Rd, Section 1, is very centrally

located near Taipei train station. Double and twin rooms cost NT$5800 and suites are NT$7000.

The *Howard Plaza Hotel* (☎ 2700-2323; fax 2700-0729; 606 rooms; *fúhuá dà fàndiàn*), 160 Jenai Rd, Section 3, is the fourth largest hotel in Taipei and has doubles for NT$5400, twins from NT$5700 to NT$7300 and suites from NT$7600 to NT$32,000.

The *Imperial Inter-Continental Hotel* (☎ 2596-5111; fax 2592-7506; *huáguó zhōujì dà fàndiàn*), 600 Linsen N Rd, is in Taipei's pub 'Zone'. Doubles cost NT$3500, twins cost from NT$3900 to NT$4800 and suites cost from NT$5500 to NT$20,000.

The *Lai Lai Sheraton Hotel* (☎ 2321-5511; fax 2394-4240; *láilái dà fàndiàn*), 12 Chunghsiao E Rd, Section 1, is the third largest hotel in Taipei and is near the Taipei train station. Doubles/twins/suites cost NT$6000/6500/10,000.

The *Leofoo Hotel* (☎ 2507-3211; fax 2508-2070; *liùfú kèzhàn*), 168 Changchun Rd, is a business hotel. Double rooms cost from NT$4000 to NT$4400, twins cost between NT$4400 and NT$4700 and suites cost NT$8000.

The *Magnolia Hotel* (☎ 2712-1201; fax 2712-2122; *zhōngtài bīnguǎn*), 166 Tunhua N Rd, is famous for its Kiss La Boca disco, one of Taipei's largest. Doubles and twins cost NT$4800 and suites cost NT$11,800.

The *Miramar Hotel* (☎ 2505-3456; fax 2502-9173; *měilìhuá dà fàndiàn*), 2 Minchuan E Rd, Section 3, has doubles/twins/suites for NT$3800/4000/5600.

The *President Hotel* (☎ 2595-1251; fax 2591-3677; *tǒngyī dà fàndiàn*), 9 Tehuei St, is in Taipei's pub area ('the Zone'). Doubles cost from NT$3800 to NT$4500, twins cost from NT$4600 to NT$5000 and suites are from NT$5800 to NT$8500.

The *Rebar Holiday Inn Crowne Plaza* (☎ 2763-5656; fax 2767-9347; *lìbà huángguàn dà fàndiàn*), 32 Nanking E Rd, Section 5, has it all. Doubles/twins/suites cost NT$5600/6300/8000.

The *Grand Formosa Regent Hotel* (☎ 2523-8000; fax 2523-2828; *jīnghuá jiǔdiàn*), 3 Lane 39, Chungshan N Rd, Section

2, has doubles from NT$6700 to NT$7000, twins from NT$7500 to NT$8500 and suites from NT$10,000 to NT$60,000.

The *Ritz Landis Hotel* (☎ 2597-1234; fax 2596-9223; *yǎdū lìzhì dà fàndiàn*), 41 Minchuan E Rd, Section 2, has doubles/twins for NT$6000/6400 and suites from NT$7500 to NT$36,000.

The *Hotel Riverview* (☎ 2311-3131; fax 2361-3737; *háojǐng dà jiǔdiàn*), 77 Huanho S Rd, Section 1, is true to its name, though it's hard to imagine why anybody would want a view of a polluted cesspool like the Tamsui River. Doubles/twins/suites cost NT$3500/4400/8000.

The *Riviera Hotel* (☎ 2585-3258; fax 2596-5160; *ōuhuá jiǔdiàn*), 646 Linsen N Rd, is a business hotel. Doubles/twins cost NT$5000/5500 and suites cost between NT$6500 and NT$12,000.

The *Hotel Royal* (☎ 2542-3266; fax 2543-4897; *lǎoyé dajiudian*), 37-1 Chungshan N Rd, Section 2, has doubles for NT$5000, twins from NT$6000 to NT$6400 and suites from NT$8000 to NT$30,000.

The *Santos Hotel* (☎ 2596-3111; fax 596-3120; *sāndé dà fàndiàn*), 49 Chengte Rd, Section 3, is a complete international business hotel. Doubles and twins cost NT$4000 and suites cost from NT$6000 to NT$12,000.

The *Sherwood Hotel* (☎ 2718-1188; fax 2713-0707; *xīhuá dà fàndiàn*), 111 Minsheng E Rd, Section 3, is within walking distance of Sungshan domestic airport. Doubles cost NT$8000, twins cost from NT$7800 to NT$8800 and suites cost from NT$12,000 to NT$58,000. The hotel is notable for its old world European décor.

The *United Hotel* (☎ 2773-1515; fax 2741-2789; *guólián dà fàndiàn*), 200 Kuangfu S Rd, is priced as an international tourist hotel though is a bit lean on facilities. Doubles/twins cost NT$3900/4250 and suites cost from NT$9450 to NT$13,400.

Places to Eat

Looking for places to eat in Taipei is like looking for leaves in a forest. Restaurants are everywhere and and ever-changing. Keeping up to date with the literally thousands of restaurants is nearly impossible.

Two good sources of information about restaurants and entertainment facilities are the monthly publications *Taipei Pocket Guide* and *This Month in Taiwan*. Both are free handouts, supported by advertising. The *Taipei Pocket Guide* has a superb map while *This Month in Taiwan* has a list of clubs and associations – if possible, try to pick up both publications. You can usually find copies at the ROC Tourism Bureau, pubs frequented by foreigners, and five-star hotels.

Cafes & Cheap Eats Inexpensive Chinese food is ubiquitous. Many cheap noodle shops and cafeterias can be found in the small lanes and alleys off the main streets. It is possible to enjoy a filling meal of noodles or dumplings from around NT$50 to NT$70. A cafeteria meal with meat, vegies and rice typically costs about NT$70. Keep your eyes open for cafeterias where you can just point to what you want. Restaurants on the main boulevards are, of course, more expensive – you're paying for the prime real estate.

Generally, where you find students, you find cheap restaurants. About 400m south of Taipei train station is Wuchang St, home of the numerous 'cram schools' that coach students to pass Taiwan's rigid university entrance exams. The high concentration of schools and students guarantees an infinite choice of cheap eateries in this area.

Cheap restaurants also surround Taiwan University and Taiwan Normal University. Don't forget the universities themselves – no student ID is needed to eat in the student cafeterias.

Across the street from the Mandarin Training Centre (Taiwan Normal University), in the basement of the dormitory, is a superb cafeteria – for NT$45 you get a mountain of rice and three dishes that would cost twice as much elsewhere. If you eat in the university cafeterias, you have to be on time – lunch runs from 11.30 am to 12.30 pm, and dinner is from 5.30 to 6.30 pm.

There is a large collection of cheapish restaurants in a place called the *Food Circle (yuánhuán)*, at the intersection of Chung-ching N and Nanking W Rds. As well as the Food Circle itself, street vendors appear at night in the side streets adjoining the circle. This is the closest night market to the Taipei train station. Taipei's other night markets are great places to eat. Not only do they offer great cheap food but they also provide all the people watching opportunites you could want. For more information see the Markets section earlier in this chapter.

Food Courts The basements of most major department stores have food courts (see Self-Catering later in this section for addresses). These can be interesting places to eat as they offer considerable variety, but they're never too expensive (NT$100 for a good meal is typical). Menus are seldom a hassle as you can just point to what you want. Food courts tend to be packed out during lunch hours – arriving during off-peak times makes it much easier to get a seat.

The 2nd floor of the Taipei train station has a food court, thought it pales in comparison to the basement food court of the nearby Mitsukoshi Department Store (one block south of the station). SOGO Department Store to the north-east of the Chunghsiao-Fuhsing intersection in east Taipei also has excellent food. Also take a look at the basement of the Far Eastern Department Store in the south-west part of the Jenai-Tunhua circle.

Restaurants Taipei has restaurants catering for all tastes and you certainly won't go hungry here. For more details on some of the particular styles of cooking given here see Food in the Facts for the Visitor chapter.

Taiwanese Traditional Taiwanese food largely consists of endless courses of exotic seafood, which is very expensive. One of Taipei's better known Taiwanese restaurants is *Hai Pa Wang* (☎ 2552-1482; *hǎi bà wáng*), 7 Hsining N Rd. There are several branches, including 59 Chungshan N Rd, Section 3 (☎ 2594-4737) and 199 Sungchiang Rd (☎ 2502-9111).

Another of Taipei's famous houses with many branches is *Shin Yeh* (☎ 2596-3255; *xīnyè cāntīng*) in the 'Soho' district at 34-1 Shuang Cheng St. There is another branch in east Taipei (☎ 2776-9305) on the 2nd floor at 125 Hsinsheng S Rd, Section 1.

Cantonese In Hong Kong and China's Guangdong province, dim sum is usually served for breakfast and lunch. In Taiwan, it's mostly served for lunch and occasionally dinner. In the evening there are various other Cantonese dishes on offer, though much of it is seafood.

East Taipei has quite a few Cantonese eateries, most of them high class and expensive. One to try is the *Haoyuan Restaurant* (☎ 2715-4929; *háo yuán cāntīng*), 232 Tunhua N Rd. A bit further to the south is the *Sun Tung Lok Restaurant* (☎ 2700-1818; *xīntónglè cāntīng*), 34 Tunhua S Rd, Section 2. Another nearby is *City Star Restaurant* (☎ 2741-2625; *jīngxīng cāntīng*), 2nd floor, 216 Tunhua S Rd, Section 1.

Sichuan If you like this spicy hot cuisine, a good choice is *Lotus Garden* (☎ 2715-3921; *lián yuán cāntīng*), 230 Tunhua N Rd. There is also the *Charming Garden* (☎ 2521-4131; *xiāng yuán cāntīng*), 2nd floor, 16 Nanking E Rd, Section 1, and the *Seasons Garden* (☎ 2708-3110; *jì yuán cāntīng*), 324 Tunhua S Rd, Section 1.

Beijing The *Taoranting* (☎ 2778-7805; *táo-rántíng cāntīng*), 2nd floor, 86 Fuhsing N Rd, is named after a famous park in Beijing. *Peking Do It True* (☎ 2720-6417; *běijīng dùyīchù*), 506 Jenai Rd, Section 4, has better food than the name suggests. The food is just heavenly at *Celestial* (☎ 2563-2380; *tiānchú cāntīng*), 2nd floor, 1 Nanking W Rd.

Korean Fine Korean food can be found for mid-range prices at the *Seoul Korean Barbecue* (☎ 2511-2326; *hànchéng cāntīng*), 1 Lane 33, Chungshan N Rd, Section 1.

Western *Grandma Nitti's* (☎ 2369-9751) advertises 'home cookin' – just like Granny used to make'. It's at 8 Lane 93, Shihta Rd, and is open from 9 am until midnight. It's become a popular venue with the all-night disco crowd – some of whom come here at breakfast time to drink coffee and nurse their hangovers. The waffles are outstanding.

The *G'day Cafe* (☎ 2727-5927), 180 Hsing'an St, gives Grandma Nitti a run for her money. The menu includes pancakes, omelettes, tacos, hamburgers, meatloaf, mashed potatoes, salad, cheesecake and just about anything else that grandma used to make. The slogan here is 'home-cooked meals', and it's hard to disagree. The G'day is open daily from 10 am until 10 pm (it closes on the last Monday of each month).

Jake's Country Kitchen (☎ 2871-5289) serves exotica such as blueberry pancakes, tacos, pizza and cheesecake. The address is 705 Chungshan N Rd, Section 6, Tienmu, Shihlin district. The kitchen is open from 7 am until midnight, but the bar continues to stay open till 2 am.

The *Lulu Bar & Restaurant* (☎ 2713-2250), 9 Lane 113, Minsheng E Rd (behind the Sherwood Hotel) has superb desserts, Californian and Italian cuisine, and Starbucks coffee.

The *TU Cafe* (☎ 2369-4905), 91 Wenzhou St, does pancakes and waffles for breakfast and serves elaborate western meals with wine in the evening.

The *Dan Ryan's Chicago Grill* (☎ 2778-8800), 8 Tunhua N Rd, is a lunch and dinner place with great décor and 'Chicago-style' steak, ribs and seafood.

Peppers (☎ 2517-5065), 187-1 Sungchiang Rd, sounds like a great name for a Mexican restaurant, but in fact it's an American grill specialising in steaks and seafood.

If you've got enchiladas, tacos and margaritas on your mind, a great little Mexican restaurant is the *Santa Fe Cafe* (☎ 2394-2181), 150 Chaochou St, which stays open until midnight.

Tequila Sunrise Restaurant (☎ 2362-7563), 42 Hsinsheng S Rd, Section 3, does western-style lunches and serves Mexican dishes for dinners and late-night snacks. It's open from 11 am until 10 pm.

YY's Kitchen & Steak House (☎ 2592-2868) at 49 Chungshan N Rd, Section 3, claims to be Taipei's only kosher restaurant. Eating gefilte fish with chopsticks can be tricky, but if you're having trouble with the matzo balls (slippery little suckers) then just use a single chopstick and spear them.

The *Hollywood Baby Diner* (☎ 2713-2113), 2 Alley 1, Lane 56, Minsheng E Rd, Section 4, dishes up things like pizzas, salads, burgers, steaks, seafood and ribs. It's open from 7.30 am until 'late'. Nice features here are videos and mellow background music.

The place to go for good German food is *Zum Fass* (☎ 2531-3815), 55 Lane 119, Linsen N Rd.

If you've been yodelling for Swiss food, check out *Ticino Swiss Restaurant* (☎ 2876-1101) at 2 Lane 82, Tienmu E Rd.

One fine Italian restaurant that's been around for a while is *Antonio's Pizzeria* (☎ 2872-6734), 56 Tienmu W Rd, Tienmu. Another is *L'Amico Restaurant* (☎ 2712-7190), 10 Lane 55, Minsheng E Rd, Section 4.

Kudos goes to *Capone's Dinnerhouse* (☎ 2773-3782), 312 Chunghsiao E Rd, Section 4, an Italian-American restaurant which boasts live music daily from 9.30 pm until 12.30 am.

Yet another venue for fine Italian cuisine is *Pasta West East* (☎ 2776-5216), 7 Anho Rd, Section 1. Roughly in the same area is the *Ciao Pasta House* (☎ 2736-7369) at 75 Hoping E Rd, Section 3.

The *Post Home Restaurant* (☎ 2835-6491) at 31 Lane 35, Chungshan N Rd, Section 6, is home to the American Legion. It's also the place for heavy-duty steak and potato dinners. A lot of expat clubs and associations have monthly get-togethers at the meeting room upstairs.

Fine French food isn't cheap; dinner for two – *sacré bleu* – is a cool NT$800 or more. *Paris 1930* in the Ritz Landis Hotel has some of the best French fare in town. Many other pricey hotels have French restaurants, including the *Brother*, *Howard Plaza*, *Lai Lai Sheraton*, *Rebar Holiday Inn*, *Riviera* and *Royal*. See Places to Stay earlier in this chapter for addresses.

TGI Friday's (Thank God It's Friday's; *xīngqīwǔ měishì cāntīng*) bills itself as an 'American bistro', though Mexican dishes dominate the menu. The food is excellent if somewhat pricey, and it's certainly popular – at lunch and dinner times you may have to queue for a table. There are currently six branches in Taipei: Tunhua Store (☎ 713-3579), 150 Tunhua N Rd; Chunghsiao Store (☎ 711-3579), 2 Lane 49, Chunghsiao E Rd, Section 4; Tienmu Store (☎ 874-7021), 34 Chungshan N Rd, Section 7; World Trade Centre Store (☎ 345-2789), 7 Keelung Rd, Section 2; Chungching Store (☎ 389-3579), 94 Chungching S Rd, Section 1; and Hsimen Store (☎ 388-0679), 45 Omei St.

Tony Roma's Restaurant (☎ 2719-0992), 156 Minsheng E Rd, Section 3, advertises itself as 'a place for ribs'. As yet, Tony only has one eatery in Taipei, but the chain has spread far and wide in Asia and elsewhere.

Malibu Cafe (☎ 2776-4963), 5 Lane 91, Jenai Rd, Section 4, is named after the famed home of 'muscle beach' in Los Angeles. Surf is up Monday to Saturday from 11.30 to 3 am, and from 6 pm to 3 am on Sunday.

Another place influenced by California is *Skylark Restaurant*, 544 Chungshan N Rd, Section 4, Shihlin district. Get your healthy cheese and salad with bean sprouts on wholewheat here. And don't forget the Napa Valley wine.

Indian The *Taj Palace Restaurant* (☎ 2567-2976), 2nd floor, 270 Sungchiang Rd, is good for fine Indian food. It's next to the Golden China Hotel.

Another place where you can get your curries is the *Lanka Restaurant* (☎ 2832-0153), 48 Chungyi Rd (opposite Yangming Hospital in Tienmu).

Vegetarian Taipei's vegetarian restaurants offer amazing variety and can even produce dishes which look like meat – some even put fake chicken (made from soybeans) onto chicken bones!

Close to the Taipei train station is the *Meilin Vegetarian Restaurant* (☎ 2391-0833; *méilín cāntīng*), 14 Peiping E Rd. Not far from there is the *Chuansheng Vegetarian Restaurant* (☎ 2541-9075; *quánshěng cāntīng*), 111 Linsen N Rd.

Close to Sungshan airport in east Taipei is the *Fahua Vegetarian Restaurant* (☎ 2717-5305; *fǎhuá cāntīng*), 132 Minchuan E Rd, Section 3. Another option is the *Kuanshihyin Restaurant* (☎ 2595-5557; *guānshìyīn cāntīng*), 29 Minchuan E Rd, Section 2, near the Ritz Landis Hotel.

Fast Food Expatriates living in Taipei call it the 'US embassy', but most of us know it as *McDonald's (màidāngláo)*. There seem to be branches (consulates?) everywhere in the city.

Pizza Hut (bìshèngkè) also has numerous branches around town; a convenient one is at 130 Chunghsiao E Rd, Section 4.

Pizzas can be delivered to your home (dispatched by motorcycle) if you ring *Domino's Pizza (dáměilè bǐsà diàn)* which has a central branch at Taipei train station (☎ 2581-1100), 12-2 Chang'an E Rd, Section 1, and several more around town.

Subway Sandwiches has a Tienmu branch (☎ 2871-4855) at 467 Chungshan N Rd, Section 6; and a Fuhsing branch (☎ 2517-5174) at 346 Fuhsing N Rd.

The fast food isn't always fast but it's certainly good at *Round Table Pizza (yuán zhuō wǔshì xīcān)*. There are numerous outlets in Taipei.

There are *Swensen's (shuāngshèng xīcàn)* at 218 Tunhua N Rd; 109 Jenai Rd, Section 4; 685 Chungshan N Rd, Section 5, Shihlin; 48 Tienmu E Rd, Tienmu; and a number of other spots. It's famous for ice cream, but does full western meals too.

Buffets These are common in all the big tourist hotels such as the *Lai Lai Sheraton, Hilton, Sherwood, Grand Hotel* etc. If you want to get your money's worth, head straight for the steak and seafood because Taipei's hotel buffets are no bargain at around NT$750 per head.

The *Tandoor Indian Restaurant* (☎ 2509-9853), 10 Lane 773, Hochiang St, serves excellent Indian food and has a bargain buffet lunch every Saturday and Sunday. The restaurant is between Minsheng E and Minchuan E Rds, near Lungchiang Rd (behind the Saab dealership).

Coriya (*kěliyà*) is a mixed Chinese-Korean style barbecue and buffet restaurant. For all you can eat, the tariff runs to something like NT$300, depending on whether it's lunch or dinner time. There are three branches of this deservedly popular restaurant: Nanking branch (☎ 2757-9560), 299 Nanking E Rd, Section 5; Chienkuo branch (☎ 2740-9458), 48 Chienkuo N Rd, Section 1; and Roosevelt branch (☎ 2369-3653), 79 Roosevelt Rd, Section 2.

Pub Grub Many pubs are excellent places to eat and drink. Taiwan's pubs usually serve food until midnight, but the bar may stay open until 2 or even 4 am. See Pubs under the following Entertainment section for details.

Self-Catering Convenience stores like *7-Eleven*, *Circle K* and others offer gourmet delicacies such as hot dogs, steamed meat buns and frozen delights that you can heat in the convenient microwave oven. There's no need to wait to be seated, nor do you have to tip the waiters. Virtually all of these places are open 24 hours.

The Hong Kong chain *Wellcome Supermarket* has several strategically placed branches in Taipei. Prices here are good and the selection of items is very thorough. The second basement of the *SOGO Department Store* on the north-east corner of Fuhsing S Rd and Chunghsiao E Rd also has a fine supermarket. Other places to try include:

Asiaworld
    50 Chunghsiao W Rd, Section 1 (opposite Taipei train station)
    337 Nanking E Rd, Section 3
Evergreen
    6 Nanking E Rd, Section 2
    246 Tunhua S Rd, Section 1
Far Eastern Department Store
    68 Jenai Rd, Section 4
    32 Paoching Rd (near Chunghua Rd)

Lai Lai
    77 Wuchang St, Section 2
Ming Yao
    200 Chunghsiao E Rd, Section 4
Mitsukoshi
    12 Nanking W Rd (near Chungshan N Rd)
Rebar
    14 Nanking W Rd
    110 Yenping S Rd
Shin Shin
    247 Linsen N Rd
Sincere
    1 Chingcheng St (cnr Fuhsing and Nanking Rds)
Sunrise
    15 Fuhsing N Rd
Today's
    54 Omei St
Tonlin
    201 Chunghsiao E Rd, Section 4

Moving upmarket, the *Tienmou Yuehou Grocery Store* (☎ 2871-0189/2871-4828; *tiānmǔ yìhé shāngdiàn*), 39 Chungshan N Rd, Section 7, specialises in imported western groceries.

Another speciality shop in the Tienmu area is *Uli's Euro Deli* (☎ 2831-2741), 17 Kehchiang St. This is a good source of western snacks, meats, coffee beans and sandwiches.

Mami Store (☎ 2369-9868; *māmī shāngdiàn*), 1 Lane 135, Shihta Rd, offers many imported western gadgets and food.

Coffee Shops There are plenty of coffee shops in Taipei, but most are expensive. One that is more reasonably priced is *Doutor's Coffee Shop* (*luóduōlún kāfēi diàn*), a fine place for a morning shot of caffeine and a side order of pastry. Doutor's has several branches around town: Po'ai shop (☎ 388-2526) 63 Po'ai Rd (near the GPO); Nanking shop (☎ 567-1497), 77 Nanking E Rd, Section 2; Chunghsiao shop (☎ 741-4996), 295 Chunghsiao E Rd, Section 4; and Chienkuo shop (☎ 515-1371), 208 Nanking E Rd, Section 2.

Kona Connection has expresso coffee, waffles and sandwiches. One notable feature is the 'cookie buffet' from 7 to 10 pm, Monday to Friday – all the biscuits you can eat free with the purchase of any large coffee! The main branch (☎ 2708-9594) is at 142

Tunhua S Rd, Section 2, opposite the Far Eastern Plaza Hotel. The Tienmu branch (☎ 2874-7816) is attached to the Eslite Bookstore at 34 Chungshan N Rd, Section 7. The Chang'an branch (☎ 2752-2814) is in the basement at 219 Chang'an E Rd, Section 2 near the Sunrise Department Store.

If you're in the Shihlin district, check out *Black Beans* (☎ 2883-1125), 527 Chungshan N Rd, Section 5.

Teahouses There are plenty of teahouses in Taipei, though most are plagued with the usual problem of going out of business quickly. One which is reliable is *The Traditional Chinese Tearoom* on the 4th floor of the National Palace Museum.

There is a mannequin decked out in scholar's garb in the middle of the tearoom. Small birds – real, not like the stuffed scholar – flit about in bamboo cages and provide light music; walls of windows provide a great view of the woods surrounding the museum. One can stay as long as one wishes, and there is even a collection of art books one can peruse while one's leaves steep; the books can be found on a wooden shelf on the far wall (copies of some are on sale in the gift shop downstairs). It's surprisingly inexpensive, considering the location and atmosphere; an afternoon splurge on myself and a friend did not cost more than approximately US$15, including pastries.

N Leavitt

You might also want to check out *Shann Garden* (☎ 2894-7185), 32 Yuya Rd, Peitou district. Built in a former Japanese officers' club on a hill, it's in the complex with the Taiwan Folk Arts Museum and a Mongolian barbecue restaurant.

The *Teye Teahouse* (☎ 2396-8036; *déyé chálóu*), 4 Lane 11, Linsen S Rd, is central and easy to find. The same applies to the *Hsiehlan Teahouse* (☎ 2561-7711; *xièlán chálóu*), 85 Chungshan N Rd, Section 2, and the *Suiyuanchu Teahouse* (☎ 2571-2995; *suíyuán jū*), 51 Nanking E Rd, Section 2.

Ice Cream If you're looking to cool off during Taipei's torrid summers, you might want to stop for a break at *Haagen Dazs* (☎ 2776-9553), 173 Tunhua S Rd, Section 1.

Entertainment

Taipei is still a good city for nightlife, even though puritan Mayor Chen Shuibian has put a dent in it by shutting down karaoke places (KTVs) and dance halls.

The daily *China News* publishes a supplement every Friday called *Weekend*. This is a valuable reference for exploring Taipei's nightlife.

There is also a schedule of cultural events published monthly which is available from the ROC Tourism Bureau.

Tickets for events such as concerts, operas, baseball games etc can be purchased from a central ticket outlet. The main agent is Era Tickets (☎ 2341-9898; *niándài shòupiào gōngsī*), 46 Pateh Rd, Section 1. Don't expect them to be able to speak very much English there.

Major bookstores such as Caves, New Schoolmate Books and Eslite also sell tickets.

Cinemas The largest concentration of movie theatres lies on Wuchang St, Section 2, near the Lai Lai Department Store. See the English-language newspapers – *China News* and *China Post* – for a current movie selection:

Ambassador
    (☎ 2361-1222; *guóbīn xìyuàn*) 88 Chengtu Rd
Capitol or *Governor*
    (☎ 2741-5991; *shǒudū/zǒngdū xìyuàn*) 2nd floor, 219 Chang'an E Rd, Section 2
Changchun
    (☎ 2507-4149; *cháng chūn xìyuàn*) 172 Changchun Rd
China
    (☎ 2331-2305; *zhōngguó xìyuàn*) 127 Hsining S Rd
Chunghsiao
    (☎ 2721-4555; *zhōngxiào xìyuàn*) 5th floor, 201 Chunghsiao E Rd, Section 4
Great Century
    (☎ 2362-9629; *dà shìjì xìyuàn*) 325 Roosevelt Rd, Section 3
Hoover
    (☎ 2331-5067; *háo huá xìyuàn*) 89 Wuchang St, Section 2
Hsimen
    (☎ 2371-3579; *xīmén xìyuàn*) 5th floor, 144 Chunghua Rd, Section 1
Lai Lai
    (☎ 2933-0333; *lái lái xìyuàn*) 403 Roosevelt Rd, Section 6

Lux
(☎ 2311-8628; *lèshēng xìyuàn*) 83 Wuchang St, Section 2
Majestic
(☎ 2331-2270; *zhēn shàn měi xìyuàn*) 7th floor, 116 Hanchung St
New Oscar
(☎ 2361-1691; *aòsīkǎ xìyuàn*) 3rd floor, 115 Omei St
New World
(☎ 2331-2752; *xīn shìjiè xìyuàn*) 116 Hanchung St
Oriental Pearl
(☎ 2511-4686; *dōngfāng míngzhū xìyuàn*) 5th floor, 14 Nanking W Rd
Oscar
(☎ 2711-8298; *jīn xiàng jiǎng xìyuàn*) 3rd floor, 215 Chang'an E Rd, Section 2
President
(☎ 2388-5576; *zǒngtǒng xìyuàn*) 4th floor, 59 Chunghua Rd, Section 1
Shin Shin
(☎ 2537-1889; *xīn xīn yǐngchéng*) 3rd and 4th floors, 247 Linsen N Rd
Sun
(☎ 2331-5256; *rìxīn xìyuàn*) 87 Wuchang St, Section 2
Ting Hao
(☎ 2711-9305; *dǐnghǎo xìyuàn*) 1 Lane 126, Fuhsing S Rd
Tung Kuang
(☎ 2541-9300; *dōngguāng xìyuàn*) 413 Linsen N Rd
Tung Nan Ya
(☎ 2368-6839; *dōngnán yà xìyuàn*) 3 Lane 136, Roosevelt Rd, Section 4
Universal
(☎ 2746-7021; *quánqiú yǐngchéng*) 200 Nanking E Rd, Section 5
Warner Village
(☎ 8780-5566; *huá nà wēi xiùchéng*) 18 Sungshou Rd (near City Hall), Taiwan's largest cinema complex

Discos Taipei's discos are known for their steep cover charges, which rise even higher on weekends and holidays – there's not much choice but to grin and pay up. However, there are often special deals available – a 'ladies night' where women get in free, a 'foreigners night' when all the big noses don't have to pay and there are even group discounts on offer (if four people show up, then one gets in free). One disco offers free admisson to anyone dressed in fluorescent clothes, another grants free admission for see-through clothing. Some discos offer prizes for best dressed (or best undressed). The

freebies and gimmicks are subject to change – call ahead to learn the latest dispensation.

A place which continues to draw foreigners like a magnet is the *Spin Disco Pub* (☎ 2394-8600), in the basement at 91 Hoping E Rd, Section 1. This place features dancing and loud music and is open from 8 pm until 4 am. The cover charge is NT$200 on weekdays, NT$250 during weekends. Tuesday is foreigners night, Wednesday is ladies night.

One of Taipei's largest discos is *@live* (☎ 2396-3155), 3rd floor, 15 Hoping W Rd, Section 1. The cover charge is NT$350 on weekdays, NT$500 on weekends, NT$800 when live bands are on duty and NT$1200 when big-name bands are employed. It's open from 8.30 pm until 4 am.

An interesting new spot is *911* (☎ 2772-6588), 119 Liaoning St, off Fuhsing S Rd/Nanking E Rd. It's a small, but very lively, disco. Admission costs NT$250 on weekdays, rising to NT$400 on Saturday and NT$300 on Sunday. Wednesday is 'free night' and Sunday is 'ladies night'.

Another large, slick disco is *Kiss La Boca* (☎ 2712-1201), on the 3rd floor of the Magnolia Hotel, 166 Tunhua N Rd. Admission is NT$350 from Monday to Thursday rising to NT$500 on Friday and Saturday.

Fever (☎ 2578-2022), basement, 2 Pateh Rd, Section 3, is named after a Madonna song and is notable for its flashing neon. Sunday to Friday are all 'foreign students nights' where foreign students studying in Taipei (with ID to prove it) get in free. There is no cover on Monday and Wednesday, but other nights cost NT$200.

Chinese Opera There are not very many places left in Taipei where you can see traditional Chinese operas *(píngjù)* – for that you're better off going to Beijing. However, it is possible to track down a bit of this Chinese culture at the *Fuhsing Dramatic Arts Academy* (☎ 2796-2666, ext 711). At the time of research there were performances every Monday, Thursday and Saturday from 11 am to 12.30 pm. Admission costs NT$400 but you should check with the Academy beforehand to confirm prices and timings. Some hotels can make the booking for you. The academy is way out in the north-east part of town at 177 Neihu Rd, Section 2. Most visitors make the journey by taxi, but bus Nos 247 and 287 go there.

Chinese opera requires the performers to wear elaborate costume and dramatic stage makeup, especially as they often have to portray the opposite gender.

Classical Music Almost every weekend Taipei hosts to a classical music concert, play or opera. The performance venue is mostly the *Chiang Kaishek Cultural Centre* (☎ 2343-1637; *zhōngzhèng wénhuà zhōngxīn*), inside the grounds of the Chiang Kaishek Memorial. The 'cultural centre' is actually two buildings; the National Concert Hall (☎ 2343-1566; *guójiā yīnyuè tīng*) and the National Theatre (☎ 2343-1587; *guójiā xìjù yuàn*), also known as the Recital Hall.

There are occasionally small-scale performances held at the *Sun Yatsen Memorial Hall* (☎ 2758-8008; *guófù jì niàn guǎn*). Another possible venue for seeing performances is the *Armed Forces Cultural Activity Centre*

(☎ 2311-4228; *guó jūn wényì huódòng zhōngxīn*), 69 Chunghua Rd, Section 1. Major events like rock concerts are occasionally staged in the Municipal Stadium on the south-east corner of Tunhua N and Nanking E Rds. The Tourism Bureau should be able to provide more information on forthcoming events.

MTV A few MTV places do still exist in Taipei, the best of which is *Barcelona*, which has several branches around the city: Hsinyi branch (☎ 2701-2174), basement, 173 Hsinyi Rd, Section 4; Minsheng branch (☎ 2536-8276), 6th floor, 381 Linsen N Rd; Nanking branch (☎ 2521-3990), 2nd floor, 2 Nanking E Rd, Section 1; and Chungshan branch (☎ 2753-2328), 4th floor, 656 Pateh Rd, Section 4.

Viewing a movie typically costs NT$250 per person, depending on the length of the film. There are discounts if you have a VIP or membership card (NT$200) which can be issued on the spot. On selected evenings you get free popcorn with each drink purchased from the snack bar.

KTV Karoake bars are everywhere – you'll be tripping over the KTV signs wherever you go so there's little need to make recommendations. Most of these places don't interest foreigners, but if you're desperate to find one, all the major tourist hostels can direct you to a suitable place.

Night Markets A trip to Taipei wouldn't be complete without a visit to one or more of the city's colourful night markets. These are great places to eat, drink, shop and get your pocket picked. Markets are most lively on weekends if the weather cooperates. See the Markets section earlier in this chapter for more details.

Pubs Some of Taipei's pubs have live music so enforce cover charges, while others have no cover but require you to spend a minimum amount on food and drinks. At special times such as New Year's Eve there may be a special cover charge – if this concerns you, then call ahead and ask about any charges imposed.

A favourite place with budget-conscious foreigners is *DV8* (☎ 2393-1726) at 223 Chinhua St. It's a little hard to find – Chinhua St is the lane just to the east of Lucky Bookstore (129-1 Hoping E Rd, Section 1) – look for the Heineken sign. This place does good pizzas and sandwiches, and the DJ takes requests. There's a billiards table downstairs, and you're allowed to leave your mark by writing on the walls (and ceilings) in the basement! There is no cover charge.

The *Opium Den* (☎ 2705-8922), basement, 32 Jenai Rd, Section 3, is certainly one of the city's more popular night spots. The music tends to be 'acid jazz', but other tastes are catered for. Admission is free on weekdays but you've got to spend a minimum of NT$300 on food or drinks. Admission on Friday and Saturday night costs NT$500 and includes two drinks.

Another interesting place is *2 Kinky* (☎ 2504-1968), basement, 33 Sungchiang Rd. The weekday cover charge is NT$250, rising to NT$350 on Friday and Saturday night. However, there are all sorts of ways to get in free, including a Tuesday 'foreigners night', a Wednesday 'ladies night' and even a 'black suit night'. Enquire at the bar to find out about the latest promotion. The pub is open daily from 9 pm until 5 am.

The *TU Pub* (☎ 2704-7290), in the basement at 249 Fuhsing S Rd, Section 1, features jazz and blues music, and a 'ladies night' every Wednesday. The cover charge is NT$200 on weekdays and NT$300 on Friday and Saturday night.

Hats go off to the *Pig & Whistle* (☎ 2874-0630), 78 Tienmu E Rd, which offers a congenial atmosphere, good pub grub and fine live music. It's open from noon until 2 am with live music starting at 9.40 pm. There is no cover but a minimum charge of NT$350 for food and drinks is payable on weekdays that feature live music. Entry is NT$450 on Friday and Saturday night, when there is always music.

Just next to the Pig is the *Green Bar* (☎ 2873-3263), 84 Tienmu E Rd, which boasts cheap beer and late hours (until the last person leaves).

The *Q Bar* (☎ 2771-7778), 16 Alley 19, Lane 216, Chunghsiao E Rd, Section 4, boasts pool tables, a crooked bar and grilled jalapeno cheeseburgers. It's open from 11.30 am until 3 am.

Mongolian barbecue is so good in Taiwan it's hard to believe it can be so bad in Mongolia. One of Taipei's most famous venues for this type of cuisine is the English-style pub the *Ploughman's Inn* (☎ 2773-3268), 8 Lane 232, Tunhua S Rd, Section 1. It's open from 5.30 pm until 2 am.

Shuang Cheng St (*shuāng chéng jiē*), just to the east of Chungshan N Rd in north-west Taipei, and the adjacent alleys are sometimes referred to as 'the Zone' or 'Taipei's Soho', though this is something of a Tourism Bureau slogan. Soho or not, there are a number of expat pubs here. One place in this neighbourhood is *The Farmhouse* (☎ 2595-1764), 5 Lane 32, Shuang Cheng St, which features live music every night from 9.30 pm to 12.30 am (the cover charge ranges from NT$200 to NT$400). Almost next door at No 3-1 is the very popular *My Place* (☎ 2591-4269). The same management also runs *My Other Place* (☎ 2718 7826), 303 Fuhsing N Rd (near the Sherwood Hotel).

The *Malibu West Bar* (☎ 2592-8228), 9 Lane 25, Shuang Cheng St, is another popular place in the Zone. It's open from 11.30 am until 3 am but gets a later start on Sunday (4 pm).

The famed *Hard Rock Cafe* (☎ 2712-2828), 115 Minsheng E Rd, Section 3, has live music from 9.30 pm until 12.30 am.

The Source (☎ 2368-8797), 190 Nankang Rd, Section 2, is a gay bar known among the foreign crowd.

The *45 Pub* (☎ 2321-2140) is so named for its address at 45 Hoping E Rd, Section 1 (on the 2nd floor). The cuisine offered here is mostly American style. This place keeps long hours – 11 am until 4 am.

When in between bars, you can drop in at the *In Between Cafe* (☎ 2362-2860), 1 Lane 92, Shihta Rd. There is live jazz from 10.30 pm until 1 am on Friday and Saturday night.

Opening hours are from 10 am until 1 am (3 am on weekends).

One of the most interesting places to visit in Taipei is *Indian Beer House* (☎ 2741-0550; *yìndì'ān*), 196 Pateh Rd, Section 2. It's hard to define what this place is – it's a pub and a restaurant with a difference. There is a skeleton of a dinosaur on the roof and the sides of the building. The interior follows the same design scheme – dinosaur bones stick out of the walls, ceiling and floor. The waiters and waitresses join in too by sporting dinosaur bone shirts. Beer is served from large wooden kegs. The place definitely has character and is usually packed with customers, both foreign and Taiwanese.

Things to Buy
Arts & Crafts The Chinese Handicraft Mart (☎ 2321-7233), 1 Hsuchou St, is the place to go for local arts and crafts. Even if you don't buy anything, there are interesting displays here. It's open from 10 am until 6 pm, Sunday to Tuesday.

Backpacking Gear The place to go for backpacking gear is Taipei Landscape (*táiběi shānshuǐ*), 12 Chungshan N Rd, Section 1, north of the intersection with Chunghsiao Rd. A few doors up is another excellent shop, The Mountaineers Friend (☎ 2311-6027; *dēng shān yǒu*), 18 Chungshan N Rd, Section 1. Both shops have a wide selection of gear for hiking, climbing and camping, but even if you don't indulge in these, they're good places to replace a worn out backpack.

Bicycles Bike shops are scattered all round the city. Most are small, but there are a few big ones. One large shop specialising in KHS bikes is Jimmy's (☎ 2700-5572) at 17 Chienkuo S Rd, Section 2. Nearby is a Giant dealer simply called 102 Bike Shop (☎ 2700-0788) at 102 Hsinyi Rd, Section 3.

Cameras Taipei's 'photography street' is Po'ai Rd, around the intersection with Kaifeng St. There are more than a dozen camera shops here and prices are about as low as you can find in Taiwan. Unlike Hong Kong, the shops here actually honour their warranties.

Computers The NOVA Computer Arcade (*NOVA zīxùn guǎngchǎng*) is on the southwest corner of Chunghsiao W Rd and Kuanchien Rd, almost directly opposite the Taipei train station. Both hardware and software are sold in abundance, though most of the computer programs available are the Chinese versions.

Very similar to the NOVA is the nearby TT Station Computer Arcade (*TT zhàn zīxùn guǎngchǎng*). It's on Chunghsiao W Rd, on the east side of the Hilton Hotel.

T-Zone Computer Store (*tàipíngyáng diànnǎo diàn*) is one of Taipei's best, and each branch even has a small cybercafe. There are three branches in Taipei: the Chunghsiao store (☎ 2392-2122), 54 Chunghsiao E Rd, Section 1; the Heping store (☎ 2364-3455), basement and 1st floor, 100 Roosevelt Rd, Section 2; and the East Taipei store (☎ 2721-8200), 225 Tunhua S Rd, Section 1.

Macintosh dealers seem to come and go quickly in Taiwan. One of the longest surviving is Support & Solutions (☎ 2876-2020; email taiwanmac@aol.com). This place, also known as AppleShop, sells Mac hardware, both PC and Mac software and does general computer consulting work. The staff speak English very well. AppleShop is on the 2nd floor at 48 Tienmu E Rd (just above Swensen's) in Tienmu, and is open weekdays from 9.30 am to 6.30 pm and weekends from 10 am to 4 pm.

Motorcycles Assuming you have the necessary resident visa, you can purchase new or good used motorcycles with a full six month warranty from Zhengcheng Motorcycle Shop (☎ 2933-3834), 27 Roosevelt Rd, Section 5. The owner, Mr Chen, has a good name among foreigners for being impeccably honest.

Music Tapes & CDs These are sold all over the place, but Tower Records (*táoér chàngpiàn háng*) has the best selection by far. The original, spacious branch (☎ 2389-2025) is

Airline Booking Offices in Taipei

Air France
(☎ 2718-1631; *fǎguó hángkōng*) c/o Dragon Van Lines, 13th floor, 167 Fuhsing N Rd

Air Macau
(☎ 2717-0377; *aòmén hángkōng*) 6th floor, 134 Minsheng E Rd, Section 3

Air New Zealand
(☎ 2516-9025; *niǔ xīlán hángkōng*) 12th floor, 65 Sungchiang Rd

Air Nippon
(☎ 2501-7299; *rìkōng hángkōng*) 3rd floor, 63 Sungchiang Rd

Ansett Airlines
(☎ 2567-8956; *ānjié hángkōng*) 8th floor, 146 Sungchiang Rd

British Asia Airlines
(☎ 2541-8080; *yīngyà hángkōng*) 5th floor, 98 Nanking E Rd, Section 2

Canadian Airlines International
(☎ 2503-4111; *jiānádà guójì hángkōng*) 4th floor, 90 Chienkuo N Rd, Section 2

Cathay Pacific Airways
(☎ 2715-2333; *guótài hángkōng*) 12th floor, 129 Minsheng E Rd, Section 3

China Airlines
(☎ 2715-1212; *zhōnghuá hángkōng*) 131 Nanking E Rd, Section 3

Continental Airlines
(☎ 2719-5947; *měiguó dàlù hángkōng*) 3rd floor, 167 Fuhsing N Rd

Dragonair
(☎ 2543-5083; *gǎnglóng hángkōng*) 7th floor, 18 Chang'an E Rd, Section 1

EVA Airways
(☎ 2501-1999; *chángróng hángkōng*) basement, 63 Sungchiang Rd

Garuda Indonesia Airlines
(☎ 2561-2311; *yìnní hángkōng*) 66 Sungchiang Rd

Japan Asia Airlines
(☎ 2776-5151; *rìyà hángkōng*) 2nd floor, 2 Tunhua S Rd, Section 1

KLM Asia Airlines
(☎ 2711-4055; *hélán hángkōng*) 9th floor, 2 Tunhua S Rd, Section 1

Malaysia Airlines
(☎ 2514-7888; *mǎláixīyà hángkōng*) 102 Tunhua N Rd

Mandarin Airlines
(☎ 2717-1230; *huáxìn hángkōng*) 13th floor, 134 Minsheng E Rd, Section 3

Northwest Airlines
(☎ 2772-2188; *xīběi hángkōng*) 9th floor, 2 Tunhua S Rd, Section 1

Philippine Airlines
(☎ 2506-7255; *fēilǜbīn hángkōng*) 11th floor, 139 Sungchiang Rd

Qantas Airlines
(☎ 2522-1001; *aòzhōu hángkōng*) 5th floor, 98 Nanking E Rd, Section 2

Royal Brunei Airlines
(☎ 2531-2884; *huángjiā wènlái hángkōng*) 11th floor, 9 Nanking E Rd, Section 3

Singapore Airlines
(☎ 2551-6655; *xīnjiāpō hángkōng*) 148 Sungchiang Rd

Swissair
(☎ 2507-2213; *ruìshì hángkōng*) 8th floor, 61 Nanking E Rd, Section 3

Thai Airways
(☎ 2717-5200; *tàiguó hángkōng*) 2nd floor, 150 Fuhsing N Rd

TransAsia Airways
(☎ 2972-4668; *fùxīng hángkōng*) 9th floor, 139 Chengchou Rd

United Airlines
(☎ 2325-8868; *liánhé hángkōng*) 12th floor, 2 Jenai Rd, Section 4

Vietnam Airlines
(☎ 2517-7177; *yuènán hángkōng*) 5th floor, 59 Sungchiang Rd

at 12 Chengtu Rd on the roundabout on Chunghua Rd in the Hsimenting area. The newer branch (☎ 2741-4891) is on the 2nd floor, 71 Chunghsiao E Rd, Section 4 between Fuhsing S and Tunhua S Rds.

Pharmaceuticals You can get your every-day needs from vitamins to sunscreen lotion at the chain stores Watson's (*qū chén shì*) and Manning's (*wànníng*). Watson's has the larger market share and is found all over Taiwan, but Manning's is often cheaper.

Toys Neighbourhood toy shops are everywhere, but if you're looking for that special something to keep the toddlers out of mischief, check out Toys R Us (☎ 2521-9025) at 28 Hsinsheng N Rd, Section 2.

Getting There & Away

Air Taipei is well served with international and domestic connections. You won't have trouble getting tickets on weekdays except during major holiday periods. Seats can sometimes be scarce on weekends too.

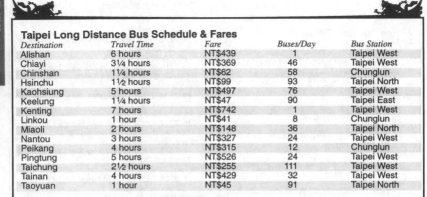

Taipei Long Distance Bus Schedule & Fares

Destination	Travel Time	Fare	Buses/Day	Bus Station
Alishan	6 hours	NT$439	1	Taipei West
Chiayi	3¼ hours	NT$369	46	Taipei West
Chinshan	1¼ hours	NT$62	58	Chunglun
Hsinchu	1½ hours	NT$99	93	Taipei North
Kaohsiung	5 hours	NT$497	76	Taipei West
Keelung	1¼ hours	NT$47	90	Taipei East
Kenting	7 hours	NT$742	1	Taipei West
Linkou	1 hour	NT$41	8	Chunglun
Miaoli	2 hours	NT$148	36	Taipei North
Nantou	3 hours	NT$327	24	Taipei West
Peikang	4 hours	NT$315	12	Chunglun
Pingtung	5 hours	NT$526	24	Taipei West
Taichung	2½ hours	NT$255	111	Taipei West
Tainan	4 hours	NT$429	32	Taipei West
Taoyuan	1 hour	NT$45	91	Taipei North

Although travel agents are the cheaper sources of international air tickets (see Travel Agencies earlier in this chapter), you must contact the airline offices directly to reconfirm your flight. This can be done over the phone or in person. It's important to remember than some international airlines fly under a different name in Taiwan to avoid 'offending China' – thus, British Airways is transformed into British Asia Airways, Japan Airlines is Japan Asia Airways and Qantas becomes Australia Asia Airlines. International airlines with booking offices in Taipei are listed in the Airlines Booking Offices in Taipei boxed text.

There are direct domestic flights between Taipei and Chiayi, Hualien, Kaohsiung, Kinmen, Makung, Matsu, Pingtung, Taichung, Tainan and Taitung. Every domestic carrier has either an office in Taipei or a counter at Sungshan airport. The domestic airlines are:

China Airlines
    (☎ 2715-1212; *zhōnghuá hángkōng*) 131 Nanking E Rd, Section 3
Daily Air
    (reservation ☎ 2546-6835; airport ☎ 2712-3995; *déān hángkōng*) 10th floor, 170 Minchuan Rd, Section 3
EVA Airways
    (☎ 501-1088/2515-5166; *chángróng hángkōng*) 63 Sungchiang Rd

Far Eastern Air Transport
    (☎ 2361-5431; *yuǎndōng hángkōng*) 36 Kuanchien Rd
Formosa Airlines
    (☎ 2514-9636; *guóhuá hángkōng*) Sungshan airport
Great China Airlines
    (☎ 2356-8000; *dàhuá hángkōng*) 38 Jenai Rd, Section 1
Taiwan Airlines
    (☎ 2717-6277; *táiwān hángkōng*) Sungshan airport
TransAsia Airways
    (☎ 080-066880; *fùxīng hángkōng*) 10th floor, 167 Fuhsing N Rd
U-Land Airlines
    (reservation ☎ 2718-3322; airport ☎ 2514-2821; *ruìlián hángkōng*) 5th floor, 186 Nanking E Rd, Section 4
Uni Air
    (reservation ☎ 2515-5166; airport ☎ 2718-7188; *lìróng hángkōng*) Sungshan airport

Bus There are four important bus stations near the train station and another one about 2km to the east. Probably the most important is the West bus station (☎ 2311-9466; *táiqì kèyùn xīzhàn*), 173 Chunghsiao W Rd, Section 1, where you can catch government-operated (Taiwan Bus Company) highway buses to major west coast cities, including Taichung, Chiayi, Tainan and Kaohsiung. There are also buses from here to a few of the major resorts areas like Kenting and Alishan.

The East bus station (☎ 2311-7629; *táiqì kèyùn dōngzhàn*) is almost right in front of the train station on Chunghsiao W Rd and is operated by the Taiwan Bus Company. From here you can take buses to CKS airport and Keelung.

The North bus station (☎ 2559-5698; *táiqì kèyùn běizhàn*), 4 Chengteh Rd, also operated by the Taiwan Bus Company, is on the north side of the train station. Buses from here go to Changhua, Chiaohsi Hot Springs, Chungli, Hsinchu, Hualien (transfer in Suao), Ilan, Keelung, Lotung, Lukang, Miaoli, Puli, Suao, Sun Moon Lake and Taoyuan.

At the north-east corner of Chengteh and Chang'an Rds, one block north of the North bus station, is the Tonglien bus station (☎ 2555-1114; *tǒnglián kèyùn*). There are three entrances to the station at Nos 31, 48 and 55 Chengteh Rd, Section 1. Tonglien is Taiwan's leading private bus company. Departures for all the major west coast cities are frequent.

The Chunglun bus station (*táiqì kèyùn zhōnglún zhàn*) is yet another branch of the Taiwan Bus Company. The station is on the south-west corner of Pateh and Fuhsing Rds, 2km east of the train station. To get there, take city bus No 57, 205 or 276 from Chunghsiao W Rd (in front of the Asiaworld Department Store). Important departures from Chunglun station include buses to Chinshan Beach, Yehliu, Linkou, Fengyuan and Peikang.

Train There are three train stations in Taipei, but the most important is the enormous Taipei train station, a palatial multistorey building that looks like a temple (from the outside at least). The ground floor is where you buy tickets; you catch your train in the basement, and upstairs there are numerous restaurants and shops which you might want to visit if you have time to kill.

Taipei train station is the most foreigner-friendly in terms of its English signage and English-speaking staff. All trains stop at both Taipei and Sungshan train stations, but many

Taipei Train Travel Times & Fares

Destination	Class	Travel Time (hours)	
Taoyuan	Ziqiang	0.30	NT$66
	Juguang	0.36	NT$51
	Fuxing	0.40	NT$43
	Putong	0.45	NT$31
Hsinchu	Ziqiang	1.06	NT$180
	Juguang	1.15	NT$139
	Fuxing	1.17	NT$116
	Putong	1.48	NT$84
Miaoli	Ziqiang	1.25	NT$257
	Juguang	1.50	NT$198
	Fuxing	2.00	NT$165
	Putong	2.51	NT$120
Taichung	Ziqiang	2.25	NT$384
	Juguang	2.43	NT$296
	Fuxing	3.00	NT$247
	Putong	4.37	NT$180
Changhua	Ziqiang	2.28	NT$425
	Juguang	2.53	NT$328
	Fuxing	3.16	NT$274
	Putong	4.23	NT$199
Chiayi	Ziqiang	3.06	NT$609
	Juguang	4.22	NT$469
	Fuxing	4.27	NT$392
	Putong	6.20	NT$285
Tainan	Ziqiang	3.53	NT$747
	Juguang	5.10	NT$576
	Fuxing	4.20	NT$481
	Putong	7.31	NT$349
Kaohsiung	Ziqiang	4.30	NT$854
	Juguang	5.40	NT$658
	Fuxing	6.00	NT$549
	Putong	7.52	NT$399
Pingtung	Ziqiang	5.25	NT$902
	Juguang	6.22	NT$695
	Fuxing	6.57	NT$580
Keelung	Ziqiang	0.34	NT$66
	Juguang	0.45	NT$51
	Fuxing	0.47	NT$43
	Putong	0.55	NT$31
Ilan	Ziqiang	1.30	NT$223
	Juguang	1.40	NT$172
	Fuxing	1.53	NT$144
	Putong	2.53	NT104
Hualien	Ziqiang	2.50	NT$445
	Juguang	3.39	NT$343
	Fuxing	3.44	NT$287
	Putong	5.42	NT$208
Taitung	Ziqiang	5.40	NT$815
	Juguang	7.00	NT$629

trains do *not* stop at Wanhua. Taipei train station does *not* handle any freight – if you're shipping things in the baggage car, you must go to Wanhua train station, in the east part of

TAIPEI

Taipei, or Sungshan in the south-west part of town.

Getting Around

If you get lost in Taipei you can always bail out and take a taxi, but most of the drivers don't speak English. It's a good idea to be prepared with your hotel name and address written down in Chinese characters so that you can at least get back there. Another tactic is to have the words for train station (*huǒchē zhàn*) written down, as they make good reference points when using a map.

To/From the Airport Two airports serve Taipei: Chiang Kaishek (CKS) international airport, near the city of Taoyuan (40km south-west of Taipei) and Sungshan domestic airport (practically in the heart of Taipei).

The government-owned and operated Taiwan Bus Company (*táiqì kèyùn*) runs two buses from CKS airport to Taipei – both buses cost NT$115. One bus goes to the Taipei train station and the other connects CKS airport to Sungshan domestic airport. The majority of travellers will want to go to the train station. Save your ticket stub – you need to return it to the driver when you disembark from the bus.

Train Station Bus This runs once every 10 minutes between 6.30 am and 10.30 pm. There are two stops en route from the airport – just stay on until the last stop for the train station. If you've got luggage and want to put it in the undercarriage compartment, it's important to make sure you use the correct compartment (for passengers travelling to the train station, this is usually the one nearest the front of the bus). To prevent theft, the three compartments are individually reserved for the luggage of passengers getting off at each particular stop. Therefore the driver only has to unlock one compartment at each stop. The driver will explain all this to you (in Chinese). Going from the train station to the airport there are no stops so it doesn't matter where you put your luggage.

When heading into town, the bus will drop you off on Chungching N Rd, which is in fact

one long block west of the train station (about a five minute walk). When going to CKS airport from the city, the place to board the bus is different – you catch it from the Taiwan Bus Company East station (*táiqì kèyùn dōngzhàn*) which is on Chunghsiao W Rd opposite the train station.

Sungshan Airport Bus This bus is very straightforward – it makes no stops en route so it doesn't matter which compartment you store your luggage in. The bus both arrives and departs from the same place, a small bus terminal at the western end of Sungshan domestic airport. Departures are every 15 minutes from 8 am to 10 pm. Bus No 262 connects Sungshan airport to the Taipei train station. Depending on the traffic, the journey should take about 45 minutes.

Airbus This is a new service operated by the privately owned Toward You Bus Company (☎ 2706-1223; *dàyǒu bāshì*). The buses operate on one route only, between CKS airport and two hotels in east Taipei (the Howard Plaza and Grand Hyatt).

Coming from the airport, the airbus stops directly in front of the Howard Plaza Hotel but on the return trip it stops on the opposite side of Jenai Rd – a bit confusing. There is no such problem at the Grand Hyatt, which is the last stop (or first stop when heading towards the airport).

The airbus runs once every 30 minutes between 6.30 am and 9.30 pm from Taipei and 8 am and 11 pm from the airport.

Taxi You'll find taxis lined up at both the domestic and international airports, but they impose an extra service charge on top of the metred fare. Taxis waiting at CKS international airport charge an extra 50%, making the fare from the airport to central Taipei about NT$1500. Going the other way, from Taipei to the airport, the drivers are only supposed to charge you the metered fare. Taxis from Sungshan domestic airport impose an extra NT$50 surcharge, but you can circumvent this by walking out of the airport exit onto Minchuan E Rd and hailing a cab there.

Limousine If you are staying at one of the better hotels in Taipei, they may offer a limousine service from CKS airport directly to your hotel. The price varies but is not horribly expensive – usually it's chcapcr than a taxi. You can find out if your hotel offers a limousine service at the service desk in CKS airport.

Helicopter There is also a helicopter service operated by Daily Air (☎ 2546-6835; *déān hángkōng*) which connects Taipei's airports.

Bus Taipei's bus network is run by a consortium of private companies which operate at a profit, and one government bus company which loses money. On most routes, the buses are frequent and the service is good. However, bus drivers rarely speak English and the destination is written in Chinese characters. Armed with a street map, your destination written in Chinese characters and maybc a compass, you should be able to manage.

If you've been studying Chinese characters for a while, you can take advantage of the Chinese-language bus route guidebooks. These can be purchased from kiosks near bus stops or from bookshops for NT$60 each. These guides have different titles – just ask for a *gōngchē zhǐnán* or *gōngchē shǒucè*. Unfortunately, if you can't read Chinese, they're of little use.

There is a freebie bus guide (in Chinese) available from Taipei City Hall, but these guides are often out of print so may not be available while you are there. Best of all, there is a reasonably good English bus guide available from Lucky Bookstore and Caves Books for NT$100, though it was a bit out of date at the time of writing.

The standard bus fare is NT$15, though this can be doubled or even tripled, depending on the number of zones you travel through. Between 11 pm and 1 am, there are just a few (very few) night buses (*yèjiān gōngchē*) which cost NT$22 per journey.

If you'll be in Taipei for a while, purchase a bus card from a convenience store or the kiosks near the bus stops (the same places that sell bus guides, newspapers and betel nut). These cards are sold in different denominations, but the smallest entitles you to at least 10 rides. There are no discounts for using these cards, therefore 10 rides would cost NT$150.

Sometimes you pay the driver when you board the bus, but usually you pay when getting off. Sometimes you must pay both when you get on and when you get off, but only if you have crossed two zones. Sometimes the driver hands you a ticket with a number on it as you get on the bus. Save it, you must return it when you get off. The ticket tells him which zone you were in when you got on. The various systems seem unnecessarily confusing, but this reflects the fact that there are numerous companies operating bus routes and each company has its own way of doing things.

Somewhere near the driver there should be a sign in Chinese or a red light telling you whether you need to pay when you get on (*shàng*) or when you get off (*xià*). Figuring out when you are supposed to pay can be confusing even for the Taiwanese.

Most bus services begin at 6 am and end at around 11.30 pm. Some buses return on the same route, while others take a circular route. Routes change periodically and the step-by-step opening of the Metropolitan Rapid Transit (MRT) is slowly forcing buses to reroute – some services may eventually cease operating completely.

MRT The Metropolitan Rapid Transit has been a long time coming. First planned in 1975, construction was delayed until 1988 because of repeated design changes and bureaucratic wrangling. Plagued by leviathan cost overruns, it's believed to be the world's most expensive mass transit system. The Taiwanese press has had a field day, with countless tales of corruption, faulty design, technical difficulties and considerable delays. Numerous MRT scandals were a major factor in the humiliating electoral

TAIPEI

TAIPEI METROPOLITAN RAPID TRANSIT (MRT) (UNDER CONSTRUCTION)
捷運系統

Tamsul Line
淡水捷運線
T1 Taipei Train Station
台北車站
T2 Chungshan
中山站
T3 Shuanglien
雙連站
T4 Minchuan W Rd
民權西路站
T5 Yuanshan
圓山站
T6 Chientan
劍潭站
T7 Shihlin
士林站
T8 Chihshan
芝山站
T9 Mingteh
明德站
T10 Shihpai
石牌站
T11 Chili An
唭哩岸站
T12 Chiyen
奇岩站
T13 Peitou
北投站
T14 New Peitou
新北投站
T15 Fuhsingkang
復興崗站
T16 Chungyi
忠義站
T17 Kuantu
關渡站
T18 Chuwei
竹圍站
T19 Hung Shulin
紅樹林站
T20 Tamsui
淡水站

Hsintien Line
新店捷運線
H1 Taipei Train Station
台北車站
H2 Taiwan University Hospital
台大醫院站
H3 Chiang Kaishek Memorial
中正紀念堂站
H4 Kuting
古亭站
H5 Taipower Building
台電大樓站
H6 Kungkuan
公館站
H7 Wanlung
萬隆站
H8 Chingmei
景美站
H9 Tapinglin
大坪林站
H10 Chichang
七張站
H11 Hsintien Government Office
新店公所站
H12 Hsintien
新店站

Mucha Line
木柵捷運線
M1 Chungshan Middle School
中山國中站
M2 Nanking E Rd
南京東路站
M3 Chunghsiao-Fuhsing
忠孝復興站
M4 Ta-an
大安站
M5 Technology Building
科技大樓站
M6 Liuchangli
六張犁站
M7 Linkuang
麟光站
M8 Hsinhai
辛亥站
M9 Wanfang Hospital
萬芳醫院站

M10 Wanfang Community
萬芳社區站
M11 Mucha
木柵站
M12 Taipei Zoo
動物園站

Panchiao Line
板橋捷運線
P1 Taipei Train Station
台北車站
P2 West Gate
西門站
P3 Lungshan Temple
龍山寺站
P4 Chiang Tzu Tsui
江子翠站
P5 Hsinpu
新埔站
P6 Hansheng
漢生路站
P7 Panchiao
板橋站

Nankang Line
南港捷運線
N1 Taipei Train Station
台北車站
N2 Shantao Temple
善導寺站
N3 Chunghsiao-Hsinsheng
忠孝新生站
N4 Chunghsiao-Fuhsing
忠孝復興站
N5 Chunghsiao-Tunhua
忠孝敦化站
N6 Sun Yatsen Memorial
國父紀念館站
N7 City Hall
市政府站
N8 Sungshan
松山站
N9 Houshan Pi
後山埤站
N10 Kunyang
昆陽站
N11 Nankang
南港站

defeat of Taipei's former mayor, Huang Tachou (he received only 25% of the vote despite having the president's endorsement). The project is still not completed and no one is quite sure when, or even if, it ever will be.

Many experts have been scratching their head as to why the Fuhsing line has been designed with a unique 90° turn in its route. Then there was the problem of the concrete support columns cracking within weeks of

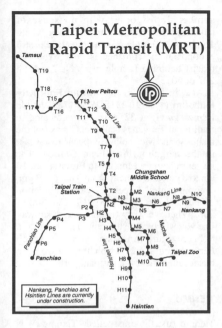

Taipei Metropolitan Rapid Transit (MRT)

Tamsui
T19
T18
New Peitou
T15   T13
T17   T16   T12
T11   Tamsui Line
T10
T9
T8
T7   T6
T5
T4   Chungshan Middle School
Taipei Train Station   T3
T2   M2   Nankang Line   N10
P2   N2   M3   N6   N8   N9
P4   P3   H2   N4   N5   N7   Nankang
P5   H3   M4
Panchiao Line   H4   M5   Mucha Line
P6   H5   M6
Panchiao   H6   M7
H7   M8   Taipei Zoo
H8   M9   M10   M11
H9
H10
H11
Hsintien Line

Nankang, Panchiao and Hsintien Lines are currently under construction.

Hsintien

renamed. The Mucha line is open from 6 am to 10 pm, and trains run at least every five minutes; the Tamsui line is open from 6 am to 10.30 pm with trains every six to eight minutes. MRT tickets cost between NT$20 and NT$60 depending on the journey. The tickets are magnetic cards which should be purchased from machines (with instructions in English) in the stations. There are also stored-value tickets available for multiple rides which come in NT$300 and NT$500 denominations. Smoking, eating and chewing gum on the MRT is punishable by a NT$6000 fine. Pulling the emergency handle without a valid reason can cost up to NT$30,000.

completion. There's been lots of finger-pointing at the Ministry of Transportation, heads have rolled, lawsuits have been filed and a special committee has been investigating the project for eons. In a dispute over money, an arbitrator ordered the Department of Rapid Transit Systems (DORTS) to pay MATRA (the French contractor) US$37 million for losses caused by delays. The city managed to weasle its way out of paying and so MATRA has withdrawn its maintenance staff (the Taiwanese have assumed this responsibility). Just why the mass transit project has become such a circus has been summed up by its engineers in one word – bureaucracy.

The good news is that, at the time of writing, two lines were open and two more should become operational in the next couple of years. Refer to the Taipei MRT map in this chapter to help you navigate the system but be aware that this map is still somewhat tentative – the stations may be

Car Driving around Taipei is hectic and not to be advised until you are completely familiar with this chaotic city. However, if you're feeling confident there are a number of car-rental places with English-speaking staff, catering to the foreign market in Taipei. Car-rental places are listed in the *China Post* and *China News*. Some to try include:

Central Auto Service
(☎ 2832-1000) 164 Chengte Rd, Section 4
China Rent-A-Car
(☎ 2500 6088) 506 Mintsu E Rd
Chuan Chia Fu
(☎ 2523-6001) 78 Hsinsheng N Rd, Section 1
International Auto Service
(☎ 2833-1225/2834-1225) 37 Tehsing E Rd, Shih-lin district, Tienmu
Tung Shin Auto Leasing
(☎ 2586-5036; fax 2591-9411) 8th floor, 27 Chungshan N Rd, Section 3
VIP Car Rental
(☎ 2713-1111; fax 2713-0000) 148 Minchuan E Rd, Section 3 (close to Sungshang airport)

Motorcycle There is no motorcycle or bicycle hire available in Taipei.

Taxi English-speaking radio dispatchers can summon a taxi for you if you call ☎ 2301-4567/2746-9988, but this doesn't mean that the driver will be able to speak English. Alternatively, you can simply flag one down in the street, but make sure you have your destination written down in Chinese to show the driver.

Around Taipei

KUANTU TEMPLE
(guāndù gōng) 關渡宮
The impressive Kuantu Temple is on the main road between Peitou and the suburb of Tamsui. The outside may not look like much, but inside there's a striking 100m-plus tunnel carved through the mountainside, displaying statues of various gods and demons. The temple was first built in 1661 and is dedicated to Matsu, goddess of the sea.

The easiest way to reach the temple is via the Tamsui subway line to Kuantu station.

PEITOU
(běitóu) 北投
A hot-spring resort area 13km north-west of central Taipei, Peitou was at one time known as a red light district. Nowadays, Peitou has been 'cleaned up' – the prostitutes are still there but maintain a very low profile to avoid tarnishing the community's family image.

Peitou still has many nice upmarket inns and spas; they are a legacy of the Japanese occupation during which time Peitou was known as one of Taiwan's big luxury hot-spring resorts.

Peitou may have lost some of its former glory, but it still retains a certain charm. Wellington Heights is one of the more affluent neighbourhoods and has a large number of well-to-do foreign residents. Even for the less well-to-do, there are a couple of unusual sights in the area which cost little or nothing to visit.

One such place is **Hell Valley** *(dìyù gǔ)*, an enormous spring with scalding hot water. This is no place to go bathing, but it is certainly interesting. The locals seem to get a kick out of boiling eggs here. It's to the north-east of Peitou Park, off Chungshan Rd.

Another place worth a visit if you are in the area is **Chaoming Temple** *(zhāomíng gōng)*. Known at one time as the Lovers' Temple *(qíngrén miào)*, romantic couples flocked here to swear their undying love to each other. The building was then sold to

another Taoist order with no sense of humour, who renamed it Chaoming (Clear Tomorrow) Temple. The architecture is still exotic, but the romance is gone. You can reach Chaoming Temple on bus No 223, 224, 277 or 601.

Also in Peitou is the **Taiwan Folk Arts Museum** (☎ 2891-2318/2893-1787; *běitóu wénwù guǎn*) at 32 Yuya Rd, dedicated to traditional Taiwanese culture. Check out the teahouse and Mongolian barbecue restaurant in the neighbouring Shann Garden. The museum is open Monday to Friday from 10 am to 8 pm, and Sunday from 9 am to 10 pm.

From central Taipei, you can reach Peitou on bus No 216, 217, 218, 219, 223, 302 or 308. Whenever they finish the new subway line you will be able to use it to get to Peitou.

From Yangmingshan, you can reach Peitou by bus No 230, which leaves from the bus terminal near the national park.

TIENMU
(tiānmǔ) 天母
Tienmu (usually misspelled 'Tienmou') is not exactly a renowned tourist attraction. Rather, some think of it as the foreigners' ghetto in the Shihlin district of northern Taipei.

Tienmu is the place to find imported western foods, especially treats from the USA like instant mashed potatoes, artificial whipped cream, frozen dinners, cheese in a spray can, microwave popcorn and other plastic foods. If you need a dose of these things while you are in Taiwan, Tienmu is the place to shop.

As far as I'm concerned, one of the most pleasant things to do in Tienmu is to take a hike up to the **Chinese Cultural University** in Yangmingshan. To do this hike, take a bus to the last stop at the big roundabout, the highest point you can go by bus in Tienmu. There are two streets leading uphill from the roundabout. Take the one to the right and walk steeply uphill until you reach the end of the road where you'll find stone steps leading up into the forest. It's signposted as being a 1.8km hike from here. Head up the steps. After a while you'll come to a fork, either path leads uphill to the university.

Buses from central Taipei to Tienmu include Nos 220, 224, 267, 268, 601 and 603. All these buses lead to the big roundabout at the top end of Chungshan N Rd.

YANGMINGSHAN
(*yángmíngshān*) 陽明山

Perhaps the most scenic place within the Taipei city limits, Yangmingshan is a mountain range that dominates the northern end of the capital. The area is noted for its beautiful flowers, especially in spring (February to April) when the cherry blossoms and azaleas are in bloom. The cherry trees are concentrated in **Chungshan Park**, which is part of the Yangmingshan National Park area.

Many wealthy Taiwanese and westerners live on the lower slopes of Yangmingshan, preferring life in the cooler, cleaner mountain air. Real estate developers have recently moved into the lower slopes erecting ultra-expensive US-style housing projects with names like 'Taipei California'. Fortunately, most of the mountain is protected by a national park and no further construction is allowed.

The park itself offers many opportunities for hiking and provides a welcome relief from Taipei's bustle. The only bad thing about this place is that on Sundays it tends to be packed out with hordes of people trying to get away from it all, especially during the blossom season. On rare occasions the higher slopes of Yangmingshan get dusted by snow. If this occurs on a weekend, you'll be able to witness the greatest pilgrimage of

A Politically Correct Matsu

As Queen of Heaven and Protector of Seafarers, Matsu is the most popular goddess in Taiwan. She is, in fact, the deification of a real person born between 900 and 1000 AD on Meizhou, an island in China's Fujian province. After her death, a Matsu cult spread southwards along the coast of China and down into South-East Asia. In Macau she is known as 'Ah Ma', in Hong Kong as 'Tin Hau', in Singapore as 'Ma Chu Po' and in Vietnam as 'Thien Hau'.

Reproductions of Matsu's figure have been manufactured and put on display in Taoist temples throughout Taiwan. But true believers pine to see the Meizhou Matsu, the 'Primitive Original Matsu', from Fujian province which is said to be over 1000 years old. Taiwanese believers finally had their chance to fufil this longing in 1996, when the Meizhou Matsu was removed from her resting place in China to embark on a 100 day tour of Taiwan. She was warmly welcomed by millions of loyal Taiwanese Matsu worshippers. It was a fine example of officials in mainland China cooperating with their Taiwanese counterparts to promote religious freedom among the Chinese people. Surely there could be no sinister financial or political motive for the tour – or was there?

A number of critics in Taiwan denounced the Matsu tour as being anything but holy. They were suspicious of the presence of Chinese politicians as 'escorts' of the goddess figure. Commentators in the Taiwan Independence Party denounced the Meizhou Matsu as being used as a 'political tool' by China to court the allegiance of the Taiwanese. 'Why else' one critic noted 'would a bunch of atheistic, Communist officials accompany a religious statue?' Their argument was further supported by the fact that some of the mainland officials were brandishing phrases such as 'the spirit of Matsu is unification'.

Others rained on the parade by suggesting that the Meizhou Matsu may in fact be a fake, as it appears to be in remarkably good shape for a deity created over 10 centuries ago. Indeed, the colour and general condition of the figure gives it an almost new appearance. Taiwan has a number of its own Matsu icons, believed to be about 300 years old, and they are in far worse shape than the Meizhou Matsu. Furthermore, most of China's religious artefacts were destroyed during the Cultural Revolution in the 1960s – it's hard to understand how the Meizhou Matsu was spared unless she was 'politically correct'.

Politics aside, it is possible that officials in Fujian province could be raking in the cash from Matsu worshippers. Since the lifting of martial law in 1987, the Taiwanese have flocked to Meizhou on religious pilgrimages, spending millions of US dollars there on the 'maintenance' of the temples and 'buying incense'. More than a few Taiwanese people suspect that much of this cash has gone towards projects that have had little to do with religion. ∎

Chinese people, all vying for a play in the snow, since the Long March.

There is a restaurant in the park and a large, impressive Chinese-style building called the **Chungshan Building** (*zhōng-shān lóu*), the site of high level KMT meetings. You can admire the building from the outside, but getting inside requires the highest connections.

Yangmingshan has hot-spring resorts similar to those in nearby Peitou (see the earlier Peitou section). One of the roads that connects Yangmingshan to Peitou is called Shamaoshan Hudi Rd – which passes through the **Hushanli Hot Springs** (*hú-shānlǐ wēnquán*) area which is lined with resorts. Bus No 230 (running from Peitou to Yangmingshan) uses this route. The resorts are open until late into the evening but you should avoid the place on weekends. Further up the slopes of Yangmingshan is the **Matsao Hot Springs** (*mǎcaó wēnquán*) area with yet more bathing resorts.

One of the more interesting thermal areas is **Sulphur Valley** (*liúhuáng gǔ*). It's not suitable for bathing, but it's a totally undeveloped spring with an eerie appearance. One traveller wrote 'it's one of the weirdest things this boy has ever seen'.

If you would like a moderately strenuous hike, climb **Chihsingshan** (*qīxīngshān*), meaning 'Seven Star Mountain'. At an elevation of 1120m, it's the highest peak within Taipei's city limits. From the summit, you can look down one side of the mountain and see Taipei – the ocean is visible from the other direction. Other notable peaks are Mientienshan which still has a well formed crater at its summit and Shamaoshan, an extinct bell-shaped volcano.

The weather up here can be unpredictable – no matter how sunny and warm it is in the city, be prepared for rain, wind and cold.

Staying in Yangmingshan may not be as convenient as being in central Taipei, but offers something Taipei doesn't have – breathable air. Accommodation is not very expensive in comparison with Taipei, but then Taipei isn't cheap either. There are no dormitories for budget travellers; however,

there are organised camping areas like the *Chingshan Camping Ground* (*jīngshān yíngdì*), or you can camp in the national park, where you won't see another soul, for free.

You can get to Yangmingshan from central Taipei on bus No 301 or 260, which run along Chungshan N Rd. Minibus No 9 also goes to the park. From Peitou you can catch bus No 230. Stay on the bus till the very last stop at the top of the mountain. From there it's about a 10 minute walk to the park entrance – follow the footpath behind the bus terminal.

By far the most interesting way to see Yangmingshan is by bicycle or motorcycle, assuming you can beg, borrow or buy one. This is the only way to really get into the backwaters, although reaching the high peaks will still require some walking. Equip yourself with a good Taipei city map and the free Yangmingshan map, available from the Taiwan ROC Tourism Bureau, and then start exploring.

PISHAN TEMPLE
(bì shān sì) 碧山寺

The Pishan (Green Mountain) Temple, also known by its more formal name of *bì shān yán kāi zhāng shèng miào*, is one of the finest sights in Taipei. Perched on the side of a mountain with breathtaking views of Taipei, the temple gets surprisingly few visitors, at least on weekdays. The scenery is great and the area is peppered with hiking trails. You can even stay overnight in the temple for a NT$500 'donation' but food costs extra.

The nearby *Pishan Camping Ground* (*bì shān lùyíng chǎng*) is a good place to stay, even if you're not particularly interested in temples, as coming up here is a great way to escape the chaos of Taipei.

The Pishan Temple is in the Neihu district in north-east Taipei. The temple is on a long loop road through the mountains, and buses stop at both ends of the loop; the temple is at the northern end of the loop, so be sure to get off at that end. It's best to take a bus to the **Golden Dragon Temple** (*jīnlóng sì*), which is also on the loop road near Pishan Temple. While Golden Dragon Temple is worth looking at, don't mistake it for your ultimate destination which is farther up the mountain. Buses to the Golden Dragon Temple include Nos 240, 247, 267 and 604. Probably the most useful is No 247, which runs there from the Hilton Hotel area (Taipei train station). From the Golden Dragon Temple, you will have to walk uphill along a paved road. There are minibuses (No 2) along the loop road which go all the way to Pishan Temple. A taxi from Neihu to Pishan Temple should cost around NT$150.

SUNGSHAN NATURE RESERVE
(sōngshān zìrán bǎoyù qū) 松山自然保育區
If you look south-east from the steps of the World Trade Centre, you can see some moderate sized hills in the distance. While this may not look like much from far away, it's one of the loveliest spots in Taipei. The Sungshan Nature Reserve is a huge, heavily forested and mountainous park laced with hiking trails and dotted with temples.

Within the reserve there are 'four animal mountains' *(sì shòu shān)*, so named because someone with a good imagination reckons that's what the peaks look like from a distance. Two of the mountains have adopted other nonanimal names.

Elephant Mountain *(xiàngshān)* is the smallest of the four mountains (strange that an elephant should be the smallest). Climbing this easy peak is a good way to warm up the muscles for the other more strenuous hikes. Along the hiking path are various exercise machines – parallel bars, chin-up bars, sit-up ramps and the like.

The third highest peak is Governess Finger Mountain *(mǔzhǐshān)* – not exactly an animal, but it does resemble a finger.

Tiger's Head Mountain *(hǔtóu shān)* is the second highest peak with an elevation at the summit of 325m. Nine-Five Peak *(jiǔwǔfēng;* 374m) has nothing to do with Taipei's working hours, but refers to a feat accomplished by Yu Hui who climbed the peak aged 95, auspiciously on the fifth day of the ninth month in 1915. This is the highest peak of the lot and the summit is

decorated with fancy calligraphy commemorating Yu Hui's accomplishment.

There are many approaches to the reserve. Probably the easiest way to get here is to take a train to the Sungshan train station (one stop past the Taipei train station heading towards Keelung). From Sungshan station, you need to head south for 1km along Sungshan Rd to where it intersects with Hsinyi Rd, Section 6. You can walk or take one of several buses (Nos 279 and 286, among others) which run south along Sungshan Rd. South of Hsinyi Rd, Sungshan Rd changes from a busy urban street to a winding mountain road, eventually ending at the magnificent **Sheng'en Temple** *(shèng'en gōng)*. There are numerous hiking trails heading up into the hills from the temple.

NANKANG TEA PARK
(nángǎng guānguāng cháyuán)
南港觀光茶園
Similar to Mucha Tea Park (see later in this section), the Nankang Tea Park is less developed, but is still very interesting. There are a number of hiking trails here winding through the forested hillsides, plus there are small temples dotted around the area.

Bus No 6, operated by the Chihnan Bus Company, follows a scenic route from Mucha Zoo to Golden Dragon Temple in Neihu, via the Nankang Tea Park.

TAIPEI-MUCHA ZOO
(mùzhà dòngwù yuán) 木柵動物園
The zoo (☎ 2938-2300) is in the south-east section of Taipei. This area is officially called the Wenshan district, but was formerly known as Mucha (Wooden Fence) and that's the name still usually applied to the zoo. It's Taiwan's best zoo by far, but it isn't really large by world standards. Limited space also prevents the creation of a very natural environment for the animals.

There is an excellent adventure playground at the far end of the zoo. It's set among bamboo groves in the hills, and all the apparatus is made of chunky logs and sturdy rope. It's ideal for kids aged six and over, although parents need to keep a watchful eye as some of the equipment is a bit too thrilling (aka dangerous).

The easiest way to reach the zoo is to take the Mucha subway line to the southernmost stop. Opening hours are from 8.30 am to 4.30 pm daily, and admission costs NT$40.

MUCHA TEA PARK
(mùzhà guānguāng cháyuán) 木柵觀光茶園
This hilly park is a good walking area. As the name implies, it's also known for tea plantations and teahouses. At present, there are over 60 teahouses here, and the number keeps increasing. The teahouses serve not only tea, but also local specialities such as 'tea gelatin' and chicken baked in tea leaves. There are also several small temples in the park.

The tea park is in the Wenshan district, the very southernmost part of Taipei city. Minibus Nos 10 and 11 go to the park from Chengchih University – these buses only run about once every 30 minutes and don't operate late in the evening. To reach the Chengchih University catch either bus No 236 or 237.

CHIHNAN TEMPLE
(zhǐnán gōng) 指南宮
One of the largest temples in north Taiwan, the Chihnan Temple is 19km south-east of the Taipei train station in the Wenshan district. The temple, which is over 100 years old, is perched on a mountainside, with outstanding views of Taipei when the weather is clear. When the weather isn't clear, it's even better – who wants to see Taipei anyway?

There are several options available for getting to the temple. You can take bus No 236 or 237 to Chengchih University in the Wenshan district, then walk uphill to the temple. Alternatively, you can take buses operated by the Chihnan (CN) Bus Company *(zhǐnán kèyùn)* from the city centre. CN bus No 1 runs along Nanking E Rd, then Sungchiang Rd, Hsinsheng S Rd, Roosevelt Rd and finally on out to Mucha, ending at the Chihnan Temple. CN bus No 2 runs down Chunghua Rd, Aikuo W Rd, Roosevelt Rd and finally terminates in the Wenshan dis-

trict. Make sure you tell the driver your destination – some of the buses take a different route and terminate at the Mucha Zoo rather than the temple.

No matter which bus you take, you won't be able to see the temple from where the bus drops you off. Follow the steep stone steps up (there are 1200 steps!) until you reach a small Taoist temple. The main temple is to your right; to the left are some picnic grounds – a good place to relax, except on weekends when it's crowded.

PITAN
(bìtán) 碧潭
To the south of Taipei is Pitan (Green Lake), which is basically a park on the edge of the city. The lake is known for its rowing boats and swimming. Local daredevils impress their friends by diving from the 12m cliffs into the lake – there is a sign in Chinese saying that cliff-diving is prohibited.

The lake is adjacent to the town of Hsintien *(xīndiàn)*, which is easily reached from Taipei. I don't recommend going out of your way just to visit this place, but if you are on your way to Wulai you can stop in Pitan along the way.

Buses to Wulai operated by the Hsintien Bus Company *(xīndiàn kèyùn)* depart every 10 minutes or so from Chingtao E Rd, one block east of Chungshan S Rd and one block south of Chunghsiao Rd.

More frequent, unnumbered buses operated by the Hsintien Bus Company, marked 'Hsintien-Tamsui' in Chinese, run from Chungshan and Roosevelt Rds to Wulai.

YUANTUNG TEMPLE
(yuántōng sì) 圓通寺
This large Buddhist monastery is in the foothills of Chungho *(zhōnghé)*, a suburb to the south-west of Taipei. The monastery is slightly up in the hills, giving it a bit of a view. However, it's considerably less attractive now that a new freeway has been built next to the temple. Probably the best reason to come here is to eat at the temple's vegetarian restaurant.

From Taipei train station, you can get

there on bus No 243. Other buses going there are Nos 201, 241 and 275. It's entirely possible to include this with a trip to the Lin Gardens – a taxi ride between the two places costs around NT$130.

LIN GARDENS
(línjiā huāyuán) 林家花園
The Lin Gardens (☎ 2965-3061) are in the suburb of Panchiao *(bǎnqiáo)*, south-west of Taipei proper. These classical gardens were constructed as part of the Lin family's home in 1894. In the succeeding years the gardens were allowed to deteriorate – until 1976, when they were donated to the government. After a financial outlay of NT$157 million, the gardens were finally restored in 1987 and opened to the public.

Covering an area of only 1.2 hectares, the gardens have been declared an historic site. The grounds have numerous pavilions, arches and ponds. However, it would be stretching things to say that they're very scenic. Consider them a place to go to kill time on a rainy Taipei day.

The gardens are at 9 Hsimen St, a 15 minute walk (slightly under 1km) north-west of the Panchiao train station. You could take a train to Panchiao, and then walk to the gardens or take a taxi. Also, bus Nos 307 and 310 from Taipei pass by the gardens. You can catch bus No 310 from directly in front of the Taipei train station on Chunghsiao E Rd.

The gardens are open from 9 am to 5 pm every day, except Monday and the day after public holidays. Admission is NT$60.

ACTIVITIES
Golf
To the west of Taipei in the suburb of Linkou (Taipei County) is the Linkou Golf Course *(línkǒu gāo'ěrfū qiú chǎng)*. There are also two golf courses near Taoyuan (see Taoyuan in the North Taiwan chapter for details).

Kayaking
The area around Wulai (south of Taipei) is a favourite venue for kayaking. For further information, contact the Adventure Kayak Club (☎ 2930-1430; fax 2930-1555).

North Taiwan 台灣北部

If you want to understand why the Portuguese called this island Formosa, you'll have to get out of Taipei. Unfortunately, too many foreigners seem to get stuck in the big city and never see the rest of the island – a pity.

Within a short distance from Taipei, you can forget all about the problems of urban life and find peace and relaxation visiting some of Taiwan's mountains, beaches and hot-spring resorts. You can experience some of the pleasures of rural living, breathe air that you can't see and visit waterfalls and temples.

Taipei County 台北縣

WULAI
(wūlái) 烏來

It rains a lot in Taipei, so if you're looking for a nearby place that can be visited on a rainy day then the answer is Wulai, a mountain area 29km (a one hour bus ride) south of Taipei. Wulai has beautiful, though rather commercialised, mountain scenery, but the star attraction is its magnificent waterfall – the harder it rains, the more dramatic the falls (as an added bonus, rain scares off the tourists). Wulai also has the advantage of being a lot higher and therefore cooler than Taipei. Other attractive features of the area are aboriginal villages and a magnificent gorge, formed by the Nanshih River.

Wulai can be jam-packed with people on weekends and holidays; the Taiwanese describe this phenomenon as a 'people mountain, people sea' *(rén shān rén hǎi)*. Come on weekdays or you'll be sorry.

Wulai Hot Springs Village
(wūlái wēnquán qū) 烏來溫泉區

Perhaps this is more of a nonattraction. From where the bus lets you off, you walk across a short bridge and enter a small street which is a solid mass of souvenir shops selling

HIGHLIGHTS

- **Wulai** – hot springs, waterfalls, hiking trails and aboriginal culture, all within easy reach of Taipei
- **Fulung Beach** – a great place to surf, swim, sail, water-ski or just laze in the sun
- **Shihtoushan** – a treasure-trove of Buddhist monasteries, temples and pagodas
- **Tapachienshan** – a challenging three day hike up one of Taiwan's most beautiful peaks

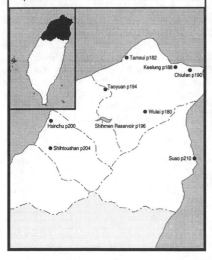

everything a tourist desires. While tacky commercialisation has taken its toll on Wulai, a brief walk through the numerous souvenir shops can be entertaining and on weekends the local aborigines put on a song and dance show (for a fee) at the Naluwan Resort Hotel (see Places to Stay later in this section). So if you'd like to pick up an alligator with a light bulb in its mouth, or a buddha with a clock in its stomach, this is the place to do it.

There are hot springs here, but they are

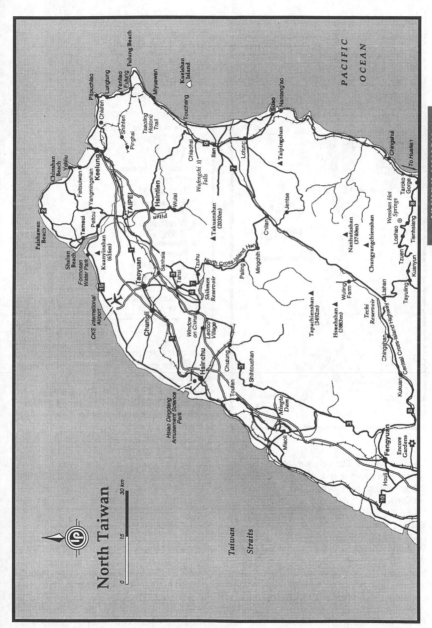

North Taiwan

NORTH TAIWAN

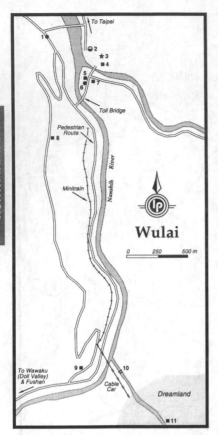

fully developed. The only way to gain access is to rent a room at one of the costly hotels in the village (see Places to Stay later in this section).

Wulai Falls
(wūlái pùbù) 烏來瀑布

When you come to the end of the street in Wulai Hot Springs Village, there is another bridge going over the river. You have to pay an admission charge of NT$50 to cross. After crossing the bridge, you will encounter a congregation of very persistent taxi drivers. Ignore them and walk up the steps. You will

soon come to the electric minitrain. For NT$30, the minitrain will whisk you away to the base of Wulai Falls. You will almost certainly see a couple of aboriginal girls in red miniskirts here. They'll invite you to take a picture of them as the pose by the waterfall, but you are expected to pay.

You can take a cable car to the top of the falls; the cost of a return ticket is NT$200 for adults. When you get to the top you will find the local equivalent of Disneyland, which is called Dreamland *(yúnxiān lèyuán)*. In spite of the amusement park atmosphere, it's fun to go there – as long as you go on a weekday, when it's not crowded.

Places to Stay

Even though most people prefer to do Wulai as a day trip, you can spend the night. There's no real budget accommodation, but discounts on weekdays are the norm. In Wulai Hot Springs Village, near the police station, there is the *Green Hill Hotel* (☎ 2661-6342;

bìshāngé dà fàndiàn), where attractive rooms cost NT$1500 to NT$3000. Close by is the *Su Shan Hotel* (☎ 2661-6446; *xiùshān dà fàndiàn*) where a room costs from NT$1500 to NT$2500. Adjacent is the *Wulai Hotel* (☎ 2661-6445; *wūlái dà fàndiàn*), a small place where twin rooms are NT$1500.

Across the toll bridge and up the hill is the friendly *Wulai Lodge* (☎ 2661-6204; *wūlái shān zhuāng*) where twins are NT$1500. It's a quiet and pleasant place to stay, but a long walk from the bus station.

Near the bottom terminal of the cable car is the *Naluwan Resort Hotel* (☎ 2661-6906; *nǎlǔwān dùjià fàndiàn*). This is a plush seven storey palace with doubles from NT$2800 to NT$3300 and twins from NT$3300 to NT$4800. The more expensive rooms have a view of the waterfall.

Ride the cable car up into the Dreamland Amusement Park to find the *Dreamland Hotel* (☎ 2661-6511; *yúnxiān dà fàndiàn*). Doubles cost NT$1000 to NT$1500, twins are NT$1350 to NT$3500, and you get a free soak in the hot springs.

Getting There & Away
Buses run by the Hsintien Bus Company (*xīndiàn kèyùn*) depart every 10 minutes or so from Kungyuan Rd on the east side of 2-28 Peace Park in Taipei. The trip takes about an hour each way.

AROUND WULAI
Fushan
(*fúshān*) 福山
Wulai Hot Springs Village, Dreamland, the minitrain and cable car are hardly representative of traditional aboriginal lifestyle. If you want to get away from the tourists and see a real aboriginal village, you can travel a further 18km (one way) south-west into the mountains to reach Fushan.

Half the fun is getting there. The twisting mountain road follows the Nanshih River (*nánshì xī*) through a scenic gorge. About 6km from Wulai Hot Springs Village you'll reach the tiny hamlet of Hsinhsien (*xìnxián*) and the nearby Hsinhsien Waterfall (*xìnxián pùbù*). Nearby is a scenic side canyon called

Wawaku (*wáwagǔ*), meaning 'Doll Valley', the Neitung Forest Recreation Area (*nèidòng sēnlín yóulè qū*) and Nahsiaoyeh Camping Ground (*nǎxiàoyě yíng dì*).

Although Fushan is an aboriginal village, don't expect to see the locals running around in loincloths and brandishing spears – they only do that in the song and dance shows staged for tourists. But Fushan is certainly representative of how many of Taiwan's rural aborigines live today.

There are a number of outstanding hikes from Fushan along rugged trails. It's even possible to walk all the way to the east coast near Chiaohsi (*jiāoxī*) in Ilan County, but finding the way will require detailed directions, if not a guide.

There are no hotels in Fushan, but it's possible to arrange a homestay (*mínsù*) by asking the villagers.

Getting There & Away To get to Fushan you'll need to obtain a mountain permit (NT$10) from the police station next to the bus station in Wulai Hot Springs Village. A passport or other ID is needed. The permit checkpoint is just outside Hsinhsien.

You can take a taxi from Wulai to Fushan, drive your own vehicle or hitch. There's no bus service. Some kayakers from Taipei take their water toys up to Fushan and float back down to Wulai and beyond.

TSUSHIH TEMPLE
(*zǔshī miào*) 祖師廟
Certainly one of the most magnificent temples in Taiwan, the Tsushih (Divine Ancestor) Temple was originally built in 1770 but was allowed to fall apart during the Japanese occupation. Restoration work began in 1947 and took some 45 years! Of particular interest (and one of the reasons why the restoration took so long) is the intricate temple art. Like most Taoist temples, Tsushih comes to life during festivals – Ghost Month is particularly good, as are the first and sixth days of the lunar month. This is a good temple for photography. Admission is free, but donations are welcomed.

It's a bit difficult to get to the Tsushih

NORTH TAIWAN

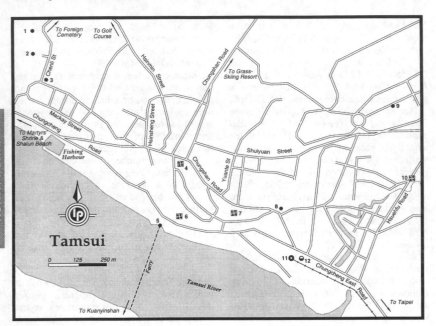

Tamsui

0   125   250 m

TAMSUI 淡水

1 Tamkang Middle
  School
  淡江中學
2 Tamsui Oxford University
  College
  淡水牛津學院
3 Fort San Domingo
  紅毛城

4 Chinfu Temple
  金福宮
5 Ferry Pier
  渡船碼頭
6 Fuyou Temple
  福佑宮
7 Lungshan Temple
  龍山寺
8 Sensaio Bookshop
  新學友書局

9 Tamkang University
  淡江大學
10 Yinshan Temple
  鄞山寺
11 Tamsui MRT
  Station
  淡水捷運站
12 Bus Station
  台汽客運站

Temple. It's in the town of Sanhsia *(sānxiá)*
about 30km south-west of Taipei. There
aren't any other tourist attractions along the
route, so it's an out-and-back trip unless you
have your own vehicle and want to visit
nearby Tzuhu. (Sanhsia itself is an historical
town with many ancient houses, some dating
back to the Ming dynasty.) The departure
point for buses from Taipei to Sanhsia is on
the west side of Chunghua Rd, between

Hankou and Wuchang Sts. Bus Nos 205 and
212 go to Sanhsia. There is also a bus to
Sanhsia from the east side of 2-28 Peace
Park. Buses between Taoyuan and Sanhsia
leave from the Taoyuan Bus Company
station in Taoyuan.

TAMSUI
(dànshuǐ) 淡水
Tamsui is a misspelling of the name Tanshui

(which means 'fresh water'). The misspelling results from the fact that *tamsui* is the Taiwanese (not Chinese) pronunciation for this place. The Taiwanese spelling has become so entrenched that it's now considered correct. Whatever this town is called, it's 20km north-west of Taipei at the mouth of the Tamsui River.

Though Tamsui was once the largest port on the island, Keelung (*jīlóng*) eventually overtook it and Tamsui was reduced to a fishing village. Fishing is only a minor (and declining) industry in Taiwan today, but the spectacular economic growth of Taipei has rubbed off on Tamsui. Today the town is a prosperous place and boasts two fine universities, a golf course and a MRT station.

Fort San Domingo

(*hóng máo chéng*) 紅毛城

The most famous historic site in Tamsui is Fort San Domingo. Its Chinese name literally means 'red body-hair city', which is an abbreviation for 'Fort of Red Body-Haired Barbarians'. The fort is a legacy of the brief Spanish occupation of north Taiwan from 1626 to 1641 and is one of the oldest buildings in Taiwan. The fort was built in 1629 and was occupied by the Dutch when they expelled the Spanish in 1641. The Dutch in turn were kicked out by the Chinese in 1661. In 1724, the fort was renovated and a wall with four gates was built around it. Three of the gates have disappeared, but the fourth gate remains.

In 1867, the fort saw the return of the Europeans one more time – it was lent to the British to establish their consulate in Taiwan. The British added considerable improvements, constructing the beautiful red-brick consul's residence (*yīngguó lǐngshì guǎn sùshè*) in 1891 adjacent to the fort. The British would probably still be there were it not for the severing of relations with the Republic of China (ROC) in 1972. The consulate was closed, but the entire structure (including the consul's residence) has now been reopened as a museum.

Admission to the site costs NT$20. To get there, follow Chungcheng Rd (which runs

parallel to the river) west from the Tamsui MRT station for 2km.

Tamsui Oxford University College

(*dànshuǐ niújīn xuéyuàn*) 淡水牛津學院

Formerly known as Tamsui Junior College (*dànshuǐ gōngshāng*), this beautiful campus with red brick buildings is Taiwan's oldest western style school. The credit for opening the college goes to Dr George Leslie Mackay, a Canadian missionary who first came to Taiwan in 1872. Within the campus is the Oxford Hall (*niújīn xuétáng*), built in 1882. Adjacent to the college is Tamkang Middle School (*dàngǎng zhōngxué*), another one of Mackay's creations.

Both schools are just up the hill from Fort San Domingo.

Tamkang University

(*dànjiāng dàxué*) 淡江大學

This university is in the hills to the north-east of town. The best sight here is the five storey Maritime Museum (*hǎishì bówùguǎn*) which is shaped like a ship. Inside are model boats (from the 15th century up to the present), model engines, a mock ship's bridge and a library. Most interesting of all is the model of Cheng Ho's 15th century treasure boat (see the Sanbao the Sailor boxed text). The Maritime Museum is open from 9 am until 4 pm daily (except Monday and some holidays). Admission is free.

Yinshan Temple

(*yínshān sì*) 鄞山寺

This is one of Tamsui's less known sights. While not a big or lively place, it's considered the best preserved Qing dynasty temple in Taiwan. It's on Hsuehfu Rd on the east side of town.

Martyrs' Shrine

(*zhōng liè cí*) 忠烈祠

Just one of many such shrines around Taiwan, this one is less militaristic and has a more tranquil setting than its counterpart in Taipei.

Shalun Beach

(shālún hǎishuǐ yùchǎng) 沙崙海水浴場
The place where the Tamsui River meets the ocean is Shalun Beach. This is one beach where surfing and windsurfing is possible. You can also go horse riding at the nearby Yuanye Chi Horse Riding Club (☎ (02) 2805-5380; *yuányě qímǎ jùlèbù*).

Tamsui Grass-Skiing Resort

(dànshuǐ huácǎo chǎng) 淡水滑草場
In the hills above Tamsui is the Tamsui Grass-Skiing Resort, one of the most convenient venues in Taiwan for pursuing this peculiar form of recreation.

Getting There & Away

Tamsui is the last stop on the Tamsui line of the MRT. This is by far the fastest way to make the journey.

The Hsintien Bus Company has lots of buses running through Taipei's centre (especially along Roosevelt and Chungshan Rds) from Hsintien in the south to Tamsui in the north. The buses do not have numbers, so you'll need to be able to read the Chinese characters saying Hsintien-Tamsui.

From Tamsui, you can continue along the coastline to Paishawan Beach *(báishāwān hǎishuǐ yùchǎng)*, Chinshan Beach *(jīnshān hǎishuǐ yùchǎng)*, Yehliu *(yěliǔ)* and Keelung, and then return to Taipei. This trip can be done in a day and in either direction.

Getting Around

If you want to explore northern Taiwan by

Sanbao the Sailor

Cheng Ho *(zhèng hé)*, also known as 'Ma Ho' and 'Ma Sanbao', was born in 1371 in China's Yunnan Province. An ethnic Hui (Chinese Muslim of Eurasian descent), Cheng is most probably the source of the famed legend of Sindbad the Sailor.

During the Ming dynasty (1368-1644), Chinese troops were sent into South-West China to expel the Mongols. Chinese soldiers were not known for their subtle methods, and one of their terror tactics to subdue the civilian population was to cut off the sexual organs of every male child they caught. Ma Sanbao was caught at age 10 and duly castrated, but he survived and demonstrated unusual intelligence. Chinese officers decided to recruit him as a eunuch servant for the Ming emperor.

It's claimed that Cheng Ho stood over 2.44m (8ft) tall. This is probably exaggerated, but theoretically his hormone deficiency (caused by his castration) could have led to excessive growth. Before age 25, he was in control of the Imperial Household Agency, overseeing the emperor's thousands of eunuchs.

Cheng Ho's fortunes really improved with the ascent of Yongle to the throne in 1402. Yongle was anxious to expand China's influence by means of foreign naval expeditions. By the Ming dynasty, China had more seafaring vessels than the rest of the world combined, as well as the world's largest ships. Chinese war junks were enormous spectacles of extravagant design, and were as long as the western ships of the day and at least twice as wide. They were coloured white, with tiger heads and dragon eyes painted on the bow to frighten enemies. In battle, the sailors wore tiger masks to look fierce.

Cheng Ho was given command of his first fleet (317 ships) in 1405. Over the next 28 years, he was to lead seven seafaring expeditions. His voyages brought him to 37 countries, as far afield as Arabia and Africa. The fact that he had grown up a Muslim and spoke Arabic no doubt helped to spread his fame in the Middle East, where the Sindbad legend originated.

The five storey ship-shaped Maritime Museum at Tamkang University houses a fantastic re-creation of Cheng Ho's treasure boat. The Chinese are more known for building walls than ships, but China was at one time the world's most important seafaring nation. For more details, see *When China Ruled the Seas – The Treasure Fleet of the Dragon Throne 1405-33* by Louise Levathes.

No one is quite sure what happened to Cheng Ho after his seventh voyage – all records were deliberately destroyed by his rivals. After Yongle's death, the Ming dynasty plunged into decline. The corrupt Qing dynasty followed and China turned inward on itself.

Cheng Ho is virtually unknown in the west, and even most Taiwanese are only vaguely familiar with his feats. His most devoted followers are Chinese communities in South-East Asia, especially in Thailand, Malaysia and Indonesia (where there are several temples named 'Sanbao'). And over on the Arabian peninsula, people still talk about a sailor named Sindbad. ■

rental car, the advantage of renting one in Tamsui is that you don't have to drive it through Taipei's traffic. A good place to try is China Rent-A-Car (☎ 809-9323) at 88 Minchuan Rd.

KUANYINSHAN
(guānyīnshān) 觀音山
This mountain, named after Kuanyin the goddess of mercy, is a pleasant half day hike in the Taipei area. The mountain is 616m high and is directly across the river from Tamsui. You can cross the river from Tamsui by taking a tiny ferry or a bus that crosses a bridge several kilometres away, but it is quicker to reach Kuanyinshan directly from Taipei. In summer, try to head up in the morning to avoid the frequent afternoon thunder showers. The trails are marked in Chinese only; inexperienced hikers should go with a mountain club.

The Sanchung Bus Company *(sánchóng kèyùn)* offers a direct bus service from Taipei. The bus station is on Tacheng St *(tǎchéng jiē)*, which is just west of the North Gate, by the GPO. The buses run about once every 20 minutes.

FORMOSAN WATER PARK
(bāxiān lèyuán) 八仙樂園
Where the slopes of Kuanyinshan meet the sea is the Formosan Water Park (☎ 2610-5200) – the literal Chinese translation is Eight Fairy Amusement Park. Although the name alone puts many foreigners off, it's not a bad place. The waterslides are the best in the Taipei area and they get chaotically busy on weekends.

To get there, you need to take a bus with no number, operated by the Sanchung Bus Company, that leaves from a stop on Tacheng St just west of the North Gate. The bus is marked in Chinese *běimén-bālǐ* which means 'North Gate-Eight Village'

PAISHAWAN BEACH
(báishāwān hǎishuǐ yùchǎng) 沙灣海水浴場
To the north of Tamsui is Paishawan, a nice beach that has surfing, windsurfing and hang-gliding facilities. Of course, it's only really enjoyable to go there during summer. There is an entry fee of NT$100 which gets you snack bars, lifeguards, changing facilities and someone to clean up the litter. There are plenty of local buses making the north coast run from Tamsui.

CHINSHAN BEACH
(jīnshān hǎishuǐ yùchǎng) 金山海水浴場
Chinshan Beach is one of the best beaches close to Taipei. It does get crowded during summer weekends, but the rest of the time it's a relaxing change of pace.

If this is your first time at a beach in Taiwan, you'll pick up an interesting fact – this may be an island, but few people can swim. An amazing number of people drown in Taiwan every year in small lakes, streams and perfectly calm sea. What most Taiwanese call 'swimming' is what I'd call wading. At Chinshan Beach, if you get into neck deep water you'll leave the crowd behind, but the lifeguards will frantically blow their whistles at you and perhaps launch a heroic rescue effort.

Admission to the beach costs NT$80. Admission to the swimming pool is NT$100. There are also hot spring baths close by, which charge NT$100 entry.

Places to Stay
Most people treat Chinshan as a day trip from Taipei, but if you want to stay, check out the *Chinshan Youth Activity Centre* (☎ 2498-1190; *jīnshān qīngnián huódòng zhōngxīn*) run by the China Youth Corps (CYC), which is right by the beach at 1 Chingnien Rd. They have two budget twin rooms costing NT$2000. Rooms for four to six persons are NT$2500. Then there are group rooms – bring along 11 friends and the whole lot can sleep snugly together for NT$3000. At the other extreme there are six bungalows costing NT$3300 each.

Getting There & Away
You can reach Chinshan very easily from Taipei by catching a bus or train to either Keelung or Tamsui (Keelung is closer), and then transferring to a local bus. Chinshan is

on the loop road that takes you through Tamsui, Chinshan, Yehliu, Keelung and back to Taipei, making a fine trip for a day or two.

A more direct approach from Taipei is to take the bus that goes over the mountains in Yangmingshan Park. You catch this bus from the Chunglun bus station *(zhōnglún zhàn)* in Taipei. If coming from Taipei, it's more appealing to take the coast road to Chinshan and the mountain road when returning.

YEHLIU
(yěliǔ) 野柳

About 10km north-west of Keelung is Yehliu Park, known for its bizarre, jagged rock formations moulded by the elements. The rocky coastline is beautiful, but don't go too near the edge – you'll see a statue that has been built in honour of a man who drowned while trying to save another drowning man at this spot.

After you've explored the main area of rock formations – frequently crawling with camera clicking tourists – continue along a footpath that climbs steeply up and towards the end of the promontory. When you reach the top you'll see a lighthouse overlooking the coastline; the view is magnificent. Continue out to the end of the promontory and you'll discover little alcoves that are nearly deserted. The area is rarely crowded, since

most of the tourists can't handle walking up the hill and prefer to hang out close to the parking lot. Admission to the park is NT$80.

FEITSUIWAN
(fěicuì wān) 翡翠灣

Feitsuiwan (Green Bay) is a small stretch of sandy beach just south-east of Yehliu. It's distinguished by the fact that it's the closest spot to Taipei that offers good surfing possibilities.

A new upmarket place to stay has opened up; the *Howard Pacific Green Bay Resort* (☎ 2492-6565; *tàipíngyáng fěicuì wān fúhuá*) has twins with an ocean view for NT$4500 and suites cost from NT$5800 to NT$10,000. Features include an indoor swimming pool, spa, fitness centre, sauna, tennis and volleyball courts, disco, bar, private beach, a 'Fisherman's Wharf', yacht club, and western and Chinese restaurants.

Local buses from Keelung frequently run to this part of the coast. From Taipei, you can get a bus directly to Feitsuiwan from Taipei's Chunglun bus station.

KEELUNG
(jīlóng) 基隆

Keelung – which really should be spelled Chilung – is better known as a container port than as a tourist attraction. It's the third

Wind and weather have shaped the rocks at Yehliu into strange formations. Some believe the shapes look like the heads of ancient tribespeople.

largest port in Taiwan, following Kaohsiung and Taichung. Taiwan's booming trade has turned Keelung into a very prosperous city, and as an international seaport, there are many foreigners who pass through.

Keelung has a pleasant atmosphere and is not that large – the population is around 350,000. The view from the green hills around the city is fine, though up close the harbour is unattractively polluted. The water has the look of cola (including the bubbles), though drinking it cannot be recommended.

During the winter months, this is one of the wettest places in Taiwan – winter visitors should bring an umbrella or plan to buy one while you're here. Sunny skies are the norm during summer, although short thunderstorms in the afternoon are a common occurrence.

Information
There are Foreign Affairs Police (☎ 2425-2787) in Keelung if you need them.

Statue of Liberty
(zìyóu nüshén) 自由女神
On the hill just behind McDonald's is a replica of New York's most famous woman. Actually, there are many such replicas in Taiwan – the Statue of Liberty and Mickey Mouse seem to be the two symbols of the USA that have really caught the imagination of the Taiwanese. While this may not be one of Keelung's most famous tourist attractions, it makes a great photograph – the golden arches of McDonald's, the Statue of Liberty and some Chinese billboards all together. You need to use a powerful telephoto lens for the best results.

Kuanyin Statue & Temple
(guānyīn miào) 觀音廟
The north-east skyline of Keelung is dominated by the huge white statue of Kuanyin, the goddess of mercy. The statue is visible from many parts of the town, so you'll have no trouble finding it. You can climb the stairs inside the statue for a splendid view, particularly at night. Adjacent to Kuanyin is a large temple built in her honour. The whole area is

surrounded by the greenery of Chungcheng Park. A series of smaller temples dot the edge of the ridge.

Sea Gate Barrier Fort
(hǎimén tiānxiǎn) 海門天險
Just a short walk north-east of the Kuanyin Temple are some old cannons and other remains of a fort that was built in the 1840s. This is said to be the only fort in Taiwan built by the Taiwanese – the others were constructed by the Spanish, Dutch and other would-be colonists.

Even if you have no particular interest in cannons, the sea views from the ridge are good and you can continue walking for a long distance.

Shihfang Tachuehchan Temple
(shífāng dàjuéchán sì) 十方大覺禪寺
The temple commands a magnificent view from its hillside location among the trees. You'll find it on the west side of town just off An-1 Rd. Buses running from Keelung to Chinshan Beach stop near the temple, though if you're feeling energetic it's possible to reach it on foot.

Places to Stay
The Longfa Hotel (☎ 2422-4059; lóngfā lǚshè), 23 Hsiao-4 Rd, is the cheapest place in town. Doubles cost NT$500.

The Yongji Hotel (☎ 2422-3570; yǒngjí dà lǚshè), 2nd floor, 31 Chung-1 Rd, costs NT$700 but isn't really worth the money.

The clean, friendly and modern Dream Palace Hotel (☎ 2422-3939; mèngdiàn dà fàndiàn), 22 Yi-1 Rd, is a good choice. Doubles are NT$880. The big sign only says 'hotel' in English, but it's easy to find – it's opposite the Hotel Kodak and just above a 7-Eleven store. The entrance is down a small alley.

The Jindongxing Hotel (☎ 2422-8206; jīndōngxīng dà fàndiàn), 58 Chung-2 Rd, charges NT$1050 to NT$2000 for a cushy twin room. Check out the circular beds.

The Huashuai Hotel (☎ 2422-3131; huáshuài dà fàndiàn), 108 Hsiao-2 Rd, is also very comfortable. Double rooms start at

NORTH TAIWAN

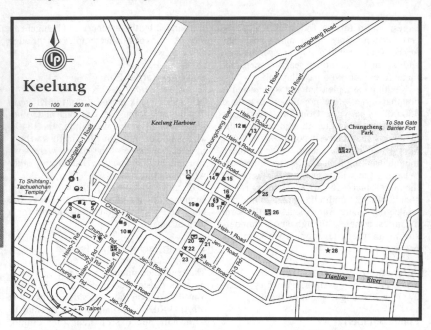

KEELUNG 基隆

PLACES TO STAY
3 Longfa Hotel
   隆發旅社
4 Yongji Hotel
   永吉大旅社
6 Jindongxing Hotel
   金東興大飯店
9 Huashuai Hotel
   華帥大飯店
10 Huaxing Hotel
   華星大飯店
12 Hotel Royal
   老爺大飯店
14 Hotel Kodak
   柯達大飯店
15 Dream Palace Hotel
   夢殿大飯店
16 Aloha Hotel
   阿樂哈大飯店
17 Beidoo Hotel
   北都大飯店

PLACES TO EAT
7 KFC
   肯德基家鄉雞
13 Domino's Pizza
   達美樂比薩店
22 Pizza Hut
   必勝客
23 McDonald's
   麥當勞
24 Temple St Night
   Market
   廟口夜市

OTHER
1 Train Station
   火車站
2 Taiwan Bus Company
   Station
   台汽客運站
5 Keelung Bus Company
   Station
   基隆客運站

8 Ching'an Temple
   慶安宮
11 Pier No 2 Okinawa Ferry
   & Matsu Ferries
   基港大樓東二碼頭
18 Bank of Taiwan
   台灣銀行
19 Cultural Centre
   文化中心
20 GPO
   郵政總局
21 Telephone Company
   電信局
25 Martyr's Shrine
   忠烈祠
26 Jile Temple
   極樂寺
27 Kuanyin Statue &
   Temple
   觀音佛像
28 Foreign Affairs Police
   警察局外事課

NT$980. Facilities include a coffee shop, restaurant, and laundry and foreign currency exchange services. The major credit cards are accepted.

The Huashuai is not to be confused with the similarly named *Huaxing Hotel* (☎ 2422-3166; *huáxīng dà fàndiàn*), 54 Hsiao-1 Rd, where rooms cost NT$1050, NT$1200 and NT$1300. Facilities include a restaurant, coffee shop and laundry service. Credit cards are accepted.

Towards the north end of town is the *Hotel Royal* (☎ 2422-4141; *lǎoyé dà fàndiàn*), 71 Yi-1 Rd. Doubles cost NT$1100. Facilities include a foreign currency exchange service, laundry service, conference room, car park and travel service.

Diagonally opposite the Bank of Taiwan is the *Aloha Hotel* (☎ 2422-7322; *ālèhā dà fàndiàn*), 292-1 Hsin-2 Rd, where doubles/twins cost NT$1080/1380. This place has a laundry service and accepts credit cards.

Opposite the Aloha is the *Beidoo Hotel* (☎ 2422-7899; *běidǒu dà fàndiàn*), 319 Hsin-2 Rd. This new, plush place has doubles starting at NT$1480. Facilities include a coffee shop, restaurant, car park and foreign currency exchange and laundry service. Major credit cards are accepted.

One of the best hotels in town is the *Hotel Kodak* (☎ 2423-0111; fax 2425-2233; *kēdá dà fàndiàn*), 7 Yi-1 Rd, where the doubles cost from NT$2200 to NT$2600, and twins are NT$2400 to NT$2800. Facilities include a coffee shop, restaurant, conference room, car park and foreign currency exchange and laundry service. Credit cards are accepted.

Places to Eat

At lunch and dinner time there are food stalls set up around the Ching'an Temple.

The *Temple St Night Market (miàokǒu yèshì)* is closed to motorised traffic in the evening and becomes one big eating orgy. Seafood is the local speciality, though snake, dog and other delicacies are available on demand. Ask the prices first – it's amazing how much someone will charge for a snake.

Domino's Pizza (☎ 2424-5522; *dámèilè*

bǐsà diàn), 86 Yi-1 Rd, is take away only and will deliver to your hotel.

Getting There & Away

Bus Buses depart for Keelung about once every five to 10 minutes from Taipei's East bus station and the fare is NT$45. The Suao *(sū aò)* to Taipei buses stop in Keelung near the ferry departure point only, rather than at the Taiwan Bus Company *(táiqì kèyùn)* bus station near the train station; make sure you get off at the ferry stop, or you could end up in Taipei!

Opposite the Taiwan Bus Company bus station are some chairs beneath a rain shelter – this is what passes as a bus station for the Keelung Bus Company *(jīlóng kèyùn)* and is the place to wait to catch the buses to Chiufen *(jiǔfēn)*.

Train Although this mode of transport helps you avoid the heavy traffic, most of the trains are slower than the buses. There are trains between Keelung and Kaohsiung (all stopping in Taipei), but departures are infrequent. As a general rule, you're better off doing the Taipei-Keelung run by bus, especially as there is practically no difference in price between the two.

Boat Keelung is the arrival and departure point for both the international ferry to Okinawa (Japan), and the ferry to Matsu (an island just off the coast of China). Both ferries depart from pier No 2 on the east side of Keelung harbour. For further information on the Okinawa ferry, see the Getting There & Away chapter. For details on the Matsu ferry see the Islands of Taiwan Straits chapter.

CHIUFEN

(jiǔfēn) 九份

An old gold-mining town in the hills east of Keelung, Chiufen is unique in Taiwan for having preserved its historic architectural beauty. Ironically, it was economic failure that accounts for Chiufen's present status as a tourist attraction. After the gold ore gave out, Chiufen's mining industry collapsed. For decades the town remained a forgotten,

NORTH TAIWAN

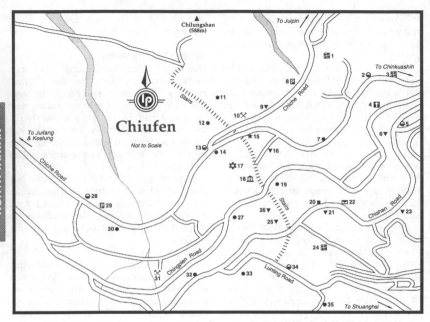

destitute backwater. It was only in the 1990s that Chiufen's residents discovered a new gold mine in the form of souvenir shops, teahouses, art galleries and fine restaurants.

The official tourist sights are the Fushan and Shengming temples, the Gold Mining Museum and the Taiyang Mining Office. However, the main thing to do here is to wander the steep, narrow alleys and stop in at any of the town's dozens of teahouses. Some of the teahouses stay open all night, especially on public holidays (or the night before holidays).

Places to Stay

While there are no hotels as such, arranging a homestay *(mínsù)* is fairly easy. Indeed, there are signs (in Chinese) advertising these places – look for them along Chishan St and Chingpien Rd.

Places to Eat

Noodles are a local specialty, and places to

try include the *Chiufeng Noodle Restaurant (jiǔfèn lǎomiàn diàn)* and *Chiutaokou Beef Noodles (jiùdàokǒu niúròumiàn)*.

For traditional Taiwanese dishes, try the *City of Sadness Restaurant (bēiqíng chéng-shì cānfīng)*.

Getting There & Away

Taipei First get to the Chunglun bus station on Pateh Rd, Section 2. Find the bus operated by the Tayou Bus Company *(dàyǒu bāshì)* heading for Chinkuashih *(jīnguāshí)* and take it as far as the Chiufen stop. The one way journey takes about two hours because these buses do not take the freeway. Buses operate on this route about once every 30 minutes from 6 am until 6 pm.

At the Chunglun bus station you can also catch the faster buses operated by the Taiwan Bus Company, but these only go as far as Juifang *(ruìfāng)*. At Juifang you can catch either a bus or taxi to Chiufen. Taxis here do *not* go by the meter, but the ride should cost

NORTH TAIWAN

CHIUFEN 九份

PLACES TO EAT
6 Chiutaokou Beef Noodles
  舊道口牛肉麵
9 Chilungshan Teahouse
  基隆山之戀
16 Yihsiang Teahouse
  藝鄉
21 Herbal Cake Shop
  草仔粿
23 Chiufeng Noodle
  Restaurant
  九份老麵店
25 Chiufen Teahouse
  九份茶坊
26 City of Sadness
  Restaurant
  悲情城市餐廳

OTHER
1 Mingsheng Temple
  明聖宮
2 Tienpantang Bus Stop
  天判堂站
3 Tienpan Temple
  天判宮

4 Protestant Church
  基督教堂
5 Chiutao Bus Stop
  舊道站
7 Tienfang Yetan Teahouse
  天方夜譚
8 Chiuhaoping Car Park
  九號坪停車場
10 Pafankeng Mine
  八番坑
11 Taiyang Mining Office
  台陽礦物事務所
12 Tourist Service Centre
  旅遊服務中心
13 Chiufen Bus Stop
  九份站
14 Chiufen General Store
  九份雜貨店
15 Police Station
  派出所
17 Peng Garden
  彭園
18 Gold Mining Museum
  九份礦石博物館
19 Folk Art Gallery
  九份民俗藝術小集

20 Shihchia Homestay
  施家民宿
22 Post Office
  郵局
24 Shengming Temple
  聖明宮
27 Shenping Theatre
  昇平戲院
28 Takanlin Bus Stop
  大竿林站
29 Takanlin Car Park
  大竿林停車場
30 Sungte Park
  頌德碑公園
31 Wufankeng Mine
  五番坑
32 Wufankeng Teahouse
  五番坑茶坊
33 Chiufen Elementary
  School
  九份國小
34 Lunting Bus Stop
  崙頂站
35 Chinhsien Junior High
  School
  欽賢國中

roughly NT$250. The journey from Juifang to Chiufen takes about 10 to 15 minutes.

Alternatively you can take an east coast train bound for Hualien and get off at Juifang. Be aware that not every train heading for Hualien stops at Juifang.

Keelung From the Keelung Bus Company stop (*jīlóng kèyùn*), catch the bus heading to Chinkuashih and get off at Chiufen. Not every bus that goes to Chinkuashih stops in Chiufen, so you'll have to ask the driver if they will be stopping there. These buses run about once every 20 minutes from 6.05 am until 10.05 pm.

LUNGTUNG
(lóng dòng) 龍洞
Taiwan's most beautiful stretch of rocky coastline lies north-east of Taipei, between Lungtung (Dragon Hole) and Pitouchiao (*bítóujiǎo*). There are no sandy beaches here, but the enterprising Taiwanese have come up

with the Lungtung South Ocean Park which has sea water swimming pools. There is also a diving school here.

The sheer cliffs surrounding the bay have made this area Taiwan's prime spot for technical rock climbing. Westerners have also started to test their skills on the cliffs. Even if rock climbing isn't your forte, the scenery is excellent.

To get there, first get yourself to Keelung. From Keelung, take a bus from the Taiwan Bus Company station to Lungtung (about a 40 minute ride). Buses depart once or twice an hour throughout the day. The bus passes Pitouchiao and then enters a tunnel. After it leaves the tunnel it stops in the town of Lungtung, which consists of a few houses and small stores. From the bus stop, walk back towards the tunnel. Just before you reach the tunnel, you will see a path dropping down to your right. Follow the path all the way down to the sea (about a 25 minute walk). When you hit the coast, turn left and continue walking until you see the rock-climbing area. As long as you go when the weather is fine, you should see climbers. During the wet winter months you probably won't see anybody.

SHIHFEN & PINGHSI
(*shífēn & píngxī*) 十分，平溪
Shihfen and Pinghsi are just two of several towns alongside Highway 106, a narrow back road that runs between southern Taipei and southern Keelung.

More interesting is the Pinghsi Railway (*píngxī xiàn*), which starts at Juifang, continues to Hutung (*hóudòng*), Shihfen, Pingsi, finally terminating at Chingtung (*qīngtóng*). The train ride takes just under an hour and is good fun. The only problem is that once you get off the train, you have no way to get around unless you've brought along a folding bicycle, so you really need private transport. Probably the most famous spot in the area is Shihfen Waterfall (*shífēn pùbù*), closely followed by Wangku Waterfall (*wànggǔ*).

The best way to get around the area and really enjoy the sights is by motorcycle, or even bicycle if you're up to the task. The road is in good nick, but it's much more enjoyable if you can avoid the weekend traffic.

FULUNG BEACH
(*fúlóng hǎishuǐ yùchǎng*) 福隆海水浴場
Fulung Beach is one of the best beaches in northern Taiwan. The east coast of Taiwan is mostly mountains and jagged rocks, but Fulung is one of the few places with a broad, white sandy beach. Surfing, sailing, water-skiing and jet-skiing are possible here.

Fulung Beach is close enough to Taipei (57km) to make it a good day or weekend trip. During summer it becomes packed on the weekends, but at other times the scenic surroundings are uncrowded.

The town of Fulung is very small, reasonably pleasant and quiet. There is a NT$100 admission fee to the main beach area. The area to the east of the broad sandy beach is free and has good coral formations for snorkelling – plus you get away from the

music that the management blasts out for the customers' enjoyment. The eastern beach has no lifeguards.

Surfers from Taipei come here. The waves are said to be good, but the riptide along the east coast can be dangerous.

Places to Stay
The *Fulung Public Hostel* (☎ 2499-1211; fax 2499-1501; *fúlóng guómín lǚshè*) is right on the beach and is the only place to stay. Actually, it's more like a complex of beach cabins and a camping ground than a hostel. The prices for twins are a heart stopping NT$3200 to NT$3500. Camping is the only cheap alternative. It's NT$300 for a camping site (tent included) or NT$250 if you supply your own tent. Sleeping bags and sleeping mats are also for rent at NT$30 each. Even portable gas stoves and cooking utensils can be rented for a price.

Getting There & Away
You can reach Fulung in less than an hour by train from Taipei's main train station, fares range from NT$62 to NT$132. Failing that, take a bus first to the Taiwan Bus Company station in Keelung and then transfer to the local bus to Fulung.

YENLIAO BEACH
(*yánliáo hǎishuǐ yùchǎng*) 鹽寮海水浴場
About 5km to the north of Fulung Beach is Yenliao, another one of the best beaches in northern Taiwan. There is a monument marking the spot where Japanese invaders first landed on Taiwan.

The nearest train station is in Fulung, and from there it's a short bus or taxi ride to Yenliao.

The Lungmen Camping Area (☎ 2499-1790; *lóngmén lùyíng dì*) is between Yenliao and Fulung.

TSAOLING HISTORIC TRAIL
(*cǎolǐng gǔdào*) 草嶺古道
This trail, near the eastern tip of Taiwan, first came into use around 1807 during the Qing dynasty. Originally it was conceived to improve local transport (at that time by horse), rather than being a hiking trail for

tourists. However, the trail gradually fell into disuse after the Taiwanese built the nearby coast road, which these days carries a considerable amount of motorised traffic.

The trail, 8.5km in length, takes about four hours to walk one way. The path connects Kungliao (*gòngliáo*) in Taipei County with Tali (*dàlǐ*) in Ilan County.

Taoyuan County 桃園縣

TAOYUAN
(táoyuán) 桃園
Taoyuan, west of Taipei, is adjacent to the CKS international airport. There is little reason to visit this city unless you need to spend the night near the airport. If you're coming up from south Taiwan, you'll probably find it easier to take the train to Taoyuan and spend the night, rather than do a mad scramble in the morning. But, if you're coming from Taipei, it's relatively easy to reach the airport and so it shouldn't be necessary to spend the night in Taoyuan. It's important to note that the airport closes at night and you are *not* allowed to sleep on the sofas even if you have a ticket for the first flight out in the morning.

Information
Tourist Office There is a tourist office at the CKS airport (☎ 383-4631) inside the reception hall.

Emergency There is a branch of the Foreign Affairs Police (☎ 333-5107) in Taoyuan if you need them.

Chiang Kaishek Aviation Museum
(zhōngzhèng hángkōng kēxué guǎn)
中正航空科學館
If you've been reading the pamphlets put out by the Tourism Bureau, you may have heard of the Chiang Kaishek Aviation Museum (☎ 398-2222). It's not a bad museum, but most travellers will find it inaccessible. It is right next to the CKS Airport Hotel, a full 2km from the airport terminal. You might

think that you could walk there, but you would have to walk on a freeway-like road with no pedestrian footpaths. Nor is there a regular shuttle bus. About the only people who get to see the museum are guests at the CKS Airport Hotel or those who drive their own cars. The museum is open from 9 am to 4.30 pm daily, except Monday, and admission is NT$50.

Big Temple
(dà miào) 大廟
Also known as the Chingfu Temple (*jǐngfú gōng*), this is Taoyuan's biggest landmark.

Activities
If you're into golf, Taoyuan can accommodate you. North of the city is the Marshall Golf Club (*tǒngshuài gāo'ěrfū qiú chǎng*) and the neighbouring Taipei Golf Club (*táiběi gāo'ěrfū qiú chǎng*).

Places to Stay
The most popular spot with backpackers is the *Taoyuan Hostel* (☎ 332-2157; *zhōngměi dà lǚshè*) at 18 Wenhua St. Rooms are in the NT$400 to NT$500 range.

As you exit the train station, the alley immediately to your left is Changshou (Long Life) St. This place has a couple of cheap and cheapish hotels. *Hangong Hotel* (☎ 332-7189; *hàngōng lǚshè*) at No 9 has doubles for NT$500. Right next door at No 7 is *Fushi Hotel* (☎ 332-4161; *fùshì dà lǚshè*), whose rooms are the same price. At No 5-1 is the better appointed *Nestle Hotel* (☎ 336-5800; *quècháo dà fàndiàn*), with rooms for NT$860 to NT$1600.

Moving upmarket, there's the *Hotel Today* (☎ 332-4162; fax 333-7778; *jīnrì fàndiàn*) at 81 Fuhsing Rd. Doubles/twin rooms go for NT$1000/1200.

The most central upmarket place to stay is the *Taoyuan Plaza Hotel* (☎ 337-9222; fax 337-9250; *nánhuá dà fàndiàn*), 151 Fuhsing Rd. Doubles/twins are NT$1800/2300.

The *Majesty Hotel* (☎ 336-6600; fax 337-4988; *dàjué shāngwù fàndiàn*), 3 Lane 106, Minchuan Rd, gets the nod from foreign business people and engineering types. The rooms are priced from NT$1500 to NT$2700.

A little way out from the city centre is the top-rated *Holiday Hotel* (☎ 325-4021; fax 325-1222; *jiàrì dà fàndiàn*), 269 Tahsing Rd. Rooms are NT$2500 to NT$4800. You'll find everything here from a gymnasium to karaoke.

There is also the *CKS Airport Hotel* (☎ 383-3666; fax 383-3546; *zhōngzhèng guójì jīchǎng lǚguǎn*). Doubles/twins are NT$2600/2800 and suites cost a mere NT$6000 to NT$20,000. Facilities include a swimming pool, KTV and tennis courts. The hotel is right in the airport area, about 2km from the terminal building, and not close to anything else.

Places to Eat

The *Night Market* in a narrow side street north of Sanmin Rd is an interesting place to eat.

The basement of the Tonlin Department Store (*tǒnglín bǎihuò*) has a *food court* serving both western and Chinese fast food.

The *Jiemei Seafood Restaurant* (*jiěmèi hǎicān*) on the corner of Sanmin and Chungcheng Rds is cheap and excellent.

Domino's Pizza (☎ 338-4877; *dáměilè bǐsà diàn*) is at 382 Chungcheng Rd.

If you're into western pub grub (including Mexican food), check out *Rodeo's Restaurant & Saloon* (☎ 331-8089) at 143 Mintsu Rd. It's Taoyuan's most popular expat club. It opens at 11 am and doesn't close until there's no one left in the place.

Entertainment

A bar/restaurant combo that appeals to business travellers is *Itzu Pub* (☎ 336-4282) at 46 Mintsu Rd. Another hot spot worth checking out is *Foxy III Disco Pub* (☎ 339-5798) at 33 Nanhua St.

Getting There & Away

Air Most international airlines serving Taiwan have booking desks at CKS airport. The main offices as listed under Getting There & Away in the Taipei chapter.

Bus & Train If you are coming from Hsinchu (*xīnzhú*), Taichung, Chiayi or other places in

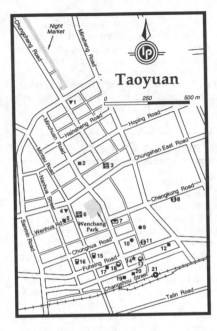

the south, you could take a train or bus to Taoyuan. The train is usually more convenient because most highway buses by-pass Taoyuan and head directly to Taipei. All north-south trains on the west coast stop in Taoyuan.

Getting Around

To/From the Airport You can reach CKS international airport (*zhōngzhèng jīchǎng*) during the day and in the early evening by buses run from the Taoyuan Bus Company (*táoyuán kèyùn*) station – fares cost NT$40. Otherwise, there are plenty of taxis swarming around the train station area. Negotiate the fare in advance and expect to pay around NT$400.

Car Thanks to the airport being here, many Taipei-based car rental agencies have branch offices in Taoyuan. A couple you can try include International Auto Service (☎ 366-6825) and Chuan Chia Fu (☎ 352-5270).

NORTH TAIWAN

TAOYUAN 桃園

PLACES TO STAY
2 Majesty Hotel
　大爵商務飯店
5 Taoyuan Hostel
　中美大旅社、
　文化街18號
12 Hotel Today
　今日大飯店
17 Taoyuan Plaza
　Hotel
　南華大飯店
19 Nestle Hotel
　雀巢大飯店
20 Hangong & Fushi
　Hotels
　漢宮大旅社、
　富士大旅社

PLACES TO EAT
1 Jiemei Seafood
　Restaurant
　姐妹海餐
4 Rodeo's Restaurant &
　Saloon
　民族路143號

OTHER
3 Big Temple
　大廟、景福宮
6 Mingde Temple
　明德宮
7 GPO
　郵政總局
8 ICBC
　國際商業銀行
9 Far Eastern Department
　Store
　遠東百貨

10 Tonlin Department
　Store
　統領百貨
11 Bank of Taiwan;
　McDonald's
　麥當勞、台灣銀行
13 Taoyuan Bus Company
　Station
　桃園客運
14 Foreign Affairs Police
　警察局外事課
15 Itzu Pub
　民族路46號
16 Foxy III Disco Pub
　南華街33號
18 Taiwan Bus Company
　台灣客運
21 Taoyuan Train Station
　桃園火車站

TZUHU
(cíhú) 慈湖

Tzuhu, which translates as 'Kindness Lake', is where the body of Chiang Kaishek is entombed. Unlike the elaborate Chiang Kaishek Memorial Hall in Taipei, the tomb at Tzuhu is simple. There is a reason for this: the site is regarded as temporary. It was always Chiang's intention – stipulated in his will – that his body be returned to his native province of Zhejiang on the mainland after China is reunited.

Chiang has been waiting since December, 1975, following his death in Taipei. In a surreal scene, thousands lined the streets of Taipei and sobbed uncontrollably. After the funeral, the president's body was transported to his 'temporary' tomb in Tzuhu, built in accordance with the principals of Chinese geomancy. Every year on the anniversary of Chiang's death, the Generalissimo's aging friends and high ranking Kuomintang (KMT) officials pay a respectful visit to their fallen leader, and wish him a speedy return home. At other times, visitors are few and growing scarcer every year. Busloads of school children are the biggest visitors.

The tomb remains tightly guarded. As the Generalissimo's political popularity has waned, fears of a nasty anti-Chiang backlash have grown. The last thing the government wants are truckloads of protesters with loudhailers, throwing eggs and bottles.

You can take photographs outside the mausoleum but not inside. You're allowed about a minute inside to view the granite case in which the body has been placed. It is customary to give a respectful bow.

Back outside, you might want to linger briefly at the lake, which is between the reception area and the tomb. There is a shop which sells drinks and snacks, but (surprisingly) has nothing in the way of Chiang memorabilia.

Getting There & Away
To reach Tzuhu from Taipei, first take a train to Taoyuan or Chungli *(zhōngli)*. From there you can get a bus directly to Tzuhu or else to the nearby town of Tahsi *(dàxī)*, from where you'll have to get another bus to Tzuhu. Buses from Tahsi to Tzuhu are not very frequent so you might have to take a taxi. Fortunately, it's not too far so it's not very expensive.

It is possible to combine a visit to Tzuhu with a trip to the Tsushih Temple and Shihmen Reservoir. However, there are no direct buses between these places even

NORTH TAIWAN

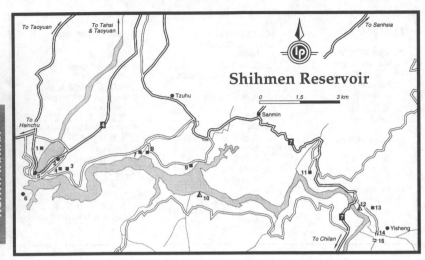

SHIHMEN RESERVOIR
石門水庫

1 Sesame Hotel
芝麻酒店
2 Asia Amusement Park
亞洲樂園
3 Hejiahuan Hotel
合家歡石門
渡假俱樂部
4 Yun Hsiao Hotel
雲霄大飯店
5 Dam
水壩

6 Fairyland
童話樂園
7 Dragon Pearl Bay Holiday
Centre
龍珠灣渡假中心
8 Lakeview Hotel
觀湖山莊
9 Shihmen Lake
Hotel
湖濱大飯店
10 Pine Forest Camping
Ground
松樹林營地

11 Fuhsing Youth Activity
Centre
復興青年活動中心
12 Grand Canyon Camping
Ground
大峽谷露營地
13 Fuchang Hotel
富場山莊
14 Hsiao Wulai
Waterfall
小烏來瀑布
15 Longku Waterfall
龍谷瀑布

though they are very close to each other. You must first go back to Tahsi, which is out of the way, and either change buses or take a taxi. The most convenient way to get around these places is to drive yourself.

SHIHMEN RESERVOIR
(shímén shuǐkù) 石門水庫
Shihmen Reservoir forms the largest lake in northern Taiwan. The Shihmen Dam, on the Tahan River, is nestled in the foothills south-west of Taipei. Construction of the dam

began in 1955 and was completed in 1964. It's an attractive area, especially for Taipei residents looking to escape the horrors of urban living. However, Shihmen Reservoir gets so congested with cars on weekends that it's a bit of an urban horror itself.

If you arrive by bus, the driver will drop you off right by the dam, the main touristy spot. From there you can join a boat tour or walk around. The road on the north shore of the lake is an attractive but very long hike – a motorcycle would be useful. Swimming is not permitted in the lake, though public fishing is allowed.

The area is thick with Disneyland clones, the largest being the Asia Amusement Park (☎ 471-2427; *yàzhōu lèyuán*) which is known for its 'spiral roller coaster'. The nearby Fairyland *(tónghuà lèyuán)* is really for children – anyone over the age of eight will find it immensely boring.

Upstream, just above the reservoir, the countryside becomes more interesting. Here you will find Hsiao Wulai Waterfall *(xiǎo wūlái pùbù)* and Longku Waterfall *(lónggǔ pùbù)*.

There is a beautiful drive between Shihmen Reservoir and Chilan *(qílán)*, via the North Cross-Island Highway (Highway 7). Details about making this trip are given in the following North Cross-Island Highway section.

Places to Stay

Shihmen Reservoir is mainly geared towards the well-to-do tourist. Camping is the most economical way to go, and some places have tents set up just waiting for you to rent them. Typical camping site rentals, with a tent (that you must use) included, cost around NT$300. Two places to pursue this sanitised form of camping include the Grand Canyon Camping Ground *(dà xiágǔ lùyíng dì)* and the Pine Forest Camping Ground *(sōngshù lín lùyíng dì)*.

At the east end of the reservoir near Hsiao Wulai Waterfall is *Yisheng Village (yìshèng)*. Homestays *(mínsù)* are available here for as little as NT$800, making it the cheapest spot in Shihmen Reservoir to rent a roof over your head.

The *Sesame Hotel* (☎ 471-4025; *zhīmá jiǔdiàn)* sets a high standard but has no view of the lake, though it does overlook the river below. There are sporting facilities, including tennis courts. Doubles cost NT$3000, twins cost NT$3600 to NT$4000 and suites are NT$4200 to NT$7200.

The *Yun Hsiao Hotel* (☎ 471-2111; *yúnxiāo dà fàndiàn)* is on a hill right next to the dam. At the time of writing, it was undergoing a major renovation that will take up to

three years to complete. When it reopens, room rates are expected to be from NT$2000 to NT$2500.

The *Hejiahuan Hotel* (☎ 471-2111; *héjiāhuān dùjià jùlèbù)* is also close to the dam. Doubles/twins here are NT$1100/2000.

The *Dragon Pearl Bay Holiday Centre* (☎ 388-4545; *lóng zhū wān dùjià zhōngxīn)* consists of a large five storey hotel and a number of wooden cabins in a park-like setting. Rooms can be rented for NT$1800, but the cabins are NT$4000.

Near the Dragon Pearl is the *Lakeview Hotel* (☎ 388-8853; *guānhú shān zhuāng)*. Rates here are NT$2000 and up.

The *Shihmen Lake Hotel* (☎ 388-5121; *húbīn dà fàndiàn)* is further into the mountains, but is so busy it has a carnival-like atmosphere. Prices begin at NT$3000.

Higher into the mountains is the *Fuhsing Youth Activity Centre* (☎ 382-2276/382-2788; *fùxīng qīngnián huódòng zhōngxīn)*. It's meant for groups, but individuals report success at getting into the dormitory on weekdays. The two twin rooms cost NT$1200, quads are NT$1000, eight-person rooms are NT$2400 (NT$300 per person), 12-person rooms are NT$2600 (NT$217 per person) and 14-person rooms are NT$3000 (NT$214 per person).

Nearby is the *Fuchang Hotel (fùchǎng shān zhuāng)*. Doubles/twin rooms cost NT$1200/2400.

Getting There & Away

To get to Shihmen Reservoir, first take a bus or train to Chungli, which is 36km southwest of Taipei. In Chungli, buses to Shihmen Reservoir are operated by the Hsinchu Bus Company *(xīnzhú kèyùn)*. Buses to the reservoir are infrequent. If you don't get one right away, you have the option of catching a bus to Tahsi and then taking either a bus or taxi, or hitchhiking up to the reservoir.

NORTH CROSS-ISLAND HIGHWAY

(běibù héngguàn gōnglù) 北部橫貫公路
Highway 7, which is also known as the North Cross-Island Highway, is a beautiful mountain road, that starts from Taoyuan and then

NORTH TAIWAN

heads up into the hills above Shihmen Reservoir. From the reservoir the highway continues to the south-east until it reaches Chilan, where it then branches: the north branch heads down to the east coast at Ilan *(yílán)* and the south branch heads still higher up into the mountains until it intersects with the Central Cross-Island Highway at Lishan. Buses operated by the Taoyuan Bus Company use the highway and the driver should drop you off at Paling and Mingchih. Cars are infrequent, so hitching is not practical except on weekends. It's a good route to drive along if you have your own vehicle.

If you stay at the Paling Mountain Hostel (see the following Places to Stay section), you can do the Lalashan Forest Reserve day hike. Just to the north-west of Paling is the mountain Takuanshan *(dáguānshān)* in the Lalashan Forest Reserve *(lālāshān shéngmù qún)* You can reach the mountain by walking 13km along the gravel road. You gain about 1000m in elevation, so you might consider hitching uphill and walking back, assuming that you see any cars. A mountain permit is needed, but it can easily be obtained at the forest reserve entrance along the way. The area is known for its giant cypress trees, some of which are more than 2500 years old. Takuanshan itself reaches 2030m above sea level.

Places to Stay

The *Paling Mountain Hostel* (☎ 391-2126; *bālíng shān zhuāng*), high up the mountains, contains only group rooms, but individuals can usually get in when it's not crowded. The 12-person dorms are NT$2400 (NT$200 per person). If you can't get into the dorm, you can always try looking for somewhere to camp, which has the advantage of being free.

At Mingchih *(míngchí)* you'll find the *Mingchih Mountain Villa* (☎ 989-4104; *míngchí shān zhuāng*), where comfortable

Taiwanese Chewing Gum

One thing you'll undoubtedly find for sale at street stalls everywhere in Taiwan is betel nut *(bīnláng)*. The locals refer to it as 'Taiwanese chewing gum', though in fact it's common throughout South-East Asia. Indeed, it's such an important cash crop in the region that many small South-East Asian farms couldn't survive without it.

The betel nut is the seed of the betel palm, a beautiful tree that resembles the coconut palm. Unlike coconuts, the flesh of the betel nut is not edible – swallow it and you'll be sorry! It's meant to be chewed. The seed is usually sold with a slit in it, mixed with lime and wrapped in a leaf. Like tobacco, it's strong stuff that you first can barely tolerate but eventually get addicted to. The first time you bite into betel nut, your whole face gets hot – chewers say it gives them a buzz.

Just like chewing tobacco, betel nut causes excessive salivation – the result is that betel chewers must constantly spit. The reddish-brown betel nut stains on the footpaths of Taipei look like freshly spilled blood (uninitiated foreigners have often been misled into believing they've stumbled across the site of a recent murder).

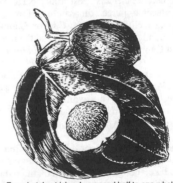

For a betel nut 'chew' you need half to one whole nut of the Areca Palm, several bites of the leaf or fruit of a betel-pepper climber and a teaspoon of slaked lime (made by burning certain seashells and corals) – a tube of good toothpaste may come in handy too.

Chewing betel nut is considered to be bad for your health, but it's good business for the dental profession. Years of constant chewing causes teeth to become stained, progressively browner and eventually nearly black. ■

doubles are NT$800. Food is available in Mingchih and Paling.

WINDOW ON CHINA
(xiǎo rén guó) 小人國

Many years ago I read a novel entitled *Slapstick* by Kurt Vonnegut. According to the story, the Chinese found that the only way they could feed their massive population was to make people smaller. Chinese scientists discovered a way to shrink people. So China closed its borders to the world and began the downsizing process. Several years later, the world was gripped by a massive killer plague. People were dying like flies. An American doctor discovered the reason why – the disease was caused by inhaling microscopic Chinese.

'Nonsense' you say? Then welcome to the Window on China (☎ 471-7211). It's an outdoor park that contains exact replicas of many of China's famous architectural wonders such as the Great Wall and the Forbidden City. And yes, miniature people too. Some of Taiwan's notable building projects are also included, such as the Chiang Kaishek Memorial, the Sun Yatsen Freeway (with miniature cars) and CKS international airport (with miniature planes). Perhaps frighteningly, more recent additions have included miniatures of monuments in Japan, Western Europe and the USA.

Everything is reduced to one-twenty-fifth of normal size. The Tourism Bureau calls it a 'world class tourist attraction'. Who says the Taiwanese don't have a sense of humour? Admission is NT$480. The Window on China is open daily from 8.30 am to 5.30 pm.

Getting There & Away

To reach the Window on China from Taipei, take a train to Chungli and then a bus from the Hsinchu Bus Company station, which is near the train station.

The Window on China is close to Leofoo Village and it is possible to visit both places on the same day. You may also want to visit Tzuhu and Shihmen Reservoir in the same trip, especially if you have your own car or motorcycle.

Hsinchu County 新竹縣

LEOFOO VILLAGE
(liùfú cūn) 六福村

The 'village' got its start as Leofoo Safari Park (☎ 587-2626). The zoo is still there, but it has been supplemented with Disney-style castles, waterslides, a children's train (far more popular than Taipei's MRT) and Taiwanese dressed up as cowboys.

At NT$650 for adults, it is still much cheaper than a real African safari. The tariff is reduced to NT$550 for those between 90 and 110cm tall, and it's only NT$350 for children under 90cm. Opening hours are from 9 am to 4.30 pm daily.

Getting There & Away

Certainly the most convenient way to get to the park is to take the bus operated by the Leofoo Hotel (☎ (02) 2507-3211; *liùfú kèzhān*) at 168 Changchun Rd, Taipei. Buses depart daily at 9 am. The price of the ticket includes the return fare, admission and a tour around the park.

You can reach the village by taking a train from Taipei to Chungli and then a bus from the station opposite the train station. There are also some buses from Hsinchu.

GOLDEN BIRD AQUATIC PARK
(jīn niǎo hǎizú lèyuán) 金鳥海族

This is basically an ocean park even though it's far from the ocean. The seals are perhaps the stars of the show. It's really a place for children. Expat families living in Hsinchu like to make weekend trips up here (along with the usual throng of Taiwanese people).

It's convenient to visit this place if you have your own car. The park is not too far south of Shihmen Reservoir, and it's possible to take in both places on the same journey. There are also buses operated by the Hsinchu Bus Company, by way of Kuanshi *(guānxī)*. From Kuanshi the buses run about each hour between 7 am and 4.20 pm. Three of these buses continue to Fuhsing on the upper end of Shihmen Reservoir.

NORTH TAIWAN

NORTH TAIWAN

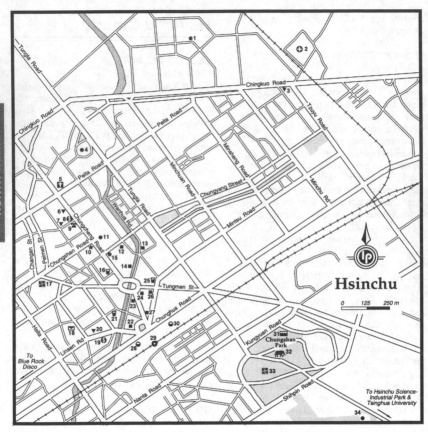

HSINCHU

(xīnzhú) 新竹

Hsinchu is a medium size city that is famous in Taiwan for its windy winter weather. The city itself is lacking in sights, and tourists are few (even Taiwanese tourists). Most visitors just use Hsinchu as a transit stop on the way to Hsiao Dingdang, Shihtoushan *(shítóushān)* or Tapachienshan *(dà bà jiān shān)*.

On the other hand, Hsinchu has a large and growing expat population. What draws them is the Science-Industrial Park, Hsinchu's economic ace of spades. As one might expect, an active pub and restaurant scene is increasingly catering to this foreign market. It's still not Taipei, but if Hsinchu has anything (besides computers) that would appeal to foreigners, it would be the nightlife.

Information

There is a branch of the Foreign Affairs Police (☎ 524-2103) in Hsinchu.

Hsinchu Science-Industrial Park

(xīnzhú kēxué yuán qū) 新竹科學園區

This is Taiwan's 'Silicon Valley', a high-technology centre with virtually nothing of interest to tourists. Perhaps you might want

HSINCHU 新竹

PLACES TO STAY
12 Chinatrust Hotel
中信大飯店
13 Sol Hotel
迎曦大飯店
14 Dong Cherng Hotel; Mer
Cady Coffee Shop
門卡迪炭燒咖啡、
東城大旅社
22 Dongbin Hotel
東賓大旅社
23 Bin-Chen Hotel
賓城大飯店
24 Hotel Central;
McDonald's
中央旅社、麥當勞
26 Moonlight Hotel
明月大飯店
27 Golden Swallow
Hotel
金燕大飯店

PLACES TO EAT
3 Restaurant 199
一九九餐廳、
經國路468號
6 Pizza Time
中正路137號

7 Boulevard Tea Shop
布雁瓦、
世界街132號
20 McDonald's; Pizza Hut
(Sunrise Department
Store)
中興百貨、麥當勞、
必勝客

OTHER
1 Graceland
光華二街1號
2 Hsinchu Provincial
Hospital
省立新竹醫院
4 Cultural Centre
文化中心
5 Cathedral
天主堂
8 ICBC
中國國際商業銀行
9 Telephone Company
電信局
10 Foreign Affairs Police
警察局外事課
11 City Hall
市政府
15 Far Eastern Department
Store
遠東百貨

16 Coach Pub
中正路5號
17 Chenghuang
Temple
城隍廟
18 GPO
郵政總局
19 Bank of Taiwan
台灣銀行
21 Nepal Pub; US Pub
大同路23巷10號、
大同路23巷2號
25 Every Day's Bar &
Restaurant
民族路33-48號
28 Taiwan Bus Company
Station
台汽客運站
29 Train Station
新竹火車站
30 Hsinchu Bus Company
新竹客運站
31 Swimming Pool
游泳池
32 Zoo
動物園
33 Confucius Temple
孔廟
34 Chiaotung University
交通大學

to visit if you're looking for a job. It's about 4km south-east of the train station, on the east side of the freeway (Highway 1).

Universities
There are two national universities here – Tsinghua University (*qīnghuá dàxué*) at 855 Kuangfu Rd and Chiaotung University (*jiāotōng dàxué*) at 100 Tahsueh Rd – that specialise in science and technology. The campuses are well manicured and serve as unofficial parks.

Hsinchu Zoo
(*xīnzhú dòngwù yuán*) 新竹動物園
As zoos go, this one's quite small. It's in Chungshan Park, behind the train station, just near the Confucius Temple (*kǒngzǐ miào*).

Chenghuang Temple
(*chénghuáng miào*) 城隍廟
The temple contains lots of artwork and is especially active during Ghost Month and on the 1st and 6th days of the lunar month. You'll find the temple near the intersection of Chungshan Rd and Tungmen St.

Hsiao Dingdang Science Amusement Park
(*xiǎo dīngdāng kèxué yóulè qū*)
小叮噹科學遊樂區
This is an outdoor science park 8km north of town. Hsiao Dingdang (named for a Japanese cartoon character) is directed more towards children than adults, but there are enough gizmos here to keep anyone amused for a few hours.

Admission for adults is NT$400, but there are discounts for students and children. It operates daily from 9 am to 5 pm. Chinese speakers can ring the park up (☎ 559-2132) for information.

The Hsinchu Bus Company station is the place to catch the bus to the park. You can take a bus to Hsiao Dingdang itself (once hourly) or Hsinfeng (*xīnfēng*; twice hourly) nearby.

Grass Lake
(qīngcǎo hú) 青草湖

The lake is east of town near the freeway. The locals seem to think it's a very impressive sight. Personally, I think it's just a small lake with grass around it.

Activities
To the north of Hsinchu is the Hsinfeng Golf Club *(xīnfēng gāo'ěrfū qiú chǎng)*.

Places to Stay – budget & middle
There is a *camping ground* in the Hsiao Dingdang Science Amusement Park (see its entry above).

The *Golden Swallow Hotel* (☎ 522-7151; *jīnyàn dà fàndiàn*) at 13 Mintsu Rd is good value at NT$550 for a double – they even have waterbeds available! Top-end rooms cost NT$1400.

The *Dongbin Hotel* (☎ 522-3162; *dōngbīn dà lǔshè*), 14 Linsen Rd, has dark doubles for NT$500 to NT$600.

The *Hotel Central* (☎ 522-4126; *zhōngyāng lǔshè*), 30-1 Chungcheng Rd, is a somewhat bleak place hidden in a small alley. The sign says NT$500, they actually ask NT$700 but will accept NT$600.

The *Bin-Chen Hotel* (☎ 526-9255; *bīnchéng dà fàndiàn*), 15 Chungcheng Rd, has doubles/twins for NT$650/1500.

The *Dong Cheng Hotel* (☎ 522-2648; *dōngchéng dà lǔshè*), 1 Lane 5, Fuhou St, is a very nice place on a quiet side street. Rooms cost from NT$700 to NT$900.

Places to Stay – top end
The *Chinatrust Hotel* (☎ 526-3181; fax 526-9244; *zhōngxìn dà fàndiàn*), 8th floor, 106 Chungyang Rd, is hidden behind the Far Eastern Department Store. Rooms are NT$2650 to NT$9900. It's decidedly upmarket, with fine facilities including a bar, business centre, conference room and (horrors) karaoke.

The *Moonlight Hotel* (☎ 523-4138; *míngyuè dà fàndiàn*), 29 Mintsu Rd, looks deceptively small – there is another branch further from the city centre with an additional 70 rooms. Both hotels are very clean and pleasant. Doubles/twin rooms cost NT$2100/2700.

The *Sol Hotel* (☎ 534-7266; fax 533-5750; *yíngxī dà fàndiàn*), 10 Wenhua St, is Hsinchu's best accommodation. This palatial place has doubles from NT$2950 to NT$3300, twins/suites cost NT$3700/6000.

Places to Eat
From noon until late at night, *food stalls* set up around the Chenghuang Temple and provide what locals claim to be the best cheap eats in Taiwan.

Restaurant 199 (yījiǔjiǔ cāntīng), 468 Chingkuo Rd (near Tzuyou Rd) is one of those all-you-can-eat firepot *(huǒguō)* buffets so popular with the Taiwanese. The cooking is done right at your table. Just pile loads of vegetables, beef, fish, mushrooms, prawns, or whatever on a plate and dump it into the pot of boiling water. The price is NT$199 for lunch on weekdays, but there is an additional 10% service charge and a weekend or night fee, so it can add up to nearly NT$300 at peak times.

Boulevard (bùluówǎ), 132 Shijie St, is a tea shop owned by a Taiwanese woman and her French husband. It's possible to drink all kinds of tea and eat good western food – the lasagne is terrific. The price range is a moderate NT$200 to NT$250 for a meal. It's open daily from 10 am to 11.30 pm.

Domino's Pizza (☎ 526-9799; *dáměilè bǐsà diàn*), 163 Chungcheng Rd, delivers right to your hotel.

The basement of the Sunrise Department Store *(zhōngxīng bǎihuò)*, 32 Linsen Rd, has a *McDonald's* and *Pizza Hut*.

Pizza Time, 137 Chungcheng Rd, adds a new twist to the definition of fast food – the cost of the pizza is apportioned to the time you spend eating it. Check it out if you're a fast eater.

Entertainment

Cinemas The cheapest place to see a film in Hsinchu is *Central Cinema* – just NT$70 for two films. The cinema in the basement of the Sunrise Department Store is probably the best in town. The line-up of cinemas in Hsinchu is as follows:

Central
    (☎ 522-2655; *zhōngyāng xìyuàn*) 27 Chang'an St
Hsinfucheng
    (☎ 524-8285; *xīnfùzhěng xìyuàn*) 26 Peimen Rd
Huayang
    (☎ 534-6752; *huáyáng dà xìyuàn*) 225 Chungcheng Rd
Hungpaoshih
    (☎ 533-2163; *hóngbǎoshí diànyǐng yuàn*) 5th floor, 72 Chingkuo Rd, Section 2
Sun
    (☎ 521-4151; *rìshèng dà xìyuàn*) 8th floor, 32 Linsen Rd
Sunrise
    (☎ 522-0220; *zhōngxīng bǎihuò*) basement, Sunrise Department Store, 32 Linsen Rd

Discos *Graceland*, 1 Kuanghua 2nd St, is a bar and disco in the Grace Hotel. It's popular with expat science-engineering types, but don't come here for a business conference – the music volume is turned way up.

Another place for loud music and liberal quantities of alcohol is *Blue Rock Disco* at 201 Chungshan Rd.

MTV If you're into MTV, check out *Barcelona* (☎ 526-5370; *bāsèluónà*) on the 6th floor at 33 Linsen Rd. It's just opposite the Sunrise Department Store.

Pubs *Mr Seven*, 28 Wenhua Rd, is a long-running expat pub, and a good place to start the nightlife marathon.

Hidden in an alley is *Nepal*, 10 Lane 23, Tatung St. Locals and expats meet here to dance and drink. The bartender does magic tricks and the owner – who is part aborigine – dances with the clients. In the same alley is *US Pub*, which draws some of the overflow clientele from Nepal.

The *Coach Pub*, 5 Chungcheng Rd, is another place where many expats can be found playing darts and sampling the local brew.

Every Day's Bar & Restaurant (☎ 525-0564), 33-48 Mintsu Rd, is a new expat wining, dining and meeting spot. It's in an alley close to the Sol Hotel.

Just around the corner from Every Day's is the *Mer Cady Coffee Shop* (☎ 524-7678; *ménkǎdí tànshāo kāfēi*), 3 Fuhou St. It's a European-style pub and restaurant with a mixed expat and Taiwanese clientele. The management says that they stay open 24 hours a day, though I admit that I didn't personally test the claim.

Getting There & Away

Hsinchu's new airport opened in 1998 (or rather, an old military airfield was converted into an airport). Currently, the only flights available are Hsinchu-Chiayi, Hsinchu-Kaohsiung and Hsinchu-Kinmen. More routes may be added later.

Hsinchu is 70km south-west of Taipei and sits right on the major west coast train line. Taipei-Hsinchu by train takes approximately 1½ hours.

The Taiwan Bus Company has frequent buses from Hsinchu to Taipei and Taichung. There are less frequent services to smaller cities such as Tainan and Chiayi.

Getting Around

If you need to rent a car, you can try China Rent-A-Car (☎ 532-6333), 231 Mintsu Rd, or International Auto Service (☎ 573-4022).

Miaoli County 苗栗縣

SHIHTOUSHAN

(shītóushān) 獅頭山

Shihtoushan, or Lion's Head Mountain, is a leading Buddhist centre in Taiwan. The name derives from the fact that the mountain vaguely resembles the head of a lion when viewed from a distance. Shihtoushan is a very restful place and draws a steady stream of pilgrims from all over Taiwan. For foreign visitors, the main attraction is the chance to visit temples and the opportunity to stay in a Buddhist monastery in beautiful natural surroundings. You can also watch the morning services at the crack of dawn. However, if you don't wish to stay in a monastery, you can still visit Shihtoushan as a day trip from Hsinchu.

Shihtoushan's temples are not very old, and indeed there were some new ones under construction when I first visited, but they are all enchanting. Spending the night in one of the monasteries can be interesting, but this is not the place for nightlife. Monks and nuns lead a spartan lifestyle and follow a rigid daily routine. They go to bed early and get up early. If you stay in a monastery you must bathe daily, usually between 3 and 6 pm (when hot water is available) which is early by Chinese standards; the monks and nuns go to bed at 8 pm. You can stay up later if you like, so long as you don't disturb those who are sleeping. Since the monks and nuns get up at dawn, you will have to as well.

SHIHTOUSHAN 獅頭山

1 Ling Pagoda
 靈塔
2 Chuanhua Hall
 (Rooms)
 勸化堂
3 Kaishan Temple
 開善寺
4 Yuankuang
 Temple
 元光寺
5 Fuhai Pagoda
 福海塔
6 Haihui Nunnery
 海會庵
7 Chuehwang Cave
 覺王洞
8 Chinkang Temple
 金剛寺
9 Linghsia Cave
 靈霞洞
10 Store
 商店
11 Wanfo Temple
 萬佛庵
12 Bus Stop
 車站
13 Store
 商店
14 Shuilien Cave
 水廉洞
15 Elementary
 School
 獅山國小

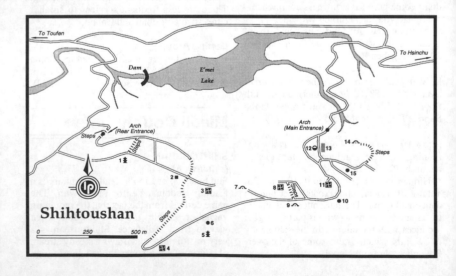

During the day, you are free to come and go as you like. The monks and nuns realise that westerners have their own peculiar customs and they are reasonably tolerant, but when you're on their turf they also want you to be tolerant and respect their religion and lifestyle. Couples cannot sleep together, even if they're married. Public displays of affection are also unacceptable. You may take photographs in the temple but don't disturb the worshippers. If the daily routine and social practices of a monastery are too confining for you, it's better not to stay there.

Miaoli County is notable for fog and wind, especially in winter, so make sure you bring a jacket as it can be really chilly at night.

Places to Stay & Eat
The most popular monastery is the *Yuankuang Temple (yuánguāng sì)*. It's near the top of the mountain, offers the best scenery and there is a caretaker who can speak English. The other monasteries that offer accommodation are *Linghsia Cave (língxiá dòng)* and *Chuanhua Hall (quànhuà táng)*. You can't book to stay at these places so just turn up and try your luck.

The more or less mandatory donation for staying in any of these places is NT$700 and this includes your dinner and breakfast. It costs another NT$100 if you stay for lunch. Expect breakfast to be served at about 5.30 am, lunch at noon and dinner at 5.30 pm. The food is good and vegetarian. Strict silence is observed while eating. Don't waste your rice! If you throw any away the monks are liable to get upset, as they believe in wasting nothing. If you need additional snacks, you can buy them from some of the vendors at the foot of the hill.

Getting There & Away
From Hsinchu, you cannot go directly to Shihtoushan – you must transfer buses. First take a bus to Chutung *(zhúdōng)*, which is a 25 minute trip. Buses run about once every 10 minutes from the Hsinchu Bus Company station, which is on the traffic island in front of the Hsinchu train station.

From Chutung there are infrequent buses to Shihtoushan (a 40 minute trip). At the time of writing, departures from Chutung were at 6.40 and 10.40 am, and at 1.55 and 5 pm. The first bus does not run on Sunday or holidays because it's used primarily to shuttle school children. On weekends, there are additional buses at 8.30 and 9.15 am and at 3.30 pm. The bus lets you off at the last stop and from here there's an hour's hike up a steep incline to the top of the mountain, so try to keep luggage to a minimum. If your backpack is overloaded, you can put the heavy items in a box and stash it in the left-luggage room at the Hsinchu train station for NT$17 per day.

KUANWU FOREST RECREATION AREA
(guānwù sēnlín yóulè qū) 觀霧森林遊樂區
Kuanwu is a beautiful, cool, forested region 2000m above sea level. The giant trees here *(shénmù)* are very impressive and look especially eerie in the fog that rolls in every afternoon. There are many good hikes in the area, most of which can be completed in two or three hours. Two popular hikes are those to Pahsien Waterfall *(bāxiān pùbù)* and Kuanwu Waterfall *(guānwù pùbù)*. There's a peak that many Taiwanese like to climb to see the sunrise, and there's a hatchery for a rare species of freshwater salmon.

The *Kuanwu Hotel* (☎ 521-8853; *guānwù shān zhuāng*) offers great scenery but not great rooms. In the high season, doubles/twins cost NT$880/1320. There are group rooms which can accommodate eight, 10, 18 and 20 people at about NT$330 per person. In the low season (winter) there are 30% discounts. When the hotel is overbooked (a problem in summer) it's possible to rent a sleeping bag for NT$100 and sleep in the TV room on a hard concrete floor. A sleeping mat would be an asset.

Two other places to stay are *Hsuehpa Farm* (☎ 585-6192; *xuěbà nóngchǎng*) and *Tapa Salmon Hatchery* (☎ 585-6239; *dàbà guīzhūn yú yǎngzhí chǎng*).

You need a class B mountain pass to visit Kuanwu, but it's easily obtained en route, at a checkpoint on the road, for NT$10 (bring a passport, ARC or some other picture ID). Kuanwu is 60km south-east of Chutung.

NORTH TAIWAN

To get there take a Hsinchu Bus Company bus from Hsinchu to Chutung and then switch to the Kuanwu bus. The Kuanwu Highway also leads to Tapachienshan (see the following section), but the trailhead for the latter is 20km further into the mountains.

TAPACHIENSHAN

(dà bà jiān shān) 大霸尖山

Tapachienshan means 'Big Chief Pointed Mountain'. Many consider Big Chief the most beautiful peak in Taiwan. At an elevation of 3492m, it's one of the jewels of Shei-Pa National Park (the 'Pa' in Shei-Pa refers to Tapachienshan).

Unfortunately, the situation here is the same as at Yushan – the whole area requires a class A mountain pass. To obtain this precious document, you are supposed to be accompanied by a licensed guide. The most practical way to climb Tapachienshan is with a mountain club. Clubs typically depart on Saturday morning and don't return until Monday, a three day journey. Some clubs also make a quick run up nearby Hsiaopa (Little Chief).

Tapachienshan's summit is shaped like a pyramid and is sheer on all sides. The government installed some metal railings to make it possible to reach the top, but after a few people fell off, going to the summit was prohibited.

The peak is not near Hsinchu, but that's more or less the starting point. Take a bus from the Hsinchu Bus Company station to the town of Chutung. From there you can get a bus to Chienshankou *(jiānshānkǒu)*, a bus stop 80km away, which is the trailhead.

From Chienshankou (1750m), it's a steep hike up to *Hut 99* (☎ (03) 522-4163; *jiǔjiǔ shānzhuāng*) at 2800m, where most climbing parties spend the night. The final assault on the (almost) summit is usually made at the crack of dawn (real enthusiasts try to reach the top in time for the sunrise). Assuming you depart Hut 99 at 6 am, you can reach Big Chief at 11 am and Little Chief at 11.30 am. You should be able to get back to the hut before 5 pm. In total, figure on about 11 hours of walking at a relaxed pace, though

speedy hikers can do it in nine hours or less. If you leave the hut the next morning at 6 am, you can get back to Chutung by afternoon and Hsinchu (or Taipei) by evening.

This hiking schedule depends on whether or not the road to Chienshankou is open. It has frequently been knocked out by landslides. To do this hike you will have to be travelling with a hiking club, presumably your leader will have made a few phone calls and checked out the situation in advance.

Ilan County 宜蘭縣

MIYUEWAN

(mìyuèwān) 蜜月灣

Also known by its English name, Honeymoon Bay, Miyuewan is a small but beautiful black sand beach at the northern end of Ilan County. This is also the home of the Honeymoon Bay Surfing Club and the Surfing Centre. Both places operate hostels with basic rooms for NT$350. Camping is also possible. There are plenty of places to eat at this popular spot, at least during summer when the weather cooperates. As at most east coast beaches, rip tides can be a problem.

You can reach Miyuewan by taking a train to Tahsi station. Only two express trains stop here daily – if you miss those, take a local train *(pǔtōng chē)* which takes about two hours from Taipei. The bus from Keelung and Taipei also stops in Miyuewan.

CHIAOHSI HOT SPRINGS

(jiāoxī wēnquán) 礁溪溫泉

Wufengchi Waterfall *(wǔfēngqí pùbù)* in the hills above Chiaohsi is the best reason for visiting this place. It's not evident at first glance, but there are in fact three cascades. The first one you confront (the bottom one) is 5m high and is decked out with Chinese pavilions and stone benches – this is as far as most Taiwanese tourists get. A trail leads up to the second falls (a much more impressive 20m in height) and then on to the third falls. If you have more ambition, follow the signs (in Chinese) or ask for directions to the

Shengmu Pagoda and then continue past it. You'll wind up on a trail that takes you to a plateau – it takes about five hours to walk the entire circuit.

Within walking distance of the waterfall is a luxury hotel complex. In winter, residents of Taipei who are weary of the city and cold come to Chiaohsi to soak in the hot springs. These springs are enclosed in hotels and you must pay to use them. There is also a horse-riding stable near the falls, but the staff prefer you to ride around the car park in circles rather than on trails through the forest.

If you want to tee off, Chiaohsi is also known for its golf course.

Places to Stay

There are dozens of hotels in the town of Chiaohsi itself, and most have signs in English so they're easy to find for the non-Chinese-speaking foreigner. However, many feel that it's only worth spending the night in Chiaohsi if you stay by the waterfall area, which is much more beautiful than the town. Near the waterfall is a complex of several luxury hotels with their own restaurants, swimming pools and other amenities.

Unfortunately budget accommodation is thin on the ground. The cheapest place is the *Vacation Hotel* (☎ 988-1511; *dùjià lǚguǎn*) on the 2nd floor above a shop. Rooms are just NT$600 but you get what you pay for.

Comfortable rooms are available at the upmarket *Wufengchi Hotel* (☎ 988-5211; *wǔfēngqí dà fàndiàn*), where twins are NT$1500 to NT$5400 but there is a 40% discount on weekdays.

Next door is the *Happy Hotel* (☎ 988-1511; *kuàilè shān zhuāng dà fàndiàn*), with twin rooms from NT$1500 to NT$6600. Discounts here are only 15% on weekdays.

There is also a little-used free camping area near Wufengchi Waterfall.

Getting There & Away

Reaching Chiaohsi Hot Springs from Taipei is easy enough. Local trains heading down the east coast stop there, as do numerous buses plying the route between Taipei and Suao. Get off the bus or train in the town of

Chiaohsi. It is about a 50 minute walk or a short taxi ride from Chiaohsi to the waterfall. You should be able to flag down a passing taxi or a hotel can call one for you.

ILAN

(yílán) 宜蘭

The largest city in Ilan County, Ilan is of no special interest to most travellers other than as a transit point. It's also an administrative centre with a Foreign Affairs Police (☎ 935-3921) branch at 23 Weishuei Rd. However, the city has won some plaudits for its efforts to protect the environment. If you have a passion for birdwatching, the Lanyang River *(lányáng xī)* just south of town is said to be a prime spot from September to May each year.

Hotels are numerous around the train station area. Budget travellers should check out the *Ilan Student Hostel* (☎ 935-3411; *yílán xuéyuàn*), 100-2 Weishui Rd. Dormitory beds are NT$200, though it may fill up with students during the school year.

Ilan is most easily approached by rail from Taipei, fares are between NT$104 and NT$223 depending on the class. Buses from Taipei and Keelung also stop here.

LOTUNG

(luódōng) 囉東

About 10km south of Ilan is Lotung, a small city notable for it's excellent parks on the edge of town – easily the finest in Taiwan.

The Lotung Athletic Park *(luódōng yùndòng gōngyuán)* is to the north-west of the centre. The park is about 40 acres in size and is the best one of its kind in Taiwan.

To the east of Lotung is Chinshui Park *(qīnshuǐ gōngyuán)*. *Chinshui* means 'near the water'. Water is a major theme here, courtesy of the Tungshan River *(dōngshān hé)* which flows through the well landscaped park. In July, Lotung hosts an International Children's Festival where imported Mongols, Latvians and Israelis all strut their stuff to traditional rhythms. It's well worth an evening out.

Lotung is a major train stop on the east

coast line and is also easily reached by bus from Ilan.

CHILAN FOREST RECREATION AREA
(qīlán sēnlín yóulè qū) 棲蘭森林遊樂區
At approximately 500m above sea level, Chilan has one of the lowest altitudes of any of Taiwan's forest recreation areas. This is not to say it isn't pretty – it's in the valley of the Lanyang River, a very attractive place. If nothing else, it should whet your appetite for some of the high altitude treats available elsewhere.

The place to stay is the *Chilan Mountain Hostel* (☎ 980-9606; *qīlán shān zhuāng*). It's an attractive place – none of the buildings are over two storeys and every room has a reasonably good view. Dormitories go for NT$400. Twins cost NT$2000 and cabins are NT$4000.

· Chilan is 39km south-west of Ilan. Buses operated by the Taiwan Bus Company depart from Ilan at 7.30, 9.30 and 11.20 am.

JENTSE, TAIPINGSHAN & TSUIFENG LAKE
(rénzé, tàipíngshān & cuìfēng hú)
仁澤，太平山，翠峰湖
Towering majestically over the scenic east coast is the sprawling Taipingshan Forest Recreation Area *(tàipíngshān sēnlín yóulè qū)*. The area is so clean, peaceful (on weekdays) and unspoiled that one could easily forget that Taipei lies only 50km away (as the crow flies).

This forest recreation area can be subdivided into three parts, based mainly on the accommodation that is available. Driving from Ilan, the first of the big three is Jentse (45km from Ilan). Jentse is a hot-springs resort at 650m above sea level. The springs can reach a temperature of 95°C, which is extremely warm. However, cold water is added to make it bearable for bathers. Like most hot springs in Taiwan, the water is pumped into hotels and there is no hope of finding a quiet spot for private outdoor bathing.

Next up is Taipingshan itself, 61km from Ilan. At 1950m above sea level, it's much cooler than Jentse and it doesn't have any hot springs. However, it's still a lovely spot for hiking. There are marked trails and the admission ticket has a map (in Chinese) on the back. More detailed topographic maps can be purchased in mountaineering shops in Taipei.

A further 18km into the mountains is Tsuifeng Lake. The lake is very small but very alpine and pretty in appearance. The road is narrow and winding, reaching an elevation of 2350m – the drive takes about 50 minutes. Many people like to walk this road, though there are additional hikes above Tsuifeng Lake – ask for details at the hotels.

There is an NT$100 admission fee to enter the Taipingshan Forest Recreation Area.

Places to Stay
The *Jentse Mountain Hostel* (☎ 980-9603; *rénzé shān zhuāng*) is the place to stay when the weather is cold. The weather is warmer at Jentse and you can enjoy a soak in the hot springs, but in summer you may prefer to go higher into the mountains. Room rates here are NT$1345 to NT$2800. Camping is permitted at Jentse for NT$200 per site with tent included, but it is strictly prohibited at Taipingshan.

In Taipingshan itself, the place to stay is the *Taipingshan Mountain Hostel* (☎ 980-9806; *tàipíngshān shān zhuāng*). Dorms are NT$450 and twins cost from NT$2000 to NT$4800.

Tsuifeng Mountain Hostel (☎ 932-2103; *cuìfēng shān zhuāng*) has dormitories only. Despite the somewhat Spartan conditions, it's not really cheap at NT$660 per person. Camping is strictly prohibited.

Getting There & Away
The Taipingshan area is a backwater and transport is a headache if you don't have your own wheels. Buses depart only once a day from Ilan at 9.30 am, stopping briefly in Lotung and then continuing to Chilan, Jentse and Taipingshan. The place to contact for transport information is the Taiwan Bus Company in Ilan (☎ 936-5441) or Lotung (☎ 956-7505). The returning bus from

Taipingshan departs at 3.30 pm. No bus goes all the way to Tsuifeng Lake – that leg of the journey you'll either have to walk, hitch or drive yourself.

In contrast to the scarce public buses, tour buses from Taipei descend on Taipingshan *en masse* during the peak (summer) season and major public holidays.

MINGCHIH FOREST RECREATION AREA

(míngchí sēnlín yóulè qū) 明池森林遊樂區

This is an area that's being newly developed for tourism, and still hasn't reached prime status. The elevation is 1240m above sea level, but it often feels colder than you'd expect because of the frequently cloudy skies (the sun shines just 60 days a year!). Although it's not the perfect place to get a suntan, the area is lush with thick forests and meadows, and hiking trails are being developed. The trails are marked in Chinese. While the area is lacking huge, challenging peaks it's still worthwhile to visit, but real mountaineers will rate Mingchih to be 'Wilderness Lite'.

Accommodation is provided at the *Mingchih Mountain Hostel* (☎ 989-4104). Twins are priced from NT$2000 to NT$4800. The entry fee to Mingchih is NT$100.

Access is from Ilan. Buses depart Ilan just once daily at 7.50 am. Going the other direction they leave Mingchih at 11.20 am.

SUAO

(sū aò) 蘇澳

Suao is more or less a transit stop for Hualien (see the East Coast chapter) but it does have a smattering of sights around the town which can keep you amused for the day.

Temples

Suao seems to have more than its share of temples. Interesting ones include the Hsienkung Temple *(xiāngōng miào)*, the Tienchun Temple *(tiānjūn miào)*, the Hsiangkuang Temple *(xiángguāng sì)* and the Chenghuang Temple *(chénghuáng miào)*.

Nanfang'ao

(nánfāng'aò) 南方澳

Suao actually has an international harbour, which is pretty amazing for such a backwater. However, the international port is hardly worth looking at. The real attraction is about 2km to the south-east at Nanfang'ao. This is an attractive fishing harbour where wooden fishing boats and steel freighters are built. Just south of the fishing harbour is a good and little-used beach *(nèipí hǎishuǐ yùchǎng)*.

However, the star of the show is neither the harbour nor the beach. Nantien Temple *(nántiān gōng)*, right on the edge of Nanfang'ao Harbour, is the town's pride and joy. Inside the temple you'll find a very impressive gold-plated statue of Matsu, goddess of the sea.

To reach Nanfang'ao, follow the road that leads out of the south side of town (part of the Suao-Hualien Highway), which takes you up a big hill. Take the left fork which brings you right into the village.

Places to Stay

Suao is a small place and all of the hotels are within walking distance of the bus and train stations.

The *Jinhua Hotel* (☎ 996-2526; *jīnhuá dà lǚshè*), 1 Lengchuan Rd, is a new place and a good choice for budget travellers. Doubles are NT$500 to NT$800.

The *Xinghua Hotel* (☎ 996-2581; *xīnghuá lǚshè*), 13 Su'nan Rd, offers doubles for NT$400 with shared bath, and NT$500 with private bath and air-con.

The *Yazhou Hotel* (☎ 996-4085; *yàzhōu lǚshè*), 18 Su'nan Rd, looks rather dumpy on the outside though it is mostly acceptable inside. Doubles are NT$700 to NT$800.

The *Suao Hotel* (☎ 996-5181; *sū aò fàndiàn*), 7 Sutung Chung Rd, is the largest hotel in town. The facilities are very good and rooms are priced from NT$1500 to NT$2400.

Places to Eat

Seafood is ubiquitous – the locals even dish up squid for breakfast. If you don't like seafood, you'll face possible starvation in Suao. Fortunately, there seems to be one place that serves up cheap rice, vegetables and meat: *Luwang Cafeteria (lùwáng zìzhù cān)* on the north-west corner of Chungshan and Chungcheng Rds. Luwang means 'deer king' – I didn't see any deer meat though.

Getting There & Away

Bus There is nobody on duty in the Suao bus station – you must purchase your ticket on the bus when it stops in the car park.

There are two bus routes between Suao and Taipei. The fastest option is to take one of the direct Taipei-Suao buses which follow a mountain route. The slower, but most scenic option is to catch a Taipei-Keelung bus and then a Keelung-Suao coastal bus.

The direct Taipei-Suao buses depart from Taipei's North bus station. There are departures in both directions about once an hour throughout the day from 6 am until 8.30 pm.

One bus departs Suao for Hualien at 1 pm each day. From Hualien, buses depart for Suao at 6.30 am. The journey takes about three hours.

Train Suao has two train stations: an old one

SUAO 蘇澳

PLACES TO STAY
6 Jinhua Hotel
  金華大旅社
9 Yazhou Hotel
  亞洲旅社
10 Xinghua Hotel
  興華旅社
13 Suao Hotel
  蘇澳飯店

OTHER
1 Chenghuang Temple
  城隍廟
2 Petrol Station
  加油站
3 Hsienkung Temple
  仙公廟
4 Hsiangkuang Temple
  祥光寺
5 Bank of Taiwan
  台灣銀行

7 Bus Station
  台汽客運站
8 Old Train Station
  蘇澳火車站
11 Post Office
  郵局
12 Luwang Cafeteria
  鹿王自助餐
14 Chungyung Temple
  忠勇廟
15 Tienchun Temple
  天君廟

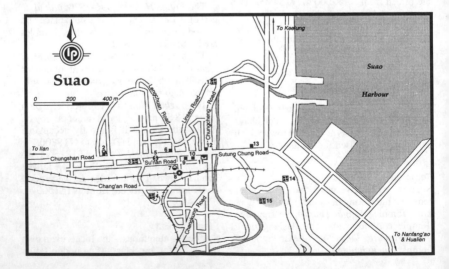

next to the bus station in central Suao and a new one 4km west of town called 'Hsin Suao' *(xīn sū aò)*. All express trains from either Taipei or Hualien stop only in Hsin Suao. The old Suao station is only served by the slow local trains. Therefore, if you arrive by express train, you have to take a bus from Hsin Suao to old Suao. You can purchase tickets on the bus, but the train station sells them too. The buses tend to follow the schedule of the train – when you arrive in Hsin Suao, there should be a bus waiting to take you into Suao. You catch the shuttle bus directly in front of the train station.

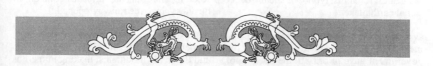

The East Coast 台灣東部

The eastern part of Taiwan presents a dramatic coastline of jagged rocks and towering cliffs, which offers a welcome change from the urban sprawl of Taipei. A mere 10% of Taiwan's population resides on the east side of the island as it is not the friendliest environment for agriculture and industrialisation. Furthermore, the east coast gets Taiwan's most powerful typhoons and it is also occasionally hit by severe earthquakes.

The east coast scenery is so stunning that it's easy to forget you're in Taiwan. The sparsely inhabited rugged landscape that characterises this area could easily pass for the coast of New Zealand.

If you don't have the time to travel all the way around Taiwan, head down the east coast to Hualien and then cut across the island over the mountains to Taichung. This is a very scenic route, although it does miss out on some of the major attractions in south Taiwan.

HIGHLIGHTS

- **Taroko Gorge** – a national park with a marble gorge, waterfalls, hikes, hot springs and aboriginal culture
- **Hsiukuluan River** – Taiwan's premier whitewater rafting venue
- **Chihpen Hot Springs** – a great place for a warm winter soak
- **Orchid Island** – a remote volcanic island where aboriginal culture still flourishes

Hualien County 花蓮縣

SUAO TO HUALIEN
(sūhuā gōnglù) 蘇花公路

The east coast of Taiwan is lined with spectacular mountains and steep cliffs. The area between Suao and Hualien is particularly dramatic, especially at a section called the **Chingshui Cliff** *(qīngshuǐ duànyaí)*; where sheer rock walls drop straight into the sea from towering mountains (over 1000m). In the 1920s, the occupying Japanese managed to carve a narrow road through this section, but ever since there has been a continuous battle between maintenance road crews and landslides, rockfalls, typhoons and the occasional earthquake.

At one time, the east coast transport system was so poor, causing a major impediment to the economic development, that the government gave priority to the opening of

a reliable railway line. Incredible as it might seem, in 1980 the Suao-Hualien railway line was finally completed, ending the isolation of the east coast. The line cost over US$200 million (in 1980!) to construct and it passes through 15 tunnels and over 91 bridges. Previously, the most reliable way to go between Taipei and Hualien was via the ferry from Keelung Harbour; the ferry has gone out of business since the railway opened.

The train is a great deal faster than the bus, but it spends much of its time going through tunnels. On the other hand, the bus climbs up and down the mountains, making numerous

EAST TAIWAN

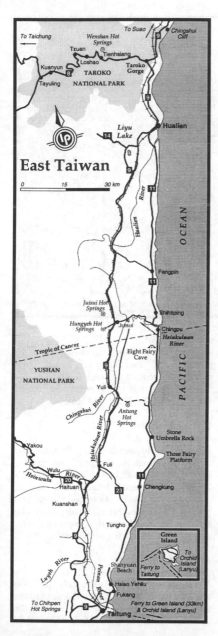

East Taiwan

0   15   30 km

hairpin turns while passing valleys, beaches and vertical cliffs.

The Suao-Hualien highway is one of the most scenic in the world, but the bus service is infrequent so you almost need your own vehicle to make the trip feasible. Cycling the route is appealing, but the traffic is a nuisance and there are some hazardous tunnels (one is 4.5km long!). If you're going to be riding a bike in the tunnels, make sure you wear bright clothing and have a rear light.

HUALIEN
(huālián) 花蓮

The largest city on the east coast, Hualien is a major transport hub that sees a fair bit of tourist traffic. It's quite a lively town, it's not too crowded by Taiwan standards.

Sugarcane was once a major export of this area, but the industry is in rapid decline as cheap imports and skyrocketing real estate prices have slashed profits. These days, tourism is the most important revenue earner, but the mining industry is also generates important income. Hualien is an international port; concrete (made from limestone) and marble are the chief exports. Unfortunately, evidence of environmental damage caused by the mining industry is all too conspicuous. Furthermore, spectacular highway crashes involving overloaded marble and cement trucks is a local specialty.

Although Hualien is worth a look, it's the impressive backdrop of near vertical mountains that excites visitors. Hualien sits in one of the most beautiful parts of Taiwan. Most visitors use the city as a gateway to the nearby Taroko Gorge National Park, considered by many as Taiwan's top scenic attraction.

Orientation & Information

You'll often hear people in Hualien refer to the 'old train station area' *(jiù huǒchē zhàn)*, even though the station disappeared around 1980. What they are talking about might better be called 'the city centre' – it's the area around Chungshan Rd, close to the sea.

The area around the new train station has been slow to develop, largely due to rampant real estate speculation which has pushed

EAST TAIWAN

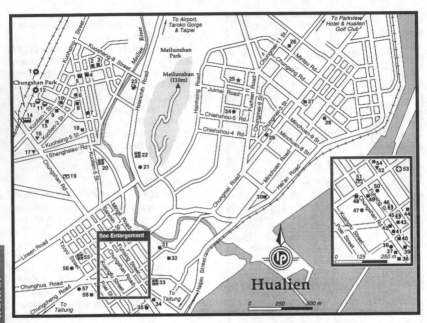

Hualien

land prices up so high that no one can afford to build there.

Hualien's third area of significance is the port district in the north-east part of town. The County Government Building, the Cultural Centre, a golf course and Hualien's most expensive hotel are found in this region.

The Foreign Affairs Police (☎ 822-4023) reside at 21 Fuchien Rd.

Beach
(hǎibiān)
For some quiet entertainment, you can stroll down to the beach. It's a pretty stretch of coastline, but like most of east Taiwan's beaches, it's stony and the surf is too rough for safe swimming.

Wood Carving Museum
(mùdiāo yìshù guǎn) 蔡平陽山地木雕藝術館
The full name of this place is the Tsai Pingyang Aboriginal Wood Carving Museum *(cài píngyáng shāndì mùdiāo yìshù guǎn).*

As the name indicates, the museum is dedicated to a Mr Tsai Pingyang, an aborigine noted for his fine wood carvings.

The museum is in the north-east part of town, next to the Xingnong Hotel.

Chihsingtan Beach
(qīxīngtán) 七星潭
Just north of Hualien (and directly east of the airport) is the obscure village of Chihsingtan. This place has one of the nicest, and still largely undeveloped, beaches on the east coast. On the south side of the village is a beautiful and large teahouse overlooking the sea. You need your own transport to get here, or you can take a taxi from Hualien.

Ami Cultural Village
(àměi wénhuà cūn) 阿美文化村
If you arrive in Hualien in the early afternoon and don't plan to visit Taroko Gorge until the next day, take time to have a look around the Ami Cultural Village (☎ 842-2734). Ami

HUALIEN 花蓮

PLACES TO STAY

2 Hotel Royal; Steak Restaurant
老爺賓館、
老爺鐵板燒

3 Sande Hotel; Dinghao Beef Noodles
三德飯店、
頂好牛肉麵

4 Dongjing Hotel
東京賓館

5 Seaview Hotel
海賓大飯店

6 Gwobin Hotel
國賓賓館

8 Hohuan Hotel
合歡大飯店

9 Chan Tai Hotel
仟台大飯店

10 Qingye Hotel
青葉大飯店

15 Yongqi Hotel
永祺大飯店

18 Naluwan Hotel
那魯灣旅店

26 Xingnong Hotel; Wood Carving Museum
興農山莊、
蔡平陽山地木
雕藝術館

27 Chinatrust Hotel
中信大飯店

29 Guanlun Motel
冠倫汽車旅館

30 Astar Hotel
亞士都飯店

31 Armed Forces Hostel
國軍英雄館

32 Hualien Student Hostel
花蓮學苑

34 Jinri Hotel
今日大飯店

36 Hotel Golden Dragon; Hualien Bus Company Station (City Centre)
金龍大旅社、
花蓮客運市中心站

37 Dashin Hotel
大新大旅社

39 Wuzhou Hotel
五洲大旅社

40 Fada & Xiangding Hotels
發達大飯店、
祥鼎大飯店

41 Longxing Hotel
龍興賓館、
福建街513號

42 Dashan Hotel
大山旅社、
復興街21號

43 Lux & Far East Hotels
天仁大飯店、
遠東大飯店

44 Marshal Hotel
統帥大飯店

54 Toyo Hotel
東洋大飯店

58 Yihua Business Hotel
益華商務飯店

PLACES TO EAT

16 Taipei Four Seas Soybean Milk King
台北四海豆漿大王

17 McDonald's
麥當勞

52 McDonald's
麥當勞

OTHER

1 Rear Entrance to Train Station
後火車站

7 Bowling Alleys
保齡球館

11 Dingdong Bus Company; Motorcycle Hire
鼎東客運站、
機車出租

12 Train Station
花蓮火車站

13 Hualien Bus Company New Station
花蓮客運站

14 Swimming Pool
游泳池

19 GPO
郵政總局

20 Tichun Temple
帝君廟

21 Martyrs' Shrine
忠烈祠

22 Hukuo Temple
護國宮

23 Petrol Station
加油站

24 County Government Building
縣政府

25 Foreign Affairs Police
警察局外事課

28 Cultural Centre
文化中心

33 Tungchingchan Temple
東淨禪寺

35 Old Railway Station Night Market
舊火車站夜市

38 Hualien Travel Service
花蓮旅行社

45 ICBC
中國國際商業銀行

46 Bank of Taiwan
台灣銀行

47 Kungcheng St Night Market
公正街夜市

48 Zhongyuan Bookshop
中原書局

49 Hung Tung Travel Service
宏東旅行社

50 Night Market
夜市

51 Post Office
郵局

53 Hualien Hospital
花蓮醫院

55 Tszshan Temple
慈善寺

56 Goushangding Night Market
溝上頂夜市

57 Far Eastern Department Store
遠東百貨

EAST TAIWAN

aboriginal song and dance shows are staged here for tourists.

Hotels and travel agents in Hualien can arrange tickets for you. Admission costs

An Ami woman wearing an elaborate
headdress of beads and pom-poms.

NT$200; a taxi from Hualien will cost an
additional NT$200. The dance shows are at
4, 5, 6, 7.20 and 8.20 pm every evening, with
the option of earlier shows on weekends and
holidays. Most tours take in the 8.20 pm show.

The village is on Highway 9, heading
south towards Taitung.

East Hawaii Amusement Park
(dōngfāng xiàwēiyí lèyuán)
東方夏威夷樂園
The volcanoes and surfboards are notably
absent, but 'Hawaii' remains the basis for
Hualien's latest theme park. Amusing attractions include grass-skiing, dodgem (bumper)
cars, dodgem boats, a bobsled course and
kayaks. Perhaps most fun are the water slides
and enormous swimming pools. When the
crowds are sufficiently large (basically
during summer weekends), you'll be enter-
tained by hula dancers and Taiwanese-
Hawaiian warriors. The restaurant is topnotch, though you won't find common
Hawaiian cuisine like *poi*.

The amusement park (☎ 835-5041) is
4km west of Hualien's new train station, and
is accessible by taxi or your own vehicle
only. Admission costs NT$300.

Liyu Lake
(lǐyú tán) 鯉魚潭
If you'd like to get out of town, Liyu Lake,
a small but very attractive lake near Hualien,
offers a nice half-day excursion. The main
activities there are boating, fishing and
hiking. There's a good walk around the lake
– follow the road all the way round. There
are also several well-marked trails leading
from the road behind the lake up towards the
summit of Liyushan (601m); a very pleasant
walk if you're up to it. Avoid Liyu Lake on
weekends when the jet-ski gorillas take over
the place.

Buses leave from the local bus stations in
Hualien about once every two hours. The
journey takes around 40 minutes, and the last
bus leaves after 6 pm.

Hsiukuluan River
(xiùgūluán xī) 秀姑巒溪
Besides the Taroko Gorge excursion, one of
the most entertaining things to do around
Hualien is to take a rafting trip on the Hsiukuluan River. This is actually 60km to the
south of Hualien, however, you need transport and equipment to go rafting, and you can
arrange the whole expedition from here.

For more information about the rafting,
see the Hsiukuluan River section later in this
chapter.

Organised Tours If you're interested in
organised tours to Taroko Gorge, the Ami
Cultural Village or rafting on the Hsiukuluan
River, there are several agents in Hualien
who would be happy to arrange them.

One of the best known is Hualien Travel
Service (☎ 835-8101; *huālián lǚxíngshè*),
137 Chungshan Rd. Another is Hung Tung
Travel Service (☎ 833-0101; *hóng dōng
lǚxíngshè*), 156 Chungshan Rd, which also
specialises in domestic and international air
tickets. Yet another with a good reputation is

Southeast Travel Service (☎ 833-8121; *dōngnán lüxíngshè*), 148 Chienkuo Rd.

Places to Stay

Hualien essentially has three hotel zones. Those near the old train station are older and more rundown, but are slightly cheaper. Everything near the new train station is less than 10 years old and in better condition; generally they will also have cable TV. The price difference between the two zones is not that large – the new station area hotels maybe charge an extra NT$200.

The third area is the port district near the east end of town. There aren't many hotels here, those that do exist are generally expensive. However, there are a few cheaper motels which are still fairly comfortable.

Places to Stay – budget

Old Train Station Area One place offering cheap dormitories is the *Hualien Student Hostel* (☎ 832-4124; *huālián xuéyuàn*), 40-11 Kungyuan Rd. Beds cost NT$200 and there are eight beds in each room.

Directly across the street is the *Armed Forces Hostel* (☎ 832-4161; *guójūn yīngxióng guǎn*), 60-1 Chunghsiao St. While it may be called a 'hostel', it's nothing more than a government-owned hotel. With prices at NT$1000 for a double it's not cheap nor particularly recommended.

The *Wuzhou Hotel* (☎ 832-4132; *wǔzhōu dà lǚshè*) has a sign outside in English saying 'Youth Hostel', but it's really just a low-rent place. There are some truly horrible singles/doubles for NT$250/350 (no bath), or you can pay NT$600 for the 'luxury hovels' which have attached bath. It's grim, and you might be better off camping. This 'youth hostel' is at 84 Chungshan Rd.

The *Yihua Business Hotel* (☎ 835-0106; *yìhuá shāngwù fàndiàn*), 85 Tzuyu St, is just behind the Far Eastern Department Store. It's a new place and really nice – recommended! Doubles are normally NT$1000 but can be easily bargained down to NT$800 during low season times.

The *Dashin Hotel* (☎ 832-2125; *dàxìn dà lǚshè*), 101 Chungshan Rd, is deservedly popular due to the extremely friendly management. Rooms are air-conditioned and clean. Doubles with private bath cost from NT$500 to NT$800.

Right next to the Hualien Bus Company bus station is the *Hotel Golden Dragon* (☎ 832-3126; *jīnlóng dà lǚshè*), 77 Chungshan Rd. The place is a bit worse for wear, but it's certainly convenient if you're catching a morning bus. Doubles with attached bath cost NT$600.

Around the corner from Chungshan Rd is Fuchien St, which has several budget places. The cheapest of the lot is the *Longxing Hotel* (☎ 832-4159; *lóngxīng bīnguǎn*) at 513 Fuchien Rd. Doubles are NT$500, NT$600 and NT$800.

The *Xiangding Hotel* (☎ 832-2132; *xiángdǐng dà fàndiàn*), 512 Fuchien St, is one of the larger and better hotels in the city centre. Doubles/twins are NT$800/1200.

Adjacent to the foregoing is the very similar *Fada Hotel* (☎ 833-0136; *fādá dà fàndiàn*) at 514 Fuchien St. Doubles here are NT$900.

Another place to try is Fuhsing St, where you'll find the *Lux Hotel* (☎ 832-3173; *tiānrén dà fàndiàn*) at No 20. It has some of the cheapest rooms around at NT$400 with shared bath. Rooms with a private bath are NT$600.

Next door at No 26 is the *Far East Hotel* (☎ 832-3136; *yuǎndōng dà fàndiàn*). It's slightly better than its neighbour and has double rooms with an attached bath for NT$700.

New Train Station Area The *Chan Tai Hotel* (☎ 833-0121; *qiāntái dà fàndiàn*), 83-1 Kuolien-1 Rd, is directly opposite the station. If you're catching a train or a bus, it could hardly be more convenient. All rooms have attached bath and cable TV. Doubles are NT$800 and twins cost from NT$1000 to NT$1200.

Equally convenient is the neighbouring *Qingye Hotel* (☎ 833-0186; *qīngyè dà fàndiàn*), 83 Kuolien-1 Rd, which is clean and comfortable. It takes a while for the hot water to come online – open the hot water tap and let it run for five minutes. Other than that, it's

EAST TAIWAN

a fine place, with comfortable beds and cable TV. Doubles/twins are NT$800/1500.

The *Yongqi Hotel* (☎ 835-6111; *yǒngqí dà fàndiàn*), 139 Kuolien-1 St, is a small, new place opposite Chungshan Park. Doubles cost from NT$800 to NT$1000, twins are NT$1200.

The *Gwobin Hotel* (☎ 835-6904; *guóbīn bīnguǎn*), 125 Kuolien-5 St, is also small but very new and quite comfortable. Doubles are normally NT$1000, but they offer a special 10% 'foreigner's discount'.

The *Sande Hotel* (☎ 836-2136; *sāndé fàndiàn*), 77 Kuomin-9 St, is one of the newest places and looks really good. There is even a fountain in the lobby, which may be a first for a budget hotel. Doubles are NT$700.

The *Dongjing Hotel* (☎ 835-6151; *dōngjīng bīnguǎn*), 212 Kuosheng-1 St, is one of the cheaper places in this neighbourhood with doubles/twins for NT$700/1200.

The *Hotel Royal* (☎ 836-2952; *lǎoyé bīnguǎn*), 51 Kuomin-9 St, is notable for its flashy steak restaurant on the ground floor. Double rooms here cost NT$1000 and twin rooms are NT$1200.

Port District If you have your own car, you might want to try the *Guanlun Motel* (☎ 823-6926; *guānlún qìchē lǚguǎn*), 67 Chungmei St, which has a car park. However, it stretches the definition of budget with doubles/twins costing NT$1000/1200.

Places to Stay – middle
Old Train Station Area The *Jinri Hotel* (☎ 832-5180; *jīnrì dà fàndiàn*), 8 Hsuanyuan St, is a little more upmarket and has cable TV. Room rates are NT$1300/2500 for doubles/twins.

New Train Station Area The *Naluwan Hotel* (☎ 836-0103; *nǎlǔwān fàndiàn*), 7-3 Kuolien-5 Rd, is new and really nice. It has an aboriginal motif, both in the lobby and the rooms. The so-called 'business suites' are NT$2000; regular doubles/twin rooms are NT$2300/2700; and the 'Naluwan suite' costs NT$3300.

The *Seaview Hotel* (☎ 822-7181; *hǎibīn dà fàndiàn*), 192 Kuolien-5 St, is one of the older places in this neighbourhood and may not be worth the price when you consider the competition. Doubles/twins cost NT$1680/1785 and suites range from NT$2205 to NT$2625.

The *Hohuan Hotel* (☎ 835-0171; *héhuān dà fàndiàn*), 105 Kuolien-5 St, is a really nice place with a computerised key system. Twins cost from NT$1500 to NT$1800.

Places to Stay – top end
Old Train Station Area The *Toyo Hotel* (☎ 832-6151; fax 833-8076; *dōngyáng dà fàndiàn*), 50 Sanmin St, is a classic place in Hualien's city centre. Doubles/twin rooms are NT$2400/2800 and suites range from NT$3200 to NT$6000.

The *Marshal Hotel* (☎ 832-6123; fax 832-6140; *tǒngshuài dà fàndiàn*), 36 Kungyuan Rd, is comfortable and proud of its karaoke facilities. Doubles are NT$2600, twins are from NT$2800 to NT$3800 and suites cost between NT$5000 and NT$9000.

Port District The *Astar Hotel* (☎ 832-6100; fax 832-4604; *yǎshìdū dà fàndiàn*), 6-1 Minchuan Rd (corner Hai'in Rd) is a sharp business hotel close to the harbour. Twins are NT$3200 and suites range from NT$4200 to NT$7000.

The *Chinatrust Hotel* (☎ 822-1171; fax 822-1185; *zhōngxìn dà fàndiàn*), 2 Yunghsing Rd, distinguishes itself by having a swimming pool and shopping arcade. Doubles are NT$2800, twins cost from NT$3100 to NT$3700, and suites cost from NT$4000 to NT$12,000.

The *Parkview Hotel* (☎ 822-2111; *měilún dà fàndiàn*) is Hualien's finest hotel. It has an attached golf course as well as a swimming pool, tennis and squash courts, a fitness centre, a sauna, a shopping arcade, a video games arcade and delicious buffets. A guy in a smart uniform rushes to open the door of your limousine as you arrive. Doubles/twins/suites cost NT$4200/4500/7800.

EAST TAIWAN

Places to Eat

There seems to be a local custom in Hualien to dump sugar into everything. Foreigners (and even some Taiwanese) complain about this, but the locals seem oblivious.

The *Old Railway Station Night Market* (*jiŭ huŏchē zhàn yè shì*) on Chungshan Rd (near the sea) is one of the least expensive eating options, and probably the most fun – with luck you should be able to find a few food stalls serving sugar-free cuisine.

There is a much smaller night market on Kungcheng St (*gōngzhèng jiē*), just off Chungshan Rd. The steamed meat dumplings look delectable, but they taste like sugar-coated pork balls.

Another place to give your pancreas a workout is the *Taipei Four Seas Soybean Milk King* (*táiběi sìhǎi dòujiāng dàwáng*), 432 Chungshan Rd. The soybean milk is so thick with sugar a spoon can stand up in it, though you can ask for it unsweetened (*bùyào tiánde*). I'd recommend you avoid the sucrose-saturated rice rolls. Oddly, the clay-oven rolls (*shāobǐng*) is one dish which proved to be sugar-free.

The eight storey *Far Eastern Department Store*, at the intersection of Chunghua and Chungcheng Rds, has a collection of Chinese food stalls on the 7th floor.

The food at *McDonald's* needs no introduction. There is a branch in the basement of the Far Eastern Department Store, next to the Toyo Hotel, and another on Chungshan Rd, close to the new train station.

Near the new train station and right next to the Sande Hotel is *Dinghao Beef Noodles* (*dǐnghǎo niúròu miàn*). Almost next door is the *Steak Restaurant* (*lǎoyé tiěbǎn shāo*) which is attached to the Royal Steakhouse.

Entertainment

Cinemas There are three cinemas here, as follows:

Haohua
(☎ 832-4380; *háohuá xìyuàn*) 41 Minyi St
Hsinmeichi
(☎ 833-8023; *xīnměiqí dà xìyuàn*) 2nd floor, 396 Chungcheng Rd

Kuosheng
(☎ 835-5719; *guóshēng dà xìyuàn*) 34 Linsen Rd

Bowling Alleys There are three bowling alleys (*bǎolíng qiú guǎn*) nicely clustered together on Kuolien-5 Rd near the new train station.

Things to Buy

Marble (*dàlǐshí*) is the main export of Hualien. It's not exactly lightweight stuff, and filling your backpack with marble souvenirs will soon cause you to exceed the 20kg weight limit imposed by the airlines (not to mention the weight limit imposed by your backbone). Considering the environmental destruction being wreaked by the mining operations, contemplate the benefits of leaving the marble in the ground.

Still, if you need to stock up on marble vases, tables and gravestones, Hualien is the place to do it. For those determined to contribute to ecological ruin, finished marble items can be bought everywhere around town. The biggest outlet for marble sales is a factory operated by the Retired Servicemen's Engineering Agency (*róngmín dàlǐshí gōngchǎng*), 106 Huahsi Rd, near the airport. Most tours offer a stop at this factory along with a trip to Taroko Gorge and the Ami Cultural Village.

Another Hualien best-buy is cement (*shuǐní*), most commonly sold in 50kg sacks at local hardware stores.

Only one bookshop in Hualien seems to offer English-language magazines (*Newsweek* etc) and newspapers. Check out the Zhongyuan Bookshop (*zhōngyuán shūjú*) at 548 Chungcheng Rd (south-east corner of Chungcheng and Chungshan Rds). This place also has a good collection of maps (Chinese-language only), including Hualien and other cities in Taiwan.

Getting There & Away

Air Hualien has air services to Kaohsiung, Taichung, Tainan and Taipei. Airline offices in Hualien include:

EAST TAIWAN

China Airlines
(☎ 834-7850; *zhōnghuá hángkōng*) 18-6 Mingli Rd
Far Eastern Air Transport
(☎ 832-6191; *yuǎndōng hángkōng*) 74 Chung-shan Rd
Formosa Airlines
(☎ 826-3989; *guóhuá hángkōng*) Hualien airport
TransAsia Airways
(☎ 080-066880; *fùxīng hángkōng*) 416-6 Chung-shan Rd
Uni Air
(☎ 826-7601; *lìróng hángkōng*) Hualien airport

Bus Hualien has three bus stations. One is operated by the Dingdong Bus Company (☎ (03) 833-1778; *dǐngdōng kèyùn*), 138-6 Kuolien-1 Rd. The other two are operated by the Hualien Bus Company (*huālián kèyùn*): at the new train station (☎ 832-3485) and at the non-existent old train station (☎ 832-3065).

There is no direct bus between Taipei and Hualien – you have to change at Suao, from where you can take the bus down the spectacular Suao-Hualien Highway. There is only one bus along this route, operated by the Hualien Bus Company. Buses leave at 2.30 pm on weekdays; there is no service on weekends. The trip takes three hours. If you arrive in Suao too late to catch the Hualien bus, there are several hotels near the bus station where you can spend the night. Going in the opposite direction, buses to Suao depart from Hualien at 10.30 am. Heading southwards to Hualien, try to sit on the left (ocean side) for the most spectacular views. The best seat is at the front.

Buses on the Hualien-Taichung route are a joint-venture between the Hualien and Fengyuan bus companies. In Taichung and Fengyuan, catch the bus at the Fengyuan Bus Company's terminals. In Hualien, catch it at the Hualien Bus Company terminal. There are two buses daily in each direction; departures from Hualien are at 7.30 and 9.30 am, from Taichung they're at 7 and 9 am. This meagre schedule is subject to change, so check on it. The one way fare is NT$519.

There is a lot more choice on the Taitung-Hualien route. The Hualien Bus Company runs buses approximately once an hour from 6.30 am until 7 pm, but all of these (except

one) use the inland route. The 1 pm departure from Taitung follows the coastal route (*hǎixiàn*). In the opposite direction, the 10.20 am bus from Hualien follows the coast road.

The Dingdong Bus Company also serves the Taitung-Hualien route, sticking exclusively to the coastal road. Departures from Hualien are at 11.45 am, 2.10 and 4.35 pm. Going the other way, departures from Taitung are at 6.10 and 8.30 am, and 2.10 pm.

Halfway between Taitung and Hualien, right on the Tropic of Cancer, is the small town of Chinpu (*jìnpú*). Local buses depart almost once an hour from both Hualien and Taitung along the coastal road to Chinpu, where they turn around and return to the city they came from. Therefore, if you're not in a hurry, you can take a local bus to Chinpu and then switch to another bus to complete the journey between Taitung and Hualien.

For information on getting to and from Tienhsiang and Taroko Gorge, see the following Taroko Gorge section.

Train As the train trip along the east coast is popular, it's best to book your train ticket a couple of days in advance, especially if you plan to travel during any weekend or holiday.

Avoid the older (cheap) trains which don't have air-conditioning. The trains spend a lot of time going through tunnels, which makes them very noisy and dirty when the windows are open. See the Taitung section later in this chapter for details on trains that pass through Hualien.

Bicycle If you are athletically inclined, a cycling trip down the east coast on a sturdy 10 speed bike offers an exciting journey. The only problem is that the stretch of highway between Suao and Hualien is so mountainous that you need to be in excellent physical condition. The ride from Hualien to Taitung and onwards to the southern tip of Taiwan is much easier.

If you want to do this beautiful trip on a bicycle, consider taking your bike on the train from Suao to Hualien. It doesn't cost much to do this. You can then ride down the coast to Taitung, from where you can either ship the bike back to Taipei or continue on to Kenting before heading back up the west coast. The west coast is not as scenic, so you can consider shipping the bike back to Taipei from Fangliao, a small city to the south of Kaohsiung.

Renting a 10 speed bicycle is not easy. You're better off buying a new or second-hand model from a Taipei bicycle shop.

Getting Around

To/From the Airport There is an airport bus from both Hualien Bus Company stations. The buses run hourly, the first departure is at 8.55 am and the last is at 6 pm. The fare is NT$25.

Most people prefer to take a taxi which costs NT$250 – there is no bargaining. If you walk outside the airport, you can sometimes catch a taxi returning to the city – these drivers should only charge NT$200.

The buses connecting Hualien to Taroko also pass by the airport. however, these are irregular and you might have to wait a while.

Bus Bus No 105 connects the new train station to the mythical old train station every 20 minutes – the fare is NT$10. The bus from the new railway station does not terminate at the old one – be sure you get off in the city centre unless you want an impromptu tour.

Car & Motorcycle Car rentals can be arranged at a number of places. Foreigners have recommended China Rent-A-Car (☎ 833-4888) at 160-3 Kuolien-1 Rd (near the train station). Other places to try include: Central Auto Service (☎ 832-5407), 6 Fuhsing St; Chuan Chia Fu (☎ 826-4489) at Hualien airport; and International Auto Service (☎ 836-0157).

Being a tourist area, motorcycle rentals are easy to find in Hualien. Most of the rental shops are right by the train station entrance on Kuolien-1 Rd. Rates are about NT$400 per day for a 125cc bike.

Taxi Hualien taxi drivers do not use meters so you must agree on the fare before you get

in. A fare to any place in town should be around NT$150 during the day and NT$200 at night or the crack of dawn. The price is fixed and is not subject to haggling. Many drivers will try to talk you into a chauffeur-driven tour of Taroko Gorge at NT$2000. If you find yourself heading out of town, stop the driver unless you want the tour.

TAYULING
(dàyǔlǐng) 大禹嶺

Inland, along the Central Cross-Island Highway, is Tayuling, the highest point on this magnificent road. This is one of the staging points for hiking trips up Hohuanshan (Harmonious Happiness Mountain) at the westernmost edge of Taroko National Park. For more information on Hohuanshan, see the Nantou County section of the West-Central Taiwan chapter.

Places to Stay

The *Tayuling Mountain Hostel* (☎ (04) 599-1009; *dàyǔlǐng shān zhuāng*) is the best known place to stay, with dorm beds for NT$200. Like all these CYC hostels in the mountains, it tends fill up in summer and during holidays. It shuts down completely in the low season, though it may open on weekends and holidays if there is snow. Take the switchback trail up the hill to reach the hostel, otherwise you'll have to walk up a long dirt driveway. Although the hostel is in Hualien county, its phone number is in Taichung county.

Just 4km to the east of Tayuling is the *Kuanyun Mountain Hostel* (☎ (04) 599-1173; *guānyún shān zhuāng*), which is supposed to be open year round. Bookings for both these hostels should be made through the Tienhsiang Youth Activity Centre (☎ (03) 869-1111).

Getting There & Away

There are four buses running along the Central Cross-Island Highway between Hualien and Taichung or Hualien and Lishan; they all stop in Tayuling.

EAST TAIWAN

Taroko Gorge

(tàilǔgé) 太魯閣

The jewel of Taiwan's national park system, Taroko Gorge is a marble canyon featuring a rushing whitewater river, towering cliffs, hiking trails and even the odd hot spring. It's widely regarded as the island's No 1 tourist attraction.

Construction of the highway running through the gorge was a major engineering feat which many thought was impossible. Work began on the project in 1956, and it was opened to commercial traffic by 1960. The road was carved out of the sheer cliffs, at a cost of some US$11 million and 450 lives. The road was built as part of the Central Cross-Island Highway which runs over the mountains to connect the east and west coasts of Taiwan.

Every so often, a boulder comes crashing down on the roof of a passing car – to help prevent this, new and better tunnels are being built. However, Taiwan's ever-growing fleet of cars insures that the road will continue to get wider, straighter and more congested.

It was during the construction of this highway that marble deposits were discovered, setting off a mineral boom in the Hualien area. For a while there was considerable pressure to mine Taroko Gorge itself. However, after much debate the government came down on the side of the conservationists and the area has now been designated a national park. An equally appalling plan to build a huge hydroelectric dam that would flood the gorge was defeated, but a smaller dam has been built.

The gorge and surrounding area was once the main stomping ground of the Atayal aboriginal tribe. The Atayals formerly enjoyed a reputation as fearsome warriors, notable for their custom of facial tattooing and cutting off the heads of their enemies. A few of the Atayals continue to live in the gorge, having found employment in tourism (you may see some mini-skirted Atayal girls posing for photos); however most have moved on to seek their fortunes in Hualien, Taipei and elsewhere.

Admission to the national park costs NT$10 on weekdays, NT$15 on weekends and holidays.

National Park Headquarters

(guójiā gōngyuán guǎnlǐ chù) 國家公園管理處

On the opposite side of the river from the arched entrance to the gorge is Taroko National Park Headquarters. Park staff have the latest news on hikes, including places to avoid (washed out by landslides), bus schedules and weather reports. The reception desk on the ground floor has some free brochures, and there is a souvenir shop upstairs (in the cafeteria) where you can purchase books and maps in English. About once an hour Chinese-language multimedia videos are screened (other languages are available on request for tour groups).

Tienhsiang

(tiānxiáng) 天祥

This is the chief resort village in the gorge area offering hotel accommodation. Other facilities include a post office, restaurants, souvenir shops and the Tienhsiang Visitor Centre which is run by the National Park Service. Tienhsiang is 19km west (towards Taichung) of the National Park Headquarters.

Tienhsiang is a beautiful place, but it tends to get overrun by tourists at times. You can leave most of the crowds behind by doing a few short hikes. There is a pagoda and temple just across the river on a hill, both easily reached by crossing the suspension bridge.

Euphrasia tarokoana is just one of the many alpine wildflowers that you may see while hiking in the Taroko National Park. There are more than 1100 species of native plants within the park, 57 of which are rare or endangered.

Places to Stay

There are *camping grounds* scattered throughout the park. See the individual walks later in this section for details. Certainly the best bargain in town (possibly the best bargain in Taiwan) is the *Catholic Hostel* (☎ 869-1122; *tiānzhǔ táng*). It's an old place, but it's clean and well maintained. A bed in a dorm costs NT$150. Doubles are NT$300 (shared bath) and twins with private bath cost NT$1500. You'll find the hostel on a hill above the Tienhsiang parking area.

At the downhill end of the Tienhsiang parking area is the five star *Grand Formosa Hotel* (☎ 869-1155; *jīnghuá dùjià jiǔidàn*). The building is not especially attractive on the outside, but inside it's everything you'd expect an international hotel to be, complete with piped music and souvenir shops. Twins/suites are NT$5500/12,000, but there are discounts of up to 30% during the low season (winter weekdays).

Continuing just a little further up the same hill will bring you to a gleaming white building which Is the *Tienhsiang Youth Activity Centre* (☎ 869-1111; *tiānxiáng huódòng zhōngxin*). This is operated by the CYC and fills up quickly on any weekend or holiday despite the fact that it has over 300 beds. Budget twins are NT$1200 but there are more opulent rooms for NT$2200. The

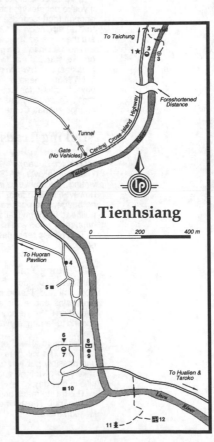

TIENHSIANG 天祥

1. National Park Police Station
   派出所
2. Bus Stop
   公車站
3. Wenshan Hot
   Springs
   文山溫泉
4. Youth Activity Centre
   天祥青年活動中心
5. Catholic Hostel
   天主堂
6. Cafeterias
   餐廳
7. Bus Station
   公路車站
8. Post Office
   郵局
9. Tienhsiang Visitor
   Centre
   天祥旅客服務站
10. Grand Formosa Hotel
    晶華渡假酒店
11. Pagoda
    塔
12. Temple
    廟

'dormitories' are in fact group rooms for eight people and cost NT$2000 (NT$250 per person). Unfortunately, when it advertises 'group rooms' it means just that, so round up seven friends (or strangers) if you want to stay here.

Places to Eat

Tienhsiang boasts a few small *cafeterias* next to the bus station. The prices are almost double those in Hualien, and the quality of the food hardly justifies it.

An alternative is to eat at the *Catholic Hostel*, where breakfast is NT$60 and lunch and dinner cost NT$120. It's advisable to purchase the breakfast ticket the night before. Meal times are fixed – breakfast is served from around 7 to 7.30 am.

It's also possible to eat at the *Tienhsiang Youth Activity Centre* even if you're not staying there, but ask first because they tend to only make enough food for those who order in advance. Meals are served from 7 to 7.30 am, noon to 12.30 pm and 6 to 6.30 pm. Prices for meals here are the same as the Catholic Hostel.

The best meals are served at the *Grand Formosa Hotel*. You can count on five star food at five star prices. The best bargain on offer is the breakfast buffet which costs a cool NT$370. Lunch is NT$600 and dinner is NT$650. These buffets are not available everyday – the lunch and dinner buffets, for example, are only prepared on weekends and holidays. Of course, the sudden appearance of a large tour group can change all that. Contact the hotel for the latest 'buffet schedule'.

Walking Trails in the Gorge

Mysterious Valley Trail

(shénmìgŭ bùdào) 神秘谷步道

This trail follows the Shakatang River *(shākădāng xī)*. At the time of writing, the trailhead was by the ticket booth at the park entrance; however, to start from here you have to first cross the river, and there is no bridge. The park service plans to extend the trail and create a new trailhead from the National Park Headquarters. Check to see if this has happened when you're there.

This hike is reasonably easy and the condition of the footpath is very good.

Tali-Tatung Trail

(dàlĭ-dàtóng bùdào) 大禮大同步道

Both Tali and Tatung are tiny aboriginal villages perched high in the mountains above the entrance to Taroko Gorge. The hike up to Tali (elevation 915m) is strenuous, and it becomes even more difficult as you ascend to Tatung (elevation 1128m) so you might have to spend the night there.

Visitors to these remote villages are few, so don't expect great facilities. The villagers may be able to sell you a few basic staple foods and possibly put you up for the night, but you shouldn't count on this. Take your own food and camping gear with you or plan to complete the hike in one day.

The trail to reach both villages runs roughly parallel to the Mysterious Valley Trail. The trailhead is about 500m south-east of National Park Headquarters.

Eternal Spring Shrine

(cháng chūn cí) 長春祠

About 2.3km above the entrance to the gorge is this shrine, which features a pavilion with a waterfall passing through it. The shrine is reached by hiking up a short hill from the highway and is well worth the walk. It was built in memory of those who lost their lives while constructing the highway – the names of the deceased are inscribed on stone tablets.

Perhaps some more names need to be added to the list. One young couple, on their honeymoon, were killed by a landslide while posing for photos in front of the shrine. Construction safety standards have improved, but injuries and occasional deaths still plague the road crews trying to mop up after big typhoons.

Pulowan

(bùluòwān) 布洛灣

About 8km above the National Park Headquarters is a turn-off for Pulowan. The road climbs steeply until it reaches a tourist village.

The theme here is aboriginal culture. There are old aboriginal women weaving traditional garments, which are sold in a nearby souvenir shop. There is also a theatre with a multimedia show and the occasional song and dance troupe routine for tour groups. A trail behind the souvenir shops climbs about another 100m to a flat area where 25 tourist bungalows were being constructed; however, a typhoon in 1997 damaged the bungalows and they are currently uninhabitable. At the time of writing there was no word on whether or not they will be repaired or torn down.

Pulowan is one place where you can see the remains of the Hohuan Old Trail *(héhuān yuèlǐng gūdào)*. Before the opening of the highway through Taroko Gorge, this was the main route crossing the island. No one is exactly sure when the path was first established, but it's over 100 years old and was probably the handiwork of the Atayal aborigines. During the 1930s, the Japanese colonial administration brought in modern machinery and began turning the trail into a highway. The highway reached as far as Tienhsiang, but the project was abandoned in 1945 following the defeat of Japan in WWII. The

Mysterious Valley & Tali-Tatung Trails

MYSTERIOUS VALLEY & TALI-TATUNG TRAILS 神秘谷、大禮-大同步道	3 Camping Ground 大禮、露營區 4 Ticket Collection Box 收費站 5 Taroko National Park Headquarters 太魯閣國家 公園管理處	6 Water Pipeline 台電輸水管 7 Parking 停車 8 Bus Stop 公車站
1 Camping Ground 大同、露營區 2 Police Check Station 檢查哨		

Kuomintang reassessed the whole project and decided to abandon it in favour of a new road through Taroko Gorge itself.

Some parts of the old trail are carved right out of the limestone cliff face which is slowly crumbling away. After the typhoons of 1997, parts of the trail were wiped out by landslides and the park service have no plans to resurrect them. New vegetation further obscures the path, making it easy to lose your way. In other words, this is a very dangerous hike and is not recommended. In 1997, a German traveller got lost for six days attempting to follow this trail and he barely survived the ordeal.

Lushui-Holiu Trail

(lǜ'shuǐ-héliú bùdào) 綠水合流步道

This trail is only 2km in length with little elevation gain, so it's an easy walk. The trail parallels the highway and there is practically no chance of getting lost. It's not possible to walk through the highway tunnel – you have to take the old cliffhanger road or the alternative 2km footpath.

If you're equipped for camping, the good news is that there is a free camping ground in Holiu *(héliú)* which is 3km below Tienhsiang (in the direction of Hualien). Buses can drop you off at Holiu, which is pretty undeveloped. Lushui, at the other end of the trail, has a shop selling all sorts of stuff and a coffee shop.

LUSHUI-HOLIU TRAIL
綠水-合流步道

1 National Park Police Station
派出所
2 Lushui Restaurant & Store
綠水餐廳商店
3 Bus Stop
公車站
4 Exhibition Site
展示館
5 Yuehwang Pavilion
岳王亭
6 Tzumu Bridge
慈母橋
7 Tzumu Pavilion
慈母亭

Paiyang Trail

(báiyáng bùdào) 白楊步道

From Tienhsiang, walk uphill along the main highway. After exactly 1km you will find a tunnel with a red gate on your left. The gate is too small to permit motor vehicles to enter, but a hiker can easily squeeze through. This is your gateway to a really fun hike, but you'll need a torch (flashlight) and plastic bag to protect your camera, as you pass through two tunnels that 'rain' inside. Walking for 2.2km will bring you to Paiyang Waterfall *(báiyáng pùbù)*, which slows to a trickle during the dry season but is a raging torrent after a storm.

About 200m beyond this is the first Water Curtain Tunnel *(dìyī shuǐlián dòng)*. Whether or not you can go inside is questionable – it was

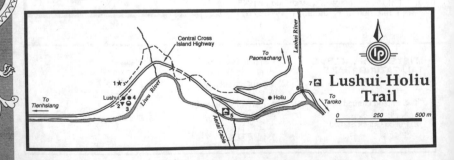

Lushui-Holiu Trail

0   250   500 m

closed off for a time because of fears that it might collapse. If it is open, then pass through and walk another 2km or so to the second Water Curtain Tunnel *(dièr shuǐlián dòng)*. The road continues up another 2km to the Small Tunnels of Nine Turns *(xiǎo jiǔ qū)*, though you might need diving gear to reach it during heavy rains. Assuming you can go the whole route, the total one way length of the hike is about 6km.

Wenshan Hot Springs

(wénshān wēnquán) 文山溫泉
From Tienhsiang, it's 2.9km up the main highway to Wenshan Hot Springs, which is 575m above sea level. You can reach the springs by

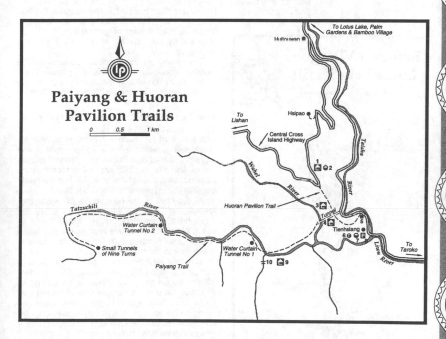

taking a bus to the national park police station. From the police station walk up the road for another 400m. Just before the first tunnel up from Tienhsiang, there are some steps leading down to the river. Walk down them and cross the suspension bridge then head along the path on the other side to reach the hot springs.

Many hot springs in Taiwan have been ruined by hotels that divert the hot water into their guest's bathtubs for private soaks. By contrast, the Wenshan Hot Springs are unique as they have untapped, outdoor pools. For a modest fee, the modest can make use of wooden changing rooms.

Huoran Pavilion Trail

(huōrán tíng bùdào) 豁然亭步道

The hike up to Huoran Pavilion is short but steep. The length of the trail is only 1.9km, but the elevation gain is 400m. There is little chance of getting lost, but if you descend by this route be extra careful if it's been raining recently.

The views from the pavilion are stunning if the weather cooperates, and this is a popular short walk. The trailhead is almost directly opposite the entrance of the Tienhsiang Youth Activity Centre.

Bamboo Village & Lotus Lake Trails

(zhú cūn bùdào) 竹村步道

The trailhead for these two hikes is Huitouwan *(huītóuwān)*, which is on a hairpin turn of the highway, 5km above Tienhsiang. The trail follows a river and is a real cliffhanger – not for the faint hearted. It's a beautiful walk which is moderately popular during weekends and holidays.

At the start of the hike you're on a trail that follows the Taisha River. You then cross the Chinghsi Suspension Bridge where the river forks. About 2.5km above Huitouwan, you reach the Chiumei Suspension Bridge which marks a major fork in the winding trail.

The trail which crosses the bridge goes a further 4.3km to Lotus Lake *(liánhuā hú)* which is 1200m above sea level. There is a small cabin at Lotus Lake run by some elderly retired soldiers. Just how much longer these guys are going to be around is anybody's guess, so be prepared with some food and a sleeping bag if you plan to stay overnight.

Alternatively, you can continue on the trail which follows the river. At a point 5.5km above Huitouwan there is another fork – the right fork leads to Plum Garden *(méiyuán)*, a few hundred metres away. There is a small orchard at Plum Garden where it's possible to camp.

It's another 3.7km from Plum Garden to Bamboo Village *(zhú cūn)*, where it's also possible to camp.

The total one way distance from Huitouwan to Bamboo Village is 9.2km.

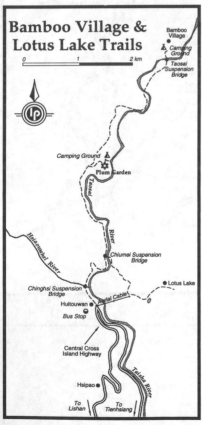

Bamboo Village & Lotus Lake Trails

Getting There & Away

Tour Bus
The Hualien Travel Service (☎ 835-8101)day tour is one of the most popular and they even have an English-speaking guide available. The tour costs NT$700 per person with lunch, an aboriginal dance show and a marble factory visit thrown in. If you forego lunch it's only NT$600, but considering food prices at Taroko Gorge you should book the lunch unless you're on a diet.

Highway Bus
If you plan to do a self-guided tour with lots of hiking, take a public bus to Tienhsiang and spend the night there. Buses from Hualien to Tienhsiang cost NT$90 and are operated by the Hualien Bus Company. You can take a bus over the Central Cross-Island Highway, all the way from Tienhsiang to Taichung on the west coast. For more details on the Central Cross-Island Highway see the West-Central Taiwan chapter.

Shuttle Bus
At the time of writing the National Park Service was running an experimental bus between Hualien and Tienhsiang. You simply purchase a bus pass which allows you to hop on and off the bus at any point along the route. The buses run about once every 30 minutes, on Sunday and holidays only. The pass costs NT$300 in Hualien, or NT$200 in the national park. The current list of bus stops are as follows: Hualien train station, Marshal Hotel, Astar Hotel, Chinatrust Hotel, Parkview Hotel, Hualien airport, National Park Headquarters, Eternal Springs Shrine, Pulowan, Tunnel of Nine Turns, Lushui and Tienhsiang. Not every bus goes into Hualien – some only operate within the gorge itself.

The whole project was introduced to do something about the horrid traffic jams that plague the park during weekends and holidays. As mentioned above, the service is experimental. If it succeeds, it may be expanded – if it flops, it may not exist by the time you get there.

Train
You can't get to Tienhsiang by train, but there is a train station in Taroko. The station's name is Hsincheng *(xīnchéng)*. Some people find it more convenient to use Hsincheng rather than backtracking to Hualien.

Taxi
Doing the gorge by taxi makes some sense if you have three or more people in your group. Considering that a day tour costs NT$600 (without lunch) per person, taking a taxi just about pays off if there are three of you. Taxi drivers want NT$1500 if you only go one way from Hualien to Tienhsiang, or NT$2000 for a return expedition. This price includes a reasonable amount of waiting time – the drivers expect that you'll want to stop off at various points and photograph the scenery. However, their patience is not inexhaustible – they will not want to spend more than four hours for the complete journey; unless they are paid more money.

Walking
Some people walk the 19km from Taroko to Tienhsiang, which takes about four hours. Doing this will give you a close-up look at the scenery, but the motor vehicle traffic can make it unpleasant. If you're going to do this walk, start out early (maybe 6 am) before the traffic gets too nasty. There aren't many shops on this route, so bring water and food with you.

The katydid has a distinctive call that can be heard throughout the Taroko National Park during the summer months.

DOWN THE EAST COAST

There are two routes between Hualien and Taitung. One route follows the coastline and the other runs through a long, narrow inland valley. Both routes are scenic, but the coast road wins the prize for being the more beautiful. If you take the inland route, you have the option of going by bus or train. The train is slightly faster and more comfortable, but it's more expensive than the bus.

The best way to enjoy the east coast of Taiwan is undoubtedly on a motorcycle or 10 speed bicycle. If you can arrange this, it is worth the effort. One option is to rent a motorcycle in Hualien, ride to Taitung on the coast road and return back through the inland valley. There are many fine, nearly deserted beaches to stop at all along the mountainous east coast. Most are rocky, but there are a few broad, sandy beaches.

If you don't have your own transport, you could consider taking the local rather than the express bus. You can get off the local bus at several places along the way which will allow you time to have a look around before you catch the next bus. This requires some patience, as the east coast buses are not very frequent, but the scenery compensates for the lack of convenience.

On the inland valley route, the scenery is rolling farm country surrounded by mountains. There are three good hot springs along the way: Hungyeh, Juisui and Antung, but they're only easily accessible if you are driving your own vehicle.

Hsiukuluan River

(xiùgūluán xī) 秀姑巒溪

About halfway between Hualien and Taitung is the Hsiukuluan River, Taiwan's premier whitewater rafting and kayaking venue.

Most travel agents in Hualien and Taipei can book these trips, which are good value at around NT$950 with transport, equipment and lunch included. A brochure by one travel agent in Hualien warns that 'sicked person heart attack are not be allowed'. Departure time is around 7 am, and you return to town at about 5 pm. If you can provide your own transport to Juisui, the price is reduced to NT$750.

The raftable portion of the river is approximately 22km in length. The actual time spent on the river is about three to four hours, depending on the water flow. These trips run mostly during the summer, and can be really exhilarating just after a typhoon. You'll get soaking wet, so take a change of clothes with you.

> My experience was that you have changing facilities at the beginning of the rafting trip, but once you change, everything you take along will probably get wet. So if you don't want those things to get soaked, leave them on the tour bus, which will meet you at the end of the trip.
>
> **Eugene Hirte**

Although the Taiwanese will probably think you're crazy, cycling along the road from Juisui to Shihtiping along the Hsiukuluan River is almost as much fun as rafting. The scenery is outstanding.

Shihtiping

(shítīpíng) 石梯坪

It's worth spending a bit of time in Shihtiping, at the mouth of the Hsiukuluan River. It has great ocean scenery, a beautiful rocky coast and an interesting cemetery. The cemetery probably explains why this area does not attract many Taiwanese tourists.

Juisui Hot Springs

(ruìsuì wēnquán) 瑞穗溫泉

Juisui is a small town on the east coast railway line, about halfway between Hualien and Taitung. The town itself is no big deal, however it's only 4km east of Juisui Hot Springs. Sadly, the springs are pumped into the nearby *Juisui Hot Springs Hotel* (☎ 887-2170; *ruìsuì wēnquán lǚshè*). The rooms here are priced from NT$1200 to NT$2500, but you can pay half this if you're just stopping to bathe for a few hours. An alternative is to continue 2km to the west to Hungyeh Hot Springs, where bathing is free.

The hot springs are most easily reached by your own vehicle. If you're limited to public transport, take a train to Juisui and then get a taxi or hitch. Juisui is a mandatory stop for *all* trains on the east coast line.

Hungyeh Hot Springs
(hóngyè wēnquán) 紅葉溫

These hot springs are 2km west of Juisui Hot Springs, or 6km west of Juisui on the main highway.

Actually, there are two hot springs, an 'inner hot spring' *(nèi wēnquán)* and an 'outer hot spring' *(wài wēnquán)*. The inner hot spring, which is further into the mountains, is more beautiful.

In either case, there are no outdoor pools. The hot spring water is piped into bath houses which are part of a hotel complex, the *Hungyeh Hot Springs Hotel* (☎ 887-2176; *hóngyè wēnquán lǚshè*). If you don't want to spend the night, you can rent a room for a few hours and use the hot springs for half the regular rates. Rooms here are priced from NT$900 to NT$2000. The hotel's restaurant dishes up delicious meals.

Antung Hot Springs
(āntōng wēnquán) 安通溫泉

Another hot spring resort just off the Hualien to Taitung inland highway, Antung is convenient for those who have their own transport. The hot springs are piped into private baths in the *Antung Hot Springs Hotel* (☎ 888-6108; *āntōng wēnquán lǚshè*). Doubles/suites are NT$1000/5000 and twins cost from NT$2000 to NT$2800.

If you have your own vehicle, the hot springs are reached by first driving 6km south of Yuli *(yùlǐ)*, then 5km to the east on a narrow road. If you want to go to Antung by public transport, first take a train to Yuli (express trains *do* stop there) and then take a taxi (NT$350, 11km) to Antung.

Taitung County 台東縣

On Sundays or holidays, tour buses from Taipei and Kaohsiung rumble up and down the east coast highway. The tour companies focus on three main attractions: Eight Fairy Cave *(bā xiān dòng)*, Stone Umbrella Rock *(shí yǔsǎn)* and Three Fairy Platform *(san xiān tái)*. At the risk of being crude, I need to explain – the Eight Fairy Cave resembles the female sexual organs. Chinese men like to stand in front of it and get their pictures taken. The Stone Umbrella Rock is a gigantic phallic symbol. Chinese women like to stand in front of it and get their pictures taken (I'm not making this up). The Three Fairy Platform is just a fancy bridge connecting some offshore rocks to the mainland – I guess that one is for the children.

From Taitung City, you can easily visit all three places in a day on a rented motorcycle.

TAITUNG
(táidōng) 台東

In the south-east corner of Taiwan, Taitung is a somewhat remote city that has escaped the feverish growth and industrialisation that characterises the north and west of the island. Taitung means 'east Taiwan' and the slow pace of development is thanks to its location on the mountainous, typhoon-battered and earthquake-prone east coast. Taitung seemed set to remain a relatively quiet backwater for a long time, but there are some ominous signs – wealthy Taipei and Kaohsiung residents have now started building villas along the east coast, causing Taitung's real-estate values to escalate dramatically. Improved air transport has brought in a rush of weekend tourists, along with five-star hotels catering to this market.

Nevertheless, Taitung is still relatively free of the traffic jams, noise and pollution which characterise Taiwan's big cities. Taitung city is the main departure point for many interesting trips, particularly to Orchid Island and Chihpen Hot Springs.

Information
There is a branch of the Foreign Affairs Police (☎ 334-756) at 268 Chungshan Rd.

Dragon Phoenix Temple
(lóngfèng fógōng) 龍鳳佛宮
Taitung's most prominent landmark is the

EAST TAIWAN

Dragon Phoenix Temple, which is on the slopes of Carp Hill *(lǐyú shān)* less than 10 minutes by foot from the old train station. Be sure to go up the stairs in the temple and climb the big pagoda. A loop path takes you to the summit of Carp Hill, a mighty 75m above sea level. On a clear day you can easily see Green Island from here.

Matsu Temple
(māzǔ miào, tiānhòu gōng) 媽祖廟，天后宮
This classic Taoist temple becomes very active at appropriate times, such as the 1st and 16th day of each lunar month. The temple is on Chunghua Rd at the north end of town.

Peinan Cultural Park
(shǐqián bówùguǎn) 史前博物館
This enormous park is devoted to the history and culture of Taiwan's aborigines. It's here where you'll find the National Museum of Prehistory (☎ 233-466), which includes an excavation site, amphitheatre and several restored buildings.

The park is about 6km from central Taitung and about 1km from the new train station. There is no public transport to the park, so you may have to take a taxi or walk. From the new train station, head out the door and turn immediately to your right, walk across the car park and you'll come to a small rural road. Turn right again, under the overpass (in fact you're going under the train tracks), and continue until you come to steps and the entrance to the park.

Beaches
(hǎibiān) 海邊
About a 10 minute walk from the centre of Taitung is a beach at the end of Tatung Rd. It looks very enticing for swimming, but can be dangerous at times. The land seems to drop straight down here, making the water

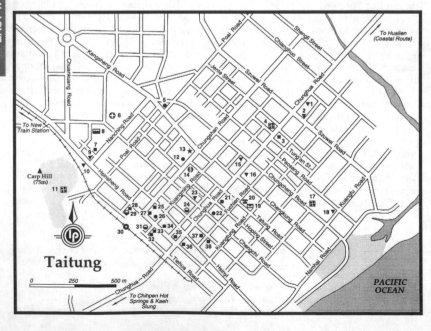

very deep just a few metres offshore. The surf is often rough and there are no lifeguards. Nevertheless, some people do swim at this beach – just be careful.

About 13km north of Taitung is an excellent beach called Shanyuan (shānyuán hǎishuǐ yùchǎng), which can be reached by bus. There is a NT$50 admission charge during the summer months, though you can avoid it if you walk to the beach just to the north. There are many sea toys available for hire, including sailboats, jet-skis and wind surfers.

Hsiao Yehliu (xiǎo yěliǔ) is just north of Fukang Harbour, about 8km by road north of Taitung. The scenery is great, but it's rocky and the surf is too rough to allow safe swim-

ming. Local residents from Taitung go there to fish off the rocks.

Swimming Pool
(yóuyǒng chí) 游泳池
The Taitung Municipal Swimming Pool at 37 Nanching Rd is a safe alternative to the beach.

Places to Stay
Most of the places listed here are within walking distance of the bus stations or old train station in central Taitung. Finding accommodation isn't usually a problem, except on Saturday night when the tour buses invade.

The *Teachers & Public Workers Hostel*

TAITUNG 台東

PLACES TO STAY
3 Woei Long Hotel
   瑋龍大飯店
7 Teachers & Public
   Workers Hostel
   公教會館
21 Fuhgwo Hotel
   富國大飯店
25 Hotel Hsin-Fu-Chih
   新福治大旅社
27 Hsin Hsin Hotel
   新新大旅社
28 Hotel Zeus
   興東園大飯店
32 Lenya Hotel
   聯亞大飯店
33 Renai Hotel
   仁愛旅社
34 Hotel Jin An
   金安旅社
35 Dongbin Hotel
   東賓旅社
36 Holiday Hotel
   假期大飯店
37 Mingyu Hotel
   明玉大飯店
38 Dongcheng Hotel
   東成大飯店

PLACES TO EAT
1 Dinosaur Buffet
   侏羅紀美食世界

2 Szuwei Rd Sunday Night
   Market
   四維路夜市
9 Texas Fried
   Chicken
   德州炸雞
10 McDonald's; Tungnung
   Supermarket
   麥當勞、
   東農超級市場
15 Vegetarian Restaurant;
   Amigo Pub
   秀羽素食館、
   ㄚㄇ一ㄍㄡ酒吧
16 Domino's Pizza
   達美樂比薩店
18 Charlie's Groceries
   信輝商行
23 Fruit Market
   水果市場

OTHER
4 Matsu Temple
   媽祖廟、天后宮
5 Orchid Island Shipping
   Office
   台東縣輪船管理處
6 St Mary's Hospital
   聖母醫院
8 Municipal Swimming Pool;
   Library; Cultural Centre
   游泳池、圖書館、
   文化中心

11 Dragon Phoenix Temple
   龍鳳佛宮
12 City Hall
   市政府
13 Police
   (Visa Extensions)
   警察局外事課
14 Bank of Taiwan
   台灣銀行
17 Haishan Temple
   海山寺
19 GPO
   郵政總局
20 Telephone Company
   電信局
22 City Market
   台東市場
24 Dingdong Inland Bus
   Station (To Chihpen Hot
   Springs)
   鼎東客運山線總站
26 Lanyu Travel Agency
   蘭嶼旅行社
29 Dingdong Coastal Bus
   Station; Hualien Bus
   Company
   鼎東客運海線總站、
   花蓮客運站
30 Old Train Station
   舊火車站
31 Taiwan Bus Company
   Station
   台汽客運站

(☎ 310-142; *gōngjiào huìguǎn*), 19 Nanching Rd, is clean and pleasant, but the real bargains are reserved for teachers and civil servants. Prices for singles/twins start at NT$610/750 (with the right credentials) and jump to NT$800/1000.

The *Dongbin Hotel* (☎ 322-222; *dōngbīn lǚshè*) at 536 Chunghua Rd, Section 1, is old and tattered, but has singles for NT$600.

The nearby *Hotel Jin An* (☎ 331-168; *jīn'ān lǚshè*), 96 Hsinsheng Rd, is also old and has singles for NT$700.

Hotel Hsin-Fu-Chih (☎ 331-101; *xīnfúzhì dà lǚshè*), 417 Chungshan Rd, is slightly nicer than the foregoing and offers singles on weekdays for NT$800.

Hotel Zeus (☎ 325-101; *xīngdōng yuán dà fàndiàn*), 402 Chungshan Rd, is another old one. Singles rooms are NT$700.

The *Hsin Hsin Hotel* (☎ 324-185; *xīnxīn dà lǚshè*), 429 Chungshan Rd, occupies a busy corner in central Taitung. Singles cost NT$800 on weekdays.

The *Lenya Hotel* (☎ 332-135; *liányǎ dà fàndiàn*), 296 Tiehua Rd, is a clean and well-run place almost directly opposite the old train station. Singles/twins are NT$800/1300 on weekdays.

The *Fuhgwo Hotel* (☎ 324-345; *fùguó dà fàndiàn*), 441 Chunghua Rd, Section 1, is on the busiest street in Taitung. If you want to be in the thick of things, look no further. Doubles cost NT$700.

The *Mingyu Hotel* (☎ 322-100; *míngyù dà fàndiàn*), 145 Fuhsing Rd, is actually quite a bargain. This new and clean place has singles for NT$800. It's down a side street but still not too far from the old train station.

Just opposite is the *Dongcheng Hotel* (☎ 322-348; *dóngchéng dà fàndiàn*), 243 Fuchien Rd, another new and pleasant hotel with singles for NT$900.

The depressing *Renai Hotel* (☎ 322-423; *rén'ài lǚshè*) is directly behind the Taiwan Bus Company Station at 283 Kuangming Rd. Singles are NT$250 with fan or NT$600 with air-con.

Moving upmarket, the *Woei Long Hotel* (☎ 311-033; *wěilóng dà fàndiàn*), 237 Chunghua Rd, Section 1, has singles for

NT$1100. The only problem with this place is that it's nearly 1km from the old train station.

The best hotel in town is the *Holiday Hotel* (☎ 348-790; fax 348-789; *jiàqī dà fàndiàn*) at 537 Chunghua Rd, Section 1. Rooms here start at NT$2200.

Places to Eat

A bunch of *noodle stalls* set up every evening in front of the Matsu Temple (*māzǔ miào*). The beef noodles are cheap and good.

On Sunday nights, the *Szuwei Rd Night Market* offers cheap eats and plenty of junk for sale.

There is a good *Vegetarian Restaurant* (☎ 350-252; *xiùyǔ sùshí guǎn*) at 245 Chungcheng Rd. It's open from 11 am to 2 pm and 5 to 8 pm.

Domino's Pizza (☎ 342-310; *dáměilè bǐsà diàn*), 341 Chunghua Rd, Section 1, offers take-away service only. There is also a *McDonald's* and *Texas Fried Chicken* in town.

If you're really hungry, check out the *Dinosaur Buffet* (☎ 351-600; *zhūluójì měishí shìjiè*), 145 Chunghua Rd, Section 1. There is no English sign, but there is no mistaking the dinosaurs out front. Lunch is only served on weekends and holidays, but the all-you-can-eat dinner is available every night for NT$235.

The *Tungnung Supermarket* is a fine place for self-catering while *Charlie's Groceries* (☎ 342-980; *xìnhuī shāngháng*) at 165 Kuangfu Rd (at the end of Paosang Rd), deals in imported western groceries – if you're starved for cheese and salami, this is the place to go.

Entertainment

The *Tatung Cinema* (☎ 322-414; *dàtóng xìyuàn*), 129 Chungcheng Rd, is the only cinema in town.

Taitung's nightlife is decidedly sedate, but there are a few local hot spots. The most popular place seems to be the *Amigo Pub* (☎ 320-618), 2nd floor, 249 Chungcheng Rd, which is open from 7 pm to 4 am.

Getting There & Away

Air Taitung's remote location makes flying a reasonable proposition. There are flights connecting Taitung with Chiayi, Green Island, Kaohsiung, Orchid Island, Taichung and Taipei.

Lanyu Travel Agency (☎ 326-111) at 130 Hsinsheng Rd offers some of the best prices on air tickets. It appears that communication between the booking offices in Taitung and Fengnien airport is poor. If you attempt to buy a ticket at the airport check-in counter, you'll often be told the flights are all full. Meanwhile, back at the ticket office in Taitung, you'll be able to buy a ticket straight away for flights departing 30 minutes later.

Airline offices in Taitung are as follows:

China Airlines
  (☎ 341-137; *zhōnghuá hángkōng*) 9 Chengchou St
Daily Air
  (☎ 352-511; *déān hángkōng*) Fengnien airport
Far Eastern Air Transport
  (☎ 326-107; *yuǎndōng hángkōng*) 241 Hsinsheng Rd
Formosa Airlines
  (☎ 329-650; *guóhuá hángkōng*) Fengnien airport
Taiwan Airlines
  (☎ 327-061; *táiwān hángkōng*) Fengnien airport
TransAsia Airways
  (☎ (080) 066-880; *fùxīng hángkōng*) 36 Kengsheng Rd
Uni Air
  (☎ 346-422; *lìróng hángkōng*) Fengnien airport

Bus There are four bus stations in Taitung. Buses to Kaohsiung originate at the Taiwan Bus Company Station (☎ 322-027; *táiqì kèyùn zhàn*). There are 14 buses per day and the bus also stops at Fengkang, where you can change buses to reach Kenting. The journey takes almost four hours and costs from NT$358 to NT$439 depending on the class.

If you're heading up the east coast to Hualien then you need the Dingdong Coastal Bus Station (☎ 327-911; *dǐngdōng kèyùn hǎixiàn zǒngzhàn*). It takes about four hours by express bus along the coastal highway and the fare is NT$352. Departures from Hualien are at 11.45 am, 2.10 and 4.35 pm.

Departures from Taitung are at 6.10 and 8.30 am and 2.10 pm.

The Dingdong Inland Bus Station (*dǐngdōng kèyùn shānxiàn zǒngzhàn*), at 184 Fuhsing Rd, serves the route to Chihpen Hot Springs and other mountain areas in Taitung county.

If you're going to Hualien on the inland route, you need the services of the Hualien Bus Company (☎ 345-398; *huālián kèyùn*).

There are no direct buses between Taitung and Taipei – you must change buses in Hualien and Suao, a complex procedure that can take two days.

From Taitung it's possible to make the spectacular trip over the mountains on the South Cross-Island Highway via Tienchih. This stretch of the highway is a popular walk for hikers, though most start in Tienchih and head downhill towards Taitung. See the South-West Taiwan chapter for details. If you wish to depart from Taitung, the bus leaves the Taiwan Bus Company Station at 8.30 am, stopping briefly in Kuanshan at 9.30 am and then continuing to Tienchih where it terminates. You can transfer to the bus to Tainan at Tienchih.

Train There are two train stations in Taitung, the 'old station' (*jiù huǒchē zhàn*) which is in central Taitung and the 'new station' (*xīn huǒchē zhàn*) which is 5km away. All trains stop at the new station but only a few stop at the old one. The old station is more convenient, so ask to see if your train goes there. If not, a shuttle bus connects the two stations, but it only meets arriving and departing trains – if you miss this bus, you're in for a long wait or a NT$200 taxi ride.

From Taipei there are eight daily trains direct to Taitung via Hualien. The fastest trains take around five hours. Unfortunately, these fast trains are only slightly cheaper than flying.

On the other hand, the train is the cheapest way to Kaohsiung. The express train takes less than three hours and costs less than the bus. There are some spectacular vistas along the way, though part of the journey is spent in tunnels.

EAST TAIWAN

Getting Around

Car & Motorcycle One place offering car rentals is Chuan Chia Fu (☎ 349-651), 327 Tiehua Rd. You can also try International Auto Service (☎ 515-457).

Motorcycles can be rented from numerous shops along Hsinsheng Rd near the old train station. There are signs everywhere (in Chinese) indicating this. Rental costs from NT$350 to NT$400 per day for a 125cc bike.

Taxi Taxi drivers charge NT$250 for the trip between the airport and city centre. Meters are not used – establish the fare in advance. There is a flat rate around central Taitung of NT$150, but it rises for anything over 2km.

CHIHPEN HOT SPRINGS

(zhīběn wēnquán) 知本溫泉

Just 30 minutes south-west of Taitung is Chihpen Hot Springs, one of Taiwan's more pleasant hot spring resorts, with opportunities for outdoor bathing, both in the springs and the river. Hiking is also possible, and there's an interesting Buddhist monastery.

All these attractions haven't gone unnoticed. Big hotels have sprouted up among the trees on the hillsides and cliffs, and on weekends the place packs out. To avoid the worst of these horrors, head directly for the upper end of the gorge – the lower end (closest to Taitung) is where most of the high rise hotels are concentrated.

There is a rumour that the hot springs are giving out due to massive exploitation. No one is quite sure when this will happen – some claim the hot springs will become cold springs within 10 years. The day may come when the hotels will have to install hot water heaters on their 'hot springs'.

Hot Springs

(wēnquán) 溫泉

The Hong Chuan Hotel has some of the

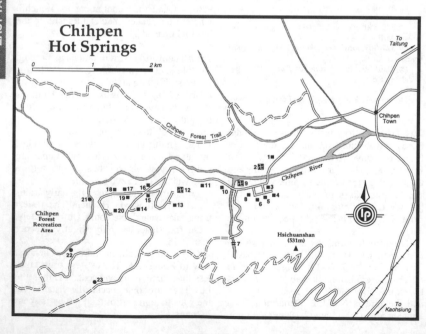

EAST TAIWAN

nicest hot springs – large outdoor pools set among the trees make this a favourite spot with the locals. You do not have to be a guest in the hotel to use the hot springs, though there's an admission charge in the evening.

There is a complex of large and pretty pools just opposite the Dongtair Hotel. Admission is NT$200.

Chingchueh Temple
(*qīngjué sì*) 清覺寺
The Chingchueh Temple is most unusual in Taiwan as it has a large white-jade Buddha from Myanmar (Burma) and a large golden Buddha from Thailand. There are some typically Chinese-looking deities off to either side. Remove your shoes before you go inside the temple.

Chihpen Forest Recreation Area
(*zhīběn sēnlín yóulè qū*) 知本森林遊樂區
At the upper end of the gorge on the north bank of the river is the Chihpen Forest Recreation Area. It costs a rather steep NT$100 to enter, though once inside there is a lovely circular hike to the top of an adjacent mountain with great views across the valley. If you hike in the early morning there's a good chance that you'll see monkeys.

The Gorge
The main road on the south side of the river continues upstream, eventually turning into a jeep trail and then a footpath. Just how far it goes, I'm not certain, but as you head upstream the river becomes a creek and the gorge narrows and becomes even more beautiful. Very few tourists make it up here, but it's certainly a worthwhile hike. During the hot summer months, sitting in the rushing creek and letting the warm water massage your back is about as close to nirvana as you can get.

Places to Stay – budget
The *Longquan Hotel* (☎ 513-920; *lóngquán shān zhuāng*) deserves a plug. This small, friendly place has rooms from NT$800 to NT$1200 on weekdays. Rooms at the rear have a spectacular view overlooking the gorge.

The *Dongquan Hotel* (☎ 510-827; *dōngquán shān zhuāng*) is another small place with a good view. Rooms start at NT$800 on weekdays.

Close by is the *Songquan Hotel* (☎ 510-073; *sōngquán shānzhuāng*), a small but new hotel with singles/twins for NT$800/1200 on weekdays.

At the less attractive lower end of the

EAST TAIWAN

CHIHPEN HOT SPRINGS
知本溫泉

PLACES TO STAY
1 Chihpen Hsiangken Hotel
   知本箱根大飯店
3 Jinshuai Hotel
   金帥大飯店
4 Longyun Zhuang Hotel
   龍雲莊大旅社
5 Xiushan Yuan Hotel
   秀山園別館
6 Victors Circle Hotel
   知本渡假飯店
8 Chihpen Hotel
   知本大飯店
10 Yunding Vacation Village
   雲頂度假村

11 Toong Shing Hotel
   統信大飯店
13 Hotel Royal Chihpen
   老爺大酒店
14 Hong Chuan Hotel
   泓泉大飯店
15 Songquan Hotel
   松泉渡假山莊
16 Dongquan Hotel
   東泉山莊
17 Hot Springs Resort
   溫泉渡假村
18 Longquan Hotel
   龍泉山莊
19 Dongtair Hotel
   東台大飯店
20 Mingchuan Hotel
   名泉旅遊山莊

OTHER
2 Temple
   廟
7 White Jade
   Waterfall
   白玉瀑布
9 Chungyi Temple
   忠義堂
12 Chingchueh
   Temple
   清覺寺
21 Footbridge
   小吊橋
22 Bridge & Tollgate
   知本森林遊
   樂區收費站
23 Chihpen Farm
   知本農場

gorge is the *Xiushan Yuan Hotel* (☎ 512-150; *xiūshān yuán biéguǎn*) and it's neighbour, the *Jinshuai Hotel* (☎ 512-508; *jīnshuài dà fàndiàn*). Both are run by the same management and offer doubles/twins for NT$800/1200 on weekdays, though prices rise to NT$1000/1400 on weekends. Adjacent to these two places is the *Longyun Zhuang Hotel* (☎ 512-627; *lóngyún zhuāng dà lǚshè*), which is even cheaper at NT$700 on weekdays and NT$1000 on weekends.

Places to Stay – middle & top end
The *Hong Chuan Hotel* (☎ 510-150; *hóngquán dà fàndiàn*) boasts some of the best hot spring facilities. It's popular with the tour groups, as the croaking sounds from the busy karaoke will demonstrate. Doubles/twins are NT$2200/3200.

The *Chihpen Hotel* (☎ 512-220; *zhībǐn dà fàndiàn*) was the first hotel to set up shop and exploit the hot springs. It was charming in the old days, but is now being transformed into a 10 storey high rise. Rooms start at NT$2000 but they will probably rise along with the new building.

Next to the Chihpen Hotel is the very fancy *Victors Circle Hotel* (☎ 510-510; *zhībǐn dùjiā fàndiàn*). On weekdays at least, the price is reasonable for such fine facilities with singles at NT$1650.

At the upper end of the gorge is the *Dongtair Hotel* (☎ 512-918; *dōngtái dà fàndiàn*). Singles/twins here are NT$2600/3000.

The *Yunding Vacation Village* (☎ 514-628; *yúndǐng dùjiàcūn*) is an upmarket high rise eyesore. Rooms here cost NT$2700. One nice feature is its sauna.

The *Toong Shing Hotel* (☎ 514-666; *tǒngxìn dà fàndiàn*) is another building that looks like it belongs in Taipei. On weekdays rooms cost NT$2560.

The *Hotel Royal Chihpen* (☎ 510-666; fax 510-678; *lǎoyé dà jiǔdiàn*) is a five star hotel and the top rated place to stay in Chihpen. It's behind the Chingchueh Temple. Doubles cost from NT$4800 to NT$5200, twins cost from NT$5200 to NT$5500, while suites cost between NT$8000 and NT$12,000.

Getting There & Away
Buses from Taitung depart from the Dingdong Inland Bus Station, Taitung. Be careful – a few buses only stop at the highway entrance to Chihpen rather than going into the hot springs area. At the time of writing there were 11 daily buses to the hot springs area, departing from Taitung at 6.20, 8, 9.10, 10 and 11.10 am, and 12.20, 2, 3.15, 4.25, 5.25 and 6.20 pm.

Buses to Taitung depart from all the major hotel areas. You can purchase tickets on the bus. The fare is NT$30.

The taxi fare from Taitung to Chihpen is NT$400.

ORCHID ISLAND
(lányǔ) 蘭嶼
Some 62km south-east of Taiwan proper is Orchid Island, a designated national park. Despite the island's name, don't come here just to see orchids, as flowers are scarce. The scenery more than makes up for this. The landscape is volcanic, resembling a Pacific island and the climate is more tropical than Taiwan.

The island is inhabited by some 2000 aborigines from the dwindling Yami tribe, whose culture is closer to that of the Philippines and Pacific islands rather than China. Many of the older islanders still wear loincloths and speak their own dialect, which is definitely not related to Chinese. They live by cultivating taro and sweet potato, raising pigs and catching fish. The women chew betel nut and, unlike Chinese women, have no fear of exposing their skin to the sun.

The traditional homes of the Yami are built underground to offer refuge from the severe typhoons that hit this region. There is no industry and the island is mostly uninhabited.

Orchid Island is very different to Taiwan, but outside influences are creeping in and the native culture is rapidly changing. Christian missionaries have done their job so well that there are now two churches in each of the six villages on the island, one Catholic and the other Presbyterian.

There are a few small Chinese businesses on the island, and modern influences like

Orchid Island

taxis, TV, radio, beer and cigarettes are all having an impact on the island culture. The elders may still wear their loincloths, but the younger generation all speak Mandarin Chinese and most have discovered blue jeans and Walkmans. Many leave to work in Taiwan and the majority never return.

Tourism has also had quite an impact – if you snap a photo of anything (even just the landscape) don't be surprised if a local resident pops up out of nowhere and asks for NT$500! Although you can buy film on Orchid Island, it's cheaper in Taitung so bring an adequate supply.

The islanders are friendly enough, but most are still very poor and will incessantly try to peddle their souvenir models of Orchid Island canoes. You'll often be asked for cigarettes and the children have learned to beg for candy. If you want to barter, it's advisable to carry a pack or two of cigarettes even if you don't smoke.

Orchid Island has excellent coastal scenery

ORCHID ISLAND 蘭嶼
1 Orchid Island Leisure Hotel 蘭嶼休閒大飯店
2 Airport 機場
3 Weather Station 氣象站
4 Lanyu Villa Hotel 蘭嶼別館
5 Lanyu Pond 蘭嶼天池

with a jagged black volcanic rock coastline. It's certainly beautiful but it makes swimming difficult. About the only beach where you can swim is south of the airport, near the Lanyu Villa Hotel.

The main pastime for tourists is walking around the island, a distance of 37km with no big hills. It's a very stiff one day, or a comfortable two day, hike.

Walking across the island near the weather station might not be all fun, because the trail is not well maintained. I nearly got impaled by a bull, who thought I was intruding, so people pitching their tent should have a good look around.

LM Kirsch

There's a very challenging hike to Lanyu Pond *(lányu tiānchí)*, a miniscule lake high in the southern mountains of the island. The 'trail' is in poor condition – it's a real bushwhack to get up there.

In winter bring a raincoat, as light rain falls nearly every day and it's also windy. In summer, carry water with you, as the island is very hot and suffers from drought. Don't attempt to go anywhere on Orchid Island during a typhoon.

Taiwanese tourists bring in plenty of cash, but do not exactly endear themselves to the local aboriginal population. City dwellers fly over to Orchid Island for a one hour tour of the island. Men dressed in suits and ties, and women in high-heels, diamond rings and *qìpào* dresses come to take pictures of each other standing in front of an Orchid Island canoe; they point and giggle at the aborigines in their loincloths, eat lunch and return to the city. They can then proudly brag to their friends that they've 'done Orchid Island' – after all, they have pictures to prove it.

Places to Stay

If you want to save some cash, it's possible to camp out next to a schoolhouse or church. You should ask permission first, though this will nearly always be granted. Sometimes you can even stay inside – you have to find the person with the key to open it and then make them understand what you want. Orchid Island is a laid-back place so you can set up a tent just about anywhere. You won't need much equipment as it's never cold, but a waterproof tent is wise. In winter, a blanket is warm enough, and in summer it's so hot you won't be able to stay in the tent.

The *Orchid Island Leisure Hotel* (☎ 732-032; fax 732-250; *lányǔ xiūxián dà fàndiàn*), in Yeyou village, is close to the harbour (convenient if you arrive by boat). Dormitory accommodation costs NT$400 and twins are NT$1800.

The *Lanyu Villa Hotel* (☎ 732-111; fax 732-189; *lányǔ biéguǎn*) has dorm accommodation for NT$400 and twins cost from NT$1800 to NT$4800. It's adjacent to what is probably the best beach on the island.

Places to Eat

Food in Orchid Island is available at the two *hotels* above – NT$120 for breakfast and NT$250 for lunch or dinner. There are a couple of reasonably priced *noodle shops* around the island, and some closet-sized *grocery shops* selling dried noodles and canned goods. Alternatively, you can buy taro roots and sweet potatoes from the locals.

Entertainment

'Aboriginal culture' makes the cash register ring on Orchid Island. A phoney aboriginal song and dance show is *de rigueur* for Taiwanese tourists. Enquire at the hotels if interested. Yeyou village has the island's best 'nightlife', which consists of a couple of noodle shops with TV sets.

Getting There & Away

Air Orchid Island's runway is too small to accommodate jet aircraft. However, Formosa Airlines and Taiwan Airlines both fly small propeller-driven aircraft to the island about once every 30 minutes throughout the day.

Both airlines also operate a flight between Kaohsiung and Orchid Island once a day.

These airlines put on as many flights as they need. The schedule is ignored, especially on holidays and weekends, if they don't have enough customers to fill a plane, they won't fly at all. Excepting holidays, you can usually get a flight for same day departure with no hassles. The contact details for these airline companies are:

Formosa Airlines
　　(☎ 732-035; *guóhuá hángkōng*) Orchid Island airport
Taiwan Airlines
　　(☎ 732-005; *táiwān hángkōng*) Orchid Island airport

Boat Boats to the island are operated by Deluxe Dragon (☎ 330-756; *lónghǎo kèlún*), 582 Szuwei Rd, Taitung. One way fares are NT$780 from Taitung and NT$636 from Green Island.

Getting Around

To/From the Airport Both hotels on Orchid Island offer a free shuttle service to and from the airport. Otherwise, transport is by rented motorcycle or foot.

Bus A bus goes around the island four times per day, twice in a clockwise direction and twice anticlockwise. The last bus makes a run between 3.30 and 4.30 pm, so don't miss it – there is practically no traffic, so you can't hitchhike. These buses are rather expensive for the short distance they travel – it costs about NT$300 to go around the island.

If there is enough demand, the two hotels will run a touring minibus around the island for NT$350 per person.

Motorcycle Motorcycles are readily available from the two hotels and other rental shops. The cost is about NT$500 per day.

Walking Walking is great for those who have the time and energy, but as the island really is quite large, many travellers prefer to opt for motorised transport.

GREEN ISLAND
(bōlìyòutǐng) 綠島

Relatively few foreign tourists make it to Green Island, even though it's closer to Taitung and cheaper to reach than Orchid Island. Green Island is more typically Taiwanese, more developed and more densely populated than Orchid Island. It is not as developed as Taiwan, of course, but it offers few surprises for those already familiar with Taiwan.

During summer it's a big hit with Taiwanese tourists. During the winter months, fierce winds and steel grey skies make the island considerably less attractive. Green Island offers interesting scenery, unspoilt beaches

The Deerly Departed

There are an estimated 300 Sika deer *(méihuā lù)* roaming Green Island, though you have to be pretty lucky to see one. The deer are not indigenous to the island; they were introduced and bred for their meat and antlers.

Although eating deer meat was once fashionable in Taiwan, pressure from animal rights activists has caused the market to decline over the years. In fact, Taiwanese attitudes towards the trade of animals have drastically changed since the mid-1990s. In 1994, the USA imposed trade sanctions against Taiwan for their failure to participate in the banning of illegal trade in rhino and tiger parts. These sanctions were lifted in 1995 (after Taiwan had reportedly lost US$20 million in trade) following a report confirming Taiwan had taken significant steps to reform wildlife conservation laws and had improved upon the enforcement and public awareness of them.

You still may occasionally see things like dog on menus, but this is becoming increasingly rare. At the same time the Taiwanese have converted from traditional Chinese to western medicine, therefore the demand for exotic animal organs is reduced. All this has contributed to the end of deer farming on Green Island.

In response to the situation, the Taiwanese government has purchased most of Green Island's captive deer and released them into the wild. However, there are still a few unlucky deer in captivity that have become a grim tourist attraction – weekend visitors from Taipei pay NT$100 a piece to snap photos of themselves 'feeding the deer'. ∎

EAST TAIWAN

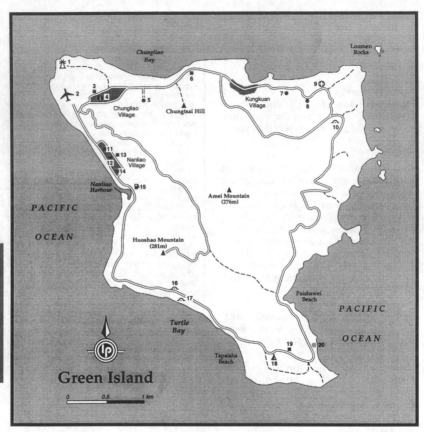

EAST TAIWAN

Green Island

0   0.5   1 km

and a chance to get away from it all – just don't arrive expecting another Tahiti.

The island is small enough to visit on a day trip from Taitung. Catch the earliest flight out to the island and the last one going back. Spending the night can also be fun, but if you're time or money is limited, then Orchid Island is more worthwhile.

Information

There is an East Coast Scenic Area Green Island Branch Tourist Office (☎ 672-027; *dōnghǎi àn guǎnlǐ chù lǜdǎo zhàn*), but just call it the 'east tourist office' (*dōgguǎ chù*).

It's opposite the entrance to the airport and has photos of the island's sights, useful pamphlets and postcards for sale, and a great aquarium. During the tourist season, a multimedia presentation, to introduce Green Island, is shown approximately once an hour throughout the day. This is also the place to make a booking for the camping ground at the south of the island.

Lighthouse

(dēng tǎ) 燈塔

In 1937, the American ship *President Hoover* sank after striking the rocks at Green

GREEN ISLAND 綠島	18 Camping Ground 露營區	8 Occupational Skills Training Centre 技能訓練所
PLACES TO STAY	19 Green Island Hotel 綠島國民旅舍	9 Military Hospital 軍醫院
3 Easy Arrival Resort 逸達山莊	**OTHER**	10 Kuanyin Cave 觀音洞
6 Guest Island Resort 賓島渡假村	1 Lighthouse 燈塔	15 Petrol Station 加油站
11 Police Hostel 警光宿舍	2 Airport 機場	16 Pahsien Cave 八仙洞
12 Green Island Resort; Tony's Diving Club 綠島渡假中心、 東尼號遊艇服務中心	4 Tourist Office 東海岸管理處綠島站	17 Lunghsia Cave 龍蝦洞
13 Songrong Hotel 松榮大飯店	5 Green Island Prison 綠島監獄	20 Chaojih Hot Spring 朝日溫泉
14 Kaihsin Hotel 凱薪飯店	7 Green Island Lodge (Former Prison) 綠洲山莊	

Island. Fortunately, none of the 500 passengers on board died, and two years later the 33.3m lighthouse was built. The original light was in fact an oil lantern. During WWII the lighthouse fell into disrepair, but when the Kuomintang took over Taiwan in 1945 a blinking electric light was installed.

Prisons
(jiānyù) 監獄
There are three prisons on Green Island which hold a morbid fascination for some.

The only prison open to the public is the ironically named **Green Island Lodge** *(lǜdǎo shānzhuāng)*. It's here that most of Taiwan's political prisoners were interned during the martial law era. Conditions in the prison were said to be horrible. Some political prisoners spent over 30 years here – after their release, many went on to become founders of the Democratic Progressive Party (DPP). With the lifting of martial law, the prison was closed; however, there is talk of turning it into a museum to remind the younger generation of the importance of Taiwan's hard-won democracy. Every so often elderly groups of former political prisoners return with TV reporters for an emotional visit. At present, all you can see is the outside of the buildings.

The **Green Island Prison** *(lüdǎo jiānyù)* is not a place for tourism – it's where Taiwan's worst Mafia chieftains are incarcerated. The third prison is the very creatively named **Occupational Skills Training Centre** *(jìnéng xùnliàn suǒ)*, which is a rehabilitation work camp for less dangerous criminals.

Kuanyin Cave
(guānyīn dòng) 觀音洞
This cave contains an interesting miniature temple with a stalagmite dressed up in a cape to represent the deity Kuanyin. Every morning incense is lit by worshipping pilgrims – some of whom have made the journey from Taiwan.

Chaojih Hot Spring
(cháorì wēnquán) 朝日溫泉
Near the southern tip of the island, right on a rocky beach is one of the world's most unusual hot springs. What makes it so extraordinary is that it's one of the only two known seawater hot springs in the world – the other is near Italy's Mt Vesuvius.

The water temperature is perfect for bathing and there are change rooms nearby.

Tapaisha Beach
(dàbáishā) 大白沙
The name of this beach means 'big white

sands', though it's actually a coral beach. It's not suitable for swimming, but snorkelling should be good.

Following the road to the north-west along the coast, you will find three beautiful caves; you can go inside two of them, but the third has too much water in it.

Fish Market
(yú shìchǎng) 魚市場
In the morning, the fishing boat harbour at Nanliao is a good place to watch the catch coming in.

Huoshaoshan
(huǒshāoshān) 火燒山
The summit of mighty Huoshaoshan, Green Island's highest peak, rises 281m above sea level. The peak is actually an extinct volcano – the lava that flowed from it created Green Island.

The climb up Huoshaoshan affords some moderate exercise and rewards you with great views of the island (when the weather cooperates). The Taiwanese like to make the ascent before dawn to catch the sunrise – you'll find it less crowded (but somewhat hotter) on the summit if you wait until later in the day.

A maintenance road leads up the mountain, but you will still have to walk the last stretch. It's better to follow the hiking trail which begins at Paishawei Beach on the south-east corner of the island. You also have the option of ascending by one route and descending by the other.

Snorkelling & Scuba Diving
(fúqián & qiánshuǐ) 浮潛，潛水
There are two companies on Green Island that charter boats and run snorkelling and scuba diving trips. Usually these companies will require a minimum of five to six people and they won't go out in bad weather. If you're with a Taiwanese tour group expect onboard KTV and lots of seasick Taiwanese passengers.

Tony's Diving Club (☎ 672-899/672-568; *dōngníhào yóutǐng fúwù zhōngxīn*) is next to the Kaihsin Hotel in Nanliao. Sanasai

Typhoons
The typhoons that hit Taiwan are usually nothing more than a large tropical storm. Outside the western Pacific Ocean region, typhoons are generally known as hurricanes or cyclones. You should not be overly concerned about these typhoons, but a few words of warning are in order.

Some typhoons are weak – basically just wind and rain – but there are other 'super-typhoons', which can uproot trees, create floods and cause landslides. As Taiwan's east coast is bordered by the Pacific Ocean, it is usually the worst hit by typhoons. Typhoons are tricky – they can change course suddenly, completely contradicting the weather forecasts. Typhoons mainly occur during summer; some years Taiwan gets no typhoons at all, but in others there could be five or more.

If a typhoon alert is issued while you are in Taiwan, be equipped to stay indoors for at least a day, maybe two. Avoid going outside as it can be dangerous – most typhoon-related injuries or deaths are caused when people go outdoors and are hit by wind-driven debris. Stock up with books and magazines, a torch (flashlight), food (canned and dried goods), candles and matches and water. Lastly, don't worry – a typhoon is just a bad storm and the worst likely scenario is that you'll get bored waiting for it to end. ■

(☎ 672-788; *shānnàsài yóutǐng lǚyóu fúwù zhōngxīn*) is by the boat harbour in Nanliao at 1 Yukang Rd *(yúgǎng lu)*.

A round-island boat trip (three hours) costs NT$700 per person at Tony's, or NT$800 at Sanasai. Tony is willing to reduce the charge to NT$500 if there are more than 20 people. A scuba diving trip will also last about three hours and costs NT$6000 for five people (dive only, not including the boat).

Glass-Bottomed Boat
(bōlí dǐ chuán) 玻璃遊艇
When there are enough tourists around, a glass-bottomed boat cruises above the coral reefs. If you want a wedding at sea, the captain is authorised to perform marriage ceremonies on board. The boat trip costs NT$200 per person. There's an additional fee for the marriage service.

The Yellow Submarine

(qiánshuǐ tíng) 潛水艇

Although it's not equipped with a periscope or torpedoes, Green Island's submarine has large windows which allows you to view sea creatures (or enemy aircraft carriers?). A cruise costs NT$2100 per person per hour with a minimum of 10 people. Real enthusiasts can book it for a round-island cruise.

The submarine is operated by the Chan'an Boat Company (☎ 672-595; *zhān'àn lúnchuán*) at the Nanliao boat harbour.

Places to Stay

There is an established *camping ground (lùyíng dì)* at the southern end of the island; you have to book your site through the tourist office next to the airport. Grass sites are NT$200 and wooden platform sites are NT$300. Tents can be rented – a two person tent is NT$300 and a six person model is NT$600. Sleeping bags can also be hired for NT$50. There are discounts in winter.

If you're interested in a homestay and you are able to speak Chinese, contact *Mr Zhen Guoxiong* (☎ 672-681).

Although it seems like an unlikely place to stay, the *Police Hostel (jǐngguāng sùshè)*. has six rooms, police get preference, but anyone can stay when there are vacancies. The facilities are good, but it's no real bargain at NT$1200 for a double. Make enquiries at the Nanliao police station.

Hotels in Green Island typically offer good discounts on summer weekdays, with even bigger discounts everyday in winter (November to February).

The *Easy Arrival Resort* (☎ 672-407; *yìdá shānzhuāng*) certainly lives up to its name – it's directly opposite the airport. It's also notable for having a beautiful log cabin design, though it isn't cheap with doubles/twins for NT$2600/4000.

Nanliao *(nánliáo)*, north of the boat harbour, has the most hotels. At 102-12 Nanliao Village is the new *Kaihsin Hotel* (☎ 672-033; *kǎixīn fàndiàn*). This hotel has good discounts on weekdays, and has dormitories for NT$500 per person. Twins without

the discount are between NT$2500 and NT$3000.

At No 42 is the comfortable *Songrong Hotel* (☎ 672515; *sōngróng dà fàndiàn*). It's clean, cheerful and friendly with twins from NT$1500 to NT$2500.

At No 102-6 is the *Green Island Resort* (☎ 672-243; *lǚdǎo dùjià zhōngxīn*), with twins for NT$2000.

In Kungkuan Village *(gōngguǎn cūn)* at No 61-1 is the *Guest Island Resort* (☎ 672-699; *bīndǎo dùjià cūn*). Twins cost from NT$1800 to NT$2200.

At the very southern tip of the island is the *Green Island Hotel* (☎ 672-314/672-244; *lǚdǎo guómín lǚshè*). Twins here cost from NT$2200 to NT$4800, with weekday discounts of around 10%. It's handy for the hot springs and Tapaisha Beach.

Getting There & Away

Air Formosa Airlines and Taiwan Airlines operate small propellor-driven aircraft on the Taitung-Green Island route. The flight takes eight minutes.

The one way fare costs NT$644. Travel agencies do not give discounts on Green Island air tickets, the price is exactly the same whether you purchase from a travel agency or from the airline directly. However, you do get a 10% discount if you purchase a return ticket, bringing the one way cost down to NT$580.

Taiwan Airlines also has at least one daily flight from Kaohsiung.

Daily Air operates a helicopter service from Taitung. This is more expensive than the plane, but it's more fun. One way tickets are officially NT$1500 but during the low season these are discounted to NT$1200.

Upon arrival at Green Island airport, be sure to reconfirm your flight back to Taiwan in person – especially at peak times.

Daily Air
(☎ 672-830; *déān hángkōng*) Green Island airport
Formosa Airlines
(☎ 672-585; *guóhuá hángkōng*) Green Island airport
Taiwan Airlines
(☎ 672-526; *táiwān hángkōng*) Green Island airport

EAST TAIWAN

Boat Four Taitung companies run boats to Green Island: Chang'an Boat Company (☎ 325-338; *cháng'ān lúnchuán*); Chan'an Boat Company (Taitung ☎ 320-413/Green Island ☎ 672-595; *zhān'àn lúnchuán*), 255-1 Hsinsheng Rd, Taitung; Deluxe Dragon (Taitung ☎ 330-756; Green Island ☎ 672-819; *lónghǎo kèlún*) at 582 Szuwei Rd, Taitung, or at Nanliao port in Green Island; and Hsinfa Boat Company (☎ 351-931; *xīnfā hángyùn*), 79 Chungcheng Rd, Taitung.

Taitung departures are from Fukang (*fùgǎng*), a small port to the north (across the bridge) from Taitung. The Green Island port is at the southern end of Nanliao village; you can purchase boat tickets from Yongjia Travel Agency (☎ 672-301; *yǒngjiā lǚxíngshè*) at the harbour.

The boat may stop at Orchid Island first – make sure that you get off at the right island.

Ticket prices vary according to which boat company you use, and the day of the week you travel. The one way Fukang fare is typically NT$275 and the Orchid Island fare is NT$636.

Getting Around

Bus There is an irregular bus service around the island but walking is probably faster.

Alternatively you can join one of the many tour buses run by the hotels. These run almost every day (maybe several times a day) during summer, but you can forget it during the low season. The cost per person for a quick, two hour, round-island tour is NT$200. Some tours race even faster around the island, only lasting 90 minutes.

Motorcycle Motorcycle rentals are available at the airport for a daily rate of between NT$350 and NT$500, though polite bargaining can sometimes yield a 10% discount. You won't have to look too hard for the bikes – people will approach you and make an offer.

Taxi A typical round-island trip by taxi costs NT$500.

Walking It's 17km around the island which means there is no problem with walking the entire route.

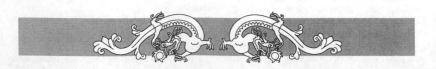

South-West Taiwan 台灣西南部

This is Taiwan's banana belt. Flat and fertile, the region has the sunniest and warmest weather in Taiwan (and is stinking hot during the long summer). The climate is favourable to tropical agriculture, and the south-west was for centuries the most heavily populated and prosperous region in Taiwan. Those honours now go to Taipei, but the south-western port city of Kaohsiung comes a close second.

The south-west coast has long been the cradle of Taiwanese culture – the old city of Tainan was the island's first capital – and much of the traditional Taiwanese way of life has been preserved here. Most of the people in this part of the island prefer to speak Taiwanese.

Of course, modern influences have made their mark. New skyscrapers and factories keep sprouting up on farms. The coast in particular has become heavily industrialised and polluted. In spite of this, south-west Taiwan is one of the more interesting parts of the island. The rural areas are endless expanses of sugar cane, rice paddies and betel nut trees. Temples are pervasive in this region, and it is in the south-west that you will find Taiwan's largest and most beautiful temples. It is not uncommon to see a huge Buddhist or Taoist festival or parade.

HIGHLIGHTS

- **Kenting** – lovely beach area, perfect for walking, cycling or just lazing in the sun
- **Maolin** – a stunning area of mountains, waterfalls, hiking trails and genuine aboriginal culture
- **Tainan** – home to the largest concentration of the most interesting temples in Taiwan
- **South Cross-Island Highway** – you have the choice of either walking or driving along this stunning and accessible mountain route

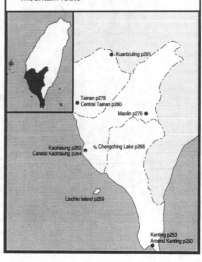

Pingtung County 屏東縣

KENTING
(kěndīng) 墾丁

On 1 January 1984, Taiwan's first national park was established at Kenting. Since then it has become a popular recreation area for both the Taiwanese and expats. More than anywhere else in Taiwan, Kenting lives or dies according to the weekend tourist trade.

Kenting is Taiwan's answer to Hawaii, the French Riviera and Australia's Gold Coast. Situated on a bay just a few kilometres from Taiwan's southernmost tip, Kenting has beautiful white sandy beaches, lush tropical forests and, not surprisingly, the warmest winter weather in Taiwan. People from Taipei and elsewhere will tell you that Kenting is horribly hot – in actual fact, Kenting's summer weather is cooler than Taipei's, thanks to the afternoon sea breeze. Although there is a chilly wind in winter, it's still warm enough for bathing throughout the year.

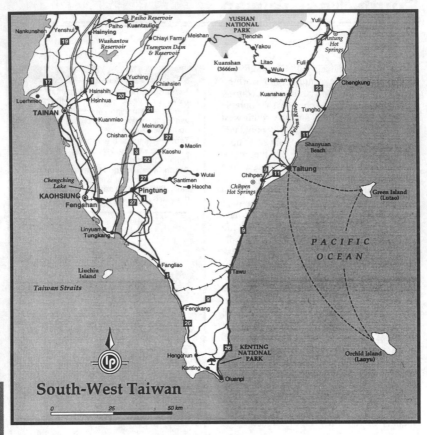

South-West Taiwan

0   25   50 km

Information

Kenting National Park Headquarters has an informative Visitor's Centre, 2km from Kenting (towards Kaohsiung). Some of the staff speak English and there are English-language books, maps and brochures on offer.

Kenting Ranch

(*kěndīng mùchǎng*) 墾丁牧場

A few hundred metres from the beach at Kenting is a ranch for raising cattle. It's open to the public and you can have a look around. Be careful of the fences as some are electrified. The voltage is low and not dangerous,

but it's still enough to give an unwelcome shock.

Frog Rock

(*qīngwā shí*) 青蛙石

All around Kenting Youth Activity Centre there are congenial walks that lead to the beach. Frog Rock is the big rock adjacent to the centre's hostel. Climbing Frog Rock used to be popular but is now prohibited.

Kenting Forest Recreation Area

(*kěndīng sēnlín yóulèqū*) 墾丁森林遊樂區

After you've enjoyed the sun and surf in

Kenting, head towards the Forest Recreation Area. The park is famous for its Botanical Gardens. Admission costs NT$50 which is payable at the entrance gate.

Just inside the park is a tall, steep, pointed peak named Taichienshan *(dàjiān shān)*. Although only 316m high, it dominates the skyline. The vertical rocky face looks like a deadly climb and, in fact, it has been closed off to prevent injuries. However, for a long time it was very popular with day trippers and even yours truly has climbed it.

Inside the park, high on a hill overlooking the area, is Kenting House – a hotel and restaurant. There is an infrequent bus that goes into the park from the park entrance gate. One of the highlights of the park is the viewing tower, from where you can see the Pacific Ocean, Taiwan Straits and Bashi Channel (which separates Taiwan from the Philippines). It's claimed that on a clear day you can even see Orchid Island and the Bataan Islands in the Philippines. Military patrol boats often cruise the channel – a reminder that this is the prime route for smuggling drugs and firearms produced in the Philippines, and for Taiwanese gangsters fleeing prosecution.

Sheting Natural Park
(shèdǐng gōngyuán) 社頂公園
Kenting National Park has two areas – the Kenting Forest Recreation Area, where you pay an admission fee, and Sheting Natural Park.

Sheting is free and relatively uncrowded, with good caves and excellent walks. It's 2km from the entrance of the Forest Recreation Area, but you will have to look for it. To the south of Kenting village you will see a sign on your left pointing to Sheting Natural Park. Walk on until you come to a parking area where vendors sell umbrellas and other junk – this is the main entrance.

Sail Rock
(chuánfán shí) 船帆石
This rock is said to look like a sail, though it's rather unlikely you'll want to place it atop your boat. The main attraction is not the rock,

but rather the small bay with the sandy beach on the northern end. There's a small collection of hotels, restaurants and places renting jet-skis and fishing gear. If you stay here, you'll find it noticeably quieter than Kenting itself.

Oluanpi
(éluánbí) 鵝鑾鼻
The southernmost tip of Taiwan, Oluanpi, is 8km south-east of Kenting, and is known for its coral gardens and big lighthouse. There is a small admission charge for the gardens, and heaps of vendors congregate near the gate to sell seashells, dried squid and other souvenirs.

As for beaches, there is a tiny stretch of sand just north of Oluanpi, but it isn't very attractive and virtually no one swims there.

Many people get up at 4 am to catch the sunrise from a scenic overlook just a few kilometres north of Oluanpi.

Chialeshui
(jiālèshuǐ) 佳樂水
On the eastern shore, north-east of Kenting, is Chialeshui (Beautiful Happy Water) – named in the interests of promoting mass tourism. The coastal rock formations are the drawcard here and are, admittedly, some of the best in Taiwan. There is a big collection of souvenir shops near the entrance gate (where you pay your NT$20 admission fee), but the inside area is mostly unspoiled.

Just south of Chialeshui is a stretch of sandy beach at Fengchuisha which is said to have good surfing, but it also has an often dangerous current. Due to the strong winds, it's also a prime venue for hang gliding.

Chialeshui can be reached by bus from Hengchun, but motorcycles or bicycles are the usual modes of transport (see Hengchun and Getting There & Away later in this section for details).

Chikung Waterfall
(qīkǒng pùbù) 七孔瀑布
Following the road from Chialeshui back to Hengchun, you pass through the small town of Hsinchuang *(xīnzhuāng)*. About 1km past

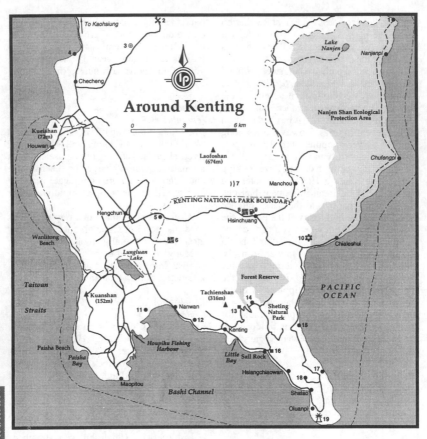

Around Kenting

0   3   6 km

KENTING NATIONAL PARK BOUNDARY

To Kaohsiung

Checceng

Kueishan
(72m)

Houwan

Laofoshan
(674m)

Lake
Nanjen

Nanjenpi

Nanjen Shan Ecological
Protection Area

Chufengpi

Manchou

Hengchun

Hsinchuang

Chialeshui

Wanlitong
Beach

Lungluan
Lake

Forest Reserve

PACIFIC
OCEAN

Taiwan

Straits

Kuanshan
(152m)

Tachienshan
(316m)

Nanwan

Kenting

Sheting
Natural
Park

Paisha Beach

Houpihu Fishing
Harbour

Little
Bay   Sail Rock

Paisha
Bay

Hsiangchiaowan

Maopitou

Bashi Channel

Shatao

Oluanpi

Hsinchuang is a turn-off on the right side
(north side) of the highway, marked only
with a sign in Chinese saying 'waterfall'
(pùbù). Follow this road until it ends (about
2km), then park your vehicle and walk, following the river upstream.

The waterfall is a series of cascades. As
you face the falls, there's a path on the right
hand side, secured with ropes, which you can
ascend from. Once past the falls, it takes
another 30 to 40 minutes to reach the top of
Laofoshan (674m). Assuming the weather is
cooperating, you should be able to see the
ocean from the summit.

Maopitou 貓鼻頭

(māobítóu) 貓鼻頭

Maopitou (Cat's Nose Head) is the peninsula
across the bay from Kenting – near the
nuclear power plant. The rugged coastline's
major attraction is its twisted coral formations. Maopitou occupies much of the
peninsula, even though the town itself isn't
very large.

There is an excellent bicycle ride along the
west coast (north of Maopitou). This route
has less traffic than the main Kenting-
Hengchun highway.

You can get there by bus from Hengchun.

AROUND KENTING
墾丁地區

1 Chiupeng Dunes
九棚沙丘
2 Shihmen Historical
Battlefield
石門古戰場
3 Szechunghsi Hot
Springs
四重溪溫泉
4 Haikou Sand Dunes
海口沙丘
5 Cemetery
墓地

6 Chennan Temple
鎮南宮
7 Chikung Waterfall
七孔瀑布
8 Lofeng Temple
羅峰寺
9 Petrol Station
加油站
10 White Banyan Garden
白榕園
11 Nuclear Power Plant
核能發電廠
12 National Park
Headquarters
國家公園管理處

13 Kenting House Hotel
墾丁賓館
14 Forest Recreation Area
墾丁森林遊樂區
15 Fengchuisha Beach
風吹砂
16 OK Hill Hotel
歐克山莊
17 Lungpan Sea Cliffs
龍磐
18 Oluanpi Recreation
Centre
鵝鑾鼻活動中心
19 Lighthouse
燈塔

Lungluan Lake

(lóngluǎn tán) 龍鑾潭

If you're a birdwatcher, grab your binoculars and head for Lungluan Lake, just north of the nuclear power plant. A large number of birds nest here – not because they are attracted to the warm glow of leaking radiation, but because this is a migratory route between the Asian mainland and the Philippines. The birds were once relentlessly hunted but are now under the protection of the park service. The 'lake' is not much more than a marsh, although it almost qualifies for lake status during the rainy season. Autumn and spring are the best times for viewing migratory species.

Nanwan

(nán wān) 南灣

This pleasant cove has a superb beach, Nanwan (South Bay) has become a mini-Kenting in its own right. Swimming and jet-skiing is popular, as is surfing and windsurfing. Snorkelling is also a possibility – the neighbouring nuclear power plant may have given birth to some unusual sea life.

Szechunghsi Hot Springs

(sìchóngxī wēnquán) 四重溪溫泉

During the time of the Japanese occupation, Szechunghsi was one of Taiwan's top three hot springs resorts (along with Peitou and Kuantzuling). These days, the springs attract busloads of weekend sightseers from Taipei. They come to get their picture taken in front of the Szechunghsi Guest House (to prove they've been there), take a quick dip in the hotel hot springs, gorge themselves on 'famous mountain food' and then throw it up on the bus heading home.

If you don't want to see tourists in their native habitat, come during the week, when the place is quiet. It's 14km from Hengchun and it's an enjoyable ride along the pretty tree-lined road. It's also a good bicycle ride with little traffic, though there's nothing to see in Szechunghsi itself.

Hengchun

(héngchūn) 恆春

There is not a lot to see in this small, bustling town, but the locals are proud of its four city gates which are still intact (rare in Taiwan). For most visitors, Hengchun is an important transit point and little else. Accommodation and motorcycle rentals (adjacent to the bus station) are available, and this is an option worth considering on weekends and holidays when Kenting itself is 'chock-a-block'. For further transit details see Getting There & Away later in this section.

Activities

During the day Kenting's main activities are swimming, sunbathing, surfing, windsurfing, snorkelling and scuba diving. You can swim and fry in the sun for free at all the beaches, except for the one next to the Kenting House Beach Restaurant, where admission is charged. There is a small, pleasant beach at Little Bay, opposite the Caesar Park Hotel. Surfing is reputedly good at the beach by the Kenting Youth Activity Centre.

The other water activities require equipment that can easily be hired. Everything from diving masks to jet-skis are available. Most of these sea toys are available from shops in central Kenting and at the beach. You won't have a hard time finding what you want; indeed, you'll be tripping over the stuff when you walk through town.

Hotel California (see the following Places to Stay entry) offers surfing classes (with equipment included) at NT$850 for a full day. Scuba gear costs about NT$750 a day to rent. A boat trip is another NT$1000 to NT$1500 per day depending on how many people are in your group.

Places to Stay

If you arrive during the week it won't take long to find a room in Kenting, but be warned that some places will ask you to leave on Saturday because another group has reserved and paid for all the rooms in advance. Weekend prices may be double, if you can get a room at all. It is possible that you may have to stay in Hengchun, a less attractive town 9km to the north. Other possible places to stay include Oluanpi, Sail Rock, Nanwan and Szechunghsi Hot Springs.

Places to Stay – budget

The vast majority of the budget places to stay in Kenting are not listed here because they simply have no name. Look for signs (in Chinese only, unfortunately) saying *tàofáng* (room with private bath), which may in fact just be a room in somebody's house. These places have to hustle for business, and indeed as soon as you step off the bus you're likely to be greeted by five or six people yelling *tàofáng* and extolling (again, in Chinese) the virtues of their particular accommodation offerings. You can negotiate with the touts if you like (remember to smile and keep it

friendly), but you'll possibly get something more suitable if you do your own exploring. Budget homestays can be as low as NT$400 per room, though quality and price vary widely.

Camping The beach south of the Lutian Disco Pub has become an informal *camping ground*. The legalities of this are questionable, but apparently many are using it and, so far, are getting away with it. The National Park Service can advise you about legal camping grounds, but these are never free.

Hostels The *Catholic Hostel* (☎ 886-1540; *tiānzhǔjiào huódòng zhōngxīn*) charges NT$800 for double rooms, however the place is geared towards groups with rooms accommodating three, four and six persons. You may get in a six-bed dorm to yourself if you arrive on a weekday – the cost for this is a mere NT$300. If you can get in, this is one of the cheapest places to stay in Kenting.

The *Teachers' Hostel* (☎ 886-1241; *jiàoshī huìguǎn*) is a good deal and you don't have to be a teacher. This is particularly recommended if you're driving your own vehicle as there is a car park within the walled compound. There are dorm beds from NT$200 to NT$250. Doubles are from NT$600 to NT$700, triples cost between NT$800 and NT$900 and quads go from NT$1000 to NT$1200.

Kenting Youth Activity Centre (☎ 886-1221; *kěndīng qīngnián huódòng zhōngxīn*) is run by the entrepreneurial China Youth Corps (CYC). It's designed to resemble an ancient Chinese village, and has become a tourist attraction in itself. Although ostensibly a youth hostel, it must have been intended for rich youths as the twins cost from NT$2500 to NT$5000. Of course, group rooms are more economical; rooms for four persons are NT$2200 (NT$550 per person) and rooms for six persons are NT$2700 (NT$450 per person). You do not necessarily need to be with a group to stay here, but groups are given preference.

Hotels The *Meixie Hotel* (☎ 886-1176; *měixié biéguǎn*) is one of the cheaper places, all the rooms are twins and cost up to

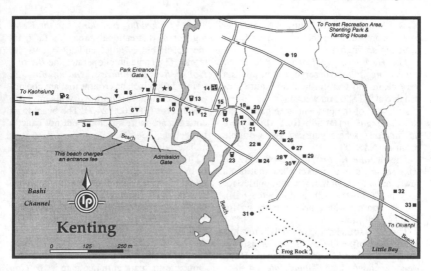

KENTING 墾丁

PLACES TO STAY
1 Kenting House Beach
   Annexe
   墾丁賓館海濱部
3 Beach Cottages
   小房子
5 Xin Taofang Hotel
   新陶芳大飯店
7 Jo Ley Hotel
   喬麗飯店
8 Gau Shang Ching Hotel
   高山青大飯店
10 A Jong Resort Hotel; KFC
   雅客之家、
   肯德基家鄉雞
17 Hiyuen Hotel
   海悅大飯店
18 Meixie Hotels
   美協別館
20 Beiping Hotel
   北平大飯店
21 South Star Hotel; Amy's
   Cucina Restaurant
   南星大飯店
22 Catholic Hostel
   天主教活動中心

24 Teachers' Hostel
   教師會館
26 Herng Chang Hotel;
   A Go Go Pub
   恒昌飯店、阿哥哥
29 Hotel California
   加州旅店
32 Caesar Park Hotel
   凱撒大飯店
33 Howard Resort Hotel
   福華大飯店

PLACES TO EAT
4 McDonald's
   麥當勞
6 Kenting House Beach
   Restaurant
   墾丁賓館海濱餐廳
11 Hollywood Chicken
   好萊屋鄉村炸雞
12 Golden Beach
   Pub/Restaurant
   金灘酒吧餐廳
15 Chingshan Papaya Milk
   Restaurant
   青山木瓜牛奶
25 Warung Didi Restaurant
   迪迪小吃

28 Linda's Cafe
   鯨魚的家
30 Dolce Vita
   Pizza
   比薩店

OTHER
2 Petrol Station
   加油站
9 Police Station
   警察局
13 Whale Bay Pub
   鯨魚灣酒吧
14 Temple
   廟
16 Open Bar
   開方啤酒屋
19 Kenting Ranch
   墾丁牧場
23 Lutian Disco
   Pub
   露天迪斯可
27 7-Eleven
   7-11便利商店
31 Kenting Youth Activity
   Centre
   青年活動中心

SOUTH-WEST TAIWAN

NT$1500 at peak times falling to NT$600 in low season. Ditto for the *South Star Hotel* (*nánxīng dà fàndiàn*).

The *Herng Chang Hotel* (☎ 886-1188; *héngchāng fàndiàn*) deserves a mention. It's very clean and well located, and quite reasonable at NT$800 on weekdays.

Just west of the park entrance gate is the *Xin Taofang Hotel* (☎ 886-1021; *xīn táofáng dà fàndiàn*), where you can get a double room for NT$700.

The *A Jong Resort Hotel* (☎ 886-1270; *yăkè zhījiā*) is an upmarket place that has a few pleasant *tatami* rooms with doubles for only NT$600 (the bath is down the hall). Fancier rooms, with a private bath, go for NT$1400 or more.

There is a solid line-up of small hotels just to the south of Sail Rock, known as Hsiang-chiaowan (*xiāngjiāowān*), or 'Banana Bay'. Recommended is the *Jinhua Hotel* (☎ 885-1340; *jīnhuá biéguăn*), where doubles/twins cost NT$800/1200.

There is no place to stay in Oluanpi itself, but there are some nearby options.

About 2km north of Oluanpi on the Oluanpi-Kenting highway is the minuscule hamlet of Shatao (*shādăo*). There are two places here with *taofang* signs. One is the *Zhongnanhai Taofang* (☎ 885-1107) and the other is the *Jinsha Taofang* (☎ 885-1155). Figure on paying from around NT$600 to NT$800.

Places to Stay – middle

The *Hotel California* (☎ 886-1588; *jiāzhōu lŭdiàn*) is popular with expats, and the manager speaks good English. Doubles are NT$1000 on weekdays and NT$1200 on weekends. Twin rooms are NT$2000 on weekdays and NT$2500 on weekends.

Next door to the Xin Taofang Hotel is the *Jo Ley Hotel* (☎ 886-1830; *qiáolì fàndiàn*), which is new and looks reasonably elegant. Twins are NT$2360 and suites are priced from NT$2600 to NT$4800.

The *Beiping Hotel* (☎ 886-1027; *běipíng dà fàndiàn*) boasts an enormous seafood restaurant, but the doubles are a steep NT$2500.

The *Kenting House* (☎ 886-1370; fax 886-1377; *kěndīng bīnguăn*) is in the Kenting Forest Recreational Area. It's far from the beach but is quiet and the views are grand. The same hotel operates the *Kenting House Beach Annexe* (*kěndīng bīnguăn hăibīn bù*), which has rooms that are considerably cramped. Doubles/twins at both places cost NT$2000/2400. The beachfront cottages are more spacious, but not exactly budget at NT$4600.

The *Oluanpi Recreation Centre* (☎ 885-1210/885-1191; *éluánbí huódòng zhōngxīn*) is in an isolated spot about 3km north of Oluanpi on the Oluanpi-Chialeshui highway. A night of recreation costs from NT$1725 to NT$3450. The hotel sits on a hill and has fine views, but it's often windy and there is no beach.

Places to Stay – top end

Opposite the park entrance gate is the *Gau Shang Ching Hotel* (☎ 886-1231; *gāo shān qīng bīnguăn*). This place is enormous and has rooms from NT$2200 to NT$5000.

The *Hiyuen Hotel* (☎ 886-2199; *hăiyuè dà fàndiàn*) looks deceptively small from the front. In fact, it's an enormous place with ocean views at the rear. Doubles/twins are NT$2800/4200, and a suite with an ocean view is NT$8000.

The *Caesar Park Hotel* (☎ 886-1888; fax 886-1818; *kăisā dà fàndiàn*) is a five star place designed to attract the Club Med crowd. Some of the amenities provided include a fitness centre, sauna, billiards hall, swimming pool, jacuzzi, tennis courts, archery range, golf practice range, beer house, KTV, organised snorkelling and scuba diving expeditions. Twins are from NT$5200 to NT$5900 and suites are from NT$10,000 to NT$40,000. If it's any consolation, the management will throw in a free baby crib if you request one. The hotel operates a shuttle bus from the Kaohsiung train station that also stops at Kaohsiung airport – the cost is NT$320. There is a moneychanging service for hotel guests only.

The neighbouring *Howard Resort Hotel* (☎ 886-2323/886-2300; *fúhuá dà fàndiàn*) looks luxurious, though the design is odd –

reaching the lobby requires going through the back entrance and walking upstairs. Once you manage to get to the check-in desk, a twin room will cost you NT$5300, or you can go for the presidential suite at NT$36,000.

OK Hill Hotel (☎ 886-1601/886-1366; *ōukè shān zhuāng*) dominates the hillside behind Sail Rock. It's a luxury resort with a disco, swimming pool and uniformed security guards who salute. The tab for a night runs from NT$3900 to NT$16,000. There is a shuttle bus to Kaohsiung for NT$320, or you can rent the hotel limousine for a mere NT$4000.

Places to Eat
There are so many seafood restaurants in Kenting that you'll be lucky not to trip over a lobster. In general, seafood is not cheap, so if you're minding the budget, look for places cooking noodle and rice dishes. There are quite a few restaurants that serve western food and have English menus.

Linda's Cafe (☎ 886-2747) is a small but friendly place, and may just be the first cafe in Taiwan to sell banana pancakes. However, Linda is most proud of her 'Bob's Breakfast' which is intended for really hungry travellers. It's also a good stop for coffee and fruit juice, and the prices are reasonable. The cafe opens at 9 am and closes late; when the customers fizzle out.

Chingshan Papaya Milk (☎ 886-1570) is known for papaya milkshakes, but also does a Taiwanese rendition of beef curry and other western dishes. There is an English menu, though at the time of writing, this place still lacked an English sign.

Warung Didi (☎ 886-1835) is unusual in Kenting as it dishes up delicious spicy Thai and Malay cuisine. Prices are very reasonable and this place is justifiably popular.

Pizza restaurants are starting to give the seafood shops some competition in Kenting. One worth trying is *Dolce Vita Pizza* (☎ 886-1679) which also serves spaghetti and steak and delivers directly to your hotel.

Pizza and spaghetti are also the basic staples at *Amy's Cucina*, though this place

has a bit more atmosphere (and somewhat higher prices) than its competitors.

If money is no object, you can get your pickles and seaweed delights at the Japanese restaurant inside the *Caesar Park Hotel*.

McDonald's and *KFC* have come to Kenting. Another competitor in the fast food business is *Hollywood Chicken (hǎoláiwū xiāngcūn zhàjī)*, which is actually pretty good if you ignore the plastic enamel decor.

There are numerous *grocery stores* where you can buy instant noodles for around NT$25.

Entertainment
One reason Kenting remains so popular is that the town offers the sort of beachside nightlife normally associated with places like Bali (Indonesia) and Pattaya (Thailand), rather than Taiwan. True, it's got a long way to go before becoming a world famous international resort, but pubs, discos and karaoke bars have sprung up, and judging from the pace of change, maybe this place really will catch up with Pattaya.

Big hotels are the venues for karaoke, if you have that particular passion. Look for the KTV signs.

The most crowded and expensive discos are in the *Caesar Park* and *Howard Resort* hotels.

Outdoor pubs broadcasting heavy rock music are conspicuous; examples being the *Open Bar*, *Whale Bay Pub* and *Golden Beach Pub*.

Getting There & Away
Air You can fly to Kaohsiung airport and catch a bus (or helicopter?) south to Kenting. Buses go right by the airport entrance and can be flagged down. Daily Air *(déān hángkōng)* has announced plans to start a helicopter service between Kaohsiung's Hsiaokang airport and Kenting, as soon as a heliport is built in Kenting. This should be forthcoming in the near future, call Daily Air (☎ (02) 2546-6835) in Taipei for details.

Bus There are a few direct buses on the Taipei-Kenting route. Additionally, all buses on the Kaohsiung-Taitung and Kaohsiung-Hengchun routes stop in Fengkang.

There is a road running directly between Taitung and Kenting via the small town of Manchou. If you have access to a car, you can indeed drive this route. The road is narrow and you'll need to show a passport or other ID at a checkpoint because the road passes through a nature reserve and a military outpost.

Car Some buses go directly to Kenting, but first stop for about 15 minutes in Hengchun, 9km north of Kenting. Many other buses terminate in Hengchun, you need to switch to another bus for the final leg of the journey. The bus station in Hengchun is on the street immediately to the left of the police station (as you face the building). Shuttle buses connect Hengchun with Kenting about every 40 minutes between 8 am and 6 pm.

Taxi You can pay NT$300 or more for the short ride to Hengchun.

Getting Around
Bus There is a daytime bus service between Hengchun and Oluanpi, via Kenting, about once every 40 minutes.

Car & Motorcycle You can hire motorcycles and 4WDs all over Kenting. You won't have any trouble finding a rental place – you'll have to climb over the vehicles just to get into some of the restaurants and hotels. Motorcycle rental is about NT$100 per hour, NT$300 for four hours, NT$500 for eight hours or NT$600 for 24 hours. Most of the bikes are 125cc – if you don't have a Taiwanese or International Driving Permit, you can hire a 50cc model (which requires no licence).

The roads around Kenting are all surfaced and smooth, so the only purpose of renting a 4WD vehicle is to drive on the beach, which causes significant environmental damage. The Taiwanese seem to find the jeeps irresistible – the reason is that they like to pose for heroic photos sitting behind the steering wheel while parked on the beach.

Bicycle There are plenty of bikes for hire in Kenting and you'll have no trouble finding a rental shop. A bicycle costs about NT$100 for eight hours, however Taiwanese bicycles do tend to be on the small side – a handicap for tall westerners.

Taxi Taxis regularly patrol the roads. Hitching is another possibility – the Kenting locals might expect payment for this, but people from Kaohsiung, Taipei and elsewhere are unlikely to ask hitchhikers for money.

PINGTUNG
(píngdōng) 屏東
The official administrative seat of Pingtung County, Pingtung is an up and coming city destined to become part of the Kaohsiung megalopolis. For all that, it's a nondescript place chiefly used by travellers as a staging post for Santimen, Wutai and Maolin. There is a branch of the Foreign Affairs Police (☎ 733-6283) at 136 Linsen Rd.

Getting There & Away
Air Pingtung has one of Taiwan's newest airports. The flight schedule is limited with two routes, Pingtung-Taipei and Pingtung-Makung. The two airlines serving Pingtung are Great China (☎ 766-5971; *dàhuá hángkōng*) and TransAsia Airways (☎ 080-066880; *fùxīng hángkōng*), both of which have offices at the airport.

Bus There are 42 daily buses between Kaohsiung and Pingtung. In Kaohsiung, they leave from the East Bus Station (see the Kaohsiung Getting There & Away section later in this chapter). The Pingtung Bus Company *(pìngdōng kèyùn)* is next to the train station in Pingtung.

Train Pingtung is on the Kaohsiung-Taitung line, which has seven trains a day, in both directions. There are also commuter trains about every 20 to 30 minutes between Kaohsiung and Pingtung. From Taitung, the train journey takes about 2½ hours; from Kaohsiung it's about 15 minutes.

SANTIMEN
(sāndìmén) 三地門

A small town where the plains dramatically meet the mountains, Santimen has peaceful surroundings and a whitewater river. The population mostly consists of Paiwan aborigines.

Santimen is made up of three areas – Santimen village, Shuimen and the popular Taiwan Aboriginal Culture Park. Shuimen is the main market town. Santimen village is on the opposite side of the river, up on a cliff hidden behind trees. Santimen village is great – an authentic aboriginal village surrounded by trees and farmland. There is a good temple overlooking the river near the bridge. Many of the people in Santimen are employed to do embroidery, as aboriginal craft has now become big business.

As you enter the Santimen area, the road is lined with tall palm tree farms. These are not coconut palms but betel nut trees.

The Paiwan tribe are renowned for their woodcarving techniques and their ancient beadwork designs, as seen in this headdress.

Taiwan Aboriginal Culture Park
(táiwān shāndì wénhuà yuán qū)
台灣山地文化園區

Just 3km south of Santimen, near the town of Machia *(mǎjiā)*, the Taiwan Aboriginal Culture Park (☎ 799-1219) is yet another aboriginal site devoted to mass tourism.

The houses are designed to look like traditional aboriginal homes, and the park has the requisite aboriginal song and dance shows at 11 am and 3 pm. All things considered, it's not bad. Admission costs NT$250 and it's open from 8 am to 5.30 pm daily.

Getting There & Away
Buses to Santimen depart from the Pingtung train station area twice daily at 6.55 am and 2.40 pm. From Santimen you can cross the suspension bridge and walk to the park. A faster alternative is to get off the bus at the town of Shuimen, before Santimen, and take a taxi or walk the 1.5km to the park. On weekends and holidays, buses go directly to the culture park.

WUTAI
(wùtái) 霧台

The town of Wutai is about 28km east of Santimen and is 1000m above sea level. The town's name means 'fog platform', a tribute to the foggy weather in these mountains. It's a remote area, inhabited by aborigines of the small Rukai tribe. About 2km north of the village is Wutai Waterfall *(wùtái pùbù)*.

Almost 18km east of Santimen, on the same road leading to Wutai, is the small community of Yila *(yīlá)*. Nearby are two waterfalls which are appropriately named No 1 Yila Waterfall *(dì yī yīlá pùbù)* and No 2 Yila Waterfall *(dì èr yīlá pùbù)*.

Very few visitors come here as you need one of those hard to get, class A mountain permits. Wutai can be reached by road and it's nowhere near 3000m high, so the excuse that the permit is necessary to prevent 'climbing accidents' doesn't hold. What is certain, is that this restriction has kept visitors away and has protected the village from tourism development.

The easiest way to get the pass is to have

a resident of the village sponsor you. You can try arranging a mountain pass and a homestay by calling the Wutai township office (☎ 790-2234/790-2260; *xiāng gōngsuǒ*) but it's unlikely that anybody will be able to speak English.

Assuming you manage to obtain all the documents, transport is available from the Pingtung Bus Company *(píngdōng kèyùn)*. Buses to Wutai also stop at Santimen. These depart from the Pingtung train station area twice daily at 6.55 am and 2.40 pm. Once there, villagers may be able to take you around by motorcycle for a reasonable fee.

HAOCHA
(hǎochá) 好茶

This is another small village nestled in the mountains, with the added attraction of nearby Shuiyun Waterfall *(shuǐyún pùbù)*. It's similar to Wutai and also requires one of those troublesome class A mountain passes.

You may be able to arrange a mountain pass and a place to stay by ringing up the Liaole Workroom (☎ 799-3001; *liáolè wēn gōngzuò shì*) or the Haocha Store (☎ 799-1128; *hǎochá shāngdiàn*).

SAI CHIA PARADISE
(sài jiā lèyuán) 賽嘉樂園

This is southern Taiwan's main venue for parasailing *(huá xiáng yì)* and ultralights *(xiǎo fēijī)* – miniaturised aeroplanes.

Sai Chia Paradise is 5km north of Santimen, on the road to Maolin. It's easy enough to find the place on weekends – just look for the aircraft floating around. Outside of hitching, there's no way to get there without your own transport.

LIUCHIU ISLAND
(liúqiú yǔ) 琉球嶼

Also known as Hsiao (Little) Liuchiu, this island is visible from Kaohsiung on a clear day. Fishing was the island's main industry, but most locals have graduated from harvesting fish to harvesting tourists. Nonetheless, the island is known for its seafood (mostly purchased from mainland China), secluded coves, coral formations and at least one good

sandy stretch of beach. The island is pretty but not stunningly beautiful. Unfortunately, it's close enough to Kaohsiung for bottles, styrofoam and other rubbish to occasionally wash up on the beaches. An effort is now being made to clean it up. The beaches are infinitely cleaner than those in Kaohsiung, and it's a wonderful, tranquil retreat from the madness of city life.

Liuchiu Island can be visited as a relaxing day trip, but it's more fun to spend the night. Indeed, the island is at its most attractive in the evening when the lights from Kaohsiung glimmer on the tranquil sea.

Near the southern end of the island is the **Seabed Zoo** *(hǎidǐ dòngwù yuán)*, a collection of aquariums that costs NT$100 to see. There are knowledgeable guides, but they are strictly Chinese-speaking only.

There is a glass-bottomed boat *(hǎidǐ bōlí chuán)* that frequently runs from Liuchiu harbour on weekends. This boat is considered to be one of the island's big attractions. The boat fare is NT$250. Sadly most of the coral formations have been damaged by collectors. You will probably get a better view of the coral at the island's souvenir shops.

Places to Stay

There are five places to stay in the Penfu Village area. Facing the harbour is the *Bailonggong Hotel* (☎ 861-2536; *báilónggōng dà fàndiàn)*. Rates here are from NT$1000 to NT$1400.

The *Fuhsing Hotel* (☎ 861-2617; *fùxīng bīnguǎn)* at 73-1 Minsheng Rd, very close to the Hsiao Liuchiu Hotel, is nothing fancy and rooms cost NT$500 on weekdays and NT$800 on weekends.

The entrance to the *Liuchiu Hotel* (☎ 861-3281; *liúqiú bīnguǎn)* faces the Lingshua Temple, while the other side looks out over the harbour. Rooms cost NT$1000 on weekends.

An alternative option is the *Nanhai Hotel* (☎ 861-1812; *nánhǎi lüshè)*, where the rooms are NT$800.

The *Hsiao Liuchiu Hotel* (☎ 861-1133; *xiǎo liúqiú dà fàndiàn)* is up the hill, one block from the harbour. This is the top place in town and charges from NT$1200 to

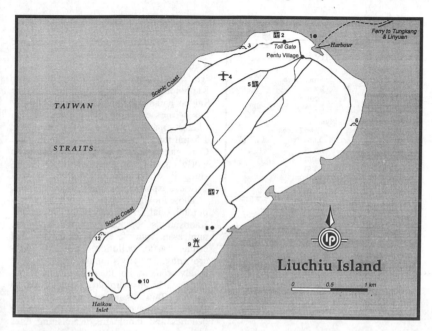

LIUCHIU ISLAND 琉球嶼

1 Coral Pinnacle
花瓶岩
2 Lingshan Temple
靈山寺
3 Beautiful People Cave
美人洞
4 Aircraft Landing Strip
機場
5 Sanlung Temple
三隆宮
6 Lobster Cave
龍蝦洞
7 Blue Cloud
Temple
碧雲寺
8 Pretty Girl Cliff
倩女塔
9 Lighthouse
燈塔
10 Cliffs
斷崖
11 Seabed Zoo
海底動物園
12 Black Ghost
Cave
烏鬼洞

NT$2500 on weekends. There is a 20% discount on weekdays.

Getting There & Away

Air The island has a small, unpaved landing strip, however it's overgrown with weeds and is only used for VIP visits.

Boat There are two ferry services to Liuchiu Island. Officially, departures from Tungkang (*dōnggǎng*) are at 8.30 am and 3 pm, returning at noon and 4.30 pm. Unofficially, boats go when they are full, which is about once an hour on weekends and holidays. The journey takes 50 minutes one way and the return fare is NT$220. Buses to Tungkang leave from the suburban bus terminal in Kaohsiung.

Chan'an Boat Company (☎ 222-2123; *zhān'àn lúnchuán gōngsī*), 65 Mintsu-2 Rd

Liuchiu Island Ferry Schedule

Weekdays

From Linyuan	From Liuchiu
8 am	9 am
10 am	noon
1.30 pm	3 pm

Weekends & Holidays

From Linyuan	From Liuchiu
8 am	9 am
9 am	noon
10 am	2 pm
11.20 am	3 pm
1.30 pm	4.30 pm

in Kaohsiung, charges NT$360 for a ticket which includes transport to the pier at Linyuan (*línyuán zhōngyún mǎtóu*) and the ferry ride both ways. If you make your own way to the pier, the ticket costs NT$280. The bus makes the trip to Linyuan harbour about eight times a day.

Getting Around

When you purchase your ferry ticket, you can also buy a pass that allows you to ride the blue trucks that drive counter-clockwise around the island. This makes more sense on weekends, when the service is frequent. You can hop off the truck at any time and catch the next one that comes along. However, the trucks are operated by different companies and they don't honour each other's passes. When you buy the pass, you'll be issued a sticker which you should stick to your shirt so the drivers can see it. The passes cost NT$100 for a full day's use.

Motorcycles can be taken on the ferry, but you can rent 50cc models on the island from a shack facing the Hsiao Liuchiu Hotel. The sign (in Chinese) says 'motorcycle rental' (*jīchē chūzǔ*).

You can walk all the way around the island in a day. Riding a bicycle is more convenient but they don't seem to be available for hire. You can take a bicycle on the ferry, though it'll cost you as much as a passenger ticket.

Kaohsiung County 高雄縣

KAOHSIUNG

(*gāoxióng*) 高雄

Kaohsiung is the second largest city in Taiwan and has the biggest seaport. The city has witnessed rapid growth and industrialisation and now has a population of over 1.5 million. The home of the China Steel Corporation, China Shipbuilding and the world's fourth largest container port, Kaohsiung is where you can really see what Taiwan's export-oriented economy is all about.

Those looking for peace, quiet and a view of traditional Taiwan may be less impressed. Kaohsiung's booming economy has some unpleasant spin-off effects in the form of crime, traffic, pollution, noise and overcrowding. The city's famous Love River is lovely no more. For many travellers, Kaohsiung will be an overnight stop on the way to some of Taiwan's major scenic attractions. On the other hand, if you'd like a break from beaches and mountains, Kaohsiung does offer pretty good nightlife. The city has a few worthwhile places to visit, but isn't likely to absorb much of your travel time.

Kaohsiung's previous name was 'Dagou' meaning 'beat the dog'. This was the name given to the place by the local aborigines long before the animal rights movement was established.

Information

Tourist Office The Travel Information Service Centre (☎ 281-1513) is on the 5th floor, 235 Chungcheng-4 Rd. The city of Kaohsiung has made it's debut on the World Wide Web. The email address for Kaohsiung Online is (www.kcg.gov.tw).

Foreign Consulates The American Institute in Taiwan (AIT; ☎ 224-0154; fax 223-8237; *měiguó zài tái xiéhuì*) is on the 5th floor, 2 Chungcheng-3 Rd. AIT serves as an unofficial consulate for the USA. It handles visas for the USA and has a notary service.

The unofficial Canadian consulate is the

Canadian Trade Office (☎ 227-0478), 10th floor, 247 Mingsheng-1 Rd.

Money There is an ICBC (☎ 201-3001; *guójì shāngyè yínháng*) at 308 Chungshan-1 Rd, very close to the train station. ICBC has another office (☎ 251-0141) at 253 Chungcheng-5 Rd. Just across the street is the Bank of Taiwan (☎ 251-5131; *táiwān yínháng*) at 264 Chungcheng-5 Rd.

There's an American Express Bank (☎ 226-3116; fax 226-2368; *měiguó yùntōng yínháng*) at 5 Chungcheng-3 Rd.

Travel Agencies Domestic and international air tickets are usually much cheaper if purchased from a travel agency. If staying at the IYHF Hostel, Ms Chen (the manager) is an authorised travel agent and can help you. Another source of international tickets is Bobby Travel Service (☎ 272-1535), 10th floor, 77 Chunghua-3 Rd. For both international and domestic tickets you can try Jupai Travel (☎ 336-6737; *jùpài lǚxíngshè*), room 1, 7th floor, 87 Linsen-2 Rd, and Three Star Travel (☎ 216-8621; *sānxīng lǚyóu*), room 4, 4th floor, 53 Chunghua-3 Rd.

Travel agencies that deal in domestic tickets include: Chienyuan Travel (☎ 336-3333; *qiānyuán lǚyóu*), 319 Chungshan-2 Rd; New Human Travel Service (☎ 323-4333), 9th floor, 28 Po'ai-1 Rd (near Chiuju Rd by the rear entrance of the train station); and Lienchiang Travel (☎ 215-4880; *liánqiáng lǚxíngshè*), room 6, 18th floor, 211 Chungcheng-4 Rd.

Medical Services Kaohsiung's biggest hospital is Chang Gung Memorial Hospital (☎ 731-7123; *cháng gēng yīyuàn*) near Chengching Lake, 7km north-east of the city centre. Bus No 60 goes there, and the hospital is the last stop.

About 1km north-east of Kaohsiung train station is the Kaohsiung Medical College (☎ 321-8753; *gāoxióng yī xuéyuàn*), 100 Shihchuan-1 Rd.

Another alternative is the Veterans General Hospital (☎ 341-9017; *róngmín zǒng*

yīyuàn), 386 Tachung-1 Rd, Tsoying (in northern Kaohsiung).

Emergency The Foreign Affairs Police (☎ 745-2830) are at 260 Chungcheng 4th Rd. There is another county branch (☎ 745-2830) at 338 Kuanyin Rd, Fengshan.

Cultural Centre The Chungcheng Cultural Centre (*zhōngzhèng wénhuà zhōngxīn*) is one of the largest in Taiwan. Architecturally, it seems to have been inspired by Taipei's Sun Yatsen Hall. It is the place to go for art exhibits, operas, exhibitions and classical performances. The cultural centre is at the intersection of Wufu-1 Rd and Hoping-1 Rd – drop by to get the current schedule of events.

Sanfeng Temple
(sānfēng gōng) 三鳳宮
Probably the best temple in Kaohsiung's city centre is Sanfeng (Three Phoenix) Temple which is hidden in a small alley to the south-west of the train station.

Tsoying
(zuǒyíng) 左營
Kaohsiung's best temples are clustered around a small lake in the district known as Tsoying, about 5km north of the city centre. The **Spring Autumn Temple** (*chūn qiū gé*) has a unique design and includes two pagodas (Spring and Autumn Pagodas) that extend into the lake.

The nearby **Confucius Temple** (*kǒngzǐ miào)* is a very tranquil place. Adjacent to the Confucius Temple is the temple library. Walking all the way around the lake is fun if you have the time.

Bus Nos 5 and 19 from Kaohsiung stop near both temples, as do hourly trains from Kaohsiung train station.

Wanshoushan
(wànshòushān) 萬壽山
Rising 355m above Kaohsiung is Wanshou-shan (Long Life Mountain). Unofficially, it's also known as Dagoushan (Beat the Dog Mountain).

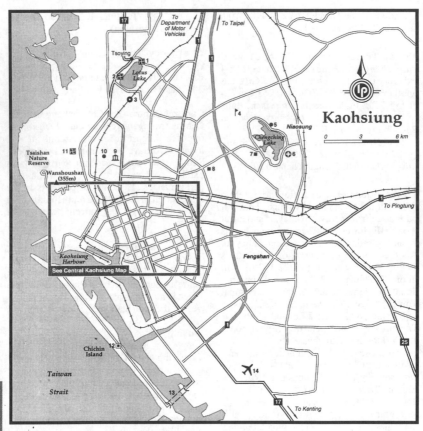

Kaohsiung

0   3   6 km

See Central Kaohsiung Map

The **Yuanheng Temple** *(yuánhēng sì)* is a good place to begin your explorations of Wanshoushan. On the ground floor there are three enormous Buddhas, and if you take the lift to the 5th floor there are three large statues of the goddess Kuanyin.

Just to the south of Yuanheng Temple is the **2-28 Memorial** *(èrèrbā jìniàn bēi)*, built to honour those killed during the anti-Kuomingtang (KMT) protests.

The **Wanshoushan Zoo** *(wànshòushān dòngwù yuán)* is worth a visit and can make a welcome break from the din of Kaohsiung's city streets.

Along the southern slopes of Wanshoushan is the **Martyr's Shrine** *(zhōng liè cí)*. It doesn't have all the pomp and ceremony of the Martyr's Shrine in Taipei, but it's still a good place to visit.

Sun Yatsen University *(zhōngshān dàxué)* is most easily reached by walking through a tunnel bored straight through Wanshoushan. The campus is pleasant and seems to serve as an unofficial park. You can see Chiang Kaishek's old limousine behind a glass showcase. At one time this campus was the Generalissimo's personal retreat. On the west side of the campus is **Hsitzuwan**

KAOHSIUNG 高雄市

1 Confucius Temple
孔廟
2 Spring Autumn Temple
春秋閣
3 Tsoying Train Station
左營火車站
4 Kaohsiung Golf Course
高雄高爾夫球場
5 Chengching Lake Youth
Activity Centre
澄清湖青年
活動中心

6 Chang Gung Memorial
Hospital
長庚醫院
7 Grand Hotel
圓山大飯店
8 Top Plaza Hotel &
Department Store
尖美大飯店、
尖美廣場
9 Fine Arts Museum
美術館

10 Chiang Chingkuo Cultural
Centre
經國文化區
11 Longchuan Temple
龍泉寺
12 25 Virtuous Women's
Tomb
二十五淑女墓
13 Cross-Harbour Tunnel
過港隧道
14 Kaohsiung International
Airport
高雄國際機場

Beach (xīziwān hǎishuǐ yùchǎng). This part of Taiwan is not exactly famous for its world class beaches, but Hsitzuwan is probably the best spot in Kaohsiung for taking a dip in the ocean. There is an NT$60 entrance fee to the beach area.

If you've got a bicycle, motorcycle or strong pair of hiking legs you can head north from the campus to the **Tsaishan Nature Reserve** (cháishān zìrán gōngyuán), which was once a military base. Aside from the views and hiking trails, the area is notable for its large population of monkeys. Bring a few goodies for the monkeys to eat – otherwise they can be pretty aggressive about stealing your lunch.

To the south of Sun Yatsen University is the northern entrance to Kaohsiung harbour. Take a look at the **Historical Relics Exhibition Hall** (shǐjī wénwù chénliè guǎn).

Nearby is the small and historical **Hsiungchen North Gate** (xióngzhèn běimén). This small gate was built by the son of Koxinga, Cheng Ching (zhèng jīng). Also in the vicinity is the Taoist **Shihpa Wangkung Temple** (shíbā wánggōng miào), a very active place of worship.

Science & Technology Museum
(kēxué gōngyì bówùguǎn) 科學工藝博物館
This, Taiwan's newest museum, is certainly one of its most impressive. There is an exhibition area and also an IMAX 3D theatre.

Admission to both is NT$100, with big discounts for students and seniors. There is a coffee shop on the 2nd floor and restaurants in the basement (reached via a separate entrance).

The museum (☎ 384-6471) is at 720 Chiuju-1 Rd and can be reached on bus Nos 60 and 73. The museum is closed on Monday.

Fine Arts Museum
(měi shù guǎn) 美術館
Close to Tsoying in the northern area of Kaohsiung is the Fine Arts Museum (☎ 316-0331). Displays are changed regularly. The museum is at 316-1 Chunghua-1 Rd. To get there take Bus No 5 from the Kaohsiung train station area.

About 100m to the west of the museum is the Chiang Chingkuo Cultural Centre (jīngguó wénhuà qū). Another 300m to the west is the Longchuan Temple (lóngquán sì).

Chienchin Cathedral
(qiánjīn tiānzhǔ táng) 前金天主堂
Also known as the Holy Rosary Cathedral (méiguì shèngmǔ yuàn), this Catholic church is the oldest in Taiwan. It was first established in 1860, and was rebuilt to its present dimensions in 1928.

The cathedral is at 151 Wufu-3 Rd just east of the Love River. English masses are held in the basement chapel at 10.30 am on Sunday.

SOUTH-WEST TAIWAN

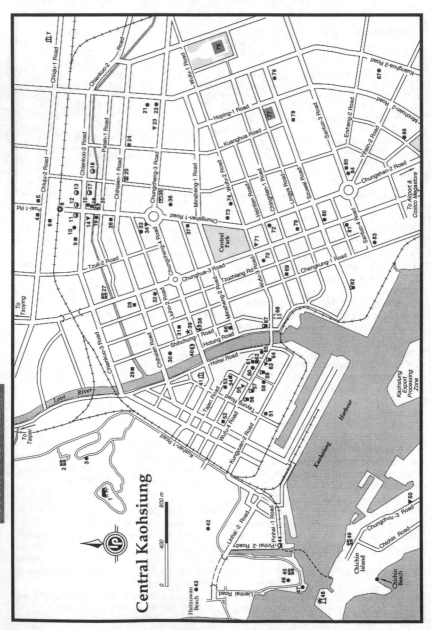

Central Kaohsiung

SOUTH-WEST TAIWAN

CENTRAL KAOHSIUNG
高雄市中心

PLACES TO STAY
4 Tian'an & King's
  Town Hotels
  天安大飯店、
  京城大飯店
5 Modern Hotel
  現代大飯店
6 Victoria Hotel
  維多利亞大飯店
9 Jui Cheng & Huang
  Pin Hotels
  瑞城別館、
  皇賓別館
15 Union Hotel
  國統大飯店
16 Himalaya Hotel
  喬山大飯店
19 Hotel Grand China
  中華大飯店
24 Howard Plaza Hotel
  福華大飯店
26 Kind Hotel
  凱得來大飯店
28 IYHF Hostel I
  文武一街120號
29 Buckingham Hotel
  白金漢大飯店
31 Hotel Holiday Garden
  華園大飯店
37 Ta Yih Hotel
  大益大飯店
51 Wen Pin Hotel
  文賓大飯店
52 Kingship Hotel
  漢王大飯店
53 Chinatrust Hotel
  中信大飯店
54 Hotel Major
  名人大飯店
61 Cheap Charlies;
  Dew Drop Inn
  新樂街81號、
  新樂街39號
62 Hotel Kingdom
  華王大飯店
66 Ambassador Hotel
  國賓大飯店
69 Grand Hi-lai Hotel;
  Hanshin Department Store
  漢來大飯店、
  漢神百貨

78 Linden Hotel
  霖園人飯店
79 IYHF Hostel II
  苓雅二路42號
81 Hotel Sunshine
  陽光大飯店

PLACES TO EAT
14 McDonald's
  麥當勞
23 Ka Ra Bour Thai Food
  卡拉包泰式餐廳
34 Box Store
  中山橫路9號
50 Jisheng Seafood
  Restaurant
  吉勝海產
55 Europe Pie Shop
  五福四路124號
63 New President Steak
  House
  新統一牛排館
71 TGI Fridays; McDonald's
  星期五美式餐廳、
  麥當勞

OTHER
1 Wanshoushan Zoo
  萬壽山動物園
2 Yuanheng Temple
  元亨寺
3 2-28 Memorial
  二二八紀念碑
7 Science & Technology
  Museum
  科學工藝博物館
8 Kaohsiung Train
  Station
  高雄火車站
10 Far Eastern Department
  Store
  遠東百貨
11 City Bus Terminal
  市公車站
12 Taiwan Bus Company
  East Station
  台汽客運東站
13 Country Buses (Taitung)
  台汽客運站(往台東)
17 Tonglien Bus Company
  統聯客運站
18 Taiwan Bus Company
  South Station
  台汽客運南站

20 ICBC
  中國國際商業銀行
21 Chan'an Boat Company
  占岸輪船公司
22 American Institute
  in Taiwan (AIT)
  美國在台協會
25 Telephone Company
  電信局
27 Sanfeng Temple
  三鳳宮
30 Baseball Stadium
  立德棒球場
32 Wenshabao Sauna
  (Men)
  溫莎堡健身廣場
33 Liuho Rd Night Market
  六合路夜市
35 GPO
  郵政總局
36 Hsinhsing Market St
  新興市場
38 ICBC
  國際商業銀行
39 Foreign Affairs Police
  警察局外事課
40 Bank of Taiwan
  台灣銀行
41 Kaohsiung City History
  Museum
  高雄市立歷史博物館
42 Martyrs' Shrine
  忠烈祠
43 Sun Yatsen University
  中山大學
44 Chichin Ferry Pier
  渡船碼頭(往旗津)
45 Shihpa Wangkung
  Temple
  十八王公廟
46 Historical Relics Exhibition
  Hall
  史蹟文物陳列館
47 Hsiungchen North
  Gate
  雄真北門
48 Chichin Lighthouse
  旗津燈塔
49 Matsu Temple
  天后宮
56 Tokyo City Pub
  五福四路145號
57 Amy's Pub II
  五福四路115號

continued over

SOUTH-WEST TAIWAN

58 OoLaLa Disco 大義街105號	70 Talee Department Store 大立百貨	80 Jurassic Park Disco 侏儸紀公園迪斯可
59 Alices II Pub; Doutor's Coffee Shop 五福四路65號、 羅多倫咖啡店	72 Rainbow's End 新田路205號 73 NOVA Computer Arcade; Pizza Hut NOVA資訊廣場、 必勝客	82 Pig & Whistle Pub 四維四路199號 83 Santuo Movie Theatres 三多大戲院 84 SOGO Department Store
60 Caves Books 敦煌書局 64 Brass Rail Tavern 五福四路21號	74 Muzhixiang Sauna (women) 沐之鄉三溫暖	太平洋崇光百貨 85 Mitsukoshi Department Store
65 Good Time Sporting Goods 好時辰運動百貨廣場 67 Rolling Stone Pub & Deli; Dew Drop Inn 五福三路152號	75 Chungcheng Cultural Centre 文化中心 76 Fashion Disco 福建街92號	新光三越百貨 86 Labourers' Recreation Centre 勞工休假中心 87 Dollars Megastore 大樂
68 Chienchin Cathedral 前金天主堂	77 City Hall 市政府	

Chichin Island
(qíjīn) 旗津

In the 1980s, Chichin Island could only be reached by boat and was devoid of cars. The mayor of Kaohsiung at that time proposed making this island into 'another Miami Beach'. It was not to be. Construction of the cross-harbour tunnel in 1985 has turned most of Chichin Island into a container port.

A belated attempt to reclaim some of the area's former charm has been attempted at the northern tip of the island. A recent innovation has been three-wheeled pedicabs *(sānlúnchē)*, formerly a common mode of transport in Taiwan. In the 1970s, pedicabs were banned in Taiwan because they were thought to be outdated and unbefitting the nation's modern image. It was only in 1995 that pedicabs were reinstated on Chichin Island, and at present this is the only place in Taiwan where they can be found. Chichin's pedicabs aren't really an effective means of public transport, but they have been a raging success with weekend tourists.

Chichin Island has a beach, and during summer there are lifeguards, ice-cream vendors and so on. Don't expect much – it's nowhere near as attractive as Kenting, let alone Bali or Phuket. However, it's good for a walk and a dip in the ocean, and it's certainly more attractive than the hot and sticky streets of Kaohsiung.

At the northern end of the island is the **Matsu Temple** *(tiānhòu gōng)*, the island's largest and most colourful temple and **Chichin Lighthouse** *(qíjīn dēngtǎ)*.

Near the centre of Chichin Island is the odd **25 Virtuous Women's Tomb** *(ershiwu shúnǚ mù)*. It was dedicated to 25 women who are said to have committed suicide to avoid being raped by pirates.

The main reason to visit Chichin Island is to enjoy the seafood restaurants (mostly clustered at the north end of the island), however seafood is not cheap here or anywhere else on the island (see Places to Eat later in this section).

You can reach Chichin by taking a short ferry ride from the fishing harbour, which is next to Sun Yatsen University. It is also possible to reach the island by driving through the tunnel.

Chengching Lake
(chéngqīng hú) 澄清湖

About 7km from the city centre, Chengching Lake is a city reservoir surrounded by a landscaped park. It's the only green spot in

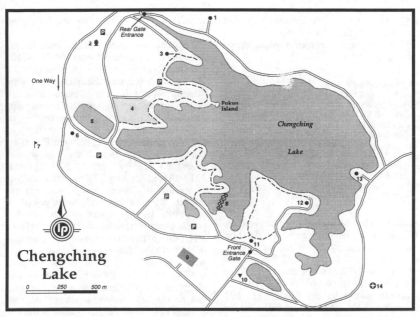

CHENGCHING LAKE
澄清湖

1 Youth Activity Centre
青年活動中心
2 Chunghsing Pagoda
忠興塔
3 Martyrs' Shrine
忠烈祠
4 Picnic Area
烤肉區

5 Rowboat Area
划船場
6 Horse Riding
騎馬場
7 Golf Course
高爾夫球場
8 Nine-Cornered Bridge
九曲橋
9 Grand Hotel
圓山大飯店

10 McDonald's
麥當勞
11 Aquarium
水族館
12 Chengching Building
澄清樓
13 Moon-Gazing Building
得月樓
14 Chang Gung Hospital
長庚醫院

Kaohsiung besides Wanshoushan. The huge Grand Hotel, which resembles a palace, overlooks the lake. Around the lake are pagodas, pavilions, a golf course and a place to hire rowing boats (NT$100 per hour).

Visit Chengching Lake anytime except Sunday and holidays when the park is inundated by a tidal wave of humanity and motor vehicles. There is an NT$80 entrance fee for the lake area plus NT$30 for motorcycles and NT$40 for cars. Bicycles are not permitted on the road around the lake because – as one of the guards at the gate explained – 'the bicycles confuse the cars and motorcycles'. To reach Chengching Lake, take bus No 60 from the city bus terminal.

Activities
If you want to play **golf**, the Kaohsiung Golf Club *(gāoxióng gāo'ěrfū qiú chǎng)* is next

to Chengching Lake. The entrance to the golf course is from the Grand Hotel.

Kaohsiung has numerous **bowling alleys** including:

gāofēng bǎolíngqiú guǎn
(☎ 717-0623) 15 Yongfeng Rd
héshēng bǎolíngqiú guǎn
(☎ 812-5111) 12 Lane 30, Wufu-2 Rd, Fengshan
jīndiàn bǎolíngqiú guǎn
(☎ 806-6099) 411 Hongping Rd
quányáng bǎolíngqiú guǎn
(☎ 381-3731) 151 Chienhsing Rd
zìyóu bǎolíngqiú guǎn
(☎ 341-5688) 240 Anchi Rd
zhōngdà bǎolíngqiú guǎn
(☎ 338-8733) 99 Linsen-3 Rd

Kaohsiung has **saunas** for men and women. Women may want to check out the Mu-zhixiang Sauna (☎ 241-9776; *mùzhīxiāng sānwēnnuǎn*), 12th floor, 192 Wufu-2 Rd, which costs NT$300. For men there is the Wenshabao Sauna (☎ 261-4977; *wēnshābǎo jiànshēn guǎngchǎng*), 6th floor, 151 Chunghua-3 Rd, which has exercise equipment and costs from NT$400 to NT$500.

If you are interested in joining a **language course**, foreigners can study Chinese at the Kaohsiung branch of the Taipei Language Institute (☎ 215-2965/215-3638; fax 215-2981), 2nd floor, 507 Chungshan-2 Rd.

Places to Stay – budget

Most budget travellers head straight for the *IYHF Hostel I* (☎ 201-2477; fax 215-6322), 120 Wenwu-1 St, one block west of Chunghua Rd and north of Chihsien Rd. This place may be full, but the overflow winds up at the *IYHF Hostel II* (☎ 339-1533; fax 336-1339) at 42 Lingya-2 Rd. Rooms cost from NT$280 to NT$380 and all have air-con. It's best to call ahead to Hostel I to see if space is available. Both hostels boast a TV sitting room, refrigerator and a place to cook simple meals.

Another option is to rent rooms from the owner of the *Box Store* (☎ 221-7265; *jiāhé shāng háng*), 9 Chungshan Heng Rd. This is not a hostel and the rooms are pretty grotty, but it's a cheap alternative. The Box Store is actually a grocery store (see the following Places to Eat section).

Towards the south end of town is the *Labourers' Recreation Centre* (☎ 332-8110/332-9110; *láogōng yùlè zhōngxīn*), 132 Chungshan-3 Rd, near the intersection with Minchuan-2 Rd. It's a huge place and occupies a city block. Single/double rooms with attached bath cost a very reasonable at NT$450/550.

Close to the Grand Hotel (see Places to Stay – top end section) is the *Chengching Lake Youth Activity Centre* (☎ 371-7181; fax 371-9183; *chéngqīng hú qīngnián huódòng zhōngxīn*). It's a mid-range, rather then budget, place to stay with twins priced at NT$1500. It only works out cheaply for youth groups: a room for four people is NT$1800 (NT$400 per person); five people is NT$2000 (NT$400 per person); and six people is NT$1600 (NT$400 per person). It's 7km from the city centre and there are plenty of activities, such as rope climbing and an obstacle course, available. Almost directly in front of the train station is the *Jui Chung Hotel* (☎ 272-5761; *ruìchéng biéguǎn*), 40 Chienkuo-3 Rd. It's a bargain by Kaohsiung standards with double rooms priced at NT$500 and NT$600.

In the same building as the Jui Cheng is the very similar *Huang Pin Hotel* (☎ 291-3173; *hua'ngbīn biéguǎn*), where doubles are NT$600.

The *Hotel Grand China* (☎ 221-9941; *zhōnghuá dà fàndiàn*), 289 Chungshan-1 Rd, is a little obscure and there's no English sign. Doubles/twins are NT$600/1500.

The *Himalaya Hotel* (☎ 237-6602; *qiáoshān dà fàndiàn*), 316 Chungshan-1 Rd, is notable for its sauna. Double rooms start at NT$860.

The *Kind Hotel* (☎ 291-9131; fax 291-9139; *kǎidélái dà fàndiàn*), 257 Chungshan-1 Rd, is a smart little business hotel near the train station. Doubles are NT$900.

The *Ta Yih Hotel* (☎ 231-2141; *dàyì dà fàndiàn*), 177 Tatung-1 Rd, is new, clean and modern, and seems a very good deal at NT$880 for a double.

Directly facing the train station is *Union*

Hotel (☎ 235-0101; *guótŏng dà fàndiàn*), 295 Chienkuo-2 Rd. This place is fairly upmarket with doubles starting at NT$980. Twins are priced from NT$1600 to NT$2200 and suites are NT$2600.

Behind the train station, the *Modern Hotel* (☎ 312-2150; *xiàndài dà fàndiàn*), 332 Chiuju-2 Rd, charges NT$780 for a double but you can get a 10% discount if you flash an International Youth Hostel Federation (IYHF) card.

If you exit the train station and cross the street the *Tian'an Hotel* (☎ 312-2131; *tiān'-ān dà fàndiàn*) is on your left (on the corner) at 1 Po'ai-1 Rd. Doubles are NT$700 and there is no English sign.

Places to Stay – middle
The *Victoria Hotel* (☎ 323-1031; *wéiduōlìyà dà fàndiàn*), 1 Chungching St, is a brand new business hotel directly behind the train station. Doubles are NT$1300.

King's Town Hotel (☎ 311-9906; fax 311-9591; *jīngchéng dà fàndiàn*), 362 Chiuju-2 Rd, is a very elegant looking business hotel behind the train station. Doubles/twins are NT$1800/2100.

The *Buckingham Hotel* (☎ 282-2151; fax 281-4540; *báijīnhàn dàfàndiàn*), 394 Chih-sien-2 Rd, is an 11 storey luxury tower west of the train station and close to the Love River. Doubles cost NT$2100, twins cost from NT$2400 to NT$3000 and suites are NT$5000.

The *Chinatrust Hotel* (☎ 521-7111; fax 521-7068; *zhōngxìn dà fàndiàn*), 43 Tajen Rd, is just one of several excellent hotels belonging to the Chinatrust chain. Doubles cost from NT$2800 to NT$4200, twins cost from NT$3400 to NT$3800 and suites cost from NT$4000 to NT$7000.

The *Hotel Major* (☎ 521-2266; fax 531-2211; *míngrén dà fàndiàn*), 7 Tajen Rd, does very nicely as a business hotel. Doubles/twins are NT$2700/3000 and suites go all the way up to NT$10,000.

The *Wen Pin Hotel* (☎ 561-2346; fax 533-8007; *wénbīn dà fàndiàn*), Tayong Rd, is one of the best places to stay if you want to be in Kaohsiung's main nightlife district. Rooms cost from NT$1350 to NT$2500.

Places to Stay – top end
The *Hotel Kingdom* (☎ 551-8211; fax 521-0403; *huáwáng dà fàndiàn*), 42 Wufu-4 Rd, is the finest hotel in Kaohsiung's hot nightlife zone. Double rooms cost from NT$3400 to NT$4300, twins cost from NT$4300 to NT$4500, and suites are between NT$7000 and NT$8500.

Kaohsiung's newest top end luxury tower is the *Howard Plaza Hotel* (☎ 236-2323; fax 235-8383; *fúhuá dà fàndiàn*). It's equipped with several fine restaurants including some that serve Chinese, Thai and western cuisine. There's a business centre, four level shopping arcade, swimming pool, jacuzzi, pay-per-view TV movies and fitness centre. Doubles cost from NT$4900 to NT$6200, twins are from NT$5200 to NT$6500 and suites rise from NT$7800 to NT$25,000.

The *Grand Hi-lai Hotel* (☎ 216-1766; fax 216-1966; *hànlái dà fàndiàn*), 266 Cheng-kung-1 Rd, is a magnificent new hotel. Facilities include a business centre, outdoor swimming pool, squash courts, fitness centre, sauna, non-smoking floor, women's floor and (count them) 26 restaurants. Standard rooms are from NT$4800 to NT$6300, deluxe rooms are from NT$5300 to NT$7100 and suites go all the way up to NT$100,000.

The *Linden Hotel* (☎ 332-2000; fax 336-1600; *línyuán dà fàndiàn*), 33 Szuwei-3 Rd, is a new and luxurious place. Amenities include numerous restaurants, a business centre, non-smoking floors, 24 hour room service, indoor heated swimming pool, jacuzzi, sauna, hair salon, clinic and dance hall. Singles are from NT$3600 to NT$4100, doubles are NT$4600, twins are NT$5200 and suites are from NT$8800 to NT$60,000.

The *Top Plaza Hotel* (☎ 385-2838; fax 385-4009; *jiānměi dà fàndiàn*), 266 Ta-chang-2 Rd, is north-east of the city centre and is attached to one of Kaohsiung's largest department stores. In house restaurants serve western cuisine, Cantonese food and Japanese *teppanyaki*. Amenities include a sauna,

SOUTH-WEST TAIWAN

beauty parlour, meeting hall and the rooftop *Sky Lounge*. Doubles are from NT$2800 to NT$3300, twins cost NT$3500 and suites cost from NT$5000 to NT$30,000.

The *Ambassador Hotel* (☎ 211-5211; fax 281-1113; *guóbīn dà fàndiàn*), 202 Minsheng-2 Rd, is an old Kaohsiung institution and is still one of the best. Facilities include a swimming pool, shopping arcade, beauty parlour, sauna, bar, business centre and rooftop garden. Rooms on the west side offer a fine view of the Love River (you can't see the pollution from a distance). Doubles cost from NT$3700 to NT$4900, twins are from NT$4500 to NT$6000 and suites cost between NT$9800 and NT$40,000.

The palatial *Grand Hotel* (☎ 383-5911; fax 381-4889; *yuánshān dà fàndiàn*), 2 Yuanshan Rd, Niaosung, is near Chengching Lake (about 7km from central Kaohsiung). It's a great place if you enjoy physical activity, as the facilities include a fitness centre, sauna, tennis courts, golf course and an outdoor Olympic-sized swimming pool. Doubles are from NT$4000 to NT$4500, twins cost from NT$5000 to NT$5500 and suites cost NT$7000.

The *Hotel Holiday Garden* (☎ 241-0123; fax 251-2000; *huáyuán dà fàndiàn*), 279 Liuho-2 Rd, once belonged to the Holiday Inn chain. Although it has changed management, it's still excellent. The restaurant is a popular venue for wedding parties. Doubles cost from NT$3800 to NT$4500, twins cost from NT$4200 to NT$4800 and suites range from NT$8800 to NT$40,000.

The *Hotel Sunshine* (☎ 332-7988; fax 332-9868; *yángguāng dà fàndiàn*), 75 Chunghua-4 Rd, is a business hotel. Doubles/twins are NT$3800/4800, which is actually a bit expensive for what you get.

Places to Eat

Night Markets Liuho-2 Rd *(liùhé èr lù)* has an active night market where the chief form of entertainment is eating. Liuho Rd is a very long street; the night market is only between Chungshan-1 Rd and Tzuli Rd. You'll find plenty of reasonably priced seafood stalls, but the snake soup and anteater may be more

interesting. The street vendors only operate in the evening, during the day Liuho-2 Rd is renowned for its steak restaurants.

The *Hsinhsing St Market (xīnxīng shìchǎng)* is adjacent to the GPO in a long alley running parallel to Chungshan-1 Rd. It operates day and night, though it's not quite open the full 24 hours. Besides cheap eats, it's a good place to look for relatively cheap clothing and shoes.

Food Courts Food courts can be found in the basements of major department stores including: SOGO, Mitsukoshi, Talee and the Far Eastern.

Restaurants As mentioned earlier, Chichin Island is famous for seafood. One of the best restaurants is the *Jisheng Seafood Restaurant* (☎ 571-9016; *jíshèng hǎi chǎn*), 186-3 Chungchou-2 Rd. It's at the northern end of the island.

Ka Ra Bour Thai Food (☎ 224-6668; *kǎlābāo tàishì cāntīng*), 54 Chungcheng-3 Rd, is one of Kaohsiung's few restaurants that serves spicy Thai food. It has a luncheon special that costs NT$180 per person.

TGI Friday's (☎ 271-3579; *xīngqīwǔ měishì cāntīng*), 25 Wufu-3 Rd, serves excellent, if somewhat costly, American and Mexican dishes.

The *New President Steak House* (☎ 551-1414; *xin tongyi niupai guan*), 31 Wufu-4 Rd, is one of the best western restaurants in town. It's almost directly opposite the Hotel Kingdom.

The *Europe Pie Shop* (☎ 551-6794) at 124 Wufu-4 Rd gets rave reviews from travellers. Pies are not the only thing on the menu – plenty of other western food is available.

Hotel food is not to be overlooked. Fine buffets cost from around NT$500 to NT$650 in Kaohsiung. Four places to pig out include the *Ambassador Hotel*, *Hotel Kingdom*, *Linden Hotel* and *Grand Hotel* (see Places to Stay earlier in this section).

Most pubs also serve food. See Entertainment later in this section for details.

Fast Food Egg McMuffins and crispy fried

The PRC, the ROC & Dr Sun Yatsen

Mainland China's Communist Party and Taiwan's Kuomingtang (KMT) agree on very little, but one thing they do agree on is that Taiwan is still a province of China, not an independent country. At least that's what they say, though many in the KMT no longer really seem to believe it. Nevertheless, as long as Taiwan officially remains a part of China, the national heroes must also remain Chinese.

All over Taiwan you can see statues and monuments honouring Chiang Kaishek, the KMT leader, and the founding father of the Republic of China (ROC), Dr Sun Yatsen. Their pictures appear on all ROC-issued coins and paper currency – they are national idols. However, in recent years a much less flattering account of Chiang Kaishek's rule has become publicly known to the Taiwanese. Many have begun to question his 'great achievements', and the Taiwanese history books are likely to be revised in the years ahead.

Mainland China is unambiguous – Chiang Kaishek is definitely not a hero to the Communists, but Sun Yatsen is. Indeed, over the years the Communist Party has been gradually downplaying the role of Mao Zedong in favour of Sun Yatsen. The PRC hopes to use Dr Sun as a national icon to rally the Chinese masses to support the great common goal of Chinese reunification.

One legacy of Dr Sun Yatsen is *The Three Principles of the People* which promoted nationalism, livelihood and civil rights. The Taiwanese government constantly enforces these principles and the book is required reading for all students, from elementary school right through to university. It is even possible to obtain a master's degree in the Three Principles. In the not-too-distant past, the Taiwanese had to pass an exam in the Three Principles before they could land a government job. Even the national anthem is titled 'Three Principles of the People'. Every city in Taiwan has a Mintsu (Nationalism), Minsheng (Livelihood), Minchuan (Civil Rights), Chungshan (Sun Yatsen) and Chungcheng (Chiang Kaishek) Rd.

Dusty English-language editions of *The Three Principles of the People* can be found in some back-alley bookshops and libraries. If you want to understand Taiwan's history, it's worth a browse; but be forewarned that the book is heavy going. Ironically, most modern-day economists would describe the book as having a Marxist bent. ■

chicken are visible from every street corner. If you need home delivery, there's *Domino's Pizza* (☎ 281-9266; *dáměilè bǐsà diàn*) at 388 Chihsien-2 Rd.

Self-Catering The place to buy preserved, canned and frozen western foods is the *Box Store* (☎ 221-7265; fax 272-7394; *jiāhé shāng háng*), 9 Chungshan Heng Rd. This is in a little alley on the north-west side of the traffic island at the corner of Chungshan-1 and Chungcheng-4 Rds.

If you're in the area of Chengching Lake, check out *Mr Li's Western Groceries* (☎ 731-2051), 2-4 Dabei Rd, which is very close to Chang Gung Memorial Hospital. It's open from 7 am until 9 pm.

Coffee Shops The *Doutor's Coffee Shop* (☎ 532-5308; *luóduōlún kāfēi diàn*) at 51 Wufu-4 Rd features something almost unheard of in Taiwan – low prices.

I Love My Home Coffee Shop (☎ 231-

9657), 258 Chungshan-1 Rd, is nice but expensive. Don't figure on getting coffee for less than NT$200. There is another branch (☎ 271-5273) at 104 Liuho-1 Rd.

Entertainment

Cinemas Kaohsiung has so many cinemas that it's a wonder that locals have time to do anything else but watch movies. The following is a small sample:

Cannes
   (☎ 321-0663; *kǎnchéng yùlè guǎngchǎng*) 161 Shihchuan-1 Rd (opposite Kaohsiung Medical College)
Great China
   (☎ 221-2972; *dà huáqiáo xìyuàn*) 4th floor, 535 Chienkuo-3 Rd
Great President
   (*hóngzǒng*) 63 Santuo-4 Rd (on Chunghua Rd)
Great Stage
   (☎ 551-4439; *dàwǔtái xìyuàn*) 199 Tajen Rd, Yencheng District

Hashin Department Store
  (☎ 216-0970; *huányì xìyuàn*) basement, 266 Chengkung-1 Rd
Hochun
  (☎ 384-7686; *héchūn dà xìyuàn*) 391 Chienhsing Rd, San Min District
Kuangfu
  (☎ 551-4290/551-2323; *guāngfù xìyuàn*) 96 Tayung Rd
Oscar
  (☎ 241-2128; *aòsīkǎ diànyǐng guǎngchǎng*) 287 Jentse St (near the corner of Wufu-2 and Chungshan-2 Rds)
Pili Palace
  (☎ 251-2095; *bìlìgōng*) 60 Wufu-3 Rd
Poai
  (☎ 311-7141; *bo'ai xìyuàn*) 21 Shihchuan-2 Rd, San Min District
Santuo
  (☎ 333-9100; *sānduō xìyuàn*) 123 Santuo-4 Rd
Tatung
  (☎ 761-8236; *dàtǒng xìyuàn*) 42 Hantai Rd
United
  (☎ 334-6285; *liánhōng yùlè*) 4th floor, 62 Tzuchiang-3 Rd

Discos *The Fashion Disco* (☎ 335-3399), 92 Fuchien St, is a trendy spot for young locals.

Jurassic Park Disco at Chunghua and Szuwei-4 Rds is another hip spot for local teenagers. It has a facade that looks like a cave and there is a big dinosaur sticking out above the doorway. Admission is NT$500.

OoLaLa Disco (☎ 561-4111), 105 Tayi St, enjoys a large share of the expat market.

Rock 22 (☎ 213-5759) is on the 22nd floor of the Grand Hi-Lai Hotel at 266 Chengkung-1 Rd. Opening hours are 8 pm to 4 am.

MTV *Kiss* is an outstanding MTV place with three branches which are down the street from one another: Kiss No 1 (☎ 272-9412) 3rd floor, 14 Chungshan-1 Rd; Kiss No 2 (☎ 281-9775) 9th floor, 4 Chungshan-1 Rd; and Kiss No 3 (☎ 291-7863) 9th floor, 165 Linsen-1 Rd (above a computer store).

Pubs The Yenchen district of Kaohsiung (near the Hotel Kingdom) is the place to look for pubs and restaurants. However, the area is a seaport and sometimes rough – a few years ago, a drunken Korean sailor was stabbed to death when he refused to pay his bar bill.

Tokyo City Pub, 145 Wufu-4 Rd, perhaps deserves top honours for atmosphere, good food and drink.

Cheap Charlie's Pub (☎ 532-1546), 81 Hsinlo St, is a hot spot with the expat crowd. As the name implies, cheap food and beer is a feature.

Alice's Pub (☎ 551-9999), 62 Wufu-4 Rd, has been around for a while, but the new *Alice's Pub II* (☎ 532-0909) at 65 Wufu-4 Rd, is even more popular.

The *Rainbow's End Pub* (☎ 201-2017), 205 Hsintien Rd, is yet another fine spot.

The *Rolling Stone Pub & Deli* (☎ 201-0574), 152 Wufu-3 Rd, is an interesting place. Aside from a great collection of 60s music, it's also the place to stock up on take away Swiss cheese, English sausages and bratwurst.

Almost next door at 39 Hsinlo St is the *Dew Drop Inn* (☎ 561-2428). Although prices are not that cheap, the food is excellent – you really do get what you pay for.

The *Brass Rail Tavern* (☎ 531-5643), 21 Wufu-4 Rd, is another pub/restaurant combination where the food is superb.

Amy's Pub II (☎ 533-0756), 115 Wufu-4 Rd, is worth a visit for the food and beer.

The *Pig & Whistle* (☎ 330-1006), 199 Szuwei-4 Rd, is a well known and somewhat upmarket place. It's open from 11.30 to 3 am (5 am on Saturdays) and upstairs there are live bands from 9 pm nightly. The western food is excellent.

Things to Buy
Camping Gear Kaohsiung boasts one of the best backpacking and camping stores in Taiwan – the Good Time Sporting Goods Department Store (☎ 551-2296; *hǎo shí chén yùndòng bǎihuò guǎngchǎng*) is at 2 Wufu-4 Rd. As its advertisement says, 'Our store believes in being honesty'.

Bookshops Caves Books (☎ 561-5716; *dūnhuáng shūjú*), 76-78 Wufu-4 Rd, near the Hotel Kingdom, has a large collection of English titles.

Also worth looking into is New School-mate Books (☎ 223-6000; *xīn xué yǒu shūjú*) at 18 Chungcheng-2 Rd. This shop is often called NSB or Sensaio Books.

Eslite Books (☎ 215-9795; *chéngpǐn shūdiàn*) is deep in the bowels (3rd basement) of the Hanshin Department Store *(hànshén bǎihuò)* at 266 Chengkung Rd, Section 1 (in the same building as the Grand Hi-Lai Hotel).

Computers The NOVA Computer Arcade *(NOVA zīxùn guǎngchǎng)*, Chungshan-1 Rd (just to the north of Wufu-2 Rd) harbours numerous hardware and software shops. Alternatively, check out T-Zone Computer Store (☎ 291-1177; *tàipíngyáng diànnǎo diàn*), 165 Linsen-1 Rd (next to the GPO), which is open from 11 am until 10 pm.

Getting There & Away
Air From Kaohsiung there are direct international flights to Hong Kong, Vietnam, the Philippines and a few other South-East Asian destinations.

Kaohsiung also has domestic air services to Chimei, Green Island, Hsinchu, Hualien, Kinmen, Makung, Orchid Island, Taichung, Taipei, Taitung and Wang'an.

Certain restrictions apply to the flights going to CKS airport in Taoyuan County. Most importantly, flights will only accept those passengers connecting with same day international flights from CKS airport. Furthermore, both incoming and outgoing passengers must clear Customs and Immigration at Kaohsiung airport. Finally, passengers travelling from Kaohsiung to CKS airport must present themselves for check-in at least 60 minutes before the flights departure (just as with any other international flight).

A number of international airlines have offices in Kaohsiung, however this does not necessarily mean that they fly into Kaohsiung, only that you can make bookings and reconfirmations here.

Air China	(☎ 231-5181)
Australia Asia	(☎ 282-3758)
British Asia	(☎ 282-3758)
Canadian Airlines International	(☎ 251-1391)
Cathay Pacific Airways	(☎ 282-7479)
Continental Airlines	(☎ 281-3346)
Delta Air Lines	(☎ 215-7286)
EVA Airways	(☎ 330-9311)
Garuda Indonesia	(☎ 251-2806)
KLM-Royal Dutch Airlines	(☎ 226-4210)
Lufthansa Airlines	(☎ 251-1403)
Philippine Airlines	(☎ 251-2315)
Qantas Airways	(☎ 282-3758)
Royal Brunei Airlines	(☎ 281-9055)
Singapore Airlines	(☎ 226-0868)
Swissair	(☎ 221-6001)
Thai Airways International	(☎ 215-5871)
United Airlines	(☎ 241-0990)
Vietnam Airlines	(☎ 227-0209)

For domestic flights, you can easily buy tickets at the airport or from travel agents. The airline representative offices are:

China Airlines
    (☎ 231-5181; *zhōnghuá hángkōng*) 81 Chunghua-3 Rd
EVA Airways
    (☎ 791-1000/330-9311; *chángróng hángkōng*) 177 Szewei-4 Rd
Far Eastern Air Transport
    (☎ 241-1181; *yuǎndōng hángkōng*) 101 Chunghua-3 Rd
Formosa Airlines
    (☎ office 332-0608/airport 806-5614; *guóhuá hángkōng*) suite 2, 9th floor, 380 Minchuan-2 Rd
Great China Airlines
    (☎ 801-7608; *dàhuá hángkōng*) Kaohsiung airport
Taiwan Airlines
    (☎ 801-3793; *táiwān hángkōng*) Kaohsiung airport
TransAsia Airways
    (☎ (080) 066-880; *fùxīng hángkōng*) 2nd floor, 148 Chunghua-3 Rd
U-Land Airlines
    (☎ 806-8348; *ruìlián hángkōng*) 2 Chungshan-4 Rd
Uni Air
    (☎ 791-1000/801-0189; *lìróng hángkōng*) 2-6 Chungshan-4 Rd

Bus The Taiwan Bus Company has two bus stations: the East Bus Station (☎ 201-8352), 310 Chienkuo-2 Rd (just east of the train station); and the South Bus Station (☎ 221-1937), 245 Nanhua Rd. The Tonglien Bus

SOUTH-WEST TAIWAN

Kaohsiung Long Distance Bus Schedule & Fares

Destination	Travel Time (hours)	Fare	No of Buses	Bus Station
Alishan	5.00	NT$270	one daily	East
Chiayi	2.00	NT$116	40 daily	East
Hengchun	2.30	NT$176	50 daily	South
Hsinchu	4.00	NT$422	four daily	East
Hualien	8.00	NT$643	four daily	South
Keelung	5.00	NT$521	six daily	East
Nantou	3.30	NT$196	four daily	East
Pingtung	1.15	NT$39	42 daily	East
Taichung	2.45	NT$288	47 daily	East
Tainan	1.30	NT$87	65 daily	East
Taipei	5.00	NT$497	75 daily	East
Taitung	3.30	NT$344	11 daily	South
Taoyuan	3.45	NT$382	14 daily	East

Company (☎ 251-6593) has a station at 263 Chienkuo-2 Rd, which is near Kaohsiung train station.

Train All the major west coast trains pass through Kaohsiung. There is also a train service to Taitung on the east coast.

Boat There are daily ferries to the Penghu Islands (see the Islands of the Taiwan Straits chapter). There are passenger ferries to Okinawa in Japan twice a month, and a ferry to Macau once or twice a week (see the Getting There & Away chapter).

Getting Around

To/From the Airport Kaohsiung's Hsiaokang international airport *(xiǎogǎng jīchǎng)* is south of the city. There is an airport bus running between the train station and the airport every 10 minutes from 6.30 am until 11 pm, which costs NT$12. There is no number on the bus, but it's marked in Chinese 'airport' (see the Language chapter).

The airport taxis add NT$50 to the metered fare. You can save this by walking outside the airport and hailing a passing taxi.

Bus City buses cost NT$10 per ride for dilapidated buses, or NT$12 for the new air-con models. You might find it useful to

buy a 10-ride bus ticket from the roadside vendors near the major bus stops.

Car Cars can most easily be rented at the airport, either inside or opposite the domestic terminal. Companies operating here include Central Auto Service (☎ 802-0800), Yongfu (☎ 801-9995/083-9641), Universal International (☎ 806-6618), Royal (☎ 806-6566) and Chuan Chia Fu (☎ 806-5013). In the city you can try China Rent-A-Car (☎ 331-1131) at 224 Chungshan-2 Rd.

LIUKUEI

(liùguī) 六龜

Liukuei, or Six Turtles, is a lovely spot northeast of Kaohsiung. The town occupies a valley, walled in by high mountains, with a whitewater river rushing by. The scenery is even better than in Santimen. Camping, hiking and rafting along the Laonung River are popular activities.

Getting There & Away

The direct bus service from Kaohsiung is not very frequent; alternatively, you can take a bus to Pingtung and then another to Liukuei. The trip is better by car or motorcycle as there are scenic spots to stop at by the river.

Just beyond Liukuei, the road continues north until it meets up with the South Cross-Island Highway at Chiahsien. This makes a

Kaohsiung Train Travel Times & Fares

Destination	Class	Travel Time (hours)	
Tainan	Ziqiang	0.30	NT$107
	Juguang	0.35	NT$83
	Fuxing	0.45	NT$69
	Putong	1.05	NT$50
Chiayi	Ziqiang	1.10	NT$248
	Juguang	1.30	NT$191
	Fuxing	1.40	NT$160
	Putong	2.15	NT$116
Changhua	Ziqiang	2.00	NT$432
	Juguang	2.40	NT$333
	Fuxing	2.50	NT$278
	Putong	2.55	NT$202
Taichung	Ziqiang	2.13	NT$470
	Juguang	2.50	NT$363
	Fuxing	3.00	NT$303
	Putong	3.15	NT$220
Miaoli	Ziqiang	3.00	NT$600
	Juguang	4.00	NT$462
	Fuxing	4.10	NT$386
	Putong	5.00	NT$280
Hsinchu	Ziqiang	3.25	NT$677
	Juguang	4.30	NT$522
	Fuxing	4.42	NT$436
	Putong	6.04	NT$316
Taoyuan	Ziqiang	4.00	NT$788
	Juguang	5.10	NT$608
	Fuxing	5.29	NT$507
	Putong	7.07	NT$368
Taipei	Ziqiang	4.30	NT$854
	Juguang	5.40	NT$658
	Fuxing	6.00	NT$549
	Putong	7.52	NT$399
Pingtung	Ziqiang	0.25	NT$48
	Juguang	0.26	NT$37
	Fuxing	0.33	NT$31
Taitung	Ziqiang	2.30	NT$364

spectacular hike (see the South Cross-Island Highway in the Tainan County section).

MAOLIN
(mào lín) 茂林

Maolin is a gem – babbling brooks, mountains, hiking trails – only a one hour drive from Kaohsiung. Tacky commercial development is (so far) absent. The road from Maolin into the mountains is about 25km long and is gradually being extended in the interests of opening new tourist sites. There are many side routes along the way that end

at scenic spots. The views are outstanding, and there are many places to stop and walk to the river. On the opposite side of the suspension bridges, you will find waterfalls.

About 15km from the entrance gate at Maolin is Tona *(duō nà)*. It's a small aboriginal village where the main industry is stone craft. Everywhere, flat and smooth stone slabs of all sizes stand against walls. Tables, chair seats and small decorative pieces are available for sale. Some of the houses are built from these stones. Simple food is available in Tona and there is one shoddy hotel. About 5km past Tona is Tona Hot Springs *(duō nà wēnquán)*, which is one of the few natural, outdoor hot springs in Taiwan that has escaped commercial development.

This place can get busy on the weekends as tour buses arrive, though it's hard to imagine how they manoeuvre the twisting, narrow mountain road. On weekdays, you'll have the place to yourself. There is a NT$60 admission charge for the area. You will need a class B mountain permit – NT$10 at the admission gate. To avoid hassle, bring a passport, driver's licence or some other form of identification. There are a few makeshift hotels, but most overnight visitors camp.

Getting There & Away
Without a tour bus or your own vehicle, transport is a bit of a problem. During the day, there are buses to Maolin about once every hour or two from either Pingtung or Kaohsiung. There are no buses to Tona.

This is one place where having your own vehicle is practically mandatory. A motorcycle is better than a car because the road is narrow, mountainous and winding. It is possible to do it on a 10 speed bicycle, but you'll need to be in good condition to tackle the hills (my condition proved to be not quite good enough). If you decide to ride, you can send the bike to Pingtung by train to save yourself the long ride through Kaohsiung's horrendous traffic.

PAOLIEN TAN MONASTERY
(bǎolián dān sì) 寶蓮禪寺

This magnificent monastery is just 2km

SOUTH-WEST TAIWAN

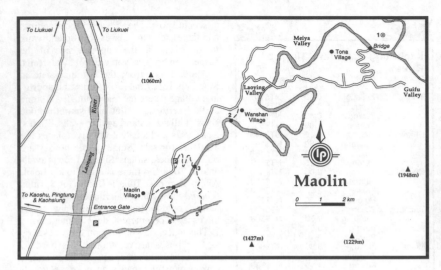

south of Maolin along the road to Santimen. It's one of Taiwan's newest temple complexes, and construction was still continuing during my last visit. There are a large number of nuns in residence. You'll need your own transport or else you will have to walk or hitch to get here.

Tainan County 台南縣

TAINAN
(táinán) 台南

Tainan is a stronghold of traditional Taiwanese culture – not surprising as this was Taiwan's provincial capital from 1663 to 1885. Today, it's the fourth largest city in Taiwan – the population is over 700,000 in the city proper, and doubles when you include suburbia. Tainan simply means 'south Taiwan'.

Tainan has a long and colourful history. The Dutch invaded Taiwan in 1624 and set up their capital and military headquarters in Tainan. In 1661, 37 years later, the Dutch were successfully expelled by Cheng Chengkung (zhèng chénggōng), known in the west

MAOLIN 茂林

1 Tona Hot Springs
   多納溫泉
2 Wanshan Fishing Bridge
   萬山吊橋
3 Maolin Valley Fishing Bridge
   茂林谷吊橋
4 Qingren Valley Bridge
   情人谷吊橋
5 Maolin Valley Waterfall
   茂林谷瀑布
6 Qingren Valley Waterfall
   情人谷瀑布

as Koxinga (guóxìngyé). Koxinga was a Ming dynasty loyalist, forced to flee to Taiwan from the mainland with 35,000 troops to escape the victorious Qing dynasty (Manchu) armies. Koxinga died in 1662 at the age of 38, only one year after ousting the Dutch. His supporters managed to maintain a Ming dynasty stronghold in Taiwan until 1683, when the island was finally captured by the Manchus.

Tainan has over 200 temples in Tainan, though many are increasingly difficult to find because they're tucked away in narrow side-alleys and hidden by the new buildings sprouting up all over the city. While some are small neighbourhood temples, others are huge, including one in the suburb of Luerhmen which is claimed to be the largest temple in East Asia. If you simply stroll around Tainan you may never see the best temples, as only a few are on the main boulevards.

Being a traditional city, there are frequent Buddhist parades and special ceremonies. At certain times in the lunar calendar, everyone worships and the air is thick with smoke from the burning of 'ghost money' and incense. Tables are set out on the street, well endowed with scrumptious food meant as offerings to the gods.

Ironically, Tainan also has the largest Christian population in Taiwan – it's claimed that Christians make up as much as 10% of the city's population.

Temples and monuments are the main attractions in this historical city. With a little effort you can see most of the really interesting ones in a day, but you need to start early. Most are within walking distance of each other, but several will require a bus or taxi trip.

Information
Tourist Office The Tainan Travel Information Service Centre (☎ 226-5681) is on the 10th floor, 243 Minchuan-1 Rd, Section 1.

Travel Agencies An agency dealing in discount domestic air tickets is Chienyuan Travel (☎ 235-7858; *qiānyuán lǚyóu*), room 2, 8th floor, 358 Tungmen Rd, Section 1 (near the intersection with Changjung Rd). Another option is Tienshun Travel (☎ 288-0857; *tiānshùn lǚxíngshè*), which has its office next to the big car park in the airport.

Emergency There is a branch of the Foreign Affairs Police (☎ 222-9704) in Tainan.

Cultural Centre Tainan Cultural Centre (☎ 269-2864; *táinán wénhuà zhōngxīn*), 375 Chunghua Rd, Section 1, is similar to the cultural centres in Taipei, Taichung and Kaohsiung. Art exhibitions and live performances of opera and classical music are held there. If you'd like to find out the current schedule of events, drop by the centre or call – however, it's unlikely that the person answering the phone will speak English.

Confucius Temple
(kǒngzǐ miào) 孔子廟
Built in 1665 by General Chen Yunghua, a Ming dynasty supporter, this is the oldest Confucian temple in Taiwan. The temple is at 2 Nanmen Rd, near the main police station. On 28 September – the birthday of Confucius – a colourful ceremony is held at dawn. You may be able to get a ticket from your hotel or a tour agency.

Directly across the street from the Confucius Temple's main entrance is a small stone archway, which forms the entrance of a busy alley. No one is certain when the archway was built, but historians estimate it was constructed in 1683 when the Confucius Temple was repaired. There are four stone archways remaining in Tainan and this is the oldest.

Kuankung Temple
(wǔ miào) 武廟
This temple on Mintsu Rd, directly opposite the Chihkan Tower, is dedicated to Kuankung *(guāngōng)*, the god of war. It looks unimpressive from Mintsu Rd, where you'll get a first glimpse of the back entrance to the temple. Walk down the narrow alley next to the temple and you'll soon find the front entrance.

Matsu Temple
(māzǔ miào) 媽祖廟
As you face the Kuankung Temple, you will see an alley on your left. Walk down this alley a short distance and you'll come to the Matsu Temple. By contrast to the Kuankung Temple, which has a very simple, conservative look, the Matsu Temple is incredibly colourful. Go around the back and have a look at the temple artwork, all of which is original. You are welcome to take photos.

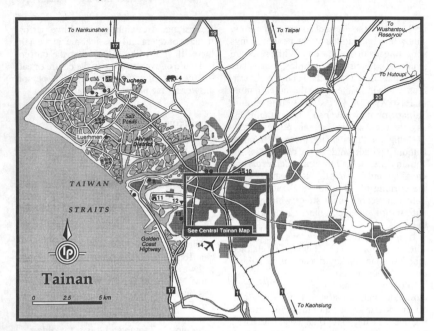

TAINAN 台南市

1 Shengmu Temple
   聖母廟
2 Koxinga Landing Memorial
   鄭成功登陸
   鹿耳門紀念碑
3 Woozland
   悟智樂園
4 Great Taiwan Magic Zoo
   大台灣奇獸樂園

5 Matsu Temple
   天后宮
6 Szutsao Temple
   四草大眾廟
7 Chiumaoyuan Amusement
   Park
   秋茂園
8 Anping Fort
   安平古堡
9 Hsiaopei Rd Night Market;
   Tuntex Department Store
   小北路夜市、東帝士

10 Kaiyuan Temple
    開元寺
11 Eternal Castle
    億載金城
12 Jiankang Snack City
    (Night Market)
    健康點心城
13 Anping Industrial Area
    安平工業區
14 Tainan Airport
    台南機場

Tien Tan Temple
(tiān tán) 天壇

This temple is more commonly known by its
local name, *tiān gōng*. It is one of the most
interesting places to visit in Tainan, and
although it is not very large, it is an extremely
active Taoist temple – reminiscent of the
Lungshan Temple in Taipei.

This temple is often packed to capacity

with worshippers, but it is best to visit on the
first and 16th days of the lunar month if you
really want to see activity. Offerings of food
are made to the ghosts, and incense and
'ghost money' are burnt. Occasionally,
someone in a trance will be possessed by a
ghost. If you visit at the wrong time, it may
be very quiet. Try to avoid dinner time, when
everyone goes home unless, of course, you

just want to photograph temple artefacts without being bothered by the crowd.

The temple is hidden away in an obscure alley just off Chungyi Rd (*zhōngyì lù*), near the intersection with Minchuan Rd.

East Mountain Temple
(*dōng yuè diàn*) 東嶽殿
This small Taoist temple is one of the liveliest, at least if you hit it at the right time. Many of the worshippers come here to communicate with dead relatives or to drive evil ghosts out of their homes.

At times, I've seen old women in the temple, with their eyes closed, pounding their fists on the table, talking rapidly, surrounded by a crowd with tape recorders trying to record their words. These women are mediums who communicate with spirits. Exorcism ceremonies also take place here occasionally. The first and 16th days of the lunar month are the busiest times.

The temple has a number of interesting artefacts. The large statues staring down at you are those of General Hsieh and General Fan. General Hsieh is the short, fat one and General Fan is tall and thin. General Fan is often depicted with his tongue hanging out because he committed suicide by hanging himself.

The story goes that General Fan and General Hsieh made an appointment to meet under a bridge by a river. General Hsieh arrived first and was drowned in a flash flood. General Fan arrived later and was so grieved to find his friend dead that he hanged himself. For this reason their statues are placed in many temples as a symbol of sincere loyalty.

The East Mountain Temple is at 110 Minchuan Rd, Section 1.

Chenghuang Temple
(*chénghuáng miào*) 城隍廟
Although the Chenghuang Temple is related to the East Mountain Temple, it is not nearly so morbid or active – it is more like other Taoist temples in Tainan. Chenghuang is the name of a god worshipped by the Hakka people, who make up 5% of Taiwan's population, and needless to say, many Hakka

people come here. The temple is at 133 Chingnien Rd.

Mito Temple
(*mítuó sì*) 彌陀寺
Constructed in 1718, this colourful temple has recently been restored. It's on Tungmen Rd just east of the train line.

On the 2nd floor of the Mito Temple is one of the best statues of Kuanyin – the Goddess of Mercy who has a thousand arms. This stature shows that the goddess is almighty. There are eyes on her hands to demonstrate that she sees all, and there are several smaller heads attached to the top of her head to symbolise her wisdom.

Fahua Temple
(*fǎhuá sì*) 法華寺
A short walk from the Koxinga Museum and Shrine, is another temple on Fahua St, which is in an obscure narrow street connecting Kaishan and Chienkang Rds. The Fahua Temple is over 300 years old and well preserved. The temple grounds are peaceful and contain many banyan trees. There are some interesting murals on the walls that are well worth photographing.

Chuhsi Temple
(*zhúxī sì*) 竹溪寺
The Chuhsi Temple is one of the largest and most beautiful temples in the city. It's in a huge park complex called the Tainan Athletic Park (*tǐyù chǎng*), just one block south of Chienkang Rd. It's a good area to go jogging, play tennis or participate in other outdoor sports, and the area is busy on weekends and holidays. However, the temple itself is rarely crowded in spite of its impressive size and beauty.

Five Concubines Temple
(*wǔfēi miào*) 五妃廟
The Five Concubines Temple is more like an altar than a temple. It's very small and is dedicated to the five concubines of Ning Ching, who was a relative of the last Ming emperor. It is said that when Ning Ching died, his five concubines committed suicide.

SOUTH-WEST TAIWAN

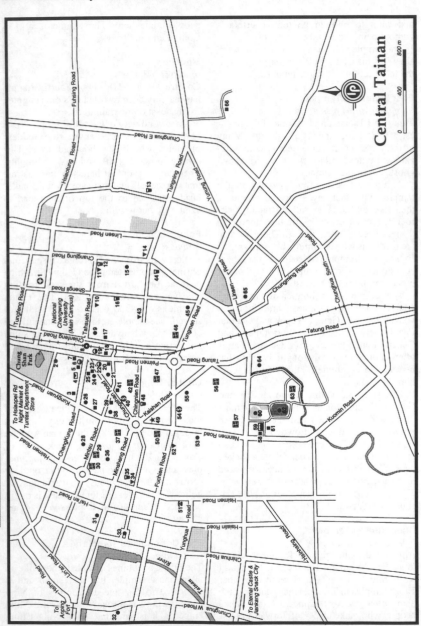

Central Tainan

SOUTH-WEST TAIWAN

CENTRAL TAINAN
台南市中心

PLACES TO STAY

3 Redhill Hotel; Napoleon
 Pub
 赤崁大飯店、
 拿破崙酒吧
5 China Ambassador
 Building
 中華國賓大樓
7 Yilou Hotel
 一樂大飯店
17 Ailisi Hotel
 愛麗思賓館
18 Chengguang Hotel
 成光別館
20 Guang Haw Hotel
 光華大飯店
23 Hann Gong Hotel
 漢宮大飯店
25 Hotel Tainan
 台南大飯店
27 Akira Top Hotel
 立人大飯店
39 Yuchilin Hotel
 玉麒麟大飯店
41 Asia Hotel
 東亞樓大飯店
58 Labourers' Recreation
 Centre
 勞工休假中心
61 Senior Citizens'
 Recreation Centre
 松柏育樂中心
66 Tainan Student Hostel
 台南學苑

PLACES TO EAT

10 21st Century
 Restaurant
 二十一世紀餐廳
11 McDonald's; 89
 麥當勞、
 八九美食漢堡店
14 Pizza Hut
 必勝客
34 Doutor Coffee Shop
 羅多倫咖啡、
 中正路311號
43 Cheese Pie Restaurant
 奇士派餐廳
52 Dragon Arch Restaurant
 龍門餐廳

OTHER

1 Chengkung University
 Hospital
 成大醫院
2 Army Surplus Stores
 軍人剩餘物
 資供應商店
4 GPO
 郵政總局
6 Local Bus Station
 市內公車站
8 Tainan Train Station
 台南火車站
9 Far Eastern Department
 Store (New Branch)
 遠東百貨
 (後火車站)
12 Our Nest Pub
 我們的窩
13 Cheers Pub
 怡東路24號
15 Mountain & Wilderness
 Service Company
 堅磊企
16 Macanna Beer House
 麥崁納
19 Taiwan Bus Company
 Station
 台汽客運站
21 Mitsukoshi Department
 Store
 新光三越百貨
22 Hsingnan Bus Company
 興南客運站
24 Caves Books
 敦煌書局
26 Shente Hall
 慎德堂
28 Chihkan Tower
 赤崁樓
29 Kuankung Temple
 武廟
30 Matsu Temple
 媽祖廟
31 Jiajia Sauna (Women)
 佳佳三溫暖
32 Indiana Disco
 中華西路二段423號
33 Chinatown
 中國城
35 Pawnshop Jazz Pub
 民生路一段181巷18號
36 Quanmei Theatre
 全美戲院

37 Tien Tan Temple
 大壇
38 Far Eastern Department
 Store (Old Branch)
 遠東百貨
 (民族路)
40 ICBC
 中國國際商業銀行
42 Chenghuang Temple
 城隍廟
44 Macanna Beer House
 麥崁納
45 Great East Gate
 大東門
46 Mito Temple;
 Dirty Roger Pub
 彌陀寺、
 東門路一段141號
47 East Mountain Temple
 東嶽殿
48 Circle Bar
 友愛東街2號
49 Police (Visa Extensions)
 警察局外事課
50 Confucius Temple
 孔子廟
51 Telephone Company
 電信局
53 Great South Gate
 大南門
54 Bank of Taiwan
 台灣銀行
55 Koxinga Shrine
 延平郡王祠
56 Fahua Temple
 法華寺
57 Five Concubines
 Temple
 五妃廟
59 Swimming Pool
 游泳池
60 Baseball Stadium
 棒球場
62 City Atheletic
 Stadium
 市立體育場
63 Chuhsi Temple
 竹溪寺
64 Martyrs' Shrine
 忠烈祠
65 Department of Motor
 Vehicles
 監理所

SOUTH-WEST TAIWAN

The temple sits in a small park just north of Chienkang Rd. There is no entrance on Chienkang Rd, so you must walk one block further north to Wufei St and enter the park from the back. It is only worth visiting if you are already at the Chuhsi Temple, which is a five minute walk away.

Kaiyuan Temple
(kāiyuán sì) 開元寺

One of the oldest and biggest temples in Tainan, the Kaiyuan Temple, is a very pleasant classical Buddhist temple with spacious, peaceful grounds, gardens, trees and pagodas. It's only problem is that it is really too far from the city centre to walk to.

To reach the temple take bus No 1, 6 or 17 from the train station. The bus ride takes about 10 minutes and you get off near the intersection of Kaiyuan Rd and Peiyuan St *(běi yuán jiē)*. Kaiyuan Rd is the big, wide, busy road and Peiyuan St is a small side street. Walk down this street for about a minute and you'll see the temple on your left.

Don't confuse the adjacent hospital with the temple itself. The hospital is a beautiful example of traditional architecture and belongs to the temple.

Koxinga's Museum & Shrine
(yánpíng jùnwáng cí) 延平郡王祠

Koxinga is not a god, but a shrine has been built in his honour. He is the national hero who successfully expelled the Dutch from Taiwan. Koxinga and his troops landed in Taiwan in 1661 with the mission of freeing Taiwan from colonial rule and returning it to China. After a six month siege, the Dutch gave up and were allowed to leave Taiwan without any reprisals, thus ending 37 years of occupation of the island.

Adjacent to the Koxinga Shrine is an interesting museum containing a large number of paintings, sculptures, costumes, a model of the Dutch Fort Zeelandia and a traditional Chinese sedan chair. Unfortunately, few of the displays have English explanations.

The museum and shrine compound is open from 9 am to 6 pm. The entrance is on Kaishan Rd – you can either walk from the Confucius Temple or take bus No 17.

Great South Gate
(dà nánmén) 大南門

Tainan used to be a walled city. The walls were built in 1723 in response to an anti-Manchu rebellion. At one time there were eight gates leading into the city, but only three remain. Of the three gates the largest, and best preserved, is the Great South Gate.

The gate is in a small park, half a block south of Fuchien Rd and the Confucius Temple. When you leave the Confucius Temple, turn right and walk south along Nanmen Rd. Pass Fuchien Rd and you'll soon come to a little alley on the right side of the street. A white sign clearly says 'Ta Nan Men' and points into the alley. The fortress-like gate is so large you can't miss it. You're allowed to climb up into the gate and walk around on the top.

The other two gates in Tainan are the Great East Gate on Tungmen Rd and the Little West Gate, which is now relocated on the campus of National Chengkung University, east of Chengkung Lake.

Chihkan Tower
(chìkǎn lóu) 赤崁樓

The Dutch built two forts in Tainan before Koxinga evicted them. One is the Chihkan Tower, also known as Fort Providentia, built in 1653. Very little remains of the original Chihkan Tower, as it was levelled by an earthquake in 1862, rebuilt in 1875, and is currently being restored.

It is at 212 Mintsu Rd, a short walk down the street from the Far Eastern Department Store, and there is a small museum inside the tower. The other fort is Fort Anping, also known by its Dutch name of Fort Zeelandia. Admission is NT$10, or free if you can prove that you are a resident of Tainan.

Anping Fort
(ānpíng gǔbǎo) 安平古堡

This is a place for history enthusiasts. The Anping Fort is also known by its Dutch name, Fort Zeelandia.

The Dutch built the fort in 1653 on what was then the coastline of Taiwan. Since then the coastline has extended several kilometres westward due to siltation, and as a result, the fort no longer commands a sea view. This is one of two forts built in Tainan by the Dutch. The other is Fort Providentia (also called Chihkan Tower, and referred to earlier in this section), which is in the heart of Tainan.

Visiting Anping Fort would be more worthwhile if it was the original building, but unfortunately this was levelled in the 1800s by a powerful typhoon. What you see today is a reconstructed fort and observation tower built in the 1970s.

Bus No 33 goes to the fort. Admission is NT$20, or free if you can prove residency in Tainan city.

Eternal Castle
(yìzǎi jīn chéng) 億載金城

The romantically named Eternal Castle was at one time a small fortress with a moat. It was built by French engineers in 1875. Today, one of the original gates remains in a 2.5 acre park. Like the Anping Fort, it's mostly of interest to history enthusiasts rather than sightseers.

From Anping Fort, it's a very short taxi ride due south. You could also walk, though you might get lost. Its address is 16 Nanwen Rd, Anping District, and bus Nos 15 and 33 go there.

Chungshan Park
(zhōngshān gōngyuán) 中山公園

After many years of enduring bulldozers, jackhammers and concrete, the park's much anticipated renovation has been completed. It's not huge as parks go, but it has a lake, pavilions, peacocks, gardens and statues. It is a relaxing spot to sit and eat a picnic lunch.

Luerhmen
(lùěrmén) 鹿耳門

Luerhmen (literally, Deer's Ear Gate), is the name of the site along the river where Koxinga landed in Taiwan on 29 April 1661. The site of the landing is actually marked, near the village of Tucheng, by the Koxinga Landing Memorial *(zhèng chènggōng dēnglù lùěrmèn niànbē)*. However, the main attraction is not the historical site, but the huge temple that has been built nearby.

Actually, there are three temples and they're only a couple of kilometres from each other. There is an interesting story which accompanies the construction of these three temples. Over the years the local people have been involved in heavy rivalry and three distinct groups have formed. They are in competition with each other as to who will build the largest temple in Taiwan. Thus the temples have never really been finished, as they are in a state of constant expansion.

The only limiting factor is money, and therefore the temples have ongoing campaigns to raise the funds for continuing construction. Should you want to support this cause, you can donate money and have your name engraved on a marble slab, column or any other temple artefact of your choice – all of the artwork in the temple is engraved, in Chinese characters, with the names of supporters.

At the forefront of the building competition is the **Shengmu Temple** *(shèngmǔ miào)*. It's adjacent to the community of Tucheng *(tǔchéng)*. The runner-up is the **Matsu Temple** *(tiānhòu gōng)*, though it looks like it has got a long way to go before it'll be No 1. Third in line, but coming up fast, is the **Szutsao Temple** *(sìcǎo dàzhòng miào)*, which has a classical Taoist appearance – take notice of the roof ornaments.

If at all possible, try to visit Luerhmen on the 15th night of the first moon – the Lantern Festival. There are brilliant displays of fireworks, but wear protective clothing (most people wear motorcycle helmets and face shields).

Right near the Shengmu Temple and the village of Tucheng is **Woozland** (☎ 257-3811; *wùzhì lèyuàn*), a park known for its amusing waterslides. It is also where one of Taiwan's well known TV shows is filmed. It's popular during the summer, and is a madhouse on weekends – the best time to visit is during the week. If you're visiting the temple anyway and the weather is hot, the waterslides are a great way to cool off. There are other entertainment machines on offer, including rides and a hologram funhouse. The tickets for all exhibits and rides cost NT$50 each, and you can buy a ticket exclusively for the waterslides. Don't forget to bring a swimsuit and towel.

Not too far away is the **Great Taiwan Magic Zoo** (dà táiwān qíshòu lèyuán). It's built on the site of the former 'Fancyland' (an amusement park) and so has a number of children's rides. This place is more geared towards children than Woozland is.

Although technically within the city limits of Tainan, Luerhmen is a long way from the city centre. It's in the Annan district, and more than 10km from the Tainan train station. Besides driving, the easiest way to get to Luerhmen is to take bus No 29 from central Tainan. Alternatively, you could take bus No 34 to the Hsimen Rd station (xīmén lù zhàn) and then change to bus No 27, 28 or 29. Tainan city bus No 27 goes to the Matsu and Szutsao temples.

Golden Coast Highway
(bīnhǎi gōnglù) 濱海公路
This is nothing more than an ocean wall crowded with lovers, food stalls and fireworks (minor) seven nights a week. It's the place to be for the Mid-Autumn Festival and, to a lesser extent, the Lovers' Festival.

The sea wall is in the south-west corner of Tainan, right on the beach. You'd have a hard time getting there by public transport at night, which is the best time to go.

Activities
Mountain clubs launch regular weekend **hiking expeditions** into the countryside surrounding Tainan. A good place to enquire about these activities is at a shop selling backpacking gear. One such place is the Mountain & Wilderness Service Company (☎ 237-3928; jiān lěi qì), at 196 Tung'an Rd, and the owner, Mr Wu Weichien, speaks English.

Despite the name, the Yukoteng Race Course (☎ 228-0325; yù oū dēng xún mǎ yuán) is not for racing – it's a riding stable

where you can hire **horses** to ride on the beach. Riding lessons are also available. The stables are in the far west of Tainan – continue past Anping Fort and you'll find it near a tacky little beachside resort area called Chiumaoyuan Amusement Park (qiūmào yuán). You can get there from the train station on bus No 15.

There are at least two places to play **golf**. In Tainan county, near the south side of Wushantou Reservoir, is the Nanpao Golf Club (nánbǎo gāo'ěrfū qiú chǎng), but closer to town near the suburb of Hsinhua is the Tainan Golf Club (táinán gāo'ěrfū qiú chǎng).

For general **health and fitness** the Arts Health Club (☎ 288-3338; yàlìshāndà jiànkāng xiūxián jùlèbù) in the basement, 117 Chungming Rd, is a deluxe establishment. There are swimming pools, saunas, a restaurant and just about everything else. It's not budget – membership costs NT$5000 per month or NT$32,000 per year. The Red Brick Sauna (☎ 220-1391/228-8569; hóngzhuān sānwēnnuǎn), 5th floor, 166 Minsheng Rd, Section 2, is for women only and is open 24 hours.

For a total of NT$800, a militantly brutal Taiwanese deep tissue massage is included, courtesy of one of the brusque, determined and efficient masseuses. It was heavenly.

Ellen Bloom

The Jiajia Sauna (☎ 220-8846; jiājiā sānwēnnuǎn), 36 Minsheng Rd, Section 2, is also for women only. It's open Monday to Saturday from 8 am to 10 pm, and Sunday from 10 am to 7 pm. The basic price without extra services (like facials, massages, pedicures and manicures) is NT$350.

All the other saunas in Tainan are for men. Probably the best is the Royal Sauna (☎ 297-5452; huángjiā sānwēnnuǎn), 133 Yunghua Rd, Section 2 (near city hall). It is open 24 hours, the basic charge is NT$400, but this increases to NT$600 if you stay past 1 am.

The Tuntex Department Store (dōngdìshì bǎihuò) has a **skating rink** and pool on the 5th floor.

Chinese **language courses** for non-native speakers are available through the Foreign Language Department at the National Chengkung University.

Places to Stay – budget
There are three hostels in Tainan offering budget accommodation. One good choice is the *Labourers' Recreation Centre* (☎ 263-0174; *láogōng xiūjià zhōngxīn*). The address is 261 Nanmen Rd, but the entrance is actually set back from Nanmen Rd on a long driveway. Immediately opposite is the *Senior Citizens' Recreation Centre* (☎ 264-6974; *sōngbó yùlè zhōngxīn*). This place is spotlessly clean. Both hostels charge the same rates – dormitories with four beds are NT$350 per bed and double rooms are NT$500. The demand for rooms is heavy so call first. From the train station, you can reach these hostels on bus No 25.

The *Tainan Student Hostel* (☎ 267-0526/268-9018; *táinán xuéyuàn*), at 1 Lane 300, Funung St, Section 1, charges NT$300 for dorm accommodation. This hostel is very clean and usually has empty beds. For a while the hostel was not accepting foreigners due to trouble with westerners using drugs. The latest word is that it is accepting foreigners again. The hostel is a fine place to stay, but there is a 10 pm curfew. To get there from the city centre take bus No 7 or 19.

Places to Stay – middle
The *Ailisi Hotel* (☎ 235-0807; *ailìsī bīnguǎn*), 200 Chienfeng Rd, is the only hotel behind the train station. This place is small and charges from NT$550 to NT$800.

The *Guang Haw Hotel* (☎ 226-3171; *guānghuá dà fàndiàn*), 155 Peimen Rd, Section 1, is certainly one of the best mid-range places. You can identify the hotel by the coffee shop on the ground floor. Doubles cost NT$760 with a free breakfast.

Just across from the train station is the *Hann Gong Hotel* (☎ 226-9115; *hàngōng dà fàndiàn*), 199 Chungshan Rd. Rooms cost from NT$680 to NT$920.

The *Chengguang Hotel* (☎ 222-1188; *chéngguāng biéguǎn*) at 294 Peimen Rd,

Section 1, is a small place just south of the train station, with doubles/twin rooms for NT$600/800.

Hotel Yilou (☎ 226-9191; *yīlè dà fàndiàn*) faces the train station. Doubles/twins are NT$780/1300.

The *Asia Hotel* (☎ 222-6171; *dōngyǎ dà fàndiàn*), 100 Chungshan Rd, is at the intersection with Mintsu Rd. Doubles/twins are NT$900/1800.

Directly across the street is the *Yuchilin Hotel* (☎ 222-0185; *yùqílín dà fàndiàn*), 117 Chungshan Rd. Doubles cost from NT$600 to NT$700.

Just opposite the train station, on the big roundabout, is a 14 storey edifice known as the *China Ambassador Building (zhōnghuá guóbīn dàlóu)*. There is no English sign identifying the building, but it's a large, ugly, brown structure that is hard to miss. The ground floor has shops and restaurants, while almost every floor upstairs has a hotel, examples being the *Audi, Golf* and *Galaxy*. It is best to take the lift to the top floor and walk down, making price enquiries. Some of these places specialise in 'short time' (two hour) rentals.

Places to Stay – top end
The *Hotel Tainan* (☎ 228-9101; fax 226-8502; *táinán dà fàndiàn*), 1 Chengkung Rd, has long considered itself to be the leading hotel in town. Doubles go from NT$2200 to NT$3000, and twins cost from NT$2500 to NT$3500.

The *Redhill Hotel* (☎ 225-8121; fax 221-6711; *chìkàn dà fàndiàn*), 46 Chengkung Rd, is where most of the expat engineers stay when they're in town. Rooms cost from NT$1980 to NT$6600.

The *Akira Top Hotel* (☎ 226-5261; fax 221-0197; *lìrén dà fàndiàn*), 88 Kungyuan Rd, is one of the newer upmarket places. Rooms cost from NT$1300 to NT$2800.

Places to Eat
Cafes & Cheap Eats The area adjacent to the National Chengkung University deserves an extra special mention as so many excellent and cheap eating establishments,

catering to the student population, surround the campus. The line-up of eating establishments begins just opposite the main entrance gate of the university and runs down the length of Tahsueh Rd *(dàxué lù)*. There are even more restaurants lining both sides of Shengli Rd.

One of the best bargains in town can be found right inside the campus of National Chengkung University itself. There are several cafeterias on campus, but you'll have to ask a student where they are since they tend to change location. Try to arrive a little early because it gets crowded and the food disappears quickly. University food isn't necessarily the best, but it's cheap. Meal times are normally from noon to 1 pm, and 5 to 6.30 pm – the greasy breakfasts aren't worth the trouble.

Night Markets Tainan's night markets are lively places, especially on Saturday nights during summer. The two largest markets are *Jiankang Snack City (jiànkāng diǎnxīn chéng)* in the south-west of the city and *Hsiaopei Rd Night Market (xiǎoběi lù yèshì)*. Unfortunately, both are too far from the city centre to walk and you'll probably have to take a taxi if you don't have your own car – both are a 10 minute drive from the city centre.

Food Courts It might seem peculiar in a Chinese town, but there is a Chinatown *(zhōngguó chéng)* in Tainan. Chinatown is contained within two large buildings and is a collection of movie theatres, shops, a skating rink and about a hundred hole-in-the-wall food stalls. It's slow during the daytime but busy at night.

As elsewhere in Taiwan, the food courts in the basements of major department stores offer considerable culinary variety at low prices. The new *Far Eastern Department Store* (behind the train station) is a good venue, as is the *Mitsukoshi Department Store (xīnguāng sānyuè bǎihuò)* at Chungshan and Mintsu Rds.

Restaurants Dim sim is the speciality at the

Diamond Restaurant (☎ 225-3100; *zhuàn shí lóu cāntīng)*. It's on the 5th floor of the old Far Eastern Department Store; take the elevator because the stairs lead to the roof, bypassing the restaurant. The old Far Eastern is on the corner of Mintsu and Kungyuan Rds.

The *21st Century Restaurant (èrshíyī shìjì cāntīng)* is a slick, multi-level chain store in southern Taiwan that specialises in roast chicken. You'll find a branch on Tahsueh Rd just opposite the main entrance to Chengkung University.

The *Cheese Pie Restaurant* (☎ 208-5623; *qǐshì pài cāntīng)*, 24 Tungning Rd, West Section, serves more than just pie. Other fine items on the menu include steak and noodle dishes. Of course, save a little room for the cheesecake – it's excellent.

The *Redhill Hotel* (☎ 225-8121; *chìkǎn dà fàndiàn)*, 46 Chengkung Rd, has several excellent restaurants on the 1st floor and in the basement, and the western buffet (available mornings and evenings) is legendary. The breakfast buffet includes: scrambled eggs, bacon, sausages, Java coffee, French toast, home-fried potatoes, and Corn Flakes with bananas and fresh fruit.

The *Dragon Arch Restaurant* (☎ 224-6332; *lóngmén xī cāntīng)*, 273 Fuchien Rd, Section 1, boasts some of the best western food in town. It's near the intersection of Fuchien and Chungyi Rds.

Fast Food During the daytime, *McDonald's* on Tahsueh Rd is worth visiting if you want to meet Tainan's expat crowd. For mysterious reasons, this place has been designated the official gathering spot for foreign English teachers.

Just next to McDonald's is *89* (☎ 237-8838; *bājiǔ měishí hànbǎo diàn)* at 24 Tahsueh Rd. The hamburgers are nothing to write home about, but the fried chicken is prime food. This seems to be the official meeting spot of trendy young locals.

Probably the thickest concentration of fast food places is around the Tuntex Department Store, where you'll find *Wendy's*, *KFC* and another *McDonald's*.

For home deliveries, there's always *Domino's Pizza* (☎ 208-7000/223-5252; *dáměilè bǐsà diàn*), with two stores in town.

Coffee Shop A good choice for breakfast or snacks is *Doutor's Coffee Shop* (☎ 229-3112; *luóduōlún kāfēi*) at 309 Chungcheng Rd.

Ice Cream Inside the 14 storey China Ambassador Building (*zhōnghuá guóbīn dàlóu*) fronting the train station is a very good ice cream shop, *Gelato Italiano* (almost beside the GPO). Lots of people swear by the papaya milkshakes (*mùguā niúnǎi*).

Entertainment

Cinemas There are numerous cinemas around town, as follows:

Chinatown
(☎ 221-5110; *zhōngguó chéng dà xìyuàn*) 72 Huanho Rd
Chuanmei
(☎ 222-4726; *quánměi xìyuàn*) 187 Yungfu Rd, Section 2
Kuohua
(☎ 226-1213; *guóhuá xìyuàn*) 3rd floor, 118 Minchuan Rd, Section 2
Mintsu
(☎ 229-3528; *mínzú xìyuàn*) 249 Mintsu Rd, Section 2
Nantai
(☎ 223-2426; *nántái dà xìyuàn*) 317 Youai St
Nantu
(☎ 222-2383; *nándū dà xìyuàn*) 138 Youai St
Prince
(☎ 228-7416; *wángzi dà xìyuàn*) basement, 323 Chungcheng Rd
Queen
(☎ 222-7761/225-4662/227-9331; *wánghòu xìyuàn*) 1st, 4th and 10th floors, 323 Chungcheng Rd
Today
(☎ 220-5151; *jīnrì dà xìyuàn*) 249 Chungcheng Rd
Tung An
(☎ 237-5650; *dōng'ān dà xìyuàn*) 18 Changjung Rd, Section 2
Tuntex
(*dōngdìshì xìyuàn*) Hsimen Rd, Section 3
Yenping
(☎ 226-1971; *yánpíng xìyuàn*) 5th floor, 120 Hsimen Rd, Section 2

Discos *Indiana Disco*, 423 Chunghua W Rd, Section 2, wins the contest for the most beloved disco in Tainan. It's near the City Hall on the west side of town.

MTV *Kiss* (☎ 241-2340) on the 9th floor at 118 Minchuan Rd, Section 2 (above Kuohua movie theatre) is a cut above any other MTV venue in Tainan. A large screen and romantic *tatami* cubicles are only half the attraction – there's also a decent bar and restaurant. All films are on laser disk.

Pubs For many years, Tainan's No 1 hot spot for foreigners has been *Dirty Roger Pub* (☎ 274-7003) at 141 Tungmen Rd, Section 1, which is very close to the Mito Temple. Operating hours are from 1 pm to 4 am, but it often stays open until sunrise on holidays and weekends.

The *Circle Bar* at 2 Youai E St is another place that packs in the expats. Ditto for the *Cosby Pub*, 128-20 Kungyuan Rd, and the *Cheers Pub* at 24 Yitung Rd. A bottle of beer costs around NT$100 in all three places.

Our Nest is in the basement at 28 Tahsueh Rd, right next to McDonald's. Although the music is very loud, students and destitute expats like the cheap beer at NT$60.

The *Macanna Beer House (màikànna)* is geared towards the student crowd at Chengkung University. There are several branches – the oldest and still a favourite is the Shengli branch (☎ 234-5882) at 117 Shengli Rd. The Changjung branch (☎ 234-1411) is at 163 Changjung Rd, Section 2.

Pawnshop Jazz, 18 Alley, 181 Minsheng Rd, is a favourite spot for live music.

Napoleon Pub (☎ 220-6479; *nápòlún jiǔbā*), 38 Chengkung Rd, is just next to the Redhill Hotel. This pub is expensive and mostly attracts foreign engineers and business people who are in town for a short junket and don't know about the cheaper bars. It's open from 8 pm to 4 am.

Things to Buy

Tainan has a collection of army surplus stores on Kungyuan S Rd on the south side of Chungshan Park. All of Taiwan's cities have these stores, but Tainan's are just about the best and are unique, in that they are all clustered together. There are some excellent buys, from backpacks to military boots. The best is at 17-1 Kungyuan S Rd, but also check out its neighbour at No 15.

The best bookshop in town is Caves Books (☎ 229-6347; *dūnhuáng shūjú*), 163 Chungshan Rd.

Getting There & Away

Air There are flights between Tainan and Hualien, Kinmen, Makung and Taipei. The airlines and their representative offices in Tainan are as follows:

China Airlines
    (☎ 235-7861; *zhōnghuá hángkōng*) room A, 6th floor, 358 Tungmen Rd, Section 1
EVA Airways
    (☎ 222-5678; *chángróng hángkōng*) 4th floor, 114 Chienkang Rd, Section 2
Far Eastern Air Transport
    (☎ 225-8111/225-8111; *yuǎndōng hángkōng*) 116 Yungfu Rd, Section 2
Great China Airlines
    (☎ 260-2811; *dàhuá hángkōng*) Tainan airport
TransAsia Airways
    (☎ 080-066880; *fùxīng hángkōng*) 55 Mintsu Rd, Section 2

Bus There is no problem reaching Tainan by public transport from the other major cities in Taiwan. It's useful to know that there are direct buses to Alishan and Kenting, and once a day, buses heading east along the South Cross-Island Highway.

Train Trains that head north to Taipei or south to Kaohsiung leave every 30 to 40 minutes from around 6 am to midnight.

Getting Around

To/From the Airport Tainan's airport can be reached by the rather infrequent bus No 36. Failing that, it's a short taxi ride.

Bus Tainan's bus system is rumoured to exist, but you'll need considerable patience to get around this way.

Car Automobile rentals are available from several agencies, including: China Rent-A-Car (☎ 226-8166), 162 Hsimen Rd, Section

3; International Auto Service (☎ 228-1770); and Chuan Chia Fu Car Rental (☎ 235-1271), 359 Tungfeng Rd.

NANKUNSHEN

(nánkūnshēn dàitiān fǔ) 南鯤身

Along with Peikang, the temple at Nankunshen is considered to be the most active, powerful, colourful and richest temple in Taiwan. The temple was built in 1662 and has been kept in fine condition. Behind the temple is a garden area.

This place is only really interesting on Sunday, especially during busy holiday weekends. At such times, thousands of enthusiastic worshippers descend on the temple and put on a sensational display of parades, fireworks, chanting, feasting and festivities. Bring lots of film and be prepared to move out of the way quickly when the firecrackers start exploding. If you visit on weekdays the place is likely to be deserted.

You may see devout worshippers practising a mild form of self-mutilation – which involves running a mace-like instrument across their back, tearing the skin and causing bleeding. The cuts are not very deep but will usually leave scars. Only men participate in this particular form of worship. Those who do are presumed to be possessed by the gods and therefore immune to pain. The whole purpose of the self-mutilation is to demonstrate the gods' power.

Other worshippers paint their faces and dress up in costumes. They march in a procession, beating gongs and drums, and often carry a Chinese-style sedan chair for a god to ride in. Meanwhile, firecrackers and skyrockets liven up the atmosphere and plenty of ghost money is burnt.

As you approach Nankunshen on the bus, you'll notice that the surrounding countryside resembles pools of mud – these are salt-evaporating ponds. Tainan County is adjacent to the sea and is the sunniest place on the island, so it is naturally Taiwan's major salt producing region.

Getting There & Away

Getting to Nankunshen is easy. From Tainan,

MARTIN MOOS   ROBERT STOREY   MARTIN MOOS

Spectacular mountain scenery (top) can be enjoyed on foot or from a car or bus. The road from Suao to Taitung, via Chingshui Cliff (bottom right) balances above sea and rocks, while the road through Taroko Gorge (bottom left) is widely acknowledged for having the most dramatic vistas. Climb the pagoda at Carp Hill (bottom centre) for more great views.

ROBERT STOREY

CHRIS TAYLOR

ROBERT STOREY

MARTIN MOOS

Top & Bottom Right: Worshippers paint their faces for one of Tainan's many street parades.
Bottom Left: 'The one who sees a thousand miles' presides over the Matsu Temple, Tainan.
Bottom Centre: Calligraphy is regarded as the highest expression of Chinese art and is a
predominant feature of many artworks, including this mural in Tainan's Kaiyuan Temple.

take a bus from the Hsingnan Bus Company station *(xīngnán kèyùn)* and get off at the last stop. There are frequent departures and the ride takes about 75 minutes. The station is about one block from the temple. To find the temple, just ask anybody for the *nánkūnshēn dàitiān fǔ*. There is also a bus from Kaohsiung.

HUTOUPI
(hǔtóubí) 虎頭埤

About 12km east of Tainan is Hutoupi, also called Hutoupei *(hǔtóubēi)*. It's basically a small reservoir, park and picnic area. Swimming in the reservoir is not permitted, but it is possible to hire a rowboat (weekends and holidays only). The area is notable for its well manicured bushes and flowers.

Admission to the area is NT$80. There are actually two entrance gates, so if you walk around the lake you have to go in twice. Save the ticket stub to get back in through the other entrance later on.

The Hsingnan Bus Company goes to Hutoupi from central Tainan. There is a *hostel* on the far side of the lake.

WUSHANTOU RESERVOIR
(wūshāntóu shuǐkù) 烏山頭水庫

Wushantou Reservoir is also known as Coral Lake *(shānhú tán)*. Like Hutoupi, it attracts picnickers, anglers and boaters. Wushantou is much larger, and high-speed motorboats zip around the lake. A bus to Wushantou departs from the Hsingnan Bus Company *(xīngnán kèyùn)* station on Chungshan Rd in Tainan.

It's doubtful you'd want to spend the night, but if you do *Wushantou Guest House* (☎ 698-3121; *wūshāntóu guómín lǚshè*) offers nonbudget accommodation. Doubles/twins are NT$1200/1800, with the most plush rooms rising to NT$3800.

TSENGWEN DAM & RESERVOIR
(zēngwén shuǐkù) 曾文水庫

Tsengwen Dam and Reservoir are in the foothills of the Central Mountains, straddling the border between Tainan and Chiayi counties. The reservoir is now the largest lake in Taiwan and it makes a nice trip if you

have the time. It is also home to a variety of birdlife including the black-faced spoonbill (see 'A Bashful Bird' boxed text on the next page). Swimming is not allowed, but boating is OK. If you want to, you can swim in the river below the dam.

Although the view from the dam is scenic, a more interesting place to visit is Chiayi Farm on the shore of the reservoir *(jiāyì nóngchǎng)*. It isn't so much a farm as a resort with fancy European houses. Entrance to the 'farm' costs NT$100.

The Tsengwen Dam area has a number of hiking trails, but few of them are marked. If you can find a Chinese person to guide you, try to do the Tsengwen Reservoir-Little Switzerland *(xiǎo ruìshì)* hike. It doesn't really look like Switzerland, but it's a good walk nonetheless.

Try not to visit Tsengwen Reservoir during the dry season, when the lake is low and has a 'bathtub ring' around it. The dry season is generally from October to April. When the lake is full it's very attractive and the water pouring from the dam's floodgates is impressive.

Places to Stay
About 2km below the dam is the *Tsengwen Youth Activity Centre* (☎ 575-3431; *zēngwén qīngnián huódòng zhōngxīn*), run by the CYC. There are 12 single rooms available at a reasonable NT$550 each or there are twins for NT$1100. If there are eight people in your group, there are dorm rooms costing NT$2400 (NT$300 per person). There is also a camping area and you can hire tents and quilts. Across the highway is a creek where you can swim.

The *Chiayi Farm Guest House* (☎ 252-1054; *jiāyì nóngchǎng guómín bīnguǎn*) is in Chiayi County. It has imitation European architecture and is a relaxing place to stay. Twins cost as little as NT$800, or you can pay up to NT$5000 for a cabin. There is also a camping ground here.

Getting There & Away
In Tainan, buses depart for Tsengwen Dam from the Hsingnan Bus Company *(xīngnán*

SOUTH-WEST TAIWAN

A Bashful Bird

The Tsengwen Estuary near Tainan is home to several species of bird, including the white stork, the short-eared owl, the Chinese egret and terns. However, one bird in particular has brought international attention to these natural wetlands – the black-faced spoonbill. This bird generally lives in north-east China and Korea, but every winter about two-thirds of the world's known population migrate south to this Taiwanese estuary. The number of spoonbills coming has increased over the years, indicating that their other migratory routes are on the decline; this greatly increases the importance of this particular sanctuary.

Many wildlife conservation groups in Taiwan, including the Wild Bird Society (Taiwan's largest and oldest conservation group), have taken action in recent years to protect the estuary and the birds nesting there. This has not always been an easy task, with many developments, including a high-tech industrial park, a garbage dump and a petrochemical and steel processing plant, proposed for the area. So far the conservationists have managed to block any such developments, often in direct conflict with the local people who would welcome the employment prospects.

The spoonbill is a notoriously bashful bird and is susceptible to even the most minimal disruption to its environment, as conservationists studying another species of spoonbill in Venezuela soon discovered. While adult birds were away from the nest looking for food, conservationists took the opportunity to carry out a census of the nests and eggs. They returned a few days later to discover a horrible smell. The adult birds had sensed the human presence and had rejected every egg and chick, all of which were discovered to be rotting or dead. This shyness has made successful studies of the black-faced spoonbill difficult, especially when trying to predict how they would coexist with the proposed developments in the Tsengwen Estuary.

The black-faced spoonbill is widely acknowledged as an endangered species and the local Tainan council has made great efforts, including the allocation of funds and government personnel, to preserve this nesting area. However, the arguments between the conservationists and developers rage on, although many are confident that the efforts made so far will help preserve this particular spoonbill and its habitat.

Joyce Connolly

kèyùn) station on Chungshan Rd. The trip takes about 1½ hours and the bus gets full on Sundays.

There was a bus service from Chiayi but it has been cancelled.

KUANTZULING

(guānzǐlǐng) 關仔嶺

Kuantzuling is an old hot springs resort which was popular during the Japanese occupation. The Japanese built charming wooden inns with tatami mats, but most of these have disappeared and given way to modern Chinese architecture. There are hot springs here, but they are rather unattractive as the water contains clay and is the colour of milk. However, it's claimed the mineral content is good for you, and so plenty of hot-springs enthusiasts still flock here.

Whether or not you care to soak in the mucky hot springs, this area in the foothills of Taiwan's mountains is pretty. The main attraction is not the hot springs but rather the temples, which are scattered throughout the area. Having a car is an advantage, but you can walk between them.

SOUTH-WEST TAIWAN

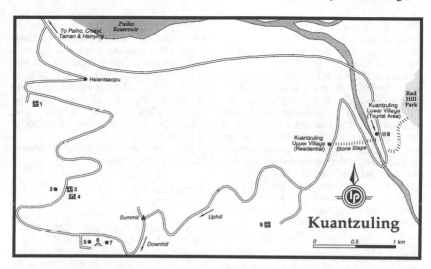

Kuantzuling

KUANTZULING 關仔嶺

1 Big Fairy Temple
   大仙寺
2 Shops
   商店區
3 Blue Cloud Temple
   碧雲寺
4 Three Treasure Palace
   三寶殿
5 Shops
   商店區
6 Water Fire Cave
   水火洞
7 Shops
   商店區
8 Hsienkung Temple
   仙公廟
9 Hot Springs
   溫泉區

The country roads around Kuantzuling are excellent for hiking, except on Sundays or holidays when tourists, in their cars, flood the area. When you arrive in town you will no doubt be greeted by a mass of taxi drivers claiming it is too far and too dangerous (with abundant snakes and tigers) for you to walk

anywhere – then offering to drive you for NT$800 or so. Hiking will take the whole day, whereas a taxi tour of the area might last for 30 minutes. You might want to take a taxi to the Water Fire Cave and then walk from there. You can also reach the Water Fire Cave by bus from Paiho (báihé).

Red Hill Park
(hóngshān gōngyuán) 紅山公園
Assuming you arrive by bus, have a look at Red Hill Park – it's up the stairs to your immediate left on the road out of town. It's a 10 minute climb to the park, which is not spectacular but is worth seeing nontheless.

Hsienkung Temple
(xiāngōng miào) 仙公廟
From Red Hill Park, go back down to the road. Either follow the road uphill or you can save some time by taking the stone steps (see the Kuantzuling map). Both will bring you to upper Kuantzuling village. Continue along the road out of the village and into the countryside for several kilometres. You'll eventually find a signposted turn-off on your left. This goes to the Hsienkung Temple, a pretty and peaceful temple sat in the forest.

Water Fire Cave
(shuǐhuǒ dòng) 水火洞

Back on the main road, continue uphill. It gets a bit steep but you'll soon reach the summit of the highway. It drops down and about 100m away you'll find a group of tourist shops. This is a good place to have lunch. Just after the first tourist shops, you can walk down to your left and you'll find the Water Fire Cave. The hot springs contain so much gas that it bubbles to the surface and ignites, giving the impression of burning water. A picture taken in 1964 shows the flame to be over 3m high; today it is much smaller, as the pressure of the gas is dropping. There is a bus from the Water Fire Cave to the town of Paiho *(báihé)*.

Blue Cloud Temple
(bìyún sì) 碧雲寺

A 15 minute walk downhill from the Water Fire Cave will take you to the attractive Blue Cloud Temple, next to the newer **Three Treasure Palace** *(sānbǎo diàn)*. From there, you again have the option of taking the bus, but if you walk downhill further you'll eventually come to the **Big Fairy Temple** *(dàxiān sì)*, which is an interesting place.

Getting There & Away

You can approach Kuantzuling from either Hsinying or Chiayi. If you are coming from the south, take a train to Hsinying *(xīnyíng)*, then take a bus from the terminal directly across the street from the train station. The buses go direct to Kuantzuling.

If you're coming from the north, first go to Chiayi and then take a direct bus from the Chiayi Bus Company *(jiāyì kèyùn)* terminal at 501 Chungshan Rd, Chiayi. If you don't get a bus to Kuantzuling right away, take one to Paiho and then another to Kuantzuling.

It's also possible to catch the bus back to Hsinying or Chiayi from Hsientsaopu *(xiāncǎopǔ)*; the bus stop is near the Big Fairy Temple.

MATOU TEMPLE
(mádòu dàitiān fǔ) 麻豆代天府

North of Tainan is Matou, a small and mostly uninteresting place except for its temple. Also known as the Five King Temple *(wǔwáng miào)*, Matou Temple is a classic Taoist place of worship, complete with firecrackers, gongs and the occasional exorcism. Adding to the festivities are the '18 Levels of Hell' and the 'Four Undersea Kingdoms of the Dragons' – a sort of attached carnival. Visit on the weekends to see the temple at its liveliest.

Buses from Tainan's Hsingnan Bus Company can take you to Matou.

YENSHUI
(yánshuǐ) 鹽水

Yenshui is a fairly ordinary town situated between Tainan and Chiayi. However, during the Lantern Festival, on the 15th day of the first moon, the whole town goes insane. The real action occurs in the square at the intersection of Chungcheng and Sanfu Rds. The activities start at 7 pm and continue past midnight. For further details see the 'A Friendly Riot' boxed text opposite.

SOUTH CROSS-ISLAND HIGHWAY
(nánbù héngguàn gōnglù) 南部橫貫公路

Running between Tainan on the west coast and Taitung on the east coast, the South Cross-Island Highway climbs into the wilderness of Taiwan's mountains. Unlike the heavily used Central Cross-Island Highway, the South Cross-Island Highway has a lot less traffic and is blessed with spectacular scenery. This route is occasionally closed due to landslides, especially during the rainy season from late May to early September, despite this, it is worth making this trip to see rural Taiwan at its best.

Most people do this trip from west to east, which makes sense if you want to hike the middle section (highly recommended) – the west side is a gentle slope and the east side drops down steeply. The hike is popular with students, so there can be large numbers of hiking groups during school holidays.

The trip can be made by car, bus or on foot. It can be done in a day from a bus, but if you want to hike the central section allow two to

A Friendly Riot

The small town of Yenshui is renowned for its celebration of the Lantern Festival, which has the most spectacular display of fireworks. There are similar fireworks displays in Luerhmen and Peikang, but nothing quite matches the grandeur of Yenshui. People from all over Taiwan converge on this town for the festival – the crowd is estimated at several hundred thousand. It can, however, be a dangerous experience.

One after another, people ignite giant cardboard honeycombs stuffed with rockets (each one costing over NT$100,000). It's open warfare – the honeycombs are often aimed right into the crowd. The fireworks will be the least of the hazards you will face. Much more dangerous are the spectators. With thousands of people standing shoulder to shoulder, the wild pushing and shoving becomes deadly. The sedan chairs charging through the crowd cause many injuries. The chance of being trampled should not be taken lightly. If you get to the front, the safest thing to do is actually to run into the firecrackers, not away from them – this way you temporarily leave the crowd behind. There are always a few fistfights, usually resulting from arguments about whose firecracker hit whose girlfriend. Even though motor vehicles are supposedly banned during the festival, there are at least a few drunken fools who enthusiastically drive their motorcycles into the crowd at high speed. The ambulances do good business and so do the pickpockets.

The best place to view the celebrations is on somebody's rooftop or terrace overlooking the square at the intersection of Chungcheng and Sanfu Rds. This is where the TV cameras are set up. To get these choice spots, you either have to know somebody or arrive early and expect to pay for the privilege. There are a few awnings that you might be able to climb onto (at your own risk), but it's not easy. Expect every square centimetre of space to be fully occupied.

A few safety measures to prepare you for the festival are wise. Wear old clothing, as the sparks can burn little holes in cloth. A motorcycle helmet with a faceshield is essential survival gear. An amazing number of people don't wear any protection at all – as any eye surgeon in a local hospital can tell you. It is possible to carry a camera, but a large one dangling from your neck is certain to get broken. A small camera that fits in your pocket would be a lot safer.

Even though it is generally cold at this time of year, it gets very hot down in the crowds. Wearing a small backpack or daypack is too inconvenient. The little packs that attach to your belt are much more secure in these crowds. Don't carry anything that you can't stuff into your pockets or beltpack, you need both hands free to manoeuvre through the crowd and keep your balance.

Everything you need can be purchased in Yenshui. Street vendors capitalise on the situation and sell motorcycle helmets and face shields.

A motorcycle or bicycle is the most practical way to get into and out of Yenshui during this festival. You can take the train to Hsinying and then walk 7km or take a taxi to Yenshui, but start out early if you're going to depend on public transport.

Perhaps the best option is to avoid Yenshui and instead visit the fireworks displays in Luerhmen and Peikang – your chances of injury are lower and you can still watch the Yenshui display on TV. It's usually broadcast several weeks later. ■

three days. Most people start walking from Tienchih.

Tienchih to Wulu

(tiānchì, wùlù) 天池 , 霧鹿

About four hours walk from Tienchih is the top of the highway at Yakou *(yăkŏu)*, at an elevation of 2728m. There is a large tunnel, about 500m in length, which you have to walk through. A torch (flashlight) is absolutely essential as the tunnel is not lit and is totally dark in the centre – it's rather spooky.

Once you are out of the tunnel, walk downhill for a short distance and you'll see the Yakou Youth Activity Centre, where you can spend the night. If you get up before dawn you can admire the extraordinary sunrise. As one traveller wrote:

Walk to the top of the pass at daybreak for lovely mountain vistas and, if conditions are good, for a beautiful display of the sea of clouds ... I stayed there over an hour in extreme wind, some rain, some sun, and saw the most spectacular cloud show I have ever seen. The ever-changing patterns and colours raced over the summit at a speed I couldn't believe.

Ruthli F Kemmerer

Walk down the road past the waterfall. It's a

SOUTH-WEST TAIWAN

full day's walk downhill to Litao *(lìdào),* about 30km or seven hours by foot. Litao is an aboriginal village at 1070m elevation which has a youth hostel.

Buses departs Litao at 8 am and 2.30 pm, heading down to Kuanshan and then on to Taitung on the east coast. If you still have the energy, you can get up early and walk for two hours from Litao to Wulu; the 9km walk takes you through a gorge that rivals the beauty of Taroko Gorge. The first bus stops in Wulu at 8.20 am, but unless you start out from Litao at 6 am you won't catch it. Of course, you can always get the afternoon bus.

Side Trips

If you want a real challenge, you can climb Kuanshan *(guānshān),* not to be confused with the small city of Kuanshan near Taitung. Kuanshan is a peak just to the south-west of the Yakou Youth Activity Centre. It's 3666m in elevation. You begin the climb from Yakou, and you will need a class A mountain pass – even though there is nobody up there to check it.

You can spend an extra night in Meishan on the west side. Meishan is a large aboriginal village with a youth hostel. There's nothing to do but relax and go for walks. There is a river nearby but the scenery is more exciting in Yakou.

Places to Stay

There are three youth hostels along this route and camping is possibile – you are allowed to pitch a tent next to a youth hostel.

Travelling from west to east, the *Meishan Youth Activity Centre* (☎ (07) 686-6166; *méishān qīngnián huódòng zhōngxīn)* is the first place you'll encounter. There's dormitory accommodation that costs NT$280 per person.

At the top of the pass is the *Yakou Youth Activity Centre* (☎ (089) 329-891; *yǎkǒu qīngnián huódòng zhōngxīn).* The dorms have 15 beds and cost NT$280 per person. There are twins for NT$2000. Bookings can be made through the Meishan centre. It's best to have reserved a room in advance. They

used to permit travellers to sleep on the dining room floor for a small fee, but recently the management have become more obstinate – you might have to beg. Alternatively, you can camp next to the hostel, but at 2500m it's cold, so bring a sleeping bag and warm clothes.

The easternmost accommodation along the highway is the *Litao Youth Activity Centre* (☎ (089) 329-891; *lìdào qīngnián huódòng zhōngxīn).* It shares a telephone number with Yakou, but bookings are made from Meishan. Dorms are NT$280 per person and twins cost NT$1500.

Places to Eat

Bring extra food along or you'll be sorry. All three *youth hostels* serve meals, but only if they are booked in advance. Some of the meals leave a lot to be desired. This particularly applies to Yakou, where for NT$50 they serve up some sort of paste that's supposed to be breakfast. If you want to eat at the hostel you either have to reserve meals in advance, or they have a little kiosk that sells cookies and other junk food.

Good food is available from the *noodle stalls* near the bus terminals in Meishan and Litao, but nothing except for biscuits and the paste is available in Yakou.

Getting There & Away

There are buses from both Tainan (west side) and Taitung (east side) that meet and terminate at the midpoint of the highway at Tienchih, just after noon. Passengers from one bus transfer to the other to complete the trip over the mountains. The buses depart about 2 pm. Hikers can get off the bus, have lunch and then start walking.

There is only one bus a day in either direction over this highway. From Tainan, buses depart at 7.30 am from the Hsingnan Bus Company *(xīngnán kèyùn)* terminal on Chungshan Rd. If you're travelling in the other direction, the bus departs from the Taiwan Bus Company Station in Taitung at 8.30 am and makes a brief stop in Kuanshan *(guānshān)* at 9.30 am.

Islands of the Taiwan Straits 台灣海峽群島

Taiwan is separated from mainland China by the stormy, windswept Taiwan Straits. The character of all the islands within these straits contrasts sharply with Taiwan. While Taiwan is densely populated and heavily industrialised, these islands are known for sandy beaches, quaint fishing villages, blue skies (in summer), turquoise seas, great seafood and no mosquitos.

The weather, however, is a major consideration. Winter brings fierce winds and surprisingly cold temperatures – it's definitely much colder here than the rest of Taiwan. The islands come alive during the warmer summer months, when Taiwanese tourists flock here by the boatload. To avoid the summer crowds, don't visit in July and August – June and September are the recommended months to plan a trip here.

Penghu Islands 澎湖

(pénghú)
The Penghu Archipelago, labelled the Pescadores (Fishermen's) Islands by Portuguese mariners, is made up of 64 islands about halfway between Taiwan and mainland China. The Dutch occupied the islands for a time during the 17th century, and they were followed by the French and Japanese.

Historically, Penghu is significant as the route used by the European invaders of Taiwan. A large fort remains on the islands as evidence of those times.

Geographically, Penghu bears little resemblance to the rest of Taiwan. While Taiwan is mountainous, wet and swathed in dense forest, Penghu is mostly flat, dry and covered with brush and grassland.

But this is not to say that Penghu isn't beautiful. During the summer months at least, Penghu is an ideal venue for beach and boating activities. From about May to October, the islands are bathed in brilliant

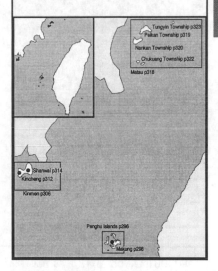

HIGHLIGHTS
• **Penghu** – make the most of the beaches and fishing and snorkelling opportunities as you hop your way around these accessible islands
• **Kinmen** – this national park island, just off the coast of China, is home to recent battlegrounds and underground military bases, offering a fascinating insight into the tenuous Sino-Taiwanese relationship
• **Matsu** – discover the way Taiwan used to be by exploring this collection of 18 scenic islands and islets just off the coast of China

sunshine reflecting a special stark beauty that defies description.

Unlike Taiwan, Penghu is not overpopulated and probably never will be as the locals tend to migrate to Taiwan in search of greater economic opportunities. Tourism is the main industry, followed by fishing and farming, but growing anything is a challenge in Penghu's harsh, windswept climate. The islanders have built coral walls to protect the crops (peanuts, sweet potatoes and sorghum)

from the fierce winter winds. However, it's likely that fishing and farming will continue to decline – Penghu's young people have little interest in pursuing such strenuous careers.

There are 147 temples in Penghu by official count and, not surprisingly, they are mostly dedicated to Matsu – goddess of the sea. Matsu is believed to protect fishermen from harm on their hazardous journeys. Many of Penghu's temples are old, but have been restored and are still worth visiting.

The main islands are served by sea and air services but visiting some of the smaller islands will require you to charter a boat or small plane.

PENGHU
(pénghú) 澎湖

The name Penghu is used to describe the area covered by Penghu, Paisha and Hsi islands and is most likely the first place you will visit in the Penghu Archipelago.

Makung
(mǎgōng) 馬公

The only city in the islands, with a population of 60,000, Makung is a picturesque town with a fishing harbour, outdoor fish markets and temples. The place retains a little 'Taiwanese flavour' (eg chaos, motorcycles), but it's more sedate and traditional than the cities on the mainland and there is virtually no air

---

PENGHU ISLANDS 澎湖

1 Chipei Sea Paradise
   Resort
   吉貝海上樂園
2 Penghu Aquarium
   澎湖水族館
3 Giant Banyan
   Tree
   通梁古榕
4 Kuahai Bridge
   跨海大橋
5 Whale Cave
   鯨魚洞
6 Hsitai Fort
   西台古堡
7 Old Fisherman's
   Lighthouse
   漁翁島燈塔
8 Fuhai Temple
   福海宮
9 Fengkuei Cave
   風櫃洞
10 Veined Stoned Exhibition
   Centre
   雅輪文石陳列館
11 Dam
   成功水庫
12 Makung Airport
   機場
13 Military Public Cemetery
   軍人公墓
14 Fenghuang Tian Temple
   鳳凰殿廟
15 Wang'an Airport
   機場
16 Chimei Airport
   機場
17 Tomb of the Seven
   Virtuous Beauties
   七美人塚

pollution. At the time of research there was not even one 7-Eleven or McDonald's in the whole place, though that is sure to change. There is a branch of the Foreign Affairs Police (☎ 927-0870) at 36 Chihping Rd, Makung.

Things to See There are a few notable historical relics in Makung. The **Matsu Temple** (*māzǔ gōng* or *tiānhòu gōng*) is 375 years old, making it the oldest temple in Taiwan. Nearby is the **Shuncheng Gate** (*shùnchéng mén*), **Shihkung Ancestral Hall** (*shīgōng cí*) and **Four Sleep Well** (*sì mián jǐng*). At the beach by Penghu Youth Activity Centre is the **Kuanyin Pavilion** (*guànyīn tíng*).

On the eastern outskirts of town are the **Martyr's Shrine** (*zhōng liè cí*) and **Confucius Temple** (*kǒng miào*).

Places to Stay There are no places to stay on Paisha and Hsi islands – everyone stays in Makung unless they're going to the outlying islands. Accommodation gets a little tight on weekends and holidays during summer, but should be easy enough to find at other times. If you will be arriving in the peak season, at least try to get on an early flight – places fill up fast after noon. Discounting is practised during the off season, but in summer you'll have to pay top dollar.

The budget market belongs exclusively to the *Teachers' Hostel* (☎ 927-3692; *jiàoshī huìguǎn*) at 38 Shute Rd, an old building which looks the worse for wear. Three bed dormitories with a shared bath cost NT$200 per person, or you can have a twin room with bath for NT$450.

Moving upmarket, the *Penghu Youth Activity Centre* (☎ 927-1124; *pénghú qīngnián huódòng zhōngxīn*), 11 Chiehshou Rd, is not especially cheap despite being labelled a 'youth hostel'. The dormitories (NT$2500 for 10 persons) are for organised groups only. Individual travellers will be steered into a double room which costs NT$650. Twins cost NT$1300. The nearby beach is the big attraction here.

The *Fu Go Hotel* (☎ 927-3861; *fùguó dà*

lǚshè), 31 Sanmin Rd, has 24 rooms with doubles/twins for NT$500/1200.

The *Hung An Hotel* (☎ 927-3832, *hóng'-ān dà lǚshè*), 16 Sanmin Rd, has 22 double/twin rooms for NT$500/1000.

The *Donghai Hotel* (☎ 927-2367; *dōng-hǎi lǚshè*), 38 Sanmin Rd, is an old and small place near the fish market. Rooms here cost from NT$400 to NT$600.

Zhongxing Hotel (☎ 926-1121; *zhōngxīng dà fàndiàn*), 82 Minchuan Rd, has doubles for NT$700.

The *Youzhi Hotel* (☎ 927-2151; *yǒuzhì dà lǚshè*), 22 Chunghsing Rd, is a small place with doubles/twins for NT$500/1200.

The *Hotel Yuh Tarng* (☎ 927-8155; *yùtáng fàndiàn*), 33 Chunghua Rd, charges NT$800 for a double. This place also has luxury rooms available for NT$2000.

The *A Seal Grand Hotel* (☎ 927-8170; *èrxīn dà fàndiàn*), 10 Minsheng Rd, is a large and well-run hotel. Doubles/twin rooms cost NT$660/1300.

The *Hotel Veined Stone* (☎ 927-2577; *wénshí dà fàndiàn*), 38 Chungcheng Rd, has rooms from NT$600 to NT$1200, plus your medical bills if you get mauled by one of the resident dogs!

At the top end of the range is the *Hwa Shin Palace Hotel* (☎ 926-4911; *huáxīn dà fàndiàn*), 40 Sanmin Rd. It's a new nine storey high rise, off Chang'an Rd, with doubles that cost NT$1200.

The *Jih Lih Hotel* (☎ 926-5898; *rìlì dà fàndiàn*), 25 Huimin 1st Rd, is a sparkling new 14 storey building. Rooms cost from NT$1280 to NT$8800.

The *Four Seas Hotel* (☎ 927-2960; *sìhǎi dà fàndiàn*), 3 Chienkuo Rd, has doubles/twins for NT$800/1800.

The *Pao Hua Hotel* (☎ 927-4881; *bǎohuá dà fàndiàn*), 2 Chungcheng Rd, is close to the ferry pier and some of the better rooms have a sea view. Doubles/twin rooms cost NT$1350/2000.

Also close to the ferry pier is the *Hotel Chang Chun* (☎ 927-3336; *chángchūn dà fàndiàn*) at 8 Chungcheng Rd. Doubles cost NT$900, breakfast included.

Penghu Royal Hotel (☎ 926-1182; *ruìfù*

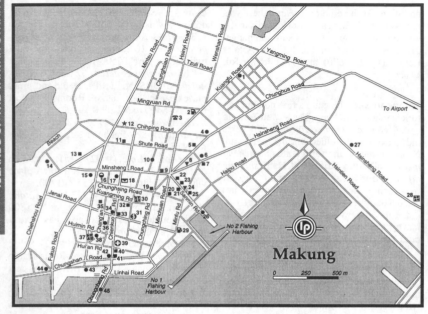

Makung

0   250   500 m

dà fàndiàn), 33 Lane 64, Hsinsheng Rd, is plush looking and rooms cost from NT$1360 to NT$2160.

Places to Eat If it's budget eats you're after, try the Wenwen Cafeteria (☎ 926-4606; *wénwén zìzhù cān*) at 9 Chunghua Rd.

Seafood is the local speciality. In Makung, the section of Sanmin Rd right near the fish market is seafood alley. One of the better known eateries here is the *Haiwangzi Seafood Restaurant* (☎ 926-3188; *hǎiwángzi hǎixiānlóu*) at 26 Sanmin Rd. Just because seafood is common in Penghu does not mean that it's cheap – always ask the price first if you're not sure.

A classier place is *Four Seas Restaurant* (☎ 927-3335; *sìhǎi cāntīng*), 3 Chienkuo Rd. The *Pao Hua Hotel* also has a notable seafood restaurant on its 2nd floor.

The *Hotel Chang Chun* has a western-style restaurant featuring steak dinners.

Veined Stone Exhibition Centre
(yǎlún wénshí chénliè guǎn) 雅輪文石陳列館
This place is a big deal for the Taiwanese, who are enthusiastic collectors of anything that's pretty, shiny or unusual. Penghu may lack forests and mountains, but it makes up for it with a geology that produces beautiful rocks with intricate veined patterns. The locals claim that only Italy matches Penghu in producing such geological treasures. If you have a passion for rocks, you may want to visit this exhibition centre which is a little over 4km east of Makung.

Lintou Beach
(líntóu gōngyuán) 林頭公園
Near the eastern end of the Island is Lintou Beach, which has beautiful white sand. On the west side is the **Military Public Cemetery** *(jūnrén gōngmù)*, a small version of Taipei's Chiang Kaishek Memorial. A short way inland is the **Fenghuangtien Temple** *(fènghuángdiàn miào)*.

MAKUNG 馬公

PLACES TO STAY
5 Hotel Yuh Tarng
  玉堂大飯店
7 Penghu Royal Hotel
  瑞富大飯店
9 A Seal Grand Hotel
  二信大飯店
11 Teachers' Hostel
  教師會館
13 Penghu Youth Activity
  Centre
  青年活動中心
19 Youzhi Hotel
  有志大旅社
20 Zhongxing Hotel
  中興大飯店
21 Fu Go Hotel
  富國大旅社
22 Hwa Shin Palace Hotel
  華馨大飯店
23 Donghai Hotel
  東海旅社
25 Hung An Hotel
  宏安大旅社
32 Four Seas Hotel
  四海大飯店
33 Hotel Veined Stone
  文石大飯店
35 Jih Lih Hotel
  日立大飯店
40 Hotel Chang Chun
  長春大飯店

41 Pao Hua Hotel
  寶華大飯店

PLACES TO EAT
8 Wenwen Cafeteria
  文文自助餐
24 Haiwangzi Seafood
  Restaurant
  海王子海鮮樓

OTHER
1 EVA Air & Great China
  Airlines
  長榮航空、大華航空
2 Petrol Station
  加油站
3 Telephone Company
  電信局
4 Far Eastern Air Transport
  遠東航空
6 TransAsia Airlines
  復興航空
10 Clothing Alley & Market
  文康街
12 Foreign Affairs Police
  警察局外事課
14 Kuanyin Pavilion
  觀音亭
15 China Airlines
  中華航空
16 Bus Station
  公共車船管理處
17 Motorcycle Hire
  機車出租

18 GPO
  郵政總局
26 Fish Market
  魚市場
27 Martyr's Shrine
  忠烈祠
28 Confucius Temple
  孔廟（文石書院）
29 Petrol Station
  加油站
30 Chenghuang Temple
  城隍廟
31 Bank of Taiwan
  台灣銀行
34 Fuhsiang Travel Service
  富翔旅行社
36 Four Sleep Well
  四眠井
37 Matsu Temple
  媽祖宮
38 Shihkung Ancestral
  Hall
  施公祠
39 Shengli Hospital
  省立醫院
42 Motorcycle Hire
  機車出租
43 Kaohsiung Ferry Ticket
  Office
  台華輪候船室
44 Shuncheng Gate
  順承門
45 Ferry Pier
  碼頭

Fengkuei Cave
(fēngguì dòng) 風櫃洞
At the south-western end of Penghu Island is Fengkuei Cave, a big attraction for Taiwanese tourists who want to see the 'dramatic coastal rock formations'. To be honest, the rocks are not that dramatic and there is often plenty of rubbish left behind by tourists.

On the way to Fengkuei Cave, you'll pass by **Chihli Beach** *(zhìlí hǎishuǐ yùchǎng)*, which is one of the finest on Penghu Island.

Paisha Island
(báishā dǎo) 白沙島
Paisha (White Sand) Island is notable for its 300 year old **Giant Banyan Tree** *(dà róngshù* or *tōngliáng gǔróng)*. The branches are

supported by latticework and walking under it is like walking through a cave.

A more recent attraction is **Penghu Aquarium** (☎ 993-3006; *pénghú shuǐzú guǎn*). A key feature here is the undersea tunnel which is (hopefully) made of unbreakable glass, allowing you to view marine life from a fish's perspective.

Hsi Island
(xī yǔ) 西嶼
Paisha is connected to Hsi (West) Island by the **Kuahai Bridge** *(kuàhǎi dàqiáo)* which, at over 5km, is the longest in Taiwan.

Hsi Island is the most beautiful of the major islands, with many hidden coves. At the very southern tip of this island is the

Hsitai Fort *(xītái gǔbǎo)*, built in 1883 under the Qing (Manchu) dynasty. It's well preserved and open to the public. It is claimed that on a clear day you can see the mountains of both Taiwan and mainland China from this fort. The air pollution generated on both sides of the Taiwan Straits is decreasing the opportunities to witness this phenomenon, though Penghu itself remains perfectly clean.

The very tiny **Hsiaomen Island** *(xiǎomén yǔ)* is connected to Hsi Island by a narrow bridge. Despite its small size, the island is very scenic. On the north side of this islet is **Whale Cave** *(jīngyú dòng)*, a natural stone arch carved by the sea.

Things to Buy

Penghu is not an industrial place and therefore offers little that you can't buy more cheaply in Taiwan. One exception is the excellent peanut candy that is sold here. There are many different varieties and they're all good. Since they usually all cost the same, you can mix many different kinds together. A Taiwanese kilogram (catty) of assorted peanut candy costs about NT$60.

The flight back to Taiwan usually reeks of the dried fish, squid and clams that the local tourists take back with them – just be glad it's only a 30 minute ordeal.

Straw hats are not made locally, but are available everywhere in Penghu and are an essential survival item in the fierce summer sun. There are also some visor caps in tourist colours (zingo-pink or dayglow-orange) in case you feel like dressing up as a clown. A small alley called Wenkang St in Makung is the place to look for modern clothing.

Getting There & Away

Air Although Penghu is a remote backwater, there are frequent flights to and from all the major cities in Taiwan. These flights are very popular and tend to be heavily booked on summer weekends and holidays. However, during the week in the off season, you might literally find yourself to be the only passenger aboard!

There are flights connecting Makung with Chiayi, Chimei, Kaohsiung, Pingtung, Taichung, Tainan and Taipei.

All airlines sell tickets at the airport check-in counters or in their Makung offices. You'll get a substantial discount by going to a private travel agency. One such agency in Makung is Fuhsiang Travel Service (☎ 926-5160), 45 Chungcheng Rd.

The following airlines have booking offices in Penghu:

China Airlines
  (☎ 927-4811; *zhōnghuá hángkōng*) 29 Fukuo Rd, Makung
EVA Airways
  (☎ 926-3111; *chángróng hángkōng*) 102 Kuangfu Rd, Makung
Far Eastern Air Transport
  (☎ 927-4891; *yuǎndōng hángkōng*) 4-2 Chihping Rd, Makung
Formosa Airlines
  (☎ 921-6966; *guóhuá hángkōng*) Makung airport
Great China Airlines
  (☎ 926-3111; *dàhuá hángkōng*) 102 Kuangfu Rd, Makung
Taiwan Airlines
  (☎ 921-1800; *táiwān hángkōng*) Makung airport
TransAsia Airways
  (☎ 080-066880; *fùxīng hángkōng*) 2 Shute Rd, Makung
U-Land Airlines
  (☎ 921-1112; *ruìlián hángkōng*) 16-1 Hsihsiang, Aimen Village
Uni Air
  (☎ 921-6350; *lìróng hángkōng*) Makung airport

Boat During the summer consider going to the islands by boat from either Kaohsiung or Chiayi and returning by air (or vice versa).

The Kaohsiung-Makung boat is known as the Taihua Ferry *(táihuá kèlún)* and is operated by the Taiwan Hangye Company. The journey takes about four hours and departures are daily during the summer months. However, the schedule gets cut back during the winter. A new ferry schedule is issued every three months, though it's in Chinese only. Taiwan Hangye will fax a copy to you if you call their office in Kaohsiung (☎ (07) 561-3866/551-5823) or in Makung (☎ 926-3030/926-4087). Or if it's convenient you can stop by their offices which are adjacent to the respective ferry piers: 5 Chiehhsing 1st St, Kaohsiung (next to Kaohsiung Customs) or 36 Linhai Rd, Makung. One-way fares at the time of research were: economy class NT$450, reclining seat NT$500, 1st class NT$700 and special class NT$1000.

There is another boat service between Putai *(bùdài)*, a port near Chiayi, and Sokang *(suǒgǎng)* on the southern end of Penghu Island. This service is called the Alishan Ferry *(ālǐshān kèlún)* and is operated by the Jiarong Sea Transport Company *(jiāróng hǎiyùn gōngsī)*. Their main office (☎ (05) 222-6859/223-3969) is in Chiayi at 692 Chungcheng Rd. There are also branches in Putai (☎ (05) 347-4878) in the Sea Transport Building *(hǎiyùn dàlóu)* and in Sokang (☎ 995-1697). The one way journey takes 100 minutes, making this the fastest boat to Penghu, and costs NT$450. The ferry departs from Putai at 10.30 am and from Sokang at 5 pm, though the schedule is subject to change so you should check with the boat company before making any plans. This boat runs during summer only. Bring sunscreen if you want to stay on the upper deck.

If you go by boat, you can take a motor-cycle or bicycle with you for half the cost of a passenger ticket. This isn't really worth the bother since motorcycle rentals in Penghu are so easy to come by.

The boat trip is wonderful! Clear water and flying fish abound, and the sunset was spectacular the day we returned.

Margit Waas

Getting Around

To/From the Airport Bus services between the airport and Makung are practically non-existent – the big buses you see parked near the airport are tour buses. Taxis waiting at the airport cost NT$300 for the 9km trip to Makung – not negotiable. If you walk outside the airport gate and hail a passing cab, the tariff is NT$200. The charge from Makung to the airport is NT$200.

Bus There are two bus services on Penghu,

both of which depart from the airport. The first travels to Lintou Beach and the other goes to Hsitai Fort. They travel along the main roads at an average rate of one per hour – you'll need a lot of patience to get around by bus.

Car & Motorcycle Given the rural nature of Penghu, the best way to get around is by motorcycle. You can bring one with you on the boat or rent one upon your arrival.

There are numerous places renting motor-cycles, mostly along Chungcheng Rd close to where the Kaohsiung ferry docks. A 50cc model should cost NT$250 per day, but you'll probably be more comfortable with a 125cc bike which will set you back NT$350.

Cars are also available from the motor-cycle hire stands or hotels. A sedan normally rents for NT$800 for five hours or NT$1300 for 24 hours. A nine passenger van costs NT$1200 for five hours or NT$2200 for 24 hours.

Bicycle Bringing a 10 speed bicycle with you is another possibility, but be warned that Penghu is large – Makung to Hsitai Fort is 35km. There are no big hills, but the sea breezes can be fierce, making cycling extremely difficult. No one seems to rent bicycles in Penghu – the Taiwanese defi-nitely seem to prefer their bikes with a motor.

AROUND PENGHU

There are quite a few islands in the Penghu Archipelago which are well worth visiting. However, the only ones with regularly scheduled boat services are Chipei, Wang'an and Chimei islands. Chimei and Wang'an even have airports.

Tachang and Yuanpei islands can be reached on foot if you are brave or foolish enough to wade through the sea at low tide. We are not recommending you do this, though apparently many people do indeed take the plunge and most (though not all) survive.

To visit the remaining islands, you'll need to get yourself aboard a chartered tourist boat. This is not difficult during the busy summer season – most of the better hotels in Makung can arrange this, if yours doesn't then ask at either the Hotel Chang Chun or Pao Hua Hotel. The cost varies enormously according to the size of the boat, the number of people on board and how many hours you want to go out for. As a rough guide, allow between NT$100 and NT$200 per hour per person.

No permits are needed to camp on the outlying islands but finding a suitable site with drinking water may be problematic.

Chipei Island

(jíbèi yǔ) 吉貝嶼

To the north of Penghu is Chipei Island, noted for its excellent **beaches** of fine coral, not sand. It has one of the best beaches in the Penghu Islands, and walking around Chipei (10km) is a good way to start your visit.

There is an excellent **fish market** here, the largest in the Penghu Archipelago outside of Makung.

Although the island is great for **swimming**, the lifeguards won't let you use a snorkel for fear of you drowning.

Places to Stay & Eat There is a resort area called *Chipei Sea Paradise* (☎ 991-1311/991-1151; *jíbèi hǎishàng lèyuán*) which charges a small admission fee; this is where most people stay. There are wooden cabins for hire – these are in fact prefabricated houses imported from Europe and North America. They have beds in dormitories for NT$250 per person, while twin rooms cost from NT$1000 upwards.

You can camp inside the resort if you bring your own tent. There are restaurants and self-catering facilities at the resort but these are very expensive so bring your own food with you. A wide-brimmed hat is essential, as there are no trees to shade under to avoid the powerful sun. At the resort you can rent jet skis, windsurfers and other water playthings.

Some other less well known but OK places include the *Bieye Hotel* (☎ 991-1278; *biéyě shānzhuāng*), the *Chipei Holiday Resort* (☎ 991-1291; *jíbèi dùjià xiūxián zhōngxīn*), the *Beizhou Hotel* (☎ 991-1116;

běizhōu lǚshè), the *Jinhai'an Holiday Resort* (☎ 991-1293/991-1290; *jīnhǎi'àn dùjià zhōngxīn*) and the *Gangbian Hotel* (☎ 991-1272; *gǎngbiā lǚshè*).

There are also two small restaurants in Chipei which rent rooms – the *Haibian Restaurant* (☎ 991-1010/991-1298; *hǎibiān xiǎochī bù*) and the *Chipei Restaurant* (☎ 991-1070; *jíbèi xiǎochī bù*). Prices are seasonal and can range from around NT$500 to NT$2000. Your room might be a tatami dormitory – check it out before handing over any cash.

Getting There & Away There are no flights to Chipei, so you have to take a boat. There is no published schedule for the boats – they run to demand when the weather is fine and tourists are abundant.

Most departures for Chipei are from Chihkan Pier *(chìkǎn mǎtóu)* on the north shore of Paisha Island. There are three companies operating boats to Chipei from Chihkan: Hawaii Boat Company (☎ 993-2237/993-2049; *xiàwēiyí chuán gōngsī*); Paisha Boat Centre (☎ 993-1917/921-2609; *báishā yóulè zhōngxīn*); and the Aimin Boat Company (☎ 993-2232/991-1145; *aìmín chuán gōngsī*).

The Chiyun Boat (☎ 991-1078; *qíyùn hào jiāotōng chuán*) runs a boat service from Houliao Pier *(hòuliáo mǎtóu)* on Paisha Island.

Tachang Island

(dàcāng yǔ) 大倉嶼

This tiny island in the middle of Penghu Bay is renowned for dramatic tides – at low tide the island is three times larger than at high tide. It's actually possible to walk the 3km across to the island during low tide though this can be dangerous; it takes about an hour to walk. The Taiwanese like to come here to dig up shells, shrimp and fish.

Yuanpei Island

(yuánbèi yǔ) 員貝嶼

This islet to the east of Paisha Island is another one of those weird places that can be reached on foot at low tide if you're willing to risk your life. The one way walk takes two hours – starting from Shakang (shāgǎng) on Penghu Island. Yuanpei is known for its pretty coral. The Yuanpei Sea Activity Centre (☎ 993-2735/993-2765; yuánbèi hǎishàng xiūxián zhōngxīn) can arrange transport, food and accommodation for a visit to the island if you're so inclined. They also have a contact number in Kaohsiung (☎ (07) 311-1070).

Hsienchiao Island
(xiǎnjiāo yǔ) 險礁嶼
Though it's very small, some say Hsienchiao is the Penghu Archipelago's most beautiful island. It's known for white sand **beaches** and is a great place to go swimming or **snorkelling**. Hsienchiao is about halfway between Paisha and Chipei islands. There are no scheduled boat services, so you have to rent one to get here. The journey from Chihkan Pier to Hsienchiao Island takes about 20 minutes depending on the speed of your boat.

Kupo Island
(gūpó yǔ) 姑婆嶼
This is the place for gathering *laver*, a kind of edible seaweed which is dried and processed. For tourists, the main interest here is the numerous birds – if you're a dedicated birdwatcher, look no further. Another interesting feature of the island is the small **saltwater lake** which contains some very beautiful tropical fish. Getting to the island is only possible by chartered boat.

Tiechen Island
(tiězhēn yǔ) 鐵砧嶼
This small rocky island, just to the east of Kupo Island, is known for a **sea cave** which is 15m wide and 7m deep – small charter boats can go inside the cave for a close-up view.

Mutou Island
(mùdǒu yǔ) 目斗嶼
This is one of the northernmost islands in the Penghu Archipelago, and is dominated by a **lighthouse** originally built during the Qing

dynasty. This tiny islet has a land area of only 210 sq metres and includes a small 'beachlet'. The shallow water attracts many tropical fish and lets you walk a long way out from the shoreline.

Chishan Island
(jīshàn yǔ) 雞善嶼
This is actually two islands. The larger one is known for its colony of sea birds while the smaller island has better scenery – the hexagonal-shaped rocks are impressive. Both islands are uninhabited and can only be reached by chartered boat.

Tingkou Island
(dìnggōu yǔ) 錠鉤嶼
The local folk like to call this place 'Little Guilin'. Guilin in mainland China is known for its dramatic rock formations – those on Tingkou Island are decidedly less extraordinary, but it's still a fun place to visit. The island is uninhabited and you will need to charter a boat to make the journey here.

Niao Island
(niǎo yǔ) 鳥嶼
The name means 'bird island', but here's the punch line – the island is nearly devoid of birdlife. At one time the fine feathered creatures were numerous – perhaps they got fed up with the tourists and flew away.

Hsiaopaisha Island
(xiǎo báishā yǔ) 小白沙嶼
This is a very tiny island with a small, white sand beach. Some people come here for swimming and snorkelling, but the island is only accessible by chartered boat.

Tongpan Island
(tǒngpán yǔ) 桶盤嶼
The hexagonal-shaped rock formations along the coastline are the main attraction of this island. The name derives from the fact that some people say the island is shaped like a big cooking pan (use your imagination). It has the distinction of recording the highest average temperatures in Penghu Archipelago. The island is inhabited and the small

village is known for its ornate **Fuhai Temple** (*fúhǎi gōng*) which attracts a steady stream of worshippers. The island is 6km from Makung by chartered boat.

Huching Island

(*hǔjǐng yǔ*) 虎井嶼

This island's name means 'tiger's well', derived from an old story that there was once a tiger on the island which hid in an old, dry well. Unfortunately, you aren't likely to see any tigers these days, if indeed there ever were any. The island is notable for its black, **volcanic rock formations**. Huching village, on the south-western corner of the isle, is notable for a few small, unnamed seafood *restaurants*. There are also some remains of a secret, underground **Japanese bomb shelter** from WWII, which are accessible to the public free of charge.

Wang'an Island

(*wàng'ān yǔ*) 望安嶼

For those who really want to get away from civilisation, there are boats and flights to Wang'an, an island to the south of Penghu. There isn't much to do here except admire the sea and surf. The island is almost devoid of trees, though the Taiwanese are enthralled with the grasslands, as they don't get to see much of that in Taipei.

On the top of the island's highest peak, Tientaishan, there is a small (very small!) crater which is said to be the footprint of a fairy. From here you can walk east to a beach and Tongdao Cave (*tōngdǎo dòng*). There are some old traditional homes here built from coral which are claimed to be 300 years old.

Places to Stay There are two places to stay on Wang'an. The cheapest is the *Wang'an Vacation Centre* (☎ 999-1200; *wàng'ān dùjià zhōngxīn*) in Dong'an Village which has beds in dorms for NT$150 and rooms for NT$500.

The *Yanchuan Vacation Centre* (☎ 999-1440; *yánchuān dùjià zhōngxīn*) is the larger place to stay. They can also arrange snorkelling trips.

Getting There & Away There are flights connecting Wang'an Island to Kaohsiung and Makung. Formosa Airlines (☎ 999-1079) and Taiwan Airlines (☎ 999-1064; *táiwān hángkōng*) both have booking offices at Wang'an airport.

There are ferries connecting Makung with Wang'an – the journey takes 1½ hours. Heng'an Boat Company (☎ 927-0334; *héng'-ān lún*) in Makung and Guangzheng Boat Company (☎ 999-1201; *guāngzhèng lún*) in Wang'an run boats according to demand.

Chiangchun'ao Island

(*jiāngjūn'ao yǔ*) 將軍澳嶼

Just 1.5km to the east of Wang'an Island is Chiangchun Island. Although this island is much smaller than Wang'an, it's actually more developed. The island's highest peak is a towering 29m. The island also boasts the **Yong'an Temple** (*yǒng'ān gōng*) which dates back to the Ming dynasty. Even larger, but not as old, are the Chiangchun Temple (*jiāngjūn miào*) and the Matsu Temple (*tiān hòu gōng*).

Small boats travel between Wang'an harbour and Chiangchun Island pier; they depart when they have enough passengers.

Tungchi & Hsichi Islands

(*dōngjí yǔ* & *xījí yǔ*) 東吉嶼，西吉嶼

These two barely inhabited islands are to the south-east of Wang'an Island. Tungchi Island has a population of 20 people and a lighthouse. The island's other claim to fame is that it's the closest in the Penghu Archipelago to Taiwan.

Hsichi Island was at one time inhabited, but everyone has now moved away. There are some old abandoned houses and a temple remaining.

Tungyuping & Hsiyuping Islands

(*dōngyǔpíng yǔ* & *xīyǔpíng yǔ*)
東嶼坪，西嶼坪

These two islands are to the south of Wang'an. Tungyuping still has a population of about 100 people, and is notable for its solar power plant.

Nobody lives on Hsiyuping Island, which

is not surprising since the entire coastline consists of steep cliffs.

Mao Island

(māo yǔ) 貓嶼

The name means 'Cat Island', which is attributed to some rock formations which supposedly look like a cat. Despite the stone cat, the island has a large bird population. Indeed, it's claimed that more migratory birds stop at this island than any other place in Asia. One theory why the birds like it so much is because the island is ringed by cliffs offering protection from predators (including humans). Birdwatchers also really seem to like this place.

Hua Island

(huā yǔ) 花嶼

This is the westernmost island in the Penghu Archipelago. There is a small, unnamed town on the south side of the island, which is a bit sheltered from the fierce north winter winds. Notable landmarks are the Tienhu Temple *(tiānhú gōng)* and the lighthouse.

Chimei Island

(qīměi yǔ) 七美島

This is the most southern of the Penghu group of islands. It was once known as Big Island *(dà yǔ)*, but the name was changed to Chimei (Seven Beauties) in 1949. According to local legend the 'Seven Beauties' were seven women who committed suicide when they saw pirate ships approaching to avoid the threat of rape. This sounds like a local adaptation of the 25 Virtuous Women's Tomb in Kaohsiung.

Though one has to sympathise with the unfortunate seven women, there are many who suspect that the whole story might have been conjured up by the Chimei Chamber of Commerce. It's certainly been a boon to the local tourist industry. Every Taiwanese tour group poses for photographs of themselves standing in front of the **Tomb of the Seven Virtuous Beauties** *(qīměi rén zhǒng)* at the southern tip of the island. You can buy Seven Virtuous Beauties ashtrays, postcards and teacups. This commercial success story has inspired the construction of several copycat 'virtuous beauty' tombs in Fujian province, making this yet another of mainland China's recent growth industries.

Another local attraction is **Wangfu Rock** *(wàngfū shí)*, said to look like a pregnant woman awaiting the return of her husband from a sea voyage.

The largest town is in the south-west of the island. At the southern tip of the island is the Chimei lighthouse *(qīměi dēng tǎ)*.

Getting There & Away You can fly directly to Chimei from Kaohsiung or Makung. The services are seasonal, so check ahead with the airline for schedules. Airline offices in Chimei are:

Formosa Airlines
　(☎ 997-1427; *guóhuá hángkōng*) Chimei airport
Taiwan Airlines
　(☎ 997-1254; *táiwān hángkōng*) Chimei airport

The ferry from Wang'an to Chimei takes three hours and is operated by the Heng'an Boat Company (☎ 927-0334; *héng'ān lún*) in Makung. There is no public transport here, however there are taxis for those who don't feel like walking.

Kinmen 金門

(jīnmén)

Occasionally Taiwan throws something at you which is totally unique and unexpected. Certainly Kinmen would fit this category.

Kinmen – formerly known as Quemoy – is an obscure island just off the coast of Xiamen, in Fujian province, in mainland China. 'Kinmen' means 'golden gate' which is an odd name given its history.

Officially, Kinmen is not part of Taiwan, but is a county of Fujian province even though it's under Republic of China (ROC) control. Kinmen and Matsu (see the following Matsu section) became famous briefly in 1958 when Chinese Communist troops started an artillery bombardment of them.

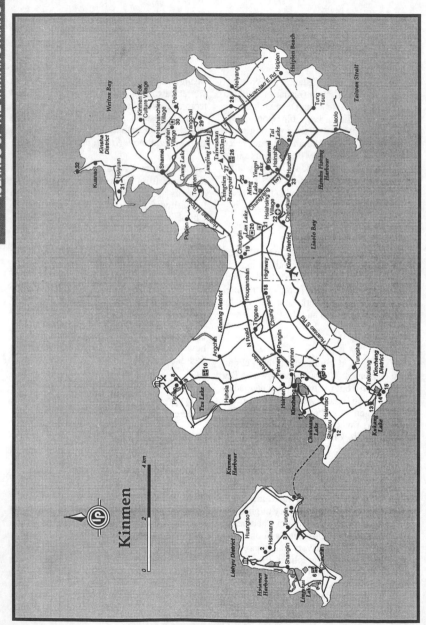

KINMEN 金門

1 Huchingtou War Museum
   湖井頭戰史館
2 Koxinga's Well
   國姓井
3 Pata Memorial
   八達樓子
4 Victory Gate
   勝利門
5 Chiukung Pier
   九宮碼頭
6 Chaste Maiden Temple
   烈女廟
7 Kuningtou Battlefield;
   War Museum
   古寧頭戰場、
   古寧頭戰史館
8 Peishan Old Western
   House
   北山古洋樓
9 Chenwei Residence
   振威第
10 Li Kuangchien Temple
   李光前將軍廟
11 Koxinga Shrine
   延平郡王祠
12 Huang Family Terrestrial
   Hall Villa; Moon Grasping
   Tower
   黃氏西堂別業、
   得月樓
13 Wentai Pagoda;
   文臺寶塔

Hsuchianghsiao Ancient
Inscription
虛江嘯臥碣
14 Kukang Tower
   古崗樓
15 Hanyingyunken Ancient
   Inscription
   漢影雲根碣
16 Mumahou Temple
   牧馬侯祠
17 Chukuang Tower
   莒光樓
18 Chungshan Memorial
   Forest; Chiang Chingkuo
   Memorial Hall
   中山紀念林、
   蔣經國先生紀念館
19 Tsai Family Shrine;
   瓊林蔡氏宗祠
   Chiunglin Tunnel;
   瓊林坑道
   Wind Lion God
   風獅爺
20 Chiu Liangkung's Tomb
   邱良功墓園
21 King Lu's Tomb
   魯王墓
22 Granite Hospital
   花崗岩醫院
23 Kinmen Pottery Factory
   金門陶瓷場
24 Chungcheng Park;
   中正公園

Chiang Kaishek Park;
中正公園
August 23 Artillery War
Memorial;
八二三戰史館
Mr Yu Tawei Museum;
俞大維先生紀念館
Banyan Garden;
榕園
Weilu;
慰廬
Chiang Kaishek Memorial
Forest
中正紀念林
25 Chingtien Auditorium
   擎天廳
26 Haiyln Temple; Stone
   Gate Pass
   海印寺、石門關
27 Don't Forget Days in Chu
   Stone Inscription
   毋忘在莒勒石
28 Forestry Department
   林務所
29 Chen Chen Memorial Arch
   陳楨恩榮坊
30 Chen Chien Ancient
   Tomb
   陳健古墓
31 Hsiyuan Salt Fields
   西園鹽場
32 Mashan Observatory
   馬山觀測站

Taiwan's troops are well dug in now, having built huge concrete bunkers which are virtually bombproof. Kinmen even boasts an underground auditorium where the off-duty soldiers can enjoy live performances and movies.

Kinmen was placed under martial law in 1949 and only returned to civilian rule in 1993. Before martial law was lifted, evening curfews had to be observed and lights could not be used at night unless the windows were shuttered. For 40 years, Kinmen (along with Matsu and Wuchiu) even had its own currency to prevent capital flight, but these days standard New Taiwan dollars are acceptable.

Until the lifting of martial law in 1993, 'entertaining the military' was Kinmen's chief source of income. Entertainment took various forms – prostitution was highly lucrative. The government reported that the closure of the military-run 831 Brothel in Kinmen in 1992 was 'to protect the health of soldiers' (831 was the brothel's telephone number).

The civilian population of Kinmen is currently 48,000. At one time there was an additional military population of 70,000, but this has been reduced to less than half that in recent years. Before martial law was lifted, Kinmen residents had a difficult time leaving – they needed permission to move to Taiwan, which was usually denied because the government feared that everyone would want to abandon the island. Now Kinmen residents

ISLANDS OF THE TAIWAN STRAITS

Tales from the Dark Side

On 31 July 1958, Nikita Khrushchev arrived in Beijing for a secret three day meeting with Mao Zedong. Khrushchev, who saw himself as something of a reformer, wanted to improve relations with the west, and he needed Mao's cooperation.

The two leaders were cordial towards each other, but Khrushchev's memoirs have made it clear that the meeting did not go well.

Mao didn't agree with Khrushchev's revisionist ideas and felt that China was as great a power as the USA and the USSR – the last thing he intended to do was 'take orders' from Khrushchev.

At 6.30 am on 23 August 1958, Mao delivered his response to Khrushchev's peace initiative. The Chinese People's Liberation Army (PLA) rained thousands of artillery shells onto the Taiwanese islands of Kinmen and Matsu. The bombardment continued unabated for 44 days, during which time Kinmen sustained hits from over 474,000 artillery shells.

The Taiwanese forces responded with a bombardment of their own. On 6 October, Mao declared a one week ceasefire. On 13 October, the ceasefire was extended for three more weeks, but when US warships entered the Taiwan Straits, the artillery bombardment resumed.

Finally on 25 October, Mao announced his deal – if US warships kept away from the Chinese coastline, the Communists would only bombard the islands on odd numbered days. The Americans and Taiwanese rejected the deal, but two years later, after continuous bombardment, it was finally accepted. By mutual agreement, Taiwan fired artillery shells on Monday, Wednesday and Friday, while the Communists launched theirs on Tuesday, Thursday and Saturday. The war was put on hold on Sunday so everyone could enjoy a holiday. This arrangement continued for 20 years until 1978, during which time 587 ROC soldiers were killed – the death toll on the Chinese side is unknown.

During the crossfire Sino-American relations had hit rock bottom. Sino-Soviet relations had also become frostier – Khrushchev reneged on a promise to provide China with a prototype atomic bomb and then sided with India in a Sino-Indian border dispute. In 1960, the Soviets removed all of their 1390 foreign experts working in China. With the experts went the blueprints for some 600 projects that the two powers had been working on together, including China's nuclear bomb program. In 1969, the Soviet and Chinese armies clashed briefly in a territorial dispute over the obscure Zhenbao (Treasure) Island on the border of Siberia and north-east China – one might even call it the 'Russian Kinmen'.

The artillery bombardment may have stopped in 1978, but a propaganda war continued until the 1990s. During this time the opposing sides saturated each other with propaganda leaflets. These were sent in canisters which were either launched by gun or carried by balloons. One balloon managed to drift all the way to Israel, where its canister was opened and the world saw the type of 'psychological warfare apparatus' being used – see-through underwear. On a more sober note, during the Tiananmen Square crisis of 1989, the balloons carried Taiwanese newspapers to inform Chinese mainlanders of the events occurring in Beijing.

The propaganda conflict also led to the construction of the world's largest neon sign on the shores of Kinmen. The sign proclaimed, in big bright lights, 'Three Principles of the People, Reunify China!', and became such a major tourist attraction that when it was finally turned off, the Xiamen city government in China made a formal complaint.

The Taiwanese army tried to erode morale further by blasting messages over gigantic loud speakers, also claimed to be the largest in the world. The Communists retaliated with loudspeakers of their own – just imagine the eardrum splitting cacophony as the two sides bombarded each other with hot air from their respective politicians.

Both the Russians and Americans are said to have considered the use of nuclear weapons against China. For his part, Mao simply didn't seem to care. As he once said 'The islands are two batons that keep Khrushchev and Eisenhower dancing, scurrying this way and that'. ∎

can leave of their own free will, the island's population is actually increasing – some Taiwanese are even making the move to Kinmen to take advantage of recent business opportunities.

Kinmen features an amazing collection of mostly reconstructed Ming and Qing dynasty architecture. The labour of soldiers plus the government's financial largesse has turned Kinmen into a place of very orderly design. Trees and flowers have been planted and potholes have been filled. The roads here are wide, hedges are regularly trimmed and hardly a scrap of paper or plastic litters the landscape. The relative absence of traffic means the island is almost free of noise and air pollution. In other words, Kinmen is considerably cleaner than Taiwan itself. Most of Kinmen's recognised tourist sights have a decidedly militaristic bent, but all things considered the island is a very rewarding place to visit.

In 1995, Kinmen was officially declared Taiwan's sixth national park. This doesn't mean that the population will be evacuated – housing construction is still permitted. The logic behind the national park scheme is to protect Kinmen's historic and cultural sites as well as the beaches and forests.

Orientation

Administratively, Kinmen is made up of Kinmen and Liehyu islands which are divided into five districts. All of these districts are primarily rural and can be further subdivided into towns or villages. There are 11 tiny islets in the surrounding waters which are under the control of the ROC military – Liehyu Island is the only one open to tourism. The largest population centre by far is Kincheng on the west side of Kinmen Island. Shanwai in the east of the island is the only other town of significant size.

Information

The Bank of Taiwan in Shanwai is the only place in Kinmen where you can change US dollars (cash and travellers cheques). The Bank of Taiwan in Kincheng does *not* offer this service, though there is an ATM there.

Things to Buy

Tourism is now Kinmen's bread and butter, but the island has several other industries of significance. In particular, Kinmen is notable for the production of Kaoliang, Taiwan's strongest liquor. Sorghum, from which Kaoliang is distilled, can be seen growing around the island. Of course you can buy Kaoliang in Taiwan too, but only in Kinmen will you find it in such a wide selection of fancy bottles. The production of fancy containers – originally for bottling Kaoliang – gave birth to a small but specialised ceramics industry. Kinmen produces Taiwan's finest

ceramics, some of which are on display in various museums around Taiwan.

Hard candy *(gòng táng)* is another Kinmen product and is popular with Taiwanese tourists. There are many varieties although not all of them are hard. The ingredients typically include peanuts, sweet potatoes and coconut. This is premium stuff, so if you've got a sweet tooth check out the local shops and stock up. It is not easy to find such good quality sweets in Taiwan.

The 20 years of artillery bombardments was a boon to Kinmen's scrap metal collectors. Local entrepreneurs took advantage of the opportunity to gather up all the metal shells which they melted down and forged into meat cleavers. For many years, meat cleavers were a major export of Kinmen. Unfortunately, the cessation of artillery duels has left Kinmen's knife manufacturers with a shortage of materials, so the meat cleavers are no longer exported, though they do remain a popular item at the many souvenir shops around the islands.

The market here sells most things, but there are also speciality shops for souvenirs and military clothing/equipment.

The Book & Newspaper Store of Quemoy *(jīnmén shūbào fúwù shè)* on Chunghsing Rd in Kincheng and the Ta Tung Book Company *(dàtǒng shūdiàn)* at 132 Fuhsing Rd in Shanwai sell English-language newspapers.

Getting There & Away

Kinmen is a military area and as such it's required that you bring your passport with you. Don't forget, otherwise you won't even be allowed to board your aircraft or ship. Taiwanese nationals must have their ID cards with them.

Air There are flights connecting Kinmen to Chiayi, Hsinchu, Kaohsiung, Taichung and Taipei. In Kincheng, discounted air tickets can be purchased at Yongxing Travel Service (☎ 24491; *yǒngxīng lǚxíngshè*) in the Lin Ge Hotel at 9 Minsheng Rd. In Shanwai, the same deals are available from the Huihuang Travel Service *(huīhuáng lǚxíngshè)* on Huanghai Rd.

Airlines offices in Kinmen are:

EVA Airways
(☎ 22207; *chángróng hángkōng*) Shangyi airport
Far Eastern Air Transport
(☎ 27331; *yuǎndōng hángkōng*) 15-6 Minsheng Rd, Kincheng
Formosa Airlines
(☎ 24605; *guóhuá hángkōng*) Shangyi airport
Great China Airlines
(☎ 22207; *dàhuá hángkōng*) Shangyi airport
TransAsia Airways
(☎ 080-066880; *fùxīng hángkōng*) 18 Minsheng Rd, Kincheng
U-Land Airlines
(☎ 22806; *ruìlián hángkōng*) Shangyi airport
Uni Air
(reservations ☎ 24481; airport ☎ 24501; *lìróng hángkōng*) Shangyi airport

Boat There are about five to six boats per month making the journey between Kinmen and Kaohsiung. The one way adult fare is NT$1350. For the latest boat information, you can call Kaohsiung (☎ (07) 521-6206) or Kinmen (☎ 29988).

Getting Around

To/From the Airport Bus No 3 runs between Kincheng and Shanwai, stopping at the airport en route. Since it only runs about once an hour, you may have a long wait.

Taxis lined up at the airport charge a flat rate of NT$200 to Kincheng or Shanwai.

Bus There are three bus stations on Kinmen; one each in Kincheng, Shanwai and Shamei. Public buses on most routes run about once an hour between 6 am and 5 pm, though a few routes have buses operating until 7 pm. It's a slow way to tour the island, the buses tend to be mostly used by off-duty soldiers. There is a published schedule available from the Kincheng bus station, though it's only written in Chinese. The island is divided into two zones – if you stay within your zone then the fare is NT$13 but if you cross into the next zone then it's NT$25.

Buses from Kincheng include Nos 2, 3, 5, 6, 7 10, 11 and 12. Buses from Shanwai include Nos 2, 3, 18, 19, 20, 21, 22, 23, 25 and 27. Buses from Shamei include Nos 5, 18, 31, 32 and 33.

There are two bus routes on Liehyu Island; a north and a south route, which run about once an hour between 6.10 am and 5.40 pm.

Car & Motorcycle Guancheng Car Rental (☎ 23390; fax 25532; *guānchéng zǔ chē*), 9 Mintsu Rd, Kincheng can put you in the driver's seat. This is also the place to book accommodation for the Royal Crown Hotel in Hsiahsing Village.

You can rent motorcycles at Laiwang Motorcycle Rental (☎ 25305; *láiwǎng jīchē háng*), 92 Mintsu Rd, Kincheng. A 50cc bike costs NT$300 per day and a 125cc costs NT$400.

Taxi Kinmen taxis have meters and in most cases the drivers will use them. They may be less willing to use the meter if they have been lined up at a taxi stand waiting for passengers – in that case, they may insist on a flat fare which will certainly be higher than the metered fare.

Flagfall is NT$70; the fare from Kincheng to Shanwai (10km) will be about NT$220.

There is a taxi stand on Fuhsing Rd in Shanwai. If you want to book a taxi for a personal tour, drivers will usually ask for NT$400 per hour.

Ferry Sailing Times	
From Kinmen	*From Liehyu Island*
April to September	
7.30 am	6.50 am
8.50 am	8.10 am
10.10 am	9.30 am
11.30 am	10.50 am
1.40 pm	1 pm
3 pm	2.20 pm
4.20 pm	3.40 pm
5.40 pm	5 pm
October to March	
8.10 am	7.30 am
9.30 am	8.50 am
11 am	10.20 am
1.40 pm	1 pm
3.20 pm	2.40 pm
5 pm	4.20 pm

Boat There is a ferry between Shuitou pier (shuǐtóu mǎtóu) on Kinmen and Chiukung pier (jiǔgong mǎtóu) on Liehyu. Please keep in mind that the ferry schedule is susceptible to change, so check times and fares with the operator beforehand just to be sure. The one way boat trip takes about 15 minutes.

KINCHENG DISTRICT

(jīnchéng zhèn) 金城鎮

The Kincheng district is in the south-western part of Kinmen Island and surrounds the largest town here, which is also called Kincheng (jīnchéng). When first arriving in Kinmen, you should probably head straight to Kincheng as it has plenty of places to stay and to arrange vehicle rentals for touring the rest of the island.

Kincheng

(jīnchéng) 金城

The town of Kincheng actually has a few interesting sights of its own. A good place to start your exploration is **Mofan St** (mófàn jiē) known for its 32 town houses with arch-shaped fronts. These were built around 1925, based on an architectural style copied from the Japanese.

In 1812 **Chiu Liangkung's Mother Memorial Arch** (qiū liánggōng mǔ jiéxiào fāng) was built to commemorate – you guessed it – the mother of Chiu Liangkung. Chiu was a governor-general of Zhejiang province in mainland China, but he also lived in Kinmen. You'll find the arch on Chukuang Rd, Section 1, in central Kincheng.

The **Kuei Pavilion** (kuí gé), on Chupu S Rd in central Kincheng, is also known as the Kueihsing Tower (kuíxīng lóu). This two storey hexagonal shaped building was constructed in 1836. Scholars once came here to pray for success in passing their civil service exams.

The **Wu River School** (wú jiāng shūyuàn) on Chupu N Rd dates back to 1780. In the backyard is the **Chutzu Shrine** (zhūzi cí) which was built to honour a scholar of the Song dynasty, Chu Hsi (zhū xī).

Places to Stay The majority of Kinmen's hotels are in Kincheng, though there are several in Shanwai and there are a few holiday resorts through the rural parts of the island.

The *Nongyou Zhijia Hostel* (☎ 21301; Nóngyǒu Zhījiā), 6 Minsheng Rd, is one of the cheapest places to stay at NT$500 for a double.

On the north side of town is the *Kinmen Youth Activity Centre* (☎ 25722; fax 28606; jīnmén qīngnián huódòng zhōngxīn). Doubles cost from NT$800 to NT$2000 and twins cost from NT$1000 to NT$2500. There are no dormitories. An advantage of staying here is its quiet location.

By contrast, the *Kinmen Hotel* (☎ 21567; jīnmén lǚguǎn), 172 Mintsu Rd, is in a bustling commercial district. Singles/doubles/twins/triples cost NT$800/1000/1200/1350 per room.

The *Six Brother Hotel* (☎ 24311; liùguì fàndiàn), 164 Chukuang Rd, is a small friendly place on a quiet side street. Single/double rooms cost NT$1000/1200.

Just around the corner from the Six Brother, the *Jindi Hotel* (☎ 23366; jīndì dà fàndiàn) at 107 Minchuan Rd is on a moderately busy street. Double/twin rooms cost NT$1000/1300.

The *Shang Bin Hotel* (☎ 21528; shàngbīn fàndiàn), 33-37 Minchuan Rd, is similar to the Jindi with doubles for NT$1000.

The *Hongfu Hotel* (☎ 26768; hóngfú dà fàndiàn), 169-175 Mintsu Rd, is in a very busy area near the market. Doubles cost from NT$1000 to NT$1200 while twins range from NT$1300 to NT$1600.

The *Lin Ge Hotel* (☎ 24823; lín gé dà fàndiàn), 9 Minsheng Rd, is beside the Kincheng bus station. Twin/triple rooms cost NT$1200/1500.

The *Haijing Hotel* (☎ 24126; hǎijǐng dà fàndiàn), 67 Minchuan Rd, is another good option with doubles for NT$1200.

Moving upmarket, the *Ta Chen Hotel* (☎ 24851; dàchéng fàndiàn) at 16 Minsheng Rd has singles/twins for NT$1500/1800.

The *Haifu Grand Hotel* (☎ 22538; hǎifú dà fàndiàn), 85 Minchuan Rd, is in the same price range with twins for NT$1580.

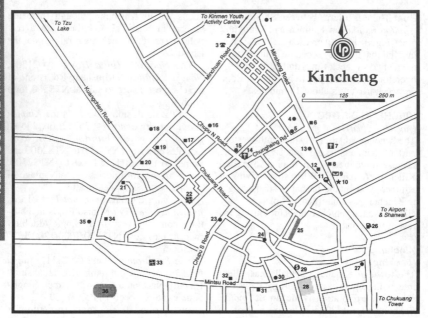

Kincheng

The *King Ring Hotel* (☎ 23777; *jīnruì dà fàndiàn*), 166 Minchuan Rd, is the largest hotel in Kinmen with 100 rooms. Twins here cost from NT$1200 to NT$1800.

Around Kincheng

About 500m into the countryside, to the south of Kincheng, one of the first tourist sites you'll stumble across is the three storey **Chukuang Tower** (*jǔguāng lóu*). It was built in 1952 as a memorial to the various soldiers who have fought in Kinmen's battles. On the 1st floor there is a multimedia show that introduces Kinmen. Bus Nos 3 and 6 stop here.

South-west of Kincheng is the **Koxinga Shrine** (*yánpíng jùnwáng cí*), which was built in 1969 and dedicated to Koxinga (*guóxìngyé*), otherwise known as Cheng Chengkung (*zhèng chénggōng*). Koxinga may be a hero to the Chinese, but Kinmenites (Kinmenese?) no doubt have less of a fondness for him – he stripped the island bare of

every tree to build ships for his navy. Much of the soil then washed away, leaving Kinmen a pretty barren place for the next 300 years until it was reafforested by the Kuomintang. Bus No 7 goes here. For more information about Koxinga, see 'Koxinga's Museum & Shrine' entry under Tainan in the South-West Taiwan chapter.

The **Mumahou Temple** to the south of Kincheng is believed to have originally been constructed during the Tang dynasty (618-907), commonly regarded by the Chinese as the most glorious period in their history. The current temple couldn't be nearly that old – it has presumably been rebuilt several times. The one storey temple is classical Taoist style and is an active place of worship.

Near the south-western corner of the island is the village of **Shuitou** (*shuǐtóu*), which is notable for its old Fujianese-style houses (though modern ones intrude too). Two of the big architectural attractions here are the **Huang Family Terrestrial Hall Villa**

KINCHENG 金城

PLACES TO STAY
2 King Ring Hotel
　金瑞大飯店
6 Ta Chen Hotel;
　TransAsia Airlines
　大成飯店、復興航空
8 Nongyou Zhijia
　Hostel
　農友之家
12 Lin Ge Hotel; Yongxing
　Travel Service
　麟閣大飯店、
　永興旅行社
17 Six Brother Hotel
　六桂飯店
19 Jindi Hotel
　金帝大飯店
20 Haifu Grand
　Hotel
　海福大飯店
21 Haijing Hotel
　海景大飯店
31 Hongfu Hotel
　宏福大飯店
32 Kinmen Hotel
　金門旅館
34 Shang Bin Hotel
　上賓飯店

OTHER
1 Kinmen County
　Government
　金門縣政府
3 Telephone Company
　電信局
4 EVA Air
　長榮航空
5 Book & Newspaper Store
　of Quemoy
　金門書報服務社
7 Catholic Church
　天主堂
9 Post Office
　郵局
10 Police Station
　警察局
11 Kincheng Bus
　Station
　金城車站
13 Far Eastern Air Transport
　遠東航空
14 Protestant Church
　中華基督教會
15 Wu River School;
　Chutzu Shrine
　浯江書院、朱子祠
16 Chungcheng Elementary
　School
　中正國小

18 Kinmen High School
　金門高中
22 Chenghuang Temple
　城隍廟
23 Kuei Pavilion (Kueihsing
　Tower)
　奎閣(魁星樓)
24 Chiu Liangkung's Mother
　Memorial Arch
　邱良功母節孝坊
25 Mofan St
　模範街
26 Petrol Station
　加油站
27 Guancheng Car Rental
　冠城租車
28 Market
　菜市場
29 Bank of Taiwan
　台灣銀行
30 Laiwang Motorcycle
　Rental
　來往機車行
33 Little Matsu Temple
　小媽祖宮
35 Kinmen Junior High
　School
　金門國小
36 Kinmen County Stadium
　金門縣立綜合運動場

(huáng shì yǒu táng biéyè) and the **Moon Grasping Tower** (déyuè lóu).

Wentai Pagoda (wéntái bǎotǎ) is a five storey granite tower with a hexagonal shape. It was built in 1387 on the orders of Chou Tehsing (zhōu déxīng), a Ming dynasty government official. On the south side of the pagoda is the **Hsuchianghsiao Ancient Inscription** (xūjiāngxiào wòjié) carved here during the Ming dynasty by General Yu Tayo (yú dàyóu). In recent times the original characters carved into the granite have been painted bright red to make them more visible. Bus No 6 goes to Wentai Pagoda.

A little to the south-east of the Wentai Pagoda is **Kukang Lake** (gǔgāng hú) and **Kukang Tower** (gǔgāng lóu). And just to the south of the lake is the **Hanyingyunken Ancient Inscription** (hànyǐngyún gēnjié). Bus No 6 travels from Kincheng to the lake.

KINHU DISTRICT
(jīnhú zhèn) 金湖鎮
This district is in the south-eastern corner of Kinmen and includes the town of Shanwai.

This district allows a good change of pace from all the militaristic sights and is home to the **Hsinhu Fishing Harbour** (xīnhú yúgǎng) on the southern coast.

Shanwai
(shānwài) 山外
There's not much to see in Shanwai itself, but the town does make a good base for exploring the surrounding area.

Places to Stay The Yingbin Hotel (☎ 32190; yíngbīn guǎn) is in a rural setting on the north side of town. Thanks to the dormitories, it's Kinmen's cheapest accommodation. They charge NT$240 per bed in a four bed dorm, while doubles/twins cost NT$900/1000.

On the eastern edge of town in a quiet setting is the *Taihu Hotel* (☎ 33399; *tàihú shānzhuāng*), 1-1 Fuhsing Rd. This is a very

attractive hotel which is reasonably priced with singles/doubles at NT$800/1200.

The *Daqing Hotel* (☎ 30461; *dàqìng lǚguǎn*), 20 Kuoshun St, is on a quiet, but ugly, alley. Singles/doubles are NT$1000/1200.

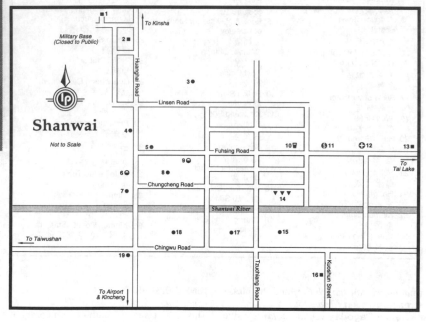

Another good option is the *Fuhua Hotel* (☎ 34333; *fúhuá dà fàndiàn*), a large place at 103-1 Huanghai Rd. Twins/triples/quads here cost NT$1500/1800/2100.

Places to Eat The *I like Pub* on Fuhsing Rd is unique for its western-style food. It's also the liveliest spot in Shanwai.

Around Shanwai

In 1962 the **Kinmen Pottery Factory** (*jīnmén táocí chǎng*) was established to produce fancy bottles for Kaoliang – the local firewater. The factory later branched out into other lines of work, producing vases and various other porcelain goods which are available for purchase.

Kinmen residents are lucky in one respect – their island is composed chiefly of granite, one of the hardest rocks around. Granite is not the stone of choice for producing fashionable jewellery, but it's geologically perfect if you're looking to build a solid bomb shelter. The **Granite Hospital** (*huāgāng yán yīyuàn*) is an underground medical facility carved out of – you guessed it – granite. Unfortunately, the hospital went into service in 1980, 22 years too late to have been of benefit to the victims of the 1958 artillery duel. Bus No 1 stops at the Granite Hospital.

To the west of Shanwai is **Chiu Liangkung's Tomb** (*qiū liánggōng mùyuán*). You can recognise it by the memorial arch which is not as fancy as the memorial arch for Chiu's mother in beautiful downtown Kincheng. Close to here is King Lu's Tomb (*lǔ wáng mù*), where bus No 1 stops.

The village of **Chiunglin** (*qiónglín*) has a number of interesting sights. Traditional Fujian style architecture is big here, a good example being the **Tsai Family Shrine** (*cài shì*). More representative of recent island history is the **Chiunglin Tunnel** (*qiónglín kēngdào*), a series of underground passages designed to be artillery-proof. This place is open to tours. The **Wind Lion God** (*fēng shī yé*) is a statue entrusted with protecting the village against evil winds.

The beautiful **Haiyin Temple** (*hǎiyìn sì*)

lies between the twin peaks of the summit of Taiwushan which, at 253m, is Kinmen's highest point. Taiwanese tourists make a big deal out of the adjoining **Stone Gate Pass** (*shí mén guān*), a stone inscription made by a Ming Dynasty military officer which says 'sea mountain No 1'.

Also close to the summit is the **Don't Forget Days in Chu Stone Inscription** (*wú wàng zài jǔ lèshí*), an inspiring slogan attributed to Chiang Kaishek.

On the south-western slopes of Taiwushan is **Chingtien Auditorium** (*qíngtiān tīng*), an underground venue for films, dance and other performances, staged to entertain Kinmen's weary soldiers. The auditorium seats 1000 people in artillery-proof comfort

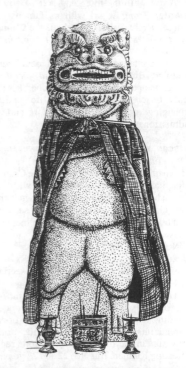

Kinmen villagers light incense in front of the wind lions, placed at the entrances and exits of their villages, to help ward off evil spirits.

and is open to the public. Ask around locally for forthcoming events.

Tai Lake *(tài hú)* is Kinmen's largest artificial reservoir, within walking distance of Shanwai. Bus No 20 stops at **Chungcheng Park** *(zhōngzhēng gōngyuán)*. Inside Chungcheng Park is the **August 23 Artillery War Museum** *(bā èr sān zhànshì jìniàn guǎn)* documenting the horrific events of 23 August 1958, when Communist China unleashed its artillery barrage against Kinmen.

The **Mr Yu Tawei Museum** *(yú dàwéi xiānshēng jìniàn guǎn)* is just opposite the August 23 Artillery War Museum. Yu Tawei was the ROC's first civilian Minister of Defence and this museum displays his belongings, photos and other memorabilia.

Adjacent to the foregoing is the **Banyan Garden** *(róng yuán)* with its famous old house, **Weilu** *(wèilú)*. Nearby is the **Chiang Kaishek Memorial Forest** *(zhōngzhēng jìniàn lín)*.

For a change of pace, you could visit **Hsibien Beach** *(xībiān hǎishuǐ yùchǎng)* which is open from May to October. It's the only beach in Kinmen with life guards, changing rooms, hot dog vendors and an admission charge.

Places to Stay The *Royal Crown Hotel* (☎ 34199; *guānchéng dà fàndiàn*) at 100 Hsiahsing Village is very close to the Granite Hospital. The hotel is associated with the Guancheng Car Rental agency in Kincheng (see Getting Around earlier in this section) and bookings can be made through them.

KINSHA DISTRICT
(jīnshā zhèn) 金沙镇
This district covers the north-eastern section of Kinmen.

The **Forestry Department** *(línwù suǒ)* is appropriately housed in a charming wooden building set among trees in a nice park. Local bureaucrats admittedly deserve the pride they take in the fine job they've done reaf-foresting Kinmen. Bus Nos 22 and 23 go past here.

The **Kinmen Folk Culture Village** *(jīn-mém mínsú wénhuà cūn)* is a collection of 18

traditional Chinese buildings. This superb village was first established in 1900 and was thoroughly renovated in 1979. Bus Nos 25 and 31 go here.

The **Li Residence** *(lǐ zhái)* in the village of Hsishanchien *(xīshānqián)* is a flashy wooden 18 room house, constructed between 1869 and 1873, which is open to the public.

Mashan Observatory *(mǎshān guàncè zhàn)* is a must-see for Taiwanese tourists. From here you can look across the water to mainland China just 2km away. There are some coin-fed high-powered binoculars here – on a clear day you can go eyeball-to-eyeball with a Communist Chinese water buffalo. Bus No 32 goes to the observatory.

Chen Chien Ancient Tomb *(chén jiàn gǔ mù)* is on a hill near Tungheng village. Chen Chien was an adviser to a Ming dynasty emperor. His father, Chen Chen, is honoured by the **Chen Chen Memorial Arch** *(chén zhēn ēnróng fáng)* nearby.

You can see saltwater evaporating ponds at the **Hsiyuan Salt Fields** *(xīyuán yánchǎng)*. Kinmen produces enough salt to supply local demand as well as a small quantity for export to mainland Taiwan.

Places to Stay The *Mantingfang Vacation Centre* (☎ 32190; *mǎntíngfāng dùjià zhōngxīn)*, 201 Yangchai Village *(yángzhái cūn)*, is a special place. The building was the former 831 Brothel. Although the rooms are small, they are said to be very comfortable.

KINNING DISTRICT
(jīnníng xiāng) 金寧鄉
This district, in the north-western part of Kinmen, is home to the **Kuningtou Battlefield** *(gǔníngtóu zhànchǎng)* which is part of the reason why Kinmen belongs to the ROC rather than the People's Republic of China. At 2 am, 25 October 1949, Communist troops invaded Kinmen. They landed on the beach on the northern shore of the island and walked straight into a column of ROC tanks. The ROC air force and navy joined in the battle, and the Communists were soon driven into the area now known as Kuningtou. After

25 hours of pounding by bombs and artillery, another battalion of mainland soldiers landed at Kuningtou to assist their beleaguered comrades. The battle lasted a total of 56 hours – by 10 am on 27 October 1949, the last surviving Communist troops had surrendered. For the ROC, it was a badly needed victory after a string of defeats on the mainland. However, victory in war seldom comes cheap – the combined death toll of ROC and Communist troops was over 15,000. The whole story is documented in the adjacent **Kuningtou War Museum** (*gǔníngtóu zhànshǐ guǎn*). Bus Nos 10, 11 and 26 go to the museum, which is 5.8km from Kincheng.

Nearby the **Peishan Old Western House** (*běishān gǔyáng lóu*) was the headquarters for the Communist troops during the 56 hour Kuningtou battle.

The **Li Kuangchien Temple** (*lǐ guāngqián jiāngjūn miào*) honours Mr Li, a hero who died in the Kuningtou battle.

The **Chenwei Residence** (*zhènwēi dì*) was built between 1789 and 1794 and served as the home of Li Kuanghsien (*lǐ guāngxiǎn*), a Ming dynasty marine officer. The largest stone lion head in Kinmen, designed to ward off evil, is in the backyard.

Tzu Lake (*cí hú*) is a saltwater lake which is a great place for birdwatchers. The lake is 6.3km from Kincheng, and bus Nos 9, 10 and 11 can take you there.

Chungshan Memorial Forest (*zhōngshān jìniàn lín*), Kinmen's largest forest reserve, is home to the Kinmen National Park headquarters. Also within the reserve is the **Chiang Chingkuo Memorial Hall** (*jiǎng jīngguó xiānshēng jìniàn guǎn*) which displays the story of the former ROC President Chiang Chinkuo (Chiang Kaishek's son). Bus No 1 covers the 4.7km from Kincheng to the Chiang Chingkuo Memorial Hall.

LIEHYU DISTRICT
(*lièyǔ xiāng*) 烈嶼鄉
Liehyu district occupies all of **Liehyu Island** (*lièyǔ*), also referred to as 'Little Kinmen' (*xiǎo jīnmén*).

The **Victory Gate** (*shènglì mén*) is a short walk from Chiukung Pier, the main access point to the island.

Almost in the centre of the island is the **Pata Memorial** (*bādá lóuzi*) honouring seven local soldiers who died here in 1933 during a battle against the Japanese. There is a petrol station here in case you need to fill up while you're on the island.

A potentially good viewing point for birdwatchers, **Lingshui Lake** (*líng shuǐ hú*) is the largest lake on Liehyu Island.

The **Chaste Maiden Temple** (*liè nǚ miào*) is based on a local legend probably invented by some not-so-chaste politicians. It is said that a young patriotic woman, Wang Yulan, fought against a group of Communist soldiers who were trying to rape her. They succeeded in killing her but did not rape her, instead choosing to dump her nude body into the sea. She floated to Little Kinmen where a soldier found her and buried her. The locals built a temple in her honour; Taiwanese tourists flock here for good fortune.

Liehyu Island is another one of those 'Koxinga Slept Here' attractions. **Koxinga's Well** (*guó xìng jǐng*) is where the great warrior took a drink, and has since become a favourite pilgrimage spot for Taiwanese tour groups.

The **Huchingtou War Museum** (*hújīngtóu zhànshǐ guǎn*) is as close as you can get to Xiamen without leaving the ROC. Telescopes have been set up here and you can see the tourists on Xiamen's Gulangyu Island staring back at you through their binoculars.

Places to Stay *Haiyang Hotel* (☎ 63338; *hǎiyáng lǚguǎn*) in Tunglin (*dōnglín*) village charges NT$1000/1500 for doubles/twins.

Matsu 馬祖

(*mǎzǔ*)
Like Kinmen, Matsu officially belongs to the Fujian Province in China and there is a heavy military presence here. Unlike Kinmen, Matsu is a genuinely remote and sleepy backwater where tourism has yet to make a

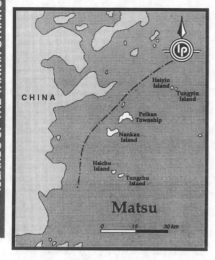

Village *(tángqí cūn)* is the island's booming metropolis. Peikan's economic curse is its mountains. True, the steep, rocky hillsides look pretty and are an advantage to the military (making it easier to hide weapons and ammunition). However, mountains make life difficult for farmers and they don't bring much joy to anyone trying to find a suitable site to build a house. As a result, Peikan is relatively undeveloped considering it's the second largest island in Matsu and the airport gateway to the archipelago.

At the eastern end of the island, **Tangwo Beach** *(tángwò hǎitān)* is close to the airport. Basically this is a flat and narrow sand spit, connecting two mountainous islands, creating an unusual looking beach. A surfaced road is built down the centre of the spit, but cars can only drive across during low tide *(tuì cháo)* as the area floods during high tide *(zhàng cháo)*.

Peikan's highest point, **Pishan** *(bìshān)* towers 298m above the island's hallowed shores. There are fantastic views from here and on a clear day you should be able to get a good view of China across the waters. A paved road leads to the summit, making it accessible by car though it's a really steep ascent. If you feel like some exercise, it can be an exhilarating walk up to the top. During winter, the winds on the summit are fierce.

Made up of 10 houses, **Chinpi Village** *(qínbì cūn)* is a preserved traditional village. The houses are all constructed from stone, which is rare in Taiwan. Chinpi is open to the public and only one house was inhabited at the time of writing.

You'll find the bright yellow **Matsu Temple** *(tiānhòu gōng)* at Panli Beach *(bǎnlǐ hǎitān)*, one of the flatter parts of the island.

In the centre of the island, **Chunghsing Park** *(zhōngxīng gōngyuán)* is notable for its Chiang Kaishek statue perched atop a white pedestal.

Places to Stay Accommodation possibilities in Peikan are limited to Tangchi Village. The *Piyuntien Hotel* (☎ 55461; *bìyúntiān lǚshè*) at 255 Chungcheng Rd seems to have the market sewn up. Four-bed dorms are

major impact on the local economy. Nonetheless, it is worth a visit – Matsu is laid-back and a great place to get an idea of the way Taiwan used to be.

There are 18 islands in the Matsu Archipelago, but even the largest of them – Peikan and Nankan – are only about 5km across at their widest points.

In terms of weather, the best time to visit Matsu is from April to October. Winter on these exposed islands is much colder and windier than in Taiwan.

PEIKAN TOWNSHIP
(běigān xiāng) 北竿鄉
Peikan Township consists of three groups of islands, of which Peikan *(běigān)* is the largest and the only one open to visitors.

Peikan Island
(běigān) 北竿
Assuming that you fly to Matsu by aeroplane (not helicopter), Peikan is the first island you'll encounter as this is where the airport is. Despite the presence of the airport, Peikan is not Matsu's most important island (that honour goes to Nankan).

Close to Peikan's eastern shores, **Tangchi**

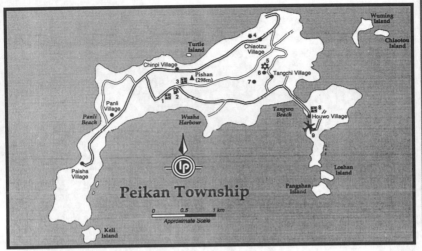

Peikan Township

PEIKAN TOWNSHIP 北竿鄉

1 Chaoyuanshui Temple
   趙元帥廟
2 Petrol Station
   加油站
3 Matsu Temple
   馬祖天后宮
4 Chukuangpao Forest
   莒光堡森林遊樂區
5 Yiyuan Vegetable Garden
   怡園
6 Yizhuqingtian Stone Pillar
   一柱擎天
7 Chunghsing Park
   中興公園
8 Yangkung Pashih Temple
   楊公八使廟
9 Peikan Airport
   北竿機場

NT$2000 and twin rooms cost NT$1300. In the very rare event that this place is full, ask around the islands for a homestay.

Things to Buy A lot of goods imported from mainland China seem to be available at the local shops in Peikan. That's curious, as there isn't supposed to be any direct trade between China and Taiwan (but then this isn't really 'Taiwan province', is it?).

Getting There & Away

The same rule applies for visiting Matsu as for Kinmen. That is, you must bring your passport with you in order to board the aircraft or boat.

Matsu's Peikan airport *(běigān jīchǎng)* is, of course, on the island of Peikan. Formosa and Taiwan airlines fly small propeller aircraft to Matsu, while Daily Air operates helicopters only. The contact information for the airlines is as follows:

Daily Air
   (déān hángkōng) Peikan airport
Formosa Airlines
   (☎ 56561; *guóhuá hángkōng*) Peikan airport
Taiwan Airlines
   (☎ 56576; *táiwān hángkōng*) Peikan airport

NANKAN TOWNSHIP

(nángān xiāng) 南竿鄉
This township is the heart of the Matsu Archipelago, and is the most populated of the

ISLANDS OF THE TAIWAN STRAITS

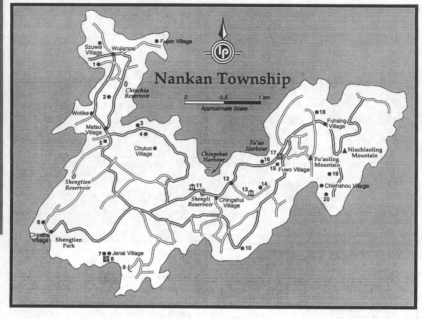

NANKAN TOWNSHIP
南竿鄉

1 Shuichan Research
   Centre
   水產試驗所
2 Chiuchia Arch
   秋佳樓
3 Four Big Diamonds
   四大金剛
4 Tienma Military Base
   天馬基地
5 Lianjiang Hotel
   連江山莊
6 Chinsha Scenic Area
   津沙風景區

7 Giant Banyan Tree
   神榕
8 Matsu Temple
   天后宮
9 Peihaikeng Tunnel
   北海坑道
10 10 Heroes Memorial
   十烈士紀念館
11 Matsu History
   Museum
   馬祖歷史文物館
12 Sanyungshih Statue
   三勇士像
13 Wenchien Museum
   文建館

14 Fushan Illuminated Wall
   福山照壁
   （枕戈待旦）
15 Fisher's Hostel
   漁民招待所
16 Yonghuailing Pavilion
   永懷領袖亭
17 Huakuang Tati Temple
   華光大帝廟
18 Matsu Distillery
   馬祖酒廠
19 Shanlong Sunshine
   Viewing Point
   山隴映日
20 County Government Office
   連江縣政府

islands. All of the main government offices are here.

Nankan Island is sometimes erroneously referred to as 'Matsu Island' because it's the largest island in the archipelago. Of course, with an area of only 10.4 sq km, that isn't saying much. It's definitely the best place to find accommodation and restaurants and to catch boats to the other islands.

Chiehshou Village (*jièshòu cūn*) at the

Kinman's architecture follows ancient styles (bottom right) and the people living here still use wind gods (bottom left) to protect their homes. However the picture postcard beaches (top) scarred with iron staves, used to slow down amphibious landing vehicles, are constant reminders of mainland China's presence a few kilometres to the west.

West-Central Taiwan is a real treat for hikers with beautiful and serene landscapes broken up by the occasional Chinese-style building or temple. Many of the trails have the added appeal of being linked by suspension bridges and/or cablecars and many pass through some otherwise remote landscapes and villages.

eastern end of the island is the main centre of commerce. There is also some activity at nearby Fuwo Village, adjacent to Fu'ao Harbour *(fú ào gǎng)* which is Nankan's main port.

In Fuwo Village there is the **Huakuang Tati Temple** *(huáguāng dàdì miào)*, built by Matsu residents 300 years ago, after they fled from mainland Chinese pirates.

The **Wenchien Museum** *(wénjiàn guǎn)* is a five storey building in the centre of the island. The 1st floor introduces the local marine life while upstairs you'll find more about the area's history and culture.

The **Fushan Illuminated Wall** *(fúshān zhàobì)* is instantly recognisable by the enormous sign of red Chinese characters on a white background. The four characters say 'sleep with one's sword ready' *(zhěn gē dài dàn)*. The sign is clearly visible from several kilometres away, and was designed to warn compatriots in mainland China that Chiang Kaishek's troops would soon be invading and reunifying China by force. The mainlanders are still waiting.

The **Chiehshou Park** *(jièshòu gōngyuán)* is dominated by the Shengli Reservoir which supplies water for local consumption. In the park is also the Matsu History Museum *(mǎzǔ lìshǐ wénwù guǎn)*, the Victory Hostel *(shènglì shān zhuāng)*, Chiang Chingkuo Memorial *(jīngguó jìniàn guǎn)* and the Victory Library *(shènglì shūzāi)*.

The **Four Big Diamonds** *(sì dà jīn gāng)* is not in fact a diamond mine, but is an 'impenetrable fortress' with big artillery cannons hidden in underground bunkers. The fortress, opposite the Tienma Military Base, was given its name on the basis that it is 'as hard as diamonds'.

The **Matsu Temple** *(mǎzǔ tiānhòu gōng)* is in Jenai Village *(rénài cūn)* overlooking the sea. It's the most lively temple in these islands and the most interesting time to visit is during Matsu's birthday (23rd day of the 3rd moon).

The **Shuichan Research Centre** *(shuǐchǎn shìyàn suǒ)* is meant to research the fishing business. It's open to the public, though there isn't a whole lot to see there.

Adjacent to Matsu's most beautiful beach, **Shengtien Park** *(shèngtiān gōngyuán)* has a pretty pavilion built in Tang dynasty style.

The **Chinsha Scenic Area** *(jīnshā fēngjǐng qū)* encompasses Chinsha (gold sand) Village, Chinsha Park and Chinsha Reservoir. Today no one actually lives in Chinsha Village, but the beautiful old traditional houses have been preserved and are open to the public.

Peihaikeng Tunnel *(běihǎi kēng dào)*, near Jenai Village, is dug deep into the bowels of the island and was constructed as an ammunition depot. You have to ask the local guards for permission to enter – don't just wander in.

The **10 Heroes Memorial** *(shílièshì jìniàn bēi)*, in the south of the island, was built to commemorate 10 people from Matsu who died in the 1911 Chinese revolution which overthrew the Qing dynasty and established the ROC. Perhaps of more historical interest is that the building next door which was Matsu's largest 'entertainment' facility, the Meishi Military Brothel *(méishí jūnzhōng lèyuán)*. It's now closed so you'll have to make your own entertainment!

The **Matsu Distillery** *(mǎzǔ jiǔchǎng)* in Fuhsing Village *(fùxīng cūn)* is famous, at least among Taiwanese drinkers. Guides will give you a tour and good explanations (in Chinese), and the visit ends with a few swigs of the potent Kaoliang. The distillery is open Monday to Friday from 9 am to 5 pm.

Places to Stay On the western side of the island is Jenai Village and the *Lianjiang Hostel* (☎ 22431; *liánjiāng shān zhuāng*). Singles/doubles here cost NT$350/1500.

The *Fisher's Hostel* (☎ 22296; *yúmín zhāodàisuǒ*) is in the Yuhui Building in Fuwo Village. Rooms cost from NT$500 to NT$1000.

Getting There & Away The 7km journey by boat between Nankan and Peikan takes either 10 or 40 minutes depending on which vessel you take. The fast boat *(xīn ài zhī chuán)* is privately owned. The military boat *(cí háng lún)* is the slow one. The Taima Boat

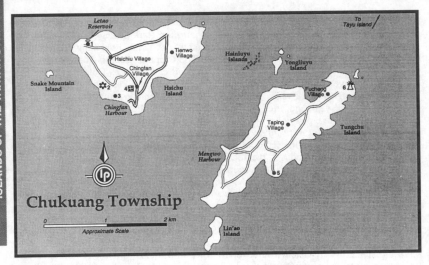

Chukuang Township

CHUKUANG TOWNSHIP 莒光鄉

1 Sea Viewing Platform
  觀海台
2 Fragrant Garden
  香圃
3 Chiang Kaishek Gate
  中正門
4 Chen Jiangjun Temple
  陳將軍廟
5 Tapu Stone Engraving
  大埔石刻
6 Tungchu Lighthouse
  東莒燈塔

Company operates services on the Taiwan-Matsu route. They have booking offices in Keelung (☎ (02) 2422-8251/2429-2117/ 2422-8267) and Nankan (☎ 22395). You need to make reservations two days prior to departure. Tickets cost from NT$600 for a bed in a large dormitory to NT$700 for a bed in a six person room. There are departures about once every two days, but the schedule is often disrupted so you must call ahead to confirm timings. Tickets can be purchased at the pier (pier 2 in Keelung) at 8 pm then you must board the boat before 10 pm.

CHUKUANG TOWNSHIP
(júguāng xiāng) 莒光鄉
This township consists of the two southern-most inhabited islands in the Matsu group, Tungchu and Hsichu.

Tungchu Island
(dōngjú) 東莒
This is the southernmost inhabited island in the Matsu Archipelago, and it's a pretty sleepy outpost. There are no places to stay, and the only food available is from the three *grocery stores* in the bustling community of Taping Village (dàpíng cūn). It's not a good

idea to camp here unless you want a run in with the military.

The main attraction is the **Tungchu Lighthouse** (dōngjú) which was built by the British during the opium wars of the mid-19th century. The lighthouse is still in use today.

The other main attraction is the **Tapu Stone Engraving** (dàpú shíkè), a carved memorial dedicated to a local hero who drove pirates away from the island about 400 years ago.

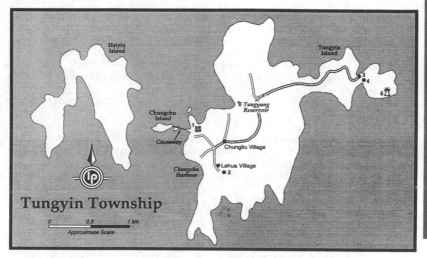

TUNGYIN TOWNSHIP 東引鄉

1 Kuanti Temple
   關帝廟
2 Tungyin Distillery
   東引酒廠
3 Martyred Righteous Woman's Hollow
   烈女義坑
4 Natural Chimney
   一線天
5 Tungyin Lighthouse
   東引燈塔

Hsichu Island

(xījú) 西莒

This island, just to the west of Tungchu, was once nicknamed 'Little Hong Kong' *(very* little) attributed to its supposedly bustling harbour. These days there's considerably less bustle, but it's still a much more lively place than Tungchu Island.

The main centre of business on Hsichu is Chingfan Village *(qīngfán cūn)*, which has some reasonably good *restaurants* but no accommodation.

The island's biggest tourist attraction is **Chen Jiangjun Temple** *(chén jiāngjūn miào)*, dedicated to a local hero. It's said that Mr Chen – who is deceased – occasionally reappears as a frog which explains the reason why it's prohibited to eat frogs around the temple.

Getting There & Away

There is a free military boat which provides daily services to both islands. It travels from Nankan to Tungchu islands, stops for two hours, then goes to Hsichu and stops for an indeterminate time before returning to Nankan. There is no schedule so you must inquire at the Nankan pier. It is also possible to charter a boat from the pier.

At the time of writing, Daily Air had announced that they would soon start a helicopter service to Tungchu and Hsichu from Peikan airport. There is no word yet on just how frequent these flights will be. The one way fare is expected to be around NT$2000.

TUNGYIN TOWNSHIP

(dōngyǐn xiāng) 東引鄉

This northernmost outpost of the Matsu archipelago is a remote place that sees few visitors. The largest island in the township is Tungyin *(dōngyǐn)* and to the west of that is

Hsiyin *(xīyǐn)*. Between the two is a barely habitable rock called Chungchu Island *(zhōngzhù dǎo)*. To enhance the local economy (and fortify the military bases against attack), the three islands are now linked together by a concrete causeway *(lián tí* or *zhōngzhù tí)*.

Tungyin Island
(dōngyǐn) 東引

Tungyin is a very windy island and therefore is almost totally devoid of trees. Grass is the main vegetation. The local population (soldiers excluded) is around 700, but military personnel far outnumber civilians.

Nan'ao *(nán ào)*, meaning 'southern inlet', is Tungyin's main population centre which can be further subdivided into Chungliu Village *(zhōngliǔ cūn)* and Lehua Village *(lèhuá cūn)*.

Tungyin is notable for its **distillery** and the infamous 'aged Kaoliang' *(chénnián gāoliáng)* and 'Tachi' *(dà qī)* are produced here. The booze is tasty thanks to Tungyin's mineral water, which is apparently the island's only natural resource (aside from stones and grass).

The **Martyred Righteous Woman's Hollow** *(liènü yìkēng)* is a cliff overlooking the sea, where a woman jumped to her death to avoid being raped by marauding pirates. Right next to this is the **Natural Chimney** *(yí xiàn tiān)*, a sea-worn gap in the stone cliffs.

The **Tungyin Lighthouse** *(dōngyǐn dēngtǎ)* was built in 1904 but has seen a bit of renovation work since then.

Places to Stay & Eat The *Fuhsing Building (fùxīng lóu)* is a military guesthouse and the main place to stay, but you'll need to get special permission which is seldom granted! Most likely, you'll have to settle for a homestay if you want to visit this isolated corner of the earth. Two places available are *Mr Chang's Homestay* (☎ 76158; *zhāng yǒnghén)* and Mr Ling's Homestay (☎ 77111; *líng rìshòu)*.

Seafood on the island is good, although it's expensive.

Getting There & Away There is a military boat going to Tungyin, but it only runs three or four times monthly. It's more likely that you'll visit if you take the boat between Nankan and mainland Taiwan because it stops overnight in Tungyin before returning to Keelung.

A new heliport has been built on Tungyin and Daily Air expects to begin service soon. A one way flight from Peikan airport should cost about NT$2000.

Wuchiu 烏坵

(wūqiū)

Between Kinmen and Matsu – and also just a stone's throw from the Chinese mainland – is a third island called Wuchiu. The island is so small and insignificant that the Communists didn't even bother shelling it. At the time of research there were only 123 civilians living on the island (the number of military personnel is classified). Wuchiu gained some recent notoriety when it was proposed as a possible nuclear waste dump site. If you can get permission to visit, there is a boat to the island every 10 days from Taichung port.

West-Central Taiwan 台灣中西部

If you have travelled down the east coast you would have already seen some of Taiwan's spectacular mountains, but the really big peaks are in this part of the country. It's here that you find Yushan, which at 3952m is the highest peak on the island. In just a few hours you can ascend by train or bus from coconut and banana groves to alpine forests.

This is where Taiwan's urban residents escape to when they have a holiday. The mountain resorts of Alishan, Tsaoling, Tungpu and Hsitou draw larger and larger crowds every year. In the foothills is Sun Moon Lake, a honeymoon resort which rivals Tienhsiang on the east coast.

The narrow coastal strip of west-central Taiwan is pancake-flat, agricultural land that is highly suited for rice-growing. This area is also rich in history and culture – it's here that you can see the enormous worship festivals at Peikang, and nearby Lukang is one of the most historical cities in Taiwan.

Chiayi County 嘉義縣

CHIAYI
(jiāyì) 嘉義

A small city in the centre of Taiwan, Chiayi is the departure point for numerous journeys into Taiwan's high mountains. If you need to get a mountain pass or extend your visa, there is a branch of the Foreign Affairs Police (☎ 223-6695) at 195 Chungshan Rd. Chiayi is also a good base for a side trip to the temple city of Peikang.

Temples

Although Chiayi's temples are not as large or as famous as the ones in Tainan, the city still has an impressive number of beautiful Buddhist and Taoist buildings.

Even if your time is limited make sure you include at least a few of the following places on your itinerary: the Chenghuang Temple

HIGHLIGHTS

- **Alishan** – walk, hike or ride a steam train through beautiful mountain scenery, or trek up Yushan, Taiwan's highest peak
- **Tungpu** – steamy hot springs and challenging hikes past waterfalls and breathtaking panoramic views
- **Hsitou** – stroll though thick fir and bamboo groves, hike up Fenghuangshan or visit Taiwan's prime tea-growing region
- **Central Cross-Island Highway** – a spectacular highway between Taroko Gorge and Taichung with stunning views of lush forests and towering mountain peaks

(chénghuáng miào), the Chennan Temple *(zhènnán gōng)*, the Hsiehan Temple *(xiéān gōng)*, the Tung'an Temple *(dōng'ān gōng)*, the Confucius Temple *(kǒng miào)*, the Titsangwang Temple *(dìcángwáng miào)*, the Wenling Matsu Temple *(wēnlíng māzǔ miào)*, the Yuanfu Temple *(yuánfú sì)*, the Yuhuang Temple *(yùhuáng gōng)*, the Wukuwang Temple *(wǔgǔ wáng miào)*.

See the Chiayi map for the exact locations of these temples.

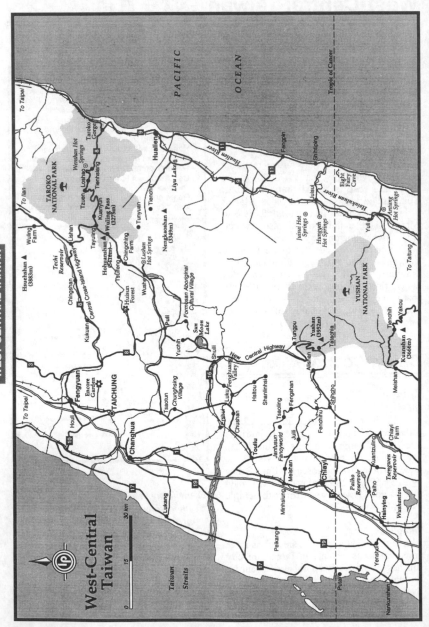

WEST-CENTRAL TAIWAN

West-Central Taiwan

Taiwan Straits

PACIFIC OCEAN

TAROKO NATIONAL PARK

YUSHAN NATIONAL PARK

Tropic of Cancer

To Taipei
To Ilan

Hsuehshan (3883m)
Wuling Farm
Techi Reservoir
Lishan
Chingshan
Kukuan
Central Cross-Island Highway
Taiyuluan
Hohuanshan (3416m)
Tsuen Loshag
Wenshan Hot Springs
Kuanyun
Wuling Pass (3275m)
Taroko Gorge
Tienhsiang
Hualien
Hualien River

Chioghing Farm
Nengkaoshan (3349m)
Tunyun
Tienchi
Liyu Lake

Huisun Forest
Wushe
Lushan Hot Springs
Formosan Aboriginal Cultural Village

Puli
Sun Moon Lake
Yuchih
Shuili

Juisui Hot Springs
Hungyeh Hot Springs
Hsiukuluan River
Juisui
Yuli
Antung Hot Springs

To Taipei
Houli
Fengyuan
Encore Garden
TAICHUNG
Tsaotun
Chunghsing Village

New Central Highway
Fenghuang Valley
Lukou
Hsitou
Shanlinhsi
Tsaoling
Fengshan
Tungpu
Yushan (3952m)
Tatachia
Alishan
Kuanshan (3666m)
Tenchih
Yakou
To Taitung
Meishan
YUSHAN NATIONAL PARK

Changhua
Tsun
Chushan
Touliu
Shihcho
Fenchihu

Lukang
Jantusan Fancyworld
Julli
Meishan
Chiayi
Paiho Reservoir
Paiho
Tsengwen Reservoir
Chiayi Farm
Quantzuling
Wushantou

Peikang
Minhsiung

Hsinying

Putai
Yenshui
Nankunshen

0   15   30 km

2-28 Peace Memorial Park

(èrèrbā hépíng jìniàn gōngyuán)
二二八和平紀念公園

This park was built to commemorate the horrific events of 28 February 1947, when Taiwan's governor Chen Yi ordered the massacre of thousands of dissidents. Chiayi is said to have suffered the highest number of casualties of any city in Taiwan, though no one will ever know what the real death toll was.

The park is in the eastern end of town on the south-east corner of Chiming and Taya Rds. The actual massacre took place in the area opposite the Chiayi train station.

Statue of Liberty

(zìyóu nüshēng) 自由女生

There are several Statues of Liberty scattered about Taiwan. The one in Chiayi stands above a roundabout about 500m south-west of the train station. Ms Liberty looks southwards, towards the Tropic of Cancer which lies several kilometres from central Chiayi. A monument marking the Tropic of Cancer can be seen on the way towards Shuishang airport.

Chungcheng University

(zhōngzhèng dàxué) 中正大學

This university is not in Chiayi, but is actually in Minhsiung *(mínxióng)*, a town 7km to the north. With its unusual campus architecture, varied flora and black swans bobbing on the lake, the campus has become a popular weekend photo-haunt for Chiayi residents. For foreigners, the main interest is the bookshop on the 2nd floor of the student activity centre which is open on weekends, and has a good stock of English-language titles. The library is also worth a visit for the same reason.

Swimming

The Wu Feng Swimming Pool *(wú fèng yóuyǒng chí)* is on the south-east corner of the intersection of Wu Feng N and Mintsu Rds.

Places to Stay

Yongxing Hotel (☎ 227-8246; *yǒngxīng dà*

lǚshè) at 710 Chungcheng Rd, with rooms for NT$400, is one of the cheapest places.

On the other side of the street at 687 Chungcheng Rd is the *Jiaxin Hotel* (☎ 222-2280; *jiā xīn dà fàndiàn*). This pleasant place has doubles for NT$500 to NT$1000.

Also a good option is the *Tongyi Hotel* (☎ 225-2685; *tǒng yī dàfàndiàn*) at 720 Chungcheng Rd, where double rooms cost from NT$550 to NT$650.

Just to the west, at 730 Chengchung Rd, is the *Jiaxing Hotel* (☎ 227-9344; *jiāxīng lǚguǎn*) – try not to confuse this with the similarly named Jiaxin Hotel. Doubles are NT$560.

A new and reasonably priced place at 621 Chungshan Rd is the *White House Hotel* (☎ 227-8046; *báigōng dà fàndiàn*). Doubles are NT$640.

Over near the International Commercial Bank of China at 283 Changjung St is *Jiazhou Hotel* (☎ 223-2077; *jiāzhōu dà fàndiàn*). It has reasonably priced doubles for NT$600.

The *Hotel Country* (☎ 223-6336; *guóyuán dà fàndiàn*), 678 Kuangtsai St, is an upmarket establishment with doubles from NT$900 to NT$1100, twins for NT$1200 and suites for NT$3100.

The *Wantai Hotel* (☎ 227-5031; *wàntài dà fàndiàn*), 46 Hsinjung Rd, is 1km south-east of the train station. It's a topnotch place with doubles/twins for NT$980/1530.

On the east side of the Far Eastern Department Store at 144-2 Chuiyang Rd is the *Jiamei Hotel* (☎ 285-3555; *jiāměi dà fàndiàn*). Doubles/twins are NT$800/1200.

To the west of the Far Eastern Department Store, at 860 Chuiyang Rd, is the *Jiabin Hotel* (☎ 229-0055; *jiābīn dà fàndiàn*). The hotel is actually on the 8th floor. Doubles/twins cost NT$1180/1520.

Places to Eat

As in most Taiwanese cities eating places are ubiquitous, but an area that deserves special mention is the *night market* on Wenhua Rd, near the Chungshan Rd roundabout. The area is active in the daytime too, but at night it really comes to life.

Chicken is the house specialty at the *21st*

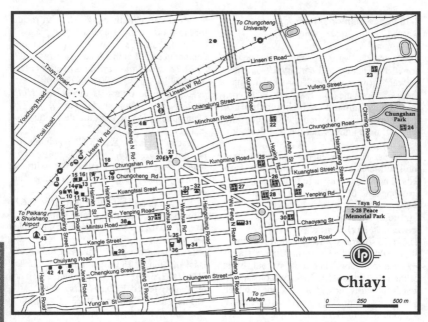

Century Restaurant (☎ 222-4282; *èrshíyī shìjì cāntīng*), 450 Chungshan Rd, which is part of the chain based in Tainan.

A good place for a snack is *Dreyer's Ice Cream* (☎ 227-5143; *zuìěrsī bīngqílín*) at 576 Jenai Rd. Aside from the ice cream, the menu includes noodle dishes.

Chungshan Rd is lined with restaurants on both sides, and various noodle and rice shops spill out into the side alleys. Chuiyang Rd is also notable for its restaurants, which includes among others a *Pizza Hut*.

Domino's Pizza (☎ 228-5511; *dáměilè bǐsà diàn*) will deliver to your hotel from its store at 495 Mintsu Rd.

Entertainment

Chiayi has many cinemas, the largest being the *Hollywood*. The line-up includes:

Chianienhua
   (☎ 225-0289; *jiā nián huá xìyuàn*) 615 Chung-shan Rd

Chiayi
   (☎ 222-2116; *jiāyì xìyuàn*) 5th floor, 155 Wen-hua Rd
Far Eastern
   (☎ 222-3312; *yuǎndōng xìyuàn*) 574 Chung-cheng Rd
Hollywood
   (☎ 229-1850; *hǎoláiwū chāojí diànyǐng yuàn*) 3rd floor, 601 Mintsu Rd
Hsinjung
   (☎ 223-7565; *xīnróng xìyuàn*) 52 Hsinjung Rd
Kuopao
   (☎ 228-6658; *guóbǎo xìyuàn*) 2nd floor, 20 Hsin-chung Market
Takuangming
   (☎ 222-2794; *dàguāngmíng xìyuàn*) 228-6 Kuo-hua Rd

The *Bird People Pub* on Kuohua St (near Chuiyang Rd) is the popular expat spot. You'll find good draft beer and Mexican food here.

Chiayi's leading MTV parlour is *Barcelona* (☎ 229-0163) on the 7th floor of 155 Wenhua Rd.

CHIAYI 嘉義

PLACES TO STAY
4 Jiazhou Hotel
  嘉洲大飯店
9 White House Hotel
  白宮大飯店
12 Hotel Country
  國園大飯店
13 Jiaxin Hotel
  嘉新大飯店
15 Jiaxing Hotel
  嘉興旅館
16 Tongyi; Yongxing Hotels
  統一大飯店
  永興大旅社
39 Wantai Hotel
  萬太大飯店
40 Jiamei Hotel
  嘉美大飯店
42 Jiabin Hotel
  嘉賓大飯店

PLACES TO EAT
10 McDonald's
  麥當勞
14 Dreyer's Ice Cream
  醉爾思冰淇淋
18 21st Century Restaurant
  二十一世紀餐廳
21 Night Market
  夜市
34 Pizza Hut
  必勝客

OTHER
1 Peimen Train Station
  北門車站
2 Cultural Centre
  文化中心
3 ICBC
  國際商業銀行
5 Tonglien Bus Company
  (Major Cities)
  統聯客運站
6 Taiwan Bus Company
  (Major Cities)
  台汽客運
7 Chiayi Train Station
  嘉義火車站
8 Chiayi County Bus
  Company (Alishan & Juili)
  嘉義縣公車站
11 Motorcycle Hire
  機車出租
17 Foreign Affairs Police
  警察局外事課
19 Chiayi Bus Company
  (Peikang & Putai)
  嘉義客運
20 Bank of Taiwan
  台灣銀行
22 Titsangwang Temple
  地藏王廟
23 Yuanfu Temple
  圓福寺
24 Confucius Temple;
  Martyrs' Shrine
  孔廟、忠烈祠

25 Tung'an Temple
  東安宮
26 Hsiehan Temple
  協安宮
27 Chenghuang Temple
  城隍廟
28 Chennan Temple
  鎮南宮
29 Yuhuang Temple
  玉皇宮
30 Wukuwang Temple
  五穀王廟
31 Wu Feng Swimming
  Pool
  吳鳳游泳池
32 Telephone Company
  電信局
33 GPO
  郵政總局
35 Petrol Station
  加油站
36 Bird People Pub
  鳥人酒吧
37 Wenling Matsu
  Temple
  溫陵媽祖廟
38 Jintsaishen Department
  Store
  金財神百貨
41 Far Eastern Department
  Store
  遠東百貨
43 Statue of Liberty
  自由女神

WEST-CENTRAL TAIWAN

Getting There & Away

Air There are flights connecting Chiayi to Hsinchu, Kinmen, Makung, Taipei and Taitung. The airline booking offices are:

China Airlines
  (☎ 223-0116; *zhōnghuá hángkōng*) room 3, 6th floor, 316 Chuiyang Rd
Far Eastern Air Transport
  (☎ 286-1956) 1 Shuishang Hsiangjung Tien Rd
Formosa Airlines
  (☎ 236-8895; *guóhuá hángkōng*) Chiayi airport
Great China Airlines
  (☎ 225-6406; *dàhuá hángkōng*) 257 Wenhua Rd
TransAsia Airways
  (☎ 080-066880; *fùxīng hángkōng*) 97 Minsheng N Rd

Bus Buses that run along the North-South Freeway pass through Chiayi, so there are frequent services to all the major points in the north and south.

In Chiayi, there are four bus stations near the train station. The station to your right as you face the train station belongs to the government-run Taiwan Bus Company (*táiqì kèyùn*), which serves major cities such as Taipei, Taichung, Tainan and Kaohsiung. Just next to this is the station of the Tonglien Bus Company (*tǒnglián kèyùn*), a privately run bus service that connects major west coast cities. The station to your left as you face the train station belongs to the Chiayi County Bus Company (☎ 224-3140; *jiāyì*

The 2-28 Incident

Japan annexed Taiwan in 1895 and ruled the island until the end of WWII. The Japanese brought considerable economic development and good social order, and crime was almost unknown. However, the tactics of the Japanese police and military were harsh, and the Taiwanese populace was genuinely fearful of them. At the close of WWII, Japanese troops were expelled from Taiwan and most Taiwanese were happy to see them go. Unfortunately, their joy was short lived.

Sovereignty was returned to China in August 1945. The new Kuomintang (KMT) governor of Taiwan, Chen Yi, proved to be far more corrupt and repressive than his Japanese predecessor. The Chinese police and soldiers brought in from the mainland were for the most part uneducated, crude and arbitrary. Even worse were the brutal criminal gangs from Shanghai, who soon took over the economy (and plague Taiwan even today). For the most part, the Taiwanese had little choice but to accept their fate silently, but resentment was building.

The spark that lit the fuse was a relatively minor event. The marketing of tobacco was a government monopoly, and as a direct result there was a good deal of smuggling of western cigarettes. On 28 February 1947, an elderly woman selling legal cigarettes (without a licence) as well as illegal smuggled ones was confronted by a policeman. She begged for mercy, but the policeman beat her with his gun, and she fell to the pavement and hit her head. An indignant crowd gathered. It's not clear who, but someone fired a shot into the crowd and somebody was killed. The '2-28 Incident', as it is now known, led to large-scale public protests the next day in front of the governor's palace. The police opened fire on the demonstrators, and news of the incident soon spread (at that time Taiwan had a thriving free press). Suddenly, there were protests erupting all over the island.

Governor Chen Yi panicked. For the next 10 days, he kept up the pretence of negotiations with the protesters while cabling Chiang Kaishek (in Nanjing, on the mainland) to send in reinforcements. The free press was silenced. On 10 March 1947, martial law was declared – it was to remain in effect for the next 40 years.

When the mainland troops arrived in Taiwan, they were ordered to immediately smash all possible resistance to the government's rule. The exact death toll is not known, but is estimated at somewhere between 18,000 and 28,000 persons. The killings took place over a period of several weeks. Especially targeted were known protesters, but this was soon expanded to include other potential 'troublemakers', including journalists, lawyers, doctors, teachers and students. Many of the victims were absolutely astounded to find themselves on the government's hit list. Although the 2-28 Incident began in Taipei, the biggest massacres were believed to have occurred in Keelung, Kaohsiung and Chiayi.

---

xiàn gōngchē zhàn), which serves mountain areas like Alishan and Juili. Don't confuse this with the Chiayi Bus Company (☎ 222-2308; *jiāyì kèyùn*) at 501 Chungshan Rd, which serves Peikang and other coastal areas of Chiayi County.

Train As it sits right on the north-south train line, Chiayi has express train services to Taipei and Kaohsiung about once every 30 minutes.

Getting Around

Bus Chiayi has a skeletal bus network – buses are tolerably frequent on big streets like Chungshan Rd but scarce elsewhere.

Car & Motorcycle One place offering car rentals is China Rent-A-Car (☎ 233-2996), 434 Jenai Rd, Section 2. You can also try Chuan Chia Fu (☎ 222-1755) at 600 Chuiyang Rd. Another option is International Auto Service (☎ 369-3651).

Renting a motorcycle is one of the real reasons to come to Chiayi. If you want to explore the backwaters, doing it by motorcycle makes sense, especially as the bus service continues to decline. There are three shops in a row with motorcycles for hire at 544, 546 and 548 Jenai Rd. The cost is NT$200 per day for a 50cc bike, but if you're heading into the mountains you'll need a 125cc model which costs about NT$350.

Taxi There are no meters and taxi drivers want a flat rate of NT$150 for any destination within the city limits. Fares beyond the city have to be negotiated.

A month after it happened, reports of the 2-28 Incident were reported in the *New York Times* and *Newsweek*, though for the most part the world knew little and cared less.

Some protesters appealed to the American consulate in Taipei for help, but even sympathetic consular officials were in no position to offer assistance, and the US government turned a blind eye to the incident. However, one official at the consulate, George H Kerr, witnessed many atrocities in person and later published his observations in 1965 as *Formosa Betrayed*.

For his role in the debacle, chief ogre Chen Yi was transferred to the mainland and promoted to Governor of Fujian Province. He was later executed on Chiang Kaishek's orders because, ironically, Chiang suspected him of colluding with the Communists. Chen Yi's replacement in Taiwan was the relatively benign Wei Daoming, China's former ambassador to Washington. Wei was soon replaced by General Chen Cheng, an intelligent man who instituted a popular land reform and helped pave the way for Taiwan's later economic boom.

After Chiang's troops lost control of the mainland and moved to Taiwan permanently, all stops were pulled out to cover up the 2-28 Incident. Taiwan's history books were carefully crafted to demonstrate that the mainlanders were great liberating heroes to the native Taiwanese. Anyone daring to publicly talk about the 2-28 Incident was prosecuted for sedition. Even the surviving relatives of those who were killed in the massacre were ostracised – banned from government jobs and frequently spied upon for signs of 'seditious behaviour'.

A whole generation of Taiwanese grew up knowing nothing about 2-28, beyond whatever rumours they might have heard. Indeed, the secret police did float rumours of their own – that the 2-28 protesters were Communists and criminals.

The truth of what really happened began to leak out in 1987, a few months before martial law was finally lifted. Dissidents attempted to publish the long-forbidden material in underground newsletters, but these were quickly banned; however, the death of Chiang Chingkuo (Chiang Kaishek's son) in 1988 ushered in a new era of openness. The lid was finally blown off by the 1989 release of the movie *A City of Sadness* by director Hou Hsiaohsien. Suddenly, everybody in Taiwan was talking about 2-28.

The Democratic Progressive Party (DPP) quickly seized on the issue. Indeed, many say they have shamelessly milked the 2-28 Incident for maximum political benefit. Some politicians still call for the public prosecution of the remaining soldiers who were involved. This seems highly unlikely, and in 1998 their favourite villain – General Peng Mengchi, the 'butcher of Kaohsiung' – died of natural causes.

In 1995, President Lee Tenghui made an official apology at the dedication of a 2-28 memorial in Taipei. In 1997, 50 years after the original 2-28 Incident, the KMT, DPP and National Party cooperated in a non-partisan effort to make 2-28 a national holiday. ∎

AROUND CHIAYI
Peikang
(běigǎng) 北港

Only about 30 minutes by bus from Chiayi, the town of Peikang is the home of the beautiful **Chaotien Temple** *(cháotiān gōng)*, the oldest and largest Matsu temple in Taiwan. With the possible exception of Nankunshen, Chaotien Temple is the most important temple in Taiwan: it has the most activities, which include parades and ceremonies, and the most money. If you find yourself in Chiayi with a few extra hours on your hands, a side trip to Peikang is definitely worth considering.

Almost any time you visit this temple there is likely to be something going on, but the best time to visit is on Sunday or holidays, when things are really jumping. The bus will be crowded on these days, but it's worth it.

If you want to witness a super-worship festival, which may have over 100,000 participants, then try to visit on the birthday of Matsu, the Goddess of the Sea, which falls on the 23rd day of the third moon in the lunar calendar. In the western solar (Gregorian) calendar, this would fall sometime between mid-April and mid-May.

Attending a super-worship festival poses some tactical problems, especially with regard to getting there and back again. Every bus, taxi, car, motorcycle, bicycle, skateboard and ox-cart will be heading into Peikang at the same time – definitely a case of 'people mountain people sea'. If you can't handle such crowds, postpone your visit to Peikang till some other time.

Another huge celebration also takes place in Peikang during the Lantern Festival, on the 15th day of the first moon, which is two weeks after the Lunar New Year – it's similar to the display at Yenshui (see the boxed text 'A Friendly Riot' in the South-West Taiwan chapter).

Places to Eat As you face the temple entrance, just to your right is a meat and fish market. It's very much in the traditional style and worth exploring even if you're not very hungry.

Getting There & Away Buses operated by the Chiayi Bus Company depart from the station on Chungshan Rd every 10 minutes. The bus stops at the temple dormitory in Hsinkang (xīngǎng) first (the dorm looks like a temple, so try not to get confused), then continues on to Peikang. The bus station in Peikang is several blocks from the temple. Just ask someone how to get to the Chaotien Temple and they'll point you in the right direction.

PUTAI
(bùdài) 布袋
On the coast, to the south-west of Chiayi, is the not-so-sleepy fishing village of Putai. The place really comes to life around lunchtime on summer weekends, when hoards of Taiwanese descend on the place in pursuit of fresh wiggling shrimps, crabs, lobsters and various other sea creatures that haven't quite given up the fight.

Putai is also one possible departure point by boat for the Penghu Islands (see the Islands of the Taiwan Straits chapter).

Getting to Putai is much the same as for Peikang – the Chiayi Bus Company serves this route. The bus journey takes just under one hour.

ALISHAN
(ālǐshān) 阿里山
Alishan is Taiwan's top-rated mountain resort and is well worth a visit. After the busy cities and the subtropical heat of the lowlands, it is literally a breath of fresh air.

At an elevation of 2190m, Alishan has impressive views in all directions. In the morning, you can look out over a 'sea of clouds' with jagged peaks sticking out like islands. In the afternoon, when the fog usually rolls in and envelops Alishan, the forest has an eerie, timeless beauty of its own. There are plenty of magnificent old cedar trees and pines, a sharp contrast to the palms and banana plants on the plains below. (Alishan attracts many tourists in the spring when the cherry trees are in full blossom.) Nearby is Yushan (yùshān), which at 3952m is Taiwan's highest mountain and one of the highest peaks in east Asia. Climbing Yushan is just one of the many interesting hikes in the Alishan area. A class A mountain permit is required to climb Yushan.

If you come to Alishan, come prepared for the cold. Even in summer, it's chilly at night. If you forget to bring a jacket, then you can hire one – several hotels rent out jackets for NT$100 a day. The jackets are usually fire-engine red, with the hotel's name in big letters on the back. The frequent afternoon thunderstorms, especially in the spring and summer, can also be a problem. If you get soaked you can freeze to death, so don't attempt any hiking in the area without proper waterproof clothing.

Finally, one thing which must be organised in advance is money; there is no bank here which means it is impossible to changes travellers cheques or foreign currency.

Given all its charms, it's no wonder that Alishan is popular. Unfortunately, it's a little too popular – definitely avoid the weekends and holidays if you can.

Alishan lies within the borders of Yushan National Park. Admission to the park costs NT$120, plus NT$40 for a car or NT$30 for a motorcycle. They charge half-price for people shorter than 145cm.

Information
Tourist Office There is a Traveller's Service Centre (☎ 267-9917; lǚkè fúwù zhōngxīn) just opposite the bus station. Staff changes are frequent – sometimes there is someone on duty who can speak English, but usually

not. There are no maps or brochures available, but the staff can give general advice about hotels, hikes and weather conditions. If you arrive on a busy day and all the hotels are full, talk to them – they might be able to help out.

Emergency There is a Public Health Clinic *(wèishēng suǒ)* on the west side of town close to the parking lot near the Catholic Hostel.

Day Hikes
The easiest hike is the **Alishan Loop Hike**, a 4km walk going in a loop past the Two Sisters Ponds, an elementary school, a few temples and a museum. It also passes the Sacred Tree, said to be 3000 years old. Although the tree is only 1.5km from Alishan village, there is a tourist train that goes there twice a day, taking five minutes each way to complete the journey. Departure times from the main train station are 7.45 am and 4.15 pm; the train returns at 7.55 am and 4.25 pm, so you get a whole five minutes to see the tree. The one way train fare is NT$10.

Another alternative is to stroll up to the summit of **Chushan** *(zhùshān)*, which is very peaceful and beautiful at any time other than the dawn rush hour (see the following Sunrise at Chushan section). You can also walk along the road leading to **Yushan**, but you cannot go further than the checkpoint without a mountain permit. The checkpoint is about a two hour hike from Alishan.

The hike to **Fengshan** *(fēngshān)*, a fantastic 10 hour or longer trek, is highly recommended. You can also walk to the resort area of **Shanlinhsi** *(shānlínxī)*. See the Hikes to Fengshan or Shanlinhsi section under Hikes Around Alishan later in this chapter for more information.

Sunrise at Chushan
The dawn trek to Chushan (Celebration Mountain) is religiously performed by virtually everybody who comes to Alishan. In fact, it's almost mandatory. Hotels will wake up all their guests around 3 to 4 am (depending on what time the sun rises) so that they can stumble out of bed and begin the one

hour pilgrimage up the mountain. It's cold at this hour, so dress accordingly and bring a torch if you have one. There are minibuses and a train for those who can't handle the hike.

If you're walking, you have the choice of two routes: the road or the stone steps. If you take the steps you will avoid the smoke-spewing minibuses with their blaring horns. When you reach the summit, you can enjoy a cheap breakfast from any of the numerous vendors with their pushcarts. Or you can have a more expensive breakfast in heated comfort at Sunrise House on the summit.

Minibuses depart from the main car park in Alishan and also from Alishan House. The buses are frequent and don't run according to any particular schedule, but they'll probably start at around 4 am during summer and a little later in winter (to coordinate with sunrise).

The train departs from the main train station and also makes a stop at Chaoping station. The departure time is about 45 minutes before sunrise – in summer figure that's 4.10 am. Inquire the day before to be sure about the time. The one way fare is NT$50 and the trip takes 30 minutes.

If you go on a weekend you'll really understand what the Chinese mean by the saying 'people mountain people sea'. By the time the sun makes its debut, there will be 5000 or more people vying for space on the summit. Just as the sun pops over the horizon, you'll hear the gentle roar of 5000 plus camera shutters all going off at the same time.

A mad stampede then begins as everyone races to be the first one back to the minibus. It's best to let them fight it out. The riot ends fairly quickly and in 45 minutes every last soul will have vacated the mountain, as if they had never been there. It's nice to linger on the summit for a while, to see the sun hanging over Yushan and to look down on the fog-filled valley below. You can then take a leisurely walk back down to Alishan.

Monkey Rock
(shíhóu) 眠月石猴
After the sunrise, many of those racing back

WEST-CENTRAL TAIWAN

WEST-CENTRAL TAIWAN

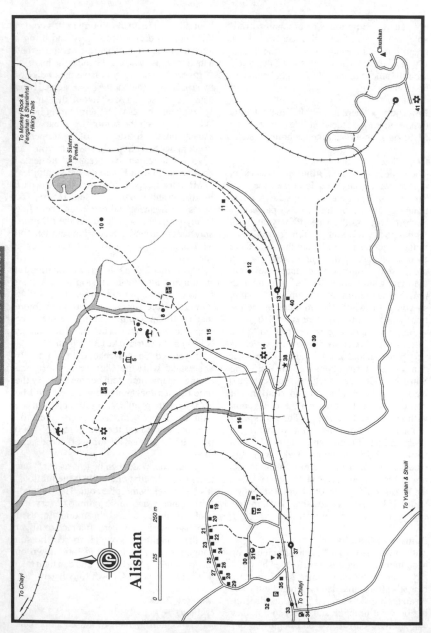

Alishan

ALISHAN 阿里山

PLACES TO STAY
11 Alishan Gou Hotel
   閣國民旅舍
15 Alishan House
   阿里山賓館
16 Forester's Dormitory
   宿舍區
17 Yingshan Hotel
   櫻山大飯店
19 Winsun House Hotel
   文山賓館
20 Kaofeng Hotel
   高峰飯店
21 Qingshan Hotel
   青山別館
22 Gau Shan Ching Hotel
   高山青賓館
23 Chenggong Hotel
   成功別館
24 Wanguo Hotel
   萬國別館
25 Dafeng Vacation Villa
   大峰渡假別墅
26 Dengshan Hotel
   登山別館
27 Wufeng Hotel
   吳鳳別館

28 Meiliya Villa
   美麗亞山莊
29 Shenmu Hotel
   神木賓館
35 Catholic Hostel
   天主堂
40 Alishan Train Hotel
   火車廂旅館

OTHER
1 Sacred Giant Tree
   神木
2 Botanical Garden
   高山植物園
3 Tzuyun Temple
   慈雲寺
4 Tree-Spirit Monument
   樹靈塔
5 Museum
   博物館
6 Junior High School
   香林國中
7 Three Generations Tree
   三代木
8 Elementary School
   香林國小
9 Shouchen Temple
   受鎮宮
10 Sika Deer Farm
   養鹿場

12 Chaoping Park
   沼平公園
13 Chaoping Train Station
   沼平火車站
14 Plum Tree Garden
   梅園
18 Post Office
   郵局
30 Traveller's Service Centre
   旅客服務中心
31 Bus Station
   客運站
32 Public Health Clinic
   村衛生所
33 Toll Gate
   大門收費亭
34 Petrol Station
   加油站
36 Restaurants; Tourist
   Shops
   商店區
37 Main Train Station
   阿里山火車站
38 Police Station
   派出所
39 Ranger's Office
   工作站
41 Flower Garden
   花園

WEST-CENTRAL TAIWAN

to Alishan want to get there in time for the morning train out to the Sacred Tree (which you can easily walk to), and after that, to Monkey Rock.

Monkey Rock itself is just a rock – it's the 9km train ride on a steam locomotive and the impressive views of the valleys below that interests the tourists. The price from either station is rather high for the short distance – NT$100 one way, NT$180 for the round trip.

You can also walk this route, but it's an 18km round trip and is somewhat dangerous. The major problem is the tunnels, which are totally black inside and dangerously narrow. Make sure you bring a torch and don't linger inside – getting hit by a train could ruin your whole day. Another danger is the railway bridges – you have to step from one sleeper to the next, and if your foot misses the target it could be a very rough landing.

Along the way you will pass a sign in English saying that you need a mountain pass. Most people ignore this. After the first bridge, but before the tunnel, you'll find a signposted trail on the right side of the tracks leading off to an aboriginal village.

At Monkey Rock train station, there is a trail that drops down steeply. This goes to Fengshan and Shanlinhsi, two resort areas covered in more detail later in this chapter. This is a fantastic hike and can be done in one (very long) day. Start early.

The trail is signposted clearly enough, but all in Chinese characters. You might want to do this with some Chinese hiking companions. During school holidays, if you catch the morning train to Monkey Rock with your gear, you will undoubtedly meet up with some student hikers heading out to Fengshan or Shanlinhsi.

Places to Stay

Your options include camping out, staying in a *tatami* closet (Japanese-style dormitory) or paying through the nose for luxury. Unfortunately, there is no official camping area, but if you roll out a sleeping bag in the forest where it's not conspicuous, no one is likely to hassle you. Remember that it often rains at night. On weekends when the hotels fill up, people occasionally sleep on the floor of the train station – you can probably get away with this if you do it late at night and get up early (about 4 am) when the station opens.

About 90% of Alishan's hotels are concentrated in one thick cluster north of the bus station. All these places charge practically the same price, usually from NT$1000 to NT$2000, but a few hotels do offer dorms.

The China Youth Corps (CYC) operated *Alishan Youth Activity Centre* (☎ 267-9874/ 267-9767; *ālǐshān qīngnián huódòng zhōng-xīn*). Unfortunately, it suffers from one fatal problem – it's in Erwanping, 6km down the hill in the direction of Chiayi. Unless you have your own transport, it is a very impractical place to stay, plus you'll have to buy another admission ticket each time you return to Alishan from the hostel. You can camp here, or stay in a room; twin rooms are NT$2400, rooms for four are NT$2500, and the eight-bed group rooms are NT$2950 (NT$369 per person).

The *Catholic Hostel* (☎ 267-9602; *tiān-zhǔ jiào táng*), at the lower end of the village just past the toll gate, has moved upmarket and at NT$1200 is no longer a bargain.

The *Kaofeng Hotel* (☎ 267-9739; *gāofēng dà fàndiàn*) is the most popular hotel with budget travellers. Tatami dormitories are NT$300 per person and come in closet size for

Wu Feng Lost His Head

The Wu Feng Temple *(wú fèng miào)*, 12km east of Chiayi, was built in honour of a man named Wu Feng. The circumstances surrounding his death have become one of the most controversial folk stories in Taiwan.

Wu Feng was born in 1699 and lived in the Chiayi area. His job was to act as the middle man in negotiations between the government and the aborigines. In the process he became a good friend of the aborigines and learnt to speak their language.

During the 18th century, the aborigines still engaged in head-hunting. Wu Feng was unable to dissuade them from continuing this grisly practice. One day, Wu Feng summoned the aborigines to his office and told them that the next morning, a man on horseback, wearing a red robe and hat, would pass by his office. He told the aborigines that they could decapitate this man, but that it would be the last head they would ever take.

The next morning a man in red robes did appear, just as he said. The aborigines duly ambushed him and quickly cut off his head, only to discover shortly afterwards that they had killed Wu Feng himself. Horrified at what they had done, the aborigines gave up the practice of head-hunting.

Until the 1990s, this story was required reading for all Taiwanese school children. But when martial law was lifted in 1987, the aborigines began to protest about what was being said about them. In the 1990s, the Ministry of Education quietly dropped the Wu Feng story from the history books.

Is the Wu Feng saga true, or was it simply a fabrication by the KMT to make the Chinese look like a civilising influence on the aborigines? This question has been the source of bitter argument for years, and there is really no way to know the truth about Wu Feng since he's not available for comment. While it is highly likely that there was somebody named Wu Feng, the legend of his heroic self-sacrifice seems rather far-fetched.

When Wu Feng was politically correct, hundreds of people in Chiayi with the surname Wu insisted that they were descendants of Wu Feng. Since the aboriginal protests, there has been a sharp decline in the number of people claiming the headless horseman as an ancestor. Nevertheless, Wu Feng has his supporters, and the temple dedicated in his honour still stands. The Wu Feng Temple is just next to the Alishan Fantasy World *(ālǐshān yóulè shìjiè)*. The fantasy world has nothing to do with the KMT's fantasies about Wu Feng – basically, it's a kiddie amusement park.

You can get to the temple and amusement park by taking a bus from the Chiayi County Bus Company station, which is in front of the train station; there's a bus about every 70 minutes. ∎

two people or in larger rooms for four people. You can also eat at the hotel for NT$150.

About 200m south-west of the Kaofeng Hotel is the *Shenmu Hotel* (☎ 267-9666; *shénmù bīnguǎn*). This place is very cagey about its prices. The lowest-priced tatami with shared bath can be had for NT$300, but it's like pulling teeth. The better rooms are the same as elsewhere in Alishan – from NT$1000 to NT$2000.

The *Meiliya Villa* (☎ 267-9745; *měilì yǎ shān zhuāng*) is intriguing in that its name means 'beautiful Asia', yet it's ugly design makes it the least beautiful hotel in town. However, the room rates are Alishan standard; NT$1000 to NT$2000.

The rest of the line-up is priced much the same. Options include the *Chenggong Hotel* (☎ 267-9735; *chénggōng biéguǎn*); *Dafeng Vacation Villa* (☎ 267-9769; *dàfēng dùjià biéshù*); *Dengshan Hotel* (☎ 267-9758; *dēngshān biéguǎn*); *Qingshan Hotel* (☎ 267-9733; *qīngshāng biéguǎn*); *Wanguo Hotel* (☎ 267-9777; *wànguó biéguǎn*); *Gau Shan Ching Hotel* (☎ 267-9716; *gāo shān qīng bīnguǎn*); *Winsun House Hotel* (☎ 267-9712; *wénshān bīnguǎn*); and the *Wufeng Hotel* (☎ 267-9730; *wúfēng biéguǎn*).

As you're facing the Alishan post office, off to the left you'll see a small road going uphill. Follow this and you'll come to the *Yingshan Hotel* (☎ 267-9803; *yīngshān dà fàndiàn*). It's one of the largest hotels in Alishan, though it's priced much the same as the others.

There are a few other pricey options in the 'upper end' of the village. These places are all far from the bus and train station area in the uphill direction which can mean an arduous trudge if you're carrying a heavy backpack. However, the top-end hotels do have minibuses to shuttle their guests – ring up the hotel to see if they'll come and pick you up. The least expensive hotel to fall in this category is the *Alishan Gou Hotel* (☎ 267-9611/267-9911; *gé guómín lǚshè*). Doubles/twins are NT$1200/1800, with the fanciest rooms rising to NT$3800.

To the south-west of the Chaoping train station is the *Alishan Train Hotel* (☎ 267-9621; *huǒchē xiāng lǚguǎn*). This one has the ultimate gimmick – it's a hotel built inside restored railway cars. Twins are NT$1800, and there are rooms for four people costing NT$2500. However, some travellers have complained that they find this place rather cramped and cold.

Also relatively isolated is *Alishan House* (☎ 267-9811; fax 267-9596; *ālǐshān bīnguǎn*). It's long been considered Alishan's top hotel, and is priced accordingly. Double/twin rooms cost NT$1700/2000 and suites are NT$3900.

If all of these are full (a possibility during holidays), consider staying in the so-called *Forester's Dormitory* (*lín wù jú yuángōng sùshè*). This is actually the housing area for Alishan's government workers, but they have some extra rooms which they'll rent out for around NT$1000, though this may be nothing more than a tatami attic. To inquire about the 'dormitory', ask at the Tourist Service Centre (*lǚkè fúwù zhōngxīn*) near the bus station.

Places to Eat

The general consensus of opinion is that Alishan has the worst food in Taiwan. Not only is it all expensive, but it's generally poor quality too.

Almost every restaurant is in the *plaza* near the bus station – all are expensive. In particular, be careful of the restaurants serving fire pot (*huǒguō*) – a stew where everything is thrown into a pot of boiling water sitting on a burner in the centre of the table. What they often do is throw a lot of things into the stew that you didn't order, and then charge you for them.

Most hotels have restaurants for their guests, but none are cheap. The cheapest way to eat in Alishan is to buy food from the two *grocery stores* on the east side of the plaza (near the post office). You can buy instant noodles and just add hot water. Most hotels have hot-water drinking fountains where the water is hot enough to make soup or really burn yourself. You'll also need chopsticks and a spoon – many hotels will give you free disposable chopsticks from the hotel restaurant. The grocery stores also sell bread, fruit and other goodies, all reasonably priced.

Besides the restaurants in the plaza, you will see the occasional roadside vendor selling food from pushcarts.

Things to Buy

There is plenty of the usual tourist junk for sale, but one thing worth buying is an Alishan bathrobe. (Actually, I've seen identical bathrobes in other mountain resorts in Taiwan, so maybe I should call it a 'mountain bathrobe'.) They are very warm, comfortable and durable – I've had one for years. A full-length bathrobe costs around NT$600.

Getting There & Away

Bus Buses connect Alishan with a number of cities all over the country.

Chiayi Although it's not as exciting as the train, the bus from Chiayi (79km to the south-west) is half the price. The trip to Alishan takes about 2½ hours (uphill), but it's much quicker going back downhill.

Theoretically, buses leave Chiayi at 6.30, 8 and 9 am, noon; 1 and 3 pm; buses depart Alishan for Chiayi at 8.30, 9.30 and 11.30 am, and at 1, 3 and 4 pm. However, these schedules will vary according to the season and to holidays. For information, call the Chiayi County Bus Company in Chiayi (☎ 224-3140) or Alishan (☎ 267-9922). At times you may find that there is nobody operating the ticket window in Alishan, in which case you purchase the ticket on board the bus.

Kaohsiung There is a daily bus from the East bus station in Kaohsiung. It departs Kaohsiung at 8 am and stops in Tainan along the way; on Saturday and holidays an additional bus departs at 9.30 am. From Alishan, the daily bus to Kaohsiung and Tainan leaves at 1.45 pm; an extra bus leaves on Sundays at 10.20 am. Travel time from Kaohsiung to Alishan is about five hours. You can call Kaohsiung for additional bus information (☎ 551-5796).

The Tax Lottery

Taiwan's Value Added Tax (VAT), otherwise known as a sales tax, affects the prices of many everyday consumer goods. The tax is already built into the retail price so you don't have to calculate it separately.

While no one likes paying taxes, Taiwan's VAT can work to your advantage as it allows you to participate in a 'tax lottery'. Everytime you buy something in Taiwan, you should receive a cash register receipt with a unique lottery number printed on it. Once a month the winning lottery numbers are announced in the newspapers – if the number on your receipt matches, the cash prize is yours.

The purpose of this system is to encourage customers to ask for a receipt, thus ensuring that shops have to ring purchases up on the cash register. This way, the government knows how much VAT to charge the store. As crazy as it sounds, this system of 'customer enforcement' actually works amazingly well. ■

Shuili There is one bus daily between Alishan and Shuili which travels the scenic mountain route via Tatachia *(tătăjiā)*. It's not terribly reliable, so don't stake your life on it. The bus departs Shuili at 9.10 am and Alishan at 2.30 pm; the journey takes three hours. You can call Shuili for additional bus information (☎ 770-041).

Taichung Buses depart Taichung daily at 8 am; with an additional bus departing at noon on Saturday and holidays. From Alishan buses depart each day at 1 pm, with an additional bus leaving at 9.30 am on Sunday. The trip takes about four hours and the buses stop in Changhua. You can call Taichung for bus information (☎ 220-3837).

Taipei An express bus departs from Taipei's West bus station at 8.30 am; on Saturday and holidays with an additional bus departing at 8.30 am. Going the other way, the bus leaves Alishan at 9 am; on Sunday an additional bus departs at 10 am. The one way journey takes at least six hours. You can call Taipei for bus information (☎ 2311-9893).

Train Long before the road was built, access to Alishan was by train only. This narrow-gauge railway was built by the Japanese during their occupation of Taiwan, and came into use around 1912. It was built mainly to exploit the timber resources of the mountains, not to develop Alishan into a resort.

Building the railway was certainly a major engineering feat. The train passes through 50 tunnels, crosses 80 bridges, and climbs from the subtropics to pine forests in just 72km. It's a very scenic train ride if you have clear weather, but many travellers have been disappointed as fog in Taiwan's mountains is so common. Your best option is to get the earliest train, as the mornings are usually clear.

If you arrive in Chiayi by train, you can get on the Alishan train and buy your ticket on board. You don't have to go into the station to buy a ticket, but doing so has an advantage – there is a better chance that you'll get a seat and not have to stand. Trains going up the mountain are more likely to be full – if that's the case, you may have better luck on the downhill run. A 15% discount is offered on round-trip tickets, though it would be far cheaper to buy a one way ticket on the bus and then a one way ticket on the train.

Despite high ticket prices and pretty heavy bookings, the train has been a consistent money loser for many years. When leaving the train station in Alishan you will be charged the NT$120 national park admission fee – there's no way to avoid this (see the Alishan Train Schedule boxed text for the schedule).

Taxi Drivers hang around the Chiayi train and bus station area and will approach any foreigner and yell, 'Alishan! Alishan!'. There is no reason to deal with them because the bus service is fine, unless you come in the evening after the last bus has departed. Expect to pay about NT$3000 for a taxi. They are only legally permitted to carry a maximum of four passengers per taxi, so the trip would cost NT$750 each between four.

HIKES AROUND ALISHAN
Yushan
(yùshān) 玉山

Yushan (Jade Mountain) is Taiwan's highest peak. At an elevation of 3952m, it's higher than Japan's Mt Fuji. Climbing it is certainly a beautiful trip, and the only thing keeping most travellers from doing so is that a class A mountain pass is needed. It takes three people to arrange a pass, and you must get it at the Foreign Affairs Police in Chiayi – you cannot organise it in Alishan.

Expect to carry a sleeping bag, food, wet-weather gear and lots of warm clothing.

The approach to Yushan is via Taiwan's New Central Highway *(xīn zhōng gōnglù)*, which runs between Alishan and Shuili. The highway's highest point is Tatachia (2610m). The bus service to Tatachia is unreliable, but theoretically there is one bus daily in each direction: departing from Shuili at 9.10 am and from Alishan at 2.30 pm. If you don't have your own wheels and the bus isn't running, your options are either to walk the 20km to Tatachia, or hitch.

At Tatachia, you'll find *Tungpu Lodge (dōngpǔ shān zhuāng)*, where you can spend the night. It tends to fill up quickly with climbing parties, so if you don't get there early to claim your bed you'll have to stake out a piece of real estate in the nearby forest. For information, call the Tatachia Visitor's Centre (☎ 702-200). Nearby is Lulin Lodge *(lùlín shān zhuāng)*, but this one is reserved for government officials and other VIPs. It's a good idea to bring supplies with you from Alishan or Chiaya as Tatachia is expensive.

The usual first-day goal is to reach the *Paiyun Hut (páiyún shān zhuāng)*, where

Alishan Train Schedule
Uphill

Chiayi	Chiaoliping	Fenchihu	Alishan
12.30 pm	2.06 pm	2.38 pm	3.53 pm
1.30 pm	3.14 pm	3.47 pm	5.03 pm

Downhill

Alishan	Fenchihu	Chiaoliping	Chiayi
12.15 pm	1.33 pm	2.05 pm	3.41 pm
1.20 pm	2.40 pm	3.13 pm	4.50 pm

WEST-CENTRAL TAIWAN

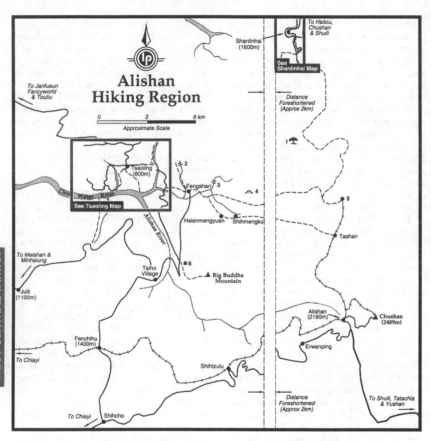

you can spend the night for NT$200. Again, don't be surprised if you have to spend the night in your tent, or sleeping in the open if you don't have one. Standard Chinese climbing procedure is to leave Paiyun Hut in the middle of the night to reach the peak in time for the sunrise. During the busy season (school holidays) you may have to line up to stand on the summit. After the requisite photo session, most climbers head straight back to Tatachia and manage to return to Taipei by the evening.

A highly recommended alternative route for the descent leads to Tungpu (*dōngpǔ*; see the Tungpu section under Nantou County, later in this chapter, for more details). You can also ascend this way, though it will be more work. If you want to come down by way of Tungpu, be sure to get your mountain pass endorsed for it and don't leave any luggage in Alishan as you won't be going back that way. While the Tungpu route is longer with a bigger elevation change, its far less crowded.

Hike to Fengshan or Shanlinhsi

There are two routes to Fengshan: one from Monkey Rock via Thousand People Cave

---

ALISHAN HIKING REGION
阿里山健行區

1 Giant Tree
　神木
2 Shihpan Valley Waterfall
　石盤谷瀑布
3 Tzuyueh Waterfall
　雌嶽瀑布
4 Thousand People Cave
　千人洞
5 Monkey Rock
　石猴
6 Taiho Mountain Hostel
　太和山莊

(qiān rén dòng) and one from Tashan via Shihmengku (shímènggǔ). The first route is more difficult, requiring 10 hours or more, while the second is easier (about six hours) but the trail is likely to be more crowded.

The hike to Shanlinhsi also passes by Monkey Rock. If you take the trail from the rock for about 1.5km you will come to a fork – the right branch leads to Shanlinhsi, the left to Fengshan. It takes about eight hours to walk from Monkey Rock to Shanlinhsi.

All three walks are good and are almost entirely downhill – Alishan is 2190m, Shanlinhsi is 1600m and Fengshan is 750m in elevation.

Monkey Rock Route You can start by either taking the train to the end of the line at Monkey Rock or walking. If you walk, start out early because it's at least a 10 hour walk from Monkey Rock to Fengshan, plus an additional two hours if you walk from Alishan.

Coming from Alishan, just off to the left of the tracks at Monkey Rock is a trail which drops steeply. If someone is around, ask them if this is the trail to Fengshan and Shanlinhsi since it's the same trail for the first few kilometres. You go down, down and down. When you reach the bottom, turn right and walk along the dirt road. You eventually come to a signposted junction in the trail. The right fork goes to Shanlinhsi and Hsitou (xītóu), the left fork goes to Fengshan. If you

take the left fork you will continue walking downhill, eventually coming to Thousand People Cave. This is a fabulous overhanging cave: it's so large that it can supposedly hold 1000 people, though they would have to be rather thin to fit in there. The cave is frequently used by hikers as shelter from the rain.

From Thousand People Cave, the trail makes another steep descent and eventually leads to the Tzuyueh Waterfall (cíyùe pùbù). When you reach the bottom of the falls, the path levels out and eventually becomes a dirt road. Follow the dirt road and after crossing the bridge over the river, you come to some farm houses and several hostels where you can spend the night.

The only bad thing about this hike is the possibility of getting lost. The trail is quite well marked in Chinese characters, but that isn't much use if you can't read them. If you hang around Monkey Rock in the morning, especially on the weekends, you'll probably meet some university students doing either the hike to Fengshan or Shanlinhsi. They will often be happy to have you join their group. However, you should be able to manage it yourself – just don't get off the main trail.

Tashan Route This is the more popular route, often crowded on weekends. Tashan (Pagoda Mountain) is along the train tracks on the way to Monkey Rock. Again, you can take the train or walk on the tracks. The trail descends steeply to the north-west from the tracks at Tashan station. The first major site you hit is Shihmengku (Stone Dream Valley), an area known for its interesting slick-rock formations. Further down the trail is Hsienmengyuan (xianmèngyuán, or Fairy Dream Garden). The trail meets up with the route from Monkey Rock just before Fengshan.

FENGSHAN
(fēngshān) 豐山
The scenery around Fengshan is superb and hiking is the main activity. In fact, you may have no other choice than to walk – there is currently no public bus service to Fengshan. The road is treacherous, but tour buses do

come up here on holidays and the quiet little village becomes a weekend carnival. The town is blissfully tranquil during the week and isn't too commercialised yet.

Hikes

Alishan Most people walk from Alishan to Fengshan (downhill) rather than the other way. See the previous Hikes Around Alishan section for details.

Around Fengshan About an hour north-east of town on the trail leading towards Alishan is Tzuyu Waterfall and about two hours south-east of town on another trail is Shihmengku (see Hikes to Fengshan or Shanlinhsi earlier in this chapter for more information). A one hour walk north-west of town will lead to the Shihpan Valley Waterfall *(shípángŭ pùbù)*, a series of six small waterfalls.

You can also easily hike 5km south to the Taiho Hostel and from there do several other walks (see the Taiho Hostel Area section later in this chapter).

Tsaoling The busy and bustling tourist resort of Tsaoling is perched on a neighbouring mountainside. The hike to this town is highly recommended, and indeed you may have no other option given the lack of bus services from Fengshan.

There are two routes. The less interesting way is to simply follow the road. This is the longer route, but it's safer and offers the option of hitching if a vehicle comes along. While traffic on this road is very light, it may increase when the road gets improved (it's presently in horrible condition). The road was only opened in 1995, just in time to be washed away in a typhoon in 1996. The repair job seems to be taking a very long time.

The more interesting alternative is to follow the Alishan River. As the river meanders through a canyon, you have to cross it about five times. However, this route is only feasible during the dry season from October to about March or April. It is very dangerous during the wet season, which begins around April and continues until September. The river becomes a raging torrent at times. Even during the dry season, the fast-moving water can sometimes be thigh deep if it has rained recently. A rope or bamboo pole can be useful. Never attempt it during or after a thunderstorm. The walk only takes about 2½ hours in good conditions, but longer if the water is deep.

Make sure you start out early in the morning – if the river is impassable you can always just return to Fengshan. The locals usually know the condition of the river and can advise you if the walk is feasible.

The first 2km of the hike involves walking down a footpath. When you reach a tea plantation, drop down to the riverbed. As in many farming areas, there are some unfriendly dogs around the tea plantation – carrying a stick is advisable. The stick will also come in handy for fording the river. If you're a dedicated dog hater, you can avoid them completely by walking in the riverbed and bypassing the plantation. Walking through the river is interesting, but is slower and more difficult.

Fenchihu or Juili If the route to Tsaoling is impassable due to flooding, you could walk from Fengshan to Fenchihu *(fēnqĭhú)*, which is about 30km uphill on a narrow but paved road (for more information see the Fenchihu section later in this chapter). From Fenchihu you can catch the Alishan to Chiayi train. Hitching is also possible but traffic is usually light.

In the village of Taiho, the road forks. The right fork leads to Juili. The route to Juili is even further than the direct Fengshan-Fenchihu walk. (For more information see the Juili section later in this chapter.)

Places to Stay & Eat

There are six hotels in Fengshan, and there is little to choose between them. The *Fengji Hotel* (☎ 266-1363; *fēngjí shān zhuāng*) is a friendly place. Ask about the tatami dorms for NT$300 – otherwise it's NT$800/1400 for doubles/twins with private bath. The food is great – they grow it themselves.

Just down the road is the *Fengye Hotel*

(☎ 266-1197; *fēngyè shān zhuāng*), which charges NT$1200 to NT$1600.

The largest place to stay is the *Fengbin Hotel* (☎ 266-1668; *fēngbīn shān zhuāng*). Dorms are NT$350, while luxury rooms can cost up to NT$2200.

Other places to stay include the *Mingyue Hotel* (☎ 266-1246; *míngyuè shān zhuāng*); the *Fengshun Hotel* (☎ 266-1161; *fēngshān shān zhuāng*); and the *Qingyuan Hotel* (☎ 266-1274; *qìngyuán shān zhuāng*).

There is a small *grocery store* in town where you can buy instant noodles and other packaged sustenance.

Getting There & Away

There is currently no public bus service to Fengshan. If you don't have your own vehicle, then walking, hitching, signing up for a tour or renting a motorcycle in Chiayi are your only options.

TAIHO HOSTEL AREA
(tàihé shān zhuāng) 太和山莊

The small Taiho Mountain Hostel (☎ 266-1222; *tàihé shān zhuāng*) is just 5km south of Fengshan, and can easily be reached on foot in less than two hours. Don't confuse the Taiho Mountain Hostel with the village of Taiho, which is several kilometres further up the road. There are some nice hikes near the hostel, in particular the climb up Big Buddha Mountain *(dàfóshān)*. Anyone can point you towards the peak, which takes about three hours to climb.

To stay at the hostel will cost you NT$150 for a tatami, NT$800 for a double room and NT$1200 for a twin. The hostel has food available but it sees few guests and seems to totter on the brink of bankruptcy, however it's been that way for years and still manages to keep going.

FENCHIHU
(fēnqǐhú) 奮起湖

Fenchihu is a small town between Alishan and Chiayi, in a scenic, heavily forested area 1400m above sea level. Although most tourists head directly to Alishan, Fenchihu does manage to attract some of the overflow crowds, especially on the weekends when Alishan's hotels book out solid. Nevertheless, Fenchihu has got a long way to go before it becomes an international resort.

There are some nice hikes in the area and Fenchihu is pleasant, cool, forested and refreshing. City-weary residents from Taipei like to come here to relax and it's certainly a good place for that. However, those looking for spectacular vistas and steep hiking challenges should head directly for Tsaoling or Tungpu.

Big Frozen Mountain
(dàdòng shān) 大凍山

Some people seem to like getting up at 4 am to climb a mountain and view the sunrise. If you're in Fenchihu on a weekend or holiday, you might as well get up with everyone else. The best view is from the summit of Big Frozen Mountain. The mountain peak is 1900m above sea level and is about a two hour walk one way from the hotel area. When there are lots of people, some hotels run a minibus halfway up the mountain so that you only have a one hour walk. On a clear morning you can see Chiayi.

Hikes

If you want an easy hike, you can visit to the **bamboo grove** *(cuì zhúpō)*, which is a short walk uphill from the train station area. Here you can see some very rare 'square bamboo'. Look closely – the stems are almost perfectly square. The train station itself keeps an old preserved steam locomotive in a shed next door which is worth taking a look at if you're a train buff.

Among the locals, the hike that's most popular is to **Heaven Sky Chasm Cave** *(tiānqiàn qíguān)*, which is to the west of Fenchihu. The hike takes about three hours for the round trip. The caves are small and they are definitely not suitable for those with claustrophobia. You've got to crawl through on your hands and knees and a torch is mandatory. But the walk leading down to the caves is pleasant, even if you decide not to crawl in.

WEST-CENTRAL TAIWAN

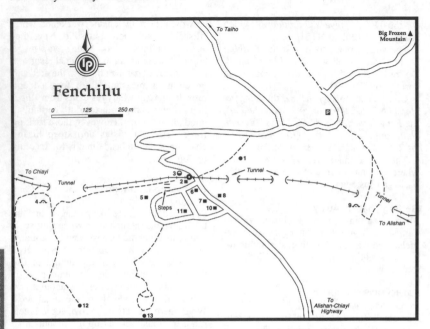

The hike I like best is to **Tomorrow Moon Cave** (*míng yuè kū*) – not a true cave, but an overhanging rock formation. The cave is steep in parts but can be very interesting to walk through.

Other nearby hiking destinations include the **Bamboo Forest** (*màzhú lín*) and **Tiger Spots Cliff** (*hǔbān qiàobì*).

Some hotels offer free, guided hiking tours of the area to all guests, but they require a group of at least 30 people. Most travellers are unlikely to be with 29 friends, but if you arrive on a weekend or holiday you can join any group of Chinese tourists.

Places to Stay

The *Catholic Hostel* (☎ 256-1035; *tiānzhǔ jiào táng*) is a very friendly place and is popular with many foreign visitors because there is usually someone around who can speak at least broken English. Dormitories with six beds cost NT$200 per person.

If you're looking for a double room, prices are lowest at the very friendly *Yahu Hotel* (☎ 256-1097; *yăhú shān zhuāng*). Doubles can be had for NT$500.

The *Jinri Hotel* (☎ 256-1233; *jīnrì shān zhuāng*) is right next to the train station and operates a good restaurant. Doubles/twins cost NT$800/1200.

The *Zhongshan Hotel* (☎ 256-1052; *zhōng-shān shān zhuāng*) is a clean-looking hotel with friendly management. Doubles/twins are NT$800/1400. The nearby *Liufu Hotel* (☎ 256-1776; *liùfú bīnguăn*) looks a bit shoddy on the outside but is OK inside. Doubles/twins are priced from NT$800/1200.

The newest hotel to rise above Fenchihu's skyline is the *Qunfeng Hotel* (☎ 256-1326; *qúnfēng shān zhuāng*). Doubles/twins are NT$1000/1200.

The most expensive place in town is the *Fancylake Hotel* (☎ 256-1888; *fènqĭhú dà fàndiàn*). Doubles are NT$1500, and twins cost NT$1800 to NT$4000.

Getting There & Away
Bus There are three buses daily between Fenchihu and Chiayi. The 55km trip takes at least one hour. Buses leave Chiayi at 7 and 10 am and at 3 pm. Buses depart Fenchihu for Chiayi at 9.15 am, 12.30 and 5.15 pm.

The Alishan to Chiayi bus does not pass through Fenchihu. If you're coming from Alishan by bus, you could get off at the rest stop at Shihcho (*shízhūo*) and then walk or hitch the 5km north to Fenchihu.

Train If you're coming by train from Alishan, it's convenient to stop off in Fenchihu. All trains make this stop, even the express. See the train schedule under Getting There & Away in the Alishan section for arrival and departure times.

JUILI
(ruìlĭ) 瑞里
Juili is a sleepy village consisting of just a few houses, an elementary school and some scattered hotels. Although the scenery isn't

quite as spectacular as that around Alishan, Juili is worth visiting as it has been barely touched by commercialism. There are pleasant hikes through bamboo forests, some nice waterfalls and a long, narrow cave to crawl through. Basically, it's a fine place for hiking and relaxing, so if you need a few days of pleasant, peaceful surroundings, come to Juili. It is also possible to hike from Juili to Taiho, Fengshan, Tsaoling or Fenchihu.

Hikes
Among the things to see around Juili are the **Cloud Pool Waterfall** *(yúntán pùbù)* and **Twin River Waterfall** *(shuāngxi pùbù)*.

The Chinese say that a journey of 1000 miles begins with a single step. There are 1600 stone steps between **Swallows Cliff** *(yànzĭyái)* and the Juili Elementary School, as you'll clearly remember if you decide to walk this route. The Swallows Cliff is an interesting overhanging rock formation – rather like a cave with one side missing.

Chinese hikers also like to visit the **Magic Cave** *(míhún gōng)*, a long narrow hole with no stalactites or other formations inside – it's not really worth the trouble. However, the walk through the bamboo forest to get there is very pleasant.

As in Alishan, crowds of people get up before dawn to hike up a mountain in order to view the sunrise. Juili's sunrise viewing spot is **Changshan**. From here it's possible to hike to Fenchihu.

You can hike from Juili to Taiho along a paved road, and from there on to Fengshan. It is also possible to hitch but traffic is very light (on weekdays) – mostly consisting of farmers on motorcycles. On weekends you won't be able to see the trees from the exhaust pipes. Hiking from Juili to Tsaoling is possible via Fengshan, but involves a dangerous river crossing (see the Fengshan section for details). It would take two days of heavy walking to reach Juili from Alishan.

Places to Stay
Ruolan Lodge (☎ 250-1210; fax 250-1555; *ruòlán shān zhuāng*) is a very friendly place with clean rooms and great food. Dorm

prices are NT$350 and twins are NT$1400 to NT$2000. There is a 20% discount on weekdays. The Ruolan Lodge is not right on the main road, but you can get off the bus from Chiaya at the Chingye Hotel and then walk about 20m down a footpath. The hotel is perched on the steep side of a mountain.

Another place to consider is the *Chingye Hotel* (☎ 250-1031; *qīngyè shān zhuāng*), which has dorm/doubles for NT$450/1200. It's fairly popular on weekends, as the blaring karaoke will make evident.

Right near the Juili Elementary School (*ruìlǐ guóxiǎo*) is the Meihua Hotel (☎ 250-1522; *méihuā shān zhuāng*), where double/twin rooms are NT$600/2200.

One of the newest hotels in the area is *Fenglin Hotel* (☎ 250-1095; *fēnglín shān zhuāng*). Doubles start at NT$1200.

The *Rey Lee Hotel* (☎ 250-1310; *ruìlǐ dà fàndiàn*) is a nine storey high rise. Without a doubt it's the largest, fanciest and most expensive hotel in town. It can be busy even on weekdays, and on weekends it's a real circus. Facilities include a disco, karaoke, coffee shop, conference room and 25 hectare car park. If you don't need all these niceties, the only real advantage it has over the competition is that it's much closer to the train station. Doubles cost NT$1800 to NT$3000, and twins cost from NT$2400 to NT$4000.

Juili

Getting There & Away
You can get to Juili by bus, train or taxi. If you take the train you'll have to do some walking to reach any of the hotels – but walking is what Juili is all about. The buses can drop you off right next to your hotel.

Bus The Chiayi County Bus Company runs a bus to Juili twice a day. The first leaves at 10.30 am, but this one only goes as far as the Rey Lee Hotel – if you want to stay elsewhere, you have to walk a few more kilometres. The second bus departs Chiayi at 3.45 pm – it terminates at the tiny outpost of Juifeng but you can get off at any hotel in Juili. Since Juili is spread out over the mountainsides, it's wise to tell the driver which hotel you want to get off at. If you're not sure

WEST-CENTRAL TAIWAN

JUILI 瑞里

1 Fenglin Hotel
  楓林山莊
2 Ancient Gravesite
  古厝
3 Chingye Hotel
  青葉山莊
4 Yuanhsing Temple
  源興宮

5 Juili Elementary School
  瑞里國小
6 Meihua Hotel
  梅花山莊
7 Ruolan Lodge
  若蘭山莊
8 Magic Cave
  迷魂宮
9 Swallows Cliff
  燕子崖

10 Twin River Waterfall
   雙溪瀑布
11 Taihsing Temple
   太興廟
12 Cloud Pool
   Waterfall
   雲潭瀑布
13 Rey Lee Hotel
   瑞里大飯店

where you want to stay, get off at the Juili Elementary School and walk from there.

When leaving Juili, the bus collects passengers from the hotels at 6.30 am. There is also an afternoon bus at 1 pm from the Rey Lee Hotel only. The bus journey takes two hours.

Train Juili is about halfway between Alishan and Chiayi and can be reached by taking the Alishan train. You can get off the train in the tiny town of Chiaoliping (*jiāolìpíng*). However, only one train a day (the local train) stops in Chiaoliping. The 1.30 pm train from Chiayi arrives in Chiaoliping at 3.04 pm. The 1.10 pm train from Alishan stops in Chiaoliping at 3.03 pm.

From Chiaoliping, get someone to point you in the right direction and walk on the paved trail that parallels the train tracks. The path quickly cuts off to the left and drops downhill into the forest. A five minute walk along the trail leads you to a road and after another 40 minutes of walking you come to the first hotel, the Rey Lee Hotel.

From this hotel, it takes over an hour to walk to the Juili Elementary School, which is in the centre of Juili. The fastest route is to take the trail that drops steeply down to the river and the Swallows Cliff, then uphill again. You have to climb 1600 stone steps if you take this route – exhausting but much shorter than the road.

Walking It is possible to walk from Juili to Taiho, a distance of 18km. Hitching also is a possibility but traffic on this road is very light. From Taiho you can reach Fengshan, Tsaoling or Fenchihu.

SHIHCHO

(*shízhūo*) 石卓

All buses travelling between Chiayi and Alishan make a 10 minute stop at Shihcho, the halfway point of the journey. As the bus approaches Shihcho from Chiayi, you will see many tea plantations. This is also the point where the weather starts getting noticeably cooler.

For most travellers, Shihcho is either a rest stop or sometimes a transit point if you're heading to Fenchihu or Alishan from Chiayi. There are also some interesting hikes in the area and aboriginal towns which can be reached on dirt roads by motorcycle, but few travellers bother.

Some people do spend the night, particularly those travelling by bicycle.

I rode my bicycle to Alishan from Chiayi. It's a good seven hour ride and I don't recommend it to anyone who's not in shape, but it's a spectacular trip. There is a small, barely travelled back road to Shihcho which is beautiful. Then the last 20km straight up to Alishan are on the main highway. The ride down was unforgettable!

Karl Krueger

Places to Stay

Linyuan Hotel (☎ 256-1523; *línyuán shān zhuāng*) is the largest hotel, with doubles/twins for NT$600/1200. Considerably more upmarket is the *Longyun Hotel* (☎ 256-1016; *lóngyún shān zhuāng*), which costs from NT$1800 to NT$2500.

Yunlin County 雲林縣

TOULIU

(*dǒuliù*) 斗六

Touliu is a small city north of Chiayi. Although the town itself is hardly a tourist attraction, it is an important transit point for travellers heading to Tsaoling, one of Taiwan's premier mountain resorts. There is also a branch of the Foreign Affairs Police (☎ 532-9033) here.

If you have an hour or two to spare in Touliu, there is an interesting temple called Shanhsiu Temple (*shàn xiū gōng*). Locals also call it the Confucius Temple (*kǒngzǐ miào*), though it's really not a true Confucian temple.

Places to Stay

Most of the hotels are either clustered around the main traffic circle or to the west near the train station.

The bottom of the market belongs to the

WEST-CENTRAL TAIWAN

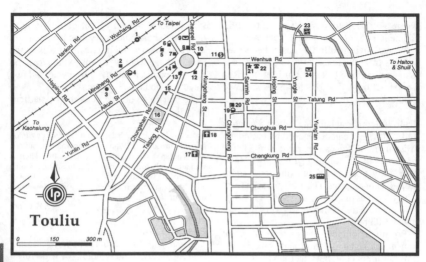

Touliu

TOULIU 斗六

PLACES TO STAY
2 Zhengang Hotel
   真岡大飯店
5 Huacheng Hotel
   華城大飯店
6 New City Business Hotel
   首都大飯店
7 Wendiser Hotel
   溫帶莎賓館
8 Guibin Hotel
   桂賓大旅社
10 Yuanhuan Hotel
   圓環大旅社
12 Taishin Hotel
   太信大飯店
13 Jincheng Hotel
   金城大旅社

14 Fortune Hotel
   福神大飯店
20 Hua Shih Hotel
   華士大飯店

OTHER
1 Train Station
   火車站
3 Sanshang Department
   Store
   三商百貨
4 Taiwan Bus Company
   台汽客運
9 Post Office
   郵局
11 Bank of Taiwan
   台灣銀行
15 KFC
   肯德基家鄉雞

16 Central Market
   中央市場
17 Protestant Church
   基督教堂
18 Catholic Church
   天主堂
19 Yongyi Tour Bus Company
   (To Tsaoling)
   永宜遊覽汽車公司
21 Foreign Affairs Police
   警察局外事課
22 Telephone Company
   電信局
23 Shanhsiu Temple
   善修宮、孔子廟
24 GPO
   總郵局
25 Swimming Pool
   游泳池

Guibin Hotel (☎ 532-4138; *guìbīn dà lǔshè*), north of the traffic circle at 1 Chenpei Rd, where doubles with private bath are NT$400 to NT$700. To the east is the *Yuanhuan Hotel* (☎ 322-637; *yuánhuán dà lǔshè*), where doubles are NT$500.

To the south of the traffic circle, on the corner of Chungshan and Taiping Rds is the *Jincheng Hotel* (☎ 532-3954; *jīnchéng lǔshè*), with singles/doubles for NT$400/500.

Moving up in price, there is the *Hua Shih Hotel* (☎ 532-4178; *huáshì dà fàndiàn*) south-east of the traffic circle at 112 Tatung Rd. This place is very close to the bus station for buses to Tsaoling. Doubles/twins cost NT$600/700.

South-west of the train station at 185-3 Minsheng Rd is the all new *Zhengang Hotel* (☎ 533-1768; *zhēngāng dà fàndiàn*) where doubles are NT$880.

The *New City Business Hotel* (☎ 532-1777; *shǒudū dà fàndiàn*) south-east of the train station at 170 Minsheng Rd (take the lift to the 5th floor) is another sharp, new place. Doubles/twins cost NT$1100/2000.

Also new is the *Wendiser Hotel* (☎ 532-8767; *wēndàishā dà fàndiàn*) on the north-east edge of the traffic circle at 1-3 Hsinghua St. Doubles/twins are NT$820/1480.

The *Huacheng Hotel* (☎ 532-4123; *huá-chéng dà fàndiàn*) to the east of the train station at 160 Minsheng Rd is on a very busy street. Doubles/twins are NT$800/1200.

To the north-west of the Jincheng is the *Fortune Hotel* (☎ 534-1666; *fúshén dà fàndiàn*), a comfortable place where doubles/twins cost NT$1000/1300.

The *Taishin Hotel* (☎ 535-2889; *tàixìn dà fàndiàn*), on the south-east edge of the traffic circle at 7 Taiping Rd, seems overpriced at NT$2700 for a 'European room'. A 'Japanese room' (sleep on the floor) is NT$3500. The hotel's entrance is on the 7th floor.

Getting There & Away

Touliu is on the west coast rail line and has frequent train departures to all points north and south. Buses travel regularly to nearby Chiayi. There are also buses to Taichung and Shuili. See the Tsaoling Getting There & Away section for information on travelling between Tsaoling and Touliu.

If you want to rent a car for the Tsaoling trip, you can try China Rent-A-Car (☎ 533-8834), 665 Yunlin Rd, Section 2.

TSAOLING
(cǎolǐng) 草嶺

Tsaoling is one of the best mountain resorts in Taiwan – at least equal to Alishan. Tsaoling offers as many hiking opportunities as Alishan. The mountains are not terribly high; Tsaoling is only about 800m above sea level, making it a good place to hike in winter. Nor

is Tsaoling shrouded in the notorious 'Alishan fog'.

One of the nice things about Tsaoling is that it caters to both the windshield tourist who likes an organised bus tour as well as the rugged individualist who prefers to scramble up and down the mountains on foot. If you want a bus tour, it can be easily arranged through the hotels.

Penglai Waterfall
(pénglái pùbù) 蓬萊瀑布

The road that runs by the Green Mountain Hotel leads to this waterfall. Ask anybody and they'll point you in the right direction. Walk about 2km down the winding road and you will eventually reach a cable car which costs NT$100 one way and NT$200 for the round trip. However, there is a trail just to the left of the cable car; the hike isn't difficult and it costs nothing.

This trail (or the cable car) takes you to the base of the waterfall, where there is another cable car that goes to the top of the waterfall. The second cable car is operated by a different owner but they charge the same prices. There is also a trail just to the left of the cable car terminal which goes to the top of the waterfall – it's a steep, 15 minute walk. It is definitely worth making your way to the top of the waterfall as the view is great.

Stone Wall
(shíbì) 石壁

From the top of Penglai Waterfall there is a hiking trail that winds several kilometres upstream to the Stone Wall. It's not actually a wall, but a riverbed of slick-rock – as slippery as greasy noodles but very interesting. Be careful if it's raining.

Water Curtain Cave
(shuǐlián dòng) 水簾洞

To get to this cave from Tsaoling village, find the Rainbow Vacation Hotel *(cǎihóng dà fàndiàn)*, which is just below the main village area. Face the entrance of the hotel and just off to the left you'll see some stone steps which descend steeply. Follow these steps and you will soon reach a bee farm.

WEST-CENTRAL TAIWAN

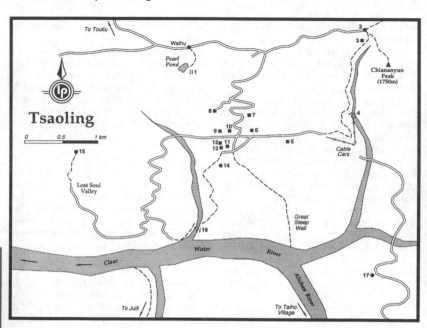

TSAOLING 草嶺

PLACES TO STAY
3 Stone Wall Hotel
  石壁大飯店
5 Shiuling Hotel
  秀嶺大飯店
6 Green Mountain Hotel
  高山青大飯店
7 Tsaoling Mountain
  Hostel
  草嶺山莊
8 Venus Motel
  愛之旅飯店

9 Sing Ming Hsiu Hotel
  新明修大飯店
10 Holiday Inn
  假期大飯店
11 Yunglih Hotel
  永利賓館
12 Tsaoling Hotel
  草嶺大飯店
13 Rainbow Vacation Hotel
  彩虹大飯店

OTHER
1 Tunghsin Waterfall
  同心瀑布

2 Stone Wall
  石壁
4 Penglai Waterfall
  蓬萊瀑布
14 Bee Farm
  蜂房
15 Spring-Autumn
  Cliffs
  斷崖春秋
16 Water Curtain Cave &
  Waterfall
  水簾洞
17 Tea Plantation
  茶園

Continue down and you will eventually come to a waterfall and cave called Water Curtain Cave. From there you can descend to the river. There are some huts there and people selling food and drinks.

From Water Curtain Cave, there are two other places you can go: the Lost Soul Valley and the Great Steep Wall.

Lost Soul Valley
(*duàn hún gǔ*) 斷魂谷
As the name implies, the Lost Soul Valley is

a little hard to find. To reach it, cross the small stream and head downstream along the river. On your right you'll find a road heading uphill. You walk uphill some way until the road forks. The left (lower) fork leads to Lost Soul Valley.

At the end of the valley is a place called **Spring Autumn Cliffs**. A bunch of food vendors have set up stalls here. Besides the cliffs, there are some small waterfalls and hiking trails. There is some quicksand near one of the waterfalls, so watch out for it. Avoid this area during the rainy season (summer) as the cliffs are unstable. In one tragic incident in 1986, over 20 hikers were buried alive by a mud slide. However, it's perfectly safe in the dry season.

Great Steep Wall
(chào bì xióng fēng)
This place is easy to find. Starting from Water Curtain Cave, head upstream along the river. You'll eventually come to a place on your left where there are some ropes set up to climb the big rock face. This place is called the Great Steep Wall. It's pretty safe and you can climb right up. You'll come to an obvious trail at the top of the cliffs; just follow it and you'll get back to Tsaoling village.

If the river has flooded, you won't be able to walk from Water Curtain Cave to the Great Steep Wall, but you can also reach the Great Steep Wall by the trail that descends from the Yunglih Hotel area.

Places to Stay
There are several good places to stay in the town itself and on the hillsides overlooking the village. On weekdays it's very easy to get into the dormitories and discounts of up to 30% are available.

The *Tsaoling Mountain Hostel* (☎ 583-1121; *cǎolíng shān zhuāng*) has comfortable dorms for NT$300, while other rooms are NT$1200 to NT$2400. There is a 20% discount on weekdays.

Another place that budget travellers can check out is the *Yunglih Hotel* (☎ 583-1012; *yǒnglì bīnguǎn*). This hotel has an old and new building. In the old building, a double

room is NT$1000. In the new building it's NT$1200. There is a 20% discount available on weekdays.

The *Stone Wall Hotel* (☎ 583-1238; *shíbì dà fàndiàn*), distinguishes itself by being far from the town. It's up high in the Stone Wall scenic area, a quiet place with lots of trees. Twins are NT$1200 on weekends, NT$1000 on weekdays.

Back in town, the *Sing Ming Hsiu Hotel* (☎ 583-1118; *xīnmíngxiū dà fàndiàn*) is a large, friendly place with dormitory beds for NT$300, doubles from NT$1200 to NT$1500 and honeymoon suites for NT$2200. The hotel has the standard karaoke, but probably more appealing to westerners is the Chin-hsuan Tea Shop. The hotel also arranges tours of nearby tea farms.

The *Venus Motel* (☎ 583-1153; *aìzīlü fàndiàn*) costs NT$1500 to NT$2000. It's way up on a hill, so it's quiet, but it's a hike to get anywhere unless you have your own set of wheels.

The *Tsaoling Hotel* (☎ 583-1228; *cǎolíng dà fàndiàn*) costs NT$1000 to NT$2500.

The *Rainbow Vacation Hotel* (☎ 583-1218; *cǎihóng dà fàndiàn*) is perched near a cliff and has particularly nice views. Twins cost NT$1400 to NT$3600, but a 30% discount is offered on weekdays.

The *Holiday Inn* (☎ 583-1397; *jiàqí dà fàndiàn*) has a name that sounds suspiciously familiar, but it's no relation to the famous international hotel chain. Rooms are excellent, with doubles/twins for NT$1500/2000. A room for six people costs NT$2600. There is a 30% discount on weekdays.

The *Green Mountain Hotel* (☎ 583-1201; *(gāoshānqīng dà fàndiàn)* is rated four stars, but the prices aren't too outrageous for this standard. Doubles/twins are NT$1500/2800. There is a 30% discount on weekdays.

The *Shiuling Hotel* (☎ 583-1222; *xiùlíng dà fàndiàn*) on the eastern edge of town is definitely upmarket. Rooms are NT$2000 to NT$3600. There are group rooms for 15 people but these are not open to individuals.

Getting There & Away
The easiest and most direct way to get to

WEST-CENTRAL TAIWAN

Tsaoling is from the small city of Touliu to the north-west of Chiayi. There are plenty of buses and trains operating between Touliu and Chiayi.

Only one small private bus company, the Yongyi Tour Bus Company (☎ 532-2388/ 532-6788; *yǒngyí yóulǎn gōngsī*) at 47 Chungcheng Rd, makes the journey to Tsaoling. The one way fare is NT$120. There is no published schedule, so you need to ring up to find out departure times – this could be a problem if you can't speak Chinese.

The alternative is to hike from Alishan to Fengshan and then on to Tsaoling. The last leg of the journey follows the river, and is beautiful but impossible during most of the wet season (see the Fengshan earlier in this chapter for details).

JANFUSUN FANCYWORLD
(*jiànhúshān shìjiè*) 劍湖山世界
Along the highway between Tsaoling and Touliu is a turn-off for Janfusun Fancyworld (☎ (05) 582-5789), a slick amusement park. You can find the usual roller coasters and Ferris wheels here; however, the most gut-wrenching ride of all is the Upchuck Tower – it lifts you up and then drops you down so fast that your kidneys wind up in your armpits.

Although it's obviously not meant for coronary patients, Janfusun Fancyworld can be a lot of fun. It's Taiwan's most serious challenge yet to Disneyland and it's hugely popular with the Taiwanese and quite a few foreigners.

Nantou County 南投縣

HSITOU
(*xītóu*) 溪頭
Hsitou – commonly misspelled 'Chitou' or 'Shitou' – is a beautiful mountain park and forest reserve south of the Sun Moon Lake area. At an elevation of 1150m, Hsitou's climate is perfect for most of the year, which makes it a prime spot for honeymooners. It's also popular with the rest of the population

and on weekends or holidays it seems like half the population of Taipei suddenly descends on Hsitou.

The forest reserve was originally established during the Japanese occupation. It is now run by the Forestry Department of National Taiwan University. Reforestation has been a major project – a highly successful one. Unfortunately, the University Forestry Department has been less successful at dissuading the central government from continuing with their massive road building and hotel development projects in the mountains.

Make sure you bring toilet paper to Hsitou. The tourist shops sell wind-up panda bears, plastic BB guns and firecrackers but mundane items like toilet paper are nowhere to be found. For information about the reserve and accommodation contact the Hsitou Restaurant Hotel (see Inside the Park under Places to Stay later in this section).

Things to See & Do
For tourists, the main attraction of the forest reserve is the opportunity to stroll through the thick groves of fir trees and bamboo. One of the great things about Hsitou is that it has a gate across the entrance which keeps most (but not all) cars and motorcycles out. However, you won't be disturbed by vehicles once you get onto the numerous hiking paths. Admission to the forest reserve costs NT$100.

From Hsitou, you can hike up to **Fenghuangshan**, a mountain about 2km to the north-east. At 1697m it's not exactly above the tree line, but the view is still good.

About 10km north-west of Hsitou is **Luku** (*lùgǔ*) – Taiwan's prime tea-growing region. The tea plantations are less noticeable these days thanks to all the new buildings, mostly tea shops catering to the tourist trade.

Places to Stay
Hsitou is expensive for hotels, though if you visit during off-peak times there are sizeable discounts to be had. If you're driving your own vehicle, you can stay a few kilometres down the mountain in the direction of Luku;

WEST-CENTRAL TAIWAN

this is somewhat cheaper and certainly less crowded.

Outside the Park Camping is the cheapest option, and indeed, might be your only option during a weekend or holiday. You have to bring your own tent, and the camping fee is NT$300. The camping area is outside the park boundary.

You may well be approached at the bus stop or (if you're driving) at the petrol station by locals offering rooms. They will usually shout out the word *tàofáng* (room with bath). More often than not, these people are renting rooms in their houses. Prices are typically in the NT$1000 range (more on weekends), but the quality of the rooms will not always be up to standard.

The *Xizhitou Muwu Hotel* (☎ 612-362; *xīzhítóu mùwū*) is one of the first places you'll encounter as you enter town. It rates only so-so as far as friendliness is concerned, but is priced reasonably at NT$1200 to NT$1500 on weekdays. The tariff rises to NT$1800 to NT$2000 on weekends and public holidays.

The *Haoshengdi Muwu Hotel* (☎ 612-177; *hǎoshèngdì mùwū*) is a relative bargain by Hsitou standards. This place resembles an American-style motel with its own car park, but the ornate wooden interiors and friendly management make it considerably more pleasant. Twins/quads are NT$1800/3000 on weekdays.

The *Mingshan Hotel* (☎ 612-121; *míngshān biéguǎn*) is close to, but still outside, the park boundary. Doubles are NT$1500 and twins are NT$2500. The hotel consists of about a dozen buildings, some of which are large wooden cabins.

About 150m south of the Haoshengdi is the *Moso Hotel* (☎ 612-131; *mèngzōng shān zhuāng*). This is a classy place with twins starting at NT$2500 and suites priced at NT$4000.

A further 150m south is the *Jinglu Hotel* (☎ 612-181; *jìnglú shān zhuāng*). Most of the rooms are in ornate wooden buildings. Twins are NT$2300 to NT$2600. A-frame cabins are NT$6000.

Inside the Park The main advantage of staying in the park is that there are fewer vehicles. Just remember that if you go outside of the park, you'll have to pay another admission fee to get back in.

The *Hsitou Youth Activity Centre* (☎ 612-161; *xītóu qīngnián huódòng zhōngxīn*) is operated by the CYC. If you can get into the eight-person group rooms (dormitories), then it's just NT$325 per person. Twins cost NT$1550. This place is about 1km from the park gate.

Everything else inside the park gate falls under the administration of the National Taiwan University Forestry Department. The *Hsitou Restaurant Hotel* (☎ 612-345; *xītóu cāntīng lǚshè*) is where you should go to find out about everything inside the forest reserve – they book the rooms. If you're coming from the bus station, the hotel is immediately to your left as you go through the gate. Their line-up of accommodation includes the *Hankuang Hotel* (☎ 645-805; *hànguāng lóu*); *Phoenix Hotel* (☎ 612-114; *fènghuáng bīnguǎn*); *Public Hostel* (☎ 612-111; *guómín bīnguǎn*); *Red Hotel (hóng lóu)*; and *The Villas (biéshù)*. Prices are in the range of NT$1000 to NT$4000.

Down the Mountain Departing Hsitou, you head downhill in the direction of Luku. There is an ever-growing number of hotels lining the highway, with prices running from very reasonable to totally outrageous. Unfortunately, most of these places to stay are only accessible if you are driving your own vehicle.

About 1km down the mountain (on the right-hand side of the highway as you go downhill) is the *Le Midi Hotel* (☎ 612-088; fax 612-031; *mǐdī dà fàndiàn*). This place is by no means geared towards budget travellers or even middle-class travellers – it positively oozes luxury. Doubles are a cool NT$5400 to NT$5700, twins cost NT$6000 and standard suites are NT$12,000. The presidential suite is a mere NT$200,000. There is a disco, pub and buffet restaurant all charging luxury prices.

Roughly 3km down the mountain on the

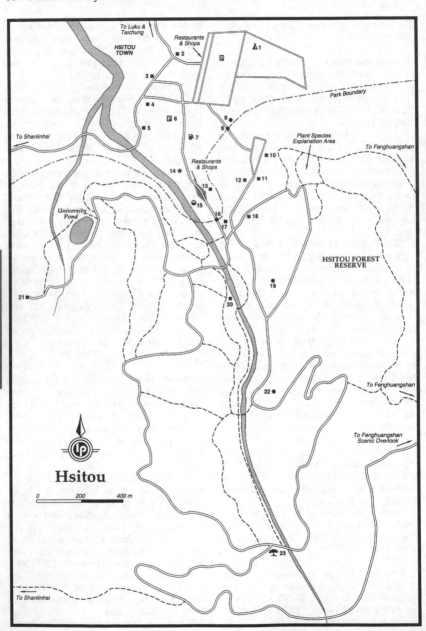

HSITOU 溪頭

PLACES TO STAY
1 Camping Area
   露營區
2 Xizhitou Muwu Hotel
   溪之頭木屋
3 Haoshengdi Muwu Hotel
   好聖地木屋
4 Moso Hotel
   孟宗山莊
5 Jinglu Hotel
   境盧山莊
10 Public Hostel
   國民旅舍
11 Phoenix Hotel
   鳳凰賓館

12 Hankuang Hotel
   漢光樓
13 Mingshan Hotel
   明山別館
17 Hsitou Restaurant Hotel
   溪頭餐廳旅舍
18 Red Hotel
   紅樓
20 Bamboo House
   竹廬
21 Hsitou Youth Activity
   Centre
   青年活動中心

OTHER
6 Motorcycle Parking
   停機車場

7 Petrol Station
   加油站
8 Gate
   大門收費亭
9 Tourist Service Centre
   旅遊服務中心
14 Police Station
   派出所
15 Bus Station
   車站
16 Gate
   大門收費亭
19 Tree Nursery
   銀杏林
22 Deer Farm
   鹿苑
23 Sacred Tree
   神木

left-hand side of the road is the *Jin Taiwan Hotel* (☎ 754-064; *jīn táiwān shān zhuāng*). Rates here for nice wooden rooms are NT$1000 to NT$1500.

About 5km down the mountain on the right-hand side is the *Mingzhu Hotel* (☎ 752-727; *míngzhú shān zhuāng*). It's one of the cheapest places to stay, and yet is still very pleasant with classy wooden cabins. It's a family-run place and the management is very friendly. On a weekday a single traveller can stay for about NT$800, or two people can stay for NT$1000. Weekend and holiday prices can be anywhere from 30 to 50% higher.

Central Luku is 10km from Hsitou. From Luku, travel downhill yet another 4km and on the right-hand side you'll find the enormous *Yuanding Hotel* (☎ 755-828; *yuándǐng dà fàndiàn*). It's a six storey concrete structure which isn't terribly attractive, but that hasn't kept the price down. Rates here are NT$2300 to NT$2800 for a western-style room, or NT$2500 to NT$2900 for 'Japanese style' (sleep on the floor). Overall, it's hard to recommend this place given the price and the concrete, but the tour groups pile in relentlessly.

About 15km from Hsitou is the *Hsiao Hsitou Resort World* (☎ 755-611; fax 755-615; *xiǎo xītóu dùjià qū*). It's also known as

the *Chungmeng Hotel (zhōngméng dà fàndiàn)*. It occupies both sides of the road, and every imaginable luxury can be found here (including a swimming pool). In the main hotel building doubles/twin rooms are NT$2800/3300. Over in the wooden cabins there are honeymoon suites for NT$3300, family suites for NT$3880 and the Japanese suite (sleep on the floor) for NT$4280.

Getting There & Away
The most frequent, direct buses are from Taichung, departing from the southbound-bus station behind the train station. The trip takes two hours. The bus is actually marked 'Shanlinhsi' (in Chinese), but it has a stop in Hsitou before continuing up the mountain.

If you are coming from southern Taiwan, you can get a bus directly from Chiayi or Touliu. No matter where you're coming from, you can always get a bus to Chushan at the base of the mountain, and then a bus from Chushan up to Hsitou.

From Sun Moon Lake, it's a little more complicated. You have to take a bus to Shuili, then a bus to Chushan and then another bus to Hsitou. You can easily get a bus from Sun Moon Lake to Shuili, but it terminates at the Taiwan Bus Company *(táiqì kèyùn)* bus station. To reach Chushan, you have to get a

WEST-CENTRAL TAIWAN

SHANLINHSI 杉林溪

1 Toll Gate
  大門收費亭
2 Green Dragon Waterfall
  青龍瀑布
3 Bus Station
  車站
4 Shanlinhsi Hotel
  杉林溪大飯店
5 Villas
  別墅區
6 Camping Ground
  露營區
7 Yen'an Waterfall
  燕庵瀑布
8 Sunglungyen Waterfall
  松瀧岩瀑布

and a cooler climate. There are plenty of hiking trails in Shanlinhsi and you can even hike to Alishan.

Brochures and advertisements for Shanlinhsi call it 'Sun Link Sea', a silly attempt to substitute an English rhyme for the Chinese words. If you ask anybody how to get to 'Sun Link Sea' they won't have the faintest idea of what you're talking about, so use the Chinese pronunciation.

Entrance to Shanlinhsi costs NT$150. This high price hasn't kept down the crowds – it looks like a tourist convention on summer weekends, but in winter you may have the opposite problem, as everything closes down and food is scarce.

Hike to Alishan
People often hike from Shanlinhsi to Alishan or from Alishan to Shanlinhsi. From Shanlinhsi to Alishan it's uphill, so of course it's easier to begin the hike from Alishan (see the Hikes Around Alishan section earlier in this chapter for details). It's a long, 27km walk that takes a full day, so start at dawn.

The beginning of the trail at Shanlinhsi is not very obvious, so you may have to ask. You have to walk up an unpaved forestry road first, then climb a steep embankment and you will find yourself on the trail. The

bus from the Yuanlin Bus Company *(yuánlín kèyùn)* bus station on Minsheng Rd, about 90m to the north of the Taiwan Bus Company station.

SHANLINHSI
(shānlínxī) 杉林溪
Hsitou actually has two sections: the forest reserve area, which is called Hsitou, and the Shanlinhsi area, some 20km away by road and considerably higher at an elevation of 1600m. If you go to Hsitou also make sure you try to make it to Shanlinhsi, as it offers different scenery, some beautiful waterfalls

trail is marked with a sign in Chinese pointing to Alishan. After eight hours of walking you reach the train tracks at Monkey Rock and then it's another 8km on foot along these tracks through many tunnels and over numerous bridges to Alishan. A torch is needed for the tunnels. (See the Alishan section earlier in this chapter for details.)

Places to Stay

Considering how much they are raking in from the admission fee, accommodation ought to be free. Unfortunately, that isn't the case. The *Shanlinhsi Hotel* (☎ 612-211; fax 612-227; *shānlínxī dà fàndiàn*) is really a complex of hotels (over 600 rooms in total!) spread around the Shanlinhsi area. All are near the bus station. If you can get into the dormitories, they cost NT$150 for a 10 person room, but you'll probably have to bring nine friends along or round up some Chinese students on the bus. Twins are NT$1500 to NT$2000, suites are NT$2100 to NT$3600.

The best deal in Shanlinhsi is the camping ground (*lùyíng qū*), where you can set up your tent free of charge. How much longer it remains free is subject to speculation.

Getting There & Away

The transport details are the same as for Hsitou. All buses going to Hsitou continue on to Shanlinhsi and there are buses connecting Hsitou and Shanlinhsi every 30 minutes. The last bus down is at 4.30 pm. Taxis are also readily available.

FENGHUANG VALLEY BIRD PARK

(fènghuáng gǔ niǎoyuán) 鳳凰谷鳥園
Fenghuang Valley has a bird park (☎ 753-100) which you can enter to watch some 280 species of birds fly around. It's nice, but touristy – not so great that you'll want to go out of your way to go there unless you're a dedicated birdwatcher.

Admission to the bird park is NT$100 and it's open from 7 am to 5 pm daily.

If you want to see Fenghuang Valley, you can get a bus from Chushan (*zhúshān*), a large town at the base of the mountain below

Hsitou. If you're already in Hsitou, you have to go back down to Chushan and then get a bus back up to Fenghuang. There are a few buses direct from Taichung.

Finding your way is easy if you're driving your own car or motorcycle, because there are many English signs pointing the way. Don't confuse Fenghuang Valley with Fenghuangshan. Fenghuangshan is a mountain next to Hsitou and is approached by a slightly different route.

SHUILI

(shuǐlǐ) 水里
Shuili is not a tourist attraction – it's an essential transit point at the south end of Sun Moon Lake. If you are travelling between Sun Moon Lake and Tungpu or Hsitou, you must go through Shuili. Cheap accommodation options make it a good place to spend the night.

If you have your own transport, it's worth stopping off at the Yushan National Park Headquarters (☎ 773-121; *yùshān guójiā gōngyuán guǎnlǐ chù*) at 112 Minsheng Rd. This places has heaps of maps and other information, some of which is in English.

Places to Stay

There are many hotels clustered around the train station, though most have signs only in Chinese.

Cheapest in town is the *Huantai Hotel* (☎ 772-137; *huántài dà lǚshè*), which is south-west of the train station at 83 Minchuan Rd. Doubles with electric fan are NT$400, while air-con pushes the tariff up to NT$800. Rooms are comfortable and clean, and all have attached bath.

About 75m south of the train station is the *Apollo Hotel* (☎ 772-110; *hóngbīn dà lǚshè*), at 140 Minsheng Rd. Rooms here cost NT$400 to NT$1000.

Another good choice is the *Long Jiang Hotel* (☎ 772-161; *lóngjiāng dà fàndiàn*), 174 Minsheng Rd, where doubles cost NT$500 to NT$600. It's somewhat grottier neighbour, the *Tongmei Hotel* (☎ 772-131; *tóngměi lǚshè*) has rooms from NT$400 to NT$600.

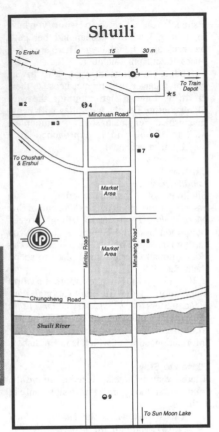

Shuili 水里

kèyùn), and it's where you catch buses to Sun Moon Lake and Puli *(pǔlǐ)*.

To reach Shuili from the major cities in southern Taiwan, first take a train to either Touliu or Ershui *(èrshuǐ)*. Ershui is closer. There are buses to Shuili from both Ershui and Touliu.

Train There is a very interesting small train that runs between Ershui and Shuili. The bus is sometimes faster, but the train is definitely more fun.

It's important to know that Shuili is not the last stop, and trains continue for another four minutes to a train depot called Chechung – be sure you get off in Shuili. Most trains leaving from Shuili terminate in Ershui, but a few continue on to Taichung.

TUNGPU
(dōngpǔ) 東埔

Tungpu is one of the best mountain resorts in Taiwan, even better than Alishan and Tsaoling. At 1120m above sea level the climate is just perfect. The area is mountainous, with many waterfalls and hot springs.

The *Yazhou Hotel* (☎ 772-151; *yǎzhōu dà lǚshè*), at 266 Minchuan Rd (about 15m west of the Huantai), has recently been renovated. Doubles/twins cost NT$1000/1200.

Getting There & Away
Bus Some confusion is caused by the fact that there are two bus stations in Shuili. The Yuanlin Bus Company (☎ 770-041; *yuánlín kèyùn*) faces the train station, and offers buses to Tungpu, Chushan and Ershui. The other bus station lies about 100m to the south-west along Mintu Rd. It belongs to the Taiwan Bus Company (☎ 770-054; *táiqì*

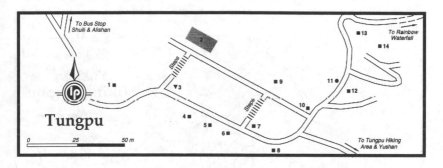

TUNGPU 東埔

1 Ti Lun Hotel
帝綸大飯店
2 Elementary School
國小
3 Daohong
Restaurant
道弘快餐
4 Tungpu Hotel
東埔大飯店
5 Samtone Hotel
山通大飯店
6 Longtai Hotel
龍泰山莊
7 Dong Guang
Hotel
東光飯店
8 Cuiluan Hotel
翠巒山莊
9 Police Hostel
警光山莊
10 Longquan Hotel
龍泉山莊
11 Store
商店
12 Hong Lin Hotel
鴻林別館
13 Shenghua Hotel
勝華大飯店
14 Aboriginal Youth Activity
Centre
原住民活動中心

WEST-CENTRAL TAIWAN

If you love hiking, Tungpu is a treat – the scenery could hardly be more spectacular. Tungpu even has a 'back door' route for climbing Yushan. There is little else to do in Tungpu but hike all day and soak those tired muscles at night in the hot springs. If you're not a hiker, you might as well skip Tungpu because there is no place for riding around in a car or tour bus. All the scenic attractions are outside the village and must be reached by walking on some fairly steep trails. The great fear of environmentalists is that this will change – let us only hope that no evil genius at the Chamber of Commerce decides to build a 'scenic freeway' to the summit of Yushan.

Tungpu is also not a place for people who fear heights, as many of the trails offer breathtaking, panoramic views from the edges of sheer cliffs. That said, try not to miss Tungpu – it's one of the most challenging hiking spots in Taiwan.

Rainbow Waterfall
(*cǎihóng pùbù*) 彩虹瀑布
If you want to take a short walk on your first day, you can hike up to Rainbow Waterfall. The path is easy to find. Just walk north-west up the main street of Tungpu (going uphill) and when you reach the Shenghua Hotel take the trail to the left. The way is obvious – rubbish left by hikers marks the route. The walk up to the falls takes about 30 minutes, but only 20 minutes to come back down.

Take a nice soak in the hot springs and get a good rest for the next day's hike, because it's a long, uphill trail.

Route to Yushan
You can't get to Yushan in one day, and you need a special permit if you want to (legally) reach the summit. However, you can hike along the Yushan trail as far as Patungkuan without a permit and even camp out along the way.

WEST-CENTRAL TAIWAN

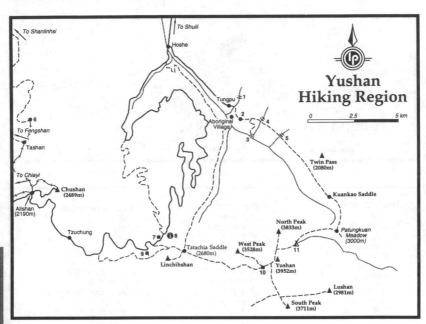

YUSHAN HIKING REGION
玉山健行區

1 Rainbow Waterfall
  彩虹瀑布
2 Father & Son Cliff
  父子斷崖
3 Happy Happy Hot Springs
  樂樂溫泉

4 Cloud Dragon Waterfall
  雲龍瀑布
5 One Girl Waterfall
  乙女瀑布
6 Monkey Rock
  石猴
7 Tungpu Lodge
  東埔山莊

8 Tatachia Visitors' Centre
  塔塔加遊客中心
9 Lulin Lodge
  鹿林山莊
10 Paiyun Hut
  排雲山莊
11 Laonung Creek
   Campground
   荖濃溪露營區

Starting from Tungpu, take the dirt road that drops slightly downhill and winds around the mountain. Before long you will come to a path on the left that goes steeply uphill. The path is well marked and has a sign in Chinese characters. (If you miss the path, you'll soon come to a village, in which case you have come too far.) Following the path uphill, you'll reach Father & Son Cliff (*fùzǐ duànyaí*). The path around here looks unstable and is not for the chicken-hearted. The

trail and nearby road collapsed during a typhoon in 1996 and although the trail has been reopened, it still looks precarious. Don't linger here too long.

Continuing past Father & Son Cliff, you'll eventually reach a fork in the trail. The right path drops steeply downhill to the river below, and is marked with a sign in Chinese. This track leads to the Happy Happy Hot Springs (*lè lè wēnquán*). However, the hot springs are not swimmable – you could take a refreshing (cold) dip in the river though. Be forewarned that it's steep climb back up to the main trail.

If you decide to bypass Happy Happy and stay on the main trail, take the left path going uphill. You'll soon reach Cloud Dragon Waterfall *(yúnlóng pùbù)* and a little later, One Girl Waterfall *(yī nü pùbù)*.

You can continue up the trail as far as Twin Pass *(duì guān)* at an elevation of 2080m. It's unlikely that you'll be able to go much further in one day and still have time to return to Tungpu. The return trip is back along the same route.

If you want to continue along the trail it leads to the Kuankao saddle *(guān'gāo)*, and then on to Patungkuan *(bātōngguān)*, a lush, green alpine meadow at an altitude of 3000m. There is a mountain hut here, but it's dirty and basic and has no water – fill up your water bottle at a stream about 15 minutes walk before the hut. You'll need a sleeping bag, and if the hut is filled by other climbing parties you may wish you had a tent too.

From Patungkuan, you could reach the summit of Yushan, Taiwan's tallest peak. However, if you plan to go higher than Patungkuan you need a class A mountain pass. It is possible to sneak in, and some people try it because this back route is not so heavily patrolled as the main route from Alishan. However there's a steep fine if you get caught without a pass.

Alternatively, you could take the easier route and climb Yushan from Alishan, then descend through Patungkuan and wind up in Tungpu. It's an exciting trip, but any such expedition is for experienced hikers only, with a mountain pass and the necessary equipment such as a heavy-duty wet weather gear and sleeping bag.

Climbing Yushan by way of Tungpu takes three days. Climbing from Alishan and back the same way could be completed in two days (see Yushan under the Hikes Around Alishan section earlier in this chapter).

Places to Stay

All of Tungpu's hotels are either on or just off the main drag.

The *Aboriginal Youth Activity Centre* (☎ 701-515; *yuánzhùmín huódòng zhōngxīn*) has dorms for NT$200 and doubles for NT$700 to NT$900. It's at the high end of town, a short but steep uphill walk. The baths use hot-spring water, a real treat.

Next door is the *Shenghua Hotel* (☎ 701-511; *shènghuá dà fàndiàn*), where doubles/ twins cost NT$1500/1700.

The *Hong Lin Hotel* (☎ 701 569/791-326; *hónglín biéguǎn*), on the north-west side of town, is excellent value (on weekdays at least). Doubles in a beautiful wooden room are NT$600 – a pleasant break from the usual concrete-box architecture of hostels.

A reasonable deal is also offered by the *Cuiluan Hotel* (☎ 701-818; *cuìluán shān zhuāng*), which is about 40m south-west of the Hong Lin. Doubles without/with private bath cost NT$500/800.

Almost exactly between the Hong Lin and the Cuiluan is the pleasant and clean *Longquan Hotel* (☎ 701-061/701-587; *lóngquán shān zhuāng*). Double rooms cost NT$700 on weekdays and NT$1000 on weekends. Nearby, about 25m to the north-west, is the *Police Hostel* (☎ 701-705; *jǐngguāng shāng zhuāng*), where rooms cost from NT$900 to NT$2400.

The *Tungpu Hotel* (☎ 701-090; *dōngpǔ dà fàndiàn*) at the lower end town is memorable for its oddly Romanised name card which dubs this the *Totong Pu* (which could be translated as 'headache market' in Chinese). Nonetheless, it's a fine place to stay, though it's not bottom-budget level. Twin rooms cost NT$1500 to NT$4000.

The *Dong Guang Hotel* (☎ 701-105; *dōngguāng fàndiàn*) is a modest five storey high rise to the north-west of the Cuiluan. Rates here are NT$1000 to NT$1800.

The *Longtai Hotel* (☎ 701-056; *lóngtài shān zhuāng*) is a new place opposite the Dong Guang. It has a few group rooms and standard doubles/twins for NT$1400/1700.

The *Samtone Hotel* (☎ 702-666; *shāntōng dà fàndiàn*) is another new place near the Longtai. Doubles are NT$2000 to NT$2500, twins are NT$2400 and suites can be up to NT$5000.

WEST-CENTRAL TAIWAN

The largest and fanciest accommodation in town is the *Ti Lun Hotel* (☎ 701-616; *dìlún dà fàndiàn*), at the lower end of the village close to the bus station. Rooms cost from NT$3000 to NT$5000.

Places to Eat

Tungpu's main drag is lined with restaurants, many serving expensive 'real mountain seafood'. One place which is very economical but still quite good is the *Daohong Restaurant (dàohóng kuàicān).*

Getting There & Away

You can catch a bus directly from the town of Shuili to Tungpu (see the Shuili Getting There & Away section for details). There are two bus companies with separate stations in Shuili, so make sure you get the right one. The bus station you want is operated by the Yuanlin Bus Company (☎ 770-041; *yuánlín kèyùn*). There are seven buses a day on weekdays and 10 a day on weekends and holidays. The first bus departs Shuili at 7 am and the last bus is at 5 pm. The trip takes about 1½ hours going uphill, and one hour coming down.

SUN MOON LAKE

(rì yuè tán) 日月潭
Sun Moon Lake is one of Taiwan's busiest resort areas, attracting a large number of honeymooners and domestic tourists. It's popular for a good reason. It's easily Taiwan's most beautiful lake, with clear and sparkling blue waters set against a magnificent mountain backdrop. The lake is 760m above sea level, giving it a pleasant climate for most of the year. Naturally, it's best to visit during weekdays to avoid the large crowds that regularly descend on the place. Even on weekdays expect to see many tour buses. There are heaps of things to see around the lake and it takes at least a full day to have a good look at this place.

Sun Moon Lake is a natural lake, but during the Japanese occupation a dam was built to raise the lake's level and generate hydroelectric power. At that time, the electric power generated was sufficient to supply all of Taiwan's needs. This dam still generates power, but with the island's heavily industrialised economy and rising standard of living, hydroelectricity can now supply only a fraction of the total demand. Today Taiwan depends on nuclear power and coal-fired plants for most of the island's electricity.

There is an NT$50 admission charge for entrance to the Sun Moon Lake area, plus an additional NT$40 if you're driving a car.

Peacock Garden

(kǒngquè yuán) 孔雀園
This is the most touristy thing to see at the lake. If you want to chase our fine-feathered friends with a camera lens, the Peacock Garden is on the north-east shore of the lake.

Temples & Pagoda

The **Wenwu Temple** *(wénwǔ miào)* is a large and beautiful structure very close to the Chinatrust Hotel. Be sure to check out the temple shop for scroll paintings and other arts and crafts.

The **Hsuanchuang Temple** *(xuánzhuàng sì)* is at the far end of the lake. It's perched up on a hill and is surrounded by a collection of souvenir shops, but it's still less touristy than the Wenwu Temple.

Within walking distance of Wenwu Temple is the **Tzuen Pagoda** *(cíēn tǎ)*. This relatively peaceful place (on weekdays at least) is well worth a visit. Climb the pagoda for a magnificent view of the lake.

Tehuashe Aboriginal Village

(déhuàshè) 德化社
This is a half-hearted attempt to give tourists an idea of what a traditional aboriginal village used to look like. The nearby Formosan Aboriginal Cultural Village is a much more sincere effort, but that one charges NT$350 while this one is free.

Water Sports

The locals say the lake has piranhas! I have my doubts, though I concede it's possible. I haven't heard of anyone being eaten lately, so you can probably relax.

There isn't any real swimming beach –

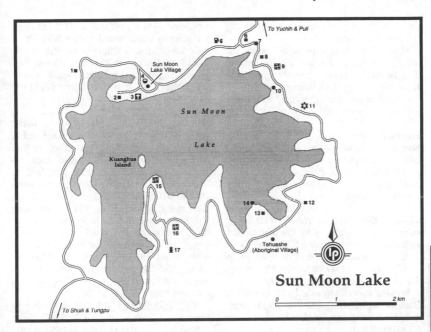

Sun Moon Lake

SUN MOON LAKE 日月潭

1 Teachers' Hostel
教師會館
2 Evergreen Hotel
涵碧樓
3 Tzuen Church
慈恩教堂
4 Bus Station
公路車站
5 Petrol Station
加油站

6 Jiulong Hotel
九龍大飯店
7 Entrance Gate
遊樂區大門
8 Chinatrust Hotel
中信大飯店
9 Wenwu Temple
文武廟
10 Chiang Kaishek Statue
蔣公銅像
11 Peacock Garden
孔雀園

12 Sun Moon Lake Youth
Activity Centre
日月潭青年活動中心
13 Yangs Wood Hotel
哲園
14 Pier
碼頭
15 Hsuankuang Temple
玄光寺
16 Hsuanchuang Temple
玄狀寺
17 Tzuen Pagoda
慈恩塔

indeed, swimming is officially prohibited except for one day of the year, when thousands flock to Sun Moon Lake to participate in a mass swim. There are numerous places where you can rent a rowing boat or canoe and no one is likely to stop you from diving overboard, especially if you do it at night.

Some Taiwanese tourists have even taken to skinny dipping at night – a cultural (not to mention legal) taboo.

You can row out to Kuanghua Island (*guānghuá dǎo*) in the middle of the lake. If rowing is too much exercise for you, there are yachts and motorised boats for rent.

There are also opportunities for water-skiing at the Asia Country Club.

Most of the boat trips originate on the south shore of the lake. Two likely places to find boats for rent are at the pier near Tehuashe and the Hsuankuang Temple.

Fishing in the lake is permitted and is very popular with the locals.

Places to Stay

Sun Moon Lake Village The main tourist area just near the bus station is a cornucopia of accommodation. Compared to most of the hotels scattered around the lake, the village is also the cheapest area.

You can start your exploration of hotel scene at the *Min Ren Hotel* (☎ 855-338; *míngrén dà fàndiàn*), 138 Chungshan Rd, with doubles/twins costing NT$800/2000.

Also downmarket is the *Honeymoon Hotel* (☎ 855-349; *mìyuè lóu biéguǎn*) at 116 Chungshan Rd. Doubles/twins are NT$800/2000.

Moving upscale, there's the *Sun Ho-Yung Hotel* (☎ 855-364; *sōnghè yuán dà bīnguǎn*) at 135-1 Chungshan Rd. Doubles/twins are NT$1000/2200.

The *Skyline Inn* (☎ 855-321; fax 855-325; *tiānlú dà fàndiàn*), perhaps so-named because it dominates the skyline of Sun Moon Lake Village has twins from NT$1800 to NT$2000, and suites for NT$2300 to NT$2800.

The *Ming Shin Hotel* (☎ 855-357; *míngshèng dà fàndiàn*), 4 Mingsheng St, has doubles/twins for NT$500/1000. Opposite is the *Hongbin Hotel* (☎ 855-381; *hóngbīn dà fàndiàn*), where rooms cost from NT$1400 to NT$2200.

Next to the Hongbin is the *El Dorado Hotel* (☎ 855-855; *shuǐshālián dà fàndiàn*). Doubles are NT$2200, twins NT$2500 and suites cost from NT$4000 to NT$6000.

There are some big (and pricey) hotels are located on a hill just west of the main village area. The *Evergreen Hotel* (☎ 855-311; fax 855-314; *hánbì lóu*), 142 Chunghsing Rd, is one of the largest places. Twin rooms cost from NT$1200 to NT$1300, and suites are NT$5000 to NT$10,000.

Almost opposite this is the *Diamond Hotel* (☎ 855-345; *zuànshí lóu dà fàndiàn*).

Doubles/twins are NT$1800/2000 but there are actually some dorm beds for NT$300.

Nearby, at 136 Chunghsing Rd, is the *Teachers' Hostel* (☎ 855-991; *jiàoshī huìguǎn*). This is a government-owned 'hostel' where the cheapest twins cost from NT$1100 to NT$1500.

Outlying Areas The outlying hotels are not really difficult to get to, but none are within walking distance of the bus station in Sun Moon Lake Village. You can reach them via the local bus which goes around the lake.

The *Sun Moon Lake Youth Activity Centre* (☎ 850-070; fax 850-037; *rì yuè tán qīngnián huódòng zhōngxīn*), 101 Chungcheng Rd, is a large and slick-looking hostel near Tehuashe on the southern shore of the lake. There are 47 dormitories here, each with eight beds. The dorms cost NT$2300 per room (NT$288 per person). There are also some twin rooms starting at NT$1600, plus wooden cabins for NT$4200.

The *Jiulong Hotel* (☎ 855-327; *jiǔlóng dà fàndiàn*), 3 Chungcheng Rd, looks a bit like a temple from the outside. Doubles/twins cost NT$800/2000.

The *Chinatrust Hotel* (☎ 855-911; fax 855-268; *zhōngxìn dà fàndiàn*), near the Wenwu Temple, has doubles/twin rooms for NT$3000/3300 and suites for NT$3800 to NT$10,000. Nearby is the Chingsheng Hotel (☎ 855-366; *jǐngshèng lóu dà fàndiàn*) where twins are NT$1600.

The *Yangs Wood* (☎ 850-000; fax 850-080; *zhéyuán míngliú huìguǎn*) is unusual in Taiwan – the all-wooden exterior is reminiscent of a Canadian mountain lodge. There is plenty of luxury here, but it comes at a price – NT$5900 for a mountain view, and NT$6900 for a lake view (and this is for standard twins). A suite with a lake view goes for a cool NT$12,000 and the presidential suite is a mere NT$16,000. This place is associated with the Asia Country Club, so you can gain access to their facilities.

Places to Eat

Sun Moon Lake is one of the most expensive resort areas in Taiwan. There are plenty of places to eat, but the emphasis is on pricey seafood restaurants. For double the usual price, you can get noodle or rice dishes in the numerous restaurants lining the street near the bus station in Sun Moon Lake Village. You might find it even cheaper to eat in some of the hotels.

Things to Buy

Although Sun Moon Lake isn't cheap for eating and sleeping, it's a good spot to hunt for arts and crafts souvenirs. Prices are low mainly because there are so many shops, and competition is good for the customer. Some polite bargaining might be possible.

Getting There & Away

There are several directions you can approach Sun Moon Lake from, but it's easiest to get there from Taichung.

In Taichung, catch buses from the Gancheng bus station. There are plenty of taxi drivers hanging around this place who will grab any westerner by the arm and yell in his/her face, 'Sun Moon Lake'. Ignore them and buy a bus ticket. The buses go directly to the lake in two hours. If you've just missed the bus and don't want to wait for the next one, first take a bus to Puli, then get a bus from there to Sun Moon Lake.

There is also a direct bus to Sun Moon Lake from Taipei which departs from the North Bus Station. The trip takes slightly more than four hours. An alternative would be to take a bus or train to Taichung or Puli first, and then transfer to the Sun Moon Lake bus.

Getting Around

If you are a hiker, you could walk from Sun Moon Lake Village to the Tzuen Pagoda at the opposite side of the lake, but it's a long way and will take most of the day. Fortunately, there are buses plying this route at the rate of about one an hour between 8 am and 5 pm. If you miss the last bus back you can take a taxi or hitch.

Sun Moon Lake looks like an excellent place to ride a bicycle. As yet, I haven't seen any bicycle rental shops that aren't attached to the hotels. Yangs Wood offers bicycle rentals to their guests, and I expect that other hotels will take note and start offering the same service.

Taking a tour by taxi is not unreasonable if you can organise a group to share the cost. The easiest way to do this is to form a group while on the bus going to the lake and include some Chinese tourists. Let them do the bargaining and don't pay until the tour is finished.

FORMOSAN ABORIGINAL CULTURAL VILLAGE

(jiǔ zú wénhuà cūn) 九族文化村
A very short distance north-east of Sun Moon Lake is the Formosan Aboriginal Cultural Village (☎ 895-361). It's an amusement park with an aboriginal theme. Although rather commercialised, the reproductions of aboriginal dwellings, arts and crafts are realistic and quite tastefully done – it's definitely worth a visit.

This woman from the Ayatal tribe is wearing a traditional headdress and layering of necklaces. The Ayatal customs are gradually declining in the face of urbanisation.

WEST-CENTRAL TAIWAN

The park is better laid out than I had expected. It is spread over a 3km circuit. There is a minibus, but it would be a shame to miss the neat suspension bridges swinging across the steep valley. Near the entrance you can watch people doing native crafts and there is an excellent permanent photography exhibition showing the changing lives of the local aboriginal tribes.

Melanie Seligman

When you first enter the grounds, you come into a large European-style garden and chateau – about as appropriate as an igloo in the Sahara Desert. They seem to have been thrown in as an added tourist attraction for locals, who don't get many opportunities to see the palaces of Europe.

Just up the hill from the gardens (you can follow either the footpath or the road up the mountainside), there is a small plaza where the aboriginal song and dance shows are performed. Just adjacent to the plaza is a museum housing aboriginal artefacts, both original and reproductions.

There are nine villages in the park and each one represents a separate tribe, except for the Tsou-Shao Village which represents two tribes. The entrance fee is NT$350, but this is not unreasonable since you can easily spend half a day here. On weekends and holidays there are continuous aboriginal song and dance shows thrown in at no extra cost. The cultural village is open daily from 7 am to 5.30 pm.

Getting There & Away

Although it's very close to Sun Moon Lake, there are no direct buses to the village. You have to take a bus from Sun Moon Lake Village to Yuchih (*yúchí*), and then another bus to the Formosan Aboriginal Cultural Village. The buses depart Yuchih at 7.30, 9.20 and 11.05 am, and 1, 2.35, 3.30 and 5 pm.

There are also direct buses from the town of Puli. They leave at 7, 8.40 and 10.30 am, and 12.20, 2, 3 and 4.30 pm.

PULI

(pǔlǐ) 埔里
Dead in the centre of Taiwan, just north of Sun Moon Lake, is the town of Puli. The town itself is hardly a tourist attraction, but it is an important transit point for many scenic areas. Many travellers wind up staying here because of its convenient location and cheapish accommodation.

One hazard to note: Puli's narrow streets, lack of footpaths and lack of traffic lights make it a bit dicey walking around. It was here that a speeding car broke its mirror against my backpack.

Things to See

The **Puli Distillery** *(pǔlǐ jiǔchǎng)* began producing rice liquor *(mǐ jiǔ)* and glutinous rice liquor *(nuòmǐ jiǔ)* in 1922, both of which tend to be rather harsh and these days are usually used for cooking. In 1952, the brewery began production of Taipai *(tàibái jiǔ)* and Shaohsing *(shàoxīng jiǔ)* liquors, considered by local booze connoisseurs to be the island's best fire water. The Taiwanese refer to these products as 'wine', but it's not wine at all – it's hard liquor. You can tour the distillery and sample the moonshine; be careful – it's deceptively potent stuff and a few cups can blast your socks off.

Assuming that you're not too hung over from the distillery, take a walk over to the **Chenghuang Temple** *(chénghuáng miào)* and the **Confucius Temple** *(kǒng miào)*.

The **Taiwan Geographical Centre Monument** *(táiwān dìlǐ zhōngxīn bēi)* marks – you guessed it – the geographical centre of Taiwan. It's about 1km north-east of Puli. To get there, follow the highway heading towards Wushe, and it will be on your right. The monument is actually more fun to visit than you'd expect because it's in a fairly scenic park and you have to climb a steep hill to reach it.

Places to Stay

One advantage of staying in Puli is that it is easy to find cheap accommodation and food, even on holidays when nearby expensive resorts like Sun Moon Lake are packed out.

In the west part of town is the *Hohuan Hotel* (☎ 984-036; *héhuān dà fàndiàn*) at 67 Chungcheng 2nd Rd. At NT$500 to NT$800

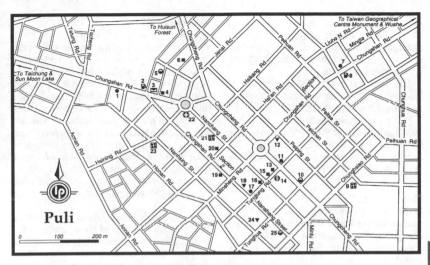

PULI 埔里

PLACES TO STAY
4 Yongfeng Hotel
　永豐旅社
6 Hohuan Hotel
　合歡大飯店
13 Jinshan Hotel
　金山大飯店
15 Xindongjing Hotel
　新東京大旅社
16 Dongfeng Hotel
　東峰大旅社
19 Sun Wang Hotel
　山王大飯店
20 Tianyi Hotel
　天一大飯店

PLACES TO EAT
12 McDonald's
　麥當勞

18 Domino's Pizza
　達美樂比薩店
24 Market
　市場

OTHER
1 Puli Distillery
　埔里酒廠
2 Petrol Station
　加油站
3 Post Office
　郵局
5 Nantou Bus Company
　Puli Station
　南投客運埔里站
7 Forestry
　Department
　林務局
8 Petrol Station
　加油站

9 Paokung Temple
　包公廟
10 Taiwan Bus
　Company
　台灣客運
11 7-Eleven
　7-11便利商店
14 Bank of Taiwan
　台灣銀行
17 Watson's
　屈臣氏
21 Chenghuang Temple
　城隍廟
22 Zonghe Hospital
　綜合醫院
23 Confucius Temple
　孔廟
25 Nantou Bus Company
　East Station
　南投客運東站

for a comfortable double, it's one of the cheapest deals in Puli.

Nearby is the *Yongfeng Hotel* (☎ 982-304; *yǒngfēng lǚshè*), 280 Nanchang St, where doubles/twins cost NT$700/1200.

If you want to be closer to the centre, the

Jinshan Hotel (☎ 982-311; *jīnshān dà fàndiàn*), 127 Tungjung St, has doubles for NT$400 to NT$800. Just next door is the *Xindongjing Hotel* (☎ 983-256; *xīndōngjīng bīnguǎn*). Doubles/twins are NT$600/1200.

Further to the south-west on the same

street, at No 103, is the *Dongfeng Hotel* (☎ 982-287; *dōngfēng dà lǚshè*) which was undergoing renovation at the time of writing. Prices for rooms had been as low as NT$500, but they are sure to rise.

The *Tianyi Hotel* (☎ 982-017; *tiānyī dà fàndiàn*) at 89 Hsi'an Rd, Section 1, offers fine rooms for NT$1000 to NT$1500.

Puli's top accommodation is the flashy *Sun Wang Hotel* (☎ 900-111; fax 900-200; *shānwáng dà fàndiàn*) at 399 Chungshan Rd, Section 2. There is even an in house disco. Doubles/twins cost NT$1600/2500.

Places to Eat
In the evening, there are plenty of cheap food stalls in the market at Tunghua Rd and Nanchang St. There's a cluster of low-priced restaurants around the Taiwan Bus Company station.

McDonald's peddles its burgers and fries in Puli, and *7-Eleven* is good for the usual microwave cuisine.

Domino's Pizza (☎ 904-567; *dáměilè bǐsà diàn*) does takeaways only and can deliver to any hotel in Puli.

Watson's, the general all-purpose pharmacy cum grocery store chain, has a branch at the corner of Tungjung Rd and Nansheng St. It's good for stocking up on chocolate bars.

Getting There & Away
There are two important bus stations in Puli. The large bus station on the corner of Tunghua and Chungcheng Rds belongs to the Taiwan Bus Company (*táiwān qìchē kèyùn*). About 150m to the south-west, on Chungshan Rd, is the Nantou Bus Company (*nántóu kèyùn*) east station. There is also a Nantou Bus Company station on the other side of town. Buses to Wushe stop at both stations.

From Taichung, direct buses to Puli leave from the Gancheng bus station. For details of how to get from Puli to places of interest in the area, refer to the Getting There & Away sections for Huisun Forest, Wushe, the Formosan Aboriginal Cultural Village and Chingching Farm.

HUISUN FOREST
(*huìsūn lín chǎng*) 惠蓀林場

To the north of Puli in a mountain valley, the Huisun Forest was originally intended as a nature reserve project for the Forestry Department of Chunghsing University in Taichung. However, it's been transformed into a picnic, camping and hiking spot. Although it's not as spectacular as Alishan, Tungpu, Hohuanshan (*héhuānshān*) and other mountain resorts in Taiwan, some consider Huisun a better place to go in the winter because it is warmer and has a milder climate. Furthermore, Huisun has not been ruined by commercialisation – at least not yet.

The valley is heavily forested with pines and there are a number of hiking trails. There is a whitewater river rushing through a canyon – some kayakers claim it's the best short whitewater run in Taiwan.

If you are on a hurried trip through Taiwan, you could bypass Huisun without feeling you've missed something important. However, if you have the time and desire to spend a couple of days in a beautiful, pine-scented valley with nice hiking trails, it's worth the trip.

Hiking is the main activity in Huisun. (Refer to the Huisun Forest map for the main trails.) The hike to Frog Rock (*qīngwā shí*) is steep but one of the best in the valley. During the week, walking along the main road through the valley is pleasant, but on weekends and holidays the traffic can be too heavy. Admission to Huisun Forest costs NT$100.

Places to Stay
There are several places to stay and everything is managed by the *Huisun Forest Hotel* (*huìsūn línchǎng guómín lǚshè*). Reservations are a very good idea on weekends and holidays; call the hotel's service centre (☎ 941-041; fax 941-340; *fúwù zhōngxīn*). Dormitory beds can be had for NT$200. Doubles/twins cost NT$1000/1600 and there are deluxe rooms for NT$2000. The other option is camping.

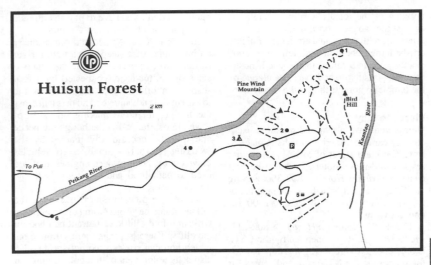

Getting There & Away

Buses to Huisun are not frequent. There are only two buses daily from Puli and the trip takes about 1½ hours. Buses leave Puli from the Nantou Bus Company station at 8.50 am and 2.15 pm; going the other way, they leave Huisun at 10.40 am and 3.55 pm. On weekends and holidays only, there are two buses from Tsaotun *(cǎotún)*, a town 17km south of Taichung. Buses leave Tsaotun at 8 am and 2.45 pm; they leave Huisun for Tsaotun at 10 am and 4.40 pm.

WUSHE

(wùshè) 霧社

At 1148m above sea level, Wushe is a cool mountain retreat with magnificent scenery. The town sits on a mountain ridge, and in the valley below there is a large reservoir. Although many tour buses come through on the weekends, you can easily escape them by walking down to the reservoir. To get there, just walk down the road through the village by the school. The reservoir, named **Green Lake** *(bì hú)*, is at its best during the spring and summer wet season. In the dry season the water level drops and a great deal of mud is revealed. Even then, the surrounding

HUISUN FOREST 惠蓀林場

1 Frog Rock
　青蛙石
2 Student Centre
　實習館
3 Camping Grounds
　露營區
4 Coffee Plantation
　咖啡園
5 Huisun Forest Hotel; Restaurant;
　Service Centre
　惠蓀林場餐旅服務區
6 Toll Gate
　大門收費亭

countryside is still magnificent, the peaceful surroundings are invigorating and the air is fresh and cool.

If you prefer a less strenuous activity to hiking down to the lake, walk down the street leading out of town. On the left side of the road there is a 'moon gate'. Walk through it, heading uphill, and you will soon come to a peaceful **temple**, surrounded by trees. This is a perfect place to sit and relax.

In 1930, Wushe was the scene of a violent

uprising of the local aboriginal population against the Japanese occupation forces. The Japanese, with their usual efficiency, quickly crushed the rebellion and left over 1000 dead. There is a mural in the youth hostel depicting this battle and there is a plaque by the temple to honour those who died.

Places to Stay
Unless you have a tent and do some back-country camping, there is no cheap place to stay. The main street of town is lined with several mid-range hotels. Perhaps the best deal is the *Wuying Hotel* (☎ 802-360; *wùyīng dà lǚshè*) at 59 Jenho Rd (the main street of town), which charges NT$1000/1600 for doubles/twins.

The *Wushe Mountain Hostel* (☎ 802-611; *wùshè shān zhuāng*), operated by the CYC, is only cheap if you're with a group. Rooms for six people are NT$1800, and rooms for eight cost NT$2400. There are also two twin rooms for NT$120. The hostel is on the hill at the end of the main street (by the market area).

Getting There & Away
Getting to Wushe is easy. There are a few direct buses a day from Taichung – if you catch one, fine, but if not just take a bus to Puli. If you are coming from Sun Moon Lake, also take a bus to Puli. The bus will drop you off by the Taiwan Bus Company station in Puli. From here walk down the street about two blocks to a hole-in-the-wall bus station operated by the Nantou Bus Company to buy a ticket to Wushe. It's a 24km trip from Puli to Wushe up a steep highway through a scenic gorge.

LUSHAN HOT SPRINGS
(lúshān wēnquán) 蘆山溫泉
Nine kilometres east of Wushe and at 1200m elevation, Lushan offers hot springs and delightful mountain scenery. Actually, most of the hot springs aren't particularly natural because they have been taken over by hotels and are simply indoor bathtubs. You don't have to stay in the hotel to use the hot baths,

but if you don't you have to pay an entrance fee if you want to 'take a rest' *(xiūxí)*.

Lushan is a village perched precariously on both sides of a steep gorge with a river rushing through the centre of town. The two sides of the town are connected by a foot suspension bridge. This feature gives the town a unique advantage as no cars can cross the bridge, therefore making one side of town almost traffic-free, although the peace and quiet is occasionally marred by the 'walking tractors' – small cargo vehicles powered by lawn-mower engines that are used to haul food and other goods to the hotels.

There is a pleasant short hike from the village along the gorge. Going upstream, you will soon find a little restaurant perched on the cliffs. There is a man there selling eggs which you can cook in the hot springs. He also sells oolong tea by the pot, so you can sit and drink tea and watch the river rush by.

If you need some more exercise, Lushan is a staging post for climbing the mighty Nengkaoshan (see the following section).

Places to Stay
There are so many hotels in this town that you begin to wonder if anyone in Lushan lives in a real house. The *Police Hostel* (☎ 802-529; *jǐngguāng shān zhuāng*) costs NT$1200, which is marginally cheaper than the competition. Police get priority, but others can stay if space is available. The hostel has hot-spring baths.

Moving upmarket, there is the *Skyline Inn* (☎ 802-675; *tiānlú dà fàndiàn*), where rooms cost NT$1600 to NT$4800. Considering the very glitzy atmosphere, it appears to be good value.

The large *Bihuazhuang Hotel* (☎ 802-326; *bìhuázhuāng lǚshè*) has doubles/twins for NT$1200/2000.

The *Honeymoon Hotel* (☎ 802-355; *mì-yuè guǎn dà fàndiàn*) is a sharp-looking place with doubles/twins costing NT$3000/3500.

Getting There & Away
Buses to the hot springs run about once an hour from Wushe. There are occasional

direct buses from Taichung and nine buses daily from Puli. Just before reaching Lushan, the bus crosses one of the highest bridges in Taiwan – this has recently become a popular site for bungy jumping.

NENGKAOSHAN
(nénggāoshān) 能高山

One of the most outstanding hikes in Taiwan is the ascent of Nengkaoshan. Aside from the great scenery, a major attraction is that you can ascend the peak from the west side of Taiwan and then continue down into Hualien county on the east coast.

Nengkaoshan's main peak reaches an elevation of 3261m, and the south peak is even higher at 3349m. Although this is a 'must climb' for Taiwanese mountaineers, it is only the 58th highest peak on the island. However, because it breaks the 3000m barrier, you'll need a class A mountain permit.

You'll also need plenty of spare time. The Lushan-Nengkaoshan-Hualien journey requires three full days of walking, and that's not including the time it takes you to reach Lushan.

Lushan is not the actual trailhead. From Lushan take a bus, taxi or motorcycle (about 1½ hours) to Tunyuan *(túnyuán)*, where your mountain pass will be checked. You'll soon reach Yunhai Hostel *(yúnhǎi shān zhuāng)*, but if the weather is fine you can push on to Tienchih *(tiānchí, or Heaven's Pond)*. Tienchih is about five hours from Tunyuan by foot, and most climbers spend the night at nearby Tienchih Hostel *(tiānchí shān zhuāng)*.

Tienchih is an important junction. The trail to the south leads to the summit of Nengkaoshan, a strenuous day hike. The trail heading east descends steeply down to a jeep road, which then continues down to Liyu Lake. From Liyu Lake, you can catch a bus to the city of Hualien. You'll need to bring a torch if you take this route, as you must pass through several unlit tunnels (the longest is nearly 1km in length!).

Assuming you want to hike up to the summit of Nengkaoshan, you'll need to get up at the crack of dawn or earlier. It's nearly

a six hour uphill slog to the summit from Tienchih Hostel, and about another five hours for the descent. On the south side of the summit is the Nengkaoshan Hut *(nénggāoshān wū)* which can provide a roof over your head and nothing else. If you make this hike you'll need to be totally self-sufficient in terms of food, water, warm clothing and rain gear.

CHINGCHING FARM
(qīngjìng nóngchǎng) 清境農場

Perched 1750m above sea level, Chingching (Quiet) Farm is undergoing a transformation from an agricultural region into a tourist resort. While on weekends the place bustles with the tour buses, cars and motorcycles carrying camera-clicking tourists, during the week it's very quiet and that's the time to visit if you wish to see this famous orchard area. However, nearby Hohuanshan is more scenic and offers better hiking opportunities.

Chingching Farm is not actually one farm, but a group of farms strewn along the highway that runs from Wushe to the top of Hohuanshan. In addition to the orchards, where you can pick your own fruit for a fee (based on weight), they also raise cows. There aren't many places in Taiwan where you can see cows and this is one of the main reasons why Chingching Farm is such a big attraction for the city folk. Also, the Chinese have a real affection for grass – not the kind you can smoke, but the kind that cows munch on. Chingching Farm has one very large pasture, and Chinese tourists flock there to take endless photos of each other standing in the grass and cow manure.

Places to Stay
Hotels fill up fast on weekends. There are several camping grounds in Chingching Farm; in the past, they used to rent out equipment but these days they expect you to supply your own.

The *Youshi Hotel* (☎ 802-533; *yòushī shān zhuāng*) is a government-owned hotel. Talk to the manager here if you want to stay in the adjacent camping ground. Double rooms in the hotel cost NT$1000.

WEST-CENTRAL TAIWAN

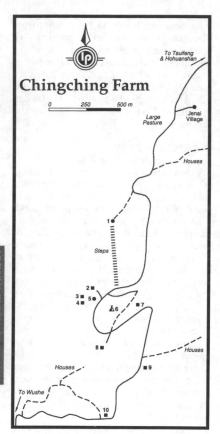

CHINGCHING FARM 清境農場

1 Chiang Kaishek Statue
蔣公銅像
2 Minsheng Guoyuan Hotel
民生果園山莊
3 Huatai Hotel
華泰山莊
4 Xintai Muwu Hotel
欣泰木屋
5 Market
市場
6 Camping Ground
露營區
7 Youshi Hotel
幼獅山莊
8 Chingching Public Hostel
清境國民賓館
9 Sunshine Vacation Villa
見晴渡假山莊
10 Yifu Hotel
億福山莊

NT$1800 to NT$2000 and suites are from NT$5000 and NT$6000. The 'dormitories' are group rooms for six people which cost NT$3000 per room.

The *Sunshine Vacation Villa* (☎ 803-162; fax 803-163; *jiànqíng dùjià shān zhuāng*) is a very elegant place. Attached to the hotel is a bar and a restaurant with outdoor tables and a spectacular view. Room rates begin at NT$1800.

A bit further down the highway is the *Yifu Hotel* (☎ 802-999; *yìfú shān zhuāng*). This is a new and pleasant place to stay. Weekday rates for twins/suites are NT$1560/1720, but on weekends and holidays prices jump to NT$1950/2150.

Getting There & Away
To reach Chingching Farm, take a bus from Puli or Wushe. It's an 8km ride from Wushe. When going up the mountain, sit on the right side of the bus for the best view.

TSUIFENG
(*cuìfēng*) 翠峰
One of the highest and coldest towns in Taiwan, Tsuifeng (2310m) is an aboriginal village.

Walk through the market and you'll find three hotels. To your right as you exit the rear of the market is the *Minsheng Guoyuan Hotel* (☎ 801-619/802-364; *mínshēng guǒyuán shān zhuāng*), which has doubles for NT$1000. To your left is the *Huatai Hotel* (☎ 801-051/802-378; *huátài shān zhuāng*) and the *Xintai Muwu Hotel* (*xīntài mùwū*), both under the same management with rooms starting at NT$1000.

The *Chingching Public Hostel* (☎ 802-748; fax 802-203; *qīngjìng guómín bīnguǎn*) is another government-owned place where doubles are NT$1500 to NT$1800, twins are

There isn't much to the town itself, which basically consists of a smattering of houses and farms. The most impressive building is the police station, which looks like a hotel.

The main reason to come here is to launch yourself at Hohuanshan, which is a six hour hike up the road.

Buses from Puli terminate in Tsuifeng, which also boasts the highest bus station in Taiwan. About 1km before the bus station is the only place to stay, the *Tsuifeng Travel Centre* (☎ 801-541; *cuìfēng lǚyóu zhōngxīn*) which is a hostel operated by the Taiwan University Experimental Forestry Department. The dormitories have four beds per room and cost NT$500 per person. Facilities are somewhat basic, but it's very clean and the manager is exceptionally friendly. The hostel has its own attached restaurant.

HOHUANSHAN
(héhuānshān) 合歡山
Many visitors to Taiwan are surprised to learn that in this subtropical island there is a ski resort. Hohuanshan (Harmonious Happiness Mountain) reaches an elevation of 3416m and the summit is well above the tree line. At this height it is cool even in summer, but in winter the night temperatures can dip well below freezing and in some years there is sufficient snowfall in January and February to permit skiing. However, the skiing isn't very good – the ski lift broke down years ago and hasn't been repaired. So 'skiing' consists of walking up the hill yourself and sliding back down.

During the rest of the year it is certainly worth visiting Hohuanshan for its magnificent views. In the morning, you can usually witness that beautiful Taiwanese phenomenon, the 'sea of clouds'. In the afternoon, the clouds rise and often envelop the summit. When this happens, it's like being inside a table tennis ball.

Hohuanshan is reached by a paved highway that connects Tayuling to Wushe. It's the highest road in Taiwan, reaching an elevation of 3275m at Wuling Pass. This is the westernmost part of Taroko National Park.

Hohuanshan is peaceful during the off

season, but when it snows everybody converges on the mountain. People in Taiwan have few opportunities to see snow, so when it falls on Hohuanshan everyone who can makes the pilgrimage there to see the white stuff. On winter weekends, it looks like a car park in Taipei.

A number of hikers use Hohuanshan as a base from which to climb **Chilaishan** *(qíláishān)* – the large, jagged-faced mountain immediately to the east of Hohuanshan. The mountain is dominated by a tremendous jagged, sawtooth ridge with several peaks, the highest one being 3607m above sea level. The 'trail' follows this ridgeline and offers numerous opportunities for hang-gliding and skydiving. If you are invited to go climbing Chilaishan, you should be aware that it's notorious in Taiwan as the site of many fatal accidents. The high body count stems from severe weather changes and a vertical, crumbly, rocky face. Also, during the frequently foggy and windy weather, hikers have been known to be blown right over the edge. A mountain permit is required to climb Chilaishan.

Places to Stay
At Hohuanshan there is only one place to stay – the *Hohuan Hostel* (☎ 802-732; *héhuān shān zhuāng*). The hostel consists of several buildings; the more upmarket one is called the *Pine Snow Lodge (sōng xuě lóu)* which was under renovation at the time of writing. The tatami dormitories can accommodate six people and cost NT$330 per person. Triple rooms cost NT$2200, but prices might rise after the renovation work is completed. Rooms at the hostel can also be booked at the service centre in Taichung (☎ (04) 588-6887/587-8800).

There are no shops in or near the hostel, so bring food, film, toilet paper, a torch and plenty of warm clothes. If you don't have a reservation, also make sure you bring a sleeping bag and sleeping mat because there is only one quilt for every guest and no extras. If all the beds are taken, you might be allowed to roll out a sleeping bag on the dining room floor when it's time for lights out, but don't count on it.

The other possibility is to not spend the night at Hohuanshan itself, but rather nearby. You can also stay in Tsuifeng (see previous section) or Tayuling (see the Tayuling section under Hualien County in the East Coast chapter).

Places to Eat

The hostel has a basic restaurant for guests, but meals have to be booked in advance. Vendors set up pushcarts in the car park, but if the weather turns foul they pack up their pick-up trucks and head down the mountain. Because food is limited and bad weather occasionally makes the access road impassable, you are strongly advised to bring extra food. Otherwise, you may have to forage for nuts and berries.

Getting There & Away

One major tactical problem with visiting Hohuanshan is that there is no bus service along the road that leads to the top of the mountain. You have two options: walk or hitch. There is plenty of traffic during the summer peak season. However, during the cold months, few come here except when the TV stations report snow at Hohuanshan – then there's a sudden fully fledged rush hour. When there is snow, huge numbers of share taxis suddenly materialise, waiting to ferry passengers up to the summit.

There are two routes, and ideally you should go up one way and down the other. Either route may be closed occasionally due to landslides, and during snowstorms tyre chains are required.

North Side Approach The north side is shorter and steeper. The highest bus stop is at Tayuling, where taxis wait for passengers whenever there is snow on the mountain. If you walk from Tayuling, it's a steep but breathtakingly beautiful walk of 9km – four hours uphill or three hours downhill. Certainly the best way to appreciate the scenery is on foot.

South Side Approach From Puli, you can get a bus from the Nantou Bus Company station to Tsuifeng and from there it's 15km, or about 6½ hours of walking. There are no taxis in Tsuifeng, but there is one place to stay (see the previous section). The next nearest place to stay is Chingching Farm. The bus from Puli passes through Wushe and Chingching Farm, and terminates in Tsuifeng (where taxis will be waiting when there is snow). Start early because the weather is usually clearest in the morning.

Changhua County 彰化縣

CHANGHUA

(zhānghuà) 彰化

The county seat of Changhua County, the city of Changhua is useful mainly as a transit stop on the way to nearby Lukang. It's also home to the county Foreign Affairs Police (☎ 726-5674). Changhua's chief claim to fame is **Pakuashan** *(bāguàshān)*, a mountain park that reaches a comparatively tiny 97m above sea level. In terms of its numbers

The Great Buddha Statue at Changhua is reputed to be the largest representation of buddha in the world.

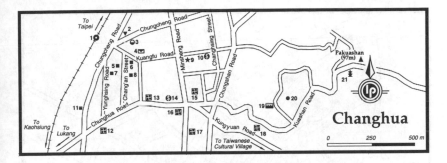

CHANGHUA 彰化

PLACES TO STAY
5 Jincheng & Hongye Hotels
   金城旅社、
   紅葉大旅社
6 Rich Royal Hotel
   富皇大飯店
7 Sanhuo Hotel
   三和大旅社
8 Ing Shan Hotel
   櫻山大飯店
11 Yongda Hotel
   永大大飯店

OTHER
1 Train Station
   彰化火車站

2 McDonald's
   麥當勞
3 Changhua Bus Company
   Station
   彰化客運站
4 Post Office
   郵局
9 Foreign Affairs
   Police
   警察局外事課
10 ICBC
   中國國際商業銀行
12 Fute Temple
   福德祠
13 Kaiyuan Temple
   開元寺

14 Bank of Taiwan
   台灣銀行
15 Confucius Temple
   孔子廟
16 Chenghuang Temple
   城隍廟
17 Tanhuafo Temple
   曇花佛堂
18 Nantien Temple
   南天宮
19 Nine Dragons Pool
   九龍池
20 Great Buddha
   Statue
   八卦山大佛像
21 Chungling Pagoda
   忠靈塔

of visitors, Pakuashan is rated as one of Taiwan's 10 most-visited tourist sites. Close to the summit of Pakuashan is the **Great Buddha Statue** (*dà fó xiàng*), which is 22m high. You can go inside and look out of the Buddha's eyes, ears, and other bodily orifices. Three hundred tons (272,000kg) of concrete were used in its construction. Adjacent to the Buddha is a temple. Also near the summit is the **Chungling Pagoda** (*zhōng-líng tǎ*) and a flower garden.

Changhua also has a **Confucius Temple** (*kǒng miào*), one of the oldest in Taiwan. It's dead quiet most of the time, but comes to life on Teachers' Day (28 September) when there is a dawn ceremony.

There are a couple of other temples around town, which are worth a look if you're spending the night in Changhua. Those to look for include the Chenghuang Temple (*chénghuáng miào*), Kaiyuan Temple (*kāi-yuán sì*), Nantien Temple (*nántiān gōng*) and Fute Temple (*fúdé cí*).

Places to Stay
There are only a small number of hotels in Changhua, a reflection of the fact that few tourists choose to spend the night here. Most travellers are drawn to nearby Taichung which offers a much richer choice of accommodation possibilities (not to mention the restaurants and nightlife).

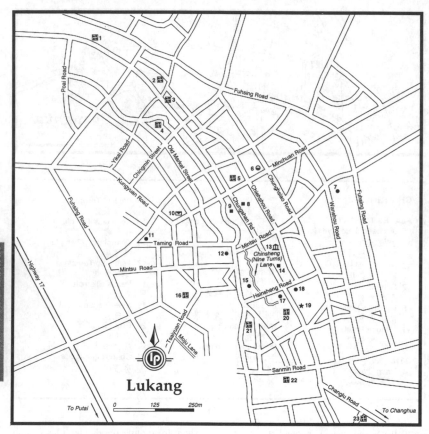

Lukang

0   125   250m

To Putai

To Changhua

The *Hongye Hotel* (☎ 722-2667; *hóngyè dà lǔshè*), 5 Lane 100, Chang'an St, has doubles with shared bath for NT$350 or with private bath for NT$500.

Next door is the *Jincheng Hotel* (☎ 722-5379; *jīnchéng lǔshè*), which has similar rooms for NT$350 to NT$500.

The *Sanhuo Hotel* (☎ 722-4646; *sānhé dà lǔshè*), 31 Lane 96, Yunghsing St, charges NT$600 to NT$1000 for a room.

The *Ing Shan Hotel* (☎ 722-9211; *yīngshān dà fàndiàn*), 129 Chang'an St, is excellent value with doubles/twin rooms for NT$600/1300.

The *Rich Royal Hotel* (☎ 723-7117; *fùhuáng dà fàndiàn*), 97 Chang'an St, is the best place to stay if you're driving your own vehicle – the car park is in the lobby! Rooms cost NT$880 to NT$1200.

The *Yongda Hotel* (☎ 722-4666; *yǒngdà dà fàndiàn*), at 120 Chungcheng Rd, Section 2, has very nice-looking doubles/twins for NT$600/1100. The lower floor is a restaurant – you have to go up the stairs to find the reception.

Activities

The Changhua Golf Club (*zhānghuà gāo'ěrfū*

LUKANG 鹿港	4 Nanching Temple 南靖宮	15 Shihyih Hall 十宜樓
PLACES TO STAY 8 Peace Hotel 和平旅社 9 Meihua Hotel 美華旅社 14 Quanzhong Hotel 全忠旅社	5 Sanshan Kuowang Temple 三山國王廟 6 Changhua Bus Company Station 彰化客運站 7 Arts & Crafts Centre 民俗藝術館	16 Weiling Temple 威靈廟 17 Remembrance Hall 意樓 18 Hsiehchai Pottery Wall 謝宅甕牆 19 Police Station 派出所
OTHER 1 Fengtien Temple 奉天宮 2 Matsu Temple 天后宮 3 Chenghuang Temple 城隍廟	10 Post Office 郵局 11 Chingyiyuan Memorial 敬義園紀念碑 12 First Market 第一市場 13 Lukang Folk Arts Museum 鹿港民俗文物館	20 Hsing'an Temple 興安宮 21 Fengshan Temple 鳳山寺 22 Lungshan Temple 龍山寺 23 Wenwu Temple 文武廟

WEST-CENTRAL TAIWAN

qiú chǎng) lies to the south-east; right next to that, is the Changhua Grass-Skiing Area *(zhānghuà huácǎo chǎng)*.

Getting There & Away
Changhua is on the major west coast train line and has frequent services to destinations in the north and south. The Changhua Bus Company *(zhānghuà kèyùn)* has a station opposite the train station and offers services to Lukang and Taichung.

In the unlikely event that you want to rent a vehicle while you're in Changhua, you can try China Rent-A-Car (☎ 761-4788) at 61 Chungyang Rd.

TAIWANESE CULTURAL VILLAGE
(táiwān mínsú cūn) 台灣民俗村
The emphasis here is on Taiwanese culture, a surprising change from the 'aboriginal cultural villages' which are rapidly multiplying around the island. Perhaps the best reason to come here is to sample the traditional Taiwanese food. There are about 300 traditional buildings on the site, well stocked with Taiwanese antiques. Rumours have persisted for years that a lot of stolen antiques have wound up here, but the allegations are so far unproven.

The Taiwanese Cultural Village (☎ 787-0088) is to the south-east of Changhua. Admission for adults is NT$530, but this is reduced to NT$350 if you stay overnight here (though that's hardly a bargain at NT$3300 for a twin!). The site is open daily from 8.30 am to 5 pm.

LUKANG
(lùgǎng) 鹿港
Lukang (Deer Harbour) is mainly of interest to historians. The town was a thriving port in the 15th century and remained so until it was closed in 1895 by the Japanese. For a glance at the past, wander through its narrow alleys. While there are many original buildings still standing, modernisation has had a big impact – don't expect to find a perfectly preserved ancient Chinese village.

The Taiwanese think Lukang is a major tourist attraction, but most foreigners find it hard to get very excited about the few crumbling relics that remain here. However, Lukang does seem to be slowly getting its act together in the interests of tourism, and there is a steadily increasing supply of 'ancient' buildings.

Arts and crafts are a better reason for a visit – Lukang has shops that make traditional Taiwanese furniture and religious artefacts.

Lukang Folk Arts Museum
(lùgǎng mínsú wénwù guǎn)
鹿港民俗文物館

One of the best sights in Lukang is the Folk Arts Museum (☎ 777-2019) at 152 Chungshan Rd. It's in an old colonial building built by the Japanese with a large collection of musical instruments, lacquerware, furniture, porcelain, a bridal sedan chair and other interesting artefacts. The entrance fee is NT$130 but students with an ID card can get in for NT$70. The entrance to the museum is not obvious from Chungshan Rd. Look for the police station, just to the left of which is a narrow alley. Follow the alley to the end, then turn left and you'll see the museum about 100m in front of you.

Alleys

By wandering through Lukang's narrow alleys, you really get an idea of what the town used to look like in the pre-motorcycle age. **Nine Turns Lane** *(jiǔ qū xiàng)* is the nickname for the narrow Chinsheng Lane *(jīnshèng xiàng)*. The narrowest lane of all is **Moju Lane** *(mōrǔ xiàng)*. **Old Market St** *(gǔ shì jiē)* is the nickname for three consecutive sections of a lane made up by Putou, Yaolin and Tayu Sts.

Temples

Lukang has numerous temples, but most are the hole-in-the-wall style. The largest is the **Lungshan Temple** *(lóngshān sì)*, dedicated to Kuanyin, the Goddess of Mercy. The runner-up is the **Matsu Temple** *(tiānhòu miào)*, dedicated to Matsu, Goddess of the Sea. Both were close to falling apart by the 1970s, but have now been restored.

Other smaller, interesting temples include the **Fengtien Temple** *(fèngtiān gōng)*, the **Chenghuang Temple** *(chénghuáng miào)* and the **Wenwu Temple** *(wénwǔ miào)*.

Places to Stay

Considering that Lukang is about the biggest tourist drawcard in Changhua County, it's interesting that there are only three hotels in town, all of them very small. Apparently most visitors do Lukang as a day trip from Changhua or Taichung.

The *Peace Hotel* (☎ 777-2600; *hépíng lǔshè*), 230 Chungshan Rd, has doubles/twins for NT$600/1000 with private bath. It looks rather tattered around the edges, but it's better (if only slightly) than sleeping in the street.

On the opposite side of the road is the *Meihua Hotel* (☎ 777-2027; *měihuá lǔshè*), where doubles are NT$500. The management claims that rooms are often full!

Quanzhong Hotel (☎ 777-2640; *quánzhōng lǔshè*) at 104 Chungshan Rd is quite new and comfortable. Doubles/twins cost NT$600/850.

Places to Eat

Lukang is famous for its good food. A local speciality is 'cow's tongue cake' *(niú shé bǐng)*, which is not really made out of a cow's tongue but resembles one in size and shape. Other sweet specialties include dried 'dragon eye biscuits' *(fèngyǎn gāo)* and 'malt biscuits' *(màiyá mǐxiāng)*. These are available everywhere, and taste best when hot out of the oven.

Things to Buy

Lukang is famous for its handicrafts. In the factories, which are easy enough to find along Chungshan Rd, you can buy statues, monuments, wood carvings, tables, paintings, embroidery, lanterns and pottery. Also worth checking out is the Arts & Crafts Centre *(mínsú yìshù guǎn)* on Fuhsing Rd near Mintsu Rd.

In many cases, you can negotiate with the artisan who made the goods, which theoretically means you should get them cheaper. If you're planning on buying something heavy, like furniture, you'll need the services of a freight forwarder to ship it abroad.

Getting There & Away

Buses run by the Changhua Bus Company travel between Lukang and Changhua once every 10 to 20 minutes. The trip takes roughly 20 minutes.

Lukang is 21km south-west of Taichung

and the Changhua Bus Company also runs buses between these two towns. The buses stop briefly in Changhua. The journey takes at least an hour and costs NT$70. The first departure from Taichung is at 6.40 am and the last departure from Lukang is 8.20 pm.

Taichung County 台中縣

TAICHUNG
(táizhōng) 台中

Taichung, which means 'central Taiwan', is the third largest city on the island. The city has prospered in recent times, and it now claims to be the heart of the island's small and medium-size manufacturing industries. The Taichung Industrial Zone is the island's second largest, as is its port. The city has also long enjoyed a reputation as an educational and cultural centre.

Many locals praise Taichung as having the best climate in Taiwan, and though you might not agree during the steamy summers, this part of Taiwan is much drier than rainy Taipei and not so stinking hot as Kaohsiung. There are many universities in Taichung and it's a good place for the study of Chinese – many expats are here for that reason. For tourists, the city offers a few attractions such as museums, some enormous shopping centres and a great nightlife. Taichung is also a major jumping-off point for trips into the spectacular Central Mountain Range.

Orientation

Taichung is rapidly becoming a place with two town centres. For most travellers, the 'real town centre' near the train station is still the best place to go – here you'll find lots of hotels, restaurants and public transport.

The new town centre is to the north-west of the centre where Taichungkang (Taichung Harbour) Rd meets the freeway. For that reason it's generally known as the Chungkang *(zhōnggǎng)* area. Lots of bus stations and upmarket hotels have established themselves here, and there are plans afoot to move

city hall and other government offices to this neighbourhood.

Taichungkang Rd is a big wide boulevard which serves as the major artery connecting the two town centres. Along this road are an ever-increasing number of hotels, restaurants and stores. Not surprisingly, there is also an ever-increasing traffic jam.

Information

Tourist Office There is a Travel Information Service Centre (☎ 227-0421) at 216 Minchuan Rd, on the 4th floor.

Emergencies

There is a branch of the Foreign Affairs Police (☎ 327-3875) in Taichung.

Useful Organisations For good English-language information on Taichung, pick up a free copy of *Compass*, the Taichung American Chamber of Commerce's bimonthly magazine. It includes a Community Calender of events, and features about new and interesting places around the city. It's readily available at expat hang-outs such as Napoli, Frog I, Fingas, La Terrasse and bigger hotels. Otherwise, give the Taichung AmCham (☎ 205-0443) a call. An online version of the magazine is also published (inside.com.tw).

Bookshops There is a Caves Books (☎ 326-5559; *dūnhuáng shūjú*) at 302 Taichungkang Rd, Section 1. There is a second Caves (☎ 227-3339) at 22-3 Taiping Rd, near the Lai Lai Department Store.

Eslite Books (☎ 221-1287; *chéngpǐn shūdiàn*) has a branch on the 13th floor of the huge Chungyo Department Store (Building C, International Hall) at 161 Sanmin Rd, Section 3. There is another Eslite branch (☎ 323-4958) in the Natural Science Museum building.

New Schoolmate Books *(xīn xué yǒu shūjú)*, also known as Sensaio Books or just NSB, has a branch beside the Lai Lai Department Store (☎ 225-7999).

On the 2nd floor of the Frog Pub I at 105 Huamei W St, Section 1, is a second-hand bookshop.

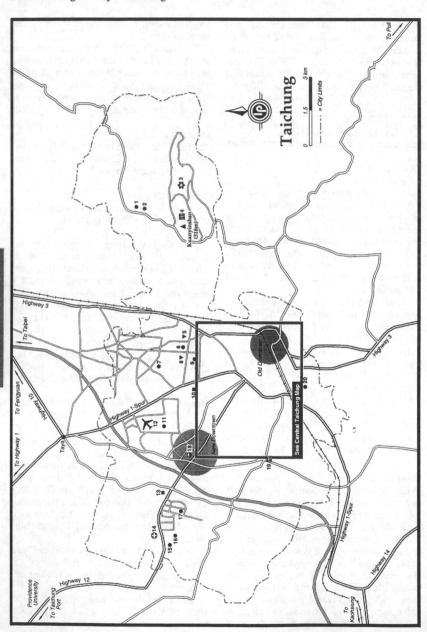

TAICHUNG 台中市

PLACES TO STAY
10 Plaza International Hotel
   通豪大飯店
13 Howard Prince Hotel
   福華大飯店

PLACES TO EAT
5 Coriya Restaurant
   可利亞
8 Sugar & Spice Bakery
   Café
   崇德路二段125號

OTHER
1 Venice Aquatic
   Amusement Park
   威尼斯水上樂園

2 Cattleya Amusement Park
   卡多里樂園
3 Encore Gardens
   亞哥花園
4 Jade Buddha Temple
   玉佛寺
6 Minsu Park
   民俗公園
7 Morrison Academy
   美國瑪禮遜學校
9 Carrefour Hypermart
   家樂福
11 Fengchia University
   逢甲大學
12 Shuinan Airport
   水湳機場
14 Veterans General Hospital
   榮總台中醫院

15 Tunghai University
   東海大學
16 Tunghai Dairy
   Farm
   東海牧場
17 Taichung World Trade
   Centre
   台中世貿中心
18 Tonglien & Taiwan Bus
   Companies
   統聯客運中港站、
   國光號站
19 Nantun Old St; Wanho &
   Wen Changkung Temples
   南屯古街、
   萬和宮、文昌公廟
20 Chunghsing University
   中興大學

Cybercafes You can surf the net at the Internet Club (☎ 310-1701 ext 24), 3rd floor, Frog Pub I, 105 Huamei W St, Section 1.

Natural Science Museum
(zìrán kēxué bówùguǎn) 自然科學博物館
This museum (☎ 322-6940) is one of the city's most highly touted attractions. It is divided into several sections with various admission fees.

Of particular interest to foreigners is the Chinese Science & Technology and Chinese Spiritual Life sections of the museum, which include excellent English and Japanese Acoustiguide systems which give self-guided tours of the exhibits.

Admission to the main exhibition hall is NT$100, while the planetarium *(tàikōng jùchǎng)* is NT$100 and the 3D theatre *(lìtǐ jùchǎng)* is NT$70.

The museum is at 1 Kuanchien Rd, near the Hotel National. It's only 10 minutes by bus from the city centre. To get there take green bus No 22, 48, 103, 106, 107 or 135, or red bus No 22, 37, 38, 45, 46, or 48 (see Taichung's Getting Around section for an explanation of the city's bus lines). The museum is open daily except Monday and the day after national holidays.

Guinness World of Records Museum
(jīnshì shìjiè jìlù bówùguǎn)
金氏世界紀錄博物館
Occasionally, Taiwan comes up with something that takes you completely by surprise. Such is the case with the Guinness World of Records Museum (☎ 259-7123). It's currently the largest such museum in the world – who would have expected to find it in Taichung? Britain's former Prime Minister Margaret Thatcher attended its opening ceremony in 1995.

World-record holders, such as the world's tallest and shortest living women, are frequently invited to the museum and stay for extended periods of time. The museum has also sponsored several record-breaking stunts – not all were successful. One stunt was to get 400 people to swim 1km at Sun Moon Lake – this was the most people to do this at one time but it didn't get into the record book because one swimmer drowned (Guinness refuses to recognise stunts that cause deaths).

The museum is at 77 Chaofu Rd, close to where Taichungkang Rd intersects with the North-South Freeway (north-west Taichung).

Confucius Temple
(kǒngzǐ miào) 孔子廟
Though not as old and rustic-looking as the

WEST-CENTRAL TAIWAN

one in Tainan, this temple is larger and more colourful. Like other Confucius temples, it has a dawn ceremony on 28 September, the birthday of Confucius. The temple is on Shuangshih Rd, about a 20 minute walk north of the train station, or you can take red bus No 10, 11, 40 or 46 there. The temple is closed on Monday.

Martyrs' Shrine
(zhōngliè cí) 忠烈祠
If you visit the Confucius Temple, it's very convenient to visit the adjacent Martyrs' Shrine. The shrine is in honour of those who died fighting for their country. On 29 March (Youth Day) a ceremony is held there.

Paochueh Temple
(bǎojué sì) 寶覺寺
A few blocks to the north-west of the Confucius Temple, at 140 Chienhsing Rd, is the Paochueh Temple. This temple features a 31m-tall Buddha who the Chinese call Milefo, a derivation of the original Indian name Maitreya. Services are held at 5 am and 7 pm and they can last for several hours. You can take green bus No 6, 14, 16 or 17 to get there.

Chingming 1st St
(jīngmíng yījiē) 精明一街
Chingming 1st St is a cobblestone street that is blocked off to traffic. Restaurants, coffee shops and tea shops have set up outdoor tables with cloth umbrellas. The street is lined with trees, arty street lamps and some cultured-looking shops reminiscent of Paris. During warm summer evenings it becomes one big street party and is a great place to hang out.

Nantun Old St
(nántún gǔ jiē) 南屯古街
While it doesn't exactly look like Ming dynasty China, this street is of moderate interest to historians and antique collectors. It's here that you can buy either genuine or imitation Taiwanese antiques. Some of this stuff is very cheap – things like handmade aluminium buckets (the modern equivalent

are plastic), wooden ladles, bamboo baskets and so on. There are also some ancient (but not stale) foods on sale, that are difficult or impossible to find elsewhere in Taiwan.

Just adjacent to Nantun Old St is the Wanho Temple *(wànhé gōng)* and the Wen Changkung Temple *(wén chānggōng miào)*.

Minsu Park
(mínsú gōngyuán) 民俗公園
Minsu (Folk) Park boasts reproductions of Taiwan's ancient architecture, including a traditional courtyard-style home and a farmhouse. There is a basement museum that displays a wide range of ancient everyday Taiwanese home and farm implements.

While the park isn't stunning, a lot of people enjoy it and it's a good place to relax for a couple of hours. There is a NT$60 admission fee.

Chungshan Park
(zhōngshān gōngyuán) 台中公園
This is a pleasant park just off Kungyuan Rd with a lake where boating is permitted.

Universities
(dàxué) 大學
Taichung has four well-known universities. As a tourist you may not have a big interest in universities, but one that is worth seeing is **Tunghai University** *(dōnghǎi dàxué)*, a private coeducational school with a beautiful campus and innovative architecture. This seems to be the unofficial city park – it's certainly larger and more attractive than Taichung's other parks. The campus is a long way north-west of the centre on Taichungkang Rd. You can get there by taking either red bus No 38 or green bus No 22 to the last stop, which is inside the campus.

The largest school in Taichung is **Chunghsing University** *(zhōngxīng dàxué)*, a public coeducational institution. **Fengchia University** *(féngjiǎ dàxué)* is a private coeducational school. **Providence University** *(jìngyí dàxué)* is a private women's college in Shalu, 8km north-west of Taichung on Highway 12.

9 am to 8 pm and is closed on Monday. Admission is NT$30.

Encore Gardens

(yăgē huāyuán) 亞哥花園

This large private garden (☎ 239-1549) is in the foothills, almost 10km north-east of Taichung train station.

The gardens are dressed up with European architecture. In terms of raking in the cash, this is one of Taiwan's biggies. Most travellers should give it a miss – it's a good escape from the city for Taichung residents rather than an international tourist attraction. There is far better natural scenery in the magnificent mountains in eastern Taichung County. In the evenings, the garden's big attraction is supposed to be the 'water dance' *(shuǐwǔ)*, a 'three-dimensional' fountain with coloured lights and music.

The Encore Gardens are heavily touted in glossy tourist pamphlets, so if you have time and don't mind the admission fee, you might want to have a look. Entry costs NT$250 and the gardens are open daily from 9 am until midnight.

Buses to Encore Gardens are operated by Fengyuan Bus Company which has a bus stop on the traffic circle in front of Taichung train station. Departing from almost the same spot is red bus No 2, which also goes to the gardens.

Kuanyinshan

(guānyīnshān) 觀音山

About 1.5km south-west of Encore Gardens is Kuanyinshan, a mountain topped by a statue of the Goddess of Mercy. It's actually a very nice, though steep, climb with plenty of stone steps. The views from the top are rewarding. On the east side of the mountain is the Jade Buddha Temple *(yù fó sì)*.

The directions for getting to Kuanyinshan are the same as for Encore Gardens.

Cattleya Amusement Park

(kăduōlĭ lèyuán) 卡多里樂園

About 3km north of Encore Gardens is Cattleya Amusement Park (☎ 239-1598). It's basically what you expect an amusement

Big Brother is Watching ...

The Chinese expression for 'cellular telephone' is *dageda*, a combination of three characters which literally mean 'big brother big'. The same phrase is used in mainland China, Hong Kong and Taiwan.

Recently arrived foreigners, in the process of learning Chinese, invariably speculate about the origins of the phrase. Some theorise that having a cellular phone with you is almost like having your big brother along as a constant companion. Others have speculated that it's because the cellular phones are a bit like the sinister 'telescreens' in George Orwell's nightmarish novel, *1984* ('Big Brother is watching you!').

The phrase does indeed have sinister origins, although it has very little to do with the dictatorial 'Big Brother' that George Orwell warned us about. In Chinese, the phrase 'big brother big' is slang for 'Mafioso'. It seems that when cellular phones made their debut in Hong Kong (and later Taiwan), the majority of the people toting them were likely to be gangsters.

The term has stuck, even though these days cellular phones are popular with taxi drivers, high school students and even geriatric grandmothers. ■

Taichung Municipal Cultural Centre

(táizhōng shì wénhuà zhōngxīn) 台中市文化中心

The cultural centre (☎ 225-7311) is similar to the ones in Taipei, Kaohsiung and Tainan. Featuring opera, art exhibits and concerts, the cultural centre will probably be of more interest to residents than travellers. To get the current schedule of events, drop by the centre or call; its address is 600 Yingtsai Rd, near Wuchuan Rd. Take red bus No 3 or green bus No 20.

Taiwan Museum of Art

(měi shù guăn) 美術館

This is one of Taiwan's best art museums. The exhibits are rotated regularly, so you'll need to call (☎ 372-3740) or pick up a schedule of events if you want to find out what's on.

The museum is at 2 Wuchuan W Rd, to the west of the cultural centre. It's open Tuesday to Saturday from 9 am to 5 pm, Sunday from

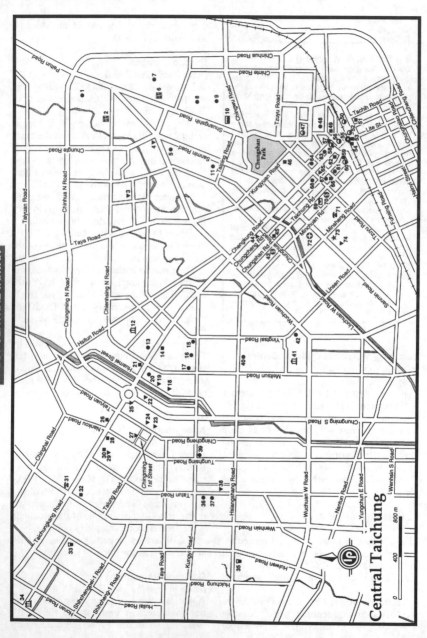

Central Taichung

CENTRAL TAICHUNG
台中市中心

PLACES TO STAY
14 Hotel National
全國大飯店
21 Grand Formosa Hotel
晶華大飯店
26 Evergreen Laurel Hotel
長榮桂冠酒店
28 Landis Hotel
永豐棧麗緻酒店
30 Provincial United Taichung Hostel
省聯合社台中會館、
大墩20街61號
32 Ful Won Hotel
富王大飯店
45 Galaxy Hotel
銀河大飯店
46 Park Hotel
敬華大飯店
49 Plaza & Crown Hotels
達欣大飯店、
王冠大飯店
51 Twinstar Hotel
雙星大飯店
53 Nan Hua Hotel
南華大飯店
54 Yeong Du Hotel
永都大飯店
57 Hotel Chance
巧合大飯店
59 Fuh Chun Hotel
富春大飯店57
62 Zhongzhou & Jiancheng Hotels
中洲旅社、
建城旅社
66 First Hotel; Chaku Chugui Tea House
第一旅社、
茶窟出軌

PLACES TO EAT
3 Frog Pub II
青蛙第二餐廳、
大德街58號
4 Coriya Restaurant
可利亞
18 Napoli Italian Restaurant
拿坡里餐廳、
華美街424號
19 PJ's Café
華美街一段392號
22 Frog Pub I
青蛙餐廳、
華美西街一段105號
23 Fingas Restaurant
風格餐廳、
精誠路17之1號
24 Fingas Deli; Frog III
風格食品店、
精誠路7號
25 McDonald's
麥當勞
27 Chunshui Tang Tea Shop
春水堂（精明一街）
29 Coffee Kitchen
大墩20街53號
38 La Terrasse French Bistro
巧味爐餐廳、
大聖街43號
44 Chunghua Rd Night Market
中華路夜市
65 Doutor's Coffee Shop
羅多倫咖啡店
74 Little Italy
四維街24-7號

OTHER
1 Department of Motor Vehicles
監理所
2 Paochueh Temple
寶覺寺
5 Martyrs' Shrine
忠烈祠
6 Confucius Temple
孔廟
7 Chungyo Department Store
中友百貨
8 Sports Stadium
體育場
9 Baseball Stadium
省立棒球場
10 Swimming Pool
游泳池
11 Lai Lai Department Store (Eslite Books)
來來百貨
12 Natural Science Museum
自然科學博物館
13 Caves Books
敦煌書局
15 NOVA Computer Arcade
NOVA資訊廣場
16 Top Mall
大廣三
17 Mei Chen Siang (Western Groceries)
美珍香、
中山路87號
20 SOGO Department Store
太平洋崇光百貨
31 Bu Bu Disco Pub
文心路三段6-5號
33 CCK Disco Pub
惠中路1段2號3樓
34 Guiness World of Records Museum
金氏世界紀錄博物館
35 Pig Pen Pub
大觀路41號
36 Carrefour Hypermart
家樂福
37 Carrefour Megamart
家樂福
39 What's Up Disco Pub
公益路363號
40 Party Animal Disco
向上北路141號
41 Taiwan Museum of Art
省立美術館
42 Taichung Municipal Cultural Centre
台中市文化中心
43 ICBC
國際商業銀行
47 Gancheng Bus Station
干城車站
48 Chienkuo Market
建國市場
50 Changhua Bus Company Station
彰化客運站
52 Taiwan Bus Company (Southbound Buses)
台汽客運南站
55 Train Station
台中火車站
56 Taiwan Bus Company (Northbound Buses)
台汽客運站
58 Tonglien Bus Company
統聯客運站

WEST-CENTRAL TAIWAN

continued over

60	Fengyuan Bus Company 豐原客運站	67	Mei Chen Siang Western Groceries 美珍香、 中山路87號	70	Bank of Taiwan 台灣銀行
61	Firefly Colony Tea Shop 火金姑殖民地			71	Telephone Company 電信局
63	First Square Shopping Plaza 第一廣場	68	Evergreen Tokyu Department Store 永琦百貨	72	Taichung Hospital 台中醫院
64	Far Eastern Department Store 遠東百貨	69	GPO 郵政總局	73	Foreign Affairs Police 警察局外事課

park to be, with lots of gentle rides for the young kids and more gut-wrenching machinery for the older ones. Most thrilling is the 360 degree roller coaster – if this doesn't make you ill, nothing will.

Admission to the park (not including rides) is NT$40. Green bus Nos 6 and 12 go there, as does red bus No 21 or 31.

Venice Aquatic Amusement Park
(*wēinísī shuǐshàng lèyuán*) 威尼斯水上樂園
Within walking distance of the Cattleya Amusement Park is the Venice Aquatic Amusement Park (☎ 239-2565). The theme is waterslides and swimming pools. Admission is NT$160 for adults, or NT$140 for students. The instructions for getting here are the same as the Cattleya Amusement Park.

Activities
Swimming There is a public swimming pool on the north-east corner of Shuangshih Rd and Chingwu Rd, opposite the rear entrance of Chungshan Park. It's only open in summer.

Bowling If you like bowling and billiards, visit the New Taichung Bowling Centre (☎ 222-8041; *xīn táizhōng bǎolíng qiúguǎn*), 14 Shihfu Rd. Another place to try is Amber Lanes (☎ 232-1177; *hǔpò bǎolíng qiúguǎn*) at 111 Taya Rd.

Taichung's newest bowling alley is at 125 Chungteh Rd, Section 2 (at Wenhsin Rd), on the 2nd floor (above the Sugar & Spice Bakery Cafe).

Golf To the north-east of Taichung near the

town of Fengyuan is the Fengyuan Golf Club (*fēngyuán gāo'ěrfū qiú chǎng*).

Saunas A good sauna for woman only is Caesar's Sauna (☎ 207-1138; *kǎiyuè sānwēnnuǎn*) in the basement at 27-8 Taya Rd (Tongling Commercial Building). Admission is NT$400 each time, or NT$6000 for a full year's membership.

For men there's Sanyang Sauna (☎ 201-5577; *sānyáng sānwēnnuǎn*) at 111 Taya Rd. Daytime admission (6 am until 9 pm) is NT$500, but you can stay from 9 pm until noon the next day with a midnight snack and breakfast included for NT$750.

Health & Fitness Centres The Arts Health Club (*yàlìshāndà jiànkāng xiūxián jùlèbù*) is open to both men and women. This is an upmarket establishment with all the latest equipment as well as swimming pools, saunas, pool table, restaurant, MTV and KTV. The cost reflects this – NT$5000 per month, or NT$32,000 per year. There are two locations: the Wenhsin branch (☎ 232-7988), basement and 1st floor, 311 Tienchin Rd (*tiānjīn lù*); and the larger Chengteh branch (☎ 230-0800), 3rd floor, 631 Chungteh Rd, Section 1 (next to Carrefour). Both branches are open from 8 am to 11 pm, Monday to Saturday, and 10 am to 6 pm on Sunday.

If you're looking for something more downmarket, there's the Modern Gym (☎ 206-4191) at 122 Taya Rd. It's fine if you just want to work out with machines, but there's no sauna or other facilities. Some have complained about vehicle exhaust fumes which come in through the open windows. Still, it's a popular place for the working class to work out. Modern Gym is open from 6 am to 11 pm, Monday to Saturday, and from 1 to 6 pm on Sunday. It's normally crowded between 6 and 8 pm.

Places to Stay – budget

If you're willing to stay in a closet-sized room and use a shared bath, the most economical place in town is Zhongzhou Hotel (☎ 222-2711; zhōngzhōu lǚshè) on the 2nd floor of 129 Chienkuo Rd, just opposite the train station, between Chungcheng and Chungshan Rds. Singles/double rooms cost NT$200/300. The management is not particularly nice and the best thing that can be said for this place is that it's cheap. Next door is a narrow alley called Lane 125 – here you'll find the Jiancheng Hotel (☎ 222-2497; jiànchéng lǚshè). Doubles/twin rooms cost NT$250/500 – the cheaper rooms have a shared bath.

The Fuh Chun Hotel (☎ 228-3181; fùchūn dà fàndiàn), 1 Chungshan Rd, is one of the best deals in town with doubles from NT$530 to NT$980 and twins from NT$880 to NT$1200. Even the lower-priced rooms are perfectly clean, have a private bath and are air-conditioned. The hotel's restaurant is also a good, cheap place to eat.

The First Hotel (☎ 222-2205; dìyī lǚshè), 51 Chikuang St (jìguāng jiē) is cheaper than the Fuh Chun, but it's showing its age. However, the management is friendly and rooms have an attached bath. Doubles are from NT$350 to NT$450.

As you emerge from the underpass stairs at the rear of the train station, you find yourself in an alley. Immediately ahead (still in the alley) is the Yeong Du Hotel (☎ 222-6418; yǒngdū dà fàndiàn). Doubles are NT$450 and NT$550; twins cost NT$600 to NT$800.

Another place behind the train station, at 133 Fuhsing Rd, Section 4, is the Nan Hua Hotel (☎ 223-1061; nán huá dà fàndiàn). Doubles/twins cost NT$600/1050.

Immediately to your right as you leave the train station at 180 Chienkuo Rd is the Plaza Hotel (☎ 229-3191; dáxīn dà fàndiàn). Twin rooms cost from NT$700 to NT$1650.

Almost next door to the Plaza is the Crown Hotel (☎ 229-2175; wángguān dà fàndiàn), where excellent singles are NT$550 and doubles/twins cost NT$750/950.

Opposite these two at 163 Chienkuo Rd is the Hotel Chance (☎ 229-7161; qiǎohé dà fàndiàn). Double rooms cost from NT$840 to NT$980.

If you're looking for a cheap (but very comfortable) hotel a little bit further out in the direction of the freeway, check out the government-owned Provincial United Taichung Hostel (☎ 325-9836/325-9581; shěng liánhé shè táizhōng huìguǎn), 61 Tatun 20th St. Double/twin rooms are NT$450/550 and triples are from NT$700 to NT$780. Tatun 20th St is one block south of Taichungkang Rd – the hotel is between Tatun and Tunghsing Rds. Buses passing nearby are red bus Nos 9, 19, 38, 39 and 48, or green bus Nos 22, 47, 48, 103, 106 and 107.

Places to Stay – middle

The Galaxy Hotel (☎ 229-1191; yínhé dà fàndiàn), 206 Mintsu Rd, is a straightforward business hotel. Doubles/twins cost NT$1440/1920.

The Park Hotel (☎ 220-5181; fax 222-5757; jìnghuá dà fàndiàn), 17 Kungyuan Rd, is near (you guessed it) the park. Doubles are NT$1600 to NT$1900, twins cost NT$2100 to NT$2300 and suites are NT$2800 to NT$3800. It's about the most luxurious hotel within reasonable walking distance of the train station.

The Ful Won Hotel (☎ 326-5463; fùwáng dà fàndiàn), 636 Wenhsin Rd, Section 2 (at Taichungkang Rd) is a great business hotel. Amenities include a business centre, travel service, coffee shop, piano bar and restaurants. Doubles are NT$2350 to NT$2700, twins are NT$2900, and suites cost NT$4000 to NT$15,000.

Behind the train station at 58 Fuhsing Rd is the impressive Twinstar Hotel (☎ 226-1811; shuāngxīng dà fàndiàn). Doubles/twins cost NT$1200/1500 but the 'tycoon suite' is NT$2200.

WEST-CENTRAL TAIWAN

Places to Stay – top end

The *Landis Hotel* (☎ 326-8008; fax 326-8060; *yǒngfēngzhàn lìzhì jiǔdiàn*), 9 Taichungkang Rd, Section 2, is one of the city's newest hotels and positively oozes luxury. Doubles are from NT$4800 to NT$5200, twins are from NT$5500, studios are from NT$5800 to NT$6800 and suites are from NT$7200 to NT$25,000.

The *Evergreen Laurel Hotel* (☎ 328-9988; fax 328-8642; *chángróng guìguān jiǔdiàn*), 6 Taichungkang Rd, Section 2, is another everything-under-one-roof sort of place. Doubles cost NT$4500 to NT$5100, twins are NT$4700 to NT$5300 and suites are NT$8300.

The Japanese Nikko chain runs the *Hotel National* (☎ 321-3111; fax 321-3124; *quánguó dà fàndiàn*) at 257 Taichungkang Rd, Section 1. Features include a business centre, sauna, coffee shop, indoor swimming pool and restaurants. Doubles and twins are from NT$3200 to NT$4500, and suites cost from NT$8000 to NT$20,000.

The *Howard Prince Hotel* (☎ 251-2323; fax 251-5566; *fúhuá dà fàndiàn*), 129 Anho Rd, is west of the freeway in the 'new town centre'. Facilities include a business centre, nonsmoking floors, executive floor, fitness centre, sauna, disco and rooms for disabled persons. Doubles/twins are NT$4300/4900 and suites cost NT$10,000 to NT$30,000.

The *Plaza International Hotel* (☎ 295-6789; fax 293-1122; *tōngháo dà fàndiàn*), 431 Taya Rd, features a business centre, roof-top swimming pool, fitness centre, sauna and children's playground. For golfing enthusiasts, there are also organised excursions to a nearby golf course. Doubles/twins cost NT$3600/3900 and suites are NT$5700 to NT$26,000.

The *Grand Formosa Hotel* (☎ 323-8909; *jīnghuá dà fàndiàn*), 1037 Chienhsing Rd, is Taichung's newest pleasure palace. It occupies the upper floors of a 32 storey building – the lower floors are taken up with the Daimaru Department Store. Doubles cost from NT$6700 to NT$7000, twins cost from NT$7500 to NT$8500, and suites cost from NT$10,000 to NT$60,000.

Places to Eat

Food Courts The best are those in the basements of the following large department stores: *SOGO (tàipíngyáng bǎihuò)* at Taichungkang Rd, Section 1, and Chungmei Rd; the mega-sized *Chungyo (zhōngyǒu bǎihuò)* at 161 Sanmin Rd, Section 3; and *Lai Lai (láilái bǎihuò)* at 125 Sanmin Rd, Section 3.

Night Market The best *night market* stretches along the length of Chunghua Rd. The local speciality is seafood but you can buy just about anything.

Restaurants *Fingas Restaurant* (☎ 327-5450; *fēnggé cāntīng*), at 17-1 Chingcheng Rd, is superb. The food is basically Italian but the chef can cook anything you like, including vegetarian meals. The menu changes every week. Prices can range from NT$250 to NT$750 – the higher-priced dishes include such things as pigeon and venison. The restaurant is open from 11.45 am to 10.30 pm; it's closed on Monday.

La Terrasse French Bistro (☎ 325-6982; *qiǎowèilú cāntīng*), 43 Tasheng St, is run by an amiable expat and serves up great French meals.

Napoli Italian Restaurant (☎ 325-3174; *nápōlǐ cāntīng*), 424 Huamei St, Section 1, is popular with both the locals and expats.

Before you leave Taiwan you should give *TGI Friday's* a try. The American chain (☎ 322-7769; *xīngqīwǔ měishì cāntīng*), 421 Yingtsai Rd, offers superb (though not cheap) western food.

The *Coffee Kitchen* (☎ 310-8116), 53 Tatun 20th St, has a deceptive name since it's really more than a coffee shop. It's great for low-priced Italian food, and has a charming warm atmosphere.

Little Italy (☎ 221-8581), 24-7 Szuwei St, has a name which basically says it all. It's yet another expat hang-out boasting a marvellous atmosphere and low-priced Italian cuisine.

Coriya Restaurant (kēliyà cāntīng) is notable for it's superb Korean-style all-you-can-eat barbecues. There are three branches in Taichung: Tzuyu Store (☎ 226-1241), 88-8 Tzuyu Lu, Section 2; Wuchuan Store (☎ 201-0863), 409 Wuchuan Rd; and Wenhsin Store (☎ 242-4618), 815 Wenhsin Rd, Section 4.

Fast Food *McDonald's* is everywhere. If you'd rather have the food come to you, ring up *Domino's Pizza (dámĕilè bǐsà diàn),* which has three stores scattered around town: Meitsun (☎ 322-5252), 364 Meitsun Rd, Section 1; Hsitsun (☎ 255-5252), 79-30 Hsitsun Rd, Section 3; and Peitsun (☎ 296-5252), 156 Shanhsi Rd, Section 2.

Taichung has more fast-food places around the train station than anywhere else I've seen. Good for those of us on a budget who want a cheap caffeine kick, or want to build the McDonald's cardboard models.
J Tolor

Pub Grub The *Frog Pub I* (☎ 321-1197; *qīngwā cāntīng*), 105 Huamei W St, Section 1, has become a Taichung institution. It serves decent spaghetti, sandwiches and 1L beers (so heavy you can barely hold the glass!). There is also a great noticeboard, book exchange and even computers for Net surfing. The pub actually occupies three floors – don't forget to look upstairs.

Business at the Frog I must be good, because there is now a *Frog Pub II* (☎ 203-0182) at 58 Tateh St. It's a very modern pub with Mexican food and décor. And yes, another great noticeboard. Operating hours are from 9 am until 2 am.

Close by Frog I is *PJ's Cafe* (☎ 325-2457) at 392 Huamei St, which calls itself 'a real American bar'. It's the brainchild of an expat Californian and is notable for its Tex-Mex food, submarine sandwiches, steaks and cheap beer.

Self-Catering If you're looking for an American grocery store and bakery, check out *Mei Chen Siang (mĕi zhēn xiāng)* which has two branches: (☎ 222-4258/222-8558) 87 Chungshan Rd; and (☎ 321-5327/321-5328) 116 Meitsun Rd, Section 1 (near Kungyi Rd).

The place to go for all sorts of superb foreign delectables (bread, cheese, salami etc) is *Fingas Deli* (☎ 327 7750) at 7 Chingcheng Rd. Be sure to check out the ice cream, which is so good that they sell it to the airlines. The deli is open from 10 am to 8 pm, but it's closed on Monday.

Coffee Shops The *Sugar & Spice Bakery Cafe* (☎ 242-6066), 125 Chungteh Rd, Section 2 (at Wenhsin Rd), is a super coffee shop that is supremely popular with expats for either coffee and dessert or meals.

Doutor's Coffee Shop (☎ 221-0311; *luóduōlún kāfēi diàn*), 77 Chungcheng Rd, is part of the Japanese chain and is certainly great for breakfast, coffee, cakes and snacks.

Entertainment
Cinemas See the English-language newspaper, the *China News* for movie listings in Taichung. The current line-up includes:

Chin Chin
  (☎ 231-9111; *qīnqīn xìyuàn*) 14 Peitun Rd
David Broadway
  (☎ 206-3636; *dàwèi dào xìyuàn*) 365 Chinhua N Rd
First Square
  (☎ 223-1703; *dìyī yǐngchéng*) 4th floor, 135 Luchuan W St
Great Earth
  (☎ 224-2588; *quánqiú xìyuàn*) 1-1 Chunghua Rd, Section 1
Hoover
  (☎ 224-2588; *háo huá xìyuàn*) 62 Kuangfu Rd
One Plus One
  (☎ 227-3796; *yī jiā yī yǐngchéng*) 87 Tzuyu Rd, Section 2
Sunrise
  (☎ 224-8953; *rìxīn xìyuàn*) 58 Chunghua Rd, Section 1

Discos *Party Animal Disco* (☎ 325-4247), 141 Hsiangshang N Rd, is a long-running Taichung hot spot. There is a NT$350 cover charge which includes two beers.

The *Bu Bu Disco Pub* (☎ 329-1358), 6-5 Wenhsin Rd, Section 3, is a little more pub than disco, with a jazz bar on the 2nd floor. The cover charge is normally NT$350, but men pay NT$500 on Thursday while women get in free. Friday is 'lovers night', where couples dressed in identical garb get in for free. On Saturday and holiday evenings, the cost rises to NT$600.

CCK Disco Pub (☎ 254-9688), 3rd floor, 2 Huichung Rd, Section 1, is close to the Guinness World of Records Museum. It's a large place with plenty of dance floor space and three bars. There is live music from 10 pm until 1.30 am. Cover charge is NT$350, but it rises to NT$500 on Saturday and holiday nights.

The *What's Up Disco Pub* (☎ 320-6676), 363 Kungyi Rd (at Tunghsing Rd), is an enormous, somewhat outrageous disco. Saturday night is 'Cross-Dresser's Night'.

The *Pig Pen* (☎ 383-4456), 41 Takuan Rd (near Hsiangshang Rd), is expensive but fun. It was once part of the Pig & Whistle chain before a falling out with the foreign joint-venture partner. Friday night has been designated 'foreigner's night'. Décor on the ground floor is British style and the food is basically Mexican. Up on the 2nd and 3rd floors is a disco. Cover charge in the upstairs disco is NT$300, but rises to NT$400 on Saturday and holidays. The Pig is open daily from 11.30 am to 3 am.

Concerts & Plays Most of Taichung's operas, plays and concerts are staged at the *cultural centre* next to the Museum of Art.

Strange as it sounds, on the 2nd floor of the Frog Pub I is the *Xiang Theatre* (☎ 632-0718), where there are various weekend performances. Tickets are available from the Frog.

Teahouses A popular place in the centre for foreigners and locals alike is *Chaku Chugui* (☎ 223-5481) at 51-53 Chikuang St, almost adjacent to the First Hotel. Look for the set of train tracks running through the shop (they're fake though, there's no trains). The teahouse's name cards are designed to look like Taiwanese train tickets. Besides tea, this place also serves beer and snacks.

Across the street is *Firefly Colony* (☎ 221-7887; *huǒjīngū zhímíndì*), which is a tea shop of similar design.

In the evenings, a really great place to go is *Chunshui Tang* (☎ 327-3647; *chūnshuǐ*

táng) at 9 Tatun 19th St on the corner of Chingming 1st St. Aside from tea you can also order noodles and beer.

MTV First Square Shopping Plaza (*dìyī guǎngchǎng*), 135 Luchuan W St, seems to be a stronghold of MTVs, including *U2 MTV* (☎ 220-2500) on the 7th floor.

Things to Buy
The Chienkuo Market (*jiànguó shìchǎng*) is a fascinating place to wander around, even if you don't buy anything. There are some good priced tools, though if you want to keep your backpack light you'd better avoid buying a jackhammer, air compressor or hydraulic press. Less bulky but useful items on sale here include key chains and pocket knives.

The Jack Wolfskin Outdoor Equipment Shop on the elegant 61 Chingming 1st St sells quality backpacks, tents and various kinds of hi-tech gear suitable for an assault on Mt Everest.

NOVA Computer Arcade (*NOVA zīxùn guǎngchǎng*) on the corner of Yingtsai and Kungyi Rds is a great place to check out for the latest game or program.

Getting There & Away
Air Taichung's Shuinan airport suffers from a serious handicap – the runway is not long enough to accommodate commercial jets. This means that only turbo-props can land here. These small planes are slow, and the limited number of seats results in very expensive air tickets. However, several international airlines do have offices in Taichung which you can ring up to make bookings or to reconfirm your flight. These offices can be contacted as follows:

Australia Asia Airlines	(☎ 327-1243)
British Asia Airways	(☎ 327-2077)
Canadian International	(☎ 329-4322)
Delta Airlines	(☎ 225-0371)
Japan Asia Airlines	(☎ 321-7700)
Royal Brunei Airlines	(☎ 327-1243)
Swissair	(☎ 329-3151)

Currently there are flights between Taichung

and Kaohsiung, Kinmen, Makung, Matsu, Taipei and Taitung. Domestic airlines with booking offices in Taichung are:

EVA Airways
  (☎ 425-7630; *chángróng hángkōng*) 100 Minhang Rd, Shuinan airport
Formosa Airlines
  (☎ 425-4236; *guóhua hángkōng*) Shuinan airport
Great China Airlines
  (☎ 425-7630; *dàhuá hángkōng*) 100 Minhang Rd, Shuinan airport
Taiwan Airlines
  (☎ 425-7630; *táiwān hángkōng*) Shuinan airport

One agency dealing in discount domestic air tickets is Pinbao Travel (☎ 293-6945; *pǐnbǎo lǚxíngshè*), room 5, 4th floor, 241 Wenhsin Rd, Section 3.

Bus Taichung is just 105km south of Taipei on the major North-South Freeway and train line. In addition to the North-South Freeway buses, there are also buses coming over the mountains from Hualien on the east coast, via the scenic Central Cross-Island Highway. There are also direct buses to many scenic areas in central Taiwan, such as Sun Moon Lake, Hsitou, Alishan, and Wushe (via Puli).

There are three major bus stations in Taichung and at least two important minor ones. The big one (*táiqì táizhōng zhàn*) in front of the train station is for northbound buses, including those to Taipei. The bus station (*táiqì nán zhàn*) behind the train station is for southbound buses (Kaohsiung, Hsitou, Chiayi etc). For country buses to places such as Sun Moon Lake, Puli, Shuili, Nantou and Wushe, you need to go to the Gancheng bus station (*gānchéng chēzhàn*), two blocks north-east of the train station.

A useful small station behind the train station is operated by Changhua Bus Company (*zhānghuà kèyùn*); here you can catch buses to Lukang and Changhua.

Perhaps the most useful hole-in-the-wall station is for the Fengyuan Bus Company (☎ 222-3454; *fēngyuán kèyùn*). It's on the traffic circle, opposite the train station and directly adjacent to the Fuh Chun Hotel. This bus company serves Taichung County, and includes Fengyuan, Kukuan, Lishan, Encore Gardens and Kuanyin Temple. This is also where you catch buses to Hualien on the east coast.

The Tonglien Bus Company is a privately owned company, with one station directly opposite the train station and another near the intersection of Taichungkang Rd and the freeway. You can get buses here to Taipei and Kaohsiung. There is another bus station close by the freeway which is the departure point for Taiwan Bus Company routes to the north and south along the freeway.

Train It's important to note that the west coast train line has two routes in the Taichung area – the sea route (*hǎi xiàn*) and inland route (*zòngguàn xiàn*). Taichung is on the inland route, which means that you cannot assume that every train on the Kaohsiung-Taipei line will stop in Taichung. It's entirely possible that when you buy a ticket to leave Taichung, you will be sold two tickets – one to your final destination and another for the shuttle train (*tōngqín diànchē*) which runs from Hsunan (*zhúnán*) to Changhua via Taichung. In this case you have to switch trains in Hsunan (northbound) or Changhua (southbound) depending on which direction you're headed.

Getting Around
To/From the Airport Taichung's Shuinan airport is in the Hsitun district in the northwest of the city. Green bus No 36 goes to the airport.

Bus If you have a day to spend in Taichung, there are a few interesting things to see and do. Taichung has two city bus companies: the Taichung Bus Company (*táizhōng kèyùn*) which operates green buses; and the Renyou Bus Company (*rényǒu kèyùn*) which operates red buses. This can create a bit of confusion for the uninitiated. For example, a green bus No 22 goes to different places from a red bus No 22.

The exact fare of NT$15 is needed.

Car Car rentals are available from the English-speaking staff at some of the following companies:

Central Auto Service
(☎ 425-7000) 112-100 Chungching Rd
China
(☎ 205-2800) 204-1 Taya Rd, North District
Chuan Chia Fu
(☎ 425-8206) 151-23 Chungching Rd
International Auto Service
(☎ 259-2977)

YUEHMEI DISCOVERY WORLD
(yuèměi yù lè shìjiè) 月美育樂世界
Not much can be said about this place because it was under construction at the time of writing. However, it should open sometime during the lifespan of this book, and when it does it's expected to be one of the best amusement parks in Taiwan.

The emphasis here is to be on space exploration. Fortunately, the equipment will not be some tacky imitation, but the real thing built with cooperation from America's National Aeronautics and Space Administration (NASA). You will able to sit in the cockpit of a real space shuttle, as well as try out some genuine training devices which are far more stomach-churning than even the wildest roller coaster ride.

Discovery World is being built in the town of Houli, about 15km north of Taichung. Until it opens, a temporary exhibit is operating near Taichung's Guinness World of Records Museum. You can ring up for information (☎ 254-4802/254-4806). Admission is NT$360 for adults, NT$300 for students, NT$250 for children under 12 but taller than 100cm. Children under 100cm get in free.

CHUNGHSING VILLAGE
(zhōngxīng xīn cūn) 中興新村
Many of the English-language tourist maps published in Taiwan mark Chunghsing Village with a star, circle or something else to show that it's a special place, but then offer no explanation why it is so. Chunghsing Village is in fact the capital of Taiwan – that is, Taiwan province. Taipei is not Taiwan's capital – rather, it's the provisional capital of the Republic of China until 'reunification'.

Most travellers probably wouldn't want to spend their time here, but some may want to have a look as it is only a short distance away from Taichung. Frequent highway buses heading south of Taichung stop briefly in Chunghsing Village, including the bus to Sun Moon Lake.

KUKUAN
(gǔguān) 谷關
Kukuan is a small town and hot-spring resort about two hours by bus from Taichung. Being rather close to the city, it gets very crowded on weekends, but it's OK at other times. The scenery is certainly good, though not as spectacular as that higher up in the mountains.

The town is divided into two – one half is next to the highway and the other on the north bank of the river. You get to the north side by crossing a footbridge, or larger bridge (for vehicles) on the eastern (uphill) part of the village. The north side is definitely the nicer part of town, since it has little traffic because the few roads are dead ends.

The towns main attraction – the **hot springs** – are piped into hotel baths; unfortunately there are no outdoor pools. In addition to the hot springs, another attraction is the hike up to **Dragon Valley Waterfall** *(lónggǔ pùbù)*. It's an easy hike – only 3.3km for the round trip but as it's in a park, you have to pay NT$100 admission. Within the park there is also a zoo, botanical garden and souvenir vendors. To find the park, cross the footbridge near the Dragon Valley Hotel and just follow the trail.

In summer, **swimming** in the river is a big attraction. There is at least one spot under the big footbridge where the pools are deep enough to dive off the rocks, a popular activity with the local kids.

Places to Stay
Kukuan is overrun with tourists on weekends and holidays and virtually every hotel is full. On weekdays business is very slow and most

hotels offer 20% off the rates quoted here; some even offer 50% discounts.

Across the footbridge on the north bank in pleasant park-like surroundings is the quiet and secluded *Wenshan Hotel* (☎ 595-1265; *wènshān dà lǚshè*), where twins are NT$800 to NT$1300.

Also on the north bank is the *Dongguan Hot Springs Hotel* (☎ 595-1112; *dōngguān wēnquán dà lǚshè*), where twins cost NT$1700 to NT$2200. Directly across the lane and under the same management is the *Mingchih Hotel* (☎ 595-1111; *míngzhì dà fàndiàn*), which has rooms for the same price.

The *Utopia Holiday Hotel* (☎ 595-1511; *shénmù jiàqí dà fàndiàn*) is also on the north bank, with a good view overlooking the river. It's a great place to stay, and its rooms are NT$1100 to NT$9000.

On the south (busy) side of town almost directly opposite the Fengyuan Bus Company station is the *Kukuan Hotel* (☎ 595-1355; fax 595-1359; *gǔguān dà fàndiàn*). All rooms are twins and cost from NT$1000 to NT$2400. The rear patio is relatively quiet and has a good view of the river, so try to get a room on this side of the building.

The *Dragon Valley Hotel* (☎ 595-1325; fax 595-1226; *lónggǔ dà fàndiàn*) is the huge high rise right in the congested middle of town. It seems very out of place with the natural surroundings, but that certainly hasn't hurt business. Twins/suites go for NT$2400/5200.

Getting There & Away

The bus stop is at the east (uphill) end of town, right in front of the Kukuan Hotel. The buses don't stop in the centre of town and it's useless trying to flag them down there.

Buses from Taichung are frequent, starting at 6 am. Most of the buses to Kukuan are operated by the Fengyuan Bus Company. You can also catch these same buses in Fengyuan, which is to the north of Taichung and definitely closer to Kukuan. If you're coming from Taipei by train, there is no need to go into congested Taichung itself – catch

the bus in Fengyuan and you'll save yourself nearly two hours.

CENTRAL CROSS-ISLAND HIGHWAY

(zhōngbù héngguàn gōnglù) 中部橫貫公路
This spectacular highway connects Taroko Gorge on the east side of Taiwan with the city of Taichung on the west, a distance of 195km. Virtually every kilometre of this highway offers a stunning view of lush forests and towering mountain peaks, and should not be missed if you have the time. The road is occasionally closed due to landslides, especially following a typhoon – which is not surprising considering that in many places the road is carved out of sheer cliffs.

Places to Stay

Assuming you travel from west to east, you will come across CYC hostels in the following order. Unfortunately, you can't rely on these – they can be packed out to overflowing during summer and Chinese New Year, and closed during winter. Only the Kuanyun and Tienhsiang hostels stay open year round, and both offer meals as well as beds. Refer to the CYC Hostels map in the Facts for the Visitor chapter for locations.

Chingshan Mountain Hostel
  (☎ 595-1700; *qīngshān shān zhuāng*) dormitory NT$250; twins NT$1200
Kuanyun Mountain Hostel
  (☎ 599-1173; *guānyún shān zhuāng*) dormitory NT$280; twins NT$1600
Loshao Mountain Hostel
  (☎ 869-1118, 869-1167; *luòshào shān zhuāng*) dormitory/doubles NT$250/1000
Tayuling Mountain Hostel
  (☎ 599-1009; reservations ☎ 869-1167; *dàyǔlǐng shān zhuāng*) dormitory NT$250
Techi Mountain Hostel
  (☎ 598-1592; reservations ☎ 524-4103; *déjī shān zhuāng*) dormitory/doubles NT$250/1000
Tienhsiang Youth Activity Centre
  (☎ 869-1111; *tiānxiáng huódòng zhōngxīn*) dormitory NT$250; twins NT$1200 to NT$2200
Tzuen Mountain Hostel
  (☎ 869-1167; *cíēn shān zhuāng*) dorm NT$250

Getting Around

It takes slightly more than eight hours by bus to travel nonstop across the island on this

WEST-CENTRAL TAIWAN

highway. From Hualien, buses depart for Taichung at 7.35, 9.35 and 11.05 am. Going in the other direction, buses depart Taichung for Hualien at 7, 8 and 9.30 am. You can also catch the bus in Tienhsiang. Although the cross-island trip can be done in one day, it's best to take at least three days because there is plenty to see along the way. The side trips to Wuling Farm and Hohuanshan are particularly worthwhile.

For those with even more time, energy and ambition, it is possible to do this journey by foot or bicycle if you're really fit. To do the journey by foot takes at least five days and life is made easier by the fact that you can always change your mind and catch a bus. It's best to do it on weekdays, when traffic is minimal. The highest point is Tayuling, from where you can walk to Hohuanshan, one of Taiwan's most beautiful mountains.

If you prefer to walk down rather than up, you can take a bus to the summit of the highway at Tayuling and then walk downhill all the way, either towards Hualien (east) or Taichung (west). During the cold months (November to May), it's better to walk from Tayuling towards Taichung (west) because the east side of the island gets locked in by cold rain and fog. The west side is usually sunny – in fact, winter is the dry season.

If you're not heading any further south, then Fengyuan, about an hour north of Taichung, is an important western highway transit point. You can get a direct train from Taipei to Fengyuan. This saves nearly two hours on a trip from Taipei to the Central Cross-Island Highway.

LISHAN
(líshān) 梨山

Lishan, or Pear Mountain, is a small farming community along the Central Cross-Island Highway. The area is famous for growing cold-weather fruits like apples, peaches and pears, which cannot grow in the subtropical lowlands. It is also a retreat for city-bound tourists seeking refuge from the summer heat. Hiking opportunities are limited in Lishan itself as most of the land is occupied by orchards. However, the nearby area is

spectacular. It's also a good transit point for a trip to Wuling Farm and Hsuehshan.

Fruit Market
(shuǐguǒ shìcháng) 水果市場

This is what the Taiwanese come for. You'll hardly have to look for the fruit market – during the summer months, that's just about all Lishan is. The area near the bus station has the thickest cluster of stalls.

For all the fame and fanfare, the prices really aren't a bargain. The locals know about the outrageous price of fruit in Taipei and they gear their prices accordingly. However, in Lishan there's at least no doubt about the freshness – it's likely the fruit was picked the same morning. Some orchards even charge an admission fee and let you pick your own, then weigh the contents and charge you as you depart.

The dried fruits are a better deal and they make good lightweight snacks for travelling.

Lishan is also famous for its peach wine *(shuǐmìtáo jiǔ)*. You can find bottles for about NT$600 at grocery stores around town.

Lishan Culture Museum
(líshān wénwù guǎn) 梨山文物館

On the east side of Lishan is a church, and across the highway is an intersection with another road. Follow this road uphill, past the elementary school, and you'll come to the museum. From the centre of Lishan, the hike is only about 1.5km. The museum is small but interesting.

Lucky Life Mountain Farm
(fúshòushān nóngchǎng) 福壽山農場

Continuing uphill along the same road (5km from Lishan), you'll come to the Lucky Life Mountain Farm. You'll easily recognise the area by the statue in front of the small farmhouse. The area is surrounded by orchards, and the view of the surrounding mountains, from the back porch, is fantastic.

Heaven's Pool
(tiānchí) 天池

Follow the same road all the way to the

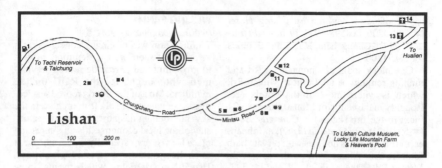

LISHAN 梨山

1 Petrol Station
  加油站
2 Lishan Guest House
  梨山賓館
3 Bus Station
  公路車站
4 Public Hostel (Closed)
  國民旅舍

5 Haowangjiao Hotel
  好望角大飯店
6 Shengxin Hotel
  聖心大飯店
7 Li Tu Hotel
  梨都大旅社
8 Guangda Hotel
  廣達大旅社
9 Fire Station
  消防隊

10 Yanhualou Hotel
   燕華樓大旅社
11 Fu Chung Hotel
   福忠大飯店
12 Guocheng Hotel
   國誠大旅社
13 Church
   教堂
14 Church
   教堂

summit of the mountain – 12km from Lishan with an elevation of 2590m. Morning is the best time to visit, when the weather is likely to be clear but cold. As long as the clouds cooperate, the view is spectacular. The pool, the house next to it and the surrounding grounds are maintained as a sort of sacred shrine – this was Chiang Kaishek's summer mountain retreat. Chiang's habit of seeking out quiet mountain retreats and pools got him into big trouble once. In China's Shaanxi Province in 1936, Chiang was kidnapped by his own generals while resting at Huaqing Pool. Coincidentally, the pool was on the slopes of a mountain also called Lishan.

Except for the odd tour bus, there are no buses going to Heaven's Pool. Hitching is a distinct possibility though.

Places to Stay

So many tour buses arrive in Lishan on weekends and holidays that it's a wonder the mountain doesn't collapse. Accommodation is very tight at these times, so you're definitely better off arriving on a weekday. The following rates are for weekdays during summer. During winter, hotels are empty and you can often bargain a 50% discount.

The cheapest place in town is the *Guocheng Hotel* (☎ 598-9279; *guóchéng dà lǚshe*) at 54 Chungcheng Rd. Doubles without/with private bath are NT$500/700.

Just west of the bus station is the *Lishan Guest House* (☎ 598-9501; fax 598-9505; *líshān bīnguǎn*). On the outside, it appears to be one of the most beautiful hotels in Taiwan. Inside, the place could do with some renovation work and prices are not nearly as high as one would expect from the ornate exterior. Singles are NT$800, twins are NT$1300 to NT$1600, suites are NT$1800 and cabins are NT$3600 to NT$4800. There is an additional 10% service charge.

Chungcheng Rd, the main drag in Lishan, is actually part of the Cross-Island Highway. It's mostly lined with restaurants, but there is one place to stay, the *Fu Chung Hotel* (☎ 598-9506, fax 598-1991; *fúzhōng dà fàndiàn*) at 61 Chungcheng Rd. It has doubles for NT$1200.

One block south of Chungcheng Rd and running roughly parallel to it is Mintsu Rd, which is where most of the hotels are. Roughly in the centre of Mintsu Rd at No 21 (next to the fire station) is *Guangda Hotel* (☎ 598-9216; *guǎngdá dà lǔshè*), the cheapest of this lot. It has doubles with private bath for NT$600. About 50m north-east, at 22 Mintsu Rd, is the *Yanhualou Hotel* (☎ 598-9615/598-9511; *yànhuá lóu dà lǔshè*), which has doubles for NT$700 to NT$800. The *Shengxin Hotel* (☎ 598-9577; *shèngxīn dà fàndiàn*), about 50m south-west of the Guangda, has doubles for NT$800. Opposite the Guangda, the *Li Tu Hotel* (☎ 598-9256, 598-9512; *lìdū dà lǔshè*) charges NT$1000 for a double. Finally, the *Haowangjiao Hotel* (☎ 598-9512; *hǎowàngjiǎo dà fàndiàn*), 52 Mintsu Rd, charges NT$1000 to NT$1200 for doubles.

Getting There & Away

Lishan is easily reached by any buses from Taichung (110km), but there are also buses from Hualien (135km) and Lotung/Ilan (110km).

From Taichung there are 14 buses daily, the first departing at 6 am and the last leaving at 2.30 pm. Most of the buses from Taichung terminate in Lishan but four of these continue onwards to Hualien. The trip takes 3½ hours. You pay less and save an hour if you board the bus at Fengyuan rather than Taichung. An additional three buses, operated by the Fengyuan Bus Company, run daily during weekends and holidays.

From Hualien, buses leave at 7.30 and 9.30 am, taking 4½ hours to reach Lishan.

There are buses connecting Lishan with the twin cities of Lotung and Ilan on the north-east coast. Buses depart Lishan for Lotung at 8.30 am and 1 pm. Buses depart Lishan for Ilan at 8 and 9 am, noon and 2 pm. Most of these buses also stop at Wuling Farm en route.

WULING FARM

(wǔlíng nóngchǎng) 武陵農場

Wuling Farm was originally conceived as a government-sponsored agricultural project to grow fruit and to resettle retired servicemen who fought for the ROC on the mainland. Most of the elderly retired servicemen have gone to the big fruit orchard in the sky, but tourism has now become the mainstay of the local economy. It's an interesting place for visitors, especially hikers who want to challenge Taiwan's second highest peak, Hsuehshan *(xuěshān)*, which means Snow Mountain. It's 3884m in elevation and one of the chief attractions of Shei-Pa National Park.

Wuling Farm is beautiful and mostly non-commercialised, though there is a NT$100 admission fee to the area.

Hikes

A mountain permit is required for **Hsuehshan**. It's about a 10 to 12 hour climb to the summit. There are two huts along the way where you can spend the night. The first hut, Chika Hut *(qīkǎ shān zhuāng)*, is a two-hour hike from the trailhead and has water. The second hut, Three Six Nine Hut *(sān liù jiǔ shān zhuāng)*, is an additional six hour climb and has no water. There are no facilities at the huts, so you'll need a sleeping bag, food, stove and other backpacking paraphernalia.

A much easier hike is to the **Yensheng Waterfall** *(yānshēng pùbù)*. It's at the top end of the valley past the Youth Activity Centre. From there you can also climb **Peach Mountain** *(táoshān)*, which reaches 3324m.

Places to Stay

There are three places to stay in Wuling. The *Wuling Guest House* (☎ 590-1183, 590-1258; fax 590-1260; *wǔlíng guómín bīnguǎn*) serves as the headquarters for booking the other two places. This one is also the classiest and most expensive. Standard twins are NT$1000 to NT$2000. There are also honeymoon suites for NT$2500 and wooden cabins for NT$2000 to NT$3000.

The *Wuling Farm Travel Service Centre*

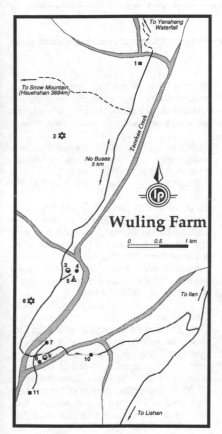

WULING FARM 武陵農場

1　Wuling Mountain Hostel
　　武陵山莊
2　Orchards
　　果園
3　Bus Stop
　　公路車站
4　Wuling Farm Travel Service Centre
　　旅遊服務中心
5　Campground
　　露營區
6　Orchards
　　果園
7　Buddha Statue
　　彌勒佛像
8　Pavilion
　　翠纓亭
9　Bus Stop
　　巴士站
10　Toll Gate
　　大門收費亭
11　Wuling Guest House
　　國民賓館

(☎ 590-1259; *wǔlíng nóngchǎng lǚyóu fúwù zhōngxīn*) is further into the park and near the final bus stop. Inquire here if you want to stay in the adjacent camping ground. No equipment is supplied so you need to bring your own.

The last option is the *Wuling Mountain Hostel* (☎ 590-1020; *wǔlíng shān zhuāng*), but it's a 5km hike up the valley road from the last bus stop. Again, ask the Wuling Guest House for details.

All hotels can be full, even on weekdays, during summer. On weekdays when kids are in school, you shouldn't have any trouble.

Places to Eat

While the *Wuling Guest House* can dish up pricey meals, the best bet for budget travellers are the instant noodles (hot water supplied) from the shop inside the *Wuling Farm Travel Service Centre*.

Getting There & Away

Wuling Farm is 25km north-east of Lishan, just off the branch highway leading down to the coast at Ilan. There are five daily buses connecting Wuling Farm and Lishan. They depart Lishan at 8.30 and 10 am and 1, 2 and 4.50 pm and Wuling Farm at 7.30 and 9.40 am, noon and 1.50 and 3.30 pm. This includes buses between Lishan and Lotung/Ilan, all of which also stop at Wuling Farm.

Buses also connect Wuling Farm with Lotung and Ilan. They depart Lotung at 7 and 11.50 am. The 7 am bus also makes a stop in Ilan. There is a bus departing Ilan for Wuling Farm at 12.10 pm.

Buses depart Wuling for Lotung at 9.20 am and 2.50 pm. Buses depart Wuling for Ilan at 10.20 am and 1.50 pm.

Language

Mandarin Chinese is the official language of Taiwan; it's spoken on TV and radio and taught in the schools. However, at least half the population prefers to speak Taiwanese at home, especially in the south and in the countryside. Taiwanese is also known as Hokkien, but is more correctly labelled the 'Minnan language' *(mǐnnánhuà)*. 'Minnan' means 'south of the Min River' – the Min River, in China's Fujian province, is where the language originated and is still spoken today. Taiwanese and Mandarin are similar in some respects, but they are still two different languages and are not mutually intelligible. Taiwanese has no written script and therefore no literature, unless you count a Romanised version of the Bible used by missionaries. While virtually all the young people can speak Mandarin, many of the older people don't speak it at all. However, many older people know Japanese as a result of the 50-year occupation of Taiwan by Japan.

The study of English is required in Taiwan from junior high school on, but few students actually learn to speak it. As a result they generally tend to read and write English much better than they can speak it, so if you need to communicate in English, try writing your message down. The reason for this is that students learn English from textbooks, without any opportunity for conversation.

Another dialect found in Taiwan is Hakka, but its use is on the wane.

Taiwan's 10 aboriginal tribes each have their own language. These languages bear no relation at all to Chinese, and are generally regarded as Malayo-Polynesian in origin.

Mandarin Chinese, Taiwanese and Hakka are all tonal languages – by altering the tone of a word the meaning is completely changed. Getting your tones wrong can have embarassing consequences – *wǒ gǎn mào* means 'I've caught a cold' while *wǒ gàn mào* means 'I copulate with cats'. Mandarin has

four tones, while other dialects can have as many as nine. For example, in Mandarin Chinese the word *ma* can have four distinct meanings depending on which tone is used:

high tone	*mā*	'mother'
rising tone	*má*	'hemp' or 'numb'
falling-rising tone	*mǎ*	'horse'
falling tone	*mà*	'scold' or 'swear'

In some words, the tone is not important. This so-called neutral tone is usually not indicated at all. Mastering tones is tricky for the untrained western ear, but with discipline it can be done. Try practising the following tongue twister: *māma qí mǎ. mǎ màn. māma mà mǎ.* ('Mother rides a horse. The horse is slow. Mother scolds the horse.').

Characters

Unlike most western languages, written Chinese does not employ an alphabet. Instead, a system of 'idea-pictures' or characters is used, each character representing a different word or syllable. Scholars claim that about 50,000 Chinese characters exist, but most are variations of the same words and have long since become archaic. About 5000 are still in use today. Of these, only 2000 are very commonly used, and this would be considered the minimum needed to read a newspaper.

To borrow from a Chinese proverb, it can take a lifetime and a little bit more to learn how to read and write Chinese. In contrast, the spoken language is not very difficult to master, apart from the problems with tones. In mainland China, a system of simplified characters was introduced to improve literacy. However, traditions die hard – in Taiwan, Hong Kong and in most Chinese communities outside mainland China, the older, more complex characters are still used. In this book we use the older characters, since these are the only kind you'll encounter in Taiwan.

Transliteration

Chinese can be written using the Roman alphabet. Unfortunately, there are three competing Romanisation systems in common use, which causes great confusion. These are Yale, Pinyin and Wade-Giles. The three systems are similar, especially for vowels, but there are some significant differences in the way Chinese consonants are represented.

Yale is the easiest system for untrained westerners to learn. It was developed by Yale University some years ago as a teaching aid, and at one time most Chinese textbooks for foreigners used it. Yale University has now dropped this system in favour of Pinyin.

While Pinyin takes more time to learn than Yale, it's the most accurate system of Romanisation so far devised for Chinese. Unfortunately, it isn't used in Taiwan, except in some Chinese textbooks written specifically for foreigners.

In Taiwan, Wade-Giles is still the official system used for street signs, maps, books, newspapers and name cards. Unfortunately, Romanisation is not taught in Taiwan's schools so most locals are unfamiliar with it and misspellings are common. For example, one street in Taipei appears alternately on maps as Tehui St and Tehhwei St; in Kaohsiung, Jeouru Rd and Chiuju Rd are the same place; a fashionable neighbourhood in east Taipei is variously spelled Dinghao, Dinghow and Tinghao.

A more serious problem with the Wade-Giles system is the use of apostrophes. For example, the city of Taipei should be written with an apostrophe *(T'aipei)* but it is almost always omitted. Without the apostrophe, the initial **t** should be pronounced (incorrectly) as a **d** *(Daipei)*. Similarly, the letter **ch'** is confused with **j**, **k'** with **g**, **p'** with **b** and so on. You should be aware of this when reading Romanised script and signs.

The presence of conflicting systems of Romanisation poses a dilemma. Since maps, street signs and all official publications in Taiwan use the Wade-Giles system, we use it for all official geographical names and names of persons. Also in line with accepted practice in Taiwan, apostrophes will not be used, so you'll see *Taipei* and *Taiwan*, not *T'aipei* and *T'aiwan*.

However, in the interests of clarity, the Wade-Giles name will be followed by the Pinyin Romanisation in italics and parentheses wherever necessary. For example, 'the second-largest city in Taiwan is Kaohsiung *(gāoxióng)*'. Whenever Pinyin is used in this text, it will always be in italics with tones shown. Other Romanised words will be written using the Wade-Giles system. Note that no tone marks will be shown with Romanised names on maps.

Pronunciation

The following is a description of the sounds produced in spoken Mandarin Chinese. The letter **v** is not used in Chinese. The trickiest sounds in Pinyin are **c**, **q** and **x**. Most letters are pronounced as in English, except for the following:

Vowels

a	as in 'father'
ai	as the word 'eye'
ao	as the 'ow' in 'cow'
e	as in 'her'
ei	as in 'weigh'
i	as the 'ee' in 'meet' or as the 'oo' in 'book'*
ian	as the word 'yen'
ie	as the word 'yeah'
o	as in 'or'
ou	as the 'oa' in 'boat'
u	as in 'flute'
ui	as the word 'way'
uo	as 'w' followed by the 'o' in or
yu	as German 'ü' – round your lips and try saying 'ee'
ü	as German 'ü'

*The letter 'i' is pronounced as 'oo' only when it occurs after **c**, **ch**, **r**, **s**, **sh**, **z** or **zh**.

Consonants

c	as the 'ts' in 'bits'
ch	as in 'church', but with the tongue curled back

h	guttural, a bit like the 'ch' in Scottish 'loch'
q	as the 'ch' in 'cheese'
r	as the 's' in 'pleasure'
sh	as in 'she', but with the tongue curled back
x	as the 'sh' in 'ship'
z	as the 'ds' in 'suds'
zh	as the 'j' in 'judge' but with the tongue curled back

Consonants other than **n**, **ng**, and **r** can never appear at the end of a syllable.

In Pinyin, apostrophes are occasionally used to separate consonants and syllables, eg *ping'an* (pronounced 'ping-an') compared with *pin'gan* ('pin-gan').

The major differences between Pinyin and Wade-Giles are as follows:

Pinyin	Wade-Giles
b	p
c	ts'
c	ch'
d	t
g	k
p	p'
q	ch'
r	j
t	t'
x	hs
z	ts, tz
zh	ch

Pronouns

I
wǒ 我
you
nǐ 你
he, she, it
tā 他
we, us
wǒmen 我們
you (plural)
nǐmen 你們
they, them
tāmen 他們

Greetings & Civilities

Hello.
nǐ hǎo 你好
Goodbye.
zàijiàn 再見
Thank you.
xièxie 謝謝
You're welcome.
búkèqì 不客氣
I'm sorry/excuse me.
duìbùqǐ 對不起

Useful Expressions

I want ...
wǒ yào ... 我要
I want to buy ...
wǒ yào mǎi ... 我要買...
No, I don't want it.
búyào 不要
Yes (have).
yǒu 有
No (don't have).
méiyǒu 沒有
I don't understand.
wǒ tīng bùdǒng 我聽不懂
I do understand.
wǒ tīngde dǒng 我聽得懂
Do you understand?
dǒng bùdǒng? 懂不懂
Wait a moment.
děng yī xià 等一下

Money

How much does it cost?
duōshǎo qián? 多少錢
That's too expensive.
tài guì 太貴
postal remittance account number
yóuzhèng huàbō zhànghào
郵政劃撥帳號

Necessities

bathroom (washroom)
xǐshǒujiān 洗手間

laundromat (laundry service)
  xǐyī zhōngxīn   洗衣中心
mosquito incense coils
  wénxiāng   蚊香
sanitary pads (Kotex)
  wèishēng mián   衛生棉
sunscreen (UV) lotion
  fáng shài yóu   防曬油
tampons
  wèishēng mián tiáo   衛生棉條
tissue paper
  miàn zhǐ   面紙
toilet (restroom)
  cèsuǒ   廁所
toilet paper
  wèishēng zhǐ   衛生紙
vape mats (mosquito pads)
  dìan wénxiāng   電蚊香

Getting Around

airport
  fēijīchǎng   飛機場
boarding pass
  dēngjì kǎ   登記卡
reserve a seat
  dìng wèizǐ   定位子
cancel
  qǔxiāo   取消
ticket
  piào   票
refund a ticket
  tuìpiào   退票
reconfirm air ticket
  quèrèn   確認
taxi
  jìchéngchē   計程車
Please use the meter.
  tiào biǎo   跳表
bus station
  gōngchē zhàn   公車站
local bus
  gōnggòng qìchē   公共汽車
highway bus
  bāshì   巴士

I want to get off ... bus/taxi
  xià chē   下車
train
  huǒchē   火車
train station
  huǒchē zhàn   火車站
Which platform?
  dì jǐ yuètái?   第幾月台?
upgrade ticket (on train)
  bǔ piào   補票
bonded baggage
  cúnzhàn xínglǐ   存棧行李
luggage
  xínglǐ   行李
luggage storage room
  xínglǐ shì   行李室
lockers
  bǎoxiǎn xiāng   保險箱
motorcycle
  jīchē   機車
motorbike hire
  jīchē chūzū   機車出租
car
  qìchē   汽車
petrol station
  jiā yóu zhàn   加油站
Fill it up.
  jiā mǎn   加滿

Directions

I'm lost.
  wǒ mí lù   我迷路
Where is the ...?
  ... zài nǎlǐ?   ... 在那裡
Turn right.
  yòu zhuǎn   右轉
Turn left.
  zuǒ zhuǎn   左轉
Go straight.
  yìzhí zǒu   一直走
Turn around.
  zhuǎn gewān   轉個彎
alley
  nòng   弄

lane
xiàng 巷
road
lù 路
section
duàn 段
street
jiē 街
No 21
21 hào 21號

Accommodation

big hotel
dà fàndiàn 大飯店
check-in (register)
dēngjì 登記
hotel name card
ǔguǎnde míngpiàn 旅館的名片
hotel (all kinds)
ǔguǎn 旅館
room
fángjiān 房間
private room
ge rénfáng 個人房
room with shared bath
pǔtōngfáng 普通房
small room with private bath
tàofáng 套房
suite
gāojífáng 高級房
reserve a room
dìng fángjiān 定房間
deposit
yājīn 押金
guesthouse
ǔshè 旅社
dormitory
tuántǐfáng/ 團體房/
duōrénfáng 多人房
mountain hostel
shān zhuāng 山莊
tatami
tātāmǐ 榻榻米
camping ground
lùyíng qū 露營區

camp site
lùyíng yíngwèi 露營營位
sleeping bag
shuìdài 睡袋
tent
zhàngpéng 帳篷

Post & Telecommunications

telephone
diànhuà 電話
telephone card
diànhuà kǎ 電話卡
telephone company office
diànxìn jú 電信局
collect call
duìfāng fùqián 對方付錢
direct dial
zhí bō diànhuà 直撥電話
international call
guójì diànhuà 國際電話
post office
yóujú 郵局
poste restante
cún jú hòu lǐng 存局候領
main post office (GPO)
zǒng yóujú 總郵局
stamp
yóupiào 郵票
aerogramme
yóujiǎn 郵簡
fax
chuánzhēn 傳真
telex
diànchuán 電傳
telegram
diànbào 電報
international express mail (EMS)
kuàijié 快捷
domestic express mail
kuài dì 快遞
registered mail
guà hào 掛號
airmail
hángkōng yùn 航空運
seamail
hǎi yùn 海運

Visas & Documents

passport
  hùzhào   護照
visa
  qiānzhèng   簽証
visa extension
  yánqī qiānzhèng 延期簽証
alien residence certificate
  jū liú zhèng   居留証
household registration report
  jūzhù zhèngmíng   居住証明
driver's licence
  jiàzhào   駕照
vehicle registration certificate
  xíngchē zhízhào   行車執照

Numbers

0	*líng*	零
1	*yī, yāo*	一, 么
2	*èr, liǎng*	二, 兩
3	*sān*	三
4	*sì*	四
5	*wǔ*	五
6	*liù*	六
7	*qī*	七
8	*bā*	八
9	*jiǔ*	九

10	*shí*	十
11	*shíyī*	十一
12	*shí'èr*	十二
20	*èrshí*	二十
21	*èrshíyī*	二十一
100	*yìbǎi*	一百
200	*liǎngbǎi*	兩百
1000	*yìqiān*	一千
2000	*liǎngqiān*	兩千
10,000	*yíwàn*	一万
20,000	*liǎngwàn*	兩万
100,000	*shíwàn*	十万
200,000	*èrshíwàn*	二十万

Time

What time is it?
  jǐ diǎn?   幾點
hour
  diǎn   點
minute
  fēn   分
now
  xiànzài   現在
today
  jīntiān   今天
tomorrow
  míngtiān   明天
yesterday
  zuótiān   昨天

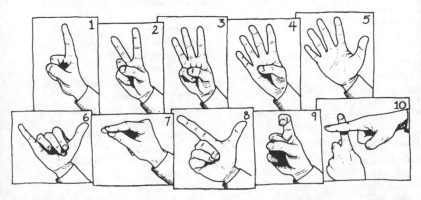

Finger counting

Emergencies

I'm sick.
wǒ shēng bìng 我生病
I'm injured.
wǒ shòushāng 我受傷
Fire!
huǒ zāi! 火災
Help!
jiùmìng a! 救命啊
Thief!
xiǎo tōu! 小偷
hospital
yīyuàn 醫院
police
jǐngchá 警察
foreign affairs police
wàishì jǐngchá 外事警察
pickpocket
páshǒu 勒戎
rapist
qiángjiānzhě 強姦者

Food Restrictions

I'm a vegetarian.
wǒ chī sù 我吃素
I don't eat meat.
wǒ bù chī ròu 我不吃肉
I don't eat pork.
wǒ bù chī zhū ròu 我不吃豬肉
I cannot eat spicy food.
wǒ bù néng chī là 我不能吃辣
I can't eat MSG.
wǒ bù néng chī
wèi jīng 我不能吃味精
I can't eat salt.
wǒ bù néng chī yán 我不能吃鹽
I cannot eat sugar.
wǒ bù néng chī táng 我不能吃糖

Bread, Buns & Dumplings 麥類

boiled dumplings
shuǐ jiǎo 水餃
clay oven rolls
shāo bǐng 燒餅

fried bread stick
yóu tiáo 油條
fried leek dumplings
jiǔ cài hézi 韭菜盒子
fried meat dumplings
guō tiē 鍋貼
fried roll
yín sī juǎn 銀絲捲
fried vegetable dumplings
shuǐ jiān bāo 水煎包
prawn cracker
lóng xiā piàn 龍蝦片
rice-meat dumplings
ròu yuán 肉圓
steamed buns
mán tou 饅頭
steamed dumplings (thick)
xiǎo lóng bāo 小籠包
steamed dumplings (thin)
zhēng jiǎo 蒸餃
steamed meat buns
bāo zi 包子
steamed sandwich
guǎ bāo, gē bāo 刈包
steamed vegetable buns
cài bāo 菜包

Noodles 麵類

soupy noodles
tāng miàn 湯麵
noodles (not soupy)
gān miàn 乾麵
fried noodles
chǎo miàn 炒麵
simple & cheap noodles
yáng chūn miàn/
yì miàn 陽春麵/意麵
sesame paste noodles
má jiàng miàn 麻醬麵
bean & meat noodles
zhá jiàng miàn 炸醬麵
wonton & noodles
hún dùn miàn 餛飩麵
seafood needles
wū lóng miàn/
guō shāo miàn 烏龍麵/鍋燒麵

fried noodles with beef
niú ròu chǎo miàn   牛肉炒麵
noodles with beef (soupy)
niú ròu tāng miàn   牛肉湯麵
noodles with beef (no soup)
niú ròu gān miàn   牛肉干麵
fried noodles with chicken
jī sī chǎo miàn   雞絲炒麵
noodles with chicken
jī sī tāng miàn   雞絲湯麵
duck with noodles
yā ròu miàn   鴨肉麵
goose with noodles
é ròu miàn   鵝肉麵
noodles, pork & mustard greens
zhà cài ròu sī miàn   榨菜肉絲麵
fried noodles with shrimp
xiā rén chǎo miàn   蝦仁炒麵
flat noodles
bǎn tiáo, kē zǎi tiáo   板條/粿仔條
sliced noodles
dāo xiāo miàn   刀削麵
rice noodles
mǐ fěn   米粉

Rice & Vegetable Dishes 飯類/菜類

plain white rice
bái fàn   白飯
watery rice porridge
xī fàn/zhōu   稀飯/粥
rice & vegetable roll
fàn tuán   飯團
salty rice pudding
wā guì   碗粿
sushi
shòu sī   壽司
Chinese salad
jiā cháng liáng cài   家常涼菜
assorted hors d'oeuvres
shíjǐn pīn pán   什錦拼盤
assorted vegetarian food
sù shí jǐn   素什錦
bean curd & mushrooms
mó gū dòu fǔ   磨菇豆腐

bean curd casserole
shā guō dòu fǔ   沙鍋豆腐
black fungus & mushroom
mù ěr huá kǒu mó   木耳滑口蘑
broiled mushroom
sù chǎo xiān mó   素炒鮮蘑
dried tofu
dòu fǔ gān   豆腐乾
fried bean curd in oyster sauce
háo yóu dòu fǔ   蠔油豆腐
fried beansprouts
sù chǎo dòu yá   素炒豆芽
fried cauliflower & tomato
chǎo fān qié cài huā   炒蕃茄菜花
fried eggplant
sù shāo qié zi   素燒茄子
fried garlic
sù chǎo dà suàn   素炒大蒜
fried green beans
sù chǎo biǎn dòu   素炒扁豆
fried green vegetables
sù chǎo qīng cài   素炒青菜
fried noodles with vegetables
shū cài chǎo miàn   蔬菜炒麵
fried peanuts
yóu zhà huā shēng mǐ   油炸花生米
fried rape in oyster sauce
háo yóu pá cài dǎn   蠔油扒菜膽
fried rape with mushrooms
dōng gū pá cài dǎn   冬菇扒菜膽
fried rice with vegetables
shū cài chǎo fàn   蔬菜炒飯
fried white radish patty
luó bo gāo   蘿卜糕
garlic & morning glory
dà suàn kōng xīn cài   大蒜空心菜
spiced cold vegetables
liáng bàn shí jǐn   涼拌什錦
spicy hot bean curd
má pó dòu fǔ   麻婆豆腐
spicy peanuts
*wǔ xiāng huā
shēng mǐ*   五香花生米
stinky tofu
chòu dòu fǔ   臭豆腐

Beef Dishes 牛肉類

beef braised in soy sauce
hóng shāo niú ròu 紅燒牛肉

beef curry & noodles
gā lí jī ròu miàn 咖喱牛肉麵

beef curry & rice
gā lí jī ròu fàn 咖喱牛肉飯

beef steak platter
niú ròu tiě bǎn 牛肉鐵板

beef with green peppers
qīng jiāo niú ròu piàn 青椒牛肉片

beef with oyster sauce
háo yóu niú ròu 蚝油牛肉

beef with tomatoes
fān qié niú ròu piàn 蕃茄牛肉片

beef with white rice
niú ròu fàn 牛肉飯

fried rice with beef
niú ròu sī chǎo fàn 牛肉絲炒飯

Egg Dishes 蛋類

1000-year egg
pí dàn 皮蛋

egg & flour omelette
dàn bǐng 蛋餅

fried rice with egg
jī dàn chǎo fàn 雞蛋炒飯

fried tomatoes & eggs
*xī hóng shì chǎo
jī dàn* 西紅柿炒雞蛋

Chicken Dishes 雞肉類

angelica chicken
dāng guī jī 當歸雞

chicken braised in soy sauce
hóng shāo jī kuài 紅燒雞塊

chicken curry & noodles
gā lí jī ròu miàn 咖喱雞肉麵

chicken curry & rice
gā lí jī ròu fàn 咖喱雞肉飯

chicken curry
gā lí jī ròu 咖喱雞肉

chicken leg with white rice
jī tuǐ fàn 雞腿飯

chicken pieces in oyster sauce
háo yóu jī dīng 蠔油雞丁

chicken slices & tomato sauce
fān qié jī dīng 蕃茄雞丁

drunken chicken
suān jī 酸雞

fried noodles with chicken
jī sī chǎo miàn 雞絲炒麵

fried rice with chicken
jī sī chǎo fàn 雞絲炒飯

fruit kernal with chicken
guǒ wèi jī dīng 果味雞丁

mushrooms & chicken
cǎo mó jī dīng 草蘑雞丁

noodles with chicken (soupy)
jī sī tāng miàn 雞絲湯麵

roast chicken
shǒu pá jī 手扒雞

sautéed chicken with green peppers
jiàng bào jī dīng 醬爆雞丁

sautéed chicken with water chestnuts
nán jiè jī piàn 南芥雞片

sautéed spicy chicken pieces
là zi jī dīng 辣子雞丁

sliced chicken with crispy rice
jī piàn guō bā 雞片鍋巴

spicy hot chicken & peanuts
gōng bào jī dīng 宮爆雞丁

sweet & sour chicken
táng cù jī dīng 糖醋雞丁

Duck Dishes 鴨肉類

angelica duck
dāng guī yā 當歸鴨

duck with fried noodles
yā ròu chǎo miàn 鴨肉炒麵

duck with noodles
yā ròu miàn 鴨肉麵

duck with white rice
yā ròu fàn 鴨肉飯

duck's blood & rice popsicle
yā mǐ xiě 鴨米血

Peking duck
běi píng kǎo yā 北平烤鴨

Pork Dishes 豬肉類

white rice & assorted meats
  sān bǎo fàn　　三寶飯
boiled pork slices
  shuǐ zhǔ ròu piàn　水煮肉片
fried black pork pieces
  yuán bào jǐ　　芫爆里脊
fried noodles with pork
  ròu sī chǎo miàn　肉絲炒麵
fried rice (assorted)
  shí jǐn chǎo fàn　什錦炒飯
fried rice Canton-style
  guǎng zhōu chǎo fàn 廣州炒飯
fried rice with pork
  ròu sī chǎo fàn　肉絲炒飯
golden pork slices
  jīn yín ròu sī　　金銀肉絲
noodles, pork & mustard greens
  zhà cài ròu sī miàn 榨菜肉絲麵
pork & fried onions
  yáng cōng chǎo
  ròu piàn　　　洋蔥炒肉片
pork & mustard greens
  zhà cài ròu sī　榨菜肉絲
pork chop with white rice
  pái gǔ fàn　　排骨飯
pork cubelets & cucumber
  huáng guā ròu dīng 黃瓜肉丁
pork fillet with white sauce
  huá liū lǐ jǐ　　滑溜里脊
pork with crispy rice
  ròu piàn guō bā　肉片鍋巴
pork with oyster sauce
  háo yóu ròu sī　蠔油肉絲
pork, eggs & black fungus
  mù xū ròu　　木須肉
sautéed diced pork & soy sauce
  jiàng bào ròu dīng 醬爆肉丁
sautéed shredded pork
  qīng chǎo ròu sī　清炒肉絲
shredded pork & bamboo shoots
  dōng sǔn ròu sī　冬筍肉絲
shredded pork & green beans
  biǎn dòu ròu sī　扁豆肉絲
shredded pork & green peppers
  qīng jiāo ròu sī　青椒肉絲

shredded pork & hot sauce
  yú xiāng ròu sī　魚香肉絲
shredded pork fillet
  chǎo lǐ jǐ sī　　炒里脊絲
soft pork fillet
  ruǎn zhá lǐ jǐ　軟炸脊肌
spicy hot pork pieces
  gōng bào ròu dīng 宮爆肉丁
spicy pork cubelets
  là zi ròu dīng　辣子肉丁
sweet & sour pork fillet
  táng cù lǐ jǐ　　糖醋里肌
sweet & sour pork slices
  táng cù zhū ròu piàn 糖醋豬肉片

Seafood Dishes 海鮮類

fried rice & seafood
  shí jǐn chǎo fàn　什錦炒飯
braised sea cucumber
  hóng shāo hǎi shēn 紅燒海參
clams
  gé lì　　　　蛤蠣
crab
  páng xiè　　　螃蟹
deep-fried shrimp
  zhà xiā rén　　炸蝦仁
diced shrimp with peanuts
  gōng bào xiā rén 宮爆蝦仁
eel
  shàn yú　　　鱔魚
fish braised in soy sauce
  hóng shāo yú　紅燒魚
fish
  yú　　　　　魚
fried noodles with shrimp
  xiā rén chǎo miàn 蝦仁炒麵
fried rice with shrimp
  xiā rén chǎo fàn 蝦仁炒飯
fried shrimp with mushroom
  xiān mó xiā rén　鮮蘑蝦仁
lobster
  lóng xiā　　　龍蝦
octopus
  zhāng yú　　　章魚

oyster
mǔ lì 牡蠣
sautéed shrimp
qīng chǎo xiā rén 清炒蝦仁
shrimp
xiārén 蝦仁
squid with crispy rice
yóu yú guō bā 魷魚鍋巴
squid
yóu yú 魷魚
sweet & sour squid roll
suān là yóu yú juǎn 酸辣魷魚卷
turtle
hǎi guī 海龜

Soup 湯類

soup
tāng 湯
thick soup
gēng 羹
bean curd & vegetable soup
dòu fǔ cài tāng 豆腐菜湯
clear soup
qīng tāng 清湯
corn & egg thick soup
fèng huáng lì mǐ gēng 鳳凰栗米羹
cream of mushroom soup
nǎi yóu xiān mó tāng 奶油鮮蘑湯
cream of tomato soup
nǎi yóu fān qié tāng 奶油蕃茄湯
egg & vegetable soup
dàn huā tāng 蛋花湯
fresh fish soup
xiān yú tāng 鮮魚湯
mushroom & egg soup
mó gu dàn huā tāng 蘑菇蛋花湯
pickled mustard green soup
zhà cài tāng 榨菜湯
seaweed soup
zǐ cài tāng 紫菜湯
squid soup
yóu yú tāng 魷魚湯
sweet & sour soup
suān là tāng 酸辣湯
three kinds seafood soup
sān xiān tāng 三鮮湯
tomato & egg soup
xī hóng shì dàn tāng 西紅柿蛋湯

vegetable soup
shū cài tāng 蔬菜湯
wonton soup
hún dùn tāng 餛飩湯

Miscellanea & Exotica 其它

betel nut
bīn láng 檳榔
cabbage roll
gāo lì cài juǎn 高麗菜捲
deermeat (venison)
lù ròu 鹿肉
dogmeat
gǒu ròu, xiāng ròu 狗肉/香肉
frog
qīng wā 青蛙
goat, mutton
yáng ròu 羊肉
kebab
ròu chuàn 肉串
Mongolian hotpot
huǒ guō 火鍋
puffed rice (or popcorn)
bào mǐ huā 爆米花
ratmeat
lǎo shǔ ròu 老鼠肉
sandwich
sān míng zhì 三明治
shaved ice & fruit
bā bǎo bīng 八寶冰
snake
shé ròu 蛇肉
spring roll (egg roll)
chūn juǎn 春捲
tofu pudding
dòu huā 豆花
vegetarian gelatin
ài yù 愛玉

Condiments 香料

black pepper
hú jiāo 胡椒
butter
huáng yóu 黃油
garlic
dà suàn 大蒜
honey
fēng mì 蜂蜜

hot pepper
  là jiāo   辣椒
hot sauce
  là jiāo jiàng   辣椒醬
jam
  guǒ jiàng   果醬
ketchup
  fān qié jiàng   蕃茄醬
MSG
  wèi jīng   味精
salt
  yán   鹽
sesame seed oil
  zhī ma yóu   芝麻油
soy sauce
  jiàng yóu   醬油
sugar
  táng   糖
vinegar
  cù   醋

Drinks Vocabulary

ice cold
  bīngde   冰的
ice cubes
  bīng kuài   冰塊
hot
  rède   熱的

Cold Drinks

water
  kāi shuǐ   開水
mineral water
  kuàng quán shuǐ 礦泉水
fizzy drink (soda)
  qìshuǐ   汽水
Coca-Cola
  kěkǒu kělè   可口可樂
lemon soda
  níngméng qìshuǐ 檸檬氣水
carrot juice
  hóng luóbo zhī   紅蘿蔔汁
orange juice
  liǔchéng zhī   柳橙汁
passionfruit juice
  bǎixiāngguǒ zhī 百香果汁
starfruit juice
  yángtáo zhī   楊桃汁

sugarcane juice
  gānzhè zhī   甘蔗汁
papaya milkshake
  mùguā niúnǎi   木瓜牛奶
pineapple milkshake
  fènglí niúnǎi   鳳梨牛奶
watermelon milkshake
  xīguā niúnǎi   西瓜牛奶
grass jelly
  xiàn cǎo   現草

Tea & Coffee

tea
  chá   茶
black tea
  hóng chá   紅茶
green tea
  lǜ chá   綠茶
jasmine tea
  mòlìhuā chá   茉莉花茶
oolong tea
  wūlóng chá   烏龍茶
hisbiscus (herb) tea
  luòshén chá   洛神茶
wheat tea
  mài chá   麥茶
coffee
  kāfēi   咖啡

Alcohol

beer
  píjiǔ   啤酒
Taiwan Beer
  táiwān píjiǔ   台灣啤酒
San Miguel
  shēnglì píjiǔ   生力啤酒
whiskey
  wēishìjì jiǔ   威士忌酒
vodka
  fútèjiā jiǔ   伏特加酒
rum
  lánmǔ jiǔ   蘭姆酒
red grape wine
  hóng pútao jiǔ 紅葡萄酒
white grape wine
  bái pútao jiǔ   白葡萄酒
rice wine
  mǐ jiǔ   米酒

Glossary

aborigines – Taiwan's earliest inhabitants who probably migrated from the Pacific Islands
aikido – martial art
Ami – aboriginal tribe
AMS – Acute Mountain Sickness
ARC – Alien Resident Certificate
Asian flu – term given to the Asian currency crisis
Atayal – aboriginal tribe

bàibài – worship ceremony
bāngdí – piccolo
big face – prestige, honour
black tea – fermented tea that most westerners are familiar with
bopomofo – Taiwan's phonetic system
Bunun – aboriginal tribe

cangjie – system that breaks every Chinese character down into four component parts to allow them to be typed into computers
catty – one catty equals 0.6kg (1.32lb)
CETRA – China External Trade & Development Council
chops – see *name chops*
CYC – China Youth Corps

dageda – Chinese expression for 'cellular telephone' which literally means 'big brother big'
dàluó – gongs (for ceremonies)
dízi – flute (horizontal)
dòngxiāo – flute (vertical)
Double 10th Day – see *National Day*
DPP – Democratic Progressive Party

EPA – Environmental Protection Agency
èrhú – two-stringed fiddle

fen – one fen equals 293.4 *pings*
fengshui – literally 'wind-water', the art of using ancient principles to maximise the flow of *chi*
finger game – a drinking game where the

loser is obliged to empty their glass; commonly played at feasts and dinner parties

gān bēi – literally 'dry glass' usually requiring you to down your drink
geomancy – see *fengshui*
ghost money – money burned to satisfy a 'hungry ghost' from the underworld (hell) so that it will not bother you or members of your family; also for a departed relative who may need some cash in heaven
god money – see *ghost money*
green tea – unfermented tea which has been steamed immediately after picking, then rolled, crushed and dried
guanxi – similar to 'relationship', advantageous social or business connections.
gǔzhēng – zither

Hakka – ethnic Chinese from the Henan province in northern China who gradually migrated into Taiwan
hánliú – monsoonal wind from Central Asia
Hokkien – name given to the Taiwanese language
Hsiao Liuchiu – the Chinese name for Taiwan from the Sui dynasty (589-618) until the Ming dynasty (1368-1644).
húqín – two-stringed viola

Ihla Formosa – name Portuguese sailors gave to Taiwan, literally meaning 'Beautiful Island'
ISP – Internet Service Provider

judo – martial art

karate – martial art
KMT – Kuomintang; political party that has controlled the ROC since its official founding in 1911

lavar – edible seaweed

mainlanders – people who came to Taiwan from mainland China after WWII

Meizhou Matsu – the 'Primitive Original Matsu', a statue from Fujian province, said to be more than 1000 years old

Matsu – Queen of Heaven and Protector of Seafarers, the most popular goddess in Taiwan

name chops – carved name seals that act as signatures

National Day – 10 October (10th day of the 10th month) sometimes called 'Double 10th Day'

neima – system that allocates every Chinese character a code number to allow them to be typed into computers

nirvana – buddhist state of complete freedom from greed, anger, ignorance and various other chains of human existence

Oolong tea – literally 'black dragon', is a partially fermented tea

opera (Chinese) – includes acrobatics, martial arts, poetic arias and stylised dance, usually performed on a bare stage, with the actors taking on stylised roles

Paiwan – aboriginal tribe

pedicab – pedal-powered tricycle used to carry passengers

people mountain, people sea – slang term used to describe very large crowd

ping – one ping equals 1.82 sq metres (5.97 sq ft)

Pinyin – the system of transliterating Chinese script into Roman characters

pípá – four-stringed lute

PLA – Chinese People's Liberation Army

PRC – People's Republic of China

Puyuma – aboriginal tribe

qiān – a box full of wooden rods found in temples. Before praying for something you desire, such as health, wealth or a good spouse you should select a rod.

qi – life's vital energy, commonly exploited in Chinese qìjōng and kungfu

qìgōng – as much an art form as a traditional Chinese medical treatment, rather like faith healing

red bomb – a wedding invitation which is invariably red, usually encouraging the obligation to present money to the newlyweds

renao – means something like 'lively', 'festive', 'happy' and 'noisy'

ROC – Republic of China. Officially, the Taiwanese agree that there is only one China, which is currently divided between the PRC and ROC, but 'someday' the Chinese nation will be reunited.

Rukai – aboriginal tribe

Saisiat – aboriginal tribe

sānxuán – three-stringed fiddle

Shao – aboriginal tribe

shimbui – kidney-shaped objects used in temple worship ceremonies

suí yì – or 'as you like', response to *gān bēi* which allows you to just take a sip of your drink

Sun Yatsen – the father of the *ROC*

suǒnà – trumpet (for ceremonies)

super worship festival – festivals occuring once every 12 years, at the end of the cycle of the 12 lunar animals. Some festivals occur only once every 60 years.

sutras – the Buddha's discourses

taekwondo – martial art

tael – one tael equals 37.5g (1.32oz)

Taijiquan – slow motion shadow-boxing, basically a form of exercise, but also an art and form of Chinese martial arts

Taiwan – meaning 'Terraced Bay'

tatami – straw mattress placed on the floor; tatami-style rooms are often cheaper alternatives to hotel rooms with beds

tax lottery – cash register receipts have unique lottery numbers printed on them for a monthly prize draw

tea-eggs – eggs boiled in tea

Three Principles of the People – nationalism, livelihood and civil rights are constantly promoted by the government

Tsou – aboriginal tribe

VAT – Value-Added Tax

Yami – aboriginal tribe

yóuzhèng huàbō zhànghào – postal remittance account numbers; a money transfer system whereby you can deposit money straight into someone's bank account

Yuan – five major branches of government
yuèqín – four-stringed banjo
Yushan – the highest peak in Taiwan and North-East Asia

Index

Thanks

Many thanks to all the travellers who wrote to us with helpful hints, useful advice and anecdotes. Your names appear below.

Douglas Berry, Ellen Bloom, Keith Bostock, T Bradford-Hunter, Donna Cabell, Joseph Caputo, T Chia-Hway, David Closs, Pat Collins, Guy Cox, Blanche & Gaetan de Brye, Claire Fentinan, Michael Fisk, Kiego Fiukatsu, Patricia Fuhrman, Roy Graff, Stephen Green, Kate Griffiths, David Hartmann, Alex & Anna Hayes, Trond Henrichsen, Maureen Holder, May Hon, Ron Hood, Nigel Jenkins, Michael Koss, Andrew Kowala, Diego Laje, Philip Lake, Sibylle Leitz, Min-Ling Liao, John Lumley -Holmes, Yung-Yu Ma, Colin Macdonald, Heather MacRae, Gill Miller, Stephanie Mills, Adrian Mills, John Andrew Moore, Stefan Moser, Chris Nelson, Captain Ni, Antje Nordmann, Patricia Oey, Daniel Packel, Jean-Francois Panis, Thomas Putsch, James Robinson, Richard Sanford, Dr Steven Schaufale, Melanie Seligman, Clive Shelley, Caleb Shen, Zdenek Slanina, S Smalley, John Soar, Gordon Spiers, John Steedman, Mark Swaim, Mimi Tan, Catherine Tingey, Goh Tong-Leng, David Tuohey-Mote, J Twitchall-Waas, Monty Vierra, Margit Waas, Uta Werlich, Dr Jon Wright and Eric Young.

LONELY PLANET

Phrasebooks

Lonely Planet phrasebooks are packed with essential words and phrases to help travellers communicate with the locals. With colour tabs for quick reference, an extensive vocabulary and use of script, these handy pocket-sized language guides cover day-to-day travel situations.

- handy pocket-sized books
- easy to understand Pronunciation chapter
- clear & comprehensive Grammar chapter
- romanisation alongside script to allow ease of pronunciation
- script throughout so users can point to phrases for every situation
- full of cultural information and tips for the traveller

'... vital for a real DIY spirit and attitude in language learning'
– Backpacker

'the phrasebooks have good cultural backgrounders and offer solid advice for challenging situations in remote locations'
– San Francisco Examiner

Arabic (Egyptian) • Arabic (Moroccan) • Australian *(Australian English, Aboriginal and Torres Strait languages)* • Baltic States *(Estonian, Latvian, Lithuanian)* • Bengali • Brazilian • British • Burmese • Cantonese • Central Asia (Uyghur, Uzbek, Kyrghiz, Kazak, Pashto, Tadjik • Central Europe *(Czech, French, German, Hungarian, Italian, Slovak)* • Eastern Europe *(Bulgarian, Czech, Hungarian, Polish, Romanian, Slovak)* • Ethiopian (Amharic) • Fijian • French • German • Greek • Hebrew • Hill Tribes • Hindi & Urdu • Indonesian • Italian • Japanese • Korean • Lao • Latin American Spanish • Malay • Mandarin • Mediterranean Europe *(Albanian, Croatian, Greek, Italian, Macedonian, Maltese, Serbian, Slovene)* • Mongolian • Nepali • Pidgin • Pilipino (Tagalog) • Portugese • Quechua • Russian • Scandinavian Europe *(Danish, Finnish, Icelandic, Norwegian, Swedish)* • South-East Asia *(Burmese, Indonesian, Khmer, Lao, Malay, Tagalog Pilipino, Thai, Vietnamese)* • South Pacific Languages • Spanish (Castilian) *(also includes Catalan, Galician and Basque)* • Sri Lanka • Swahili • Thai • Tibetan • Turkish • Ukrainian • USA *(US English, Vernacular, Native American languages, Hawaiian)* • Vietnamese • Western Europe *(Basque, Catalan, Dutch, French, German, Greek, Irish, Italian, Portuguese, Scottish Gaelic, Spanish (Castilian), Welsh)*

LONELY PLANET

Guides by Region

Lonely Planet is known worldwide for publishing practical, reliable and no-nonsense travel information in our guides and on our Web site. The Lonely Planet list covers just about every accessible part of the world. Currently there are 16 series: Travel guides, Shoestring guides, Condensed guides, Phrasebooks, Read This First, Healthy Travel, Walking guides, Cycling guides, Watching Wildlife guides, Pisces Diving & Snorkeling guides, City Maps, Road Atlases, Out to Eat, World Food, Journeys travel literature and Pictorials.

AFRICA Africa on a shoestring • Cairo • Cape Town • Cape Town City Map • East Africa • Egypt • Egyptian Arabic phrasebook • Ethiopia, Eritrea & Djibouti • Ethiopian (Amharic) phrasebook • The Gambia & Senegal • Healthy Travel Africa • Kenya • Malawi • Morocco • Moroccan Arabic phrasebook • Mozambique • Read This First: Africa • South Africa, Lesotho & Swaziland • Southern Africa • Southern Africa Road Atlas • Swahili phrasebook • Tanzania, Zanzibar & Pemba • Trekking in East Africa • Tunisia • Watching Wildlife East Africa • Watching Wildlife Southern Africa • West Africa • World Food Morocco • Zimbabwe, Botswana & Namibia
Travel Literature: Mali Blues: Traveling to an African Beat • The Rainbird: A Central African Journey • Songs to an African Sunset: A Zimbabwean Story

AUSTRALIA & THE PACIFIC Auckland • Australia • Australian phrasebook • Australia Road Atlas • Bush-walking in Australia •Cycling New Zealand • Fiji • Fijian phrasebook • Healthy Travel Australia, NZ and the Pacific • Islands of Australia's Great Barrier Reef • Melbourne • Melbourne City Map • Micronesia • New Caledonia • New South Wales & the ACT • New Zealand • Northern Territory • Outback Australia • Out to Eat – Melbourne • Out to Eat – Sydney • Papua New Guinea • Pidgin phrasebook • Queensland • Rarotonga & the Cook Islands • Samoa • Solomon Islands • South Australia • South Pacific • South Pacific phrasebook • Sydney • Sydney City Map • Sydney Condensed • Tahiti & French Polynesia • Tasmania • Tonga • Tramping in New Zealand • Vanuatu • Victoria • Watching Wildlife Australia • Western Australia
Travel Literature: Islands in the Clouds: Travels in the Highlands of New Guinea • Kiwi Tracks: A New Zealand Journey • Sean & David's Long Drive

CENTRAL AMERICA & THE CARIBBEAN Bahamas, Turks & Caicos • Baja California • Bermuda • Central America on a shoestring • Costa Rica • Costa Rica Spanish phrasebook • Cuba • Dominican Republic & Haiti • Eastern Caribbean • Guatemala • Guatemala, Belize & Yucatán: La Ruta Maya • Healthy Travel Central & South America • Jamaica • Mexico • Mexico City • Panama • Puerto Rico • Read This First: Central & South America • World Food Mexico • Yucatán
Travel Literature: Green Dreams: Travels in Central America

EUROPE Amsterdam • Amsterdam City Map • Amsterdam Condensed • Andalucía • Austria • Baltic States phrasebook • Barcelona • Barcelona City Map • Berlin • Berlin City Map • Britain • British phrasebook • Brussels, Bruges & Antwerp • Budapest • Budapest City Map • Canary Islands • Central Europe • Central Europe phrasebook • Corfu & the Ionians • Corsica • Crete • Crete Condensed • Croatia • Cycling Britain • Cycling France • Cyprus • Czech & Slovak Republics • Denmark • Dublin • Dublin City Map • Eastern Europe • Eastern Europe phrasebook • Edinburgh • Estonia, Latvia & Lithuania • Europe on a shoestring • Finland • Florence • France • Frankfurt Condensed • French phrasebook • Georgia, Armenia & Azerbaijan • Germany • German phrasebook • Greece • Greek Islands • Greek phrasebook • Hungary • Iceland, Greenland & the Faroe Islands • Ireland • Istanbul • Italian phrasebook • Italy • Krakow • Lisbon • The Loire • London • London City Map • London Condensed • Madrid • Malta • Mediterranean Europe • Mediterranean Europe phrasebook • Moscow • Mozambique • Munich • Norway • Out to Eat – London • Paris • Paris City Map • Paris Condensed • Poland • Portugal • Portuguese phrasebook • Prague • Prague City Map • Provence & the Côte d'Azur • Read This First: Europe • Romania & Moldova • Rome • Russia, Ukraine & Belarus • Russian phrasebook • Scandinavian & Baltic Europe • Scandinavian Europe phrasebook • Scotland • Sicily • Slovenia • South-West France • Spain • Spanish phrasebook • St Petersburg • St Petersburg City Map • Sweden • Switzerland • Trekking in Spain • Tuscany • Ukrainian phrasebook • Venice • Vienna • Walking in Britain • Walking in France • Walking in Ireland • Walking in Italy • Walking in Spain • Walking in Switzerland • Western Europe • Western Europe phrasebook • World Food France • World Food Ireland • World Food Italy • World Food Spain
Travel Literature: Love and War in the Apennines • The Olive Grove: Travels in Greece • On the Shores of the Mediterranean • Round Ireland in Low Gear • A Small Place in Italy

INDIAN SUBCONTINENT Bangladesh • Bengali phrasebook • Bhutan • Delhi • Goa • Healthy Travel Asia & India • Hindi & Urdu phrasebook • India • Indian Himalaya • Karakoram Highway • Kerala • Mumbai

LONELY PLANET

Mail Order

Lonely Planet products are distributed worldwide. They are also available by mail order from Lonely Planet, so if you have difficulty finding a title please write to us. North and South American residents should write to 150 Linden St, Oakland, CA 94607, USA; European and African residents should write to 10a Spring Place, London NW5 3BH, UK; and residents of other countries to Locked Bag 1, Footscray, Victoria 3011, Australia.

(Bombay) • Nepal • Nepali phrasebook • Pakistan • Rajasthan • Read This First: Asia & India • South India • Sri Lanka • Sri Lanka phrasebook • Tibet • Tibetan phrasebook • Trekking in the Indian Himalaya • Trekking in the Karakoram & Hindukush • Trekking in the Nepal Himalaya
Travel Literature: The Age of Kali: Indian Travels and Encounters • Hello Goodnight: A Life of Goa • In Rajasthan • A Season in Heaven: True Tales from the Road to Kathmandu • Shopping for Buddhas • A Short Walk in the Hindu Kush • Slowly Down the Ganges

ISLANDS OF THE INDIAN OCEAN Madagascar & Comoros • Maldives • Mauritius, Réunion & Seychelles

MIDDLE EAST & CENTRAL ASIA Bahrain, Kuwait & Qatar • Central Asia • Central Asia phrasebook • Dubai • Hebrew phrasebook • Iran • Israel & the Palestinian Territories • Istanbul • Istanbul City Map • Istanbul to Cairo on a shoestring • Jerusalem • Jerusalem City Map • Jordan • Lebanon • Middle East • Oman & the United Arab Emirates • Syria • Turkey • Turkish phrasebook • World Food Turkey • Yemen
Travel Literature: Black on Black: Iran Revisited • The Gates of Damascus • Kingdom of the Film Stars: Journey into Jordan

NORTH AMERICA Alaska • Boston • Boston City Map • California & Nevada • California Condensed • Canada • Chicago • Chicago City Map • Deep South • Florida • Hawaii • Hiking in Alaska • Hiking in the USA • Honolulu • Las Vegas • Los Angeles • Miami • Miami City Map • New England • New Orleans • New York City • New York City City Map • New York City Condensed • New York, New Jersey & Pennsylvania • Oahu • Out to Eat – San Francisco • Pacific Northwest • Puerto Rico • Rocky Mountains • San Francisco • San Francisco City Map • Seattle • Southwest • Texas • USA • USA phrasebook • Vancouver • Virginia & the Capital Region • Washington, DC City Map • World Food Deep South, USA
Travel Literature: Caught Inside: A Surfer's Year on the California Coast • Drive Thru America

NORTH-EAST ASIA Beijing • Cantonese phrasebook • China • Hiking in Japan • Hong Kong • Hong Kong City Map • Hong Kong Condensed • Hong Kong, Macau & Guangzhou • Japan • Japanese phrasebook • Korea • Korean phrasebook • Kyoto • Los Angeles • Mandarin phrasebook • Mongolia • Mongolian phrasebook • Seoul • South-West China • Taiwan • Tokyo
Travel Literature: In Xanadu: A Quest • Lost Japan

SOUTH AMERICA Argentina, Uruguay & Paraguay • Bolivia • Brazil • Brazilian phrasebook • Buenos Aires • Chile & Easter Island • Colombia • Ecuador & the Galapagos Islands • Healthy Travel Central & South America • Latin American Spanish phrasebook • Peru • Quechua phrasebook • Read This First: Central & South America • Rio de Janeiro • Rio de Janeiro City Map • Santiago • South America on a shoestring • Santiago • Trekking in the Patagonian Andes • Venezuela
Travel Literature: Full Circle: A South American Journey

SOUTH-EAST ASIA Bali & Lombok • Bangkok • Bangkok City Map • Burmese phrasebook • Cambodia • Hanoi • Healthy Travel Asia & India • Hill Tribes phrasebook • Ho Chi Minh City • Indonesia • Indonesian phrasebook • Indonesia's Eastern Islands • Jakarta • Java • Lao phrasebook • Laos • Malay phrasebook • Malaysia, Singapore & Brunei • Myanmar (Burma) • Philippines • Pilipino (Tagalog) phrasebook • Read This First: Asia & India • Singapore • Singapore City Map • South-East Asia on a shoestring • South-East Asia phrasebook • Thailand • Thailand's Islands & Beaches • Thailand, Vietnam, Laos & Cambodia Road Atlas • Thai phrasebook • Vietnam • Vietnamese phrasebook • World Food Thailand • World Food Vietnam

ALSO AVAILABLE: Antarctica • The Arctic • The Blue Man: Tales of Travel, Love and Coffee • Brief Encounters: Stories of Love, Sex & Travel • Chasing Rickshaws • The Last Grain Race • Lonely Planet Unpacked • Not the Only Planet: Science Fiction Travel Stories • Lonely Planet On the Edge • Sacred India • Travel with Children • Travel Photography: A Guide to Taking Better Pictures

The Lonely Planet Story

L onely Planet published its first book in 1973 in response to the numerous 'How did you do it?' questions Maureen and Tony Wheeler were asked after driving, bussing, hitching, sailing and railing their way from England to Australia.

Written at a kitchen table and hand collated, trimmed and stapled, *Across Asia on the Cheap* became an instant local bestseller, inspiring thoughts of another book.

Eighteen months in South-East Asia resulted in their second guide, *South-East Asia on a shoestring*, which they put together in a backstreet Chinese hotel in Singapore in 1975. The 'yellow bible', as it quickly became known to backpackers around the world, soon became *the* guide to the region. It has sold well over half a million copies and is now in its 9th edition, still retaining its familiar yellow cover.

Today there are over 350 titles, including travel guides, walking guides, language kits & phrasebooks, travel atlases, diving guides and travel literature. The company is the largest independent travel publisher in the world. Although Lonely Planet initially specialised in guides to Asia, today there are few corners of the globe that have not been covered.

The emphasis continues to be on travel for independent travellers. Tony and Maureen still travel for several months of each year and play an active part in the writing, updating and quality control of Lonely Planet's guides.

They have been joined by over 120 authors and 280 staff at our offices in Melbourne (Australia), Oakland (USA), London (UK) and Paris (France). Travellers themselves also make a valuable contribution to the guides through the feedback we receive in thousands of letters each year and on our web site.

The people at Lonely Planet strongly believe that travellers can make a positive contribution to the countries they visit, both through their appreciation of the countries' culture, wildlife and natural features, and through the money they spend. In addition, the company makes a direct contribution to the countries and regions it covers. Since 1986 a percentage of the income from each book has been donated to ventures such as famine relief in Africa; aid projects in India; agricultural projects in Central America; Greenpeace's efforts to halt French nuclear testing in the Pacific; and Amnesty International.

LONELY PLANET OFFICES

Australia
PO Box 617, Hawthorn, Victoria 3122
☎ 03 9819 1877 fax 03 9819 6459
email: talk2us@lonelyplanet.com.au

USA
150 Linden St, Oakland, CA 94607
☎ 510 893 8555 TOLL FREE: 800 275 8555
fax 510 893 8572
email: info@lonelyplanet.com

UK
10a Spring Place, London NW5 3BH
☎ 020 7428 4800 fax 020 7428 4828
email: go@lonelyplanet.co.uk

France
1 rue du Dahomey, 75011 Paris
☎ 01 55 25 33 00 fax 01 55 25 33 01
email: bip@lonelyplanet.fr
www.lonelyplanet.fr

World Wide Web: www.lonelyplanet.com *or* AOL keyword: lp
Lonely Planet Images: lpi@lonelyplanet.com.au